# THE RESTOR



The Pathway *in Time*
of
JESUS OF NAZARETH
*The Eternal* Son of God
perfectly recovered from
the Holy Scriptures

By
A. E. WARE

*PUBLISHERS*
SHILOAH MINISTRIES

This edition printed by Butler & Tanner Ltd,
Frome and London
Published by Shiloah Ministries
Obtainable from Mr C Corin
Trespassers W
Bugsell Lane
Robertsbridge
Sussex TN32 5EN
Tel 01580 880366

# CONTENTS

# PREFACE

THIS BOOK, the product of 30 years of study of the chronological framework of the ages since creation, is the work of a man, called of God, to learn from the Bible the way in which He measures time. God has not left these things to human reasoning or calculation for only He can reveal the deep and secret things which lie hidden in His word.

The Restored Vision was first printed in 1957 but to-day has lost nothing of its fascinating and instructive insights into the time measurements in relation to the life, death and resurrection of the Lord Jesus Christ.

We believe in these last days before Jesus comes to fetch His Bride, the Church, God would lead her back into an understanding of the New Testament Church and free us from some of the traditions that have come in down through the years.

This book can be read in two ways

1. By accepting the mathematical calculations checked by many and enjoying the revelations brought to light by them.
2. As a study book by those who have the capacity and desire to search out these things for themselves.

The book contains many new premises which some may find hard to accept but we offer them to you for your prayerful consideration.

There are many references in the book to the World in Liquidation. This work has been out of print for some time but we invisage getting the Fourth Paper, dealing with the time measurements since creation as revealed through the pages of the Bible, reprinted at a later date.

# THE PATHWAY IN TIME OF OUR LORD AND SAVIOUR JESUS CHRIST PERFECTLY RECOVERED FROM THE HOLY SCRIPTURES

(AS DEMONSTRATED IN "THE RESTORED VISION" BY A. E. WARE)

## A SUMMARY OF PRINCIPAL DATES

| | |
|---|---|
| THE ANNUNCIATION AND INCARNATION (AT NEW MOON) . . . . . . . . . | Jan. 23rd, 1 B.C. |
| HIS BIRTH AT BETHLEHEM AT THE FEAST OF TABERNACLES . . . . . . . . . | Oct. 29th, 1 B.C. |
| HIS CIRCUMCISION ON THE 8TH DAY OF THE FEAST . . . . . . . . . . | Nov. 5th, 1 B.C. |
| HIS PRESENTATION IN THE TEMPLE (Luke II, 22) . | Dec. 8th, 1 B.C. |
| THE VISIT OF THE WISE MEN (2ND LUNAR ANNIVERSARY) . . . . . . . . | Oct. 7th, A.D. 2 |
| AT TWELVE YEARS JESUS ATTENDS THE PASSOVER, ETC. . . . . . . . . . | Apr. 22nd, A.D. 12 |

### THE SEVEN YEARS AND SEVEN WEEKS FROM THE OPENING OF THE BAPTIST'S MINISTRY TO OUR LORD'S ASCENSION

(See Acts I, 22)

| | | |
|---|---|---|
| | JOHN THE BAPTIST COMMENCES TO HERALD THE MESSIAH . . . . . . . . . . | Apr. 25th, A.D. 26 |
| THE FIRST 212 DAYS | JESUS BAPTIZED ON DAY OF ATONEMENT (1260TH DAY) . . . . . . . . . . | Oct. 5th, A.D. 29 |
| | THE FORTY DAYS' TEMPTATION . . | Oct. 12th to Nov. 21st, A.D. 29 |
| | JESUS BEGINS HIS MINISTRY WHEN THIRTY YEARS OF AGE . . . . . . . . . . | Nov. 26th, A.D. 29 |
| | THE FIRST PASSOVER OF HIS MINISTRY (John II) . | May 4th, A.D. 30 |
| | "THREE YEARS" OF MINISTRY END (Luke XIII, 7) . | Oct. 22nd, A.D. 32 |
| THE LAST 212 DAYS | JESUS ATTENDS THE FEAST OF TABERNACLES (John VII) . . . . . . . . . . | Nov. 13th, A.D. 32 |
| | HE ATTENDS THE FEAST OF THE DEDICATION (John X) . . . . . . . . . . | Jan. 14th, A.D. 33 |
| | LAST 40 DAYS OPEN—JESUS FORETELLS HIS DEATH (Matt. XVI) . . . . . . . . . . | Mar. 23rd, A.D. 33 |
| | THE TRANSFIGURATION—33 DAYS BEFORE HIS DEATH . . . . . . . . . | Mar. 30th, A.D. 33 |
| | THE LAST PASSOVER WITH "THE TWELVE" | Thursday, Apr. 30th, A.D. 33 |
| | HIS CRUCIFIXION AND DEATH AT CALVARY | Friday, May 1st, A.D. 33 |
| | HIS RESURRECTION AT MIDNIGHT ON SUNDAY AFTER "THREE DAYS AND THREE NIGHTS" OR 57 HOURS . . . . . . . . | Sunday, May 3rd, A.D. 33 |
| | THE DAY OF THE RESURRECTION—HE APPEARS TO MANY . . . . . . . . | Monday, May 4th, A.D. 33 |
| | HIS ASCENSION INTO HEAVEN AFTER 40 DAYS | Saturday, June 13th, A.D. 33 |

The exact measurement of time between October 29th, 1 B.C., when our Lord was born, and June 13th, A.D. 33, when He ascended into Heaven, was 33 Bible Years (i.e., 354 days each) and 233 days, or 32 Solar Years and 227 days.

It is significant that the first 212 days from our Lord's Baptism and the last 212 days to His Ascension can be exactly traced in the Gospels. Between these periods there were 33 months of 28 days.

# INTRODUCTION

THE BIBLE, for the first time since the departure of the Apostles, has been allowed to yield up its deeply concealed secrets relative to the course of TIME in the earthly pathway of our Lord and Saviour Jesus Christ. Not only does the Bible reveal the actual day and date of the birth of our Lord but in the Four Gospels, as these pages will abundantly demonstrate, there exists, beneath the surface, an exact record of Time between the day of His Incarnation in the womb of the Virgin Mary and His Ascension into Heaven, from whence He had come to tabernacle among men, taking for the purpose a body of "flesh and blood", so that as our Kinsman He could accomplish our Redemption.

If, as we have affirmed, the Bible does contain a perfect record of Time covering our Lord's earthly life, how are we to account for the fact that, in spite of numberless efforts to search it out, no one until now has been rewarded with success? The reason for this in the first place is that the time had not yet come in the Divine counsels for such an unveiling; and, in the second place, that the facts had been so deeply concealed in the Scriptures that no human being could *of himself* possibly discover them. Furthermore, anyone allowed to do so would first have to acquire an exact knowledge of the Bible's faultlessly accurate Chronology (i.e. its system of measuring time and dating events) and of the operation of the Bible's lunar Calendar.

In other words, until someone could take the period of time covered by the Gospels from the birth of John the Baptist and of Jesus Christ and discern its exact place in the Bible's Chronological Plan, there would be no hope of obtaining any kind of accuracy as to the course of time in our Lord's life. No one has been able to do this because Bible chronology, until now, has never been elucidated with even an approach to accuracy. Consequently, though "many have taken in hand" to write a "life" of Jesus Christ, not one of these has ever been accompanied by a dating of events which was other than the opinion of the author based upon the admittedly sparse material on the subject to be found on the surface of the Four Gospels. (These opinions actually vary as much as eight or nine years as to the date of the Nativity, that is, from 8 B.C. to A.D. 1.)

It is, indeed, most sobering to contemplate that for eighteen hundred years no one on the earth has been able to date a single event correctly in the life of our Lord Jesus Christ, not excepting His birth or His death. That all such matters were known perfectly to the Apostles of our Lord and to the Four Evangelists is proved by their presence in the Gospels, from whence they have now been recovered in minute detail – a fact all sincere Christians who read these pages will wish to acknowledge with deep thanksgiving to God.

Many will desire to know why it pleased God to go to such lengths to conceal the Time factors of the Saviour's earthly pathway. We may rest assured that this was not mere arbitrary action, but a course dictated by a perfect foreknowledge of events in the Christian era, and by a determination, in the light of these, to preserve inviolable the many sacred facts of His Personal pathway on the earth which a true knowledge of Time would bring to light.

As all know, the Four Gospels on the surface scintillate with "all that Jesus began both to do and teach", but they are strangely silent as to any details affecting His Personal pathway. As regards His Public Ministry nothing must be concealed. All men must be allowed to know of His teaching, His miracles and His parables, as well as of His conflicts with the Religious Authorities of His day. The details of His trial, His sufferings, His crucifixion and His resurrection must be recorded with meticulous care in each Gospel so that all men may know what it cost Him to accomplish their Redemption.

Not so, however, the intimate details of His Personal path. These must remain in concealment after the departure of His Apostles because of the gross apostasy which would so soon develop in Christendom. The dates of His birth, His death and His resurrection, must therefore be hidden lest the true anniversaries of these should be desecrated by the apostates with their hideous perversions of the Christian Faith. Christendom should have its own celebration of His birth *on an invented date*, and its Easter Festival, by being linked to the vernal equinox since the

Council of Nicaea in A.D. 325, without any warrant from the Holy Scriptures, should never occur on the true anniversary of His glorious resurrection.

In His dealings with the nation of Israel God acted in a like manner, for the Bible reveals that by a secret manipulation of the Calendar He gave them days for their Sabbaths and Festivals which were one day later than those of Jehovah. This God did to preserve His own Holy Days from desecration. It was for this reason that our Lord Jesus Christ took the last Passover with His disciples one day before the Jews took their Passover. It is not, therefore, surprising that God acted as He did towards Christendom when He saw the need to preserve the Sacred Anniversaries of His Son's birth, death and resurrection from desecration by the many who would become Christians in name but not in fact.

The importance of Time in the life of our Lord Jesus Christ on earth will be the better appreciated when it is realized that His pathway here was evidently circumscribed by a predetermined Time Pattern designed for Him by God the Father. It could hardly be otherwise when the Scripture declares, "To everything there is a season, and a time to every purpose under the heaven" (Eccles. III, 1). It was our Lord's submission to this Time Pattern that constituted so perfect an expression of filial obedience. On numerous occasions He makes indirect reference to it by such words as "My time is at hand", or "My time is not yet come", or "the hour is come". His perfect knowledge of this Time Pattern shone forth brilliantly on the occasion when He said to His Mother, "Wist ye not that I must be about My Father's business?" For a reason He perfectly understood, our Lord had to be in the Temple *on that particular day*. This was the cause of the whole incident when He was twelve years of age, as we will in due course explain.

How wondrous a privilege has fallen to those responsible for this Treatise in that they have been enabled to trace out this Pattern of Time in all its perfection and are now allowed to reproduce it from the Scriptures for the benefit of their fellows, and notably for all those to whom every detail of the Saviour's sojourn among men is both sacred and of profound interest.

The Christian Faith rests upon the historic facts narrated in the Four Gospels concerning the Person of our Lord Jesus

Christ. These historic facts have now been magnificently supplemented by a true and faultlessly accurate chronology which embraces the whole era covered by the Four Gospels. Every major event in the Saviour's life has now been accorded its true date in terms of our solar calendar and of the Bible's lunar calendar. Numerous new facts of great historic importance have thereby come to light, and many events have taken on a new meaning because of the significance attaching to their dates.

So it has pleased Almighty God to restore to mankind the whole Truth concerning TIME in the earthly pathway of our Lord Jesus Christ as it was known to the Apostles and to those to whom they ministered in the first century. This is notably the case in reference to His death and resurrection in regard to which many problems of the greatest importance have until now remained unsolved.

## HOW AND WHY THE VEIL OF SECRECY AS TO TIME HAS NOW BEEN LIFTED FROM OUR LORD'S PATHWAY ON THE EARTH

As these things have been hidden from the eyes of all living for eighteen hundred years, it requires but a modicum of common sense to realize that their restoration *at this time* is no matter of chance but rather of deliberate design, if not of actual fore-planning, on the part of the Deity. It certainly is not due to any moral change on the part of Christendom, which in the middle of the twentieth century is found in the grip of the most fearful apostasy – political and religious – in the whole of its tortuous history. As in the days before the Flood, it can again be declared, "the earth also was corrupt before God, and the earth was filled with violence". The Bible perfectly accounts for the present state of things, and in the Book of the Revelation of Jesus Christ we have a vivid series of prophecies describing the judgments by which Civilization as now existing is to be "liquidated", in order to prepare the earth, and those upon it who survive, for the coming of the Kingdom of our Lord and Saviour, Jesus Christ.

It is perfectly clear that God, Who is "not willing that any should perish, but that all should come to repentance", has taken account of the increasingly hopeless state of mankind and has entered the scenes with a Testimony which directs the minds of men back again to the Holy Scriptures by restoring all the light and understanding concerning the Person of our Lord Jesus Christ with which Christianity made its first glorious entrance into the earth. In other words, by this restoration of light God is pointing men to the Person of Jesus Christ Himself because true Christianity in the first instance is a personal relationship, supernaturally wrought, between the individual and his Redeemer. It was when this fact was lost sight of that Christianity ceased to be a vital force in the world.

The authors of the present Treatise published in May 1953, a considerable volume which had as its title, *The World in Liquidation*, and as its sub-title, *The Coming of Christ at Hand.* This title and sub-title express two immeasurably solemn facts and in essence they answer the question why God has granted this recovery of light concerning His beloved Son's pathway on the earth. In this volume we narrated how in 1933 God, by a definite act, commenced the process by which He intends to accomplish the dissolution of Christendom in order to effect the establishment of the Kingdom of Christ in visible form and power over the earth.

In this former Treatise we also narrated the circumstances by which the writer and several associates were caused in 1933 to abandon all secular preoccupations and give themselves up to a comprehensive research into the Holy Scriptures, in order to elucidate their Time mysteries and find out just where we, of this day and generation, stood in the Divine plan of the ages. We were definitely conscious of being called to this service by our Lord and Master, Jesus Christ. That we were not deluded in this will, we trust, be apparent to all who will take the trouble to submit the results of our labours to a critical examination.

After mastering the principles of Biblical chronology and the operation of the calendar, we were enabled to reproduce from the Bible an exact record of its absolutely scientific and astronomically accurate chronology, from the first "evening and morning" of Genesis to the year 1933 when we began our labours. In the Fourth Paper of *The World in Liquidation* we have given a Summary of this chronology from which the indisputable fact emerged that on Monday, 12th June 1933, the predetermined Six Thousand Years of Man under probation terminated. This termination took place in the most dramatic circumstances as, for the first time in history, the whole world had on that day been representatively assembled in London for the World Economic Conference. These 6,000 years are typified by the six days of Creation and by several other Bible types.

Our readers will now understand that this present Treatise has its foundation in the considerable array of chronological facts given in our former Treatise – *The World in Liquidation* (see page 525).

As it is necessary to show our Lord's life as an era in the Bible's chronological structure, we shall give in the adjoining "Brief Summary of Facts" all measurements from Creation as they stood on the day of His birth. By this means the true dates in the Sacred Calendar of the Bible and in our Solar Calendar can be simply and accurately arrived at for all events, as well as the age of the Moon and the day of the week – every such detail being stamped with the divine impress.

## THE TIME FACTORS IN THE DEATH AND RESURRECTION OF OUR LORD JESUS CHRIST

It has long been recognized by many that the notion that our Lord rose early on the Sunday morning which followed His crucifixion on the Friday at 3 P.M. cannot possibly be reconciled with His own categorical pronouncements concerning the length of His sojourn "in the heart of the earth". Furthermore, the statements on this subject by the Four Evangelists are absolutely irreconcilable until certain hitherto concealed facts, which we shall in due course set forth, are taken into account.

We need only remark here that the whole mysterious subject of Time, as a vital factor in our Lord's death and resurrection, has now once for all been elucidated and every statement on the subject in the Bible seen to be in perfect harmony with every other statement.

There is, we believe, a very important reason for this which we will endeavour to explain.

The celebrations of the Ordinances of the Christian Faith, apart from Baptism, are all related to the time of the Death and Resurrection of Christ. When the knowledge of the actual dates of these great events was lost, and with this the knowledge of Apostolic practice in relation to them, the Churches of Christendom at the Council of Nicaea in A.D. 325 were compelled to devise a method of fixing the time for their celebration. This method has been in vogue ever since throughout Christendom.

The knowledge of the actual dates of our Lord's Death and Resurrection and of the Day of Pentecost in A.D. 33 having been restored, it became quite clear from the Bible that the Apostles and churches in the first century kept these annual Ordinances on their true solar anniversaries – the solar year being the one in use among the Gentiles. What else could be expected when all the Feasts in the Levitical economy were celebrated on anniversaries in the sacred lunar calendar? There can, indeed, be no questioning of the fact that at the beginning all the churches formed under Apostolic ministry kept the Memorial Supper, the Resurrection and the Day of Pentecost on their true solar anniversaries. To keep them at any other time is to rob them of their true significance as Divine Institutions. Not to keep them at all is to depart entirely from the plain teaching of the Apostles of our Lord.

It is not for us to discuss what Religious Christendom, as a whole, will do now that it has pleased God to restore the knowledge of the true dates upon which the Christian Ordinances should be kept. It is, however, to be hoped that all who love our Lord Jesus Christ in sincerity will realize the need to return speedily to the forsaken paths of obedience to Apostolic practice in all such matters, and so be found of Him at His now imminent Appearing.

* * *

We must now proceed with the task of recording the true historic facts of our Lord's earthly pathway as seen in the bright light of a perfected chronology – chronology forming, as it were, the backbone of history. There will be no need to embellish our pages with any human gloss, or to ignore the reticences of the

Sacred Writers when tempted to fill in a blank with invented material calculated to appeal to imaginative minds. We are not writing a "Life" of Jesus of Nazareth, but reproducing from the Gospels that which Divine Inspiration has caused to be set forth therein concerning the Pattern of Time by which His pathway was regulated and which, for reasons we have attempted to explain, has lain concealed beneath the surface of the Four Gospels for eighteen hundred years. The facts which we shall present as to the time of the major events in our Lord's life can be verified with the greatest ease as the exact course of time will be traced, without a break, from the day and hour of His birth to the day and hour of His ascension.

This recovery of Truth concerning the Person of our Lord Jesus Christ will neither be ignored nor discredited, except by those who have an ulterior motive for so doing. Without doubt, the sincerity of all in a position to influence their fellows will be put to a severe test because of the profound revolution in Christian practice which it will necessitate on the part of all who would "not be ashamed before Him at His coming" – it being remembered that it is to this end that our Lord and Master has interposed to rectify our ignorance of the Scriptures in "the things concerning Himself".

## A BRIEF SUMMARY OF FACTS ESSENTIAL TO THE UNDERSTANDING OF TIME IN THE LIFE OF JESUS CHRIST OUR LORD

1. Time and all its divisions, except minutes and seconds, originated with God. The Eternal Truth of His Word – the Bible – embraces a Plan of Time which covers Seven Thousand Years of human history.

2. Time in the Bible is reckoned exclusively by the civil lunar year of 354 days. This being so, we know that the years named in the Gospels, which have reference to our Lord Jesus Christ, are years of 354 days and not solar years of 365 days.

3. The Bible year of 354 days is divided into 12 months. The 6 months with odd numbers have 30 days each, and the 6 months with even numbers have 29 days each. This order of

months never varies in either the Old or the New Testament.

The Bible year of 354 days, with this division of months, was designed by the Creator to be an integral part of the Divine Economy. Apart from a few hours, 354 days are equal to 12 revolutions of the Moon. After the Exodus of Israel in 1639 B.C. and until our Lord's death in A.D. 33, the first month in each Bible year began at the New Moon of the Spring season.

## THE ANNUAL CALENDAR OF THE BIBLE

4. All that we need to know about the Bible Calendar, with one important exception, is found in Leviticus XXIII, where the annual Feasts of Jehovah are recorded. These Feasts or anniversaries occupy a very important place in the life of our Lord because of their typical meaning. It is therefore absolutely necessary to possess a working knowledge of them if we are to appreciate their significance in His life, not to mention their typical significance to the Christian Church. They appear in the following order.

### *The 10th day of the 1st month*

5. Reference to this date is found in Exodus XII, 3 (the exception above referred to). On this 10th day of the 1st month every household in Israel had to set aside the Passover lamb. This fact is mentioned only once in the Bible.

### *The 14th day of the 1st month at even*

6. In Leviticus XXIII, 5, we read, "In the fourteenth day of the first month at even is the Lord's passover". Thus there were four complete days from the setting apart of the Passover lamb on the 10th day to the slaying of the same "at even" on the 14th day.

7. LET THIS FACT BE CAREFULLY NOTED. These four days, during which the Passover lambs were in keeping before being slain "at even" on the 14th day, were designed to be a chronological type of the 4,000 years which elapsed *to the day and hour* between the Fall of Adam in the Garden of Eden and the Crucifixion of our Lord Jesus Christ – "the Lamb of God which taketh away the sin of the world" – at the Passover in

A.D. 33. Further reference to this fact will be found in the appropriate section of this Treatise. In II Peter III, we are told not to be "ignorant of this one thing, that one day is with the Lord as a thousand years, and a thousand years as one day".

8. As we have stated, the Bible's secular or civil year is 354 days. The Bible's Sacred or Redemption year is only 350 days. This begins, like the secular years, at the opening of the 15th day of the 1st month, with the taking of the Passover. It ends, however, on the 10th day of the 1st month in the next year, when once again the Passover lambs are set aside. The four following days, namely, the 11th, 12th, 13th and 14th of the 1st month, are totally ignored in all Sacred or Redemption years – the period being viewed as an absolute blank. The Bible provides the most perfect chronological evidence of this fact and this we have given in Paper Four of our former Treatise, *The World in Liquidation.*

Twice in our Lord's life we shall see the practical effect of the omission of these 4 days from the Sacred year. It was by this omission that God intended Israel to learn that the Passover lambs were a type of the Messiah, Whom He had set apart in the Garden of Eden to die after four "days" of 1,000 years in order to obliterate the sins of His people throughout that period. In anticipation of this, and as a sign to His people, God obliterated these four days from the Sacred Calendar every year while the Passover lambs were awaiting death. We have been obliged to enlarge upon this subject because of its immense importance in relation to the Person of our Lord Jesus Christ.

*The 15th to the 21st day of the 1st month*

9. In Leviticus XXIII, 6, we read, "On the fifteenth day of the same month (i.e., the 1st) is the feast of unleavened bread unto the Lord: seven days ye must eat unleavened bread". These seven days followed the eating of the Passover. They form a positive type of the Christian Dispensation (always marked by the number "seven") when the Church should partake exclusively of the Bread of God which came down from Heaven, even our Lord Jesus Christ. So the Apostle Paul writes, "For even Christ our passover is sacrificed for us: therefore let us keep the feast . . . with the unleavened bread of sincerity and truth" (I. Cor. V, 7 and 8).

*The Seven Weeks of Harvest*

10. In Leviticus XXIII, 9 to 22, we are informed that the seven weeks of harvest (which are another type of the Christian Dispensation) are to begin "on the morrow after the sabbath" which follows the Passover, by the presentation of "a sheaf of the firstfruits" to the Lord. This sheaf, from grain that has died in the earth, is a perfect type of Christ on the morning of His resurrection when, as "the firstfruits of them that slept", He presented Himself to God. After seven weeks comes the day of Pentecost when two loaves, called "bread of the firstfruits", are likewise to be presented to God. These two loaves are a type of the Church (Jew and Gentile) when its sleeping members – "the dead in Christ" – are raised at the end of the age. The seven weeks of harvest would always end early in the 3rd month of the Bible year with the day of Pentecost. The next Feast was not until the 7th month.

*The 10th day of the 7th month*

11. In Leviticus XXIII, 27, we read, "Also on the tenth day of this seventh month there shall be a day of atonement". We shall learn presently that our Lord Jesus was baptized of John in Jordan on the Day of Atonement in A.D. 29, and that in A.D. 31 our Lord healed a cripple who "had an infirmity thirty and eight years" on the Day of Atonement (John V).

*The 15th to the 23rd day of the 7th month*

12. In Leviticus XXIII, 34 to 44, we learn that there were two Feasts which were concurrent – the Feast of Tabernacles and the Feast of Ingathering. Both these Feasts began at 8 A.M. on the 15th of the 7th month and were of seven days' duration, followed by an eighth day – the day spoken of in John VII, 37, as "the last day, that great day of the feast". As our Lord was born at the Feast of Tabernacles, we shall take occasion to write of its typical significance when we reveal from the Bible the date of His birth. The significance of the 8th day of these Feasts we explain in section 18 of this "Summary of Facts".

This brings us to the end of these few essential remarks on the Feasts in the Bible Calendar. These should be referred to as required when the narrative is being read.

### *The difference of* ONE DAY *between the Calendar of Jehovah and the Calendar of Israel*

13. We must now call attention to a supremely important fact. It is well known that our Lord Jesus and His disciples took the Passover Supper on the Thursday night *before* His Crucifixion and that the Jews took their Passover Supper on the Friday night *after* His Crucifixion. At the Exodus God gave Moses and Aaron a new calendar (Exodus XII, 2). This made sure that each first month would occur in the Spring season and that every month would begin with a New Moon. This Calendar was absolutely scientific, though perfectly suited to civil purposes. God gave it to Israel on the day of the true New Moon, that is, the day on which the Sun and the Moon were in exact conjunction. It was, in short, the day of the astronomical New Moon. At the opening of the third month after leaving Egypt, because no Moon was to be seen in the heavens, Israel waited one day until it appeared and then started the third month (see Exodus XIX, 1). In effect, this transferred their calendar to months which started at the phasis or first appearing of the Moon instead of at the true New Moon, as ordained by Jehovah. Israel's calendar was equally scientific and accurate but it was always one day of the month *behind* the Divine Calendar of Jehovah. The word "month" in the Hebrew is CHODESH which means "new moon". The Feasts of Jehovah were to be on given days of the Moon as measured from the day of the actual conjunction. Israel's Feasts were celebrated on the correct date but in months which started at the first appearance of the Moon which was one day after the conjunction. Unless the fact is admitted that Israel delayed a day and began this third month a day late, it is impossible to affirm that the Law was given on Sinai at Pentecost, that is, on the fiftieth day after the Exodus began.

Now we know why our Lord and His disciples took the Passover on the Thursday evening before His death. It was because this was the true 14th day of the Moon and in accordance, therefore, with the Law. Furthermore, John in his Gospel speaks of "the Jew's passover" and "the Jews' feast of tabernacles" in order to distinguish them from those of Jehovah which occurred one day earlier.

All will understand from what we have said that there is a

difference of one day between the Feasts of Jehovah and the Feasts of the Jews named in the Gospels. It will be well to point out that the Passover taken by our Lord with His disciples is the only occasion named in the Gospels when He kept a Feast of Jehovah with outward expression.

*God's Sabbath and the Jews' Sabbath were also one day apart*

14. In the Wilderness Israel so desecrated God's holy Sabbath (see Ezekiel XX) that He wrought to give them their own Sabbath and so preserve His own. This God accomplished when He responded to Joshua's request that the Sun and Moon should "stand still" for a whole day of 24 hours (Joshua X). As there was only one sunset in 48 hours, Joshua and Israel treated the period as one day. Jehovah, however, regarded it as two days of 24 hours each. Consequently, from that time Israel's days of the week were one day behind those of Jehovah.

It is for this reason, as we will explain in due course, that the Evangelist Matthew records the death of our Lord Jesus as taking place on the Sabbath (XXVIII, 1); whereas the other three Evangelists clearly indicate that it occurred on a Friday. We thus possess evidence from Holy Scripture that God's Sabbath had become the Jews' Friday. As we shall learn later, Matthew is caused to adopt the Divine (i.e. Jehovah's) Calendar in his account of the death and resurrection of our Lord Jesus Christ, while the other Evangelists are caused to adopt that of Israel in their accounts.

*The Chronological Eras of the Bible during the life of our Lord Jesus Christ*

It is most important that readers of this Treatise should have some knowledge of the operation of Bible chronology during our Lord's lifetime. We shall therefore give a brief outline of the four great chronological eras which run right through the Bible. For further details of these eras we must refer readers to "The Summary of Time" which is the Fourth Paper of *The World in Liquidation*.

*The Secular Chronology* (*Anno Mundi*)

15. This begins on the first day of the Bible (4th March,

4075 B.C.) and runs an unbroken course of 354-day years to 12th October, A.D. 33, after which, in one predetermined stride of 1,960 Bible years, it reaches the date of 12th June in 1933, with a total of 6,198 years and 22 days. This is the Bible's inspired and therefore faultlessly accurate record of time and it forms the foundation of all Bible chronology. *It is the world's only such record.* Its astronomical accuracy may be proved by anyone who will take the trouble to do it. It accounts for every year, month, week, day, hour, minute and second from the first day of the Bible to the end of the 6,000 Years of Man on 12th June, 1933.

AT THE OPENING OF THE DAY OF OUR LORD'S BIRTH SECULAR CHRONOLOGY HAD REACHED A TOTAL OF 4,204 BIBLE YEARS AND 21 DAYS. This is the exact equivalent of 4,074 Solar years and 239 days.

### *The Chronology of Redemption*

16. This is an era with a fixed limit of 6,000 years. It began on the day *after* the Fall and will terminate with the setting up of the Kingdom, when the whole earth will be brought into the benefits of our Lord's Sacrifice and be delivered from its present "bondage of corruption". This era is concurrent with the Secular Chronology, except that it omits periods of years or days that are marked by circumstances incompatible with the principles of Redemption and Forgiveness, such as, for instance, the 70 years' Captivity of Judah in Babylon. The years of this era are of 350 days' length and no account is taken of the 4 days during which the Passover lambs were awaiting death. This era is measured throughout the Bible in Jubile cycles of 49 years and major cycles of 490 years. It has no value from the astronomical aspect because of its many omissions on moral grounds.

The 6,000 Years of Redemption had exactly reached the middle of the 3,888th year at our Lord's birth. This is a most significant fact for reasons we shall explain in due course.

### *The Chronology of Man (Anno Hominis)*

17. This is an era of 6,000 years reckoned in terms of the solar year of 365¼ days as used by Gentiles from time immemorial. It views the race as sinful but, nevertheless, as under probation. It is composed of the Bible's Secular Chronology converted into

solar years, but it omits the period during which our Lord "went in and out among" men from the Baptism of John to the Ascension, for reasons we will give later. This era began on the 9th day of the Bible and terminated at the close of 12th June 1933, when exactly 6,000 Julian years were completed. Thereafter "the consummation of the age" began, and this has now lasted over 23 years.

THE 6,000 YEARS OF MAN HAD REACHED A TOTAL OF 4,074 YEARS AND 231 DAYS AT OUR LORD'S BIRTH. This is 8 days less than the Secular Chronology which begins on the first day of the Bible.

### *The Years of the Messiah*

18. This is the most deeply concealed series of years in the Bible and its existence we believe has never before been recorded. It is measured in seven cycles of 888 years each. These began on the 8th day of the Bible, that is, after the first Sabbath. The number 888 is the numerical value of the letters which form the name "JESUS" in the Greek. It is no wonder, therefore, that in announcing the birth of the Messiah the Angel told the Virgin Mary to call His Name "Jesus".

As we have previously stated, the Feast of Tabernacles and the Feast of Ingathering in the 7th month each lasted for seven days to which an eighth day, having special characteristics, was added. These "eighth" days typify the Messianic Kingdom, while the seven days are typical of the seven cycles of 888 years which lead up thereto. Furthermore, we are informed in Luke's Gospel that the Transfiguration of our Lord, which is an adumbration of the Kingdom, took place on an eighth day (IX, 28).

This remarkable series of years, which runs independently of all other chronological eras in the Bible, relates exclusively to Jesus as the Messiah and to the seed through whom He was to come. We shall see how very important a part the calendar based upon these Messianic years plays in the life of our Lord. In fact, these years of the Messiah afford the clearest proof of His Messiahship ever allowed to men. In our former Treatise – *The World in Liquidation* – we present an extensive commentary on this series of years and give the date when the seven times 888 years will have run their course.

THE YEARS OF THE MESSIAH HAD REACHED A TOTAL OF 4,204 YEARS AND 14 DAYS AT THE TIME OF OUR LORD'S BIRTH. As one might expect, this figure is of the greatest possible significance. This we shall explain in our opening chapter when we shall show how the Bible establishes the date of His birth.

*The Total Number of Days and Lunations from the First Day of the Bible to the Day of our Lord's Birth*

19. It is necessary to give these figures in order to establish the day of the week and the age of the Moon for any given occasion in our Lord's life. To do this it is only necessary to add the days or lunations (i.e., revolutions of the Moon) from His birth to the following figures.

| DAYS | LUNATIONS |
|---|---|
| 1,488,237 | 50,396 lunations, 13 days, 21 hours, 43 mins. |

*Non-Biblical Chronological Eras*

20. The most important of these in the time of our Lord was the Greek era of the Olympiads which began in 776 B.C. The Olympic Games were held every four years thereafter and formed a useful basis for a chronological era.

The years from the Foundation of Rome in or about 754 B.C. formed another era in general use throughout the Roman earth This era is signified by the letters AUC – "*Anno Urbis Conditae*".

Lastly, and by an act of Providence because the Bible's faultless recording of human time was soon to cease, the great Julius Caesar on 1st January 45 B.C., was moved to inaugurate the solar calendar that bears his name. It has proved a perfect instrument for keeping time because, like the Bible year, it consists of an exact number of days (namely, 365 days and 366 every fourth year). Since its inauguration 2,000 years ago the world has possessed a calendar that has required but one adjustment and this gave us in 1582 our present Gregorian Calendar.

The Julian Calendar was, therefore, in use in Palestine when our Lord was there, and its twelve months were the same as we have them today.

### GEMATRIA *or the Numerical Value of Hebrew and Greek Words*

21. Every Hebrew and Greek letter has a number attached to it and all numbers have a spiritual significance in the Bible. We have already shown that the letters composing the Name – JESUS – in its Greek spelling (IESOUS) have a total value of 888. In the same way every Hebrew and Greek word has a numerical value and this was called by the ancients, GEMATRIA. We shall be obliged to make reference in the Narrative to the numerical value of the Names and Titles given to our Lord Jesus Christ and it will then be seen how immensely this adds to their significance. (A number of books exist on this subject of which *Spiritual Arithmetic* by R. T. Naish, and *Number in Scripture* by W. E. Bullinger, will be found most helpful.)

## FIVE CALENDARS WERE IN OPERATION DURING THE LIFE OF OUR LORD JESUS CHRIST ON THE EARTH

It will have been noted that in the foregoing Summary of Facts we have made reference to no less than four different calendars which were in operation in relation to our Lord's life. These are (I) the Calendar of Israel which lies on the surface of Holy Scripture; (II) the Calendar of Jehovah which differed from the Calendar of Israel by being one day of the month and one day of the week ahead; (III) the Messianic Calendar based upon the Years of the Messiah, and (IV) the Roman or Gentile Calendar inaugurated by Julius Caesar in 45 B.C.

To these four calendars we must add the Calendar based upon the years of His own life as measured from His birth to His Ascension. Like ourselves, our Lord had a personal chronology and this, like all Bible years, was composed of years of 354 days. The annual Feasts of Leviticus XXIII were viewed by God as also applying to this series of years, in which, for instance, the Anointing by Mary of Bethany took place on the Day of Atonement which was the 10th day of the 7th month in His 33rd year.

If the reader cares to do so, he may turn to the end of Chapter XIII, where he will find some further remarks on these

Five Calendars and a Chart showing them in operation together at the time of our Lord's death and resurrection.

NOTE CONCERNING THE ACCURACY OF THE ABOVE FIGURES

In Appendix A the reader will find a Chart giving the exact course of Time from Creation to 12th June 1933, when the 6,000 Years of Man ended and when the world entered a parenthetical era in its chronology pending the commencement of the Seventh Thousand Years or Millennial Reign of Christ. This Chart will confirm the figures we have given at the Birth of our Lord. Their accuracy is undeniable because the Bible, which is the Inspired Word of God, is their actual source. Anyone who wishes can check these measurements by reference to the Bible.

# CHAPTER ONE

## THE TIME AND MANNER OF THE INCARNATION AND BIRTH OF JESUS OF NAZARETH THE ETERNAL SON OF GOD

---

### PART ONE

THE DATE OF THE NATIVITY OF OUR LORD JESUS CHRIST UNVEILED FROM THE HOLY SCRIPTURES AFTER CONCEALMENT THEREIN FOR 1800 YEARS

THE DATE OF THE ANNUNCIATION TO THE VIRGIN MARY
THE DATES OF THE CONCEPTION AND BIRTH OF JOHN THE BAPTIST

---

### PART TWO

THE CIRCUMSTANCES OF THE INCARNATION AND BIRTH OF OUR LORD JESUS CHRIST CONSIDERED

THE IMMENSE SIGNIFICANCE OF THE VISIT OF THE WISE MEN OF THE EAST WHICH OCCURRED ON THE SECOND LUNAR ANNIVERSARY OF THE NATIVITY IN A.D. 2

---

### PART THREE

THE FACTS FROM THE HOLY SCRIPTURES WHICH LED TO THE RECOVERY OF THE DATE OF OUR LORD'S BIRTH

THE PRE-INCARNATION OF OUR LORD JESUS CHRIST AS IMMANUEL AT THE TIME OF ISAIAH'S PROPHECY OF THE VIRGIN BIRTH IN 742 B.C.

---

Read Matthew I and II; Luke I and II, 1 to 40; III, 23; XIII, 7, 8; Isaiah VII, 14 and Daniel IX, 25

---

The Time covered by Chapter One commences with the Conception of John the Baptist in August, 2 B.C., and ends in the spring of A.D. 3, when Mary and Joseph with the Child Jesus return to Nazareth from Egypt.

# PART I

## THE DATE OF THE NATIVITY OF OUR LORD RECOVERED FROM THE HOLY SCRIPTURES

AS IT WOULD be impossible to reproduce from the Four Gospels the exact "Pathway in Time" of our Lord Jesus Christ here upon earth without starting on the actual day of His birth at Bethlehem, we shall open this Chapter by giving this date in terms of the two main Bible Calendars, and of our own Solar Calendar which was in use throughout the Roman Earth during our Lord's life. Though, as these pages will prove, this date confirms itself at every chronological point given in the Gospels and could not, therefore, be other than the true date, we propose to devote Part III of this Chapter to the setting forth of the facts by which the Bible reveals it, and so avoid commencing with a number of details which will only be of interest to the most serious enquirers.

---

## THE DATE

### WHAT THE BIBLE REVEALS

THE BIRTH OF JESUS OF NAZARETH, THE SON OF GOD AND MESSIAH OF ISRAEL, TOOK PLACE AS FOREORDAINED ON THE 1ST DAY OF THE FEAST OF TABERNACLES, WHICH WAS THE 15TH DAY OF THE SEVENTH MONTH IN THE 3888TH YEAR OF THE BIBLE'S REDEMPTION CHRONOLOGY

THIS DATE IN OUR SOLAR CALENDAR WAS

FRIDAY, 29TH OCTOBER 1 B.C.

IN THE CALENDAR BASED UPON THE YEARS OF THE MESSIAH THIS DATE WAS THE 1ST DAY OF THE FEAST OF UNLEAVENED BREAD, BEING THE 15TH DAY OF THE FIRST MONTH IN THE YEAR 4205 FROM ADAM

---

It will be seen from this statement that God ordained the Birth of His Son should occur on a day which was both the 1st day of the Feast of Tabernacles and the 1st day of the Feast of Unleavened Bread, each according to its respective series of years.

* * *

As we stated in our Introduction, it would not be possible to discover the actual date of the Saviour's birth or reproduce His Pathway in terms of Time, as given in the Four Gospels, without first possessing a faultless knowledge of the Bible's chronology and of the operation of its lunar Calendar. With this knowledge it has been possible in the above statement to give the Jewish and Gentile dates of our Lord's birth, each such date constituting an unimpeachable chronological fact drawn from the Holy Scriptures, which can be verified by anyone who desires to do so.

Let it, therefore, be clearly understood that the dates given are not to be viewed as the result of a further effort to arrive at the time of our Lord's birth, but as FACTS ACTUALLY REVEALED IN THE HOLY SCRIPTURES which establish once and for all the day and date of that GREAT EVENT.

We may mention in passing that it has for long been held by many that our Lord Jesus Christ was born at the Feast of Tabernacles because of the typical significance of that Feast, and because the Evangelist John states, as given in the R. V. Margin, "The Word became flesh, and tabernacled among us" (I, 14). Furthermore, nearly all responsible authorities, including the Papacy, have held that our Lord was born in 1 B.C., as established by Dionysius Exiguus in the sixth century. This knowledge, however, though correct in itself lacked any real value because of the apparent absence of any actual proof in the Bible in support of it. Not only has this now been found, but with it, and as a result of possessing it, the ability to trace throughout the Four Gospels the exact course of Time in our Lord's life from His Incarnation to His Ascension. It will be obvious to all that the Pattern of Time by which our Lord walked when here on earth would be in error throughout if it were shown as commencing other than upon the true date. As it is, nearly every major event in our Lord's life is marked by a lunar date in the Bible Calendar which adds immensely to its significance, while the plan as a whole confirms its own absolute accuracy at every point. This could not be otherwise since the Pattern of Time itself and the recording of it in the Scriptures are the work of God's Holy Spirit.

Remembering that in Part III of this Chapter we are going to give the facts from the Holy Scriptures by which the dates of our Lord's birth in the Jewish and Gentile Calendars were recovered, after having been lost to sight for 1800 years, we will before proceeding examine these dates themselves because of the glorious light they shed upon the occasion of our Lord's entry into this world.

It will at once be realized that the date of 29th October 1 B.C., in the Solar Calendar when our Lord was born, has no Biblical significance whatsoever. Nevertheless, every true Christian believer will rejoice to possess the certain knowledge of the time in our calendar when the Saviour was born and to know that the date of 25th December is a fictitious one, never again to be honoured by association with His birth, with which it has nothing whatever to do, since it is of a purely heathen origin – a fact long acknowledged by many.

## WHY OUR LORD JESUS CHRIST WAS BORN IN THE 3888TH REDEMPTION YEAR FROM ADAM

We might well expect that the Son of God and Messiah of Israel would be born into this world in a year which was marked with a Divine significance. The Apostle Paul informs us that "when the fulness of the time was come, God sent forth His Son, made of a woman, made under the law" (Gal. IV, 4). The immense significance of the 3888th year from Adam will at once be appreciated by all who recall that (as we stated in Paragraph 18 of the Summary of Facts) the Greek spelling of the Name "Jesus" has a numerical value of 888. How truly marvellous, therefore, that God should ordain that His Son – JESUS – should be born in a year which combines the number of the Trinity of the Godhead, namely, "3", with "888", His personal number. The number "8", which bespeaks "superabundance", is indelibly associated with our Lord Jesus Christ and appears as the chief factor in the numerical value of the

Greek spelling of all His Names, including "Saviour", "Lord", "Christ", "Messiah" and "Son". God has thus marked the birth of Jesus with a chronological sign which sets Him forth as the One in Whom "dwelleth all the fulness of the Godhead bodily" (Col. II, 9).

The absolute certainty that the year 3888 in the Bible's Redemption Chronology (see Par. 16; Summary of Facts) was that in which our Lord was born is established by the following simple facts. The year 3888 ended in the spring of A.D. 1. If we add 32 years we reach the spring of A.D. 33, when our Lord died, and thereby raise the total from 3888 to 3920 years. In 3920 years there are 80 Jubile cycles of 49 years each from the Fall of Adam. Time in the Bible is measured by these Jubile cycles – each of which has a nominal value of 50 years because one Jubile year is added to each 49 years. The Bible, therefore, adds 80 years of Jubile to these 3920 years and this makes a total of exactly 4000 Redemption years from the Fall of Adam to the Death of our Lord Jesus Christ. In Paragraph 7 of the Summary of Facts we show that the 4 days from the 10th to the 14th of the 1st month, during which the Passover lambs are awaiting death, were designed to be a positive type of these 4000 Redemption years – each day for a thousand years, according to II Peter III, 8.

## WHY OUR LORD JESUS CHRIST WAS BORN ON THE 1ST DAY OF THE FEAST OF TABERNACLES AND CIRCUMCISED ON THE 8TH DAY THEREOF

The Feast of Tabernacles, details of which will be found in Leviticus XXIII, 33 to 38, like all the annual Feasts of the Bible, has a deep typical meaning, not only for Israel but for all mankind, since it embraces the whole course of human history. The basic principle which underlies this Feast is the transitoriness of human existence in this world. It views man as a sojourner tabernacling for a brief season on the earth. Like Abraham, of whom it is written, "he sojourned in the land . . . dwelling in tabernacles with Isaac and Jacob", all people in all ages who have walked in the fear of God have viewed themselves as tabernacling on the earth for a brief season before passing on to an eternal existence in the heavenly country.

In the light of these facts all can see why God ordained that Jesus, His well-beloved Son, should be born into the world on the opening day of the Feast of Tabernacles. Was not our Lord a perfect Example of a sojourner Who had for a brief season come to pitch His Tabernacle in our midst and then return to the Heavenly Country from whence He had come? With what truth He could say to an intending disciple, "The Son of Man hath not where to lay His head" (Luke IX, 58).

The Feast of Tabernacles not only had a moral significance for all mankind but a chronological one as well. This Feast was for Seven Days but these were followed by an Eighth Day which in John's Gospel is called "the last day, that great day of the feast" (VII, 37). These 7 days are a type of the 7 Cycles of 888 Messianic years each which are destined to run their course from Adam to the Messianic Kingdom; while the 8th Day typifies the era of the Kingdom. This important aspect is dealt with in Paragraph 18 of the Summary of Facts, so we need add no more on the subject here.

The question will quite properly be asked, How do we know that the 15th day of the Bible's 7th month, which was the first day of the Feast of Tabernacles, was Friday, 29th October, in the year 1 B.C.? This is a particularly pertinent question because several reputable writers have advanced the date of 29th September, which is eactly one month earlier, as that of the Feast of Tabernacles in 1 B.C.

The answer is that we possess a faultless astronomical record of time in the Bible from the New Moon of the Exodus of Israel from Egypt, which was on 28th April 1639 B.C., to the New Moon of 12th October A.D. 33, during which interval Israel possessed the luni-solar Calendar given by the Lord God to Moses and Aaron, as recorded in Exodus XII, 2. This record of time is set forth in Paper IV of our former Treatise, *The World in Liquidation*. It shows that both the Christian Church and the Jewish people, by respectively linking Easter and the Passover to the Vernal Equinox since the fourth century of our Era, have been allowed to err as to the time of the true beginning of the Bible's first month, which could never be earlier than

30th March, or later than 28th or 29th April. The Passover at the Exodus, when the new calendar started, was in the evening of 11th May and the Exodus was the next day, Friday, 12th May. May we add that it is a well-known fact that the 1st month of the Bible year in Old Testament times began later than that adopted by the Jews of the Dispersion.

The reader will not wish to be burdened with a number of lunar calculations so we will give the bare facts which are as follows. The New Moon of the 1st month in 1 B.C. was on 21st April and the New Moon of the 7th month was therefore on 15th October. The 15th day of this Moon or month was therefore on 29th October. The Feast began at 8 a.m. and our Lord, for reasons we will give later, was born at that hour. At 8 a.m. on 29th October 1 B.C., the mean age of the Moon was 14½ days or in the middle of the 15th day which was the appointed time according to the Law of Moses for this Feast of Jehovah. The Jews' Feast of Tabernacles was the next day as they reckoned their months from the first appearance of the Moon, as explained in Paragraph 13 of the Summary of Facts.

The following facts constitute a perfect witness to the accuracy both of the date of our Lord's birth and of the chronology from the Exodus of Israel upon which it is based. The day of our Lord's birth, namely, October 29th 1 B.C., as we have stated, was in Redemption Years the 1st day of the Feast of Tabernacles, and in Messianic Years the 1st day of the Feast of Unleavened Bread; whereas, the Exodus of Israel, which began on 12th May 1639 B.C., was in Redemption Years the 1st day of the Feast of Unleavened Bread, and in Messianic Years the 1st day of the Feast of Tabernacles – the two days and their events being separated by exactly 1638½ luni-solar years. By design of God the two events are interlocked by the chronology which must, therefore, be accurate to a day, otherwise the synchronism would not exist.

Like the first Adam who, with Eve, was created on the 6th day (Friday) our Lord Jesus Christ – "the last Adam" – was born on Friday, the Jewish 6th day. We must, however, remind the reader that the Jews' 6th day – Friday – was in Divine Time God's Sabbath, as explained in the Summary of Facts; Paragraph 14. As Jesus was also crucified on the Jews' Friday, we therefore know that in Divine Time He both entered the world and departed out of it on God's Holy Sabbath. In this connection it is important to remember that the birth of Israel as a nation took place at the Exodus from Egypt, and that the expression, "Out of Egypt have I called My Son", which Matthew applies to our Lord Jesus Christ, is taken from the prophecy of Hosea where it is applied to the nation of Israel (Matt. II, 15, & Hosea XI, 1).

As we shall make reference to our Lord's Circumcision in later pages, we only need to point out here that the 8th day from His birth, when according to the Law He must be circumcised, was current with the 8th day of the Feast of Tabernacles, namely, Friday, 5th November – the reckoning being an inclusive one. In this we again note a perfect design and realize how God in ordaining this Feast foreknew that it would embrace the first eight days of our Lord's life on the earth and thus mark Him out as the One *above all others* Who exemplified the principle which the Feast of Tabernacles was designed to set forth, namely, that man is a mere sojourner, tabernacling on the earth – Time itself being but a brief interval between two eternities.

Finally, let the fact be taken account of that on 28th October, 1019 B.C., which was the 1st day of the Feast of Tabernacles, Solomon, King of Israel, dedicated the Temple he had built according to the Divine Pattern given to him by his father, King David. It was on that day that Jehovah came down to tabernacle in the midst of His people – the occasion being marked by the descent of a cloud of glory which filled the House of the Lord (II Chron. V, 14). The One Who then descended on the 1st day of the Feast of Tabernacles was the same One – "the Word made flesh" – Who, 1018 years later was born of the Virgin Mary into this world on the 1st day of the Feast of Tabernacles, and concerning Whom John declares, "We beheld His glory, the glory as of the only begotten of the Father" (I, 14).

The Scriptures, therefore, not only reveal that Jesus of Nazareth, the Son of God, was born on Friday, 29th October, 1 B.C., because it was the 1st day of the Feast of Tabernacles, but also why that Feast had to be honoured by His birth on its 1st day and His circumcision on its last or 8th day.

# THE DATE OF OUR LORD'S BIRTH IN THE YEARS OF THE MESSIAH PERFECTLY CO-ATTESTS AND FINALLY SEALS THE FACT THAT IT TOOK PLACE ON FRIDAY, 29TH OCTOBER, 1 B.C.

Nothing is more clear than that Almighty God intended, when the time arrived, not only to restore to mankind the knowledge of the date of the birth of our Lord Jesus Christ, but to do so in such a way as to remove the subject from any further possible human speculations. So, in addition to ordaining that our Lord should be born on the first day of the Feast of Tabernacles in the 3888th Year of Redemption Chronology, He further ordained that, in the Calendar based upon the Seven Times 888 Years of the Messiah, He should be born on the 15th day of the 1st month, which is the first day of the Feast of Unleavened Bread.

In the Summary of Time (Par. 18) we showed that on the day before our Lord's birth this series of 354-day Bible Years (which are divided into twelve months of 30 and 29 days alternately, like all Bible years) had reached a total of 4204 years and 14 days. These 14 days are, therefore, the first 14 in the 1st month of the 4205th year from Adam. Our Lord was born the next day which was the 15th of the 1st month and, therefore, the first day of the Feast of Unleavened Bread, as stated in Leviticus XXIII, 6 and Numbers XXVIII, 17, etc.

What a wealth of deep meaning attaches to the fact that God ordained that His well-beloved Son should be born at the Feast of Unleavened Bread, the seven days of which typify the Christian Dispensation when the people of God are called upon to feed upon the One Who declared, "The bread of God is He which cometh down from heaven, and giveth life unto the world . . . I am the bread of life . . . he that eateth Me, even he shall live by Me" (John VI, 33, 35, 57).

No wonder, therefore, we read in Paul's first letter to the Corinthians, "For even Christ our passover is sacrificed for us: therefore let us keep the feast . . . with the unleavened bread of sincerity and truth" (V, 7, 8).

So it happens, but by Divine ordering, that this Series of Years which relates exclusively to the Person of our Lord as THE MESSIAH furnishes a date in its Calendar in perfect keeping with so momentous an event as His Birth, when, as a helpless Babe He enters a world so dominated by Evil that with His Mother and Joseph, His step-father, He very soon becomes a Fugitive, lest idolatrous Rome's overlord in Immanuel's Land should succeed, as Satan's tool, in slaying Him at birth (Matt. II, 13 and Rev. XII, 4).

In our later pages we shall show from the Scriptures that our blessed Lord and Master also laid down His life on the first day of the Feast of Unleavened Bread in the year A.D. 33, when He died for us as the Sin-Offering of that day, as required by the Law (Numbers XXVIII, 17 and 22). The fact, therefore, emerges that He was both born and died on that day – the 15th of the 1st month – which opened with the eating of the Passover and which was the beginning of Israel's Sacred and Regnal years.

* * *

In the light of the foregoing facts, no serious person could deny that our Lord Jesus Christ was born of the Virgin Mary into this world on Friday, 29th October, 1 B.C., which in the Bible's Chronology of Redemption was the 3888th year from the Fall of Adam. Neither could any deny that this Friday, 29th October, being both the first day of the Feast of Tabernacles and the first day of the Feast of Unleavened Bread, each according to its respective series of years, is stamped with a Divine impress as the day appointed for the emergence of the Son of God into this world. This is that to which the Holy Scriptures bear witness and as such it must silence for ever any further debate upon this sacred subject.

## A FEW CHRONOLOGICAL FACTS

The date of Friday, 29th October, 1 B.C., was 4,074 Solar years and 239 days from 4th March 4075 B.C., which was the first "evening and morning" of Genesis I.

This period contains 1,488,237 days.

The Years of the Messiah began after the first seven days of the Bible and this reduces the total number of days to 1,488,230. If we divide these days by 354, which is the number of days in a Messianic year, we shall find the result is 4,204 years and

14 days over. The Nativity was the next day – the 15th of the 1st month of the year 4205.

Another perfect proof of the accuracy of these measurements is to be seen in the following facts. The Bible clearly reveals, as we demonstrate in Paper IV of our former Treatise, that the Fall of Adam took place after a probationary period which lasted 40 days, like that of "the last Adam", our Lord Jesus Christ. Redemption Chronology began the next day which was a Monday – the Fall being viewed as taking place on the 8th day, a Sunday. The order of the days of the week has never changed from the start of the Bible's Redemption Chronology. If we take the 7 days of Creation and the 40 days of Adam's testing from the above total of 1,488,237 days, the result will be 1,488,190. If we divide this number by 7, the result will be 212,598 weeks and 4 days. As these weeks began with a Monday, they end with Sunday. The 4 days reach to Thursday. The Nativity was the next day – a Friday.

## THE DATE OF THE ANNUNCIATION AND INCARNATION OF OUR LORD JESUS CHRIST AT THE NEW MOON OF 23RD JANUARY, 1 B.C.

### THIS COMPLETES THE WITNESS OF THE HOLY SCRIPTURES AS TO THE DATE OF THE NATIVITY BEING FRIDAY, 29TH OCTOBER, 1 B.C.

To suggest that in bearing the Son of God the Virgin Mary was other than the normal period of 40 weeks or 280 days would be to infer that the Creator, Who, for very good reasons designed this interval between conception and birth in the human family, failed to respect it in the birth of His only begotten Son. Therefore, we may be quite sure that the circumstances surrounding our Lord's birth were perfectly normal and that He was born to the day (and probably the hour) 280 days from the Annunciation by the Angel Gabriel. The date, as we might expect, carries its own confirmation.

If we measure back 280 days from the morning of 29th October 1 B.C. (a leap year), we arrive at the morning of 23rd January, which therefore was the date of the Incarnation and doubtless also of the Annunciation. As in 280 days there are an exact number of weeks, the day must also have been a FRIDAY, like that of the birth. In Divine time that day was God's Sabbath.

It would be impossible to contemplate God commencing A NEW ERA except at a New Moon, since all Bible time is lunar. The Bible opens on the day of the New Moon. God gave Moses His instructions about the Passover and the Exodus at the New Moon of April, 1639 B.C.

The Bible reveals and lunar tables confirm (see Note below) that the Moon was new about midnight on 22nd January in 1 B.C. The Bible day called 23rd January opened at 6 P.M. on the 22nd, so that there can be no doubt that the 23rd was the day of the New Moon which was that of the 11th month. It is therefore evident that the Angel Gabriel appeared to the Virgin Mary at Nazareth at the New Moon of 23rd January 1 B.C. Neither can there be any doubt that the miraculous conception was wrought immediately after the Angel Gabriel had departed – the Virgin Mary having accepted her vocation with the words "Behold the handmaid of the Lord; be it unto me according to thy word" (Luke I. 38).

Not only had the Angel Gabriel appeared about five months previously to Zacharias, the father of John the Baptist, but in 537 B.C. he had appeared to the prophet Daniel to unfold to him the great Messianic Prophecy of the "Seventy Weeks" which would elapse to the cutting off of the Messiah (Daniel IX). This Angel evidently had the high and holy office of directly ministering on God's behalf to those on earth who, in any way, were called to have part in the Advent of the Messiah; and notably so in the case of the Israelitish Virgin of the Royal Davidic house whose womb was to be the vessel for His Emergence – "the Word (being) made flesh" therein.

How perfectly this *New Moon* date of 23rd January 1 B.C., for our Lord's Incarnation in the Virgin's womb accords with His Birth date 280 days later, at the *Full Moon* of 29th October which was the first day of the Feast of Tabernacles in the 7th month.

### NOTE ON THE MOON'S AGE AT THE INCARNATION

If anyone wishes to check the age of the Moon on 23rd January 1 B.C., or at any other time prior to May, A.D. 33, he must take account of the fact that the Bible reveals the existence of a lunar phenomenon during the death of our Lord Jesus Christ, by which the Moon's revolution was suspended for two whole days. The date of this phenomenon, as we shall prove in due course, was May 2nd and 3rd, A.D. 33. Therefore the date of any New Moon given in Lunar Tables must be placed two days earlier than what is stated. There is astronomical proof that such a phenomenon did occur, but this we will set forth later.

## THE DATES OF THE CONCEPTION AND BIRTH OF JOHN THE BAPTIST

29th August 2 B.C. – 280 days – 4th June 1 B.C.

It is beautiful to behold God in operation in relation to the birth of His only begotten Son into the world. Neither the will nor power of man has a place in the matter at all. All is planned in Heaven and executed by the power of the Holy Ghost, or by a heavenly messenger, Gabriel "that stand(s) in the presence of God", and who is sent direct from the Throne of God.

This being so, we find there is an exquisite order in relation to it all. Everything begins with Gabriel's appearance in the Temple at Jerusalem, when he is sent to tell Zacharias that his prayer for a son has been heard and will now be answered by a miraculous conception in the womb of the aged and faithful Elisabeth, his wife. Elisabeth was beyond the age for child-birth, so divine power would be in operation, as in the case of Sarah with the birth of Isaac. The offspring of these two aged parents – Zacharias and Elisabeth – would be no ordinary child. His name must be "John" which means, "the favour of Jehovah". Concerning Him the Angel declares, "He shall be great in the sight of the Lord, and shall drink neither wine nor strong drink; and he shall be filled with the Holy Ghost, even from his mother's womb. And many of the children of Israel shall he turn to the Lord their God. And he shall go before Him in the spirit and power of Elias . . . to make ready a people prepared for the Lord" (Luke I, 13 to 25).

The coming King – our Lord Jesus Christ – must be heralded by one who was capable of shaking the religious self-complacency of Israel and of bringing at least a section of this people to a deep consciousness of their sinful departure from God. According to the prophecy of Isaiah, John was "the voice of him that crieth in the wilderness, Prepare ye the way of the Lord, make straight in the desert a highway for our God" (Isai. XL, 3).

There is no need to recount the details of the birth of John the Baptist. They are all to be found in the first chapter of Luke. When we reach the point of time when John the Baptist opens his Testimony to the Messiah in A.D. 26, we shall of necessity have to make reference both to him and his mission.

The conception of our Lord took place at a New Moon and His birth at a Full Moon. It was exactly the same with the conception and birth of John the Baptist. Here, as we have remarked, we may note the perfection of the divine order.

The Bible never records what is indefinite chronologically, as such generalities would have no value. In the present case we are told Elisabeth "hid herself five months . . . and in the sixth month the angel Gabriel was sent from God . . . to a virgin espoused to a man whose name was Joseph". Gabriel's visit to Nazareth was at the New Moon of 23rd January 1 B.C. Five lunar months had passed since Elisabeth conceived the Baptist. In five lunar months there are 147 days and these extend back to 29th August 2 B.C., which was the day of the New Moon of the Bible's sixth month.

If we measure forward the normal 280 days of gestation from 29th August 2 B.C., when John was conceived, we reach 4th June 1 B.C., as the date of his birth, which of necessity is exactly five months or 147 days prior to 29th October, when our Lord was born. 4th June 1 B.C., was the day of the Full Moon of the Bible's second month.

It is a fact of great interest that John the Baptist was conceived and born on a Friday exactly like the Messiah, our Lord Jesus Christ. What is the significance of this? Undoubtedly, all time measurements relating to John, owing to his high calling, were reckoned according to the Divine Calendar which, until the Lord's death, was one day ahead of the Jewish and Roman calendars (see Par. 13 of the Summary of Facts). Therefore, in God's sight the Fridays on which John, and later Jesus, were conceived and born were all holy Sabbaths. Our Lord therefore also died on God's Sabbath in the Divine Calendar.

# HOW WE KNOW THAT OUR LORD WAS BORN AT THE HOUR OF 8 – 9 A.M.

Not only was Jesus born at 8 A.M., but all the days of His Personal Years – those dated from His birth – began at the hour of 8 – 9 A.M. This was the third hour according to Jewish reckoning, which measures the day from 6 A.M. to 6 P.M., and the ninth hour according to Roman reckoning which measures the day from Midnight to Noon and from Noon to Midnight.

In the time of Isaiah and Hezekiah, King of Judah, God, as a sign, caused the shadow of the Sun to return "ten steps" on the steps of Ahaz, which formed a kind of timepiece. Each step was designed to mark an hour of the day. (The word translated "degree' in the A. V. should have been translated, as in the R.V., "step".) The effect of this phenomenon, which caused celebrities to come from Babylon, "to enquire of the wonder that was done in the land", was to make time, as reckoned by the Moon, 10 hours ahead of time, as reckoned by the Sun, which had been retarded by that amount. Thereafter, each period of 24 hours ended at 8 A.M. instead of 6 P.M. As all Sacred Time is lunar, naturally our Lord's days began at 8 A.M. (See II Kings XX; II Chron. XXXII, 31, and Isaiah XXXVIII.) This may be inadequately expressed, nevertheless, these facts provide the reason why, in Divine reckoning, all the days of our Lord's life began at 8 A.M. The number "eight" is indelibly associated with Him throughout Scripture, as we have previously stated. The number "six" is essentially the number of man as falling short of the glory of God.

One further fact must be mentioned on this subject. In Hebrews X, 5 we read of our Lord Jesus Christ that "when He cometh into the world, He saith, Sacrifice and offering Thou wouldest not, but a body hast Thou prepared Me". At the time of our Lord's birth, namely, the third hour – 8 to 9 A.M. – the Morning Sacrifice was being offered in the Temple. This, however, had now descended to being an empty formality; hence the above words of our Lord, quoted by the Spirit, from the 40th Psalm. The fact stands out, therefore, that our blessed Lord and Master entered this world at the hour of the Morning Sacrifice – 8 to 9 A.M. – and that He made His exodus out of it at the hour of the Evening Sacrifice, which was 2 to 3 P.M., after which the Body prepared for Him was to be seen hanging lifeless upon a Tree between two malefactors, in a place called Golgotha.

## PART II

## THE INCARNATION OF THE SON OF GOD

"God sending His own Son in the likeness of sinful flesh"
(Romans VIII, 3)

O mighty stoop,
Unmeasured and immeasurable, when
Th' Eternal Son, in grace beyond all grace,
Emptied Himself of glory, and came down,
And was incarnate in the Virgin's womb!
(*Lyra Christi*, A. E. K.)

WE HAVE dealt in Part I with the date of the Incarnation, but not with the event itself. As our later pages will set forth the pathway on earth of our Lord Jesus Christ in terms of Time, it will be well for us to take serious account of its inception – namely, the occasion when He left the splendours of the Glory in which He had dwelt for eternal ages with His Father and entered the womb of the Virgin that He might take part in "flesh and blood" and, like those He had come to redeem, experience what it means to be "made in secret, and curiously wrought in the lowest parts of the earth" (Ps. CXXXIX, 15).

The fact that our Lord Jesus Christ – the Jehovah of the Old Testament – became incarnate in the womb of the Virgin Mary and was duly born of her into this world at Bethlehem in Judaea, as foretold by the Prophet Micah, is the corner stone upon and around which true Christianity is built – for if this were not true, as some have dared to suppose and others have blasphemously declared, the rest is not worth telling because our Lord, though utterly superior in all respects as a MAN, would be but another figurehead of one of earth's many "religions".

We must now briefly call to remembrance the circumstances of the Incarnation. The Angel Gabriel suddenly, and without notice, appears to an unknown maiden, in the notably corrupt town of Nazareth in Galilee, with the salutation (as it should be translated), "Hail, thou that art endued with grace, the Lord is with thee" (Luke I, 28, R.V. Margin).

Mary, with Joseph her espoused husband, was one of the small select circle of those in Immanuel's land who, amidst a decaying Judaism, were watching for Israel's redemption and the Coming of the Messiah, according to the time prophecy of Daniel IX. Endued with exceptional grace from God and, though unknown to herself, a ward of Heaven, she had been kept from all contamination with evil, a virgin – pure, pious and unaffected. Nevertheless, like all other children of Adam, she had inherited a sinful nature.

The Angel then proceeds to make his official pronouncement:

> "Fear not, Mary: for thou hast found favour with God. And, behold, thou shalt conceive in thy womb, and bring forth a Son, and shalt call His name JESUS. He shall be great, and shall be called the Son of the Highest: and the Lord God shall give unto Him the throne of His father David: and He shall reign over the house of Jacob for ever; and of His Kingdom there shall be no end"
>
> (Luke I, 30 to 33).

Such an address could leave no single doubt in the Virgin's mind that she had been called of God to be the mother of the long-awaited Messiah, Who would redeem Israel from all his enemies and restore the Kingdom. Nevertheless, the biological difficulty presents itself to her mind and this prompts her to enquire of the Angel, "How shall this be, seeing I know not a man?" This most reasonable enquiry provides occasion for the final revelation by the Angel who meets her difficulty with this awe-inspiring explanation:

> "The Holy Ghost shall come upon thee, and the power of the Most High shall overshadow thee: wherefore also that which is to be born shall be called holy, the Son of God"
>
> (Luke I, 35, R. V.).

The Virgin would understand from this that the natural order was to be wholly set aside and a miraculous conception was to take place in her womb. The first prophecy in the Bible had declared that the Seed of the woman "shall bruise" the serpent's head (Gen. III, 15). Therefore, He that should come forth from the Virgin's womb would triumph over the one who led the first woman – Eve – into the transgression, by lying about God. A child born in the natural order would be the man's seed and not the woman's. Our Lord Jesus Christ, and He alone, is the Seed of the woman, as none other has ever been, or will ever be, miraculously born of a virgin.

King David in the Psalms declares concerning himself, "Behold, I was shapen in iniquity; and in sin did my mother conceive me" (LI, 5). But our Lord's conception was not so. It was immaculate, and sin did not enter into it – man's will and natural generation being wholly set aside. It was not a case of bringing into being, by procreation, a new personality; but Eternally-existing Deity becoming incarnate – Jehovah Himself being organically clothed in the womb of the Virgin with a body of "flesh and blood". Consequently, it is written of Him:

> "Wherefore it behoved Him in all things to be made like unto His brethren, that He might be a merciful and faithful high priest in things pertaining to God, to make propitiation for the sins of the people. For in that He Himself hath suffered being tempted, He is able to succour them that are tempted"
>
> (Hebrews II, 17 and 18, R. V.).

Man, by natural generation, could not provide the race with a saviour because one sinner could not make propitiation to God for the sins of other sinners – "for all have sinned, and come short of the glory of God" (Rom. III, 23). Nevertheless, the law of God righteously demanded that one who had sold himself to be a slave could only be redeemed by a kinsman (Levit. XXV, 48, 49 et seq.). In a very real sense Eve, who, unlike Adam, was deceived and was "in the transgression" (I Tim. II, 14), sold the race to Satan – so without exception her progeny has been a race of sinners – a sinner being one who consciously or unconsciously obeys Satan and who disobeys God and His Law. For this reason, when our Lord was commissioning the Apostle Paul to go to the Gentiles, at the time of his conversion on the Damascus road, He told him "to open their eyes, and to turn them from darkness to light, and from the power of Satan unto God, that they may receive forgiveness of sins" (Acts XXVI, 18).

In becoming our Redeemer, our Lord Jesus Christ had to start where we started, namely, "in the lowest parts of the earth", that is, the womb of His Mother. Like ourselves, He had to be born a helpless Babe in utter dependence upon His Mother. He had to be a Child, an Adolescent, and a Man; and as a Man – a Representative Man – He had to fulfil Man's whole duty to God perfectly and also to His neighbour (Luke X, 27). This He did not only because He was perfect Man and could never be less than perfect, but because He was "made like unto His brethren" in order to meet those responsibilities to God and their neighbour, which the Law required, and which they had proved themselves utterly incapable of doing.

The essence of the Incarnation is that our Lord Jesus Christ came into our circumstances so that He might, *on our account*, perfectly glorify God in the keeping of His Law. But that was not all. He came to die in our stead and so remove our guilt by making propitiation for our sins. Again, we are told that He "took part" in flesh and blood "that through death He might destroy (annul) him that had the power of death, that is, the devil" (Hebrews II, 14).

More we need not say. The Incarnation of our Lord and Saviour, Jesus Christ, in the womb of the Virgin Mary is the central fact of the whole Bible narrative because only thus could He be our Redeemer and only thus could He annul the power of "that old serpent, called the Devil, and Satan, which deceiveth the whole world" (Rev. XII, 9).

A Christian is one who has accepted the testimony of the Bible concerning our Lord Jesus Christ. That testimony opens with a precise account of how He was born into this world of the Virgin Mary, following a miraculous and sinless conception in her womb. This was His starting-point as far as this earth is concerned, but let it never be forgotten that, prior to this, He eternally existed in the Godhead as the only begotten Son with the Father. Neither dare we for a moment forget that though He became Man, and for a while voluntarily laid aside His Godhead power and glory, humbling Himself even unto the death of the Cross, He was none the less God – God manifest in flesh, God our Saviour. With what solemn right then can He address those He came to redeem with the warning, "If ye believe not that I am He, ye shall die in your sins" (John VIII, 24).

## THE BIRTH OF JESUS OF NAZARETH AT BETHLEHEM IN JUDAEA

Samuel anointed David to be King over Israel in Bethlehem, the native place of his father Jesse. The Angel Gabriel had affirmed to the Virgin Mary, in whose veins ran the blood of the Royal Davidic dynasty, through Nathan, that God would give her Firstborn Son "the throne of His father David". It was to be expected, therefore, that "great David's Greater Son" should be born at Bethlehem in Judaea, exactly as appointed by God through the Prophet Micah who declared, "But thou, Beth-lehem Ephratah . . . out of thee shall He come forth unto Me that is to be Ruler in Israel; Whose goings forth have been from of old, from everlasting" (V, 2). The means that God employed, namely, the Augustan decree, to cause Joseph to take the Virgin, then "great with child", the seventy or more miles from Nazareth to Bethlehem is recorded by Luke (chap. II) and is too well known to require comment.

From the humane aspect, nothing could have been more unfortunate than that Mary should have had to leave home with what comforts it provided, not to mention relatives and friends, and go to a place where, as it proved, she could not even obtain the sanctity of an apartment when giving birth to her Royal Firstborn Son, Whom, we are told, she wrapped "in swaddling clothes, and laid . . . in a manger; because there was no room for them in the inn" (Luke II, 7).

Mary, however, had been yoked to one of God's mightiest purposes and no doubt received grace and help in the trying circumstances in which she found herself. But what a significance all this gives to our Lord's words on the last evening of His life, when He said, "A woman when she is in travail hath sorrow, because her hour is come: but as soon as she is delivered of the child, she remembereth no more the anguish, for joy that a man is born into the world" (John XVI, 21).

No doubt, transcendent joy was Mary's portion as she held the Child Jesus in her arms. Truly she could again say, "He that is mighty hath done to me great things; and holy is His Name".

It is important to remember that because the Saviour was born at the Feast of Tabernacles in the 7th month, multitudes had gathered from all over the land of Israel, as the law required that all men should come to Jerusalem three times in the year – for the Feast of the Passover, the Feast of Weeks or Pentecost, and the Feast of Tabernacles (Deut. XVI, 16). Bethlehem was only six miles from Jerusalem and, like all other places contiguous to the Holy City, would have been overflowing with pilgrims. It was this fact that caused Joseph to have to accept what was nothing more than the shelter afforded by a stable or out-house for the accouchement of the Virgin.

Nevertheless, God allowed all these circumstances in connection with the birth of our Lord Jesus Christ, Who, though a King and presently to be "King of kings", must be born in the humblest manner conceivable, and take His place among the poorest in Israel, as an expression of His thoughts about the pomp and glory of a world that lived joyfully in total alienation from its Creator, and which, acting characteristically, provided His Son with nothing better than a stable for a birthplace, because "there was no room for them in the inn" – a fact the Spirit of God carefully places on record. It will be said that those in the inn did not know Mary was going to give birth to "the Son of God – the King of Israel". Truly enough, they had no idea of such a thing, and if the lowly pair had intimated it, they would have been laughed to scorn. No, indeed, if God acts in the world, He takes good care that His actions are apart from the world. It was only an elect few who were in the secret that the Messiah had been born and was alive on the earth.

If the world remains totally unaware that the Greatest Event in the history of the Universe has just transpired in the birth of the Son of God upon the earth, Heaven takes full cognizance of the fact and sends an angel, not to the high and mighty, but to a few lowly and despised shepherds, to announce the "good tidings of great joy, which shall be to all people" for, said the angel, "unto you is born this day in the city of David a Saviour, which is Christ the Lord" (Luke II, 10 and 11). And, as if to confirm the message, "suddenly there was with the angel a multitude of the heavenly host praising God, and saying, Glory to God in the highest, and on earth peace, good will toward men". The faith of these shepherds is rewarded and they are the only strangers to see "the Babe lying in a manger". It is a humbling thought for Israel that these lowly shepherds were the only ones to receive a direct communication from God concerning the Advent of the Messiah in the midst of His people. Perhaps this was because the Babe they had beheld was Himself none other than "the Shepherd of Israel" Who had come to gather His flock and feed it in green pastures of His own providing (Isaiah XL, 11).

We are told that "the shepherds returned, glorifying and praising God for all the things they had heard and seen" and that they "made known abroad the saying which was told them concerning this Child" (Luke II, 17 and 20).

As the visit of the "wise men from the East" clearly took place no less than two years after our Lord's birth, we will comment upon it, and the flight into Egypt, after our remarks on the Circumcision and Presentation of the Infant Jesus in the Temple.

## THE CIRCUMCISION OF THE INFANT JESUS

*Date: Friday, 5th November* 1 B.C.

We are told that our Lord, as the Son of God, was "made of a woman, made under the law" (Gal. IV, 4). (The word "made" signifies "came into being".) Therefore the whole scene of our Lord's birth is Jewish. The Law made circumcision absolutely obligatory on the "eighth day" (Lev. XII, 3). This is because the Fall of Adam is viewed in the Bible as occurring on the 8th day; and in a spiritual sense circumcision is the renouncing of the Fall.

We read in Luke II, 21, "And when eight days were accomplished for the circumcising of the Child, His name was called JESUS, which was so named of the angel before He was conceived in the womb". No doubt, in the secret counsels of the Most High, our Lord, with His incarnation in view, was named Jesus before the ages began, because the Seven cycles of 888 Messianic years which began on the 8th day from Creation are founded upon the numerical value of His Name – IESOUS – according to the Greek spelling. Jesus is our Lord's Name in the days of His humiliation – "Jesus of Nazareth". Yet how many millions there are to-day who have learnt to know Him as

JEHOVAH THE SAVIOUR, and who rejoice to sing, "How sweet the Name of Jesus sounds in a believer's ear".

On the surface the Bible gives us no details about our Lord's circumcision, save that it was then that He formally received the Name – Jesus. We have already demonstrated the fact that our Lord was born on the first day of the Feast of Tabernacles, which was the 15th of the 7th month. As He was circumcised on the eighth day from His birth, this must have occurred on the 8th day of the Feast – that which on a later occasion John calls "the last day, that great day of the feast" when "Jesus stood and cried, saying, If any man thirst, let him come unto Me, and drink" (John VII, 37). This fact reveals how closely our Lord was identified with the Feast of Tabernacles. The Roman or Gentile date was Friday 5th November 1 B.C. So the first eight days of our Lord's life on the earth had now passed. How deeply humbling it is to realize that these eight days were spent with His Mother and Joseph, living in a stable with a manger doing service in place of a cradle. How literally true, therefore, are the words, "Ye know the grace of our Lord Jesus Christ, that, though He was rich, yet for your sakes He became poor, that ye through His poverty might be rich" (II Cor. VIII, 9).

## THE PRESENTATION TO GOD OF THE INFANT JESUS IN THE TEMPLE

Date: Wednesday, 8th December 1 B.C.

We are told that "when the days of her (Mary's) purification according to the law of Moses were accomplished, they brought Him (i.e., Jesus) to Jerusalem, to present Him to the Lord" (Luke II, 22). The days of purification when a son was born were forty – that is, thirty-three days after the Circumcision. As our Lord was born on the morning of Friday, 29th October, the 40 days of Mary's purification would end on the morning of Wednesday, 8th December. Directly that day was reached, Mary and Joseph brought the humblest of the offerings allowed for that occasion, namely, "a pair of turtledoves, or two young pigeons" (see Leviticus XII).

The doing of this provided an opportunity to fulfil another ordinance of the Law which required that "every male that openeth the womb shall be called holy to the Lord". So Jesus is brought into the Temple to be presented to God, and in an incipient degree this was the fulfilling of the prophecy, "the Lord, whom ye seek, shall suddenly come to His temple" (Mal. III, 1). It becomes a great occasion and the Holy Ghost uses it to form a link between the faithful remnant in Jerusalem and the Infant, Jesus, Who is at once acknowledged by them as the Messiah – the Salvation of God.

It is of the utmost importance to take note of the fact that, howsoever evil the mass may be, whether in Israel or in Christendom, the Spirit of God always has human vessels for His use in a remnant that is faithful to God and His revealed Truth, and which stands apart from all people and things that have become apostate. The Virgin Remnant in Judah came into being in the days of Isaiah the prophet and continued to exist right through until the time of our Lord's birth – the Virgin Mary herself and Joseph being of their number.

On the occasion of the Lord's presentation in the Temple, the Holy Ghost rewards these faithful ones, among whom Simeon and Anna are named, by allowing them actually to see the Child – Jesus – or to hear first-hand from those who had seen Him (Luke II, 25 to 38).

The aged Simeon, who had received a precious promise from the Holy Ghost that he should behold the Christ before his death, is guided to enter the Temple just when Mary is presenting Him according to the Law. The Spirit then uses Simeon to declare that Jesus is the One of whom Isaiah prophesied, "A light to lighten the Gentiles, and the glory of Thy people, Israel" (see Isaiah XLII, 6).

Furthermore, the Holy Ghost uses Simeon to utter a most solemn prophecy concerning the Child, Jesus. This he does in these terms while bestowing His blessing on Mary and Joseph, our Lord's legal father:

> "Behold, this child is set for the fall and rising again of many in Israel; and for a sign which shall be spoken against; (yea, a sword shall pierce through thy own soul also,) that the thoughts of many hearts may be revealed".

In the light of our Lord's rejection by Israel and of the sword that pierced through Mary's soul, when she beheld her first-born Son hanging on a Tree between two malefactors, we can discern the poignant accuracy of Simeon's prophecy.

In this connection we may mention a most remarkable sequel to this prediction in recent history. The session of our Lord in death, as we shall perfectly establish in due course, was two days and nine hours. This period finds symbolical expression in chronology throughout the Bible in various forms – in this case a thousand years being typical of one day (II Peter III, 8) and one year being typical of one hour. The date of Simeon's prophecy was 8th December 1 B.C. Two thousand Bible years (of 354 days) thereafter was 17th May 1939, the day Britain abrogated the Palestine Mandate and presented to Parliament the infamous White Paper forbidding any more Jews to return to the Land of Israel after 1944. (This measurement excludes the two complete days our Lord was in death.) Nine years later, on 17th May 1948, Russia gave *de jure* recognition to the State of Israel which had been resurrected at Midnight on 14th May when it was instantly given *de facto* recognition by the United States. Russia's act sealed the resurrection of the Nation of Israel as it meant that the two greatest Powers had officially recognized her as an independent State. So we see that to the day the State of Israel was raised into being after Two "Days" of 1000 years and Nine "Hours" (or years) from Simeon's prophecy concerning "the fall and rising again of many in Israel". It will be easier to appreciate the immense significance of this measurement when we have shown from the Bible that two days and nine hours was the actual period between our Lord's death and His resurrection. But all can see how it links Simeon's prophecy with that of Hosea who declared concerning Israel, "after two days will He revive us: in the third day He will raise us up". (Hosea VI, 2.)

## WISE MEN FROM THE EAST COME TO WORSHIP THE NEW-BORN KING OF THE JEWS

### THE IMMENSE SIGNIFICANCE OF THIS EVENT WHEN OUR LORD WAS TWO YEARS OF AGE

Read Matthew II, Luke II, 39 and Zechariah XIV, 16

When all the facts connected with the Visit of the Wise Men

of the East to Jerusalem are brought to bear upon the event it will be seen for what it was, namely, a direct act of God with a deep symbolical significance.

From whatever country in the East they came, it is clear that they were men of the highest rank whose arrival in Jerusalem was an event of no little importance. The object of their visit was stated in the most precise terms, as follows:

> "Where is He that is born King of the Jews? For we have seen His star in the east, and are come to worship Him".

They did not ask if the King of the Jews had been born because they had received a Divine intimation of that fact on the day of His Birth by the appearing of His Star in the heavens, as they affirmed. Their one enquiry was limited to the present whereabouts of the King born to the Jews, so that they could pay Him homage and present Him with their gifts.

The nature and urgency of their enquiry was such as to remove all uncertainty from the minds of the Jewish Authorities, and word to this effect reached the ears of Herod, so we read, "When Herod the king had heard these things, he was troubled, and all Jerusalem with him".

It is quite clear that through these Gentiles from the East God was giving to official Jewry and its Idumean monarch the first positive intimation that "MESSIAH THE PRINCE" of Daniel's prophecy (IX) had been born into the world.

The very suggestion that One had already been born who could lay claim to the allegiance of the Jews and a right to the royal Davidic Throne filled Herod with the utmost dismay and determined him to take steps to forestall any such catastrophe. Without in any way disclosing his purpose, Herod "gathered all the chief priests and scribes of the people together" (i.e. the Sanhedrin) and "demanded of them where (the) Christ should be born". Having no notion of what was in Herod's mind, they inform him that Bethlehem of Judaea is the place foretold by the Prophet Micah for the birth of Israel's Messiah. They quote Micah's prophecy in support of this fact, "And thou Bethlehem, in the land of Juda . . . out of thee shall come a Governor, that shall rule My people Israel" (Matt. II, 6 and Micah V, 2).

That was all Herod wanted to know for it put him in the position to answer the enquiry of the Wise Men as to the place where Judah's King must have been born. We know from

Revelation XII, 3 and 4, that it was Satan who was directing and inspiring Herod's actions in this matter. We are not, therefore, surprised that Herod acted with great cunning. Without letting anyone know (i.e. "privily") he called the Wise Men and "enquired of them diligently (lit. precisely) what time the star appeared". Having learnt the exact time, he directs them to go to Bethlehem to "search diligently for the young Child . . . that I may come and worship Him also".

Satan may have been at the back of Herod, but God was at the back of these Gentile Wise Men, for no sooner had they left Herod and started for Bethlehem than "the star, which they saw in the east, went before them, till it came and stood over where the young Child was" and "when they saw the star, they rejoiced with exceeding great joy", that is, they were exultant at receiving a Divine confirmation of so positive an order concerning the Advent of Judah's King.

Before taking account of the Wise Men's actions on reaching "the house" where Mary and Joseph and "the young Child" lived, it is necessary to take careful note that when later Herod carried out his Satanic device of slaying all the children in Bethlehem in the hope of destroying the young King of the Jews, he decreed that these were to be "from two years old and under, *according to the time he had diligently enquired of the wise men*" (v. 16). From this fact we know that the Wise Men must have told Herod that the Star which was given to bear witness to the birth of Judah's King had appeared "two years" before their visit to Jerusalem. They had doubtless given Herod to know the exact day when they saw the Star and received a Divine intimation as to the object of its appearance. Herod, guided by this accurate information, decreed that all children from "two years old and under" were to be slain.

Once the significance of these "two years" is seen this whole incident takes on a new meaning, for this is one of a multitude of incidents in our Lord's earthly pathway in which the Time factor proves to be the key by which access is gained to facts otherwise inaccessible. To start with, Mary, with the Infant Jesus and Joseph, returned to Nazareth directly after the Presentation in the Temple on 8th December, 1 B.C., as stated in Luke II, 39. For this reason, when God saw the Wise Men setting out for Bethlehem He caused the Star to appear again and by its movement directed them to Nazareth, until it rested over the very house where "the young Child with Mary His mother" dwelt. The Wise Men, therefore, never went to Bethlehem as is so often erroneously stated.

God, for a most perfect reason, had moved the Wise Men to delay their visit to Jerusalem for about two years. By that time the Infant King would have become "the young Child", as our Lord is always called in this chapter. A boy of two years and able to walk is very different from an infant in arms.

As we well know, our Lord was born on the first day of the Feast of Tabernacles in 1 B.C. When all the facts are considered it becomes perfectly evident that God planned that these Gentiles should arrive at Nazareth and accomplish their mission of worshipping the King of the Jews on the second lunar anniversary of His birth, that is, on the 1st day of the Feast of Tabernacles in the year A.D. 2 – the date of which was 7th October.

Now these first "two years" of our Lord's life were designed by God to be symbolical of the whole Christian Dispensation which everywhere in the Bible is viewed as being two "days" of a thousand years each. (See the following types: Joshua III, 4, Hosea VI, 2, and Luke X, 35.) In actuality, as we demonstrate in our former Treatise, *The World in Liquidation*, the 2,000 Bible years of the Christian Dispensation ran their course from 12th October A.D. 33, to 12th June 1933, when, as we there prove, the Six Thousand Years of Man ended and the world entered "the consummation of the age", which is an extra-dispensational chronological hiatus leading up to the establishment of the Kingdom of God over the earth.

It is revealed by the Prophet Zechariah that when the Kingdom is established Gentiles are to come every year to Jerusalem at the Feast of Tabernacles to do exactly what the Wise Men did on the first day of that Feast when our Lord was "two years" old.

In Zechariah XIV, 16, we read, "Every one that is left of all the nations . . . shall even go up from year to year to worship the King, the Lord of hosts, and to keep the feast of tabernacles". And of the Wise Men we read that they said, "Where is He that is born King of the Jews? . . . we . . . are come to worship Him". Who could doubt for a minute that it was God Who had planned that Gentiles should be found worshipping His King at the Feast of Tabernacles after these two symbolical years – the first two in our Lord's life – had elapsed.

It is very clear that these Wise Men were impelled in their quest by knowledge gained through the Jewish Scriptures. This would have come to them from Jews who had been dispersed through the East at the time of the Assyrian and Babylonian captivities. Daniel, whose prophecy of the coming of "Messiah the Prince" these Wise Men must have known, was himself Head of the College of Wise Men in Babylon in his day. Balaam's prophecy, "There shall come a Star out of Jacob, and a Sceptre shall rise out of Israel", must also have been known to them (Numbers XXIV, 17). It is, indeed, almost certain that these Wise Men acted upon the prophecy of Zechariah from which they would learn that it was obligatory upon Gentiles to go up to Jerusalem every Feast of Tabernacles "to worship the King, the Lord of hosts" (Zechariah XIV, 16).

Let note also be taken of this fact. In referring to Herod's action in the slaughter of all children under two years old, Matthew quotes Jeremiah's prophecy, "In Rama was there a voice heard, lamentation, and weeping, and great mourning, Rachel weeping for her children, and would not be comforted, because they are not". When we turn to Jeremiah XXXI, where this utterance is found (v. 15), we find the context relates to the time when Israel is being gathered back to their land (v. 10) – an event fulfilled before our eyes since 1933, when the 2000 years of the Christian Dispensation ended, as mentioned above. And could not Jeremiah's prophecy be applied in reference to Hitler's terrible holocaust when 6,000,000 of Rachel's children were done to deaths too terrible to contemplate? Surely, between 1942 and 1945, when this terrible work was accomplished, there was "lamentation and bitter weeping: Rachel weeping for her children . . . because they were not". Who can say whether this was not the actual fulfilment of this prophecy which had its incipient fulfilling in the slaughter of the innocents?

The record in Matthew II states concerning the arrival of the Wise Men at Nazareth:

> "And when they were come into the house, they saw the young Child with Mary His mother, and fell down, and

worshipped Him (lit. did homage): and when they had opened their treasures, they presented unto Him gifts; gold, and frankincense, and myrrh" (v. 11).

So the object of the Wise Men, by the ordering, grace and guidance of God, was perfectly accomplished and they were evidently the first Gentiles to be allowed to see and do homage to God's King; and their act formed a perfect symbol of that day when Gentiles from all over the earth will come to Jerusalem at the Feast of Tabernacles, "to worship the King, the Lord of hosts".

It is to be noted that on this occasion there is no mention of Joseph being present during the visit of the Wise Men to Nazareth. This is to be explained by the fact that he had gone to Jerusalem to keep the Feast of Tabernacles, as required by the Law applying to all males (Deut. XVI, 16).

## THE FLIGHT OF JOSEPH AND MARY WITH THE YOUNG CHILD INTO EGYPT

As all know, God visited Joseph in a dream and told him to "take the young Child and His mother, and flee into Egypt . . . for Herod will seek the young Child to destroy Him". Here again we see how God countered Satan's moves through Herod, for though it was the children in Bethlehem who were massacred, word might be passed to Herod's minions that Joseph and Mary with a Child born in Bethlehem had later left for Nazareth. Be that as it may, there was a prophecy which necessitated that our Lord, like the elect nation among whom He arose, must sojourn for a while in Egypt. That prophecy (Hosea XI, 1) quoted by Matthew was "Out of Egypt have I called My Son".

We have seen how the birth of Israel as a nation is interlocked chronologically with our Lord's birth – both occurring, in their respective Calendars, at the Feast of Tabernacles and the Feast of Unleavened Bread. Now we shall see that just as Israel anticipated the above prophecy by being called "out of Egypt" at the Passover in 1639 B.C., so Jesus, God's beloved

Son, was likewise called "out of Egypt" at the Passover in the year A.D. 3, when it was on 3rd May, which was the 14th of Nisan in that year.

The Bible reveals, therefore, that the death of Herod the Great took place just before the Passover of A.D. 3, and profane history, *when understood*, confirms this fact.

There were exactly Seven Months between the Feast of Tabernacles in A.D. 2 and the Passover in A.D. 3, due to the fact that there was an intercalation of one month in that year. These seven months, apart from the hasty journey thereto, were spent in Egypt and the period is once again a symbolical one which we will briefly attempt to explain.

We have seen that by design of God our Lord's first two years are symbolical of the two thousand years of the Christian Dispensation from A.D. 33 to 1933. Just as His two years were followed by seven months in Egypt, so the 2000 years (apart from the present hiatus) are followed by the seven years of the Book of Revelation (see chapters XI and XII), when a remnant of the Jews are driven out of their land by a tyrant who, like Herod, will be Devil-inspired. The XIIth chapter of the Revelation links our Lord's birth and Satan's effort to destroy Him with this coming tyrant's success in driving a remnant of the Jews, who will then believe in our Lord as their Messiah, from their land. The 1260 days of verse 6 and the "time, times and half a time" of verse 14 make up the 7 years.

It is clear that, as the prophecy "Out of Egypt have I called My Son" applied both to Israel and to our Lord, He, like Israel, must have made His exodus from Egypt with Mary and Joseph at the Passover. Once it is seen that all movements connected with our Lord were according to a pre-ordained Pattern, it requires but little faith or spiritual intelligence to fill in the detail – the capacity to do which depends upon one's knowledge of the Pattern.

We know, therefore, that the return to Nazareth from Egypt took place in early May, A.D. 3, as we read, "an angel of the Lord appeareth in a dream to Joseph in Egypt, saying, Arise, and take the young Child and His mother, and go into the land of Israel". Matthew, after certain details, closes his account of this wondrous episode with these words:

"And He came and dwelt in a city called Nazareth: that

it might be fulfilled which was spoken by the prophets, He shall be called a Nazarene".

## THE TIME PATTERN OF OUR LORD'S LIFE AS RECORDED IN THE GOSPEL BY LUKE

### THE SUBLIME SIMPLICITY OF THE CHRONOLOGY OF THE FOUR GOSPELS

We shall now very briefly give the reader a bird's-eye view of the years of the Saviour's life on the earth. When a few simple but very important facts are taken into account the whole subject of Time in His life becomes clear and devoid of all complexity.

Up to the Exodus of Israel from Egypt TIME in the Bible is only recorded in terms of the civil lunar year of exactly 354 days, irrespective of the Sun, Moon or Seasons. Just before the Exodus, as we have already stated, God gave to Moses and Aaron a new Calendar. This was luni-solar, that is, it retained the civil lunar year of 354 days but, as this was short of a solar year by over 11 days, every 3 or 2 years an extra month of 30 or 31 days was added, so as to delay the start of the next year until the Spring season. This luni-solar Calendar remained in operation until 12th October A.D. 33, and was, therefore, in vogue when our Lord was on the earth. It is this Calendar which lies on the surface of the Bible after Exodus XII.

It did not, however, please God to measure the years of our Lord's personal pathway, as recorded in the Bible, by this luni-solar series of years with their intercalated thirteenth months, because the Sacred Years of the Bible are exclusively of 354 days and totally ignore all intercalations. All will readily appreciate that God could not allow any of the days of His Son's sinless life to be unrecorded or ignored, since to Him every day and hour was redolent with a fragrance arising from an unfaltering obedience, not one minute of which could be lost to God, His Father, or to man, His fellow.

Accordingly, the life of our Lord Jesus is given only in terms of straight unbroken years of 354 days each, exactly like the years of the Patriarchs up to the Exodus. *God evidently determined that our Lord's life should have a chronology of its own, measured as a series of pure Sacred Years of 354 days each.* Let it, therefore, be clearly understood that any chronological reference in the Scriptures to the Person of our Lord is expressed in terms of His own personal chronology, which began at the hour of His birth, on 29th October 1 B.C., and continued to the day and hour of His Ascension into Heaven on 13th June A.D. 33 – His age then being 33 years and 233 days, or in solar terms, 32 years and 227 days.

## OUR LORD'S PERSONAL CHRONOLOGY IS RECORDED EXCLUSIVELY IN THE GOSPEL BY LUKE

It was given to the Evangelist Luke to mark out the chronological era covered by the Four Gospels and this he does by adopting the years of our Lord's Personal Chronology. John gives chronological order to the years of our Lord's Public Ministry – his characteristic expression being, "after these things".

Luke's references cover an unbroken series of 34 years of 354 days each, which are measured from the day of our Lord's birth on 29th October 1 B.C., to the end of 11th October A.D. 33, when, as we will later reveal, the martyrdom of Stephen took place and when, as a result of the rejection of Peter's appeal for its repentance, the Jewish nation was "cut down" and the era termed "the times of the Gentiles" began.

Luke composes these 34 years in the following order. His most important reference to time in our Lord's life is found in Chapter III, verse 23, which the Revised Version accurately translates thus:

> "And Jesus Himself, when He began *to teach*, was about thirty years of age".

In Luke XIII, verse 7, our Lord is heard to say concerning Israel:

> "Behold, these three years I come seeking fruit on this fig tree, and find none: cut it down; why cumbereth it the ground?"

In Luke XIII, verses 8 and 9, the One addressed replies,

"Lord, let it alone this year also, till I shall dig about it, and dung it: and if it bear fruit, well: and if not, then after that Thou shalt cut it down".

In these verses we have positive reference to 34 consecutive years of 354 days each. We say "positive" because the Bible indulges in no indefinite time references as they would be quite useless. Neither need any think that Luke's use of the word "about", when referring to our Lord's age of 30 years when He began His public life, implies indefiniteness, for, as Prof. Sir W. M. Ramsay writes in his book *Was Christ born at Bethlehem?* "It is a characteristic usage in Greek to employ this vague expression, when there is no intention to imply doubt as to the age" (Chapter X). Our Lord was to the day and hour, 30 Bible years of age when He emerged from private life to take His place publicly as the One of Whom God speaks in Isaiah XLII, 1, "Behold My Servant, Whom I uphold" (cf. Numbers IV, 3, 23, 30, 39, 47; Genesis XLI, 46, etc.).

Thirty Bible years of 354 days from 29th October 1 B.C. reach to 26th November A.D. 29 – being equivalent to 29 Solar years and 28 days. On this 26th November A.D. 29, as recorded in John I, 35 to 39, our Lord opened His public Ministry and was joined by two disciples.

Three years of 354 days from 26th November A.D. 29, reach to 23rd October A.D. 32. This was the 1st day of Israel's 7th month and in it our Lord uttered the words quoted in Luke XIII, 7. For exactly 3 years He had striven with His own nation but without reaching its hardened conscience. No fruit had Israel yielded to God and, therefore, the Messiah purposes there and then to cut the nation down. Being reasoned with, and still hoping the antitypical "fig tree" would respond to the treatment of the Dresser of the Vineyard, our Lord grants *one further year of clemency* to Israel. If there was then no response He would cut the fig tree down.

"This year also" was the year of 354 days from 23rd October A.D. 32 to 11th October A.D. 33. In that year, between 1st and 4th May, our Lord died and rose, and on 13th June ascended into Heaven – the Holy Ghost descending upon the believing Jews at Pentecost which was 22nd June. For three or four months after this the Apostles of our Lord pleaded with their nation and sought its repentance, but without avail. On the last day of this year, that is, on 11th October, as we will later show, Stephen was killed and the nation of Israel was "cut down" for the Gentile age which began the next day, namely, 12th October A.D. 33.

It was thus that the 34 Bible years from our Lord's birth were completed – the period being just 18 days short of 33 Solar years.

We have not made mention of the twelve years named in Luke II, 42, when as a Youth our Lord went up to Jerusalem with His parents for the Passover.

It will thus be seen that Luke gives a sequence of four dates in our Lord's life which may be tabulated thus:

| | |
|---|---|
| Our Lord Jesus Christ born 29th October 1 B.C. | — |
| Luke II, 42. Our Lord Jesus Christ, 12 years 16th June A.D. 12 | 12 years |
| Luke III, 23. Our Lord Jesus Christ, 30 years 26th November A.D. 29 | 18 years |
| Luke XIII, 7. Our Lord Jesus Christ, 33 years 23rd October A.D. 32 | 3 years |
| Luke XIII, 8, 9. 1 year, 11th October A.D. 33 | 1 year |
| The period from 29th October 1 B.C. to 11th October A.D. 33 | 34 years |

Our Lord died when He was 33 years and 191 days and He ascended 42 days later when He was 33 years and 233 days of age.

Luke, therefore, with the utmost precision accounts for every day in these 34 years as the Bible year of 354 days has no fractions. It is quite simple to convert these years into our Solar years or the Bible's luni-solar years at any point of time.

Apart from the visit of the Wise Men when our Lord was but Two Years of age, and the incident in Luke II when He was Twelve Years of age in A.D. 12, there is no named point of time in the Bible until the opening of John the Baptist's Ministry, as recorded in Luke III, at which date a period of Seven Years and Seven Weeks or 49 days opens to our Lord's Ascension into Heaven.

As we shall see in the course of our narrative, John's testimony to Israel began on 25th April A.D. 26, which is the most heavily emphasized date in the Bible. John's sole Ministry continued to 5th October A.D. 29 – a period inclusively of 1,260 days – when our Lord was baptized, the day being Israel's Day of Atonement. After an interval of 51 days, which included 7 days with John and the 40 days of the Temptation, our Lord, being 30 years of age, began His Ministry on 26th November A.D. 29. From 26th November A.D. 29, to His Ascension on 13th June A.D. 33, was a period of exactly 3 Solar years and 200 days – the last 40 being His Resurrection Ministry.

We are indebted to John's Gospel for the chronological framework of our Lord's public Ministry. In John II, 13, we have the Passover of A.D. 30. The Feast of John V is the Day of Atonement in A.D. 31. John VI, 4 gives the Passover of A.D. 32, and John VII, 2, the Feast of Tabernacles in A.D. 32. John XI, 55, gives the Passover in A.D. 33, when the Saviour died. The Passover of A.D. 31 is not mentioned. The Lord's Public Ministry, therefore, embraced Four Passovers. He only attended at Jerusalem for that of A.D. 30.

It will be appreciated by all from the foregoing facts that the Four Gospels contain an absolutely perfect chronological record from the Conception and Birth of John the Baptist to the Ascension of our Lord Jesus Christ into Heaven.

Without any question, this period of years was the most important in human history but more notably so the last Seven Years and Seven Weeks which embraced the Testimonies of our Lord Jesus Christ and of John His faithful Herald.

# PART III

## THE FACTS FROM THE HOLY SCRIPTURES WHICH PERFECTLY ESTABLISH THAT OUR LORD JESUS CHRIST WAS BORN AT THE FEAST OF TABERNACLES IN 1 B.C.

### HOW THE ERRONEOUS DATE OF 4 B.C. CAME TO BE ACCEPTED BY MANY

IN THIS brief section of our Treatise we have simply to show

how the Bible reveals that our Lord Jesus Christ was born in the year 1 B.C., and not, as generally accepted, in 4 B.C. The actual day and date of His birth in 1 B.C. is arrived at by means of the quite obvious assumption that it took place at the Feast of Tabernacles. This assumption would not, however, be obvious to any but those students of the Bible who have a knowledge of the typical significance of these Levitical anniversaries.

It will be seen as we proceed that a limited amount of knowledge of Biblical Prophecy is also essential in arriving at the actual year of the Saviour's birth. The date of His birth is, however, nowhere prophesied but there is one positive chronological prediction as to the year when John the Baptist would commence his testimony to Israel concerning the Appearing of the Messiah and this is the foundation date of the New Testament, that upon which its whole chronological structure rests.

Because of the difficulties of Bible chronology and the apparent paucity of information on the subject in the Gospels, people, in seeking the truth as to the time of the Lord's birth, have to the greatest extent confined themselves to fields of research extraneous to the Scriptures. The writings of the early Church fathers have been carefully canvassed and compared; but these are so vague and so often at variance with one another that no one has been able to discover the true date. It is only fair to state, however, that deductions from this source have clearly indicated that our Lord was born in 1 B.C., but these though accurate, were always open to challenge because of the absence of actual proof from the Bible itself.

The Bible is a self-contained series of Books that have God as their Author. It is always self-confirmatory and requires no kind of confirmation as to its accuracy from outside sources. Archaeology, profane history, the early fathers, etc., etc., may all contribute facts which agree with what is in the Bible, but they do not confirm the Bible – rather is it that the Bible confirms them. To suggest otherwise is to infer that statements in the Bible must be confirmed from independent sources before being accepted. This is infidelity *ad nauseam* and such views have turned myriads away from the simple faith held by our forefathers that the Bible is the inspired Word of God – a fact which this Treatise will abundantly confirm.

## THE FOUNDATION DATE OF THE NEW TESTAMENT IS A.D. 26 WHEN "THE WORD OF GOD CAME UNTO JOHN"

Luke informs us that our Lord was born in the reign of Augustus Caesar (II, 1) and that John the Baptist opened his testimony to the Messiah in "the reign" of Tiberius Caesar.

In Luke III, 1 and 2, we find what is by far the most heavily underscored date in the whole Bible.

It is as follows:

> "Now in the fifteenth year of the reign of Tiberius Caesar, Pontius Pilate being governor of Judaea, and Herod being tetrarch of Galilee, and his brother Philip tetrarch of Ituraea and of the region of Trachonitis, and Lysanias the tetrarch of Abilene, Annas and Caiaphas being the high priests, the word of God came unto John the son of Zacharias in the wilderness".

It will be obvious to all that Luke was caused by way of emphasis to give the complete category of Roman overlords who dominated the land of Israel "in the fifteenth year of the reign of Tiberius Caesar" because, on a given day in that year, John the Baptist commenced his appointed task of preparing "the way of the Lord".

Isaiah had foretold John's arrival with the words, "the voice of him that crieth in the wilderness, Prepare ye the way of the Lord, make straight in the desert a highway for our God" (XL, 3). Three hundred years later Malachi again foretells John's arrival with the words, "Behold, I will send My messenger, and he shall prepare the way before Me" (III, 1). With such predictions concerning the one who was to precede the Messiah and prepare His way, it is not surprising that the Scripture lays the utmost emphasis on the date when they were fulfilled and when John actually first lifted up his voice in the Wilderness of Judaea with the words, "Repent ye: for the kingdom of heaven is at hand".

Before quoting the great Messianic time prophecy of Daniel IX which foretells the actual year when John the Baptist would commence his ministry in Israel of preparing "the way of the Lord", we will give the evidence of profane history as to the year in the Solar calendar which was current with "the fifteenth year of the reign of Tiberius Caesar".

Augustus Caesar died in August, A.D. 14, and was then succeeded by Tiberius his step-son as sole ruler of the Empire. In this case the 15th year of Tiberius's reign would be from August, A.D. 28, to August, A.D. 29. When, however, we examine Luke's statement, we find that with the utmost precision, because perfectly cognisant of the facts, he uses the Greek word HEGEMONIA in relation to the 15th year and not the common word for "reign" which is BASILEIA. The word HEGEMONIA which means "rulership" or "leadership" is nowhere else in the Bible translated "reign". If the translators had used the word "rulership" or "government" instead of "reign" they would have saved much confusion. Luke referred to the 15th year of the "rulership" of Tiberius because he was reckoning from the date that Augustus took Tiberius into a joint-rulership of the Empire. It is a perfectly attested fact of Roman history that this was towards the end of A.D. 11. Luke, therefore, knew that the 15th year of Tiberius's rulership would be from the latter end of A.D. 25 to the same point in A.D. 26. It was, indeed, on the 21st day of the 1st month in the Bible year which began in the spring of A.D. 26 that John first began his epoch-making testimony to the Messiah. In our calendar, as we shall show in later pages, the date was Thursday, 25th April.

We have, therefore, unassailable evidence from profane history that "the word of God came unto John" in the year A.D. 26. We will now show that the Bible itself predicted the start of John's ministry in the year A.D. 26 and the death and resurrection of our Lord in A.D. 33.

## THE GREAT MESSIANIC TIME PROPHECY OF THE SEVENTY WEEKS OR 490 YEARS WHICH IS RECORDED IN DANIEL IX

Daniel, more than any other of the prophets, punctuates his predictions with statements as to the time of their fulfilment. In Chapter IX the greatest Messianic Time prophecy in the Bible is recorded. It is called the prophecy of the "Seventy Weeks", as it begins with the words, "Seventy weeks are determined upon thy people and thy holy city". It had a near fulfilment in exactly 70 weeks or 490 days from the day in 537 B.C. when Daniel, in answer to his earnest prayers, received it from the Angel Gabriel who was sent from God for the purpose. That fulfilment was on the Day of Atonement in 536 B.C. when the returned remnant of Judah again commenced the worship of Jehovah at Jerusalem (Ezra III). The main object of the prophecy, however, related to events connected with the Messiah which would begin with the appearing of His Herald. In this aspect the 490 days were typical of 490 years. This is the prophecy: "Know therefore and understand, that from the going forth of the commandment to restore and to build Jerusalem UNTO THE MESSIAH THE PRINCE shall be seven weeks, and threescore and two weeks" (v. 25). In these 69 weeks there are 483 days. Therefore 483 years would elapse between the giving of the commandment mentioned and the fulfilment of the event implied by the words, "unto the Messiah the Prince".

The "commandment" referred to was given to Nehemiah verbally in 458 B.C. and the details are to be read in Chapter II of his book. It is the only commandment or decree which refers exclusively to the rebuilding of Jerusalem. It was given by Artaxerxes in the 20th year of his reign to Nehemiah his Jewish cup-bearer. It has been proved that in the Years of the Messiah (Summary of Facts, Par. 18) the actual day Nehemiah was addressed by the King was the 1st day of the year 3733. This date was the 26th day of the 1st month of the Jewish year 458 B.C. – our 26th of April. It is perfectly confirmed by the fact that these 490 years terminated at the opening of the 26th day of the 1st month in A.D. 33, when the risen Lord, with the positive object of marking the event, appeared "after eight days again" to the disciples, with Thomas present, in order to show him His wounded hands and feet – a symbolical act pregnant with deep meaning for the nation of Israel in a future day when, like Thomas, they shall look upon Him "Whom they have pierced" (Zech. XII, 10). This date was to the day 490 years in Israel's Calendar from "the commandment" given to Nehemiah in 458 B.C. The Bible, therefore, reveals the actual days on which the Prophecy of the Seventy Weeks or 490 Years began and ended.

It will be well to explain here that the prophecy of the Seventy Weeks really has a dual ending. Chronologically it terminated on the day our Lord revealed Himself to Thomas, eight days after His resurrection; but owing to the Jews' rejection of their Messiah the object of the prophecy was not attained and its fulfilment was deferred until after the 2,000 years of the Christian Dispensation when Israel's unbelief, like that of Thomas, will fade away at the sight of our Lord's pierced hands and feet. This second ending is described in Zechariah XII, 10 to 12 and XIII, 6, and Thomas's repentance and confession of faith are typical of Israel's at that time.

It is self-evident that if the Seventy Weeks or 490 Years of Daniel's prophecy terminated in A.D. 33, the Sixty-nine Weeks (7+62) or 483 Years "unto the Messiah the Prince" must have terminated in A.D. 26, when, as we have shown, "the word of God came unto John" in the 15th year of "the rulership" of Tiberius Caesar.

There is, therefore, *prima facie* evidence that Daniel's expression, "Unto the Messiah the Prince", signified the opening of John the Baptist's testimony to the Messiah which took place in A.D. 26. This is not surprising, as John opened his ministry in the Wilderness of Judaea with the words, "Repent ye: for the Kingdom of Heaven is at hand"; and as there could be no such Kingdom without THE KING it is obvious that John's words also implied that He was present. This fact is perfectly established by the Apostle Peter when, after our Lord's Ascension, the question had to be settled as to who would fill the place of Judas as the twelfth Apostle. Peter specifies that the candidate must "have companied with us all the time that the Lord Jesus went in and out among us, beginning from the baptism of John, unto that same day that He was taken up from us". Only on these terms, says Peter, could "one be ordained to be a witness with us of His resurrection" (Acts I, 20 to 22). In these words Peter perfectly defines the exact two limits of the seven years and seven weeks or 49 days which elapsed between the opening of "the baptism of John" and the Ascension of our Lord. The expression "the baptism of John" is used to express John's whole mission and is so adopted by our Lord Himself when He challenges the Jews as to its origin (Matt. XXI, 25).

It is clear from Peter's statement that our Lord at once attached Himself to John as an obedient Israelite – John being a man "sent from God". Though present with John our Lord did not yet disclose His identity to anyone but afterwards all knew that He had gone "in and out among" them from the very start of John's ministry.

More we need not add to make it plain that the expression in Daniel's prophecy, "Unto the Messiah the Prince" is a reference to the start of John's ministry in A.D. 26.

It is a matter of simple arithmetic to see that if our Lord died and rose in A.D. 33, as proved by Daniel's prophecy of the Seventy Weeks, He must have been born in the Autumn of 1 B.C. He began His ministry, as stated by Luke, when He was 30 Bible years of age, which equal 29 Solar years and 28 days. John's Gospel shows His public Ministry lasted just about three Solar years and a half. If we add these 3½ Solar years to the 29 Solar years, we have a total of 32½ years. If we measure back 32½ years from the Passover in the Spring of A.D. 33, we arrive at the Autumn of 1 B.C. when our Lord was born of the Virgin Mary at the Feast of Tabernacles which in that year was on Friday, 29th October.

(The date of Nehemiah's rebuilding of Jerusalem in 458 B.C. under the command of Artaxerxes (Longimanus) in his 20th year is perfectly established by the chronology of the Bible, as we prove in our former Treatise, *The World in Liquidation*. The 490 years from 458 B.C. to A.D. 33 form one of the major cycles of Bible Chronology. This being so, profane history must adjust the chronology of the Kings of Persia which, as to the date of Artaxerxes' reign, is at variance with the Bible by several years though, we understand, Ussher's original date was only about 3 years in error.)

## HOW THE ERRONEOUS DATE OF 4 B.C. WAS ARRIVED AT

The utterly false notion that our Lord was born in 4 B.C., and that the Christian Era was shown by Dionysius Exiguus to have started four years too late, came into being through the assumption that our Lord Jesus Christ was "thirty years" of age in the 15th year of the rulership of Tiberius Caesar, that is, in A.D. 26. It was also assumed that our Lord's 30 years at the opening of His Ministry are Solar years when in fact they are Sacred Lunar years of 354 days and measure only just over 29 Solar years. Thirty Solar years back from A.D. 26 would of course reach to 4 B.C.

Luke however, infers nothing of the kind, though the 15th year of Tiberius and our Lord's "thirty years" are to be found in the same chapter (III).

We have already shown that the prophecy of the Seventy Weeks proves that there was one "week" of seven years between A.D. 26, when the 483 years ended, and A.D. 33, when the 490 years ended. We have also shown that our Lord's Ministry covered the last 3 years and 6 months of this "week". Therefore, the Ministry of John the Baptist must have occupied the first three years and six months of the same. As previously mentioned, our Lord was baptized on the 1,260th day of John's Ministry.

Another simple proof that John's sole Ministry lasted 1,260 days or 3½ years is to be seen in the following facts. Our Lord, when speaking to the disciples about John, says, "If ye will receive it, this is Elias, which was for to come" (Matt. XI, 14). It is well known that Elias is one of the "two witnesses" of Revelation XI who are to testify for "a thousand two hundred and threescore days, clothed in sackcloth". John heralded the Kingdom which did not materialize, while Elias will, with another (Moses), herald the Kingdom that will be set up after "the coming of the great and dreadful day of the Lord" (see Malachi IV, 5).

Therefore to assume that our Lord Jesus Christ was 30 years of age in A.D. 26 is incorrect. His age was 25 Solar years and 178 days when John the Baptist began on 25th April in A.D. 26, and He was "thirty years" of age on 26th November, A.D. 29. This allows John the Baptist a period of 3½ years for his Ministry of heralding the Messiah. There is, therefore, not a vestige of authority for naming 4 B.C. as the year of our Lord's birth, as is so generally done by those who are not in possession of all the facts.

It is only right that we should render honour to the faithful Abbot of Rome, Dionysius Exiguus, who in the sixth century of our Era gave to Christendom a system of reckoning years which made the birth of our Lord the turning point in chronology. No doubt with the help of valuable material then at his disposal, Dionysius proved that our Lord was born in the year A.U.C. 753 which became the year 1 B.C. under the system he inaugurated of dividing the chronology of the world into years before Christ (B.C.) and years of Christ (A.D.). The Bible confirms the accuracy of the reckoning of Dionysius Exiguus as to the year of Christ's birth. It was in 1 B.C. and 63 days and 16 hours before the Midnight of 31st December at which point the Christian Era began with Saturday, 1st January A.D. 1.

## THE PRE-INCARNATION OF OUR LORD JESUS CHRIST AS IMMANUEL IN 742 B.C. – THE DATE OF ISAIAH'S PROPHECY OF THE VIRGIN-BIRTH

We have already noted that our Lord was set apart for death as "the Lamb of God, which taketh away the sin of the world", in the Garden of Eden at the time of the Fall of Adam and Eve. We have stated (the proof we have given in our former Treatise, *The World in Liquidation*) that our Lord died, to the day and hour, 4,000 years from the Fall in the Chronology of Redemption (Summary of Facts, Pars. 8 and 16).

Now we must make a brief allusion to the year 742 B.C. when the Prophet Isaiah uttered the words, "Behold, a virgin shall conceive, and bear a son, and shall call his name IMMANUEL" (Isaiah VII, 14).

The context shows that this son was to be a sign to King Ahaz and the people of Judah that their enemies, Syria and Samaria, would be destroyed as kingdoms before this child was about three years old. The Virgin's child in a literal sense was our Lord – a fact confirmed by the Evangelist Matthew who says the birth of Jesus was the fulfilment of Isaiah's prophecy (Matt. I, 22 and 23). The question at once arises: How could this fulfilment, which was 741 years later, be a sign to Judah and her king of the promised deliverance which was to occur about three years after the prophecy was uttered?

This is one of the deep mysteries of the Bible and it has completely baffled commentators. Its solution is a chronological one, as we have proved. The details, for want of space, we dare not set forth now, but they are to be found in the Third Paper of *The World in Liquidation.* The year 742 B.C. was 3,333 years from Adam and it was a year of immense chronological significance. Isaiah's prophecy was not literally fulfilled until 29th October 1 B.C., and, as we have said, this could not be a sign to people living in 742 B.C. Did Isaiah prophesy falsely, or was there a mysterious significance attaching to his prediction which was uttered with the direct authority of God?

Our Lord as Immanuel (the name means "God with us") first manifested Himself to and with the faithful remnant that stood with Isaiah at the time of the prophecy. This is proved by Isaiah's statement to the nation (VIII, 10): "Take counsel together, and it shall come to nought . . . for God is with us" (IMMANUEL). This identification of our Lord as "Immanuel" with the remnant in Judah (in contradistinction to the nation) continued right through to the days of His birth when the Virgin Mary, one of their number, became the vessel chosen of God to fulfil Isaiah's prophecy *in a literal sense.*

The normal interval between the conception and birth of a child is 280 days. We have proved (and have given the full facts in our former Treatise) that from the day of Isaiah's prophecy, when our Lord became mystically incarnate in the remnant of Judah, to His actual birth was 280 cycles (or "days") of 888 days each. Many times "the virgin, the daughter of Zion" is spoken of in one way or another and *in the mystical sense* she was "the virgin" to whom Isaiah referred. In other words, our Lord became mystically incarnate in this faithful remnant which ultimately gave birth to Him through the person of the Virgin Mary. With the utmost precision this Pre-Incarnation was timed to last a symbolical period of 280 cycles or "days" of 888 days each – 888 being the numerical value of the Name – JESUS.

To complete our all-too-brief reference to this amazing feature of our Lord's birth, we must make two facts plain. The first is that our Lord as Immanuel did literally present Himself in and with the faithful Remnant in Judah from the day of Isaiah's prophecy to His actual birth by the Virgin Mary in Bethlehem on 29th October 1 B.C. The second fact is that a royal child, in every respect *typical* of Immanuel, was conceived on that day in the womb of a maiden whom Ahaz, King of Judah, had just married. This child was Hezekiah, and before he could "refuse the evil, and choose the good", the promised overthrow of Syria and Samaria, of which he was the "sign", took place. Hezekiah became King of Judah and his actions, as such, in every respect proved him to be indwelt by IMMANUEL (II Chronicles XXIX to XXXII).

* * *

We now bring this lengthy first chapter of our Treatise to an end. We have sought to bring into it every really important fact provided by the Bible in relation to TIME as it affected the Incarnation and Birth of our Lord and Saviour, Jesus Christ, Who Himself declared, "I am come a light into the world, that whosoever believeth in Me should not abide in darkness" (John XII, 46). It is the Holy Scriptures that have spoken to us in these pages, revealing the actual dates of our blessed Lord's Incarnation and Birth in such a way as to be a cause for praise and thanksgiving in that all further discussion or controversy on this sacred subject is excluded. Our Lord became Incarnate in the womb of the Virgin Mary at the New Moon of Friday, 23rd January 1 B.C., and was born at the Feast of Tabernacles in Bethlehem of Judaea on Friday, 29th October 1 B.C., at the hour of 8–9 a.m. And let all who revere the Holy Scriptures say so too!

# CHAPTER TWO

## THE DARK SHADOW OF CALVARY CROSSES OUR LORD'S PATH AT TWELVE YEARS OF AGE

### GOD'S TIME PATTERN FOR HIS SON REQUIRES HIS PRESENCE IN THE TEMPLE AT JERUSALEM INDEPENDENTLY OF HIS MOTHER AND JOSEPH

### THE CHRONOLOGY OF THE BIBLE GIVES TO THIS INCIDENT AN ENTIRELY NEW SIGNIFICANCE

---

Read Luke II, 40 to 52
Friday, 22nd April, to Sabbath, 18th June A.D. 12

AT THE close of our first chapter we had commented on events in the life of Jesus Christ our Lord up to His return with His Mother and Joseph from Egypt, when they again settled in Nazareth, where, as all know, our Lord spent His childhood and early years as a Man (Matt. II, 19 to 23).

We are told no details regarding this phase of the life of God's Son on the earth, and this, doubtless, because God did not wish men to occupy with His Humanity so much as with His Deity. We are, however, informed that "the Child grew, and waxed strong, filled with wisdom: and the grace of God was upon Him" (Luke II, 40, R.V.).

The Son of God, as Jesus of Nazareth, had assumed true humanity; consequently His physical and mental development as a Child had to take place in a perfectly natural environment – in His case the humble abode of Mary and Joseph His legal father who was a carpenter by trade.

It is useless to disregard the reticences of the Inspired Gospels touching our Lord's life at Nazareth by drawing upon our imaginations, as did the infamous writers of the Apocryphal Gospels. Jesus was the Son of God, and as such He could not be less than perfect as a Man in every phase and aspect of His life on earth. Therefore, in the home at Nazareth He glorified His Father in Heaven by exhibiting perfect obedience as a Child to His parents. He could no more fail there than He could when later He became the Subject of immense public interest. All that He did and said in His Nazareth home was not only known to God but was to Him as a sweet fragrance ascending from an earth which was peopled by those whose boast, for over four thousand years, had been in their independence of the One Who created them and Who "giveth to all life, and breath, and all things" (Acts XVII, 25). In the remarkable incident when our Lord was 12 years of age, which we are about to consider, we are forced to take account of the fact that His Deity in the sphere of knowledge was entirely unaffected by His having taken a body "of flesh and blood". Knowledge with Deity is intuitive and not acquired by the exercise of the mind. Our Lord had not parted with Deity on becoming Jesus of Nazareth, that is, when "the Word was made flesh". Consequently, it is written of Him, "Jesus did not commit Himself unto them, because He knew all men, and needed not that any should testify of man: for He knew what was in man" (John II, 24 and 25).

Our Lord had willingly laid aside for the time the exercise of His Omnipotence when He assumed a true Humanity; hence it is written of Him, "He was crucified through weakness" (II Cor. XIII, 4). He also laid aside His official Glory and "took upon Him the form of a servant, and was made in the likeness of men" (Phil. II, 7). There is not, however, a hint in Holy Scripture that He ceased on becoming Man to be Omniscient – there is, in fact, perfect evidence to the contrary. Therefore, to talk of our Lord as One Who had to *learn* anything in the sphere of knowledge is at once to deny His Deity, since Omniscience is the very essence of Deity. Let the early verses of the first chapter of John's Gospel be pondered by anyone anxious to know our Lord in His essential Being prior to the Incarnation. There we learn that He was "THE WORD" that was "WITH GOD" and that "WAS GOD" before being called to create the Heavens and the Earth named in Genesis I, 1. Elsewhere our Lord is referred to not only as Creator but as the One for Whom the Universe was created, as the following words indicate: "all things were created by Him, and for Him: and

He is before all things, and by Him all things consist" (Col. I, 16 and 17). While we contemplate the earthly pathway of "THE MAN CHRIST JESUS" may we ever keep in mind that before His Incarnation He was the Eternally-existing Son of God and co-equal with the Father Whom He came to make known.

## THE VISIT OF MARY AND JOSEPH WITH JESUS TO JERUSALEM FOR THE PASSOVER ON FRIDAY, 22ND APRIL, A.D. 12

It must have occurred to many that the facts relating to this incident which appear on the surface in Luke's Gospel do not constitute the whole story. On this occasion, as so often in the Bible, the real truth is concealed beneath the surface for the benefit of those who care to search it out. In the present instance, however, the key of understanding lies in the chronology of the Bible; and no one could penetrate the veil of secrecy with which God has hidden the true objective of this incident apart from the possession of a faultless knowledge of this much neglected subject. To start with, the first essential in this case is the knowledge of the actual day of our Lord's birth, because without this no one could know the date upon which He attained twelve years of age. Furthermore, it is the calendar based upon the Years of the Messiah (see Summary of Facts, Par. 18) that marks this incident with so solemn an emphasis; and no one until now has even suspected the existence of such a chronological era. It is, therefore, manifestly clear that, as neither the date of our Lord's birth nor the existence of the Years of the Messiah has been known to anyone for eighteen hundred years, the real truth concerning our Lord's visit to Jerusalem, when He was 12 years old, has had to remain in concealment until such time as it pleased God to grant someone light on these two kindred subjects. There are, indeed, many clear indications in the Holy Scriptures that God would interpose with light therefrom before this Dispensation ended. We shall shortly refer to a pre-eminent example of this, namely, our Lord's first sign-miracle at Cana in Galilee, when we commence to trace out the days of His Public Ministry.

The Evangelist Luke, who alone records this incident, states that our Lord's parents "went to Jerusalem every year at the feast of the passover". Joseph was obliged by the Law to attend the three great annual Feasts of the Passover, Pentecost and Tabernacles (Deut. XVI, 16). Mary evidently accompanied him, and on the occasion in question Jesus also went up to Jerusalem with them.

In order to obtain the true meaning of Luke II, verses 42 and 43, it is necessary to give the literal translation of the Greek, which is as follows:

> "And when He was twelve years old, having gone up after the custom of the feast and having completed the days, as they returned, the boy Jesus remained behind in Jerusalem, and His parents knew it not".

The ordinary English translation of these verses clearly implies that our Lord was 12 years old when Mary and Joseph took Him with them to Jerusalem for the Passover. This was not the case, neither is it what Luke states or implies. The Bible reveals that our Lord only attained 12 years of age some weeks later when the extremely significant event which was the real objective of the whole incident took place.

It will be clear to all from what happened to Mary and Joseph when, unknown to them, our Lord remained behind in Jerusalem, that a moment had come when He must begin to fulfil His Mission as the Son of God on the earth. If this meant wounding His Mother and Joseph, it was only that they might begin to realize that His first concern in life was the doing of the Will of His Father in Heaven Who had sent Him into the world. Mary, His Mother, must be made conscious that there was One above Whose prior claim upon her First-born Son must henceforth be a vital factor in her relationship to Him.

The chronology of the Bible reveals the following facts concerning this visit of Joseph and Mary to Jerusalem for the Passover. In A.D. 12 the 1st month of the Bible year began on 9th April – the Moon being new the previous day. The Feast of the Passover began at even on the 14th day which was Friday, 22nd April. This fact raises an immediate difficulty but, as so often in the Bible, it is one which leads to the discovery of hidden facts.

The years of our Lord's life, like all Bible years, were composed of 354 days. They followed one another in unbroken succession without any reference to the sun, the moon or the seasons.

Our Lord Jesus Christ, as we have revealed from the Bible, was born on Friday, 29th October 1 B.C. Twelve years of 354 days from this date terminate on Wednesday, 15th June A.D. 12. (In 12 Bible years there are 4,248 days, or 11 solar years and 231 days.)

It, therefore, becomes perfectly evident that our Lord was not 12 years of age until several weeks after the Passover which was on 22nd April in A.D. 12. This is in keeping with Luke's statement which clearly implies that our Lord was 12 years old at the time He was "lost" – an event which forms the central theme of the whole episode.

As our Lord Jesus Christ was not 12 years old until 15th June in A.D. 12, the fact at once emerges that Mary and Joseph must have remained in Jerusalem after the Passover for the seven weeks to Pentecost. It is for this reason that we are told that they returned "when they had fulfilled the days" – that is, the 49 days of the Harvest which end with the Feast of Pentecost or Weeks (see Leviticus XXIII, 16). The journey from Nazareth to Jerusalem would take a caravan about a week, so it is evident that Joseph and Mary preferred to abide for the seven weeks in the Holy City rather than make the return journey twice. As a true Israelite Joseph had to be present in Jerusalem at Pentecost.

The Harvest or seven weeks to Pentecost began on "the morrow after the sabbath" which followed the Passover (Lev. XXIII, 15). In A.D. 12 the Passover was on Friday, 22nd April. The seven weeks would therefore begin on Sunday, 24th April, and end on Sunday, 12th June, which was the day of Pentecost. After so long an absence from home, Joseph and Mary would not delay a day after they had fulfilled the claims of the Law, and therefore without doubt the "company" which they joined left Jerusalem for Nazareth on Monday, 13th June – the day after Pentecost.

In order that the period of time involved in this incident may be easily comprehended, we will tabulate the days from the Passover to the day that Jesus was found by His parents in the Temple "sitting in the midst of the doctors". It is most important to take account of the fact that verses 45 and 46 make it perfectly clear that Mary and Joseph were "seeking" Jesus for "three days" after they returned to Jerusalem and that these do not include the two days occupied with journeying from and to Jerusalem.

## THE EXACT ORDER OF THE DAYS WHEN JESUS WAS "LOST" TO HIS PARENTS

| | | | |
|---|---|---|---|
| Friday, | 22nd | April, | The Passover at Jerusalem. |
| Sabbath, | 23rd | ,, | |
| Sunday, | 24th | ,, | The Seven Weeks to Pentecost begin on "the morrow after the sabbath". |
| Sunday, | 12th | June, | "The feast of weeks" or Pentecost (Deut. XVI, 10). |
| Monday, | 13th | ,, | Mary and Joseph join the caravan for Nazareth. Jesus remains in Jerusalem unknown to them. |
| Tuesday, | 14th | ,, | Mary and Joseph "turned back again to Jerusalem". |
| Wednesday, | 15th | ,, | JESUS ATTAINS 12 YEARS OF AGE (at 6 P.M.). 1st day of "seeking Him" by Joseph and Mary. |
| Thursday, | 16th | ,, | 2nd day of "seeking Him" by Joseph and Mary. |
| Friday, | 17th | ,, | 3rd day of "seeking Him" by Joseph and Mary. |
| SABBATH, | 18th | ,, | "AFTER THREE DAYS THEY FOUND HIM IN THE TEMPLE" (Luke II, 46). |

This tabulation of days enables us to see that this sudden disappearance of Jesus was a more serious and tragic experience for His Mother and Joseph than appears on the surface. Altogether He was absent from them for at least five days. Mary must have suffered great anguish as for "three days" they searched Jerusalem for Him. Doubtless she and Joseph chided themselves for their carelessness in leaving for Nazareth without Him. And when they did find Him and sought to blame Him for His treatment of them, He expressed surprise ("How is it that ye sought Me") that they did not know that He must be in His "Father's House" (R.V.) at that time. The statement that "they understood not the saying which He spake unto them" carries the inference that Mary and Joseph had in some measure lost, perhaps through a lack of faith, the reality of having the Son of God, in the Person of Jesus, Mary's First-born Son, in their family circle.

It is most important to keep in mind that the underlying cause of this incident lay in the fact that God intended to mark our Lord's twelfth birthday in a most significant and solemn manner; and that for this purpose He must be in the Temple – His Father's House – for the occasion. We must not, therefore, attribute to Mary and Joseph a too serious lack of concern for the boy – Jesus – in that they actually went a day's journey before finding out that He was not in the company. Rather must we view it as a permitted lapse made necessary by the purpose God had before Him. On our Lord's part, He must be willing to allow this sharp passing sorrow to overtake His Mother and Joseph because He had come into the world to do His Father's will, and on this occasion this necessitated His acting independently of those whom He loved and to whom He was always subject in the normal course.

Thus far we have only considered the human aspect of this incident. We must now consider what the purpose was that God had before Him which made it necessary for Mary and Joseph to suffer so tragic an experience as to "lose" the boy Jesus for no less than five days.

## "IN A FIGURE" AT TWELVE YEARS OF AGE OUR LORD DIES AS THE PASCHAL LAMB AND RISES AGAIN "AFTER THREE DAYS"

The day upon which our Lord Jesus Christ completed the first twelve years of His life on the earth was one of immense significance to His Father in Heaven – and to Himself, as perfectly understanding its significance. This understanding was the logical outcome of the unbroken communion which ever existed between our Lord, as the Son of God on the earth, and His Father in Heaven.

We stated in the Summary of Facts (Par. 18) that the chronological era termed "the Years of the Messiah" played a very important part in the life of our Lord on the earth. It is not a matter of surprise, therefore, that it is to the calendar founded upon this series of years that we have to turn if we would learn the true secret of what transpired at the close of the day on which our Lord attained 12 years of age, and in the following days when His parents were "seeking Him".

It will be remembered that in Israel's Calendar our Lord was born at the Feast of Tabernacles on the 15th day of the 7th month in 1 B.C., and that in the Years of the Messiah He was born on the 15th day of the 1st month at the Feast of the Passover and Unleavened Bread in the Messianic Year 4205 from Creation. As the Years of the Messiah and the years of our Lord's life were both of the same duration, namely, 354 days, it stands to reason that He must have attained 12 years of age on the 15th day of the 1st month in the Messianic year 4217 (4205+12) from Creation.

To be more exact, if our Lord was born in the Years of the Messiah on the 15th day of the 1st month, then His every year thereafter would terminate at the close of the 14th day of the 1st month which was the appointed hour for the slaying of the Passover lambs in the Temple. This being so, we know that Wednesday, 15th June A.D. 12, when Jesus completed 12 years of His age, was the day of the Passover in the Messianic Calendar and that at 6 p.m., which was the close of the day, the hour had arrived for the Paschal sacrifice to be offered.

It was for this reason that our Lord was in the Temple at the very hour when He had completed the first 12 years of His life on the earth. When 12 years old, a boy in Israel reached the age of responsibility. The time had therefore now come in our Lord's life when He was able to offer to God, His Father, a perfect token of His willing acceptance of His Vocation as "the Lamb of God, which taketh away the sin of the world" (John I, 29).

## THE TWELVE YEARS OF PREPARATION

The number "12" in the Bible frequently bespeaks preparation in relation to the events which follow (see Genesis XIV, 4). Notably is this the case with the twelve hours (6 a.m. to 6 p.m.) of what the Bible terms "the day of the preparation" which preceded the Passover and the Sabbath (Mark XV, 42). It is, furthermore, a fact that the 12 hours of "the day of the preparation" for the Passover were designed by God to be a positive type of our Lord's 12 years of preparation before He could present Himself for the first time to God as the Antitypical Paschal Lamb – in the manner we are about to relate. This is proved by the following facts. Our Lord took the last Passover in A.D. 33 with His disciples at 6 p.m. on Thursday which was therefore "the day of the preparation" for Jehovah's Passover. He died at 3 P.M. the next day – Friday – which was "the day of the preparation" for the Jews' Passover (Matt. XXVII, 62). The actual period of our Lord's Passion began, therefore, at 6 A.M. on Thursday. After 12 hours, that is, at 6 P.M., He sat down with His disciples to eat the Passover. At 3 P.M. on Friday, that is, after a further 21 hours, He died upon the Cross. From 6 A.M. on Thursday to 3 P.M. on Friday was 33 hours. These 33 hours are a type of our Lord's 33 years which were divided thus – the 12 years of preparation to A.D. 12 and the 21 years to His death in A.D. 33. We have mentioned these facts now in order to make it perfectly plain that the 12 hours of "the day of the preparation" for the Passover are a type of the 12 years of preparation in the life of our Lord Jesus Christ which ended, in Messianic Years, with His presenting Himself to God in the Temple at the hour of the Passover as the true Antitypical Paschal Lamb.

"So they went both of them together"
(Genesis XXII, 6 and 8)

The incident we are considering provides a most touching picture of God the Father and God the Son in action together in reference to the Redemption of the world. Though our Lord was but 12 years of age as regards His Humanity, He was, as the Son of God, in full understanding of the purpose for which the Father had sent Him into the world. He could look back to the Garden of Eden when sin first entered into the world "by one man's disobedience" and when, as the result, He was set apart as "the Lamb of God, which taketh away the sin of the world" to die after four "days" of a thousand years. Now He was in the world, the sin of which He was to bear. For the purpose He had taken upon Himself "the likeness of sinful flesh" and having attained the age at which, in the human sphere, responsibility begins, He seals His acceptance of His

Vocation by presenting Himself before His God and Father in the Temple at the hour of the Paschal Sacrifice, *as ready to die* for "the sin of the world". Yet He was but a Lad of twelve years as regards His Humanity.

There was no human eye to perceive what was transpiring when Jesus, having just completed His 12 years of preparation, appeared alone in the Temple at 6 P.M. on Wednesday, 15th June A.D. 12, because in that series of years which relate exclusively to Him as Messiah the day and hour of the Paschal Sacrifice had once again been reached. But the ever-watchful eye of God the Father beheld the scene as the youthful Jesus, His well-beloved Son, presented Himself FOR DEATH as the Lamb of God, and as knowing Himself to be the true Antitype of every Paschal Offering. If the hour for *actual death* as such had not arrived, the whole tragedy of Calvary is, nevertheless, foreshadowed for the Father and the Son on this occasion; for "*in a figure*" Jesus does die and "after three days" rises again and is found by His Mother and Joseph in the Temple "sitting in the midst of the doctors".

The expression "in a figure" (or, "in a parable", R.V.) is used in Hebrews XI, 19 in reference to Abraham's offering up of Isaac – an event which is a perfect type of God the Father giving His only-begotten Son to die upon the Tree at Calvary. How truly can it be said of this occasion when Jesus, as a Lad of 12 years, offered Himself to God as ready to die for "the sins of the whole world", that "they went both of them together". The whole scene, as we have said, was a perfect, though figurative, foreshadowing of Calvary. It was the Father and the Son acting together alone and in perfect communion in regard to the salvation of a lost world – a world which "God so loved . . . that He gave His only begotten Son, that whosoever believeth in Him should not perish, but have everlasting life" (John III, 16).

## THIS OCCASION FORMS A PERFECT CHRONOLOGICAL TYPE OF OUR LORD'S DEATH AND RESURRECTION IN A.D. 33

The Bible abounds in chronological types of the Death and Resurrection of our Lord Jesus Christ. The occasion we are considering is a notable example of these. The key is found in the expression, "after three days they found Him" – a statement which perfectly accords with our Lord's words in Mark VIII, 31, "The Son of Man must . . . be killed, and after three days rise again".

In the present instance we find that God so planned as to cause that our Lord's death and resurrection "in a figure" should occur on precisely the same days in the 1st month of the Messianic year 4,217 as His literal death and resurrection did in the 1st month of Israel's year in A.D. 33. We will therefore tabulate these days, setting those of A.D. 12 alongside those in A.D. 33.

THE DEATH AND RESURRECTION OF OUR LORD JESUS CHRIST IN A.D. 33 FORESHADOWED IN THE THREE DAYS HE WAS "LOST" IN A.D. 12

| | A.D. 12<br>MESSIANIC YEAR 4217<br>*1st month (Nisan)* | | A.D. 33<br>THE CALENDAR OF ISRAEL<br>*1st Month (Nisan)* |
|---|---|---|---|
| 11th | The Day of Pentecost | 11th | |
| 12th | Mary and Joseph leave for Nazareth without Jesus. | 12th | |
| 13th | Mary and Joseph return to Jerusalem "seeking Him". | 13th | "Day of the preparation" for Jehovah's Passover. |
| 14th | THE PASSOVER. Jesus, now 12 years old, dies "in a figure". | 14th | The Jews' Passover. Jesus dies. |
| 15th | The three days Joseph and Mary were | 15th | The "three days and three nights in the |
| 16th | "seeking Him". | 16th | heart of the earth" (Matt. XII, 40). |
| 17th | "AFTER THREE DAYS THEY FOUND HIM IN THE TEMPLE" (The Sabbath) | 17th | "AFTER THREE DAYS SHALL RISE AGAIN". |

In giving above the days in Israel's 1st month in A.D. 33,

when our Lord Jesus Christ died and rose again, we have been obliged to anticipate facts which we will perfectly establish in due course in the appropriate section of this Treatise.

This then is one of the many occasions in our Lord's life in which Bible chronology lifts the veil of secrecy and allows us to peer behind the scenes and behold an event in His Personal Pathway which otherwise we should know nothing about, since no hint of it appears on the surface. Some may not be able to enter in and appreciate the poignancy of such a scene as we have just sought to present. But to spiritual minds which are able to comprehend the essential sacredness of an event in which God the Father and God the Son are seen in action together over the stupendous issue of Man's Redemption, the reward will be great, and the heart be bowed in worship and thanksgiving for being allowed to contemplate a scene which so perfectly sets forth "in a figure" the literal death and resurrection of our Lord Jesus Christ at the Passover in A.D. 33.

It will be appreciated that our Lord's actions when He attained twelve years of age were exclusively for the eye of His Father in Heaven. Probably no human being even knew of the existence of a chronological era which related exclusively to Jesus as the Messiah; but doubtless to God the Father and God the Son this was the foremost of all the Bible's time measurements. It will be understood that when the Feasts of Jehovah occurred in the Years of the Messiah, as in the case of the Passover when our Lord was 12 years of age, there was no external manifestation of the fact such as took place when the Feasts occurred in Israel's Calendar. It was solely that God wished to mark the occasion with the spiritual significance attaching to the Feast at which it took place. As Jesus was God's Passover Lamb and the Antitype of every Paschal Offering, it was fitting to the last degree that in the Years of the Messiah He should be born on the day which opened with the slaying of the Paschal lambs; and that His every year thereafter should open at a like point of time in that Calendar. We shall presently see that our Lord opened His Public Ministry at 30 years of age on the day of the Passover in this Calendar and that this was accompanied by another chronological expression of His death and resurrection.

Our curiosity would perhaps lead us to enquire how and

where Jesus spent the days when He was "lost" to His parents. That is a secret known only in Heaven. He certainly was not with relatives or friends known to His parents. Possibly, as later in life, He went out to the Mount of Olives at night. No doubt each day was spent in the Temple in holy contemplation of the Scriptures which foretold His sufferings and Death and in communion with the One in Whose House He was abiding.

How strange a sight for Mary and Joseph to find the lost One quite unperturbed, "sitting in the midst of the doctors, both hearing them, and asking them questions". He was not there to teach, though He could have done so if it had been the time. He certainly was not there to learn. Speaking in all reverence, it was the Son of God travelling *incognito*, and no wonder "all that heard Him were astonished at His understanding and answers".

So for a brief moment the silence of 30 years has been broken and the veil of secrecy, which covers the Saviour's life until His Baptism, lifted. How filled with meaning are His first recorded words, "How is it that ye sought Me? Wist ye not that I must be about my Father's business?" And how they accord with His last recorded words uttered on the Cross, "IT IS FINISHED".

This narrative closes with a statement which sets forth the perfection of our Lord in His Humanity. For several days He had been involved in tremendous issues with His Father in Heaven. The whole purpose of His Incarnation has been before Him and His ultimate decease as the Antitypical Paschal Lamb has been prefigured and chronologically expressed. For the moment all this must be laid aside and He must return to the path of humble duty. So it is recorded, "He went down with them (His parents) and came to Nazareth, and was subject unto them . . . and Jesus increased in wisdom and stature, and in favour with God and man".

From this point of time, namely, A.D. 12, the Gospel Records are silent for 14 years, that is, until A.D. 26, when the Voice of the King's Herald – John the Baptist – is lifted up, summoning Israel to repentance because "the kingdom of heaven is at hand".

# CHAPTER THREE

## "THE BEGINNING OF THE GOSPEL OF JESUS CHRIST, THE SON OF GOD"

MARK I, I

---

FOURTEEN YEARS OF SILENCE END WITH THE TESTIMONY OF JOHN THE BAPTIST TO THE MESSIAH, OUR LORD JESUS CHRIST, ON THURSDAY, 25TH APRIL A.D. 26

---

THE BIBLE'S IMMENSE EMPHASIS UPON THIS DATE AND THE SUBSEQUENT SEVEN YEARS AND FORTY-NINE DAYS LEADING UP TO THE ASCENSION OF THE RISEN CHRIST INTO HEAVEN AT 8 A.M. ON THE SABBATH – 13TH JUNE A.D. 33

---

OUR LAST Chapter ended with the date of 18th June A.D. 12 – a Sabbath – when Mary and Joseph found our Lord Jesus Christ in the Temple, His Father's House. No doubt the return to Nazareth began the next day, 19th June, a Sunday. From that date to 25th April A.D. 26, when John the Baptist began his Testimony to Jesus, as the Messiah, was 13 Solar years and 310 days. As far as we know, the Bible does not make any direct or indirect reference to any event connected with our Lord between these two points of time during which He passed from adolescence to manhood and became known as "the carpenter, the son of Mary, the brother of James" (Mark VI, 3). No doubt the counsels of God decreed that His Son should remain completely hidden from view until the hour arrived when Daniel's time prophecy of the "seven weeks, and threescore and two weeks", or 483 years, "UNTO THE MESSIAH THE PRINCE" should be fulfilled by the appearing of John the Baptist, His herald (Daniel IX, 25).

Our Lord's age on 25th April A.D. 26 was, in Bible terms, 26 years and 105 days and, in Solar terms, 25 years and 178 days. John the Baptist, who was 5 months, or 147 days, older than our Lord, was therefore, in Solar terms, 25 years and 325 days old when he began his Testimony to Israel.

We mention these facts first as our main objective in this Treatise is to set forth the Pathway in Time of our Lord Jesus Christ. We shall, therefore, at each stage continue to give our Lord's age in both Bible and Solar years. In this way the figures can easily be checked and error be excluded. If there were an error, even of one day, the whole Time Pattern designed by God for His Son's earthly pathway would be marred throughout, as the various calendars would never synchronize in the manner we have already demonstrated at our Lord's birth and when He was 12 years of age.

The period of Seven Years and Forty-Nine Days, between the opening of John the Baptist's Testimony to Israel and the Ascension of the Risen Christ into Heaven, stands by itself as absolutely unique in the whole history of the human race. As already fully explained, the expression "unto Messiah the Prince", in the great Messianic time prophecy of Daniel IX, was fulfilled on the day that John the Baptist first sounded his clarion call of repentance to the Jewish nation. The date of this momentous event was 25th April A.D. 26. It is most important to understand that the Bible treats these Seven Years and Forty-Nine Days as the period during which our Lord was moving about among men.

The statement of the Apostle Peter from Acts I, 20 to 22, which we quoted fully in Part III of our first chapter, makes it perfectly certain that our Lord at once identified Himself with John the Baptist. As a true Israelite ("made under the law") He would at once attend upon John – "a man sent from God". Until His Baptism by John, He remained absolutely unknown but afterwards all the Apostles, who themselves likewise attended upon John, must have realized Who it was – even Jesus the Messiah – Who had been going "in and out" among them from the very start of John's Ministry. Even John, His cousin, did not know Him, as he positively declares (John I, 31, 33). It hardly needs stating that had our Lord, as the Messiah, allowed His identity to become known before the Baptist's appointed season of Testimony had run its course, confusion would have resulted. The essence of John's teaching is found in the words, "I indeed baptize you with water; but

One mightier than I cometh, the latchet of whose shoes I am not worthy to unloose: He shall baptize you with the Holy Ghost and with fire" (Luke III, 16 and Matt. III, 11).

The Evangelist Mark opens his Gospel with the words, "The beginning of the gospel of Jesus Christ, the Son of God; as it is written in the prophets, Behold, I send My messenger before Thy face, which shall prepare Thy way before Thee". Mark, it is to be noted, is thus caused by the Spirit of God to state that the Gospel of Jesus Christ began with the Testimony of the herald – John the Baptist.

The Scriptures, therefore, make it perfectly plain that we are to identify our Lord, as the Messiah, with the whole period of the Seven Years and Forty-Nine Days and not only with the latter half when He was publicly manifested to the Jewish nation, following His Baptism and Temptation.

When we have traced the course of these seven years and forty-nine days in its various stages to our Lord's Ascension, we shall then set forth some extremely solemn facts relating to the way God cancelled the whole period chronologically as the result of the rejection of the Testimonies rendered by our Lord and His herald.

We must now proceed to consider events from the beginning of John the Baptist's Testimony to Israel.

## THE TESTIMONY OF 1260 DAYS OF JOHN THE BAPTIST FROM THURSDAY, 25TH APRIL A.D. 26, TO THE BAPTISM OF OUR LORD JESUS CHRIST ON WEDNESDAY, 5TH OCTOBER A.D. 29

"Now in the fifteenth year of the reign (rulership) of Tiberius Caesar . . . the word of God came unto John the son of Zacharias in the wilderness." The third chapter of Luke's Gospel opens with this pronouncement which for the Jewish nation meant the breaking of a silence on God's part which had lasted for about 400 years. Malachi, the last of the post-exilic prophets, had foretold the coming of God's messenger – John the Baptist – and now he was present in the midst of the people to whom the Messiah was about to be manifested. Not only had Malachi prophesied of John's arrival, but Isaiah, Israel's most eminent seer, had also plainly declared his coming with the words, "The voice of one crying in the wilderness,

Prepare ye the way of the Lord, make His paths straight" (Luke III, 4). The prophet Daniel, on his part, was caused to reveal *the time* of John's appearing, namely, 483 years after Nehemiah's return to rebuild Jerusalem in 458 B.C., that is in A.D. 26 – the 15th year of the rule of Tiberius Caesar.

This was a tremendous moment in the history of Israel and for a time the complacency even of the religious leaders was disturbed by the cry, "Repent ye: for the kingdom of heaven is at hand" (Matt. III, 2). This utterance was the essence of John's Ministry and it made it manifestly clear that no one could pass into the new dispensation – the reign of the Heavens – without repenting of the sins, both personal and national, which found the elect nation far from God and sunken in a dead and formalistic profession of a faith that had lost all reality through the introduction of a mass of human traditions which made "the word of God of none effect" and robbed it of all its spiritual value.

In the first chapter of this Treatise it was necessary, in establishing the date of our Lord's birth, to make considerable reference to the Messianic Time Prophecy of Daniel IX. It is not, therefore, needful to rehearse again the facts which prove that the expression in that prophecy, "unto the Messiah the Prince", was fulfilled by John in A.D. 26. We will, however, state the facts which establish that the Baptist's testimony officially began at 8 A.M. on Thursday, 25th April, in that year.

The prophecy of the Seventy Weeks or 490 years is measured in the Bible in both solar years and luni-solar Bible years. The reason for this is that our Lord was not only Israel's Messiah but also the World's Redeemer. It is natural, therefore, that this vastly important time prophecy should be expressed in Gentile solar years as well as Israel's luni-solar years. We have shown in Chapter One that in the latter the terminating date was the 26th of Israel's 1st month in A.D. 33, when our Lord after His resurrection met with Thomas.

As the 483 solar years "unto the Messiah" began on 26th April 458 B.C., the period ended with 25th April A.D. 26 – that is, 25th April would be the last day of the 483 solar years. The 490 solar years ended on 25th April A.D. 33 – a Sabbath – when the Lord was in Jericho and abiding in the house of Zacchaeus – "a son of Abraham". This event, as we will explain in due course, was of the utmost significance (Luke XIX, 1 to 10).

The date of 25th April A.D. 26, was in Israel's calendar the 21st day of the 1st month, which is the last of the Seven Days of the Feast of Unleavened Bread. In Divine time, which was then one day of the month and one day of the week (see the Summary of Facts, Pars. 13 and 14) ahead of Israel's time, the 25th of April A.D. 26, was the 22nd of the 1st month – the day after the close of the Feast of Unleavened Bread.

The Bible definitely reckons John the Baptist's time according to the Divine method and not Israel's. John was sent from God – a man "filled with the Holy Ghost, even from his mother's womb". It is natural, therefore, that time relating to him should be reckoned in the same terms as that of the Holy One Whom he had been sent to herald.

In Chapter One, under the heading, "Why our Lord was born at 8 A.M.", we showed why all the days of our Lord's life began at that hour. John's days, being according to Divine reckoning, are likewise viewed as starting at 8 A.M. Therefore the official starting-point of John the Baptist's Testimony was 8 A.M., Thursday, 25th April A.D. 26. For very important reasons which will appear later, we must here state that it proved absolutely necessary to know the exact hour of the beginning of John's Ministry because it directly affects every chronological era in the Bible, except purely Secular Years.

The very fact that from 8 A.M. on 25th April A.D. 26, when John began his testimony, it was exactly 7 years and 7 weeks to 8 A.M. on 13th June A.D. 33, when our blessed Lord ascended into Heaven, is almost in itself evidence of the correctness of both dates. The matter is, however, settled by the fact that from 25th April A.D. 26, there are exactly 1260 days to and including 5th October A.D. 29, which, it is manifestly clear, was the date of our Lord's Baptism and therefore the end of John's sole witness to the Messiah Who was now to be revealed to Israel in Person.

Our Lord, by His various statements on the subject, made it perfectly plain by implication that the testimonies of John the Baptist and Elias (Elijah) were identical in purpose and length of time. They were in a sense interchangeable testimonies. In speaking of Elias, we do not refer to his original testimony of three years and a half (James V, 17) but to his coming testimony referred to in Revelation XI, 3 in these words, "I will give power unto My two witnesses, and they shall prophesy a thousand two hundred and threescore days, clothed in sackcloth". Not only does the Old Testament end with the promise "I will send you Elijah the prophet before the coming of the great and dreadful day of the Lord" (Mal. IV, 5), but our Lord Himself declared, "Elias truly shall first come, and restore all things" (Matt. XVII, 11). In other words, Elias is one of the "two witnesses" who with Moses is to return to Israel and prophesy for 1,260 days.

Finally, on two occasions our Lord deliberately called John the Baptist "Elias" in order to make it plain that John's testimony was so completely in the spirit and power of Elijah's coming testimony as to make them identical in purpose – the former adumbrating the latter. In Matthew XI, 3, we have the account of how John sent to Jesus this message, "Art Thou He that should come, or do we look for another?" Jesus sent a reassuring and tender message in reply – John being then in prison and suffering grievous hardship. Our Lord thereupon gave to the multitudes a beautiful dissertation on John's very high calling in these words, "A prophet? yea, I say unto you, and more than a prophet . . . Among them that are born of women there hath not risen a greater than John the Baptist". Our Lord then declared, "For all the prophets and the law prophesied until John. And if ye will receive it, this is Elias, which was for to come" (verses 13 and 14).

Again, after the Transfiguration, when John had been beheaded, our Lord spoke on this subject to Peter, James and John. These are His words: "Elias truly shall first come, and restore all things. But I say unto you, That Elias is come already, and they knew him not, but have done unto him whatsoever they listed. Likewise shall also the Son of Man suffer of them. Then the disciples understood that He spake unto them of John the Baptist" (Matt. XVII, 10 to 13).

We shall not delay to comment on all that the Scriptures narrate as to the person and ministry of John the Baptist as it would require a small volume to do so. Though Israel remained nationally unaffected, and rejected the baptism of John, yet, nevertheless, he did "prepare the way of the Lord" in the lives of a considerable remnant among whom were the twelve

Apostles of the Lamb. Presently, John's testimony will be taken up again by the prophet Elijah and the seven years, A.D. 26 to 33, will again be brought into the calendars of Israel and the Gentiles; this time, not in the terms of lowly grace and entreaty, or even of warning, but in those of the retributive judgments of the Apocalypse of John, the seer of Patmos; for in the time periods of the Revelation, namely, 1260 days and 42 months (Chap. XI, 1 to 3) we have a chronological replica of the seven years, A.D. 26 to 33, when John the Baptist first and then our Lord Jesus Christ were rendering testimony to Israel for like periods.

The last of the 1260 days of John's testimony was Wednesday, 5th October A.D. 29, and it was on that day that our Lord was baptized, as the Scripture declares, "then cometh Jesus from Galilee to Jordan unto John, to be baptized" (Matt. III, 13).

Henceforth our pages will be devoted to recording the steps of Jesus, the Son and Christ of God, as He trod His way for a further 3 years and 252 days to His Ascension amidst the wreckage of over 4,100 years of human sin and wickedness; yet, nevertheless, going "about doing good, and healing all that were oppressed of the devil; for God was with Him" (Acts X, 38).

# CHAPTER FOUR

## THE COURSE OF TIME BETWEEN THE BAPTISM OF OUR LORD JESUS CHRIST AND HIS FIRST SIGN-MIRACLE AT THE CANA WEDDING

---

A PRELUDE OF SIXTY-TWO DAYS EMBRACING HIS BAPTISM AND ANOINTING – HIS ABIDING WITH JOHN THE BAPTIST FOR SEVEN DAYS – HIS TEMPTATION – HIS BEGINNING AT THIRTY YEARS OF AGE – HIS MANIFESTATION BY JOHN THE BAPTIST – THE WEDDING AT CANA

THIS PRELUDE IS AN EXPRESSION IN MINIATURE OF THE WHOLE COURSE OF THE AGES TO THE SECOND ADVENT OF CHRIST

TIME

Wednesday, 5th October, to Monday, 5th December A.D. 29 (inclusively)

## PART I

UNTIL His Baptism in the river Jordan by John the Baptist on 5th October A.D. 29, our Lord Jesus Christ had been able to live as a PRIVATE INDIVIDUAL, because His identity as the Son of God and Messiah of Israel had remained hidden from all, except His Mother and Joseph. At His Baptism God revealed our Lord's identity to the Baptist who in turn made Him known to a prepared Remnant of the Jews, five of whom at once became our Lord's disciples. It was not until seven months later that our Lord embarked upon His Public Ministry and this, as might be expected, was in Jerusalem.

In Bible terms our Lord Jesus Christ was 29 years (of 354 days) and 302 days old on 5th October A.D. 29. In Solar terms He was 28 years and 341 days old – that is, just 24 days less than 29 Solar years. These figures can be confirmed by adding

1,260 days to our Lord's age (as previously given) on 25th April A.D. 26, when John the Baptist began his Testimony.

From now onwards we shall see how brilliant a light an accurate knowledge of time sheds upon events in our Lord's life. Notably is this the case in the Prelude of 62 days between His Baptism and the Cana Miracle – a period which was filled with events of the utmost significance in relation to His Person because preparatory to His Public Service as God's Anointed Servant – the Messiah.

It pleased God so to design the divisions of this Prelude of 62 days that, taken together, they would form a perfect expression of the whole course of time from Creation to the Second Advent when our Lord will come as the Bridegroom to claim His Bride, the Church. For that reason the period ends with a wedding which typifies the Christian Dispensation, during which the Gentile Bride of Christ is, like Eve for Adam, being formed of and for her Bridegroom. The details of this aspect of the 62 days we intend to give at the end of this chapter. The Bible abounds from end to end with chronological types and antitypes but these reach a positive crescendo in the days of our Lord's earthly life. Indeed, God's manipulation of time in the Bible and the manner in which He has engrafted His Eternal Truth into a perfectly-designed Plan of Time must be numbered among His mightiest works, since it proves Him to be (in all reverence) the Supreme Master Mathematician of the Universe. In our former Treatise *The World in Liquidation* we give a Summary of Bible Chronology and this conveys some idea of the perfection of the main stream of Time which runs right through the Bible and terminates on 12th June 1933, with the completion of man's 6,000 years of sinful failure. Let it be remembered that this tracing of our Lord's life in terms of Time has only been made possible by the possession of this faultless reproduction of Bible chronology as a whole.

The question will arise in many minds as to how we know that our Lord's Baptism and Anointing took place on 5th October A.D. 29. This can be quite simply explained.

We know that 30 Bible years of 354 days from our Lord's birth on Friday, 29th October 1 B.C., terminated on Friday, 25th November A.D. 29. Our Lord's 30th birthday was the next day – a Sabbath – 26th November. The Bible, as we are about to demonstrate, accounts for every day between this 26th November and 5th October A.D. 29, which was the Jews' Day of Atonement. Actually, in our researches on this subject, we discerned the truth by acting on the assumption that our Lord's Baptism was on this Day of Atonement because of its proximity to His 30th birthday when, as Luke informs us, He began His Ministry. Furthermore, we knew that all the major events in the Saviour's life occurred on Feast Days. We also knew that His Baptism in Jordan, in one aspect, speaks typically of His atoning death, and that no day in the Calendar of Sacred Feasts was more suited to this occasion than the great Day of Atonement.

## THE BAPTISM AND ANOINTING OF OUR LORD JESUS CHRIST WITH THE HOLY GHOST

### JESUS ABIDES WITH JOHN THE BAPTIST FOR THE SEVEN DAYS OF HIS CONSECRATION AS GOD'S HIGH PRIEST

5th October to 12th October A.D. 29

No words of man could possibly convey the limitless importance to God and the whole Universe of that which transpired by the banks of the Jordan when John baptized Jesus in its waters and when the Spirit of God descended as a "dove" and abode upon Him. There has been much discussion as to why the sinless Son of God should come to John whose baptism with water was unto repentance for sin. We shall learn that our Lord's baptism was not of that order at all, though His coming to John may have signified His identification with the faithful in Israel who had hearkened to John's summons to repent because the Kingdom of Heaven was at hand.

Let us at once say that a perfect understanding of Time in our Lord's earthly pathway has brought much to light on this subject concerning which there is no inkling on the surface of Scripture.

Before proceeding we will record Matthew's account of the

Baptism of Jesus. All four Gospels give substantially the same accounts of this great event. (See Mark I, 9 to 11; Luke III, 21 and 22; John I, 32 to 34.)

"Then cometh Jesus from Galilee to Jordan unto John, to be baptized of him.

"But John forbad Him, saying, I have need to be baptized of Thee, and comest Thou to me? And Jesus answering said unto him, Suffer it to be so now: for thus it becometh us to fulfil all righteousness. Then he suffered Him. And Jesus, when He was baptized, went up straightway out of the water: and, lo, the heavens were opened unto Him, and He saw the Spirit of God descending like a dove, and lighting upon Him: and lo a voice from heaven, saying, This is My beloved Son, in whom I am well pleased." (Matthew III, 13 to 17.)

The immense importance of this occasion may be gleaned from the fact that this is the first time in the Bible when the Three Persons of the Godhead – the Father, the Son and the Holy Spirit – are to be seen in action together. The occasion, as the Bible makes perfectly clear, is the Consecration of Jesus of Nazareth, the Son of God, as God's High Priest, in fulfilment of the word, "The Lord hath sworn, and will not repent, Thou art a priest for ever after the order of Melchizedek". (Psalm CX, 4.)

Our Lord, of course, perfectly understood why He must come to John and be baptized. Therefore when John sought to hinder Him, He replied, "Suffer it to be so now: for thus it becometh us to fulfil all righteousness" – that is, "the righteousness of the law" in relation to the consecration of the High Priest and his sons, as given in Leviticus VIII, etc. Aaron was a type of Christ and as High Priest nearly all the holy ritual of his consecration as such was typical of that which would mark the Consecration of our Lord as God's High Priest.

This subject is far too vast to develop in these pages but to understand exactly what took place at our Lord's Baptism we must name the salient features. In Leviticus VIII, 6 we are told, "Moses brought Aaron and his sons, and washed them with water". In verse 12 we are told, "He (Moses) poured of the anointing oil upon Aaron's head, and anointed him, to sanctify him". It is obvious that the counterpart of Aaron's "washing with water" was our Lord's Baptism in the Jordan and that the counterpart of the "anointing oil" with which Aaron was anointed was the Spirit of God Who descended "like a dove" upon our Lord as, praying, He "went up straightway out of the water".

At His Baptism our Lord was nearly thirty years of age but He had never before been anointed by the Holy Ghost. Nevertheless, as the Son of God, Whose conception in the womb of the Virgin Mary was wrought by the power of the Holy Ghost, Jesus had lived and walked in the ordinary circumstances of our human life in unbroken communion with His Father in Heaven, ever delighting in everything to do His will. Now the hour had come when our Lord must, as Man, offer Himself as ready for the fulfilment of all God's counsels in having sent Him to save the world. It has been rightly said that at His Baptism our Lord Jesus Christ accepted His Vocation or, we might say, sealed His acceptance of His Vocation, namely, that He had come to lay down His life in order to accomplish our redemption.

Our Lord's Baptism was a positive prefigurement of His death and resurrection – the Jordan river always being a type of death as the end of human life, and the coming up out of Jordan being therefore a type of resurrection unto eternal life (Joshua IV, 19). To God the Father our Lord's baptism was, therefore, a sublime expression of His willing obedience to take up and complete the purpose for which He had come into the world. ! To do this He must as Man be anointed with the Holy Ghost for it is as God's High Priest He must die and rise again in "the power of an endless life". This fact is best explained by the following quotation from the Hebrew Epistle on the subject – "Christ being come an high priest . . . by His own blood . . . entered in once into the holy place, having obtained eternal redemption for us. . . . How much more shall the blood of Christ, Who through the eternal Spirit offered Himself without spot to God, purge your conscience from dead works to serve the living God?" (Heb. IX, 11 to 14.) Let it be noted that our Lord's service as God's High Priest is by virtue of His anointing with the Holy Spirit, through Whom also He makes the offering of Himself to God. It is the same with all true believers in Christ. Our service, if acceptable to God, is by virtue of the anointing of the Holy Spirit (II Cor. I, 21 and 22; I John II, 27).

Our Lord's Baptism, as we have stated, took place on 5th October A.D. 29, which was the Jews' Day of Atonement. This was perfectly in keeping with the Scripture just quoted. Aaron, as High Priest, once a year on the day of Atonement, went into the holy place of the Tabernacle with the blood of the typical sacrifices "which he offered for himself, and for the errors of the people" (Heb. IX, 7, and see Leviticus XVI). It is not, therefore, surprising that God fixed on the Day of Atonement for the consecration of our Lord Jesus Christ as High Priest; and the more so when it is remembered that His Baptism prefigured His atoning death and glorious resurrection. Our Lord's Priesthood was in every sense an eternal one and founded upon His resurrection figuratively accomplished at His Baptism, and actually so on "the third day" after His death at Calvary.

All this very imperfectly explains why, as Jesus came up out of the water, the Spirit of God descended and abode upon Him as a dove. Our Lord was there and then consecrated as God's High Priest; and Aaron's typical consecration then found its Eternal Antitype, as it is declared, "Thou art a priest for ever after the order of Melchisedec". Again, of this anointing of Jesus with the Holy Ghost it is written in Psalm XLV, "God, Thy God, hath anointed Thee with the oil of gladness above Thy fellows"; and yet again, John the Baptist declared, "God giveth not the Spirit by measure unto Him" (John III, 34). We would commend the following Scriptures to the attention of those who desire more fully to enter in to the essential significance of our Lord's Baptism and Anointing as High Priest – Leviticus VIII and XVI; Hebrews V to IX and Psalm CX.

We cannot pass on without reference to God's own part at our Lord's Baptism. To our Lord the Heavens are opened and the Voice of God Himself is heard to declare, "This is My Son; My beloved in Whom I am well pleased" (Matt. III, 17, R.V. Margin). What a testimony to our Lord Jesus Christ after nearly 30 years of life on the earth as the Son of God. Our Lord's life had ever been a sweet fragrance to His Father Who now on one of three occasions causes His Voice to be heard from Heaven in glowing testimony to His well-beloved Son (cf. Matt. XVII, 5 and John XII, 28).

# THE SEVEN DAYS OF OUR LORD'S CONSECRATION AS GOD'S HIGH PRIEST SPENT WITH JOHN THE BAPTIST "BEYOND JORDAN"

In tracing the days between 5th October A.D. 29, and 26th November when our Lord attained "thirty years of age", we were at a loss to account for seven days. The Temptation absorbed 40 days and the days from its end to our Lord's return to the Baptist, as narrated in the 1st chapter of John, could be accounted for, as we will show, by means of the Years of the Messiah; but not so these seven days after the Baptism. Then light was granted as to the true significance of the Anointing of the Lord with the Holy Spirit and that caused us to turn to Leviticus VIII where we read in verses 33 to 35:

> "Ye shall not go out of the door of the tabernacle of the congregation in seven days, until the days of your consecration be at an end: for seven days shall he consecrate you. . . . Therefore shall ye abide . . . day and night seven days, and keep the charge of the Lord, that ye die not."

Here was the answer to the problem of the seven days, which are not named in the Gospels. In fulfilling "all righteousness" our Lord well knew that He must abide seven days at the place of His Baptism and Anointing with the Holy Spirit and that His consecration must be "for seven days" – night and day – "that ye die not". Our Lord in this, as all else, upheld God's unchangeable Law which, said He, "I am not come to destroy, but to fulfil" (Matt. V, 17).

The existence of these seven days of our Lord's Consecration brought to light a new and very precious fact, namely, that He and John must have spent this time together in holy converse. On the surface, our Lord's communications with John are limited to His remarks before His Baptism and the message He sent to John in prison which ended, "And blessed is he, whosoever shall not be offended in Me" (Matthew XI, 2 to 6). Now, however, we know that John must have been in the company of our Lord Jesus for seven days, and this fact is perfectly confirmed by the following remark made to John by his disciples, "Rabbi, *He that was with thee beyond Jordan*, to whom thou barest witness, behold, the same baptizeth, and all men come to Him" (John III, 26). The Scripture here, as always, confirms itself.

We need not speculate as to the nature of the communications which passed between Jesus and His herald during these days but we know from Isaiah XL the gist of their converse. In verses 3 to 5, John's mission as "the voice of him that crieth in the wilderness" is referred to. In verses 6 to 8, "the voice" says to our Lord, "Cry". Our Lord replies, "What shall I cry?" John gives answer, "All flesh is grass, and all the goodliness thereof is as the flower of the field . . . the grass withereth, the flower fadeth: but the word of our God shall stand for ever".

These words clearly indicate the manner in which John handed over responsibility to our Lord because now "He must increase" while John himself "must decrease". We therefore now know how close was the link of fellowship between the Messiah and His herald – the faithful Spirit-filled John. This accounts for the Baptist's last testimony to Jesus found in John III, 27 to 36. This contains expressions concerning our Lord and the Father which it would appear are the result of John's direct contact with the Lord, as they are unlike any other of his utterances.

It is of great interest to note that the seven days of our Lord's Consecration as High Priest, having begun on the Day of Atonement which was the 10th day of the 7th month, must have ended on the 17th day of the same. It was on this day that the Ark rested on Mount Ararat – a fact which betokened resurrection (Gen. VIII, 4). Furthermore, as we shall demonstrate later, in our Lord's Personal Chronology, that is, in the years of His own life dated from His birth, He was anointed by Mary of Bethany on the 10th day of the 7th month, that is, the day of Atonement, and rose from the dead on the 17th day of the 7th month in His 34th year. It is also a fact of great and solemn significance that the seven days of our Lord's Consecration as High Priest are separated from the seven days of His Passion (i.e., from His anointing by Mary of Bethany to His Resurrection) by exactly 1300 days. As all know, the number "13" is clearly marked in the Bible as expressing sin and rebellion. It is the main factor in the numerical value of many of Satan's names, and remarkably enough it is the same in our Lord's Old Testament names (Jehovah, Adonai, Ha-Elohim and Messiah), all Hebrew and Greek letters having a numerical value. This is explained by the fact that our Lord in order to be our Redeemer had to identify Himself with our fallen race, and to be "numbered with the transgressors" (Mark XV, 28). We thus learn why the first seven days of His life after His Anointing by the Holy Spirit are separated from the last seven days, those of His Passion, by 1300 days (5th to 12th October A.D. 29, to 26th April to 3rd May A.D.33).

It is also to be noted that the first verse of Leviticus IX opens with the words, "And it came to pass on the eighth day". This fact shows that the 7 days of consecration are viewed as a "death" period and that the first day thereafter typifies "resurrection". This is exactly the position of the 7 days of our Lord's Passion – they were followed by an "eighth day" – called in the Bible, according to the true translation, "the first day of the sabbaths", that is, the seven sabbaths or weeks to Pentecost (Leviticus XXIII, 15-16). It would, indeed, be difficult not to believe that Aaron's days of consecration as High Priest were designed by God to be a type, not only of our Lord's Consecration as High Priest, but also of the seven days of His Passion at the end of which, "after the power of an endless life", He entered upon His High Priestly service.

We must make brief reference to certain other features of our Lord's Baptism.

As the Baptism was on the Jews' Day of Atonement, all the people would have been engaged in its solemnities. Furthermore, it was a special "Sabbath of rest". This would mean that our Lord's Baptism and Anointing were not witnessed by the vulgar crowds that normally stood around at John's baptisms –

"Ambition's slaves
And Pleasure's jaded dupes from Herod's court
With Scribes and Pharisees, whose flowing robes
And broad phylacteries on arm and brow –
Badge of the hypocrite – compel the gaze."

We question whether anyone but John was present when our Lord, in His deep humility and grace, went down into the Jordan that with John He might "fulfil all righteousness". It was an occasion when Heaven came down to the earth and when God the Father unbosomed Himself in regard to the infinite pleasure He found in His well-beloved Son.

Mark's account of our Lord's Baptism informs us that "Jesus came from Nazareth of Galilee, and was baptized of John in

Jordan". It is a matter of interest to note that our Lord Jesus Christ never again returned to Nazareth to live but only to pay His one last visit, when the people were so enraged that they attempted to kill Him (Luke IV, 29). We read next of our Lord's Mother and brethren being at Cana and, after the wedding, of their going down together to Capernaum (John II, 12). Matthew informs us that when our Lord began His Galilean Ministry, "leaving Nazareth, He came and dwelt in Capernaum" (Matt. IV, 13). No doubt, Joseph being dead, our Lord encouraged His Mother to close the Nazareth home when He, of necessity, would be moving about hither and thither. Furthermore, the later attitude of the people of Nazareth to the One Who had grown up in their midst perfectly bore out the truth that "No prophet is accepted in his own country" (Luke IV, 16 to 30).

### ANOTHER ASPECT OF OUR LORD'S ANOINTING WITH THE HOLY SPIRIT

The aspect of Christ's anointing that we have been considering is one which relates to His Service for God as High Priest. It would be a gross omission not to refer to the aspect which concerns His relationship to His fellows. As Perfect Man our Lord fulfilled the first commandment, "Thou shalt love the Lord thy God with all thy heart, and with all thy soul, and with all thy mind, and with all thy strength". There also was, He said, a second commandment, namely, "Thou shalt love thy neighbour as thyself" (Mark XII, 30 and 31).

These two aspects of man's duty are typified by two of the Levitical Offerings – that which is to God by the Burnt Offering and that which is to man by the Meal Offering (Leviticus I and II, R.V.).

The "fine flour" of the Meal Offering is a type of Christ, as we have already mentioned, because of the perfect evenness which marked Him in all His ways and works. The Meal Offering expresses Christ fulfilling man's duty to his neighbour and doing so at immense personal sacrifice. God holds man responsible to love his neighbour as himself and He will judge all men for not doing so. When our Lord sets up His Kingdom, the world will be peopled by those who love their neighbour as themselves and peace and righteousness will reign on the earth as a consequence.

It is impossible on this occasion to give an exposition of the Meal Offering as a type of Christ in His Humanity, but reference to Leviticus II, 5 and 6 reveals that it was composed of "fine flour unleavened, mingled with oil". This typifies our Lord as the One born of the Virgin Mary to whom the Angel said, "The Holy Ghost shall come upon thee, and the power of the Highest shall overshadow thee". This was the "fine flour" of Christ's humanity, "mingled with oil" which typifies the Holy Spirit. We are next told that this Meal Offering is to have "oil" poured upon it. It is this which typifies what took place at our Lord's Anointing with the Holy Spirit because He was now coming forth to offer Himself as a Servant to His fellows. So we hear the Apostle Peter declare to the company assembled in the house of the Roman centurion, Cornelius, upon whom the Holy Spirit fell, "God anointed Jesus of Nazareth with the Holy Ghost and with power". But Peter went on to declare the effect of this in these words, "Who went about doing good, and healing all that were oppressed of the devil; for God was with Him" (Acts X, 38). That is a perfect expression of our Lord anointed by the Holy Spirit for the purpose of loving His neighbour as Himself. We know that in the end the doing of this cost Him His life. These remarks but poorly touch the fringe of a great subject to which, in effect, we merely call attention because of its immense importance.

# PART II

## THE FORTY DAYS OF TEMPTATION WHICH FOLLOWED OUR LORD'S ANOINTING AS GOD'S HIGH PRIEST

---

### HIS RETURN TO JOHN THE BAPTIST AT BETHABARA "BEYOND JORDAN"

---

### THE TRIUMPH OF "THE LAST ADAM" OVER THE DEVIL OR SATAN

---

A PERIOD OF 44 DAYS

12th October to 21st and 25th November A.D. 29

---

Read Matthew IV, 1 to 11; Mark I, 12 and 13; Luke IV, 1 to 13

THE SCRIPTURE reveals by means of its chronology that directly the seven days of our Lord's Consecration as God's High Priest ended, He was "led up of the Spirit into the wilderness to be tempted of the devil". The days of our Lord's life all began at 8 A.M. and the seven days of His Consecration are to be measured from 8 A.M. on Wednesday, 5th October, to 8 A.M. Wednesday, 12th October. The "forty days and forty nights" of His Temptation began, therefore, at 8 A.M. on 12th October and terminated at 8 A.M. on 21st November – a Monday.

We noted that Aaron and his sons entered upon their new service on "the eighth day" and according to this type our Lord, as God's High Priest, on the eighth day after His Baptism and Anointing, was driven by the Spirit into the wilderness to be "tempted of Satan" and to be "with the wild beasts" (Mark I, 12 and 13).

We shall at once do well to consider the cause for so tremendous an anticlimax as overtook our Lord in the circumstances of His path on this occasion. To have been the Subject of the anointing of the Holy Spirit and to have heard at the same time the Voice of God from Heaven declaring Him to be His beloved Son in Whom He was "well pleased", and immediately thereafter to find Himself apparently deserted, and the prey of wild beasts in a foodless wilderness, constituted for our Lord an anticlimax calculated to put His faith to a severe test and to cause Him to call in question the possibility of any success as regards His mission in the earth – at least, that is how the Adversary would present it to His mind. In this connection it will be well to quote a passage in the Hebrew Epistle which makes it perfectly clear that our Lord, having taken a body of flesh and blood, experienced our infirmities – "We have not an high priest which cannot be touched with the feeling of our infirmities; but was in all points tempted like as we are, yet without sin" (IV, 15).

While we know as a fact of history that our Lord Jesus Christ did not fail, but emerged unscathed from the ordeal of His Forty Days' Temptation in the wilderness at the hands of Satan, we must not allow it to weaken our apprehension of what it cost Him in the way of agonizing suffering to accomplish this triumph over His and our Adversary the Devil. If He had not so suffered, it could not have been written of Him, "in that He Himself hath suffered being tempted, He is able to succour them that are tempted" (Heb. II, 18).

The first fact to be noted is the positive emphasis in each of the three accounts that it was the Holy Spirit of God that "led" or drove Jesus into the wilderness for 40 days to "be tempted of the devil". Our Lord did not go of His own volition, neither did the Devil have any say in the matter whatever. It was God, acting through the Spirit, Who deliberately placed His Son in circumstances which He knew the Devil would take immediate advantage of in an effort to tempt Him to disobedience or to independent action.

In all reverence let it be said that God had no alternative to this course of action if Christ was to be our Redeemer. His well-beloved Son was here as Man (i.e. "made of a woman") to deliver the Adamic race from the thraldom of Satan in which He found it as the result of sin – sin being Satan's weapon for the enslavement of mankind. This being so, it was absolutely vital in the first instance that our Lord should not only show Himself proof against Satan's lying deceptions but that He should also show Himself to be a Man Who, by wholly trusting God and His written Word, was capable of complete victory over Satan. How otherwise could He deliver those whom Satan held in his power? On a later occasion our Lord perfectly expressed what we have just stated, in these words, "How can one enter into a strong man's house, and spoil his goods, except he first bind the strong man? and then he will spoil his house" (Matt. XII, 29).

Until our Lord appeared on the earth Satan was the undisputed Prince of this world – ruling it through sin which had made entrance into the race through the disobedience of "the first man Adam" – for "by one man's disobedience many were made sinners". Our Lord is spoken of as "the last Adam" in order to make it plain that, like the first Adam who was head of the race he brought down into ruin through disobedience, He is the Head of a new race which will triumph over Satan, sin and death through His own obedience – for "by the obedience of one shall many be made righteous" (Rom. V, 19).

The Bible reveals that directly after their creation Adam and Eve were placed by God on a probationary test of Forty Days. This plainly means that before God could hand over the dominion of the Earth to Adam, whom He had created for the purpose, he must give proof of being willing to own God's sovereign rights by acting in entire submission to Him in all things.

It is not stated on the surface of Scripture that Adam was placed on probation for 40 days, but that it was so is made perfectly certain by the chronology of Genesis. In our former Treatise, *The World in Liquidation* (Paper Four), we show from the Bible that prior to Adam's 130 years at the birth of Seth (Gen. V, 3), there was a period of 47 (7+40) days without which it is impossible to make the age of the Moon at the Flood agree with the chronology. Furthermore, without bringing in these 47 days before Adam's 130 years, it would not be possible to make the age of the Moon at any point in the Bible agree with the chronology. As it is, the Bible reveals that Adam and Eve began a 40 days of probation on the 8th day, that is, on the day following the first Sabbath of Creation. The date was 11th March 4075 B.C., and the 40 days terminated on 19th April which was the day Satan lured Eve into disobeying God—a disobedience in which Adam at once participated. *It should be noted that the temptations both of our Lord and of Adam began on an "eighth" day.*

With these facts before us, we are the better able to appreciate why it was righteously necessary for God to cause our Lord Jesus Christ to have to pass through a season of 40 days of agonizing temptation at the hands of Satan before He could be confirmed in the Headship of the New Creation. "The first man Adam" had failed miserably under a test conducted in the most *favourable* circumstances (that is, the Garden of Eden) conceivable to the human mind. Our Lord, as "the last Adam", is required of God to pass through a 40 days of Temptation in the most *unfavourable* circumstances conceivable to the human mind, that is, in the barren and rocky wilderness of Judaea, the haunt of predatory beasts, and far removed from all His fellow men and from all creature comforts.

We shall presently show that there is a most remarkable chronological correspondence between Adam's 40 days' temptation and that of our Lord Jesus Christ. It is, indeed, a fact that no one could really understand either of these periods of temptation apart from the other. Adam, we are told, "is the figure of Him that was to come" (Rom. V, 14); so that it is not surprising that our Lord's 40 days of Temptation were the positive counterpart of Adam's 40 days.

Watching closely the actual text of Scripture, we may learn the following facts about our Lord's Temptation.

The period appointed by God was 40 days and 40 nights – no more and no less. During this period our Lord fasted but He did not hunger, or Scripture would not state "when He had fasted forty days and forty nights, He was afterward an hungered" (Matthew), or, as in Luke, "And in those days He did eat nothing: and when they were ended, He afterward hungered". (Note. Some MSS. omit Luke's "afterward".)

It should hardly need stating that as our Lord, *after the 40 days were ended*, declared to Satan, "Man shall not live by bread alone, but by every word that proceedeth out of the mouth of God", He had been putting into practice this most precious principle enunciated by Moses as recorded in Deuteronomy VIII, 3. It is as clear as words in the Bible can make it that our Lord did not hunger in the 40 days because He was "living" on the Word and Words of God. When God's allotted span of 40 days was ended, then "He afterward hungered". In the 40 days it was God Who was allowing our Lord, as Man, to be tested by Satan.

What took place after the 40 days was not part of our Lord's Temptation as ordained by God, but an effort of Satan which God allowed in order to manifest our Lord's complete mastery over the Adversary through the use of "the sword of the Spirit, which is the word of God" (Ephes. VI, 17).

It is, therefore, necessary to make a sharp difference between the 40 days and those that followed when Satan thrice openly challenged our Lord in regard to the three subversive principles by which he had held the human race in enslavement for the 4,000 years since the Fall of Adam.

In the 40 days God allowed Satan to tempt our Lord and Master with every wile and fiery dart known to his evil and cunning mind. Of the nature of these temptations nothing appears openly upon the surface of Scripture. They were not of an order understandable by anyone who has not been actually engaged in conflict with the powers of darkness as the result of maintaining the rights of Christ in a sphere dominated by "the prince of this world" – the one who is also termed "the prince of the power of the air, the spirit that now worketh in the children of disobedience". There is no doubt that many of the Psalms give expression prophetically to our Lord's thoughts during His Temptation. At such a time the heavens would appear to be like brass and a deep sense of being forsaken would be present to the heart and mind. Psalm CXIX contains a great many expressions of our Lord's faith in the face of great adversity. There are many others which must also have been a source of infinite comfort to our Lord in the face of the unceasing assaults of the Adversary.

How good it is to realize that our blessed Lord and Master passed through the whole 40 days unscathed, His obedience to the Word of God and His submission to the Will of God being unimpaired so that at the end He had NOTHING with which to reproach Himself; and, above all, so that His Father in Heaven, Who had ordained the test, knew that the One He had sent into the world was proof against the wiles and fiery darts of its Prince (Ephesians VI, 11 and 17).

The 40 days of our Lord's Temptation made it manifest, therefore, that there was One Man on the earth Whom Satan could not tempt into disobedience or distrust of God, no matter how subtle his wiles or how well-aimed his fiery darts. This, however, was a negative result which left the "strong man" – Satan – in complete control of "his palace". Our Lord had, indeed, withstood the assaults of the Adversary but thus far the

Adversary's power remained unimpaired. If the strong man's palace was to be invaded and his spoils divided, the strong man must be defeated and bound by One Who was "stronger than he" (Luke XI, 21, 22, etc.).

In the 40 days there is no suggestion that Satan made any direct approach to our Lord. Satan's power to the greatest extent lies in his presence remaining undetected, while he levels his assaults upon the mind, the soul or the spirit of his victim who may remain quite unaware of the source from which his foreboding fears and questionings arise. This conflict with Satan and the powers of darkness is described for Christians in Ephesians VI as a warfare with unseen and physically intangible foes.

When, however, God's part in the Temptation of our Lord was completed at the end of the 40 days during which He, having been "led by the Spirit into the wilderness", was "tempted of the devil", an entirely new phase in these proceedings began – the phase in which our Lord's complete mastery over Satan was established by His bold use of the Word of God – the Sword of the Spirit – as an offensive weapon. In the 40 days Jesus not only lived by the Word of God but His "loins" were "girt about with Truth" used defensively in meeting the assaults of the Adversary. In other words, Truth, that is, the Word of God, enwrapped our Lord and was His protection in that it entirely governed His heart and directed His every step, so that as none other He could say "by the word of Thy lips I have kept me from the paths of the destroyer" (Psalm XVII, 4). Before briefly considering how our Lord acted in driving off His Adversary in utter defeat, we must refer to a most important chronological fact which has a direct bearing upon the day our Lord emerged from the Temptation – that is, the last of the 40 days.

### THE CHRONOLOGICAL SIGNIFICANCE OF THE FOUR DAYS BETWEEN THE END OF THE FORTY DAYS OF TEMPTATION AND THE RETURN TO JOHN THE BAPTIST.

21st to 25th November A.D. 29

Once again the calendar of the Years of the Messiah sheds its enlightening rays upon our Lord's earthly pathway. In Israel's calendar 21st November was the 27th day of the 8th month, and 25th November the 2nd day of the 9th month – neither of which dates has any Biblical significance.

In the calendar founded upon the Years of the Messiah (see Summary of Facts, Par. 18) the 21st of November, which was the last of the 40 days of the Temptation, was the 10th day of the 1st month in the year 4,235 from Creation. This being so, the 22nd, 23rd, 24th and 25th of November were the 11th, 12th, 13th and 14th of the 1st month. We need hardly remind readers that the Paschal lambs were set aside on the 10th of the 1st month and slain on the 14th day at even, that is, at 6 P.M.

In the Summary of Facts (Pars. 5, 7 and 8) we explain the reason why the 4 days, the 11th, 12th, 13th and 14th of the 1st month, while the Passover lambs are awaiting death, are viewed as an absolute blank in the Sacred Years of the Bible. It is for this reason that there is no mention whatever of the 4 days between the 21st of November when the 40 days of the Temptation ended and the 25th of November when our Lord returned to John the Baptist at Bethabara "beyond Jordan". This is the more remarkable because, with the exception of these 4 days, the Gospels directly account for every one of the 62 days between the Lord's Baptism and the end of the Wedding at Cana in Galilee.

It will be remembered that when referring to the occasion when Jesus was twelve years of age we pointed out that in the Years of the Messiah every year of His life ended at 6 P.M. on the 14th day of the 1st month, that is, at the exact hour when the Passover lambs were sacrificed. At 6 P.M. on Friday, 25th November which, as we have already stated, was the 14th of the 1st month in the calendar based upon the Years of the Messiah, our Lord had attained 30 years of age in Bible terms.

On that day, and in all probability at its close when the hour had arrived for the Passover to be killed, our Lord returns to John at Bethabara. So we read in John I, 29:

> "The next day John seeth Jesus coming unto him, and saith, Behold the Lamb of God, which taketh away the sin of the world."

By this statement John the Baptist marked out our Lord to his disciples as THE ANTITYPE of every Passover lamb ever offered in Israel – Jesus being God's Passover Lamb Who had come to take away the sin of the world. This pronouncement of John and the day upon which it was made are quite inseparable. In the Chronology of the Messiah it was the day and hour of the Paschal Sacrifice and such a pronouncement could not be made on any other day in the year with any true relevance.

We shall not at this point make any further reference to our Lord's visit to John, as it will come up for full consideration at the opening of Part III of this Chapter. We have been obliged to refer to the matter thus far in order to bring out the fact that the 4 days between the end of our Lord's 40 days of Temptation and His return to John are the 4 unreckoned days of the Bible's Sacred Year, which form the most brilliant type in the Bible of the 4,000 Years of Redemption between the end of Adam's 40 days of testing (the transgression was on the 40th day) and the death of Jesus Christ our Lord at the Passover in A.D. 33.

It was in these 4 days, the 11th, 12th, 13th and 14th of the 1st month in the Messianic year 4,235, that the three final assaults of Satan upon our Lord, as recorded by Matthew and Luke, were made. We may well ask, Are these facts related? Satan knew perfectly well that Jesus was the Messiah, and that these 4 days were a type of the 4,000 years at the end of which He – the Seed of the Woman – would bruise the serpent's head; even though he – Satan – might bruise His heel, in fulfilment of the first Bible prophecy (Genesis III, 15).

Perhaps, then, if we briefly consider these three final assaults of the Adversary, we may discover their relevance.

### WHY OUR LORD'S THREE TEMPTATIONS TOOK PLACE IN THE FOUR DAYS WHICH TYPIFY THE 4,000 YEARS FROM ADAM.

It is a fact glaring in its significance that the 40 Days of Temptation of "the first man Adam" were followed by the 4 "days" of 1,000 years each to the death of Christ – "the last Adam"; and that the 40 Days of Temptation of "the last Adam" were similarly followed by the 4 days in the Bible's Sacred Year which so positively typified these 4,000 years. In this we see a perfect design and one by which God expresses Himself as to the relationship of "the last Adam" – our Lord Jesus Christ – to "the first man Adam" who brought his race down into ruin by his one act of defiant disobedience which was induced by Satan on the last of his 40 days of testing.

We may therefore be sure that the three assaults upon our Lord have a typical bearing upon Satan's relationship to the human race in the 4,000 years from Adam to Christ. In other words, these three assaults represent the three great subversive principles by means of which Satan had held mankind in enslavement ever since the Fall of Adam and Eve in the Garden of Eden.

After the Fall the needs of man's spirit and soul were submerged beneath the more clamant needs of his body, the appetites of which must be satisfied before all else. It was this principle that Satan worked on in seeking to persuade our Lord (since He was hungry) to consider His bodily needs by the performance of a miracle from which He alone would benefit, and by which He would endorse the evil principle that man's bodily needs must be his primary consideration. Our Lord at once exposed Satan by quoting a divine principle from the Word of God, "Man shall not live by bread alone, but by every word that proceedeth out of the mouth of God" (Matt. IV, 4 and Deut. VIII, 3). This principle forms a primary element in our Lord's teaching. In the Sermon on the Mount, we hear Him say, "Take no thought for your life, what ye shall eat, or what ye shall drink . . . Is not the life more than meat . . . ? Therefore take no thought, saying, What shall we eat? or, What shall we drink? . . . (for after all these things do the Gentiles [nations] seek;) . . . but seek ye first the kingdom of God, and His righteousness; and all these things shall be added unto you" (Matt. VI, 25 to 33).

The second assault, when Satan took our Lord to Jerusalem and proposed that He should put God to the test by casting Himself off a temple pinnacle is, as the Lord showed, the evil principle of tempting God. This principle is seen to be much in evidence with the people of Israel, and our Lord quoted a Scripture which refers to their conduct at Massah because they thought they were going to die of thirst. This incident is recorded thus: "He called the name of the place Massah . . . because they tempted the Lord, saying, Is the Lord among us, or not?" (Exodus XVII, 7). In Psalm LXXVIII, verses 18, 41 and 56, it is thrice stated that the people of Israel tempted God. Satan was always at the back of the scenes when Israel tempted the Lord God. In effect, to tempt God was an effort to force Him into a course of action of some kind and carried with it the aspersion that He was failing to keep His Word with His people. Our Lord repelled this assault by quoting the divine rule, "Thou shalt not tempt the Lord thy God".

In the final assault the Adversary laid bare his motive which involved the principle of giving to him the worship due only to God. Had he not succeeded through idolatry in drawing to himself the worship of men from the very beginning? All the idols of the heathen were and are but forms of Satan-worship. On this account God said to Moses, referring to the people of Israel, "they shall no more offer their sacrifices unto devils, after whom they have gone a whoring" (Lev. XVII, 7). Joshua challenges Israel with these words, "Choose you this day whom ye will serve; whether the gods which your fathers served that were on the other side of the flood (lit. Euphrates), or the gods of the Amorites, in whose land ye dwell: but as for me and my house, we will serve the Lord" (Joshua XXIV, 15). The Apostle Paul declares, "The things which the Gentiles sacrifice, they sacrifice to devils, and not to God" (I Cor. X, 20). Here then was another evil principle with which Satan had enslaved the human race for 4,000 years, namely, that by deceit and by the promise of imaginary benefits, he had turned men away from the worship of the only true and living God, so that they might worship him. Consequently God warned Israel in the most solemn terms about idolatry and it is this which our Lord quoted from Deuteronomy VI, 13 to 15:

> "Thou shalt fear the Lord thy God, and serve Him, and shalt swear by His name. Ye shall not go after other gods, of the gods of the people which are round about you . . . lest the anger of the Lord thy God be kindled against thee, and destroy thee from off the face of the earth."

With this final assault upon our Lord Satan encompasses his own defeat and earns the stern rebuke, "Get thee hence, Satan: for it is written, Thou shalt worship the Lord thy God, and Him only shalt thou serve."

Thrice defeated and exposed, Satan, "the strong man", is

brought low by "the Stronger than he". Now our Lord can go forward! "The last Adam" has triumphed, and the deceiver of the first Adam has been bound by the One Who will now enter "his palace", spoil his goods and free his captives (Luke XI, 21 and 22).

These remarks may, because all too brief, very imperfectly show the relationship between the three final assaults of Satan upon our Lord and the four typical days when these took place; but that they represented principles upon which Satan had enslaved mankind for 4,000 years none can doubt.

It is important to take account of the fact that Israel's 40 years of temptation in the wilderness of Sinai terminated on the 10th day of the 1st month (Joshua IV, 19), exactly as did our Lord's 40 days of Temptation in the Years of the Messiah.

It is also worthy of note that our Lord's Temptation began on 12th October A.D. 29, and that four years later on 12th October A.D. 33, the Christian Dispensation began chronologically and ran its course for 2,000 Bible years (which include 40 years of Jubile) to 12th June 1933. The true Christian Church is the Body of Christ and its whole history has been a conflict with Satan and the powers of darkness, so that our Lord's Temptation may be viewed as a type of His Church's sojourn in the Wilderness of this world.

We shall now proceed to Part III of this chapter and show how the Bible accounts for the 11 days from 25th November A.D. 29, when our Lord returned to John the Baptist, to the end of the Wedding at Cana in Galilee on December 5th – an event of deep typical significance in the present hour.

# PART III

## OUR LORD JESUS CHRIST, NOW THIRTY YEARS OF AGE, TAKES HIS PLACE AS MESSIAH IN THE MIDST OF A REMNANT OF THE JEWS "PREPARED" BY JOHN THE BAPTIST

---

### FIVE DISCIPLES OF JOHN ATTACH THEMSELVES TO JESUS WHOM THEY OWN AS THE MESSIAH

---

### OUR LORD'S MINISTRY OPENS WITH A SYMBOLICAL EXPRESSION OF HIS DEATH AND RESURRECTION – AN EVENT WHICH FORMS THE KEY TO THE GOSPEL OF JOHN

---

### THE WEDDING OF ONE OF OUR LORD'S BROTHERS AT CANA ON "THE THIRD DAY"

---

TIME

Saturday, 26th November, to Monday, 5th December A.D. 29

Read John I and II to verse 12

---

IF IT WERE not for the first four chapters of the Gospel by John the world would be totally ignorant of all the events in the life of Jesus Christ our Lord between the end of the Temptation on 21st to 25th November A.D. 29, and the Autumn of A.D. 30, when He returned into Galilee, through Samaria, after learning "that John was cast into prison". Matthew, Mark and Luke each write as if our Lord commenced His Galilean Ministry directly after His Temptation. John, writing last, is caused to correct this unfounded impression, and this he does as an eye-witness of the events he records. Matthew was not "called" until after the Autumn of A.D. 30 when Jesus was ministering in Galilee (Matt. IX, 9) and so could be no witness of events prior thereto.

Our present considerations will therefore be drawn exclusively from Chapters I and II of John's Gospel as this is the sole source from which to glean our knowledge of events from the beginning of our Lord's Ministry on 26th November A.D. 29, to the end of the Cana Wedding on 5th December, when the prelude of 62 days from His Baptism was completed.

It will be remembered that we are not writing a Dissertation on the Gospels or "a Life of Christ", but that we are reproducing from the Scriptures the course of our Lord's earthly pathway in terms of Time. This being so, we shall not be expected to give an exposition of these two chapters with which John is caused to open his Gospel, but merely to select therefrom that which has a positive relationship to our main objective.

We know that the Spirit of God caused John in writing his Gospel to present our Lord Jesus Christ as THE SON OF GOD – THE WORD MADE FLESH – tabernacling among men, "full of grace and truth" (I, 14). In this aspect, therefore, John's Gospel presents our Lord in His life on the earth like the other Gospels, but with this difference, that John maintains throughout an order which is strictly chronological. By means of John's Gospel we have been able to set up a calendar for the whole period of our Lord's life from the opening of His Ministry on 26th November A.D. 29, to His Ascension on 13th June A.D. 33 – a period of precisely 3 solar years and 200 days.

We shall see that in its most important aspect, John's Gospel is a prefigurement of the Christian Dispensation, that is, of the period between the Lord's Ascension and His Return when He fulfils the promise, "I will come again, and receive you unto Myself; that where I am, there ye may be also" (John XIV, 3). In this aspect, all the eight Sign-Miracles of this Gospel are prophetic of events at the end of this Dispensation – four relating to the Christian Church and four to the people of Israel. We shall have reason to refer to each one of these in due course.

## OUR LORD'S DEATH AND RESURRECTION PREFIGURED IN THE "PASSOVER" AT WHICH HIS MINISTRY OPENED ON 26TH NOVEMBER A.D. 29

### HE NOW ATTAINS THIRTY YEARS OF AGE

We are indebted to Luke, "the beloved physician" and intimate companion of the Apostle Paul, for the vital information that our Lord began His Ministry when He was thirty years of age. This was the age according to the Law, as repeated many times in Numbers IV, when Levitical service began. Luke's statement, according to the Sinaitic and Vatican Codices, reads, "And Jesus Himself was, when He began, about thirty years of age" (Luke III, 23). It will be recalled that in Chapter One we explained that the word "about" does not imply indefiniteness in the Greek where numbers are concerned.

The Gospel of John reveals that our Lord began His Ministry at "the tenth hour" (9-10 A.M.) on 26th November A.D. 29, and this was *to the hour* exactly 30 Bible years of 354 days from the 9th hour (8-9 A.M.) on 29th October 1 B.C., when He was born of the Virgin Mary into this world at Bethlehem in Judaea. In effect, this means that our Lord began His public service for God the Father at the very first hour the Law allowed.

The immense importance of the occasion to God is made known to us in John's Gospel by what transpired on the previous day, 25th November. This calls for careful examination.

In Part II of this Chapter, when writing on the Temptation and our Lord's return to John the Baptist, we showed that in the Years of the Messiah (see Summary of Facts, Par. 18) 25th November A.D. 29, was the day of the Passover, namely, the 14th day of the 1st month. This 25th of November was the last day of the Lord's 30th year and, like every year of His life, in the calendar of the Years of the Messiah it ended at the actual hour when the Passover lambs were killed, that is, 6 P.M. (In all such measurements the Bible adopts the day beginning and ending at 6 P.M.)

As Jesus approached him, John, moved to do so by the Spirit of God, proclaims:

> "Behold the Lamb of God, which taketh away the sin of the world". (John I, 29.)

This is another occasion, like that which occurred when He was but twelve years of age, when our Lord presents Himself as the Antitypical Paschal Lamb. Only His death could take "away the sin of the world" and rehabilitate the human race before God, so that "whosoever believeth in Him should not perish, but have everlasting life".

Therefore, "in a figure" Jesus is viewed as dying there and then as the Antitypical Paschal Lamb. As was the case when our Lord was 12 years of age, this was only as seen by God. It was again the Father and the Son acting together in relation to the Redemption of the world. It was Calvary being anticipated. Again, it was our Lord, at the opening of His Service for God, reaffirming His acceptance of His vocation as the Lamb of God set apart in the Garden of Eden to die at the end of four "days" of a thousand years in order to take "away the sin of the world".

Where the Lord is concerned there can be no death, even symbolically, without resurrection. Hence we read:

> "Again the next day after John stood, and two of His disciples; and looking upon Jesus as He walked, he saith, Behold the Lamb of God!" (John I, 35, 36.)

This was said between 8 and 9 the next morning, the hour when the sheaf of firstfruits (the type of Christ risen) was waved before the Lord (Levit. XXIII, 11). What a glorious testimony John gives to our Lord's accomplished sacrifice. He sees Jesus now as the slain Lamb risen from the dead and "the sin of the world" taken away. He, therefore, exclaims only "Behold the Lamb of God!" In vision, as it were, John has heard the triumphant cry, "It is finished". Man may now be "reconciled to God by the death of His Son" (Rom. V, 10).

All this may appear deep and filled with mystery to those who do not comprehend the true perspective of the Gospel of John which, as we have said, is a prefigurement, both as a whole and in its specific parts, of the Christian Dispensation. In verse 11 of chapter I, our Lord's rejection by Israel is viewed as an accomplished fact – "He came unto His own (neuter: things or place), and His own (masc: people) received Him not". This fact, coupled with our Lord's death and resurrection "in a figure", is absolutely essential to that aspect of this Gospel which constitutes it a prefigurement of the Christian Dispensation which, as everyone knows, actually began after Israel's rejection of our Lord and His death upon Calvary's Tree.

In John's Gospel our Lord is presented as the Son of God – "the Word . . . made flesh". But from the beginning of His Ministry He is viewed as the Son of God *in resurrection* and as such the Dispenser of "eternal life". He could not take that place in the $3\frac{1}{2}$ years of His Ministry without first having passed through death "in a figure", and this to the perfect satisfaction of "God, Who quickeneth the dead, and calleth those things which be not as though they were" (Rom. IV, 17).

We will now make reference in turn to each day named in the 1st and 2nd chapters of John's Gospel to the end of the Wedding at Cana.

THURSDAY – 24TH NOVEMBER A.D. 29 – *13th of 1st month, Messianic Year 4235*

The events of this day are recorded in John I, 19 to 28. A deputation of Priests and Levites sent from Jerusalem waits upon John the Baptist, pressing him to unveil his identity, which he does, saying, "I am the voice of one crying in the wilderness, Make straight the way of the Lord, as said the prophet Esaias". John then positively declares the Messiah present, saying, "There standeth One among you, Whom ye know not; He it is . . . whose shoe's latchet I am not worthy to unloose". It is to be noted that John the Baptist renders this final testimony to official Jewry concerning the Messiah two days before He begins His Ministry, having attained 30 years of age.

24th November A.D. 29, is 1,310 days from 25th April A.D. 26, when John the Baptist began his testimony as the Herald of the Messiah.

FRIDAY – 25TH NOVEMBER – *14th of 1st month, Messianic Year 4235*

The events of this day are given in John I, verses 29 to 34. We have explained in previous pages that our Lord is here viewed as dying "in a figure". In the latter part of these verses John the Baptist bears testimony to his own disciples concerning events at our Lord's Baptism. God Himself had informed John that He on Whom the Spirit descended and remained was "He which baptizeth with the Holy Ghost". John concludes with the words, "And I saw, and bare record that this is the Son of God".

SABBATH – 26TH NOVEMBER – *15th of 1st month, Messianic Year 4235*

The events of this day are given in John I, 35 to 42. We have already pointed out that the Lord, having died "in a figure" on the 14th of the 1st month as God's Passover Lamb, is viewed the next morning by John the Baptist as having been raised from the dead – "the sin of the world" having been taken away.

We trust we have said enough to show that our Lord's death

and resurrection "in a figure", as recorded at the opening of John's Gospel, is a divine foreshadowing of Calvary, for it is this fact which forms the key to the true understanding of this Gospel.

"Rabbi . . . Master, where dwellest thou?"

Finding Himself followed by two of John's disciples, Jesus addresses them (His first public utterance) with the enquiry, "What seek ye?" The disciples reply, "Rabbi . . . where dwellest Thou? He saith unto them, Come and see. They came and saw where He dwelt, and abode with Him that day: for it was about the tenth hour".

Let it be realized that this was the first act of the "risen" Christ. At once our thoughts go to the day of His actual resurrection when He walked to Emmaus with another two of His disciples and opened to them the Scriptures (Luke XXIV).

In each case only one of the two disciples is named. Clearly, each pair typifies the Church – Jew and Gentile. In the case of the two disciples in John I, the day was Israel's Sabbath and God's "first day of the week". Plainly, therefore, in these two disciples we have a symbolical expression of the Church abiding with Christ in the Millennium – the Earth's coming Sabbath.

The mention of "the tenth hour" (9 to 10 A.M.) is most illuminating because previous to this there had been two days and nine hours named by John. As we shall reveal from the Scriptures in due course, our Lord was in death for exactly 2 days and 9 hours. Therefore, "the tenth hour" is the resurrection hour, and as such it is brought into the Scripture here in order to emphasize that in this Gospel our Lord Jesus Christ is to be viewed as having died and risen again. In this aspect, therefore, John's mention of this "tenth hour" constitutes the key to the whole Gospel. (The 10th hour in Jewish time would be 4 P.M. But all John's "hours" are Roman and are measured from Midnight to Noon and from Noon to Midnight, just like our own.)

In his Gospel John tells us that Andrew, Simon Peter's brother, was "one of the two which heard John speak". Manifestly, the Apostle John was himself the companion of Andrew on this occasion. Nothing could be more clear than that John is giving a first-hand or eye-witness's account of events in the days we are considering. John never brings himself into the picture but in Chapter XXI he says, "This is the disciple which testifieth of these things, and wrote these things". The word "testifieth" in the Greek signifies "to bear witness" and it is used 33 times in John's Gospel. It is, indeed, blessed to contemplate that "that disciple whom Jesus loved" was one of the first to be drawn to the Master and to receive the invitation to spend the Sabbath with Him.

After a day in the Master's Presence, Andrew "findeth his own brother Simon" (no doubt that evening) whom he addresses thus, "We have found the Messias . . . the Christ". When Jesus beheld Simon Peter, He said, "Thou art Simon the son of Jona: thou shalt be called Cephas, which is by interpretation, A stone".

And so our Lord's first day of ministry closed with John, Andrew and Peter – three future Apostles – at His side and owning Him as the Messiah – God's Anointed One.

The month of November when our Lord began His Ministry is the time for sowing in Palestine. This is in perfect keeping with His statement in the Parable of the Wheat and Tares – "He that soweth the good seed is the Son of Man; the field is the world". Verily, therefore, it may be said of Him, "Behold, a sower went forth to sow" (Matthew XIII, 3 and 37).

SUNDAY – 27TH NOVEMBER – *16th of 1st month, Messianic Year 4235*

In John I, 43, we read, "The day following Jesus would go forth into Galilee, and findeth Philip, and saith unto him, Follow Me". The expression "would go forth" simply means that Jesus had planned to go into Galilee for the wedding at Cana which, as we shall see presently, He was under obligation to attend for family reasons, and also for reasons of a much higher order since the event was to form a perfect type of the Christian Dispensation.

There is no intermediary in the case of Philip's call. He is the first whom the Lord Himself seeks and calls. How clear it becomes that our Lord and Master must have been moving about all the time within the circle of John's disciples and knew each one and yet was unknown to any.

Considerable detail is supplied in John I, verses 45 to 51, in relation to the call of Nathaniel who is not heard of again until the Fishing Episode of John XXI.

## "THE THIRD DAY THERE WAS A MARRIAGE IN CANA OF GALILEE"

### "THIS BEGINNING OF HIS SIGNS DID JESUS"

Tuesday, 29th November, to Monday, 5th December A.D.29.

John II, 1 to 11 (R.V.)

The Wedding at Cana in Galilee is only mentioned by the Evangelist John and it forms the first of the Eight Sign-Miracles recorded by him in his Gospel. As we have already pointed out, John's Gospel as a whole, and in many of its parts, prefigures the Christian Dispensation. To this end the Gospel opens with the assumption that our Lord has been rejected by His own nation (I, 11) and with His figurative death and resurrection as "the Lamb of God, which taketh away the sin of the world". The Wedding at Cana attended by our Lord and five of His disciples is the first of these prefigurements.

This is not the occasion to embark upon a detailed exposition of this first "sign" of John's Gospel, but it would be out of keeping with the purpose of this Treatise not to call attention to its great significance as a type of the Dispensation in which we live and which, in one aspect, has already come to an end, as we shall explain.

Before referring to the typical significance of this Marriage, it will be well to note some features of its domestic setting. In the first place, it must be recognized that, like all Bible weddings, this one lasted for a whole week. It is this fact that makes it a type of the Christian Dispensation which is always marked by the number "seven". Jacob's "week" of nuptials for his marriage with Leah is another such type. (See Genesis XXIX, 27, and Judges XIV, 12 and 17.)

The position occupied by our Lord's Mother makes it perfectly clear that it was an affair of her own family and probably the marriage of her eldest son by Joseph, who by then had evidently been gathered to his fathers. Mary was obviously the presiding Hostess at this Wedding and to suggest otherwise would be to infer that in concerning herself about the failure of the wine, and in her giving of commands to the servants, she was stepping out of her place. Being responsible it was natural that she should turn to our Lord, her first-born Son, to assist her in what was a real dilemma, namely, the absence of any wine for the wedding-guests.

It is important to note that while this Cana Wedding is a type of the Christian Dispensation as a whole, it was the miracle of the water turned to wine that constituted the "sign". This fact calls for explanation.

In the Revised Version we read:

> "And when the wine failed, the mother of Jesus saith unto Him, They have no wine. And Jesus saith unto her, Woman, what have I to do with thee? Mine hour is not yet come" (II, 3, 4).

There is hardly a passage of Scripture which has caused commentators more exercise than this. Why did our Lord address His Mother in these terms when almost at once He responded to her appeal for help in so mighty a manner? The answer is that our Lord, knowing all things, was perfectly well aware that this Wedding was a type of the then coming Christian Dispensation, and that the failure of the wine at that given point of time was a prophetic intimation that the Dispensation would end in failure through the apostasy that would set in. He knew, furthermore, that the time would come when He would have to act out of Heaven and not only restore "the wine" that had failed but provide an abundant supply, even better in quality than that with which the Dispensation began; as only thus could the Divine objective for the Dispensation be attained, namely, the gathering out from the nations of a people to form the Body and Bride of Christ (see Acts XV, 14; Ephes. V, 32). Our Lord, therefore, addressed His Mother as one filling a typical role in a wholly typical setting, as we are about to explain.

In this instance, as so frequently in our Lord's pathway, it is chronological knowledge that provides the key to the understanding of this episode.

This Wedding, the Bible shows, started on "the third day" after our Lord "began". The date was Tuesday, 29th November, as He "began" on the 26th – a Sabbath. The Christian Dispensation began in the third year after our Lord's death and resurrection in A.D. 33, that is, in A.D. 36, when the Holy Ghost first fell on the Gentiles, as recorded in Acts X and XI. In conformity with its antitype the Wedding at Cana had to start on "the third day". The Christian Dispensation is viewed, however, in the Bible as starting over three years, as Pentecost at Jerusalem in A.D. 33 and Pentecost at Caesarea in A.D. 36, as recorded in Acts II and X, respectively, are treated as *one descent of the Holy Ghost* – the interval of 3 years being viewed as a chronological hiatus.

We have already pointed out, when referring to the first two years of our Lord's life, that the Christian Dispensation is everywhere in the Bible viewed as being 2,000 years in length. The "two thousand cubits" of Joshua III, 4, the "two days" of Hosea VI, 2 and the "two days" of our Lord in Samaria, of John IV, 40, are but three of many chronological types of the 2,000 years of the Christian Dispensation which began on 12th October A.D. 33 (when the additional year of clemency to Israel, named in Luke XIII, 8, ended) and ran an unbroken course to 12th June 1933.

In our former Treatise, *The World in Liquidation*, we not only show how these 2,000 years are measured, but explain fully that the date of 12th June 1933 was also the last day of the predetermined 6,000 Years of Man of which the first 6 days of the Bible are a type. We furthermore explain that the world then entered *an extra-dispensational era* which our Lord on four occasions termed "*the consummation of the age*" (Matt. XIII, 40; XXIV, 3, etc., R. V. Margin).

Our Lord also referred to these 2,000 years of the Christian Dispensation as "the times of the Gentiles" – the period when Jerusalem would be under Gentile rule (Luke XXI, 24).

It has been essential to give these facts about the Christian Dispensation in order to explain the typical aspect of the Cana Wedding and of our Lord's words to His Mother – "Woman, what have I to do with thee, Mine hour is not yet come". How simple it is to see that in this instance "the mother of Jesus" is addressed by her Son in her typical capacity, as representing

Israel, "of whom as concerning the flesh Christ came" (Romans IX, 5).

During these 2,000 years of the Christian Dispensation Israel is "Lo-ammi" (Not My people – Hosea I, 9). How obvious it was that when they ended on 12th June 1933, the Dispensation had failed of its purpose for sheer want of "the wine" of true Christianity which, through the gross apostasy of Religious Christendom, had ceased to flow.

When "the mother of Jesus" said to our Lord, "They have no wine", He immediately looked on to the end of the Dispensation and, as it were, heard Israel announcing that, "the times of the Gentiles" having ended in utter failure, it was now time for Him to show them the same mercy as He had to the Gentiles over these 2,000 years (Romans XI, 25 to 32). But what is our Lord's response! In effect, the words He addressed to His mother in her typical capacity as Israel were of this order: "Not so, the time has not yet arrived for Me to revive you nationally and restore you! Even though the Christian Dispensation has ended chronologically, there are yet several years before it can end actually, and in this extra-dispensational era, which exists for the purpose, I intend to act in sovereign grace to restore for a very brief season 'the wine' of true Christianity, the absence of which has brought the Dispensation to so abrupt an end! I will, in fact, grant a supply of 'wine' even better in quality than that partaken of in the beginning and thus ensure that while the Dispensation has irremediably failed through human perversity, its Divine objective will be attained through My sovereign intervention and the Church, which is My body, be thus brought to fullness, and, as My Bride, unite with the Holy Spirit in summoning Me – the Bridegroom – to 'come' to take her to My Father's House" (Rev. XXII, 17).

All this is implied in our Lord's words to His Mother and in His subsequent act of turning the six waterpots of water into that superb cordial which caused the ruler of the feast to declare to the Bridegroom,

> "Every man at the beginning doth set forth good wine; and when men have well drunk, then that which is worse: but thou hast kept the good wine until now" (John II, 10).

We have said enough to show the importance of this episode

in the present hour. It will be obvious to many that this extra-dispensational era is liable to close abruptly and at short notice. Then our Lord will say to Israel, now unconsciously awaiting Him in their own land, "Mine hour is come", for, "the fulness of the Gentiles (is) come in" (Rom. XI, 25).

It may be asked, What does the "wine" in this wondrous episode typify? First we must recall our Lord's words, "No man putteth new wine into old bottles . . . new wine must be put into new bottles" (Luke V, 37). The "new wine" was the truth of Christianity, or that which composed Christianity. The "new bottles" were the Gentiles. After the Holy Ghost fell upon the Gentiles, when Peter first preached the Gospel to them in the house of Cornelius, Christianity spread world-wide. The "wine" that ran out in the Cana Wedding is a type of all that joyous blessedness that has come to mankind through the life, death, resurrection and ascension of our Lord and Saviour, Jesus Christ, as revealed by the power of the Holy Ghost through the Holy Scriptures. "Wine", we are told, "maketh glad the heart of man" and so filled with joy and gladness were the Apostles at Pentecost that onlookers declared, "These men are full of new wine" – a very truth uttered in mockery (Acts II, 13).

The fact stands out that the Marriage at Cana ended on a joyous note, the guests being regaled with wine such as they never before had tasted, and this as the fruit of the fiat of the will of the Son of God, Whose power is such that the water that filled the six waterpots up to the brim was converted into the "good wine" which called forth the high commendation of the ruler of the feast and made glad the hearts of all the guests. It was thus that our Lord "manifested forth His glory" and no wonder "His disciples believed on Him" (II, 11).

In verse 9 we are told in a parenthesis that only "the servants which drew the water knew" the secret as to the origin of the "good wine" and its abundant supply. It was "the servants" who heard our Lord's Mother say to them, "Whatsoever He saith unto you, do it". In this connection we trust it will not be out of place to mention the following facts as we have postulated action since 1933 by our Lord Jesus Christ which would be the counterpart of His turning the water into wine at the Cana Wedding.

In our former Treatise, *The World in Liquidation*, we explain how in 1933 it pleased God to call the writer and five associates – six in all – to undertake a comprehensive and prayerful study of the whole Bible. It was made clear to us that, if we would return to primitive Christian principles, it was the Lord's intention to grant a completely new unveiling of the Holy Scriptures and to restore much divine truth possessed by our fellow-Christians in apostolic times, and lost very soon thereafter. We were shown that the key to this recovery of light lay in a perfect understanding of TIME in the Bible. Consequently, our first exercise was to trace the exact course of time right through the Scriptures. We then learnt that on 12th June 1933, the great Six Thousand Years of Man had ended. This knowledge of Time had brought to light numerous new facts throughout the whole Bible. We realized we must know "the former things, what they be" if we were to "know the latter end of them" in this our day (see Isaiah XLI, 22; XLIII, 9). Our former Treatise covers this ground.

Our present Treatise constitutes a complete recovery of apostolic light on our Lord's earthly pathway. This has lain concealed in the Scriptures for 1,800 years. That it should now have been unveiled may be taken as first-hand evidence that since 1933 our Lord has been secretly working with a few "servants" to prepare a testimony of His own so that, for *a very brief season* before the Dispensation finally closes by His Second Appearing, "whosoever will" may partake of "the good wine" He has reserved for the end, as typified by "this beginning of signs" which He performed at the Cana Marriage.

(The preceding statement is not made lightly or in self-exaltation. If the light concerning His pathway has been granted by direct act of our Lord, it should be received as such and be acted upon. No one is in a position to judge this who has not read this Treatise through with the Holy Scriptures in hand.)

The last of the seven days of the Cana Wedding was 5th December A.D. 29, and this was exactly 6 Solar years and 200 days to Pentecost, A.D. 36, (22nd June) when the Holy Ghost descended in anointing power on the Gentiles and when the antitype of the Cana Wedding actually commenced by our Lord accepting the redeemed from among the Gentiles as

His heavenly bride and helpmeet. We are deeply conscious of the inadequacy of these remarks on our Lord's first "sign" but we have said enough to allow any who wish to enter into the subject in greater detail.

# CHAPTER FIVE

## OUR LORD JESUS CHRIST AS THE SON OF GOD AND MESSIAH OF ISRAEL OPENS HIS PUBLIC TESTIMONY IN JERUSALEM AT THE PASSOVER OF A.D. 30

HIS FIRST ACT IS TO CLEANSE THE TEMPLE – HIS FATHER'S HOUSE.

HIS AUTHORITY AT ONCE CHALLENGED BY JEWISH LEADERS WHO ASK FOR A SIGN.
HE REPLIES WITH A VEILED REFERENCE TO HIS DEATH AND RESURRECTION.

THE TYPICAL "TWO DAYS" IN SAMARIA ON LEAVING JUDAEA TO RETURN TO GALILEE IN THE AUTUMN OF A.D. 30.

"THE SECOND SIGN" – THE NOBLEMAN'S SON IS HEALED.

TIME

4th May A.D. 30, to the Autumn of A.D. 30
Read John II, 13 to IV, 54.

OUR LORD'S first sign-miracle was not a public act but one wrought in the circle of His own kindred and their friends. In thus acting He "manifested forth His glory; and His disciples believed on Him".

The next named point of time in our Lord's pathway after the Cana Wedding is the Passover on 4th May A.D. 30 (John II, 13). Our Lord had then attained the age of 30 Bible years and 160 days, or 29 Solar years and 188 days.

Between the end of the Cana Wedding on Monday, 5th December A.D. 29, and the Passover on Thursday, 4th May A.D. 30, there were 150 days, and as far as Holy Scripture is concerned there is not a word mentioned about the Lord's activities during this interval except that, after leaving Cana,

He made a brief stay in Capernaum. In John II, 12, we read:

> "After this He went down to Capernaum, He, and His mother, and His brethren, and His disciples: and they continued there not many days."

The expression "after this", gives no indication as to how soon after the Cana Wedding this departure of the Lord for Capernaum took place. Cana had no doubt for the time become the home of our Lord's Mother and doubtless He and all her family remained for some time there.

Early in A.D. 30 our Lord, accompanied as stated, goes down to Capernaum. In the Greek the word "they" does not appear and the Alexandrine Codex adopts the reading "He continued there not many days". No doubt about this time our Lord and His disciples parted company with His Mother and brethren, as He was about to embark upon His public Ministry. Neither is there any evidence that He again made His home with them.

Our Lord, as the Son of God from Heaven, had now to set aside His ties of earthly kinship in favour of relationships which were eternal. This fact He makes perfectly clear when, on a certain occasion, He is informed that His Mother and brethren desire to speak with Him. It is recorded that "He stretched forth His hand toward His disciples, and said, Behold My mother and My brethren! For whosoever shall do the will of My Father which is in heaven, the same is My brother, and sister, and mother" (Matt. XII, 49 and 50).

On leaving Capernaum, our Lord and His disciples commenced the journey south because of His intention to be present at Jerusalem for the Passover.

## OUR LORD JESUS CHRIST OFFICIALLY PRESENTS HIMSELF TO ISRAEL AS THE MESSIAH AT THE PASSOVER OF A.D. 30

In John II, 13 we read,

> "And the Jews' passover was at hand, and Jesus went up to Jerusalem."

At last the long-awaited moment had come when our Lord as the Son of God and Messiah of Israel must make His first contact with His nation and its rulers. With this purpose in view

He goes up to Jerusalem. In due course He enters the Temple and at once acts in His capacity as God's Anointed Servant. The sight of trading and money-changing which He beheld called for prompt judicial action as it was one which glaringly set aside the holiness of God's House. Neither did He delay in order to raise the issue with the rulers, for the offence was not merely condoned by them but encouraged as a source of profit.

Our Lord does not conceal His identity but uses words which mark Him out as the Messiah by calling the Temple "My Father's house", thus declaring Himself to be the Son of God.

Our Lord's manner of acting in the cleansing of the Temple was not likely to ingratiate Him with either the people or the Temple authorities; but He was here to glorify His Father in Heaven Who had sent Him into the world, and His first public act is to uphold the sanctity of His Father's House. No doubt our Lord's action on this occasion would be heartily approved by that remnant of the Jews which mourned over the back-sliding state of the nation and was looking for the Messiah to appear (Mal. III, 16 to 18).

All this trading took place in the court of the Gentiles – "oxen and sheep and doves" being sold for purposes of sacrifice. The money changers were an avaricious body of men who exchanged foreign coins for the half-shekel of the Sanctuary which had to be paid by all pilgrims from the many lands to which the Jews had been scattered. Our Lord dealt with these men with the utmost severity. We are told He "poured out the changers' money, and overthrew the tables". To them that sold doves, He said, "Take these things hence; make not My Father's house an house of merchandise" (John II, 16).

With His "scourge of small cords" in His hand and by virtue of the awe His Presence created, not to mention the guilty consciences of those who well knew the seriousness of their offence, our Lord's action is not contested for a moment and He clears the Temple courts of all these traffickers in merchandise. The Prophet Malachi had declared, "The Lord, Whom ye seek, shall suddenly come to His temple . . . but who may abide the day of His coming? and who shall stand when He appeareth?" (Mal. III, 1 to 3). Surely the cleansing of the Temple was an incipient fulfilling of this prophecy, for not a murmur is raised in opposition and none dare to resist the One Whose

Presence and Authority fill all with a sense of the righteousness of His actions. In this same Gospel it is recorded that those who came with Judas to take our Lord, "went backward, and fell to the ground", when He said unto them, "I am (He)" (ch. XVIII, 6). This shows that there were times when our Lord's Presence was so overwhelming that evil-doers and opposers were rendered impotent. Neither must we forget that the day is near when myriads of all classes of His despisers and rejectors will call upon "the mountains and rocks", saying, "Fall on us, and hide us from the face of Him that sitteth on the throne, and from the wrath of the Lamb: for the great day of His wrath is come; and who shall be able to stand?" (Rev. VI, 15 to 17.)

As there is a close relationship between the cleansing of the Temple which we are now considering and that which is recorded by Matthew, Mark and Luke on the occasion of our Lord's last visit to Jerusalem when He died, we shall be obliged to consider them briefly both together.

## THE TWO OFFICIAL ENTRIES OF OUR LORD JESUS CHRIST INTO JERUSALEM AND THE TWO CLEANSINGS OF THE TEMPLE IN A.D. 30 AND A.D. 33

The Gospels reveal that our Lord's public Ministry to Israel covered a period of exactly Three Solar Years and that at its opening and its close He made official visits to Jerusalem as the Messiah, on each occasion entering the Temple and driving out from it all who were using its sacred courts for the sale of merchandise or the exchanging of money (see Matt. XXI; Mark XI, and Luke XIX). All our Lord's other visits to the Holy City were of a markedly unofficial character (see John V and VII).

As the result of the first cleansing of the Temple the Jewish rulers demand of our Lord a sign. In John II, 18, we read that they said to Him,

> "What sign showest Thou unto us, seeing that Thou doest these things?"

Our Lord's reply, which to them was enigmatic in the extreme, was,

> "Destroy this temple, and in three days I will raise it up."

To this the Apostle John adds,

"But He spake of the temple of His body."

In effect, the Jewish rulers demand from our Lord a sign that He is the Messiah, as no one not claiming to be the Messiah would take upon himself to act and speak as He had done in the cleansing of the Temple.

In reply our Lord gives to the Jews this chronological sign of His death and resurrection. This is perfectly in keeping with His reply on a later occasion when they again asked for a sign. He then said, "There shall no sign be given . . . but the sign of the prophet Jonas: for as Jonas was three days and three nights in the whale's belly; so shall the Son of Man be three days and three nights in the heart of the earth" (Matt. XII, 39 and 40).

Our Lord's statement to the Jews at the Passover in A.D. 30 was both profound and solemn. It was made at the Passover on 4th May, and exactly three years later on 4th May A.D. 33, He rose in triumph out of death. It is, therefore, clear that the sign He gave was a veiled reference ("each day for a year") to the three years of His public Ministry between A.D. 30 and A.D. 33. For these three years He would walk in "the valley of the shadow of death"; and in a figurative sense they would be to Him just what, in a literal sense, the three days of His actual death would be. If at His first presentation of Himself the Jews called His Messiahship in question by asking for a sign, how certainly would they in the end rise up and destroy "the temple of His body". Thus, for the three years, A.D. 30 to 33, our blessed Lord and Master was like a man in "the condemned cell" awaiting the day of his execution. We are told that on several occasions the Jewish rulers "sought to destroy Him", so in a very real sense our Lord's life was always in jeopardy (see Matt. XII, 14; Mark III, 6, XI, 18, etc.).

We will now give the facts which make it clear that our Lord's official entry into Jerusalem and His cleansing of the Temple at the Passover in A.D. 33, when He died, was a chronological repetition of that which took place at the Passover in A.D. 30.

In Ecclesiastes I, 9, the divine principle of repetitive action, so frequently seen in Scripture, is expressed thus:

> "The thing that hath been, it is that which shall be; and that which is done is that which shall be done."

The Triumphal Entry into Jerusalem in A.D. 33 was on the

10th day of Nisan, the first Bible month, and the date was our 27th April. The cleansing of the Temple took place the next day, Nisan 11th – our 28th April (Mark XI, 15). Three days later on Nisan 14th, our 1st May, which was the day of the Passover, our Lord Jesus Christ died. Yet another three days later, on 4th May, He rose from the dead. All these dates will be perfectly confirmed when we are considering this period in our Lord's pathway.

We know that the Passover of A.D. 30 was on 4th May which was the 14th of Nisan. On the principle of repetitive action we may safely believe that our Lord entered Jerusalem for the Passover in A.D. 30 on the same day in the Jewish calendar as in A.D. 33, that is, on the 10th of Nisan, when the Passover lambs were set apart for death. Our Lord, as the Antitypical Paschal Lamb, would wish to be in evidence in Jerusalem four days before the Passover. It appears obvious on the same principle that the cleansing of the Temple took place on the next day, the 11th of Nisan – our 1st May. Three days later, namely, the 14th of Nisan and our 4th May, was the Passover, when the Jews asked our Lord for a sign of His authority and received the answer, "Destroy this temple, and in three days I will raise it up".

Without doubt, when our Lord made this statement on 4th May, He was not only looking back three days to 1st May when He cleansed the Temple (the event which prompted the request for a sign) but was also looking forward three years to the same three days, 1st to 4th May in A.D. 33, when the Jews would be allowed to destroy "the temple of His body" which "in three days" He would raise up again.

We will tabulate the dates in A.D. 30 and A.D. 33 to which we have been referring.

A.D. 30

| | | |
|---|---|---|
| JESUS ENTERS JERUSALEM | (30th April) | NISAN 10TH |
| CLEANSING OF THE TEMPLE | (1st May) | NISAN 11TH |
| THE PASSOVER, "DESTROY THIS TEMPLE" | (4th May) | NISAN 14TH |

A.D. 33

| | | |
|---|---|---|
| THE TRIUMPHAL ENTRY | (27th April) | NISAN 10TH |
| CLEANSING OF THE TEMPLE | (28th April) | NISAN 11TH |
| THE PASSOVER – JESUS DIES | (1st May) | NISAN 14TH |
| THE RESURRECTION | (4th May) | NISAN 17TH |

The Apostle John brings his account of this solemn episode at the Passover of A.D. 30 to a close with this statement:

> "When therefore He was risen from the dead, His disciples remembered that He had said this unto them; and they believed the Scripture, and the word which Jesus had said" (Ch. II, 22).

No doubt to John as an eyewitness, and to all the disciples who were present with the Lord in Jerusalem at the Passover in A.D. 30, His resurrection brought this whole incident vividly to their remembrance and to a realization of the solemn significance of His words uttered on this occasion.

As we have said, this visit of our Lord to Jerusalem for the Passover in A.D. 30 was an official one. By this we mean that as the Messiah it was necessary that He should make official contact with Israel's rulers in Jerusalem, and that the people should know Who He was and the purpose for which He had come into the world. His cleansing of the Temple was not done to display His power but was accomplished to show His Messianic Authority in a sphere where His Father's rights were being trampled under foot.

Our Lord as the Messiah must also make contact with the people of Israel and they must be allowed to see that the One now in their midst in all respects fulfilled that which was written of Him in the Law of Moses, the Prophets and the Psalms. Consequently we are told that He performed many miracles on this first visit to Jerusalem and that as a result, "many believed in His name". In John IV, 45, we are told that when our Lord went back into Galilee "the Galileans received (i.e. welcomed) Him, having seen all the things that He did at Jerusalem at the feast". Whatever effect our Lord's actions had upon the Jews of Jerusalem, these had left so deep an impression on the simple Galileans that they welcomed Him into their midst, with the result that their country became the scene of His mightiest displays of grace and power as He went hither and thither bestowing His rich favours upon all who came to Him with their needs, whether of spirit, soul or body.

## OUR LORD JESUS CHRIST COMMENCES HIS TEACHING MINISTRY

"Thou art a teacher come from God"

Read John III, 1 to 21

The Second Chapter of John ends with a statement by the Apostle in reference to the important principle which governed our Lord's attitude toward those who made profession of faith in Him as the result of seeing His miracles. In verses 24 and 25, we read,

> "But Jesus did not commit Himself unto them, because He knew all (men), and needed not that any should testify of man: for He knew what was in man."

This principle finds its logical development in our Lord's conversation with Nicodemus, as recorded in John III. Furthermore, His teaching on this occasion goes right to the heart of all human failure and shortcoming and establishes the principle upon which all man's future relationships with God must be based, whether in the Christian Dispensation or in the Kingdom of God when it is established in visible form and power over the earth.

Nicodemus, a Pharisee and Master of Israel, was one of those who had come to believe on Christ by virtue of the miracles which He did at the Passover in A.D. 30. As already a gulf of distance had been formed between the Jewish rulers and Jesus, Nicodemus, being one of them, is afraid to go to Him openly *as a learner*, so makes his approach under cover of darkness – "by night".

Our Lord takes advantage of the occasion to explain why He did not "commit Himself" to man by exposing what man's nature is in essence. Nicodemus might "believe" in Jesus but if that belief were submitted to a real test it would be found to be "that which is born of the flesh" – a mere mental belief – and not, therefore, a belief which rested on an abiding foundation; for "that which is born of the flesh is flesh" (verse 6).

The purpose which brought our Lord Jesus Christ into the world was an absolute proof that man in "the flesh", that is, in his natural state, was sinful and corrupt *beyond remedy*. As the

Psalmist declares, "Verily every man at his best state is altogether vanity" (XXXIX, 5).

Our Lord is at pains to lead Nicodemus the Pharisee into the understanding that He had come into the world to establish A NEW ORDER – THE KINGDOM OF GOD. In that new order the corrupt natural man, thinking and acting in the flesh, would have NO PLACE whatsoever. In fact, until a man has been BORN AGAIN, that is, from above – from heaven – he "cannot see the kingdom of God", much less participate in it (verse 3).

This assuredly is the central and most revolutionary fact in the whole of our Lord's revelation to the human race. Consequently, He develops the matter further. This new birth is not like that which brings a man into the world, for "except a man be born of water and of the Spirit, he cannot enter the kingdom of God. That which is born of the flesh is flesh; and that which is born of the Spirit is spirit" (verses 5 and 6).

This "water" to which our Lord refers is THE WORD OF GOD in its cleansing power (see John XV, 3 and Ephesians V, 26). This truth is confirmed by the Apostle Peter in these words, "Being born again, not of corruptible seed, but of incorruptible, by the word of God, which liveth and abideth for ever" (I Peter I, 23 to 25).

From henceforth all, whether Jew or Gentile, who would be brought into relationship with God and His Kingdom must experience an INCORRUPTIBLE BIRTH, founded upon THE WORD OF GOD and conceived by the quickening action of the Spirit of God. This, however, was not to be experienced by following some abstruse formula or religious curriculum, but *by believing the testimony of the Word of God* concerning the Person and Work of the Son of Man, our Lord Jesus Christ.

It was one thing to believe in Jesus as the Performer of the miraculous, but quite another to believe on Him as the One Who, like the brazen serpent in the Wilderness, must be "lifted up" to die on Calvary's Tree to make expiation for our sins if we, the sinners, would be reconciled to God. This latter belief involves an admission of our sinfulness and of the fact that, apart from the lifting up of Jesus, we are *without hope* as regards eternal life and salvation. This is too much for the natural man, so many prefer to evade the issue by adopting as a "religion" a system of ordinances with a veneer of

"Christianity" which leaves "the flesh" in undisturbed possession of the life and the lifting up of Jesus at Golgotha as "much ado about nothing".

At His first Advent our Lord found Judaism lying in ruins because the Law of Moses, though perfect in itself, found in man no capacity to keep its precepts. So, instead of the Law giving life ("This do, and thou shalt live"), it brought all men under condemnation by exposing the utter sinfulness, as well as the weakness, of man in his natural state. Therefore, as regards man in that condition, our Lord had no remedy to offer, "for He knew what was in man" and that "the flesh" could never be anything but what it is, namely, sinful, corrupt and weak.

The New Order – the Kingdom of God – could, however, since the coming of Jesus into the world, be seen by all who were "born from above" (ch. III, 3, Margin) and entered now by all "born of water and of the Spirit", as the result of "believing" in the Son of Man, as the One Who must be "lifted up" as "Moses lifted up the serpent in the wilderness" (Numbers XXI, 8).

> "For God so loved the world, that He gave His only begotten Son, that whosoever *believeth in Him* should not perish, but have everlasting life" (ch. III, 16).

As we have stated previously, John's Gospel prefigures the Christian Dispensation. Consequently, the very first subject of our Lord's Teaching Ministry, as recorded therein, is the absolute necessity of a NEW BIRTH, since without it no man, however moral or pious, can enter the Kingdom of God or become a member of the Church, which is the mystical body of Christ.

Without doubt, our Lord's teaching reached the heart of Nicodemus for when, in fact, Jesus was lifted up in the manner He had foretold, he came out into the open as a disciple and with Joseph of Arimathaea took part in removing our Lord's body from the Cross and preparing it for burial in the new sepulchre wherein they laid Him (John XIX, 38 to 42).

## OUR LORD AND HIS DISCIPLES LEAVE JERUSALEM FOR "THE LAND OF JUDAEA"

### John III, 22.

Our Lord, as we know, was in Jerusalem for the Passover of A.D. 30 which in that year was on 4th May. In verse 23 of John II (R.V.) we read:

> "Now when He was in Jerusalem at the Passover, during the feast, many believed on His name, beholding His signs which He did."

Reference to this is again made in John IV, 45, where we are told that the Galileans welcomed Jesus because of the signs or miracles He wrought on this occasion, "for they also went unto the feast".

While it is not a matter of any particular importance, it would be safe to assume that our Lord and His disciples remained in Jerusalem for the seven weeks to Pentecost which in A.D. 30 was on 25th June. We know that Joseph and Mary went up for the Passover but remained in Jerusalem for Pentecost in A.D. 12, though we are only told that "they went up to Jerusalem after the custom of the feast". Doubtless in A.D. 30 many of the Galileans stayed in Jerusalem for Pentecost or the Feast of Weeks. It is not likely that all the signs or miracles which Jesus did were performed in the Seven Days of the Feast of Unleavened Bread.

In John III, 22 to 24, we read:

> "After these things came Jesus and His disciples into the land of Judaea; and there He tarried with them, and baptized.
>
> "And John also was baptizing in Ænon near to Salim, because there was much water there: and they came, and were baptized. For John was not yet cast into prison."

All this information is exclusive to the Gospel of John, who, no doubt, was an eyewitness and participator in the events.

Our Lord, having borne a full and faithful testimony in Jerusalem, now moves out into the province of Judaea. Not far away at Ænon John was still baptizing and preaching the Gospel of the Kingdom. Jesus Himself did not baptize (John IV, 2) but His disciples did so on His behalf and no doubt this baptism was, like John's, "unto repentance" because the Kingdom was at hand.

The context informs us that so many came for baptism by our Lord's disciples that John's disciples felt constrained to tell him of the success of our Lord's Ministry and that "all men come to Him" for baptism. John thereupon, in perfect self-abnegation, utters his last testimony to Jesus as the Messiah, the key phrase being, "He must increase, but I must decrease" (John III, 27 to 36).

If our Lord commenced His testimony in the land of Judaea after Pentecost in A.D. 30, He must have "tarried" there a considerable time before the results became a subject of discussion both with John's disciples and also with the Pharisees (John IV, 1). This being so, it becomes clear that our Lord and His disciples could not have left Judaea for Galilee until the Autumn of A.D. 30, that is, in the month of either September or October.

The Bible reveals that it was *before* the next Feast which was that of Tabernacles, for if not the statement in John IV, 45, which is an obvious reference to our Lord's miracles at the Passover in A.D. 30, when the Galileans were present, could not have been made without it being wrongly inferred that the Lord had acted similarly at a later Feast, of which there is no mention in Scripture. The Feast of Tabernacles in A.D. 30 was on 29th October. We know, therefore, that our Lord left Judaea prior to this, and that it was about the same time that Herod cast John the Baptist into prison (Matthew IV, 12; Mark I, 14), thus bringing to an end the brief but blessed era during which the testimonies of John and of Jesus were being rendered at one and the same time, and only at a short distance from one another.

## OUR LORD JESUS CHRIST SPENDS TWO DAYS IN SAMARIA

"He left Judaea, and departed again into Galilee."
John IV, 1 to 45

To understand the beautiful incident at the Well of Sychar and our Lord's stay of Two Days in Samaria, it is most essential to grasp its dispensational character as expressed by its chronological features. These "two days" in Samaria, like the Cana Wedding and the Fishing Episode of John XXI, form a manifestly clear type of the Christian Dispensation.

In the first place, it must be noted that our Lord's visit to Samaria was after "He left Judaea" – an expression in perfect keeping with the fact that the Christian Dispensation only began when, following His rejection by the Jews, He turned His back upon them "for the age", as typified by the cutting down of the Fig Tree which continued to cumber the ground throughout an extension of clemency lasting one year (see Luke XIII, 6 to 9). On the very day after this one year terminated, "the times of the Gentiles", which is but another name for the Christian Dispensation, began to run their course of two "days" of 1,000 years each to 12th June 1933.

In the Third Chapter of John we have seen how our Lord set forth the vital need of a New Birth if anyone would enter the Kingdom of God.

In the touching incident narrated in the Fourth Chapter, our Lord adds to His teaching of the New Birth the need for the indwelling of the Holy Spirit Who is typified by "living water". Unless sustained from within by the unceasing ministration of the Holy Spirit, our New Birth could not thrive and we would die in infancy. But the Holy Spirit is God's gift to all who have been "born from above". Our Lord, therefore, says to the Samaritan woman, "If thou knewest the gift of God, and who it is that saith to thee, Give Me to drink; thou wouldest have asked of Him, and He would have given thee living water" (verse 10).

This is not the occasion to dwell at length upon our Lord's teaching concerning the gift of the Holy Spirit or to enlarge upon the wonderful grace with which He revealed Himself to this humble sin-conscious woman of Samaria. In fact, the language of this chapter is so clear and plain and our Lord's words so full of grace to one who had to be brought "out of darkness into His marvellous light" that little could be added with any profit.

The woman herself in her immoral course is a type of the Samaritan people, and her five "husbands" typify the five "gods" named in II Kings XVII, 24 to 41. There was no blessing for her until she realized that she had to do with One

Who knew the wretched story of her past life, concerning which she needed but to be reminded in order that her conscience might do its own work of conviction as a preparation for the glorious revelation that she was in the presence of "Messias . . . which is called Christ" – hearing from His own lips the words, "I that speak unto thee am He". From that moment her heart was won for Him and unashamedly she went forth to be a witness of His saving grace.

### THE TYPICAL SIGNIFICANCE OF OUR LORD'S TWO DAYS IN SAMARIA

"The Samaritans . . . besought Him that He would tarry with them: and He abode there two days. . . . Now after two days He departed thence, and went into Galilee" (John IV, 40 to 43).

At the beginning of this Treatise we called attention to the fact that our Lord Jesus Christ walked here on earth according to a Pattern of Time designed for Him by God the Father. Already we have traced much of this Pattern, step by step, from the day of His birth on 29th October 1 B.C. Our Lord was now very nearly 30 solar years of age – a point of time which would be reached on 29th October A.D. 30.

As we have said, our Lord left Judaea for Galilee in the Autumn of A.D. 30. The journey to Galilee through Samaria would take at least 3 days apart from His stay of "two days". Jews going to Galilee would often cross the Jordan into Peraea in order to miss Samaria, because they so despised the Samaritans; but not so our Lord Who, in infinite grace, would invite the Samaritans, as all others, to become partakers of eternal life – the free gift of God.

The Samaritans and their country typify what is called Christendom, that is, the sphere in which people profess the Christian religion. The Samaritans were Gentiles who, because they had been placed in the land of Israel, had adopted the Jewish religion and made it conform to their own idolatrous religion. All this is explained in II Kings XVII.

Christendom is peopled by those who, having been born in the sphere where the Christian Religion is practised, have themselves adopted it as such, in the same way as others adopt Hinduism, Buddhism or Mohammedanism, if born in a sphere where one of these is practised. In other words, Christendom is peopled in the main by those who have accepted Christianity as their Religion, but have evaded or are ignorant of the teaching of Christ as to the absolute necessity of a New Birth, by means of which alone an unregenerate Gentile can become a Christian – an appellation which in the Bible is applied only to those who are actual disciples of Jesus Christ (see Acts XI, 26).

Once it is realized that Samaria in the Bible is a type of Christendom, it is simple to see the typical significance of the Two Days during which our Lord "abode" there. All know the statement of the Apostle Peter who informs us "that one day is with the Lord as a thousand years, and a thousand years as one day" (II Peter III, 8). It is, therefore, perfectly obvious that our Lord's stay of "two days" in Samaria, after "He left Judaea", was symbolical of the two "days" of a thousand years each during which He made His abode in Christendom.

These 2,000 years, which are Bible years of 354 days, are composed of 4 cycles of 490 years, making a total of 1,960 years, to which 40 years of Jubile are added. This makes a nominal total of 2,000 years.

When, therefore, our Lord said, "Say not ye, There are yet four months, and then cometh harvest?" (IV, 35), He was again making chronological reference to the Christian Dispensation in that these "four months" are a type of the 4 cycles of 490 years into which the Bible divides these 1,960 years. In another place our Lord said "the harvest is the consummation of the age" (Matt. XIII, 40, R.V. Margin). His predictive declaration has therefore been perfectly fulfilled. The "four months" or 4 cycles of 490 years ran their course from 12th October A.D. 33, to 12th June 1933, when "the harvest" which is "the consummation of the age" began. This fact, which no one can possibly refute, is of immeasurable solemnity to all mankind as it accounts for all that has taken place in the world since 1933.

Our Lord, however, because of the nature of the Dispensation, made it perfectly clear to the disciples that it was wrong to wait for "the harvest" because "the fields . . . are white already to harvest". In other words, while God's harvest time would be at the end of the age, as revealed in Revelation XIV, 14 to 20, the reaping of souls could be done throughout the Dispensation by faithful labourers, since "He that reapeth receiveth wages, and gathereth fruit unto life eternal" (IV, 36).

It is most illuminating to notice the way in which the Apostle John is caused by the Spirit of God to apply our Lord's words in the Synagogue at Nazareth to the Two Days in Samaria (Luke IV, 24). We read in John IV, 43 and 44:

> "Now after (the) two days He departed thence, and went into Galilee. For Jesus Himself testified, that a prophet hath no honour in his own country."

Not seen in its typical setting, no one could possibly account for the fact that John brings in this saying of Jesus at that point. But, seen in its typical light as referring to our Lord's long identification with Christendom, its presence there is full of deep and solemn significance. Our Lord for 2,000 years has made Christendom "His own country". Familiarity has bred contempt, and nothing is more obvious than that the honour Christendom accords to Christ is only nominal – He has no real honour or His teaching would be obeyed.

In this connection, let us not forget that our Lord presents Himself typically as "a certain Samaritan" in the Parable of Luke X, or that the Jews said to Him, "Say we not well that Thou art a Samaritan, and hast a devil?" (John VIII, 48). To the Jews during this Dispensation our Lord Jesus Christ is One wholly identified with Christendom, and it is not surprising, in view of its dispensational character, that it is in John's Gospel we find this latter statement.

Finally, let it be said that the declaration of the men of Samaria concerning our Lord again proves the typical character of this whole episode. The woman herself typifies the Samaritan people who cling to the Jewish hope of a coming of the Messiah. Consequently, our Lord reveals Himself to her in that capacity. The men of Samaria who come to believe on our Lord during His two days' stay typify believers in Christendom and consequently their testimony is, "This is indeed . . . the Saviour of the world". (Unfortunately, and in contradiction to the reading of all the leading Manuscripts, including the Sinaitic and Vatican, the Authorized Version inserts the words, "the Christ", before "the Saviour of the world". The Revised

Version, however, corrects this error.) So to the men of Samaria our Lord is not One limited to the fulfilment of Jewish hopes, but One Who meets the needs of all mankind – He to them, as to Christendom, is "the Saviour of the world".

### OUR LORD JESUS CHRIST RETURNS TO GALILEE AND AGAIN VISITS CANA "WHERE HE MADE THE WATER WINE".
John IV, 46 to 54

We have already pointed out that when the Saviour left Judaea and entered Galilee, after passing through Samaria, He was welcomed by the Galileans because of the signs or miracles He had wrought at the Passover in Jerusalem in A.D. 30.

It is at this point in our Saviour's pathway that the three synoptic Gospels – Matthew, Mark and Luke – commence their accounts. Before turning to these we must refer to our Lord's second sign which He wrought in Cana on His return into Galilee, as recorded in John IV, 46 to 54. It is certain that our Lord went direct to Cana; at least, such a conclusion is warranted by the wording, "So Jesus came again into Cana of Galilee, where He made the water wine", which immediately follows the statement of His arrival in Galilee.

It will be recalled that we have shown that our Lord's Mother and His brethren had moved from Nazareth to Cana, where the wedding of one of Mary's sons took place, when our Lord performed His first sign. Our Lord had been in the South, that is, in Jerusalem and Judaea, for over six months and it was natural that on His return to Galilee He should first visit Cana where His Mother dwelt. It would be difficult to imagine that He would do otherwise.

That our Lord went first to Cana is borne witness to by the following facts. The nobleman, whose son was "at the point of death", came from Capernaum because he had "heard that Jesus was come out of Judaea into Galilee" and was to be found at Cana. Matthew, in Chapter IV, 13, informs us that when our Lord returned to Galilee "He came and dwelt in Capernaum". This clearly means that our Lord made Capernaum His centre; but evidently He first visited Cana. If our Lord had gone straight to Capernaum when He arrived in Galilee the nobleman would not have needed to journey to Cana at a time when to leave his son must have been painful in the extreme.

### THE NOBLEMAN'S SON HEALED – OF WHAT IS THIS A SIGN?

One thing is certain, namely that our Lord's Second Sign, being wrought after leaving Judaea and arriving in Galilee, has nothing to do with the Jews. It must, therefore, be related to the Gentiles and like our Lord's First Sign, when He turned water into wine, it must relate to this Dispensation. As it follows the typical "two days" in Samaria, it evidently refers to an event *after* the 2,000 years of the Christian Dispensation which ran from 12th October A.D. 33, to 12th June 1933. This reduces the time when the antitype of this sign must be fulfilled to the present brief era called "the consummation of the age". Already 23 years have passed since this began, but so far no event in Christendom has occurred which could possibly answer to the quickening touch of Divine Power which was manifested in the restoring to health of the nobleman's son, as described in the latter verses of John IV. It is, therefore, certain that this second sign of our Lord Jesus Christ has yet to witness its counterpart in our own day.

Without attempting to examine the details of this incident which lie on the surface of this Scripture, we may say that it appears to us quite clear that the nobleman, being a Royal Personage (as the Greek word used implies), is a type of the Holy Spirit and that the son is a type of the Church, which is the Body of Christ, at the end of the age. Every member of the Body of Christ has been "born of water and of the Spirit" and every such one has been baptized "by one Spirit . . . into one body, whether we be Jews or Gentiles" (I Cor. XII, 13).

Anyone with a discerning eye, who is instructed in the Holy Scriptures, and who knows what the Church of Christ was at the beginning, must realize that it is now, at the end of the age, "at the point of death", because of the division of its members into numberless sects and with this the most abominable disunity of thought in all matters of doctrine and the practice of the ordinances. As so few lament this dishonouring state of things, it will be only a few who realize how near to the "point of death" the Church is. Are we to regard our Lord's prayer in John XVII as uttered in vain, or may we still believe that His prayer for the unity of His own members will be answered before He returns to take them to the "place" He went away to prepare? We will quote one verse of that prayer and in the light of it ask ourselves where the Church stands today in regard to it:

> "That they all may be one; as Thou, Father, art in Me, and I in Thee, that they also may be one in Us: that the world may believe that Thou hast sent Me" (verse 21).

To deny that the Church, which is the Body of Christ, is "at the point of death" is to deny what is obvious even to people of the world. Furthermore, not only has this sign to be fulfilled which will restore the Church to being a living and vitalized organism, but there are many more Scriptures that hold out the same hope, not the least of which is the return of the Prodigal Son from the far-off land to the Father's House (Luke XV).

The name Capernaum, from whence the nobleman came, means "the village of the Comforter". All will know that our Lord referred to the Holy Ghost as "the Comforter". No doubt, therefore, Capernaum may be viewed typically as representing the present sphere of the Holy Spirit's activities, namely, Christendom. After the nobleman knew that his son had been healed, we are told that "himself believed, and his whole house" (verse 53).

In view of our Lord's statement, "Except ye see signs and wonders, ye will not believe" (verse 48), it is reasonable to expect a great revival of life in the Church, which is the body of Christ, before our Lord's Second Advent (obviously now imminent) and that this will be effected by some action on His part in response to the pleading of the Holy Spirit.

We shall now for a while leave the Gospel of John that has been the exclusive source of our information since our Lord's Temptation, and pick up the narrative as recorded by the Evangelists, Matthew, Mark and Luke.

# CHAPTER SIX

## OUR LORD JESUS CHRIST, IN THE AUTUMN OF A.D. 30, COMMENCES HIS MINISTRY IN GALILEE

### HE PREACHES "THE GOSPEL OF THE KINGDOM"

### JOHN THE BAPTIST, HAVING REBUKED HEROD, IS CAST INTO PRISON

### PETER AND ANDREW, JAMES AND JOHN FINALLY ABANDON THEIR SECULAR CALLINGS AND FOLLOW JESUS

TIME

The Autumn of A.D. 30 to the Autumn of A.D. 31

OUR LORD and Saviour, Jesus Christ, after He left Judaea in the Autumn of A.D. 30, came into Galilee after passing through the province of Samaria and, as we know, was received with honour because many Galileans had witnessed His miracles at the Passover in Jerusalem in the previous Spring. As we shall presently show from the Gospels, our Lord remained in Galilee for a whole year, as His next appearance in Jerusalem was not until the Autumn of A.D. 31 when He was present at the unnamed Feast mentioned by the Apostle John in verse 1 of Chapter V of his Gospel.

Matthew (IV, 12) and Mark (I, 14) both inform us that the Lord returned into Galilee as soon as He heard that John the Baptist had been imprisoned by Herod. This wicked act was at the request of his unlawful wife Herodias – John having told the King, "It is not lawful for thee to have her" (Matt. XIV, 4).

It was not until John's Ministry was finished that our Lord first commenced *to preach*. Mark states:

> "Now after that John was put in prison, Jesus came into Galilee, preaching the gospel of the kingdom of God."

This statement is immediately followed by a clear definition of the terms of this Gospel:

> "Saying, The time is fulfilled, and the kingdom of God is at hand: repent ye, and believe the gospel" (Mark I, 14 and 15, cf. Matt. IV, 17 and IX, 35).

Up to that time John the Baptist had been preaching this same Gospel of the Kingdom for about four years and a half, that is, from the Spring of A.D. 26 to the late Summer of A.D. 30. It is clear from Matthew X, 7 that the Twelve Apostles were commissioned by our Lord to proclaim this Gospel. Furthermore, we learn from Matthew XXIV, 14 that "this gospel of the kingdom" is to be preached throughout the world "for a witness" by our Lord's Jewish disciples after the Church, which is the body of Christ, has departed to its eternal dwelling-place in Heaven (cf. Matt. X, 23). The Gospel of the Kingdom is purposed to prepare people for the Millennial Reign of Christ *on the earth*; while "the gospel of Christ" or, as it is called, "the gospel of the grace of God" is purposed to prepare people for their eternal inheritance *in heaven* (I Peter I, 4).

It is a solemn fact that our Lord Jesus Christ did not commence to preach until, for the time, He had turned His back upon official Jewry and come amongst the humble and often despised Galileans – those whom the prophet Zechariah speaks of as "the poor of the flock that waited upon me" (XI, 7, 11). It was these Galileans who received the Son of God, Israel's Messiah, and who witnessed and experienced His mighty power. So we find it recorded:

> "Jesus went about all Galilee, teaching in their synagogues, and preaching the gospel of the kingdom, and healing all manner of sickness and all manner of disease among the people. And His fame went throughout all Syria" (Matt. IV, 23, 24; IX, 35).

Matthew informs us that when our Lord began His Galilean Ministry He "dwelt in Capernaum". This we are told was in fulfilment of a prediction uttered by Isaiah in reference to "the land of Zabulon, and the land of Nephthalim" in "Galilee of the Gentiles". This was the first part of the land of Israel to be conquered by Tiglath-Pileser, King of Assyria, about 758-738 B.C. Its inhabitants were the first captives to be taken to Assyria. Isaiah prophesied that this very region should be the one to witness the activities of Immanuel and consequently our Lord fulfilled the prophecy and "the people which sat in darkness saw great light" (Isaiah IX, 1, 2, and Matt. IV, 13 to 16).

The Gospel by Luke, unlike those by Matthew and Mark, begins our Lord's Galilean Ministry with a long account of His visit to the Synagogue at Nazareth "where He had been brought up" (Luke IV, 16 to 30). Before this Luke gives a general statement in these terms:

> "And Jesus returned in the power of the Spirit into Galilee: and there went out a fame of Him through all the region round about. And He taught in their synagogues, being glorified of all."

This statement clearly infers that before His Nazareth visit our Lord had already become famous throughout Galilee. This is in accord with the accounts given by Matthew and Mark, each of whom place our Lord's visit to Nazareth at a much later point in their accounts. Some get over the difficulty by allowing that our Lord twice visited His former home town. As in part similar wording is used in all three accounts, we find it very hard to accept that our Lord ever returned to Nazareth after the events recorded in Luke IV. He could hardly have twice made reference to the fact of a prophet receiving no honour in his own country. (See Matthew XIII, 53 and Mark VI, 1.)

It will be well to state here that as we are not attempting to write a "Life" of our Lord or to give an exposition of the Four Gospels, we do not conceive it to be in our province to attempt any kind of a "harmony" or to allocate events or sayings to any particular period of time, except where this may be done under the direct authority of the text. The Spirit of God caused the Evangelists to adopt an order which was in keeping with a Divine design for each account. All know that Matthew presents our Lord as King, in accordance with Jeremiah XXIII, 5, which says, "I will raise unto David a righteous BRANCH, and a King shall reign and prosper". Mark sees our Lord as the Servant of Jehovah, and so omits a genealogy. His account has in view Zechariah III, 8: "Behold, I will bring forth My Servant THE BRANCH". Luke beholds our Lord as "the Man Christ Jesus" and so traces His genealogy back to Adam. He has in view Zechariah VI, 12: "Behold the Man whose name is THE BRANCH". John knows our Lord to be the ever-existing One – the Word made flesh – Jehovah Himself manifested in human form. Consequently, he writes in the light of Isaiah IV, 2, "In that day shall the BRANCH of the Lord (Jehovah) be beautiful and glorious".

These four Accounts of our Lord's earthly pathway are simply four aspects of His life among men. Together, they present ONE DIVINE RECORD of all that God requires men to know of our Lord's life in all its varied aspects. As we have stated already, John alone conforms to a strictly chronological order, though Luke is caused to provide the chronological framework which embraces the whole period of our Lord's earthly life, as we shall presently demonstrate.

### THE CALL OF THE FOUR FISHERMEN

It is most blessed to note the simplicity of the call of Peter, Andrew, James and John. This is recorded in Matthew IV, 18 to 22 and Mark I, 16 to 20. It is, of course, evident that up to their call they were "part-time" disciples. With His return to Galilee our Lord began at once to formulate His plans and these, as we know, included the appointment of Twelve Disciples as Apostles to whom were given power over evil spirits and to heal "all manner of sickness and all manner of disease" (Matt. X, 1).

To Peter and Andrew our Lord's promise was, "Follow Me, and I will make you fishers of men". James and John are called on the same occasion, "And they immediately left the ship and their father, and followed Him". In each case there was an instantaneous response to our Lord's summons and a total abandonment to the service of Him who said, "He that loveth father or mother more than Me is not worthy of Me" (Matt. X, 37).

### A DEEPLY CONCEALED DATE IN LUKE'S GOSPEL

"And it came to pass on the second sabbath after the first"
(*Luke VI, 1*)

It is a cause for thanksgiving that Luke marks out one point of time – the only one in the Four Gospels – in the course of the year of our Lord's Galilean Ministry between the Autumn of A.D. 30 and that of A.D. 31.

Matthew (XII, 1), Mark (II, 23), and Luke (VI, 1), all record the occasion when, on a certain Sabbath, the Lord and His disciples passed through a cornfield when the disciples plucked the ears of corn and ate them. This was an absolutely lawful act in itself (Deut. XXIII, 25), but to do it on the Sabbath was to the Pharisees most unlawful. Our Lord chooses the occasion to declare Himself "Lord also of the sabbath."

Luke (VI, 1) informs us that this event took place "on the second sabbath after the first". To commentators of all schools this has proved to be one of the most difficult statements in the Four Gospels. Neither could it possibly be correctly understood apart from the knowledge that our Lord kept two Sabbaths in each week, namely, the Sabbath of Jehovah and the Jews' Sabbath. The reason for this is fully explained in the Summary of Facts (Paragraph 14) which precedes Chapter One of this Treatise.

The first point to note is that this incident was in the Seven Weeks of Harvest, as the grain was ripe (see Leviticus XXIII, 15 and Deut. XVI, 9). These seven weeks began on the next Sunday after the Passover. They contained seven Sabbaths, and Pentecost, or the Feast of Weeks, was on "the morrow after the seventh sabbath".

The occasion in question must have been on the first of the seven Sabbaths to Pentecost. There were, however, *two* "first" Sabbaths, namely, that of Jehovah and that of the Jews. As this was the Jews' Sabbath which was the day after Jehovah's Sabbath (the Jews' Friday), Luke, with perfect accuracy, calls it "the second-first Sabbath". To express this he adopts a compound of two Greek words, "deutero" and "prōtos", which as one word can only be translated "second-first".

Some commentators have tried to interpret this unusual expression by assuming that the first day of Unleavened Bread, which opened with the Passover, was *a Sabbath* and that the day in question was the next weekly Sabbath. In all relevant Scriptures the first and last days of Unleavened Bread are called "holy convocations" which term is used in order to distinguish them from Sabbaths which only apply to the three Feasts of the 7th month (see Levit. XXIII). The Feast of Unleavened Bread, like that of the Firstfruits and Pentecost, is typical of the Christian Dispensation in which Sabbaths have no place.

It is clear from the context in the Gospels that this event in the cornfields was during the seven weeks of harvest in A.D. 31 – that is, about six months after our Lord began His first Ministry in Galilee in the Autumn of A.D. 30.

In A.D. 31 the Passover was on Monday, 23rd April. The seven weeks of harvest began on Sunday ("the morrow after the Sabbath"), 29th April. The *two* "first" Sabbaths were the next Friday and Saturday, 4th and 5th May. The event named in Luke VI, 1 was therefore on Saturday, 5th May, and it is this day which with perfect propriety is called by Luke "the second-first Sabbath".

There can be no doubt that the Spirit of God guided Luke to introduce this remarkable word "second-first" in order to bring out the fact that our Lord kept the holy Sabbath of Jehovah as well as the Sabbath God gave to the Jews. Matthew, as we shall see later, brings out this fact by calling the Jews' Friday, the day on which Jesus died, the Sabbath (XXVIII, 1). Furthermore, if it were not that the date of Saturday, 5th May A.D. 31, for the "second-first" Sabbath of Luke VI, 1, was ascertainable there would be a whole year of our Lord's life without a dated event. This date, linked as it is with the Passover of A.D. 31, enables us to know that the Gospels mark out the Four Passovers of A.D. 30, 31, 32 and 33. The Gospel of John makes no reference to the Passover of A.D. 31 but names those of A.D. 30, 32 and 33.

It may be a disappointment to many that the Gospels contain no material by which it is possible to assign even approximate dates for the many events in our Lord's earthly pathway after He returned to Galilee in the Autumn of A.D. 30. Apart from the date of 5th May in A.D. 31, which we have just given, we know of no datable event in the course of the year ending in the Autumn of A.D. 31, when, as we are about to show, the Saviour again went to Jerusalem for the "feast" of John V.

It appears from the following facts that the principle which the Spirit of God adopted with the inspired writers of the Four

Gospels was that they should only provide chronological data when it related specifically to the Person of our Lord and not to events in His Public Ministry, except when these were on, or adjacent to, a named annual Feast of the Jews.

### THE TWO MARKED PERIODS OF 212 DAYS AT THE BEGINNING AND ENDING OF OUR LORD'S PUBLIC LIFE

From our Lord's Baptism on Saturday, 5th October A.D. 29, it is possible to trace *every day* in our Lord's life to 4th May A.D. 30, when He was present at Jerusalem for the Passover. This is a period of 212 days and it is divided into 62 days from the Baptism to the first Sign-miracle at the Cana Wedding on 5th December and 150 days thereafter to 4th May A.D. 30. What is so remarkable is that every one of the last 212 days of our Lord's life to His Ascension can likewise be perfectly traced. These latter 212 days begin on 13th November A.D. 32, which is the day called in John VII, 37, "the last day, that great day of the feast", and they terminate on 13th June A.D. 33, when our Lord ascended into Heaven. Furthermore, as in the former 212 days, this period is also divided into 62 and 150 days. The 62 days end on 14th January, A.D. 33, which is the date of the Feast of Dedication in John X, when "in a figure", as we shall later explain, Jesus was stoned "to death" by the Jews.

Both these periods of 212 days at the beginning and the ending of our Lord's public life were filled with events related to His Person, and consequently every day can be accounted for and all the leading events given their true dates in Bible and solar years. Between these two periods of 212 days there is an interval of 923 days (4th May A.D. 30, to 13th November A.D. 32) during which, apart from the annual Feasts, no events appear to be dated because not directly connected with the Person of our Lord Jesus Christ.

Having given these facts, it may be helpful at this stage to view our Lord's public life as a period of 1,347 days, as follows:

| | |
|---|---|
| 5th October A.D. 29, to 4th May A.D. 30 | 212 days |
| 4th May A.D. 30, to 13th November A.D. 32 | 923 days |
| 13th November A.D. 32, to 13th June A.D. 33 | 212 days |
| The Baptism to the Ascension, Total: | 1,347 days |

There is a great significance attaching to these 1,347 days in our Lord's public life, but this we will allude to when we have traced their course in the Gospels.

How perfectly all these facts reveal the existence of a predetermined Time Pattern in our Lord's life on the earth; and with what thankfulness to the One Who designed it should we, with unshod feet, trace it out in all its precious detail. The measure of our zeal in doing this will, however, depend upon the measure in which the One, Whose pathway we are tracing, had attracted our hearts to Himself.

We might have made a brief review of the leading events in our Lord's first Galilean Ministry, but many books exist with this in one form or another. Most, however, will prefer to obtain this direct from the Gospels of Matthew, Mark and Luke.

# CHAPTER SEVEN

## OUR LORD'S THIRD SIGN-MIRACLE AT THE UNNAMED FEAST OF JOHN V

### THE MAN WITH AN INFIRMITY THIRTY-EIGHT YEARS "MADE WHOLE" ON THE DAY OF ATONEMENT, THE SABBATH, 13TH OCTOBER A.D. 31

### THIS SIGN RELATES TO THE NATION OF ISRAEL NOW RESTORED TO THEIR LAND

### OUR LORD'S AGE IN BIBLE YEARS WAS NOW 31 YEARS AND 333 DAYS AND IN SOLAR YEARS, 30 YEARS AND 349 DAYS

Read the Gospel of John – Chapter V

THE FIFTH Chapter of John opens with the words, "After this", or, more correctly, "After these things". This expression, which does not imply that what is to follow is part of the same sequence of events, embraces all that had taken place in Galilee from our Lord's arrival there in the Autumn of A.D. 30, after His visit of two days in Samaria. We read in verse 1 (R.V.):

> "After these things there was a feast of the Jews; and Jesus went up to Jerusalem."

When we have ascertained which of the Feasts is referred to in this verse, we shall know the time Jesus left Galilee and went up to Jerusalem. As everyone who studies the Bible is aware, there has been much divergence of views as to the identity of this Feast. Some think it was one of the three great Feasts, and others that it was either Purim or the Feast of Dedication. All these are mere guesses as there is no material in the Bible to support any one of them.

All admit that a true knowledge of what this Feast of John V was is essential if an accurate chronology of this Gospel is to be established.

It being in the counsels of God that His people should once again possess a perfect knowledge of time in our Lord's earthly pathway, it pleased Him to enable us to discern that the required knowledge lay in a more accurate translation of the Greek text. In other words, it appears that if the translation of certain Greek words had been a strictly literal one, others, like ourselves, might have detected how, by a simple deduction this knowledge could be obtained.

As we will presently demonstrate from the text, the Feast of John V was the Day of Atonement in A.D. 31. In that year the 10th day of the Jewish 7th month was Saturday, 13th October. We therefore know that Jesus left Galilee early in October A.D. 31. This was almost exactly one year from when He arrived in Galilee and went to Cana, where He wrought His second Sign-Miracle (John IV, 46).

The healing of the man "which had an infirmity thirty and eight years" was our Lord's Third Sign-Miracle recorded by John. It relates exclusively to the people of Israel and is the first of the eight "signs" of John's Gospel to do so. It is followed by "Jesus walking on the sea" in John VI, by the giving of sight to the blind man in John IX and by the raising of Lazarus in John XI. These four Sign-Miracles, namely, the third, fifth, sixth and seventh, are all prophetic of Israel at the end of the age and they are all now in course of having their complementary fulfilments.

Apart from the healing of this "impotent man" and the discourse addressed to the Jewish leaders as the outcome of our Lord having performed this miracle on the Sabbath, there is no record in the Gospels of any other events connected with this visit to Jerusalem. Our Lord must therefore have travelled from Galilee – a distance of over 80 miles – for this one purpose – a fact which gives both to this sign and the discourse that followed it *an exceptional importance.*

It is to be noted that our Lord made the approach without any request on the part of "the impotent man" to whom He addresses the question, "Wilt thou be made whole?" As so often throughout Scripture, there is a number connected with this incident which has a most important typical significance. In this case the number forms the key to the understanding of what the incident signifies.

We are told that among the "multitude of impotent folk" lying by the pool of Bethesda waiting for the troubling of the water, there was "a certain man . . . which had an infirmity thirty and eight years". This man explains his predicament to our Lord Who then addresses him thus:

> "Rise, take up thy bed, and walk."

The record continues,

> "Immediately the man was made whole, and took up his bed, and walked" (verses 8 and 9).

This number "thirty-eight" as the period of this man's infirmity at once directs our thoughts to Deuteronomy II, 14, where Moses states that "the space in which we came from Kadesh-barnea, until we were come over the brook Zered, was thirty and eight years". Moses is addressing Israel at the end of the Wilderness Journey from Egypt to Canaan and, in effect, he is telling them that the period of their "wanderings" was 38 years. The whole wilderness period was 40 years, but of these only 2 years were required by God for the necessary preparation of the redeemed nation to enter the Land of Promise. The 38 years of wandering constituted the penalty for their sinful unbelief in accepting the adverse report of the ten (out of twelve) spies sent into Canaan to search out the land.

This numerical correspondence between the period of this man's infirmity and Israel's wanderings in the Wilderness, as the direct result of their sin, enables us to know that this sign has a positively Jewish significance. At once the question arises, What relation have these facts to the people of Israel at the end of the Christian age? The answer is perfectly simple. The period of the wanderings of the people of Israel for 38 years before entering the Land of Canaan under the leadership of Joshua forms a perfect chronological type of the world-wide Dispersion of the Jewish people after the Fall of Jerusalem in A.D. 70, following upon their rejection of their Messiah, our Lord Jesus Christ. Both "the wanderings" and the Dispersion were the results of sinful unbelief.

Let the following facts be carefully noted. The Forty Years' Wilderness Journey from Egypt to Canaan is a chronological type of the 49 times 40 years of the Christian Dispensation and of the rejection of the Jewish nation between 12th October

A.D. 33, and 12th June 1933, when "the times of the Gentiles", named by our Lord, as recorded in Luke XXI, 24, ended, and "the consummation of the age" began. But the Jews were not dispersed in A.D. 33, because it suited the purpose of God that they should remain intact as a nation for a further 38 years, that is, until A.D. 71. This was the year after the Fall of Jerusalem when the whole Jewish nation was dismembered – those not slaughtered by crucifixion being carried as captives into Egypt from whence 1,709 years previously (i.e. 1639 B.C.) they had as a nation been led forth in triumph by the mighty hand of God.

We have seen that it was 49 times 40 years from A.D. 33 to 1933 when "the times of the Gentiles" ended chronologically. Now the extremely important fact emerges that from A.D. 71, *when the Dispersion of the Jews actually began*, it was 49 times 38 years to 1933. Thus the typical 40 years and the typical 38 years of Israel in the Wilderness respectively found their antitypes in the 1,960 Bible years from A.D. 33 to 1933 and in the 1,862 solar years from A.D. 71 to 1933.

It needs to be remembered that it was the rise of Hitler in 1933 and the events which followed that ultimately led to the resurrection of the State of Israel in 1948.

It is absolutely necessary to take note of these facts if we are to understand the true significance of our Lord's act in raising up the impotent man in John V. This man does not typify the nation of Israel in the Wilderness wanderings *but the nation of Israel (i.e. the Jews) in their Dispersion over the earth from A.D. 71 to 1933*, when, as we reveal in our former Treatise *The World in Liquidation*, "the times of the Gentiles" ended by the nations of Christendom being "cut off", as forewarned by the Apostle Paul, for their non-continuance in "the goodness . . . of God" (Rom. XI, 22); and when also the Six Thousand Years of Man terminated to the hour on 12th June.

Our Lord made two separate contacts with this "certain man" of John V. He first made him whole so that he took up his bed and walked. Later He met him and gave him a word of most solemn warning in these terms (verse 14):

> "Behold, thou art made whole: sin no more, lest a worse thing come unto thee."

Our Lord's first contact with this man, when unasked He

healed him of his infirmity, had its counterpart or antitype in the raising up again of the people of Israel to nationhood in the year 1948, when, at the midnight of 14th-15th May, which was the 3,586th anniversary of the night they crossed the Red Sea on leaving Egypt in 1639 B.C., the State of Israel came into being simultaneously with the "death" of the British Mandate at that significant hour.

The resurrection of the new State of Israel brought the Dispersion to an end, as any Jew in the world from that time was at liberty to return, bag and baggage, to the land of his Fathers. Already some 8-900,000 have entered the Land since May 1948; but unfortunately many of these, through the extreme cruelty of certain nations, returned with neither bag nor baggage.

It was the sin of unbelief in regard to their Messiah that sent the Jews into Dispersion; but when 1933 was reached, and they had expiated their sin by 49 times 38 years of wandering among the nations, the hour had come when Divine Mercy, not to mention Divine foreplanning, must operate to heal their impotence and cause them to "walk" once again as an independent nation. No doubt the hour is about to come when the people of Israel in and out of the Land will be willing to recognize Who it was that allowed and empowered them to rise again as a nation. They will then know that it was the One Who raised "the impotent man" at the pool of Bethesda and Who now, as the Risen Christ, has been appointed of God to be the Supreme Governor of the Universe (Matt. XXVIII, 18).

Our Lord's final contact with the impotent man whom He had made whole was "in the temple". We have already quoted verse 14 with its words of solemn warning. It was "sin" that had caused this man to suffer his infirmity for 38 years and it was sin that caused the Jewish nation to be dispersed over the earth for 49 times 38 years, that is, from A.D. 71 to 1933.

Who cannot detect in our Lord's words, "Thou art made whole: sin no more, lest a worse thing come unto thee", a warning to the people of Israel of the utmost solemnity in the present hour? What does it imply? Clearly this: that lying ahead there is a danger of their falling into a yet greater sin than that which caused the Dispersion. And who can doubt that this warning has to be linked with a verse (43) later in this same chapter in which our Lord states, "I am come in My

Father's name, and ye receive Me not: if another shall come in his own name, him ye will receive"? More we are not at liberty to say, but the Law and the Prophets, not to mention the teaching of our Lord and His Apostles, especially that of the Apocalypse, are full of instruction for Israel in the present dark hour of human history. Indeed, this transitional era since 1933, called "the consummation of the age", occupies a place of transcendent importance prophetically throughout the Holy Scriptures.

In the light of these facts no one could be surprised to hear that our Lord's raising up of "the impotent man" in John V was on the Day of Atonement. Obviously the raising up of the nation of Israel in 1948 signified that they had paid the penalty for the sin for which they had been punished by their Dispersion over the earth. But that does not mean that their sin had been atoned for and that they were "at one" with God again. He Who raised "the impotent man" later became the Antitype of the Sin-Offering of the Day of Atonement by the laying down of His own life: and it is He Who has made propitiation for Israel's sin, as He has for the sin of "the whole world" (I John II, 2). For this reason our Lord chose the Day of Atonement to perform this typical sign of Israel's national resurrection after 49 times 38 years of Dispersion.

We must briefly refer to the text to explain how it reveals that this Feast was the Day of Atonement (see Levit. XXIII, 27).

In verse 9 a new sentence begins with the words, "And on the same day was the sabbath". The literal translation of the Greek is "Now on that day was *a* sabbath". Such a wording, as many commentators have noticed, could only be used in order to make it clear that the writer is not referring to *the* Sabbath, which always signifies the weekly Sabbath. In verse 10 the words, "It is the sabbath day", have no warrant in the Greek. The verse should read, "It is *a* sabbath: it is not lawful for thee to carry thy bed".

Again, in verse 16, the words, "on the sabbath day", should read "on *a* sabbath".

These three corrections, which can be confirmed by reference to any literal translations of the Greek, make it obvious that the Apostle is stressing the fact that this happened on one of the Feasts which was *a* Sabbath. The three Feasts of the

7th month, namely, those of Trumpets, the Day of Atonement and Ingathering, were all special Sabbaths, on whichever day of the week they occurred (see Levit. XXIII, verses 24, 32 and 39).

How were we to discover which of these three Feasts is referred to in John V, 1?

In verse 18 we read, "Therefore the Jews sought the more to kill Him, because He not only had broken *the* sabbath, but said also that God was His (own) Father, making Himself equal with God". Now in this verse the translation of the words "the sabbath" is strictly in accord with the Greek text. The words "the sabbath" can only refer to the weekly Sabbath which the Pharisees guarded with such pious exactitude. It therefore became clear from the text that the Feast of John V was both *a* Sabbath and *the* Sabbath. In other words, it was one of the three Feasts which was *a* Sabbath and which occurred on *the* (weekly) Sabbath.

With this information it was not difficult to establish that the Day of Atonement, which was Israel's 10th day of the 7th month, in A.D. 31 was on the Sabbath Day, the date of which was 13th October. So in rendering his account of the incident of John V the Apostle thrice refers to the day as *a* Sabbath, because the Day of Atonement was a Sabbath, and he wished to emphasize the fact. When, however, he refers to the attitude of the Pharisees or Jewish rulers, he calls attention to the feature which had so enraged them, namely, that Jesus had wrought this miracle on *the Sabbath day* and allowed the man to carry his bed. Doubtless, if it had only been *a* Sabbath their ire would have been far less vehement, but when it came to being the Sabbath day that had, in their estimate, been broken, their wrath was unrestrained and they "sought the more to kill Him". (The law of the Sabbath in Exodus XXXI, 12 to 17, only applied to the Sabbath Day because it was the seventh day and a type of the Kingdom and of God's Rest which must not be broken. This law, they well knew, could not be applied to a Sabbath other than the weekly day of rest.)

A year later our Lord and Master is again in Jerusalem for the Feast of Tabernacles, as recorded in John VII. He then refers back to His raising of "the impotent man" of John V. In each reference (see verses 22 and 23) He refers, as shown by the Greek text, to *a* Sabbath and not "the sabbath day" as in our translation. He argues that if in keeping the Law of Moses in regard to the eighth day the Jews circumcise a male infant on a Sabbath, that is, on one of the three Feasts which is a Sabbath, why should they be angry and seek to kill Him "because", as He says, "I have made a man every whit whole on a sabbath" (verse 23, literal trans.). It must be remembered that the Day of Atonement was the most important and solemn day in the whole of Israel's calendar and yet circumcision had to be performed if it was an eighth day. Surely then the Lord was free to perform a work of mercy on a day of Atonement, even though it was a Sabbath.

It is quite clear that our Lord's act of raising the impotent man on the Day of Atonement in A.D. 31 led to the Jews' determination to get rid of Him, that is, to kill Him. His discourse to them in John V, from verse 19 to the end, was plainly intended to set before them His full Messianic claims. This He does by persistently referring to His relationship to God as His Father. There is a fourfold witness as to His Messiahship. This was John the Baptist (verse 33), His own works (verse 36), God the Father Who at His Baptism declared, "This is My beloved Son" (verse 37), and, finally, the Scriptures (verse 39).

This discourse, while putting the Jewish leaders under direct responsibility, which it was intended to do, reveals our Lord to all men as co-equal with the Father. To Him had been given the power to communicate life and also to execute judgment. With this comes the solemn declaration, "He that honoureth not the Son honoureth not the Father which hath sent Him" (verse 23).

Our Lord apparently returned to Galilee soon after this Feast of the Day of Atonement. He may have lingered for the Feast of Tabernacles which began four days later and continued for eight days. There is, however, no reference in the Gospel regarding any other activities of our Lord in Jerusalem at that time. So it is a well-founded assumption that He returned to Galilee and took up His Ministry there to "the poor of the flock" among whom He found a welcome and upon whom He could lavish many expressions of His boundless love and grace as He "went about doing good, and healing all that were oppressed of the devil; for God was with Him" (Acts X, 38).

# CHAPTER EIGHT

## THE SECOND YEAR OF OUR LORD'S MINISTRY IN GALILEE

### THE MURDER BY EXECUTION OF JOHN THE BAPTIST

### THE FEEDING OF THE FIVE THOUSAND – THE FOURTH SIGN-MIRACLE OF THE GOSPEL OF JOHN

### JESUS WALKS UPON THE WATER – THE FIFTH SIGN-MIRACLE

TIME

October A.D. 31 to November A.D. 32

THE ACCOUNT of the visit of our Lord Jesus Christ to Jerusalem in the Autumn of A.D. 31 when, on the Day of Atonement (13th October) He raised up the impotent man, is exclusively recorded in John's Gospel. As the Jews sought to kill Him, our Lord must have left Jerusalem forthwith. The first verse of John VII opens with the confirmation of this fact: "After these things Jesus walked in Galilee: for He would not walk in Jewry, because the Jews sought to kill Him" (cf. John V, 18).

We may, therefore, rightly assume that the Lord returned to Galilee very shortly after the miracle of John V. This was in the month of October. We can find no word to indicate that on this visit to the South He performed any other act. Having left Judaea in the Autumn of A.D. 30, our Lord evidently again felt the need to appear in Jerusalem in order to press home His Messianic claims upon the Jewish authorities. This He did, as we have seen, in no uncertain way after raising the impotent man on the Day of Atonement.

On 4th November A.D. 31, two Bible years of 354 days had passed from 26th November A.D. 29, when our Lord opened His Ministry at the age of exactly 30 years. In Bible years our

Lord was, therefore, 32 years old on 4th November A.D. 31, and 31 solar years and 6 days had elapsed since His birth on Friday, 29th October 1 B.C.

As we have already pointed out, it has not pleased God to allow the many events and discourses of our Lord's Galilean Ministry to be dated. It is a fact that apart from the information given by John as to the time of the Feeding of the Five Thousand, namely, the Passover of A.D. 32, it is not possible to name a single date during the second year of our Lord's Galilean Ministry which began in the Autumn of A.D. 31.

We might wish to know when our Lord sent out the Twelve to preach but we are only told that they returned just before the Feeding of the Five Thousand. We cannot say exactly when it was that John the Baptist sent his rather pathetic enquiry to Jesus, "Art Thou He that should come, or do we look for another?" (Matt. XI, 3). We do, however, know that John was murdered by Herod shortly before the Feeding of the Five Thousand in the Spring of A.D. 32 (Matt. XIV, 13). As we have already pointed out, the Gospels do not date our Lord's public actions or discourses, but they do date events in His personal pathway and all who love Him will rejoice to be able to trace in the Scriptures the Pattern of Time by which He walked here on earth.

### THE FEEDING OF THE FIVE THOUSAND

(Matthew XIV, Mark VI, Luke IX and John VI)

Our Lord's fourth Sign-Miracle of John's Gospel – the Feeding of the Five Thousand – is the only one recorded in the other three Gospels. It is, in fact, the only miracle recorded in all four Gospels. This gives to it an entirely unique importance.

It is easy to discern from the Gospels, and notably from that of John, that this event took place early in May A.D. 32. John names three Passovers – the first is in A.D. 30 (II, 13), the second is in A.D. 32 (VI, 4) and the third is that of A.D. 33 (XII, 1). He does not mention the Passover of A.D. 31 but, as we have already pointed out, the incident in the corn-fields on "the second-first sabbath", named in Luke VI, 1, is related to the Passover of that year. This proves that the Gospels account for the four Passovers of our Lord's Ministry, namely, A.D. 30, 31, 32 and 33 – the last being the one at which our Lord laid down His life.

The Passover of A.D. 32 was on 12th May, which is the very latest date possible according to the series of luni-solar Sabbatic years which began at the Exodus. The Exodus Passover was 11th May (1639 B.C.), and the people of Israel commenced their journey out of Egypt on Friday, 12th May, which was the 15th of the 1st Month – then called "Abib" (Numbers XXXIII, 3).

In John VI, 4 we read, "And the passover, a feast of the Jews, was nigh" (i.e. at hand). From this we may conclude that the Feeding of the Five Thousand was on one of the early days of May A.D. 32 – exactly one year before our Lord died and rose again.

We learn from Matthew's Gospel that the day on which our Lord performed this sign-miracle was tinged with deep sorrow. It was, in fact, on hearing that John the Baptist had been beheaded in prison by Herod that our Lord "departed thence by ship into a desert place apart" with His disciples (Matt. XIV, 12 and 13). Mark and Luke inform us that this corresponded in time with the return of the Twelve Apostles from their preaching tour and that Jesus invited them to join Him for a season of rest after their arduous activities (Mark VI, 31 and Luke IX, 10).

It is very clear that instead of a season of quiet and rest, our Lord must have spent most of the day in healing and teaching. The multitudes discovered where Jesus had gone and followed Him. Mark records this: "And Jesus, when He came out, saw much people, and was moved with compassion toward them, because they were as sheep not having a shepherd: and He began to teach them many things" (VI, 34). Matthew adds, "And He healed their sick" (XIV, 14).

It is characteristic that in each of the first three Gospels it is recorded that the Twelve Apostles tendered the advice to the Lord that He should send the multitude away as "the day was now far spent" and the people had nothing to eat. How different was our Lord's attitude. They had come in search of Him – the One by Whom the worlds were created. He could not send them away without a practical expression of His compassion when it was in His power to meet their need. He, therefore, says to the disciples, "Give ye them to eat".

John records this. "Jesus . . . saith unto Philip, Whence shall we buy bread, that these may eat? And this He said to prove him: for He Himself knew what He would do." Philip replies by saying that "two hundred pennyworth of bread" would be inadequate. Then, as we know, a lad was found who had "five barley loaves, and two small fishes". These Jesus took "and when He had given thanks, He distributed to the disciples, and the disciples to them that were set down; and likewise of the fishes, as much as they would" (John VI, 5 to 11). This was an occasion when it could truly be said, "He hath filled the hungry with good things".

In each account we are informed that "twelve baskets" of fragments were taken up of that "which remained over" after this bounteous meal had been partaken of by our Lord's guests, who numbered "five thousand men, beside women and children". Luke informs us that the desert place belonged to Bethsaida which was evidently near, and this accounts for the great number who came out in search of our Lord.

There can be no doubt that the Feeding of the Five Thousand was a tremendous occasion and that our Lord's miraculous powers were never seen in greater display or, indeed, His compassion for the multitude. There was, however, a predictive element in this display of power which extended far beyond the confines of its immediate setting. It is for this reason that the Apostle John is caused to insert it as one of the Sign-Miracles of his Gospel. In other words, this great event was prophetic of action by our Lord at the end of the Christian Dispensation. As we have said previously, all the Sign-Miracles of John's Gospel are to be fulfilled or have their antitypes in the brief era called "the consummation of the age" which began after the 6,000 Years of Man and the 2,000 Years of the Christian Dispensation had terminated, on 12th June 1933, as fully explained in our former Treatise.

In the first Sign-Miracle of John II, when our Lord turned the water into wine, we have predictive evidence that at the end of the age the pure truth of Christianity is to be restored for a brief season, not only in abundant supply, but even of a better quality than at the beginning of the Dispensation. Here, in this fourth Sign-Miracle of John VI, we have a prediction that our Lord Jesus Christ is to be manifested at the end of the age as the Bread of God which came down from Heaven, and that as such He will miraculously meet His people's needs at a time when spiritual hunger grips them because, like those He fed in the desert near Bethsaida, they "have nothing to eat".

Furthermore, after abundantly meeting the needs of the Church, which is His body, there will be enough remaining over for the believing remnant of the Twelve Tribes of Israel which is to be sealed by the Holy Ghost after the Church has departed to its heavenly home (see Revelation VII, 1 to 8). That is the meaning of the "twelve baskets of fragments". Thus the Church on its departure leaves a legacy to Israel.

The Feeding of the Five Thousand, like the first sign of John II, 11, and the second sign of John IV, 46, supposes the failure of this Dispensation and the necessity of our Lord meeting the occasion by a display of His sovereign grace and power to bring about a recovery before He appears "a second time". The hunger of the Prodigal Son and his return to the Father's House where the fatted calf is killed, not to mention the jealousy of the Elder Son – Israel – is but another aspect of the Church's brief recovery at the end of the age through the sovereign grace of God the Father and our Lord Jesus Christ.

## THE FIFTH SIGN-MIRACLE OF JOHN'S GOSPEL

"JESUS WALKING ON THE SEA"

A SIGN RELATING TO ISRAEL

John VI, verses 15 to 21

It has to be admitted that the Eight Signs of John's Gospel are clothed with considerable mystery and that any interpretation of them must needs be but a faint marking of the reality which they portend. This is particularly so in regard to the Fifth Sign-Miracle which presents "Jesus walking on the sea" and coming to the Twelve disciples in their ship during a storm which had arisen "by reason of a great wind that blew".

The Feeding of the Five Thousand, as we have shown, denotes a coming act of our Lord Jesus Christ towards Christendom – a positive revelation of Himself as "the Bread which came down from heaven". The miracle itself created such an impression that the people proposed to "come and take Him by force, to make Him (a) king". His response to this impulsive desire was to withdraw "again into a mountain Himself alone".

In the meanwhile His twelve disciples had "entered into a ship", and they "went over the sea towards Capernaum". Darkness came on and with it "the sea arose by reason of a great wind that blew". The record continues, "So when they had rowed about five and twenty or thirty furlongs, they see Jesus walking on the sea, and drawing nigh unto the ship: and they were afraid. But He saith unto them, It is I; be not afraid. Then they willingly received Him into the ship: and immediately the ship was at the land whither they went."

It is perfectly clear that the twelve disciples in the ship, like the twelve baskets of fragments, typify that section of the twelve tribes of Israel, referred to in Revelation VII, who come to believe in Jesus after the Church, which is Christ's body, has ascended up to its heavenly home at the Second Appearing of our Lord, when the Christian Dispensation finally ends.

As we have fully explained in our former Treatise in Paper V, our Lord Jesus Christ at His Second Appearing is coming down from Heaven to be with His Church on the earth for nine days – the period which, with the 40 days after His resurrection, completes the 49 days to Pentecost, when He will summon her to meet Him in the air (see I Thess. IV, 13 to 18). It is clear that the antitype of the Feeding of the Five Thousand is an act which prepares His Church for His return and for her departure with Him to His Father's House.

The Parable of the Ten Virgins informs us that when He is about to return as the Bridegroom, the whole of Christendom, which the Ten Virgins represent, rises to trim its lamps. It seems that when our Lord returns for His Church the world will desire then and there to make Him its King, but He will not have come for that purpose. Therefore, His act in going up "into a mountain" appears to signify His return to Heaven *with the Church which is His body* prior to the opening of the Seven Years of the Apocalyptic Era.

The storm that overtook the twelve disciples, when "the sea arose by reason of a great wind", clearly speaks of the "wars and rumours of wars" which beset mankind in these seven years. At that time this faithful remnant of the Twelve Tribes of

Israel will become the object of a diabolical persecution (Revelation XII, 13); but at a given point of time their Messiah, our Lord Jesus Christ, will appear for their relief – His "walking on the sea" denoting His dominance over the nations and His power to protect His people of Israel from being overwhelmed by the untold calamities of the Apocalyptic Era.

The link between the two sign-miracles of John VI is to be clearly seen in the fact that what is represented typically by the food with which our Lord fed the Five Thousand avails first for His Church as a preparation for His Second Appearing and then, in the twelve baskets of fragments, as that which sustains the faithful in Israel during the Apocalyptic Era which precedes His Third Appearing, when He comes to save them from destruction and to set up His Kingdom over the whole earth. It is well to remember that in Matthew's Gospel we are told it is for the sake of this elect remnant that the days of "the great tribulation" are to be shortened (XXIV, 21, 22). It is, therefore, clear that, however faint the markings, this Fifth Sign-Miracle relates to Israel in the near future.

## OUR LORD'S DISCOURSE IN JOHN VI, 22 to 71

Those whom our Lord Jesus Christ had fed miraculously seek Him out again "the day following". He then takes occasion to discourse to them at length, saying, "the Bread of God is He which cometh down from heaven, and giveth life unto the world" (verse 33). Previously He said to them:

> "Labour not for the meat which perisheth, but for that meat which endureth unto everlasting life, which the Son of Man shall give unto you: for Him hath God the Father sealed" (verse 27).

The effect of this solemn Discourse on the Bread of Life was to sort out the unbelievers among our Lord's professed followers. These said, "Is not this Jesus, the son of Joseph, whose father and mother we know? How is it then that He saith, I came down from heaven?" (verse 42).

It was one thing to receive of our Lord's bounty in the form of bread and fishes, but quite another to be told, "Except ye eat the flesh of the Son of Man, and drink His blood, ye have no life in you" (verse 53). "Many therefore of His disciples, when they heard this, said, This is an hard saying; who can hear it?" (verse 60).

No wonder Jesus said, "There are some of you that believe not" (verse 64). Finally, the record states, "From that time many of His disciples went back, and walked no more with Him" (verse 66.)

Our Lord then challenges the twelve, who formed the inner circle of His followers, with the question, "Will ye also go away?" To this Peter, speaking for the others, says, "Lord, to whom shall we go? Thou hast the words of eternal life. And we believe and are sure that Thou art that Christ, the Son of the living God" (verses 68 and 69). Our Lord then acquaints the twelve disciples with the fact that one of them is a devil (i.e. an adversary). He is, of course, referring to Judas Iscariot who "should betray Him, being one of the twelve" (verse 71).

Who knows how near we may be to witnessing the antitypical fulfilment of these Fourth and Fifth Sign-Miracles of John's Gospel? How blessed to recall that these events are not merely history but signs of forthcoming acts of our Lord Jesus Christ prior to His return which evidently is at hand.

# CHAPTER NINE

## THE LAST PHASE OF OUR LORD'S EARTHLY PATHWAY OPENS

HIS "THREE YEARS" OF SEEKING FRUIT
FROM ISRAEL TERMINATE ON 22ND OCTOBER A.D. 32

OUR LORD ATTENDS THE FEAST OF TABERNACLES
AT JERUSALEM IN NOVEMBER A.D. 32.
WHY HE WENT UP "ABOUT THE MIDST OF THE FEAST"

THE MARKED 212 DAYS FROM "THE LAST DAY" OF THE FEAST
ON 13TH NOVEMBER A.D. 32,
TO THE ASCENSION INTO HEAVEN ON 13TH JUNE A.D.33.

THE SIXTH SIGN-MIRACLE OF JOHN'S GOSPEL.
A MAN BORN BLIND RECEIVES SIGHT.
ITS TYPICAL SIGNIFICANCE FOR ISRAEL.

On 13th November A.D. 32, our Lord's age in Bible Years was 33 years and 22 days, and in Solar Years, 32 years and 16 days.
Read the Gospel of Luke, Chapter XIII, 6 to 9, and
the Gospel of John, Chapters VII, VIII and IX.

AT THIS point in our narrative we must again draw attention to the Parable of the Barren Fig Tree in the 13th chapter of Luke's Gospel, because it contains the most important chronological statements in the Four Gospels. In doing this we shall of necessity have to repeat much on this subject already recorded in Chapter One, but its great importance warrants this measure of repetition.

In this Parable, like that of "A Certain Householder" in Matthew XXI, 33 to 45, our Lord Jesus Christ reveals Himself as having come into the world in search of "fruit" from the nation of Israel, which is represented in the Parable as "a fig tree planted in His vineyard". Addressing the Keeper of His vineyard, He represents Himself as saying:

> "Behold, these three years I come seeking fruit on this fig tree, and find none: cut it down; why cumbereth it the ground?" (verse 7).

As the Bible does not contain indefinite or inexact chronological data – because this would be quite useless – the implication to be drawn from this utterance is that it was made on the day after our Lord's first three years of Ministry to Israel were completed. Year by year for three years He had sought in vain to obtain fruit from this particular fig tree, that is, from the Jewish nation. Our Lord's Ministry began on Saturday, 26th November A.D. 29. These three Bible years of 354 days ended on Wednesday, 22nd October A.D. 32, and our Lord's utterance must have been made the next day, Thursday, 23rd October, which was the 1st day of the Jews' 7th month (Tishri) in A.D. 32.

Our Lord's suggestion is that the Jewish nation should there and then be "cut down". Why should it longer cumber the ground, He asks the Dresser of His vineyard, whom we may assume typifies the Holy Spirit? The Dresser pleads for a further period of clemency in these terms:

> "Lord, let it alone THIS YEAR ALSO, till I shall dig about it and dung it: And, if it bear fruit, well: and if not, then after that thou shalt cut it down" (verses 8 and 9).

There is an immense significance attaching to this expression: "Let it alone this year also". The year referred to would run inclusively from 23rd October A.D. 32, to 11th October A.D. 33. In that year our Lord would lay down His life as an atoning Sacrifice for sin, and rise again "after three days". On the Day of Pentecost the Holy Spirit would descend in mighty power upon the Remnant of the Jews which believed in Jesus as the Messiah, and Peter, with the other eleven Apostles, would proclaim Him as now risen and ascended into Heaven. An official intimation would be made to the Jewish nation that, if it would repent, the rejected Messiah would return and bring in "the times of refreshing", that is, the Kingdom (Acts III, 12 to 26). In other words, during this one further year of clemency the Holy Spirit would use every means to save the Jewish nation from reaching that point when mercy would be withdrawn, and the full penalty be exacted for its sinful rejection of the Messiah – God's well-beloved Son.

We shall, in the appropriate section, disclose what Scripture reveals concerning events at the end of this one year of clemency, when the Jewish nation was "cut down", but the whole world knows that the period availed nothing and that the Jewish rulers at once came out in open enmity against the Apostles whom they resisted with every means at their disposal (Acts IV to VII).

As we stated in Chapter One, it is of the utmost importance from the chronological aspect of the Gospels to take note of the fact that Luke names altogether 34 consecutive Bible years of 354 days each. In Chapter III, verse 23, we read in the Revised Version, "And Jesus Himself, when He began (to teach), was about thirty years of age". These 30 Bible years began with His birth on 29th October 1 B.C., and ended on 25th November A.D. 29, after which the "three years" of Luke XIII, 7, began. As we have shown, "these three years" ended on 22nd October A.D. 32, when the year of clemency ("this year also") opened and ran its course to 11th October A.D. 33, when the Jewish nation was "cut down" following the stoning to death of the martyr Stephen.

This sequence of years did not, however, stop there for on 12th October, that is, on the day after the year of clemency to Israel ended, "the times of the Gentiles" began and ran an unbroken course of 1,960 (4×490) Bible years to 12th June, 1933, when, as narrated in our former Treatise, *The World in Liquidation*, the Gentiles – like Israel in A.D. 33 – were "cut off" for their non-continuance in the goodness of God (see Romans XI, 22), and "the consummation of the age" began. The Bible, therefore, reveals an unbroken sequence of 1,994 Bible years from the day of our Lord's birth to 12th June, 1,933, when the Christian Dispensation or "times of the Gentiles" ended *chronologically*.

We will tabulate this sequence of years thus:

| | | |
|---|---|---|
| The Nativity to the Ministry, | | |
| 29th Oct. 1 B.C., to 25th Nov. A.D. 29 | .. | 30 years |
| "These three years", | | |
| 26th Nov. A.D. 29, to 22nd Oct. A.D. 32 | .. | 3 years |

| | | |
|---|---|---|
| "This year also", | | |
| 23rd Oct. A.D. 32, to 11th Oct. A.D. 33 | .. | 1 year |
| "The times of the Gentiles", | | |
| 12th Oct. A.D. 33, to 12th June A.D. 1933 | .. | 1,960 years |
| The Birth of our Lord to "the consummation of the age" | .. .. .. .. .. | 1,994 years |

We are indebted to the Gospel of Luke for this complete record of time in Bible years from the birth of our Lord Jesus Christ to the end of "the times of the Gentiles" – a phrase which appears nowhere else in Scripture. It was uttered by our Lord in His Olivet Discourse, as recorded by Luke, in the following context:

> "They shall fall by the edge of the sword, and shall be led away captive into all nations: and Jerusalem shall be trodden down of the Gentiles, until the times of the Gentiles be fulfilled" (XXI, 24).

Jerusalem was the Jewish capital when our Lord uttered these words and remained so until its fall to the armies of Rome under Titus in A.D. 70, when it began to be "trodden down of the Gentiles". "The times" or seasons of grace to the Gentiles had begun on 12th October A.D. 33, the next day after the end of the year of clemency to Israel on 11th October when the Jewish nation was "cut down" by our Lord, as the Dresser of the vineyard had counselled – "after that (i.e. the year of clemency) Thou shalt cut it down". For obvious reasons Luke does not mention that "the times of the Gentiles" would last for 1,960 Bible years. The Bible, however, reveals this in that human history to the Kingdom is manifestly divided by it into three such periods of 1,960 years, as follows: from Adam to Abraham (the Times of the Patriarchs); from Abraham to the Death of Christ (the Times of Israel), and from A.D. 33 to 1933 ("the times of the Gentiles") see *The World in Liquidation*. These "times of the Gentiles" have nothing whatever to do with the "seven times" or 2,520 years of Gentile governmental supremacy which began in 588 B.C. with the fall of the Kingdom of Judah, in the days of Nebuchadnezzar, King of Babylon (Daniel IV).

## OUR LORD VISITS JERUSALEM FOR THE FEAST OF TABERNACLES IN A.D. 32

### (John VII)

This Chapter opens with a record of the altercation between our Lord and His brethren after the flesh, of whom it says, "For neither did His brethren believe in Him". They would have Him go to Jerusalem and make a display at the Feast of Tabernacles. Our Lord's statement in verse 6: "My time is not yet come: but your time is alway ready", is both solemn and important. In the first place He shows, in speaking of Himself, that He perfectly understood that His pathway on the earth was according to a Pattern of Time designed for Him by God the Father. For Him it was impossible to fail to walk in exact conformity with that Pattern, since not to do so would have been to disobey His Father in Heaven and that, at the least, would have been an evidence of a lack of communion, if not of actual sin. Our Lord knew that *for a particular reason* He had to arrive in Jerusalem "about the midst of the feast". His brethren knew nothing about this but sought to persuade Him to do what was out of Divine order, judging that He ought to act as they did.

What our Lord says to them, as to all who walk in self-will and in disregard of the fact that there is "a time to every purpose under the heaven" (Eccles. III, 1), is, "Your time is alway ready". This is most solemn, because in effect it means that all who do not walk in strict obedience to the ordered path of God's will and keep to His pattern of time for them, know no restrictions upon their liberty but go hither and thither *at times of their own choosing* and in total disregard of any need to keep step with the Master. How often such conduct has led to confusion, or even to catastrophe, with the people of God, is a matter of all too common knowledge.

> "About the midst of the feast Jesus went up to the temple, and taught" (verse 14).

There is a very great deal to be gleaned from the fact that our Lord did not attend at the Feast of Tabernacles in A.D. 32 until "the midst of the feast". We have already noted that He had had to rebuke His brethren who urged Him to go up at once, by saying, "My time is not yet come".

The question arises, What actually did our Lord mean by this statement? It obviously indicated that there was a reason why He should arrive in "the midst of the feast", and not before. What then was His reason? To answer this we must briefly explain what the Scriptures reveal about the Feast of Tabernacles. All will recall that our blessed Lord and Master was born on the first day of the Feast of Tabernacles in 1 B.C. and that He was circumcised on the 8th day – the day which this chapter speaks of as "the last day, that great day of the feast" (verse 37).

In Leviticus XXIII, 33 to 36, we read, "The fifteenth day of this seventh month shall be the feast of tabernacles for seven days unto the Lord . . . on the eighth day shall be an holy convocation unto you". In other words, like the concurrent Feast of Ingathering (verse 39), Tabernacles was a Feast which lasted for seven days but to which was appended an "eighth" which was "an holy convocation" – the feature which made it the "great day of the feast".

The Feast of Tabernacles embraces the whole course of human history and envisages man as a sojourner on the earth, like Abraham "dwelling in tabernacles with Isaac and Jacob" (Hebrews XI, 9). As this Feast had seven days and an eighth, so the whole course of time in accordance with it is divided into seven parts with an eighth part to follow it.

It is common knowledge with students of the Bible that the six days of Creation, and the hallowed seventh day which followed them, are a type of the 6,000 years of man which are to be followed by a seventh thousand years, commonly called the Millennium or Era of the Kingdom. This fact rests on Peter's words in his Second Epistle: "that one day is with the Lord as a thousand years, and a thousand years as one day" (III, 8). These words, however, cannot refer to time as it is viewed in the Feast of Tabernacles, since the "holy convocation" is an eighth day and not a seventh. In the concurrent Feast of Ingathering the eighth day was a Sabbath (Levit. XXIII, 39).

In the Summary of Facts (Par. 18) we give some details of a deeply-concealed chronological era which runs right through the Bible and which is divided into seven "days" or cycles of 888 years each. The number 888 is the numerical value of the Greek spelling of the Name – Jesus. As fully explained in our former Treatise, we discovered that the calendar based upon this series of 888 years only speaks with any meaning when it is in relation to events connected with Jesus as the Messiah, or the seed through which He was to come. For instance, the day Abraham left Haran for the Promised Land (Gen. XII, 4) which was the beginning of "the sojourning of the children of Israel", named in Exodus XII, 40, was the first day of the Feast of Tabernacles in this series of years, as also was the Exodus of Israel from Egypt 430 years to the day afterwards. The outstanding example in this series of years is, however, our Lord's birth which was on the 15th day of the 1st month, the 1st day of Unleavened Bread. For this reason we named this series the "Years of the Messiah" as they run their course from the 8th day of Creation to the establishment of the Messianic Kingdom at the opening of the 8th cycle of 888 years.

The essence of all we have said is that the 8 days of the Feast of Tabernacles typify 8 "days" or cycles of 888 Messianic Years each, and that in this aspect the whole course of man's time on the earth in its present form is viewed as 8 times 888 years.

As the Feast of Tabernacles typifies the whole course of human history on this present earth, the point of time at which our Lord, as "the Word . . . made flesh", commenced to tabernacle in our midst must obviously agree with the point of time in the Feast of Tabernacles in A.D. 32 when He appeared in the Temple.

In the Years of the Messiah our Lord was born on the 15th day of the 1st month in the year 4205. This was during the fifth "day" or cycle of 888 years from Adam. Consequently, we know that it was in the fifth day of the Feast that Jesus "went up into the Temple and taught".

Why did our Lord so act? It must have been God's way of emphasizing that the Feast of Tabernacles represented the whole course of human history on the earth, divided into eight Messianic "days" or cycles of 888 years each. It is probable that our Lord chose the Feast of Tabernacles in A.D. 32 because the 80th Jubile year from Creation had begun only a few days before, on the 10th day of the 7th month. At this 80th Jubile the Kingdom should have been proclaimed but the Lord's rejection by Israel made this impossible.

If all our Lord's disciples in this Dispensation had been sojourners on the earth, "tabernacling" as He did, instead of becoming its citizens, the difference between a Christian disciple and a non-Christian would have stood out with an emphasis like that which marked the Nazarite of old. But as it is there is now, with few exceptions, no difference to be seen between believers and unbelievers, as the former unashamedly display the fact that, like other people, their roots run down deep into the world and that its possessions and riches, its comforts and customs, are as much for them as for those on the broad road that leads to destruction.

"The Last Day, that Great Day of the Feast" (John VII, 37).

The date of the last or eighth day of the Feast of Tabernacles in A.D. 32 was Thursday, 13th November. In Bible terms it would be measured from 8 A.M. on the 22nd day of the 7th month to 8 A.M. on the 23rd day of the same. This "eighth" day was "an holy convocation" as it formed a type of the era when the Kingdom of God will be established over the earth.

We are told that it was on this day that Jesus stood and cried, saying,

> "If any man thirst, let him come unto Me, and drink. He that believeth on Me, as the scripture hath said, out of his belly shall flow rivers of living water" (verses 37 and 38).

The date of 13th November A.D. 32, was inclusively exactly 222 days prior to 22nd June A.D. 33, which was the day of Pentecost and 50 days after the resurrection of our Lord Jesus Christ on 4th May. It is not, therefore, surprising that the Apostle John introduces a parenthetical statement, immediately after this utterance of our Lord, in these terms:

> "(But this spake He of the Spirit, which they that believe on Him should receive: for the Holy Ghost was not yet (given); because that Jesus was not yet glorified)" (verse 39).

On the day of Pentecost, when the Holy Ghost descended, the Apostle Peter declared, "This is that which was spoken by the prophet Joel . . . in the last days, saith God, I will pour out of My Spirit upon all flesh" (Acts II, 16 and 17).

If we deduct the two complete days of our Lord's session "in the heart of the earth" from the 222 days between 13th November A.D. 32, and 22nd June A.D. 33, we have a total of 220 days. This corresponds to the 220 cubits (20 × 11) of the "porch" of the Ezekiel Temple (see Ezekiel XL, 49).

A porch is the entrance to a building and it appears that these 220 days to the day of Pentecost, signified that the hour was approaching for the Spirit to be poured out on all flesh, according to Joel's prophecy. This, however, supposed Israel's repentance and restoration. Nevertheless, there is only one day of Pentecost, namely, that on which the Holy Spirit descended fifty days after the death and resurrection of our Lord Jesus Christ. Every subsequent descent of the Spirit must be on that one day, that is, on the solar anniversary of it, as appointed by God. Thus, in A.D. 36 the Holy Ghost was bestowed upon the Gentiles on 22nd June which was the third anniversary of His descent at Jerusalem.

## THE LAST 212 DAYS OF OUR LORD'S EARTHLY PATHWAY

We have already called attention to the fact that from 13th November A.D. 32, to 13th June A.D. 33, when our Lord and Master ascended into Heaven to sit on the right hand of the Majesty on High, is a period of 212 days, every one of which can be accounted for in the Gospels. These 212 days, like the 212 days at the beginning of His public life from His Baptism on 5th October A.D. 29, to the Passover on 4th May A.D. 30, are filled with events related to the Person of our Lord, rather than to His public acts.

As the enmity of Israel's rulers towards our Lord increased, His pathway became narrower and more restricted until finally that enmity, which so often would have destroyed Him, had it been the time, burst all bounds and was allowed to display itself in all its hideousness and cruelty at the Passover on 1st May A.D. 33.

This Treatise will therefore now be occupied with tracing out these last 212 days, which God has been pleased to mark out so clearly at the close of our Lord's earthly pathway.

# THE SIXTH SIGN-MIRACLE OF JOHN'S GOSPEL

## A MAN BORN BLIND RECEIVES HIS SIGHT

## THE THIRD SIGN RELATING TO ISRAEL

Read John IX

Our Lord's act in giving sight to "a man which was blind from his birth" is recorded only by the Evangelist John and this in great detail. This is because, as a sign relating to Israel at the end of the age, it is of the greatest significance – a fact which can be better appreciated when Paul's statement – "blindness in part is happened to Israel, until the fulness of the Gentiles be come in" – is taken into account (Romans XI, 25).

In verse 3 we are told that this man's affliction was due neither to his own nor his parents' sin, "but that the works of God should be made manifest in him" – an expression which corresponds with our Lord's statement about Lazarus, "This sickness is not unto death, but for the glory of God". In both of these cases we witness God acting sovereignly to effect His purpose in the giving of a sign which is predictive of an event related to Israel in the latter days.

Like the healing of the cripple who had been afflicted for thirty-eight years, the man in John IX received his sight on the Sabbath day (verse 14). This fact alone would be proof that these signs relate to Israel to whom God gave the Sabbaths, apart from the fact that they were performed in or near Jerusalem. It is quite clear from the context that the incident in John IX took place on the Sabbath day which followed the Feast of Tabernacles in A.D. 32. The eighth day of that Feast was 13th November – a Thursday; therefore the Sabbath in question would have been 15th November.

Our Lord's act was in two parts. He first covered the man's eyes with clay made from His spittle and earth and then sent him to "wash in the pool of Siloam". We are informed that the man "went his way therefore, and washed, and came seeing" (verse 7).

This incident, like the raising of Lazarus, called forth a display of diabolical hatred by the Jewish leaders towards our Lord Jesus Christ. Being confronted with the fact that a mighty miracle had been performed which they could not deny, the Pharisees resorted to an effort to discredit the One Who had performed it by alleging that He was a Sabbath-breaker. This was after they had failed to prove that the man who had received his sight was not the beggar who had been born blind (verses 18 to 23). The parents of the man refuse to admit openly to the Pharisees that it was Jesus Who had healed their son, "for the Jews had agreed already, that if any man did confess that He was Christ, he should be put out of the synagogue" (verse 22).

In this incident we have a divine illustration of the time, now at hand, when a reserved remnant of the Jewish people will have their eyes opened as to who Jesus of Nazareth was and is. This remnant will know that it is He, acting in sovereign grace, Who has removed the veil that is upon their hearts, so that they can with the eyes of a living faith see and own Him as the Son of God, their rejected Messiah (see II Corinth. III, 14 to 16). This man in John IX is a positive type of this believing remnant.

It is to be noted that our Lord's act in this case wrought a sharp division in Jewry and that it will be so again when this sign has its counterpart. Some said that the One Who performed the miracle could not be of God "because He keepeth not the sabbath day. Others said, How can a man that is a sinner do such miracles? And there was a division among them" (verse 16).

The boldness of the man who received sight is most refreshing to behold and it stands out the more boldly when seen against the background afforded by the slippery and tyrannical efforts of the Pharisees, first to discredit our Lord and then to discredit the man himself when he had taunted them with their vain attempts to dislodge his faith in the One Who had healed him, by asking them, "Will ye also be His disciples?"

No word in this chapter should be missed and the final words of the healed man to the Pharisees in verses 30 to 33 are a model of unassailable reasoning. In fact, their logic so irritated the Pharisees that, stung by their defeat, they cast him out of the synagogue.

In all this, as we have said, we have a prediction of that fearful division which will again arise between those in Israel who repent of the sin of their nation and believe on our Lord Jesus Christ and those who will still adhere to their present refusal to recognize that the One Whom they crucified was the Son of God and their own Messiah. The Scriptures frequently refer to this coming division both in the Old and New Testaments (see Isaiah LXV, and Matthew X and XXIV, etc., etc.).

One question of great importance remains to be answered. Why did our Lord send the blind man to the Pool of Siloam to wash in order to receive his sight? To answer this question fully, for it is both a solemn and most important one, would require a lengthy dissertation on Israel's history at the time when they went into captivity to Assyria in 720 B.C. On this occasion we can only state the essential facts.

The pool of Siloam was fed by a conduit made by Hezekiah, King of Judah (726 to 697 B.C.) in order to bring water into Jerusalem from outside the Holy City. These waters, called "the waters of Shiloah", ran quietly and unseen and as such they formed a type of Immanuel Whose unceasing flow of love and power had from the beginning been the unseen source of Israel's strength. That this is so is proved by the following utterance of God through the prophet Isaiah, addressed to Israel:

> "Forasmuch as this people refuseth the waters of Shiloah that go softly, and rejoice in Rezin and Remaliah's son . . . behold, the Lord bringeth up upon them, the waters of the river, strong and many, even the king of Assyria, and all his glory: and . . . shall fill the breadth of Thy land, O Immanuel" (VIII, 6 to 8).

In effect, this simply means that Israel, instead of trusting in Immanuel, and His unseen but ever present power, preferred to trust to an alliance between their King, Pekah, the son of Remaliah and Rezin, King of Syria. God only could have averted the oncoming assault of the armies of the mighty King of Assyria but as Israel had turned to idols and preferred an alliance with Syria to dependence on the God of Israel, He would allow things to take their course. Consequently, first Syria was overthrown and annexed and then Israel, whose people were taken as captives to Assyria – a captivity and exile which only ended in 1948, when the present State of Israel came into existence.

Israel's refusal of Immanuel, Who in the person of Hezekiah, King of Judah, pleaded with them to return to the worship of the God of Israel, is recorded in II Chronicles XXX, where we learn from verse 10 that "they laughed them (i.e. Hezekiah's messengers) to scorn, and mocked them".

Our Lord's act in causing the blind man to wash in the Pool of Siloam before he could receive his sight is therefore A SIGN to every Israelite in the present day that, when the nation refused Hezekiah's invitation to return to the God of their fathers, they were in fact refusing IMMANUEL Whom Hezekiah represented and typified. By washing in the Pool of Siloam the blind man signified that he no longer refused "the waters of Shiloah" which speak of Immanuel's power. Directly he had done so, he received eyesight. But not only so, for the veil fell from his heart and he instantly stood out in bold defence of the One Who had healed him. This led to an open breach with his nation's professed leaders until they cast him out. So will it be with the faithful ones in coming days who own Jesus as their Messiah. But to all such, as to this formerly blind man, this will lead to a personal revelation of the Messiah: for the record informs us that our Lord openly revealed Himself as the Son of God, when He said, "Thou hast both seen Him, and it is He that talketh with thee". The man at once became a worshipper. He had found His God. (This subject is referred to in greater detail in Paper III of *The World in Liquidation.*)

# CHAPTER TEN

## THE DISCOURSE OF JOHN X AT THE FEAST OF DEDICATION. OUR LORD REVEALS HIMSELF AS THE TRUE SHEPHERD OF ISRAEL

THE JEWISH LEADERS, WHO ARE THE HIRELING SHEPHERDS, FINALLY REJECT HIM AND "IN A FIGURE" STONE HIM TO DEATH. HE WILL NOW LEAD "HIS OWN SHEEP" OUT OF THE "FOLD" OF ISRAEL THAT THEY MAY BE JOINED TO THE GENTILES – HIS "OTHER SHEEP" – IN ONE FLOCK

TO EXPRESS HIS REJECTION BY ISRAEL, OUR LORD RETURNS TO THE PLACE WHERE JOHN "AT FIRST BAPTIZED"

TIME

Wednesday, 14th January A.D. 33
the Jews' 25th of the 9th Month (Kisleu)
Our Lord's age is now 33 Bible Years and 83 Days, or 32 Solar Years and 77 Days

Read the Gospel of John – Chapter X

THE DISCOURSE and subsequent events recorded in the tenth Chapter of John's Gospel took place, we are told in verse 22, at the Feast of Dedication which in A.D. 33 was on Wednesday, 14th January. In Bible time it was the 25th day of the 9th month. This is the only mention in the Canonical Scriptures of this Feast which was inaugurated in the days of the Maccabees (165 B.C.) in celebration of the cleansing and rededication of the Altar in the Temple after its desecration by Antiochus Epiphanes, three years to the day previously. That it is so mentioned, and that our Lord Jesus Christ was present in the Temple at its celebration, affords Divine sanction for its existence even though it was instituted in the interval of 400 years, during which the Bible is silent, between the end of the Old Testament and the start of the New Testament. (See I Maccabees IV, 36 to 56 and II Maccabees X, 1 to 8.)

There is a very important reason why the events of John X are dated, but it will suit our purpose better to give this after a brief examination of the contents of the chapter.

Though sixty days had elapsed since the healing of the blind man, as recorded in the ninth chapter of John, the tenth chapter opens as if it were a continuation of the ninth. This, doubtless, is because the Discourse of the Good Shepherd forms the logical sequel to events at the end of the ninth chapter, where the Jewish rulers cast out from the Synagogue the man whom the Lord had healed because he refused to denounce his Benefactor.

By way of illustrating what He has to say, our Lord adopts a similitude familiar to all. At night it was customary for several shepherds to bring their flocks into a common fold which was watched over by a porter. In the morning each shepherd would enter the fold by the door and call the sheep of his own flock to follow him out. Each flock knew its own shepherd's voice and would not respond to the voice of a stranger.

In this chapter, therefore, the people of Israel are viewed as a sheepfold containing different flocks of sheep. Our Lord is the true Shepherd of Israel, so when He came and presented Himself to the Porter Who typically is the Spirit of God, He was able to enter into the sheepfold by the door because His credentials as the Messiah were in perfect accord with what had been written concerning Him in the Scriptures of Truth. Therefore, "to Him the porter openeth" (verse 3).

There were, however, false shepherds who had got inside the fold by illicit means – "some other way" – because they could not stand before the scrutiny of the Porter who kept the door. These were "thieves and robbers" whose object was to exploit the sheep for their own benefit. This was a manifestly clear allusion to the Pharisees and rulers of Israel who posed as shepherds of the flock of God but who in fact were "hirelings" who had no real care for the sheep, but only for their own aggrandizement and material profit. Those in Israel who were not His sheep responded to the voices of these false shepherds and joined heartily with them in disclaiming the rights of Him

Who was the true Shepherd of God's flock and Who had entered in by the door into the sheepfold.

In this beautiful chapter, then, our Lord is seen presenting Himself as the true Shepherd of Israel in contradistinction to the false hireling shepherds who were lording it over the flock of God for their own gain. These false shepherds had existed from the start of Israel's apostasy and in Ezekiel XXXIV God addresses them in terms of the severest condemnation, the which must have been in the mind of the Lord when He uttered the Discourse of John X.

In this Jewish sheepfold there were those whom our Lord could call "His own sheep". These knew His voice and He called each one of them by name. Furthermore, He knew that the hour had come when He must forsake His heritage in Israel for a long season and that He was now to become "a light to the Gentiles" and God's "salvation unto the end of the earth" (Isai. XLIX, 6). As "the good Shepherd" He must therefore call upon "His own sheep" to leave the Jewish sheepfold, as He Himself was about to do. So we read:

> "He calleth His own sheep by name, and leadeth them out. And when He putteth forth His own sheep, He goeth before them, and the sheep follow Him: for they know His voice" (verses 3 and 4).

These Jewish sheep are the elect Remnant which followed the Lord out of Judaism. They do not know *where* He is leading them *but they know Him*. It is to them that He says, "Verily, verily, I say unto you, I am the door of the sheep. All that ever came before Me are thieves and robbers: but the sheep did not hear them" (verses 7 and 8). This plainly means that HE WAS THE DOOR by which "His own sheep" must pass out of Judaism. There was no other exit save Himself. The sheep must leave with the Shepherd.

Our Lord has now made reference to TWO doors. He had entered the Jewish sheepfold by its one and only entrance and to Him the Porter had opened. Once within, He, the Shepherd of Israel, had found Himself estranged from the majority of the sheep because the hireling shepherds, namely, the Pharisees and rulers, had declared Him to be an impostor and not the Messiah. They did not know His voice because they were not His sheep (verses 26 and 27). This situation was without remedy. For three years in succession as the true Shepherd of Israel He had contested the false claims of the hireling shepherds, but to no avail.

One course only remained open and that was for Him to separate "His own sheep" from the main flock. The Shepherd and His sheep must therefore together abandon the sheepfold of Israel which presently (i.e. in A.D. 70) would be swept out of existence – the sheep being left shepherdless to wander among the nations and become a prey whithersoever they might go. (See Ezekiel XXXIV, 8).

In verse 9 our Lord speaks of yet another "door". He says, "I am the door: by Me *if any man* enter in, he shall be saved, and shall go in and out, and find pasture". If our Lord was the Door out of the Jewish sheepfold, He was also the Door into the Kingdom of God. All who passed into the Kingdom through that Door would be saved. In other words, our Lord was THE DOOR OF SALVATION, not only to His Jewish sheep but to ANY MAN who could say with the Apostle Peter, "Neither is there salvation in any other: for there is none other Name under heaven given among men, whereby we must be saved" (Acts IV, 12). All such could "go in" to the presence of God to worship, "and out" into the world to serve Him; and the Good Shepherd would see that His flock fed in pastures of His own choosing.

Our Lord then explains in solemn terms how all this would be made possible. First, the Shepherd must die, so He declares:

> "I am the good Shepherd: the good Shepherd giveth His life for the sheep" (verse 11).

Our Lord had not only come to give life but to give it more abundantly. A hireling shepherd would not risk his own life if the sheep were in danger but would leave the sheep and flee "because he is an hireling". But He, the Good Shepherd, would lay down His life for the sheep (verse 15), as only thus could He make them co-sharers with Himself of eternal life.

Directly our Lord has declared that He will die "for the sheep" (as without His death such a thing would be impossible), He announces His intention of enlarging His flock to include the Gentiles, saying,

> "And other sheep I have, which are not of this fold: them also I must bring, and they shall hear My voice; and they

shall become one flock, one Shepherd" (verse 16, R.V.).

This is, of course, a positive intimation of our Lord's purpose to unite His Jewish sheep and His Gentile sheep into one body – the Church. Our thoughts in this connection at once go to Ephesians II, 14 to 18, where we read:

> "For He is our peace, Who hath made *both* one . . . that He might reconcile *both* (i.e. Jew and Gentile) unto God in one body by the cross . . . for through Him we *both* have access by one Spirit unto the Father."

Finally, our blessed Lord and Master declares that it was not in the power of man to take His life from Him. When He died, He would be laying down His life of Himself; for He had received a commandment from His Father by which He could both lay down His life and take it again (verses 17 and 18). This was but to reiterate His original statement when, asked by the Jews for a sign at the Passover of A.D. 30, He had declared, "Destroy this temple, and in three days I will raise it up".

We shall reveal presently that there is a most important chronological relationship between the date of the Passover in A.D. 30, namely, 4th May, and the date of 14th January, A.D. 33, when the events of John X took place.

### THE CLIMAX IN JEWISH HATRED OF OUR LORD IS REACHED

### THEY PURPOSE TO STONE HIM TO DEATH

The tenth Chapter of John ends on a most solemn note. Our Lord's Discourse had caused a division "among the Jews". Some said He was mad and had a devil and others that this was impossible in one who could give sight to the blind (verses 19 to 21).

The Jews again challenge our Lord to declare plainly if He is the Messiah (verse 24). He replies that His works bear adequate witness to this fact, but they did not believe because they were not His sheep. He then declares:

> "My sheep hear My voice, and I know them, and they follow Me: and I give unto them eternal life; and they shall never perish, neither shall any man pluck them out of My hand" (verses 27 and 28).

Our Lord then states that His sheep were the gift to Him of His Father Who "is greater than all". And, finally, He says, "I and My Father are One".

It was this statement that precipitated the final crisis and which sealed the Jews' rejection of Jesus as their Messiah. So great was the hatred that welled up in them against Jesus that they "took up stones again to stone Him" (verse 31).

Challenged by our Lord as to why they stone Him, the Jews declare, "Because that Thou, being a man, makest Thyself God". After a last appeal to His works as a proof that He was the Son of God, "they sought again to take Him: but He escaped out of their hand" (verse 39). *This was the final act and all was now over for the Jewish nation as regards their Messiah* until after the 2,000 years of the Christian Dispensation. Had it been the appointed time and way, our Lord would there and then have been stoned to death by the Jews; but, as it was, He died "in a figure" or, as we would say, figuratively.

Our Lord Jesus Christ acknowledged this final rejection of Himself by the Jews in a most solemn way. We are told that after He had escaped out of their hands, He

> "went away again beyond Jordan into the place where John at first baptized; and there He abode" (verse 40).

By this act our Lord intended to convey to all, that He knew that *His Mission,* which began seven years previously on 25th April A.D. 26, with the Ministry of John the Baptist, *had failed.* The Kingdom, which John had proclaimed as "at hand", would not now be realized because the King – Israel's Messiah – had been disowned and rejected by his own people (John I, 11).

It is impossible to exaggerate the importance of the events recorded at the end of John X. To understand them it is necessary to go back to the great Messianic time-prophecy of the "seventy weeks" in Daniel IX. Of these "seventy weeks" or 490 years, sixty-nine "weeks" or 483 years had expired on 25th April A.D. 26, when John opened his testimony to the Messiah. This left one "week" or 7 years to the completion of the 70 "weeks", when the Messianic Kingdom would be set up. John the Baptist's sole testimony continued for the first half of these seven years; after which our Lord was publicly manifested to Israel to whom He rendered a faithful testimony until the events recorded in the end of John X. This was on 14th

January A.D. 33, when the seven years or last "week" of the "seventy weeks" was drawing to a close.

Our Lord knew that His rejection by Israel would cause God to cancel these seven years, A.D. 26 to 33, because they had failed of their object, namely, the ushering in of the Messianic Kingdom. Not only had Israel rejected the Herald – John the Baptist – but now they had rejected the King, Whose Kingdom John had proclaimed as "at hand". With this knowledge it is easy to understand why our Lord, following the events at the end of John X, "went away again beyond Jordan into the place where John was at the first baptizing" (verse 40, R.V.). This act, as we have said, was a confession that His Mission to Israel had failed through their hard-hearted rejection both of His claims and of His gracious overtures, whereby He had hoped to gather the tribes of Israel together into "one flock". But Israel would have none of Him – resenting His overtures, despising His claims, and hating Him without a cause.

When our Lord and Master left the Temple and the Holy City, having escaped out of the hands of those who would kill Him, He must have wended His way beyond Jordan with feelings of the deepest sorrow as He looked back over the years to the time when John began his testimony, and when "Jerusalem, and all Judaea, and all the region round about Jordan" went out and "were baptized of him in Jordan, confessing their sins" (Matt. III, 5 and 6).

The Prophet Isaiah foresaw this occasion and foretold our Lord's inmost thoughts in these words:

> "Then I said, I have laboured in vain, I have spent my strength for nought, and in vain: yet surely my judgment is with the Lord, and my work with my God. . . . Though Israel be not gathered, yet shall I be glorious in the eyes of the Lord, and my God shall be my strength" (Isai. XLIX, 4 and 5).

To this lament our Lord received this answer from God:

> "It is a light thing that Thou shouldest be My servant to raise up the tribes of Jacob, and to restore the preserved of Israel: I will also give Thee for a light to the Gentiles, that Thou mayest be My salvation unto the end of the earth" (Isai. XLIX, 6).

With these words in mind the rejected Messiah of Israel

found relief for His sorrow of heart that His beloved nation had rejected Him and must remain estranged from Him until the far-off day when they should say to Him, "Blessed is He that cometh in the name of the Lord" (Matt. XXIII, 39). In the meanwhile, "through their fall salvation is come unto the Gentiles" (Rom. XI, 11), and our Lord Jesus Christ has become God's "salvation unto the end of the earth".

Beyond Jordan, we are told, many resorted to our Lord Jesus Christ because they realized that all that John the Baptist had said of Him was true. And "many believed on Him there" (verses 40 to 42).

After a brief stay beyond Jordan, where John at first baptized, our Lord must have returned into Galilee where His mighty works had been done, for it was from thence that He took the three disciples – Peter, James and John – up into a high mountain for His Transfiguration, which was late in the following March and several weeks after His arrival beyond Jordan.

### THE CHRONOLOGICAL RELATIONSHIP BETWEEN 4TH MAY A.D. 30, AND 14TH JANUARY A.D. 33, WHEN THE JEWS "IN A FIGURE" STONED JESUS TO DEATH

The Bible from beginning to end contains varied chronological expressions of our Lord's Death and Resurrection. These take different forms, the commonest of which is "three days". Another to be met with several times is symbolic of the Two Days and Nine Hours during which our Lord was "in the heart of the earth". That this was the actual period of His "death" we shall presently demonstrate from the Scriptures in a manner so clear as to remove the subject from further discussion.

From 4th May A.D. 30, to 14th January A.D. 33, there are 2 solar years and 255 days. These 255 days consist of 9 "months" of 28 days each, with a surplus of 3 days. As a chronological type always possesses numerical affinity with its antitype, these 2 years and 9 months form a symbolic expression of the literal Two Days and Nine Hours between our Lord's death and His resurrection. The Bible adds 3 days, or (where the design is in years) 3 years, as every chronological expression of our Lord's death must be accompanied by a token of His resurrection.

These 3 additional days or years nearly always lead to resurrection in manifestation.

What is to be learnt from this? On 4th May A.D. 30, our Lord said to the Jews, "Destroy this temple, and in three days I will raise it up". From that day forth our Lord walked in the shadow of death. At the end of these 2 years and 9 months plus 3 days, "the Jews took up stones again to stone Him". Figuratively speaking, our Lord then died at the hands of the Jews and His resurrection is expressed by the fact that "He escaped out of their hand".

Thus in the interval of time between 4th May A.D. 30, and 14th January A.D. 33, when finally the Jews rejected their Messiah, and "in a figure" stoned Him to death, we have a symbolical expression of our Lord's death and His resurrection.

As we shall later prove from the Scriptures, our Lord rose from the dead on 4th May A.D. 33, which, to the day, was 3 years from His declaration – "Destroy this temple, and in three days I will raise it up".

We trust that in spite of inadequate explanations, for want of space, many will appreciate from the little we have said that "these are parts of His ways" and parts, indeed, of that secret Pattern of Time, designed by God the Father for the pathway on earth for His well-beloved Son, our Lord and Saviour Jesus Christ.

# CHAPTER ELEVEN

## THE TRANSFIGURATION OF OUR LORD JESUS CHRIST AND ITS PRELUDE

## THE LAST FORTY DAYS OPEN ON MONDAY, 23RD MARCH A.D. 33

THE OCCASION IS MARKED BY THREE SIGNIFICANT EVENTS,
(I) PETER'S CONFESSION OF FAITH "THOU ART THE CHRIST"
(II) OUR LORD'S FIRST ANNOUNCEMENT OF HIS IMPENDING DEATH AND RESURRECTION
(III) THE MYSTERIOUS APPEARING ON EARTH OF MOSES AND ELIJAH WHO ARE SENT OF GOD TO BE HIS WITNESSES OF OUR LORD'S SUFFERINGS, DEATH, RESURRECTION AND ASCENSION. THE CLEAR WITNESS OF THE GOSPELS TO THIS FACT

THE TRANSFIGURATION OF OUR LORD TAKES PLACE ON MONDAY, 30TH MARCH A.D. 33, EXACTLY 33 DAYS BEFORE HIS DEATH. MOSES AND ELIJAH ARE AGAIN PRESENT.
PETER, JAMES AND JOHN BECOME "EYEWITNESSES OF HIS MAJESTY"

THE FINAL DEPARTURE FROM GALILEE

Our Lord's age at the Transfiguration was 33 Bible Years and 158 days or 32 Solar Years and 152 days

Read Matthew XVI, 13 to XVII, 13, and XIX, 1; Mark VIII, 27 to IX, 13 and X, 1; Luke IX, 18 to 36 and 51; XXIV, 4, and Acts I, 10

### THE PRELUDE TO THE TRANSFIGURATION

AT THE end of our previous chapter we recorded that our Lord Jesus Christ left Jerusalem and Judaea and wended His way in deep sorrow of heart across the Jordan to the place in Peraea where John first began His Ministry. The expression in John X, 40, "and there He abode", clearly indicates that our Lord made a stay at this place of at least some weeks. This is confirmed by the words, "And many resorted unto Him . . . and many believed on Him there" (verses 41 and 42). Our Lord left Jerusalem on or just after 14th January A.D. 33, which was the date of the Feast of Dedication named in John X, 22.

The next dated event in our Lord's pathway is one of the greatest significance because it was exactly *Forty Days* prior to His death. That to which we refer is the Apostle Peter's Confession that Jesus was the Christ and our Lord's first announcement of His rejection, death and resurrection. This we are told in Luke's account was "about an eight days" before the Transfiguration which, inclusively, was 33 days before our Lord's death – a fact we will support in due course with clear evidence from the Holy Scriptures.

After a stay of some weeks beyond Jordan, our Lord and His twelve disciples, whom He named Apostles, moved North into Galilee. It appears that they first visited "the parts of Dalmanutha" where the Pharisees ask for a sign (Matt. XVI, 1 and Mark VIII, 10 and 11). They then crossed the Sea of Galilee (Mark VIII, 13 to 22) and arrive at Bethsaida where our Lord heals a blind man whom He leads out of the town because He had already consigned it to judgment for its rejection of Himself after He had wrought so many mighty works in it (Matt. XI, 21).

We next learn from Matthew XVI and Mark VIII that our Lord and the twelve disciples come "into the coasts of Caesarea Philippi" which was about thirty miles north of Bethsaida and the Sea of Galilee. It was here at Caesarea Philippi that the last 40 days leading up to our Lord's death opened and this with events of incalculable importance. The date was Monday, 23rd March A.D. 33, and it was the Vernal Equinox. Our Lord had just left the sign-seeking Pharisees with the words, "O ye hypocrites, ye can discern the face of the sky; but can ye not discern the signs of the times?" (Matt. XVI, 3).

Following a season of prayer (Luke IX, 18) our Lord Jesus challenges the disciples with the questions, "Whom do men say that I the Son of man am?" and "Whom say ye that I am?" It was given to Peter to answer the second of these questions. (See

Matthew XVI, 13 to 16; Mark VIII, 27 to 30, and Luke IX, 18 to 21.)

We will quote from Matthew XVI:

"Simon Peter answered and said, Thou art the Christ, the Son of the living God. And Jesus answered and said unto him, Blessed art thou, Simon Bar-Jona: for flesh and blood hath not revealed it unto thee, but My Father which is in heaven" (verses 16 and 17).

The deep conviction with which Peter uttered this transcendently important declaration of faith concerning the Person of our Lord Jesus Christ made it obvious to Him that Peter had been made the subject of a Divine revelation. Such a declaration could not flow from human reasoning. In effect, Peter acclaims Jesus of Nazareth as the long-awaited MESSIAH, Who could be none other than "THE SON OF THE LIVING GOD".

As the result of Peter's confession of faith our Lord makes His first disclosure concerning that which He calls "My church". That He should do this at the opening of the last Forty Days and at the same time announce His rejection by the Jewish rulers speaks for itself. In other words, as the seven-branched Candlestick of Israel was now to be removed, the Seven Golden Candlesticks representing the Church begin to come into view.

In His discourse recorded in John X our Lord had already intimated that He had "other sheep" to bring. These He would unite into one flock with those sheep (the Jewish believers) whom He was about to lead out of the Jewish fold. This flock of Jewish and Gentile believers He now names "My church" (i.e., an assembly of called-out ones). The meaning of our Lord's words, "Upon this rock I will build My Church", is fully explained by the Apostle Peter to whom they were uttered. In his first Epistle, Chapter II, he says:

"The Lord . . . a living Stone, disallowed indeed of men, but chosen of God, and precious, Ye also, as lively stones, are built up a spiritual house, an holy priesthood. . . . Unto you therefore which believe He is precious: but unto them which be disobedient, the Stone which the builders disallowed, the same is made the head of the corner, and a Stone of stumbling, and a rock of offence, even to them which stumble at the word, being disobedient" (verses 3 to 8).

When our Lord made reference to His "church", the Jews

had finally rejected Him – "being disobedient". He Whom they had disallowed would, after His death and resurrection, become the chief Corner Stone of His Church against which "the gates of hell", that is, the forces of Satan, who until then had the power of death, should never prevail.

As regards Peter himself, our Lord confers on him the right to hold "the keys" of the Kingdom; and, as everyone knows, it was Peter who *first* proclaimed the Gospel to the Jews and was the means of three thousand being brought into the Kingdom on the day of Pentecost in A.D. 33. It was also Peter who *first* preached the Gospel to the Gentiles in the house of the Roman centurion Cornelius, as recorded in Acts X, and thereby unlocked to them the gates into the Kingdom. (See also Acts VIII for Peter's visit to Samaria.) Concerning this event Peter declares, "God made choice among us, that the Gentiles by my mouth should hear the word of the gospel, and believe" (Acts XV, 7).

We need hardly remark that Peter's confession and our Lord's response constituted events of immense significance; and that they occurred exactly *Forty Days* before our Lord's death gives to them a greatly added importance because His Church could only be built after He had triumphed over death and thereby annulled "him that had the power of death, that is, the devil" (Heb. II, 14). It was, indeed, to this end that our blessed Lord had taken part in "flesh and blood". This being so, it might be expected that, in view of its imminence, He would make known to His disciples that the time was approaching when He would have to lay down His life. So we read that after charging them to "tell no man that He was . . . the Christ", He began

> "to shew unto His disciples, how that He must go unto Jerusalem, and suffer many things of the elders and chief priests and scribes, and be killed, and be raised again the third day" (Matt. XVI, 21; Mark VIII, 31 and Luke IX, 22).

Peter, perhaps now with an exaggerated sense of his own importance or out of natural affection, seeks to dissuade our Lord from following such a course and earns the sharpest rebuke ever uttered by Him to a disciple. These were its terms, "Get thee behind Me, Satan: thou art an offence unto Me: for thou savourest not the things which be of God, but those that be of men" (Matt. XVI, 23).

Following this rebuke to Peter, our Lord takes the opportunity to press home upon the hearts and consciences of His disciples what it will cost them to follow Him. He had just told them what obedience to God was going to cost Him, namely, the giving up of His own life. On their part, if they did what Peter had advised Him to do, that is, *consider Himself*, they could not follow Him. Rather must each "deny himself, and take up his cross . . . for whosoever will save his life shall lose it: and whosoever will lose his life for My sake shall find it". (See Matt. XVI, 24; Mark VIII, 34 and Luke IX, 23.) No doubt these words proved to be a solemn test to the twelve, as they have been to all disciples down through this age who have honestly faced their implications. Our Lord then reminds the disciples that He will be coming again "in the glory of His Father with His angels" and that everyone will then be rewarded "according to his works".

Before proceeding, we desire to direct attention to the fact that by design these last 40 days of our Lord's life synchronize chronologically with the first 40 days of the same.

Our Lord was born on 29th October 1 B.C. After 7 days, that is, on the 8th day, He was circumcised. After a further 33 days (the first of which was this 8th day) He was presented in the Temple, whither His Mother had come according to the Law of Moses. So we see that our Lord's life opened with a period of 40 days which was divided into two parts, namely, 7 days and 33 days. These last 40 days are likewise divided into two parts, namely, the 7 days prior to the Transfiguration, which was on the 8th day according to Luke, and the 33 days (the first of which was this 8th day) to His death. We have already pointed out that there is another such synchronism in the 212 days from our Lord's Baptism on 5th October A.D. 29, to the Passover on 4th May A.D. 30, and the 212 days from 13th November A.D. 32, which was "the last day, that great day of the feast" of John VII, 37, to 13th June A.D. 33, when our Lord ascended into Heaven. As previously stated, the Bible accounts for every day in both these periods of 212 days. From 13th November A.D. 32, to 30th March A.D. 33, when the Transfiguration took place, 137 days had elapsed of the latter period of 212 days.

# THE APPEARANCE ON THE EARTH OF MOSES AND ELIJAH AT THE OPENING OF THE LAST FORTY DAYS

## A DISCLOSURE OF SOLEMN SIGNIFICANCE TO ISRAEL IN THE PRESENT HOUR

"There be some standing here, which shall not taste of death, till they see the Son of Man coming in His kingdom" (Matt. XVI, 28; Mark IX, 1, and Luke IX, 27)

Our Lord Jesus Christ brought His "sayings" at the opening of the last Forty Days before His death to a close with the above statement which Matthew, Mark and Luke each quote with only slight variations. To assume that our Lord was referring to Peter, James and John, who a few days later were to witness His Transfiguration, even though that event was a glorious manifestation of Christ in His Kingdom, is entirely to miss the significance of an utterance so designedly mysterious in its content. To emphasize the importance of this statement the Saviour prefaced it with, "I tell you of a truth" or "Verily I say unto you".

The Scriptures reveal that when our Lord made this statement His eye was resting upon "two men" who, unseen by any human eye, were "standing" among those He was addressing. These "two men" were Moses and Elijah who had been sent of God from Heaven *to fulfil a commission of the utmost importance.*

It is common knowledge that Moses and Elijah "appeared" with our Lord on the Mount during His Transfiguration, as the fact is clearly stated by Matthew, Mark and Luke. The Gospels, however, reveal beneath the surface much more than this, namely, that the great Lawgiver of Sinai and the mighty Prophet of Carmel appeared on the earth at the opening of the last Forty Days and that, following the Transfiguration, they remained here *to witness* our Lord's death on Calvary; and, furthermore, that they again appeared *to witness* His Resurrection and remained for a second Forty Days *to witness* His Ascension.

Before alluding to the Scriptures which reveal the nature of the commission Moses and Elijah were sent from Heaven to perform we will refer very briefly to the evidence in the Gospels from which the above facts are derived. The complete evidence will appear later in the course of our comments on our Lord's Transfiguration, Resurrection and Ascension.

It was mainly given to the Evangelist Luke to disclose that Moses and Elijah were present on the earth during the two periods of Forty Days above referred to. This he does by making several references to the presence of "two men" of celestial status. In Luke IX Moses and Elijah are twice referred to as "two men" (verses 30 and 32). In Luke XXIV, 4, we learn that certain women, who came to the Sepulchre on the morning of the Resurrection, were addressed by "two men . . . in shining garments". It is from the statement these "two men" make to the women that we know that they were present in Galilee when our Lord announced to His disciples that He was going to die and rise again the third day. These are their words: "He is not here, but is risen: remember how He spake unto you when He was yet in Galilee, saying, The Son of Man must be delivered into the hands of sinful men, and be crucified, and the third day rise again. And they remembered His words" (Luke XXIV, 6 to 8). Our Lord spoke thus to His disciples twice when in Galilee. The first time was at the opening of the last Forty Days and the second time was just after His Transfiguration (see Matt. XVI, 21, XVII, 22; Mark VIII, 31, IX, 31; Luke IX, 22 and 44).

It is obvious from the words of these "two men" to the women that they were present when the Lord made His first announcement about His death and resurrection, and it was of this that they reminded the women who must also have been present. The quotation by the "two men" was a faithful paraphrase of exactly what our Lord said when He first spoke of His impending death and resurrection. Bishop Christopher Wordsworth in commenting on the words, "remember how He spake unto you", says, "Hence it would seem that (they) had been invisible hearers and spectators of Christ's intercourse with His disciples" (Commentary on the Four Gospels).

Finally, at the Ascension Luke, in Acts I, 10, refers to "two men . . . in white apparel" who addressed the disciples in reference to the return of "this same Jesus . . . in like manner as ye have seen Him go into heaven".

We can, on this occasion, only give this brief outline but the full evidence of Holy Scripture which we will unfold in stages will leave no room for doubt that Moses and Elijah were present on earth with the Lord during the whole of the last Forty Days; that they witnessed His death on Calvary, were present at the Sepulchre to witness His resurrection, and at the end of the Forty Days were present to witness His ascension into Heaven.

We will now proceed to show from Holy Scripture why God commissioned Moses and Elijah to be present with our Lord during these two periods of Forty Days.

Apart from holding converse with our Lord and addressing the women at His resurrection and the eleven disciples at His ascension, neither Moses nor Elijah took any part in the solemn events which they witnessed in their eighty-day sojourn on the earth. What then was the object of their visit? Manifestly it had reference to some future day.

The Old Testament ends with these words, "Behold, I will send you Elijah the prophet before the coming of the great and dreadful day of the Lord", etc. (Malachi IV, 5). Answering an enquiry of the disciples, our Lord, on the way down from the Mount after His Transfiguration said, "Elias truly shall first come, and restore all things" (Matt. XVII, 11). There can be no doubt, therefore, as regards Elijah that what he witnessed, with Moses, in these two periods of Forty Days is related to his return "before the coming of the great and dreadful day of the Lord" – Elijah's return being an event to which all orthodox Jews look forward and particularly so at the Passover festival.

There is no prophecy in the Old Testament relating to the return to the earth of Moses, but in the Book of Revelation there is a manifestly clear inference that Moses is to return with Elijah and that they are to bear a joint testimony for God in the land of Israel. Let us at once say that the visit of Moses and Elijah during the two periods of Forty Days was in anticipation of this testimony which they are yet to bear to their own nation concerning events touching our Lord Jesus Christ which they then witnessed.

We must now refer readers to the eleventh chapter of the Apocalypse, verses 3 to 12. We cannot quote so lengthy a passage in full though it should be read by all who wish to understand the reason for Moses' and Elijah's visit to the earth in the two periods of Forty Days.

In verses 3 and 6 we read:

> "And I will give power unto My two witnesses, and they shall prophesy a thousand two hundred and threescore days, clothed in sackcloth. . . . These have power to shut heaven, that it rain not in the days of their prophecy: and have power over waters to turn them to blood, and to smite the earth with all plagues, as often as they will."

It was Elijah who shut up the heavens in the days of Ahab, "and it rained not on the earth by the space of three years and six months" (James V, 17); and it was Moses who turned the waters into blood and brought numerous plagues on the Egyptians before Israel's exodus from Egypt (Exod. VII, 20 etc.).

Moses and Elijah, though not named, are here termed by God, "My two witnesses", and it will be noted that they are to be endued with terrifying power – a power so great as to hold evil in the world in check for 1,260 days. But that is not their first office which relates to bearing witness to their own nation – Israel – in order to convict it of having been party to the murder of the Messiah, God's beloved Son. Under the Law of Moses a minimum of two first-hand witnesses had to be provided before an Israelite could be convicted of murder (Deut. XVII, 6; XIX, 15). From this simple but solemn fact we learn why Moses and Elijah came down from Heaven and were present with the Lord from the opening of the last Forty Days and *why they witnessed His Death, Resurrection and Ascension.* Confronted as they will be by the powerful first-hand testimony of the "two men" – Moses and Elijah – who actually witnessed every event connected with the Messiah's death and resurrection in A.D. 33, the people of Israel will be divided into two parts, namely, those who fear and repent and those who prefer the immediately easier but fatal course of rejecting the testimony borne to them by God's faithful witnesses. The 11th to 13th chapters of the Book of Revelation refer to the supreme crisis of human history – a period of seven years. The testimony of Moses and Elijah occupies the first three and a half years of these seven years, in the same way that the testimony of one witness – John the Baptist – occupied the first $3\frac{1}{2}$ years of the seven years, A.D. 26 to 33.

It will be seen from Revelation XI, 7, that Moses and Elijah, after their testimony is completed, "taste of death" at the hands of one called "the beast", who is better known as Antichrist, and who receives his power from Satan (XIII, 2 to 4). Before God's two witnesses "taste of death", as described in this chapter, a certain period of time elapses and it is during this interval that our Lord Jesus Christ as the Son of Man is invested with the Kingdom in Heaven, as described in Daniel VII, 13 and 14. Then it is that the latter part of Revelation XI is fulfilled and "great voices in heaven" are heard to proclaim "The kingdoms of this world are become the kingdoms of our Lord, and of His Christ; and He shall reign for ever and ever".

It is at some point of time following this great event in Heaven that Moses and Elijah are overcome and killed by "the beast" who makes "war against them" and against all the faithful of that day (Rev. XIII, 7 and Daniel VII, 21, 25).

In this manner the words of the Lord to His disciples – "There be some standing here, which shall not taste of death, till they see the Son of Man coming in His kingdom" – shall be fulfilled. Nor can we doubt that in uttering them the Saviour knew they would remain sealed until the end of this Christian age when they would take on a meaning of intense solemnity for the people of Israel and, indeed, for all mankind, because "the great and dreadful day of the Lord" would then be "at hand" – the Church, which is Christ's mystical body, having left the earth in fulfilment of I Thessalonians IV, 13 to 18.

May we conclude this all-too-brief survey of the Scriptures on the subject of our Lord's words quoted at the head of this section by saying, that the Bible, by its perfect chronology, reveals that the hour is at hand when Moses and Elijah shall again appear in the land of Israel; and that it is for this reason that this deeply-concealed mystery has been unveiled.

NOTE: Elijah, it will be remembered, was translated to Heaven without dying (II Kings II), and Moses' body was secretly buried by the Lord in the land of Moab (Deut. XXXIV). The contest between Michael and Satan over the body of Moses must have been at the time of Moses' resurrection (Jude 9).

# THE TRANSFIGURATION OF OUR LORD JESUS CHRIST

> "For we have not followed cunningly devised fables, when we made known unto you the power and coming of our Lord Jesus Christ, but were eyewitnesses of His majesty . . . when we were with Him in the holy mount" (Peter's reference to the Transfiguration in his 2nd Epistle, Chapter I).

The Transfiguration of our Lord Jesus Christ is recorded in the Gospels of Matthew, Mark and Luke. The event itself formed a perfect typical expression of the Messianic Kingdom when our blessed Lord will be seen in all His glory reigning over the whole earth, with the Church as His Bride, and restored Israel and the saved nations as His willing subjects.

It is extremely important to understand why Matthew and Mark state that the Transfiguration was "after six days", while Luke states that it was "about an eight days after these sayings" (IX, 28). As Scripture never contradicts itself, it is obvious that on one basis of reckoning the Transfiguration was "after six days", which means on the seventh day, and that on another basis of reckoning it was on an eighth day.

Luke's reckoning of the days is inclusive and embraces all the day (23rd March) of "the sayings" and the day of the Transfiguration – the 8 days being 23rd March to 30th March. Matthew and Mark adopt the exclusive principle and name the "six days" *from* the "sayings" to the opening of the day on which the Transfiguration took place – the 6 days being 24th, 25th, 26th, 27th, 28th and 29th March. Thus, in one aspect the Transfiguration was on the seventh day, that is, "after six days", and in another aspect it was on an eighth day.

It is common knowledge that the Bible by various types, such as the Sabbath or seventh day, the seventh month and the seventh or Sabbatic year, positively indicates that the Messianic Kingdom of our Lord Jesus Christ will be the seventh thousand years of human history. The first seven days of the Bible form a type of these seven thousand years and to this Peter directs our attention when he declares "that one day is with the Lord as a thousand years, and a thousand years as one day" (II Peter III, 8).

Our Lord, therefore, put His own seal of authority on these facts by causing Matthew and Mark to date the Transfiguration (which was the Kingdom in miniature) "after six days" which means at the opening of the seventh day.

Luke's reference to the eighth day, as that on which the Transfiguration occurred, is of great significance because it is one of the few occasions when the Bible adopts the reckoning of time according to the Years of the Messiah (see Summary of Facts, Par. 18). In this series of years each "day" consists of 888 years, in contradistinction to the better known "day" of 1,000 years. Until now (as the result of light afforded by the Spirit of God) there has not been any knowledge of the existence in the Bible of this important series of years, as far as we are aware.

As we have pointed out, Time in Messianic Years is composed of seven "days" or cycles of 888 years each, with an eighth "day" which is a type of the Kingdom. So when the Spirit of God caused Luke to measure time in days to the Transfiguration, He caused him to name an "eighth day" for that event, because in the Years of the Messiah the Kingdom will be the eighth "day" of 888 years. We need hardly remind the reader that the Calendar based upon the Years of the Messiah is the most important of all in the Personal Pathway of our Lord. We have seen it in operation at His Birth, again when He was Twelve Years of age, and at the opening of His Ministry on 26th November A.D. 29, not to mention occasions yet to come.

## THE DATE OF THE TRANSFIGURATION RECOVERED

It appears that many commentators have supposed that our Lord's Transfiguration took place much earlier than it did because of the position it occupies in the Gospels.

The expression used by Luke (as correctly given in the Revised Version), "His decease which He was about to accomplish at Jerusalem" (IX, 31), constitutes a very clear inference that our Lord's death was actually at hand.

The Transfiguration, figuratively speaking, was a return to Heaven for, as Peter tells us, our Lord "received from God the

Father honour and glory . . . when we were with Him in the holy mount". This followed His 33 years of life on the earth. Our Lord's descent from the mount of Transfiguration was therefore like a new beginning, but this time for a symbolical period of only 33 days.

The Holy Scriptures provide clear evidence that the Transfiguration took place on Monday, 30th March A.D. 33. Our Lord was crucified, as we will later establish, on Friday 1st May A.D. 33, which inclusively is 33 days from 30th March.

In presenting the evidence of Scripture as to the date of the Transfiguration we shall be obliged to make a brief excursus into a most important and illuminating subject, namely, the use made by God of the numerical value of the various names attaching to the Person of His well-beloved Son (Summary of Facts; Par. 21).

Every Hebrew and Greek letter represents a number and the adding together of the numbers which the letters represent gives us the numerical value of any word. Nothing in the whole realm of Biblical exposition is more clear than that God Himself designed and ordained the numerical value of our Lord's many names or titles. The Name JESUS in the Greek has 6 letters and the total of the 6 numbers represented by these letters is 888. The number "8" in the Bible signifies either "superabundance" or "resurrection".

We have also just pointed out that God regards a cycle of 888 Messianic years as "one day". For this reason He also regards "37" years as an "hour" because it is a 24th part of a "day" of 888 years.

The number "37", which for reasons we cannot delay to explain represents "the Word of God", appears as the prime factor in the numerical value of many of our Lord's Names or Titles. These we will now give, as follows:

| | |
|---|---|
| JESUS | $= 888 = 37 \times 8 \times 3$ |
| GODHEAD | $= 592 = 37 \times 8 \times 2$ |
| CHRIST | $= 1{,}480 = 37 \times 8 \times 5$ |
| SON OF MAN | $= 2{,}960 = 37 \times 8 \times 10$ |

It will be noted that each of these totals has the numbers 37 and 8 as its main factors. We must call attention also to the following remarkable features which attach to these figures. If the numbers of JESUS and GODHEAD are added together, the result is 1,480 which is the number of CHRIST. Again, if the numbers of JESUS, GODHEAD and CHRIST are added together, the result is 2,960 which is the number of SON OF MAN. In all this the hand of God may be seen in operation in relation to our Lord Jesus Christ Who, though of the "Godhead", is also the "Son of Man". (We are indebted to *Spiritual Arithmetic* by R. T. Naish for the above facts.)

Now we must relate these figures to the date of our Lord's Transfiguration on 30th March, A.D. 33.

Between 29th October 1 B.C., when our Lord was born, and 30th March A.D. 33, there are 32 solar years and 152 days. In this period there are 11,840 days.

If we take the number 1,480, which is the value of the Name CHRIST, and divide 11,840 by it, we shall find it goes 8 times without remainder. The "8" here expresses the fact that the Transfiguration was essentially a "resurrection" scene.

Taking the number of JESUS (888) and adding it to the number of CHRIST (1,480) we find it gives a total of 2,368 which goes 5 times into 11,840 without remainder. The "5" being the number in the Bible for "grace" testifies to "the grace of our Lord JESUS CHRIST" in these 11,840 days to His Transfiguration.

If we take the number of SON OF MAN (2,960) and divide 11,840 by it, it goes 4 times without remainder. The "4" represents the Son of Man in His Universal capacity as "the Saviour of the World".

Finally, if we take the total of the numbers of JESUS, GODHEAD, CHRIST and SON OF MAN, which is 5,920, we find this figure goes TWICE into 11,840 without remainder.

Much more might be said on this subject but in all these facts and figures we can at least see how God has indelibly stamped with the impress of His Son the 11,840 days between His Birth and His Transfiguration, when from Heaven He declared, "This is My beloved Son: hear Him".

One further marking of the date of 30th March A.D. 33, demands attention.

From 26th November A.D. 29, when our Lord began His Ministry, to 30th March A.D. 33, there are inclusively reckoned 1,221 days. The figure 1,221 is composed of 33 times 37 days. As stated above, 37 days are regarded in the Bible as "one hour" because they are a twenty-fourth part of 888 days.

We thus see that from the opening of the Lord's Ministry to the Transfiguration there were 33 symbolical "hours" of 37 days each. We need not again comment on the significance of such a measurement as it speaks for itself to anyone in possession of the above facts.

All those who love our Lord Jesus Christ in sincerity will rejoice that it has pleased God to restore the knowledge of the actual day when, with Peter, James and John, He ascended the Mount of Transfiguration to receive from God the Father honour and glory in the presence of the highly favoured representatives of the Old and the New Covenants.

## THE EVENT ITSELF

The proximity of Mount Hermon to Caesarea Philippi and the fact that the Lord led the three disciples "up into an high mountain apart" would indicate that it was the scene of this wonderful meeting between the Lord and His disciples and the two heavenly visitants – Moses and Elijah – who, having come to the earth eight days previously, were present for the purpose of holding converse with the One Whom their nation had now rejected and Who was about to lay down His life in order to accomplish our Redemption and become the Mediator of the New Covenant (Heb. IX, 15 R.V.).

Mount Hermon is a great height, being over 9,000 feet, so the journey up and down would have called for considerable effort. Matthew tells us that our Lord Jesus Christ

> "was transfigured before them: and His face did shine as the sun, and His raiment was white as the light" (XVII, 2).

It was the same lowly and humble Jesus Whom the three disciples gazed upon but for the moment a mighty transformation had taken place and His whole body and clothing became transfigured by an outshining of celestial Glory – the Glory which He had had with the Father before the earth was formed (John XVII, 5).

This was His official Glory which He had laid aside or veiled when He took part in flesh and blood and which for the moment He took again at the Transfiguration. It was this Glory which the three disciples witnessed and which must have been ever before their hearts and minds in the fearful tragedies they were so soon to witness in relation to the One Whom they had seen transfigured. Nevertheless, the occasion was to remain an untold secret in their own bosoms "until the Son of Man be risen again from the dead" (Matt. XVII, 9).

We will now quote from Luke IX, 30 and 31 (R.V.):

> "And behold, there talked with Him two men, which were Moses and Elijah; who appeared in glory, and spake of His decease which He was about to accomplish at Jerusalem."

Moses, now raised from the dead and clothed with a body of glory, and Elijah, who was translated to Heaven in a chariot of fire, are the great representatives of the Law and the Prophets. Their presence on the Mount of Transfiguration was of most solemn importance as may be gleaned from the fact that they spoke with our Lord "of His decease which He was about to accomplish at Jerusalem". The Greek word (EXODOS) used by Luke and translated "decease" might much better have been translated "exodus" as there is a wealth of meaning attaching to it when applied to our Lord's death.

Moses had led the people of Israel at their Exodus from Egypt in 1639 B.C. and knew that the occasion was, by design, a perfect type of the Lord's impending exodus out of this world. The nation of Israel took the Passover, like our Lord and His disciples, on a Thursday evening (11th May 1639 B.C.). They commenced their exodus the next day, Friday – the day our Lord made His Exodus from Calvary. Israel crossed the Red Sea during the night of Sunday and saw their Egyptian pursuers completely vanquished by the hand of God; while at Midnight on Sunday our Lord, having accomplished our Redemption, rose in triumph over death and all His and our foes. In other words, Israel's Exodus, from the taking of the Passover to the crossing of the Red Sea, was both a chronological and spiritual type of our Lord's death and resurrection from the last Passover taken with His disciples. This will become more apparent when we unfold from the Scriptures the long-concealed truth concerning these great events.

We are given three separate accounts of events on the Mount during our Lord's Transfiguration and there is, therefore, no need to pass further comment on such well-known facts.

What an immense responsibility is placed upon the whole human race in that men, such as the Apostles Peter, James and John, have borne witness to having actually heard the Voice of the Living God say concerning Jesus of Nazareth, "This is My beloved Son, in Whom I am well pleased; hear ye Him" (Matt. XVII, 5).

As the three disciples "came down from the mountain, Jesus charged them, saying, Tell the vision to no man, until the Son of Man be risen again from the dead".

So our Lord's Transfiguration ended. And how well for us that He did not there and then leave the earth and return to Heaven from whence He had come. He could not yet say, "I have finished the work which Thou gavest Me to do". Before doing so, He must suffer and die as "the Lamb of God, which taketh away the sin of the world".

# CHAPTER TWELVE

## THE FINAL DEPARTURE FROM GALILEE

## THE RAISING OF LAZARUS AS THE SEVENTH SIGN-MIRACLE OF JOHN'S GOSPEL

Our Lord's age on 20th April A.D. 33, was in Bible Years, 33 years and 179 days, and in Solar Years, 32 years and 173 days.

Read Matthew XIX, 1 and 2; Mark X, 1; Luke IX, 51; also John XI, 1 to 57

THE RAISING of Lazarus took place on Monday 20th April A.D. 33, exactly 3 weeks or 21 days from Monday, 30th March, which was the date of the Transfiguration. We will explain later how the date of the raising of Lazarus was ascertained from the Scriptures.

It is quite clear from several Scripture statements that our Lord and His disciples left Galilee soon after the Transfiguration. Before leaving, however, He again took occasion to press upon His unresponsive disciples the fact of His approaching death. In Mark IX, 30 to 32, we read:

> "And they departed thence, and passed through Galilee; and He would not that any man should know it. For He taught His disciples, and said unto them, The Son of Man is delivered into the hands of men, and they shall kill Him; and after that He is killed, He shall rise the third day. But they understood not that saying, and were afraid to ask Him."

Parallel passages are to be found in Matthew XVII, 22 and Luke IX, 43 to 45. A little later our Lord used even more emphatic words on this subject, as may be learnt from Matthew XX, 17, Mark X, 32 and Luke XVIII, 31. It becomes painfully manifest from the Luke reference that the twelve disciples were totally unable to grasp the significance of their

Master's words because they were ignorant of those Scriptures which foretold His sufferings and death. They were, in fact, wholly occupied with another point of view to that of their Master.

Before leaving Galilee the extremely important teachings recorded in Matthew XVII and XVIII and Mark IX were uttered by our Lord. It was also at this time that He performed the miracle of the Tribute Money.

In the light of His long and gracious Ministry to the Galileans our Lord's final departure from their country was a most solemn event. Matthew records the fact in these words:

> "And it came to pass, that when Jesus had finished these sayings, He departed from Galilee, and came into the coasts of Judaea beyond Jordan; and great multitudes followed Him; and He healed them there" (XIX, 1 and 2).

In Mark X, 1 there is a corresponding statement as to this final departure from Galilee after the Transfiguration. Neither Matthew nor Mark give any details of the journey from Galilee. Luke, however, does do so. In chapter IX, 51 we read:

> "And it came to pass, when the time was come that He should be received up, He stedfastly set His face to go to Jerusalem" (cf. Isaiah L, 7).

The journey to Jerusalem which took the Lord through Galilee and Samaria (Luke XVII, 11) led first to "the coasts of Judaea beyond Jordan". Luke marks the various stages, as may be seen from the following passages – XIII, 22; XVII, 11; XVIII, 31; XIX, 28.

It is quite clear from Matthew XIX, 1 and 2, and Mark X, 1 that our Lord engaged in much public teaching and healing while He was in Peraea "beyond Jordan" before He received the information from Martha and Mary that their brother Lazarus was sick. His arrival in Peraea was in the early days of April, A.D. 33, and His departure therefrom was on 19th April when He left with His disciples for Bethany.

# THE SICKNESS, DEATH AND RESURRECTION OF LAZARUS

## THE FOURTH AND LAST SIGN-MIRACLE IN JOHN'S GOSPEL RELATING TO THE PEOPLE OF ISRAEL

It is not a little remarkable that three of the four Sign-Miracles of John's Gospel which relate to Israel, namely, the healing of the man who had been impotent for 38 years, (John V), the giving of sight to the blind man (John IX) and the raising of Lazarus (John XI), were each in turn events which acted like a potent fuel to the fire of official Jewry's hatred of our Lord. This reached a white-hot heat as a result of the raising of Lazarus from the dead and caused Israel's rulers, in a blind fury, to determine at any price to kill Him. Consequently, we read in John XI, 53, "From that day forth they took counsel together for to put Him to death". See also John V, 16 to 18 and X, 31 and 39. And would it not be the same to-day if any-one were to rise whose influence and teaching exposed the pharisaical bigotry of religious Christendom?

As stated above, the raising of Lazarus was the fourth and last of the Sign-Miracles of John's Gospel wrought by our Lord in relation to the people of Israel. It is a fact of the utmost significance that in the raising up again of this people to Statehood in the land of Israel on 14th-15th May 1948, this pre-eminent Sign-Miracle of our Lord received in part its antitypical fulfilment. We will give the evidence of Holy Scripture in support of this fact in a Note when we have briefly examined the main features of this miracle.

When Jesus and His disciples received the message from Martha and Mary that their brother ("he whom Thou lovest") was sick, they were dwelling in Peraea beyond Jordan which was rather more than a day's journey to Bethany.

It has been possible to learn from the Scriptures the exact days in the solar calendar referred to in John XI. In the first place we learn from verse 55 that "the Jews' passover was nigh at hand". The date of the Jews' Passover in A.D. 33, when our Lord was put to death, was Friday, 1st May, and, therefore, 14th Nisan in the Jewish Calendar.

By clear inference the Scriptures reveal that the death and

resurrection of Lazarus took place exactly TWO WEEKS before that of our Lord Jesus Christ, and on precisely the same days of the week. In order to convey this fact John was caused by the Spirit of God to insert the following parenthetical statement (verse 18): "Now Bethany was nigh unto Jerusalem, about fifteen furlongs off".

No one could fail to realize that topographical information such as this is not in itself of sufficient importance to find a place in Holy Writ. It must have been inserted solely on account of its typical significance, since Bethany's proximity to Jerusalem was well known. Lazarus died and rose at Bethany and the Lord died and rose at Jerusalem. The fifteen furlongs which lie between these two places clearly typify the fifteen days which separated our Lord's death and resurrection from that of Lazarus. In this case, as with all such in the Bible, the clue to understanding is to be looked for in the numerical affinity which exists between the type and the antitype.

In Bible terms, 15 days is an inclusive expression of two weeks. Lazarus died on Friday, 17th April and rose on Monday, 20th April. Our Lord died (as we are about to reveal from Scripture) on Friday, 1st May, and rose on Monday, 4th May, in exact fulfilment of every statement He had made upon the subject. Inclusively, Friday, 17th April, is 15 days from Friday, 1st May, and Monday, 20th April, is 15 days from Monday, 4th May.

The messenger sent by the two sisters must have left Bethany on Thursday, 16th April, and reached our Lord on Friday, 17th April, which was the 29th of the 12th month (Adar) and the last day of the Bible year. When our Lord had heard about Lazarus He at once said to His disciples, "This sickness is not unto death, but for the glory of God, that the Son of God might be glorified thereby" (verse 4). Our Lord had foreknowledge of this event as He had of everything else which lay ahead in His earthly Pathway.

After receiving the sad news, we are informed that our Lord "abode two days still in the same place where He was" (verse 6). The reason for this may be learnt from the following facts. The day upon which our Lord first heard about Lazarus was Friday, 17th April. The Jews' Friday was, however, God's Sabbath in Divine time. (See the Summary of Facts – Par. 14.)

Our Lord, therefore, in accordance with the Law, abode where He was that day and also the next day which was the Jews' Sabbath. From these facts it appears evident that our Lord kept both His Father's Sabbath and the Jews' Sabbath.

On the day that the messenger reached our Lord, namely, Friday, 17th April, Lazarus died, and according to custom was at once buried in a sepulchre, with a stone at its mouth.

On Sunday 19th April (i.e., from 6 P.M. on the 18th) after the two Sabbaths were passed, our Lord said to the disciples, "Let us go into Judaea again". This causes the disciples to say, "Master, the Jews of late sought to stone Thee; and goest Thou thither again?" (verses 7 and 8). The Lord, in effect, replies that in doing His Father's will He was as one walking in the light of day and need fear no man.

After declaring plainly, "Lazarus is dead", our Lord continues, "I am glad for your sakes that I was not there, to the intent ye may believe; nevertheless let us go unto him" (verses 14 and 15). Lazarus' sickness and death were no accident but events foreknown to our Lord which had a deep symbolical significance. Furthermore, it was that the Son of Man might be glorified in the display of His power over death. The faith of all His disciples would thereby be greatly strengthened at a time when it was about to be most sorely tried by His own death. That is the meaning of the words, "to the intent ye may believe".

The eleventh of John is a long chapter wholly devoted to the incident of the death and raising of Lazarus. No mention of this event appears in any other Gospel but its importance as a vital feature in the closing scene of our Lord's pathway on earth will be obvious to all. The home of Martha, Mary and Lazarus was much blessed by the frequent presence in it of Israel's Messiah. The Lord loved each inmate of it. The sisters had a deep affection for their brother and their grief at his death was inconsolable. Furthermore, the thought persisted with both sisters that if Jesus had only been there He could have cured the malady that had caused their brother's death (verses 21 and 32). It was to yield to sheer human despair to dwell upon what appeared to be the irreparable in the Presence of the One Who could say, "I am the resurrection, and the life: he that believeth on Me, though he die, yet shall he live" (verse 25, R.V.). But Martha's faith as regards her brother's resurrection was limited to the remote future. The Lord, however, presents Himself to her as the present Source of resurrection life.

Mary rises up on hearing that the Lord has arrived and goes to the place outside the town where Martha has met Him. Weeping, she casts herself down at His feet with the same lament as her sister's – "Lord, if Thou hadst been here, my brother had not died" (verse 32). Our Lord "groaned in the spirit, and was troubled" as He beheld Mary's grief and that of those with her who were weeping. Our Lord Himself weeps as He beholds the untold sorrow that sin has wrought; for He sees death as the result of sin.

After travelling all Sunday, 19th April, it was in the morning of Monday 20th April, that our Lord arrived in the precincts of Bethany and was met first by Martha and then by Mary. In due course He and the sisters and their friends and His disciples made their way to the grave where the body of Lazarus had been buried. None but the disciples, to whom He had said, "I go that I may awake him out of sleep", knew the Lord's intentions in going to the sepulchre. Most would have judged it to be an expression of His deep sympathy with the sisters.

The thought that corruption must have taken place lays hold of Martha and with it a sense of the utter impossibility of her brother's being raised up. She, therefore, says, "Lord, by this time he stinketh: for he hath been dead four days". To this our Lord replies, as if mildly to rebuke her lack of faith in His power to keep His word, "Said I not unto thee, that, if thou wouldest believe, thou shouldest see the glory of God?" (verses 39 and 40).

Our Lord commands that the stone be removed from the cave's mouth, just as fifteen days later the stone would be removed from His own sepulchre that all might see for themselves that He was risen (John XX, 1).

Our Lord standing by the open sepulchre then gives thanks, saying, "Father, I thank Thee that Thou hast heard Me. And I knew that Thou hearest Me always: but because of the people which stand by I said it, that they may believe that Thou hast sent Me" (verses 41 and 42). These words clearly imply that the raising of Lazarus was to be the final proof of our Lord's Messiahship. We are, indeed, told that "many of the Jews that came to Mary, and had seen the things which Jesus did, believed on Him" (verse 45).

"And when He thus had spoken, He cried with a loud voice, Lazarus, come forth. And he that was dead came forth, bound hand and foot with graveclothes: and his face was bound about with a napkin. Jesus saith unto them, Loose him, and let him go" (verses 43 and 44).

Resurrection had now become a fact – a living reality – through the intervention of the Son of God and once again the Bethany home had its three occupants. The once grief-stricken sisters had learnt how good it was that the Lord was not there when their brother was sick and died. Their brother's death they now knew was that "the Son of God might be glorified". For them weeping had endured for a night but joy had come in the morning. They had indeed seen "the glory of God" and their brother's death as an event to subserve that glory.

This has not been an occasion for any lengthy comments upon this solemn episode. We have therefore attempted nothing more than to give a brief outline with the chronological data which establishes that the four days of Lazarus' death were from Friday, 17th April to Monday, 20th April, which was the Jews' 3rd of Nisan. As we reveal from the Bible in our former Treatise, this 20th April was the 4107th solar anniversary of the start of the 6,000 Years of Redemption in 4075 B.C. – the day after the Fall of Adam and Eve who, through sin, brought death into the world. Furthermore, 20th April A.D. 33 was, according to the calendar based upon the Years of the Messiah (see Summary of Facts, Par. 18), the 17th day of the 7th month which was the date upon which the Ark rested upon Mount Ararat (Gen. VIII, 4) and which is universally regarded as symbolical of resurrection. In this connection we may also mention that our Lord's resurrection, which took place on the 15th day after that of Lazarus, was, in the years of His personal chronology (i.e. years measured from His Nativity), again the 17th day of the 7th month. (See Chart of the Five Calendars, after Chapter Thirteen.)

It is, indeed, wonderful to contemplate that every event in the Bible took place on a date foreknown to God, if not actually foreplanned by Him. And are His children to ignore all such matters and never know on earth His wondrous manipulations of Time and all its divisions in the display of His Glory and in the execution of His Counsels? Nothing is more remarkable than the manner in which God has concealed the Time factors of His Word. But in this connection, how full of meaning is the Scripture, "It is the glory of God to conceal a thing: but the honour of kings is to search out a matter" (Prov. XXV, 2). That the time factors of the Bible have to be searched for is proved by the Apostle Peter's words: "the prophets . . . searched diligently . . . what, or what manner of time the Spirit of Christ which was in them did signify" (I Peter I, 10, 11).

## A NOTE

### THE TYPICAL SIGNIFICANCE OF THE FOUR DAYS LAZARUS WAS IN THE SEPULCHRE

"One day is with the Lord as a thousand years,
and a thousand years as one day"
(II Peter III, 8)

The raising of Lazarus after four days in the grave was given to be a sign that after 4,000 years the seed of Abraham would again be raised to nationhood in the land of Israel, which God gave as a perpetual possession to Abraham and his seed, as recorded in Genesis XV, 18, in these terms: "In the same day the Lord made a covenant with Abram, saying, Unto thy seed have I given this land, from the river of Egypt unto the great river, the river Euphrates". It is a fact of transcendent significance that from the day that is named in this verse, Four Thousand Solar Years of 365¼ days passed to the rise of the State of Israel in May, 1948.

It will be asked at once how we came to know the date of the covenant which the Lord God made with Abram, as recorded in Genesis XV. In the first place, it must be appreciated, as stated in the Introduction, that we possessed a perfect knowledge of Time in the Bible before writing this present Treatise, which would not otherwise have been possible. The date of Abram's leaving Haran, as recorded in Genesis XII, 4, we knew was 6th August, 2056 B.C. because it was *to the day* 430 Bible years to the Exodus on 12th May, 1639 B.C. (see Exodus XII, 40, 41). We had already learnt that 4,000 Julian

Years from this date ended on 2nd September, 1945, when the Second World War officially terminated (6,000,000 Jews having been cruelly slaughtered by Hitler and his minions).

We next noted that the animals which had to be sacrificed, when God made His covenant with Abram in Genesis XV, must each be "three years old". This appeared to be a veiled intimation that this covenant was made in the third year after Abram entered the land in 2056 B.C.

We mentioned at the end of Chapter Ten that from 4th May A.D. 30, when our Lord declared, "Destroy this temple, and in three days I will raise it up", to 14th January A.D. 33, when the Jews figuratively put Christ to death by stoning, was 2 Solar years, 9 months and 3 days – a period expressing the 2 days and 9 hours that our Lord was "in the heart of the earth". We therefore applied this measurement to the period between Abram's departure from Canaan on 6th August 2056 B.C. and the covenant of Genesis XV. After measuring 985 days (i.e. 2 Solar years, 9 months and 3 days) from 6th August 2056 B.C. we arrived at the date of 15th April 2053 B.C. It is to be noted that the making of the covenant took altogether 3 days, namely, 15th, 16th and 17th April. We then measured forward 4,000 Julian Solar years of 365¼ days and discovered that they terminated on 15th, 16th and 17th May in A.D. 1948, which were the actual days over which the State of Israel came into existence and was recognized by the United States of America and Soviet Russia, the two most powerful nations on the earth.

As it is obvious that the four days of Lazarus' session in death form a type of some sort, it would be sheer blindness to refuse to see that their antitype is the four "days" of a thousand years each which elapsed between the solemn covenant made by the Lord God with Abram concerning the land of Canaan in Genesis XV, and 15th to 17th May in A.D. 1948, when the seed of Abram again became a nation in the form of the State of Israel.

It will be seen that in the type we have our Lord's 2 years, 9 months and 3 days, followed by the typical "four days" of Lazarus (that is, as presented in John's Gospel), and in the antitype, Abram's 2 years, 9 months and 3 days, followed by the antitypical Four Thousand years to the rise of the State of Israel.

In Chapter One we showed that from our Lord's presentation in the Temple, on 8th December 1 B.C., we have another expression of the 2 days and 9 hours of His death in the form of 2,000 Bible years and 9 Solar years to 15th May 1948, when the State of Israel was formed.

It is confirmatory of the above facts that the name of Abram's steward, "Eliezer" (given in Genesis XV), is the Hebrew spelling of "Lazarus". It is also of interest that the Acting Chief Rabbi of Britain which held the Mandate over Palestine until May 1948, was also surnamed "Lazarus" at the time.

Like the healing of the cripple in John V and the giving of sight to the man in John IX, this fourth Sign-Miracle relating to Israel also has a sequel. After Lazarus had come forth "bound hand and foot with grave clothes: and his face . . . bound about with a napkin", Jesus commanded saying, "Loose him, and let him go". This clearly indicates a later stage in Israel's resurrection, when the grave clothes of the Dispersion era are removed and the ability given to see Him "Whom they have pierced".

After the raising of Lazarus our Lord "walked no more openly among the Jews; but went thence into a country near to the wilderness, into a city called Ephraim, and there continued with His disciples" (John XI, 54). This was because our Lord knew that the Jews had taken counsel to put Him to death (verse 53). When the appointed time arrived He would allow Himself to be taken but until then He must preserve Himself from becoming the victim of their precipitate action as tools of Satan.

We shall open our next Chapter with the Lord's visit to Jericho on the Sabbath – 25th April and 8th Nisan – when He abode for the day in the house of Zacchaeus (Luke XIX). This was 7 days inclusively before His death on Friday, 1st May – the Jews' 14th Nisan and the day of "the preparation of the passover".

# CHAPTER THIRTEEN

## THE LAST WEEK OPENS WITH THE VISIT OF OUR LORD JESUS CHRIST TO JERICHO ON THE SABBATH – 25TH APRIL A.D. 33

### THE IMMENSE SIGNIFICANCE OF THE CONVERSION OF ZACCHAEUS

### THIS EVENT WAS DESIGNED TO MARK THE TERMINATING DATE OF "THE SEVENTY WEEKS" OR 490 YEARS OF DANIEL IX, 24, IN GENTILE SOLAR YEARS

### JERICHO – "THE CITY OF PALM TREES" – IS THE PRE-EMINENT BIBLE TYPE OF THE GENTILE WORLD

The Age of our Lord Jesus Christ on 25th April A.D. 33, was 32 Solar Years and 178 Days, or 33 Bible Years and 184 Days.

Read Luke XVIII, 35 to XIX, 10, and Mark X, 46 to 52

THE TRUE significance of our Lord's visit to Jericho lies in knowing THE DAY and THE DATE upon which it took place. Our previous pages have demonstrated this principle over and over again. Robbed of the knowledge of the significance of the date in the Pattern of Time by which our Lord and Master walked here on earth, the story of the Conversion of Zacchaeus, and of our Lord's stay in his house in Jericho becomes one of merely passing interest; but when the true significance of the occasion is entered into it is seen to be an event foreplanned of God and of the utmost importance as a prophetic type of the Coming of Christ's Millennial Kingdom.

The very words addressed by our Lord to Zacchaeus, "To-day I *must* abide at thy house", carry with them the authority of a Royal command and are obviously related to a plan and a purpose foreknown to the One Who uttered them. The "I must" of our Lord excludes any option on the part of Zacchaeus to refuse to be host to Israel's Messiah on this obviously foreordained occasion. The fact is that our Lord Jesus Christ had already entered Zacchaeus' heart (or the latter would not have been so determined to see Him) and He now claimed the right to enter his house.

Jericho, which was a few hours' journey from Bethany and Jerusalem, is, as we stated above, a pre-eminent Bible type of THE GENTILE WORLD. It is several times called "the city of palm trees" (see Deut. XXXIV, 3, etc.) because the palm tree in the Bible is a type of the Gentiles, just as the fig tree is a type of the Jews.

As it is essential to understand that Jericho typifies the Gentile World, we will call attention to the following facts. In the Parable of the Good Samaritan (Luke X, 30) the man who fell among thieves and was left half dead, when he was going down "*from Jerusalem to Jericho*", typifies the persecuted believing remnant of the Jews after the martyrdom of Stephen. Our Lord as the Good Samaritan ministered to these and later merged them with the believing Gentiles so that together they might form the Church (EKKLESIA) which is His Body (Ephes.II, 15 and 16).

In Revelation VII a vision is recorded of a great multitude of Gentiles who are brought into the Kingdom. These hold in their hands "palms" which are symbolic of Gentiledom.

After the fall of Jerusalem and the overthrow of Judah the Romans struck a medal in celebration of their victory. This proved to be a fitting emblem for "the times of the Gentiles" during which the Jews have been in subjection to the nations. On one side of this medal was a weeping Jewish woman sitting *under* a palm tree and watched by a Roman soldier. This shows that the Romans understood the symbolic meaning of the palm tree.

This was not our Lord's first visit to Jericho because it was He, as "Captain of the host of the Lord", Who appeared to Joshua "by Jericho" and gave him instructions as to the manner of its conquest by the armies of Israel in 1599 B.C. (Joshua V and VI). Because of its remarkable relationship to the incident we are considering, we shall later make further reference to the Joshua conquest of that city. It is important also to remember that Jericho has been for years, and is still, one of the most profitable spheres of archaeological research. Recent results have brought to light many expected confirmations of Biblical history.

Our Lord Jesus Christ, hearing that they intended to kill Him, "walked no more openly among the Jews" after He had raised Lazarus from the dead but "went thence into a country near to the wilderness, into a city called Ephraim" (John XI, 54). The raising of Lazarus was on Monday, 20th April. Ephraim, the site of which is in doubt, must have been near to Jericho which the Lord reached on Friday evening, 24th April. This was the opening of 25th April, and the Jews' Sabbath.

We learn from Luke XVIII, 35, "that as He was come nigh unto Jericho, a certain blind man sat by the wayside begging". As the context informs us, our Lord had mercy on this man and bestowed sight upon him, so that he "followed Him, glorifying God".

In this connection it is important to note that as the Lord left Jericho, having spent the Sabbath in the house of Zacchaeus, He gave sight to another man, by name, Bartimaeus. Two accounts of this incident, with one variation, are to be found in Mark X and Matthew XX. It must have occurred to many to ask why, both on entering and on leaving Jericho, our Lord and Master is recorded as having healed men that were blind. In this fact we again have the testimony of Scripture that Jericho typifies the Gentile world because blindness in everything that relates to God is the outstanding moral defect of the Gentiles. It was for this reason that our Risen Lord, when He had apprehended Saul of Tarsus on the Damascus road, commissioned him to go to the Gentiles "to open their eyes, and to turn them from darkness to light, and from the power of Satan unto God, that they may receive forgiveness of sins" (Acts XXVI, 18). Furthermore, the Prophet Isaiah foretells that our Lord would Himself be "for a light of the Gentiles; to open the blind eyes" (XLII, 6 and 7). The Bible reveals that the conversion of a Gentile to faith in Christ is the direct result of the miracle-working power of the Holy Spirit Who opens his eyes to the fact that he is by nature dead in trespasses and sins and can only be saved from perdition by believing on the Lord Jesus Christ and accepting that His death upon the Cross was as his Substitute (John III, 3 to 21).

## OUR LORD ENTERS JERICHO

At the time that Jesus and His disciples reached Jericho, bands of pilgrims from all over Palestine were wending their way to Jerusalem for the Passover which in A.D. 33 was on 1st May (John XI, 55). The Lord Himself was at the head of such a band when He entered Jericho which lay in His path to Jerusalem whither "He stedfastly set His face to go" (Luke IX, 51). He Himself was the true Antitypical Paschal Lamb that must now be offered up and the time had therefore come when He need no longer keep out of sight of those who wished to apprehend Him, but could go openly and fearlessly because His hour had come.

Not only would our Lord's appearance in Jericho cause a great stir ("This is Jesus the prophet of Nazareth of Galilee", cf. Matt. XXI, 11), but the knowledge that He had just healed the blindness of a well-known beggar as He approached the city would rouse all its inhabitants to a state of intense curiosity and the hope that He would perform some further miracle in their sight. Crowds, therefore, lined the streets as the Lord at the head of His band, not only consisting of the twelve disciples but doubtless of a multitude of others that followed Him from Galilee and Peraea, made His way into the city, perfectly well aware that His Presence in it *on that day* constituted a vital feature in the Pattern of Time which His God and Father had designed for Him in His pathway through this world. But not only must our Lord be *in Jericho* on that day, He must also take up His residence in the house of one who is "a son of Abraham" if the symbolism of His visit is to reach perfection.

Acting sovereignly, God had already touched the heart of Zacchaeus, a rich chief publican or taxgatherer, because he, inwardly and outwardly, qualified to fill the part needed by the one in whose house the Lord *must* abide that day.

Luke, who alone records this incident, tells us all we need to know about Zacchaeus (XIX, 1 to 10). The sycamore tree into which he climbed in order to see Jesus is a species of fig tree which is symbolic of the Jewish nation (cf. John I, 48). Who can imagine Zacchaeus' astonishment at being addressed by name and at being summoned to receive our Lord and, no doubt, His disciples into His house. Our Lord's action in this creates a stir and many, forgetting He had come to call sinners to repentance, murmur because "He was gone to be guest with a man that is a sinner" (XIX, 7). Like all others who find themselves in the Lord's presence, the conscience of Zacchaeus became active and as he beheld his ill-gotten wealth repentance in a most practical form laid hold of him. In future, half his goods would be distributed to the poor and to anyone he had cheated "by false accusation" he would restore fourfold (see Exodus XXII, 1). (Zacchaeus, as we shall see, is a type of the repentant nation of Israel and his reference to "false accusation" and restoring "fourfold" is most remarkable because such restoration only applied to those who had killed another man's sheep. Our Lord, Who was the Lamb of God, was killed by the Jews at the end of the Seventy Weeks or 490 years named in the Prophecy of Daniel IX. That was in A.D. 33. The official period of their rejection was from A.D. 33 to 1933 which is 4 times 490 Bible years of 354 days. Here, indeed, was true repentance because accompanied by admission of wrong-doing in the past and a promise to act righteously in the future. So the Lord is able to say, "This day is salvation come to this house, forasmuch as he also is a son of Abraham".

## THE DAY AND DATE OF OUR LORD'S VISIT TO JERICHO

As we stated above, the day was THE SABBATH and the date in the solar calendar, 25th April A.D. 33. In Israel's calendar it was the 8th of Nisan, the first month.

The Sabbath, or Seventh Day, given of God by covenant to the people of Israel, is the great pre-eminent Bible type of the coming Kingdom of the Messiah, our Lord Jesus Christ, Who during the Seventh Thousand Years of human history will reign over the whole earth, which will enjoy the rest and peace which the Sabbath signifies – the word itself meaning "cessation".

Now we can begin to see the typical aspect of our Lord's visit to Jericho on THE SABBATH.

Jericho is a type of the Gentile World. The occasion of our Lord's visit is on the Sabbath day which, as we have just said, is a type of the Kingdom and a period of unbroken peace and tranquillity among the Gentiles that have part in it (see

Matthew XXV, 31 to 46). Zacchaeus and his house form a type of the repentant nation of Israel in the Kingdom and as all should know our Lord when He reigns will, as the Heir of David, be King over Israel as well as "King over all the earth" (Zech. XIV, 9). In Ezekiel XXXVII, 28, we read, "And the heathen (lit., the Gentiles) shall know that I the Lord do sanctify Israel, when My sanctuary shall be in the midst of them for evermore".

It must be remembered that the Coming of Christ's Kingdom will be the fulfilment of the hope that God has set before the human race in the Scriptures ever since the Fall of Adam over six thousand years ago. The world then, as now, will be a Gentile world and in it will be the restored and repentant nation of Israel in the midst of whom our Lord will dwell and have His Sanctuary.

The question now arises, Why did our Lord choose that particular Sabbath in which to abide in Jericho? This is a question of the greatest possible importance and one which the Bible answers by referring us to the great Messianic Time Prophecy of the ninth chapter of Daniel.

It will be recalled that in Chapter One of this present Treatise we gave a brief exposition of this prophecy in order to establish the date of our Lord's birth. Readers will do well to refresh their minds by referring to what we then set forth (see also Chapter Three). This chronological prophecy of the "Seventy Weeks" forms the keystone of all Bible prophecy and no words could possibly exaggerate its importance. In effect, it measures off a period of 490 years from Nehemiah's rebuilding of Jerusalem in 458 B.C. to the Crucifixion of our Lord Who, as "Messiah the Prince", was "cut off" in A.D. 33.

These 490 years find their type in the 490 days which formed the Seventy Weeks named in Daniel IX, 24. In Chapter One we showed that on 25th April A.D. 26, when John the Baptist opened his testimony "unto the Messiah", 69 "weeks" or 483 Solar years had passed to the day from 26th April, 458 B.C. when the period began. Between 25th April A.D. 26, and 25th April A.D. 33, when our Lord entered Jericho and abode in the house of Zacchaeus, exactly 7 years or one "week" had been added to the 483 years or 69 "weeks". This addition brought the 490 years or 70 "weeks" to their termination. (In our former Treatise *The World in Liquidation* (Paper IV) we give full details from the Bible as to how the starting date of the prophecy of the Seventy Weeks, namely, 26th April, 458 B.C., was ascertained.)

This Sabbath on 25th April A.D. 33, was therefore the last day of the great Messianic time prophecy of the "seventy weeks" or 490 years, as measured in Gentile time, and it is this fact which clothes our Lord's action on that day with such immense significance. This statement calls for explanation.

It is perfectly clear from the terms of this prophecy set forth by the Angel Gabriel in Daniel IX, 24, that the 490 years were purposed to terminate with the establishment of the Kingdom and the bringing in of "everlasting righteousness", etc. With infinite wisdom God left a blank space in the prophecy and refused to reveal (save that Messiah would be "cut off") what the course of events would be in the seven years or "one week" between A.D. 26 and 33. He foreknew Israel's rejection of their Messiah (God forbid that any should think He foreplanned it) and this in spite of the fact that both John the Baptist and, notably so, Jesus, whose ministries each covered about three and a half years, perfectly fulfilled all that was written of them in the Holy Scriptures.

Our Lord Jesus Christ from the very beginning experienced the hatred of the Jewish leaders and knew well that in spite of all His miracles and manifested grace they would reject and kill Him. This being so, it pleased Almighty God to ordain that the chronological end of the Seventy Weeks or 490 years should be marked by a symbolical expression of the setting up of the Kingdom, in the place of the literal fulfilment which would have taken place had Israel not refused their Messiah. Hence our Lord's visit to the typical Jericho and His abiding in the house of the repentant Zacchaeus on that Sabbath day which, in the solar calendar, was 25th April A.D. 33, and exactly "Seventy Weeks" or 490 years from 458 B.C. which was the starting date of the prophecy given to Daniel.

It is necessary to understand that the prophecy of the Seventy Weeks or 490 years is measured by God in solar terms, in the manner we have just set forth, because of our Lord's relation to the Gentiles, all of whose eras are expressed in solar years. (In fact, the prophecy is dated from the years of a Gentile monarch, Artaxerxes, and the 483 years are marked as ending in the years of another Gentile monarch – Tiberius Caesar.) The Jewish measurement is in luni-solar Bible years which began on the 26th day of the 1st Month in 458 B.C. The terminating date in this series of years was, therefore, the 26th of the 1st Month in A.D. 33. This, as we have already shown in Chapter One was 12th May – a post-resurrection date which was marked by our Lord with a most touching symbolical expression of Israel's ultimate repentance and recognition of Himself as the One Whom they had pierced and slain (see John XX, 24 to 29). It will have been noted from the facts we have just given that the chronological prophecy of the Seventy Weeks or 490 years is measured in the Bible in both Gentile and Jewish years. This proves that it is one of universal significance.

### THE SEVEN DAYS' ENCIRCLEMENT AND FALL OF JERICHO BY JOSHUA AND ISRAEL IN 1599 B.C. ITS TYPICAL SIGNIFICANCE AND ITS RELATION TO OUR LORD'S VISIT TO JERICHO IN A.D. 33

We cannot leave the subject of our Lord's visit to the house of Zacchaeus in Jericho without reference to the occasion when He appeared to Joshua, and gave him instructions as to the conquest of Jericho after seven days, because of its relationship to the subject we are now considering (see Joshua VI).

In our preceding pages, when writing of the seven years, A.D. 26 to 33, which began with the testimony of John the Baptist and ended with the Death, Resurrection and Ascension of our Lord Jesus Christ, we have stated that the Scriptures make it manifestly plain that because of what took place, namely, the rejection of the testimonies of both John the Baptist and our Lord Himself, whose joint ministries covered these seven years, God cancelled the whole period chronologically and determined that it should be relived after the Christian Dispensation had run its course. For this reason the Book of the Revelation after Chapter III is seen to cover a period of Seven Years, divided into 1,260 days and 42 months – a division which is exactly similar to that in the seven years, A.D. 26 to 33 (Rev. XI and XII).

We have just shown that our Lord's visit to Jericho on the Sabbath of 25th April A.D. 33, was to mark the end in solar terms of the seven years from 25th April A.D. 26. Instead of the fulfilment of the Seventy Weeks' prophecy of Daniel IX being marked by the inauguration of the Kingdom of the Messiah, in accordance with its terms, we have only witnessed a symbolical fulfilment. This fact in itself proves that the seven years, A.D. 26 to 33, which formed the last "week" of the prophecy, had failed of their object which was the national repentance of Israel and the restoration of the Davidic Kingdom under the Messiah – "great David's greater Son" – our Lord Jesus Christ.

One week after our Lord was in Jericho He was crucified and this act finally sealed the cancellation of the seven years, A.D. 26 to 33, which would now have to be relived at the end of the Christian era as a period of retributive judgments, the desolating nature of which the Apostle John received by revelation from our risen Lord and recorded in the Apocalypse.

The seven days' encirclement of Jericho by Joshua and Israel and its fall on the seventh day, when the walls came crashing down, constitutes the most brilliant type in the Bible of these relived seven years at the end of which the great Gentile World System will be demolished by the Appearing of our Lord, as described in Revelation XIX, 11 to 21, and at the end of Daniel II, where He is the One typified by a "Stone" that falls upon the Great Gentile Image and grinds it to powder.

We have proved from the Bible that the Fall of Jericho took place on the Sabbath Day of 12th May 1599 B.C. (As stated above, it was 12th May A.D. 33, when the Seventieth Week ended in Luni-solar years.) The Bible itself states that it was on "the seventh day" that the walls of Jericho fell. This event proves conclusively that the Kingdom, of which the Sabbath is an ever-recurring type, will be inaugurated by a catastrophic act of judgment which will sweep Gentile governmental sovereignty from the earth, so that the Kingdom of Christ, Who is the "Stone" of Daniel II, 34 and 35, which smites the Image, may become a Great Mountain (i.e., Empire) which fills "the whole earth".

We thus see that in our Lord's visit to Jericho and His stay in the house of Zacchaeus on the Sabbath Day, 25th April A.D. 33, we have a symbolical expression of the Kingdom over which He will reign. In the encirclement of Jericho for seven days, we have a perfect type of the Seven Years of the Book of

Revelation which are the relived seven years, A.D. 26 to 33, and in the Fall of Jericho (typically the Gentile World) on the seventh day or Sabbath we have a perfect type of the inauguration of the Kingdom by means of a vast catastrophic act of judgment which will remove "out of His kingdom (i.e., the world) all things that offend, and them which do iniquity" (Matthew XIII, 41).

In our former Treatise, *The World in Liquidation*, we have established from the chronology of the Bible (which for the first time in human history has been faultlessly reproduced therein and shown to be a scientific and astronomically-perfect recording of Time from Genesis I) that the Second Advent of Christ, when He comes as defined in I Thessalonians IV, is at hand and that the Seven Years of the Apocalypse are about to open. We mention these solemn facts for the sole reason of inducing any who have not obeyed the call of God to repentance for their sins to do so and to believe in the One Whose pathway on earth we have been tracing and Whose Death and Resurrection *according to the Scriptures* we are, by the Grace of God, about to unfold.

## IMPORTANT NOTE

### WHY IT WAS ORDAINED OF GOD THAT FIVE CALENDARS SHOULD BE IN OPERATION TOGETHER DURING THE LIFE ON EARTH OF OUR LORD JESUS CHRIST

EVERYONE who fears and respects Almighty God knows that He does nothing without a reason. That it was absolutely necessary in the Divine Counsels that no less than Five separate Calendars should be in operation at one time in order to express in the Life of our Lord the true significance of certain events, which took place on particular days in one or more of these calendars, is proved by the fact of their existence in the Bible and of the vital part they fill in the Bible's calendarial economy, as expressed in Leviticus XXIII.

We have drawn the attached Chart in order to show these Five Calendars in operation in the Life of our Lord from the death of Lazarus to Pentecost, A.D. 33. In actual fact, apart from the solar month dates, our attention while setting forth the time factors related to the death and resurrection of our Lord will be directed almost exclusively to the calendar of Israel (which is the only one to appear in the text of Holy Scripture) and to the Divine Calendar which up to the Cross was always one day of the week and one day of the month ahead of Israel's calendar. The reason for this difference of one day we explain in the Summary of Facts – Paragraphs 13 and 14 – which should be carefully read.

Our blessed Lord and Master must Himself have perfectly understood the relationship of these Five Calendars to events in His own life. Take the occasions we have already considered when He was 12 years of age and 30 years of age. In the calendar based upon the Years of the Messiah, both these important anniversaries of His birth fell on the 14th day of the 1st month which was the Feast of the Passover. For this reason, in the case of the 30th anniversary when our Lord began His Ministry, John the Baptist could view Him as the Paschal Lamb and say, "Behold the Lamb of God, which taketh away the sin of the world". Divine order would never have permitted John so to speak of our Lord except it had been on the day of the Passover when the Paschal lambs were sacrificed. In this instance the date in Israel's calendar was the 2nd day of the 9th month which has no significance.

Let us recall again that 29th October 1 B.C., when our Lord was born, was, in the Divine Calendar, the 15th of the 7th month which is the first day of the Feast of Tabernacles, while in the Years of the Messiah, it was the 15th day of the 1st month which is the first day of the Feast of Unleavened Bread. In Israel's calendar this date was the 14th of the 7th month which again has no significance.

We are about to see that the day on which Mary of Bethany anointed the Lord was marked by a great significance in two of these Calendars and it is this which clothed her act with such an immense meaning in the eyes of the One she anointed. One of these Calendars is based upon the Years of our Lord's own life as measured from His birth. That there should be such a series of years is not in the least remarkable since every individual can boast of a personal chronology – a fact which becomes evident upon each anniversary of one's birth.

Let the fact be honestly faced that the secrets of eighteen hundred years' duration connected with the Saviour's death and resurrection have now been unveiled by God solely through the granting of understanding of how He manipulated these various calendars in order that the Scriptures might be fulfilled in every detail and our Lord's Messiahship be thereby perfectly established.

It is both the privilege and solemn duty of every sincere believer in our Lord Jesus Christ to go again to the Scriptures and confirm therefrom the facts we are about to set forth. These have lain concealed since the departure of the Apostles because of the apostasy that then set in. That they have now again been brought to light should be a cause for deep thanksgiving on the part of all who have found peace with God through our Lord's atoning Sacrifice on Calvary's Tree.

## CHART SHOWING THE FIVE CALENDARS IN CONCURRENT OPERATION AT THE TIME OF THE DEATH AND RESURRECTION OF OUR LORD JESUS CHRIST

A.D. 33

| EVENT | DAY OF THE WEEK | SOLAR MONTH DATE | JEWISH MONTH DATE | DAY AND MONTH IN DIVINE CALENDAR | | 4238TH YEAR OF MESSIAH MONTH DATE | OUR LORD'S YEARS: MONTH DATE IN 34TH YEAR | OUR LORD'S YEARS: AGE |
|---|---|---|---|---|---|---|---|---|
| Death of Lazarus | Friday | 17 April | 29 XIIth | Saturday | 1 Ist | 14 VIIth | 29 VIth | 33 yrs. 177d. |
| | Saturday | 18 April | 1 Ist | Sunday | 2 ,, | 15 ,, | 1 VIIth | ,, 178 |
| | Sunday | 19 April | 2 ,, | Monday | 3 ,, | 16 ,, | 2 ,, | ,, 179 |
| Lazarus raised | Monday | 20 April | 3 ,, | Tuesday | 4 ,, | 17 ,, | 3 ,, | ,, 180 |
| | Tuesday | 21 April | 4 ,, | Wednesday | 5 ,, | 18 ,, | 4 ,, | ,, 181 |
| | Wednesday | 22 April | 5 ,, | Thursday | 6 ,, | 19 ,, | 5 ,, | ,, 182 |
| | Thursday | 23 April | 6 ,, | Friday | 7 ,, | 20 ,, | 6 ,, | ,, 183 |
| | Friday | 24 April | 7 ,, | Saturday | 8 ,, | 21 ,, | 7 ,, | ,, 184 |
| The Lord in Jericho | Saturday | 25 April | 8 ,, | Sunday | 9 ,, | 22 ,, | 8 ,, | ,, 185 |
| Mary anoints the Lord in Bethany | Sunday (1) | 26 April | 9 ,, | Monday | 10 ,, | 23 ,, | 9 ,, | ,, 186 |
| Triumphal Entry into Jerusalem | Monday (2) | 27 April | 10 ,, | Tuesday | 11 ,, | 24 | 10 ,, | ,, 187 |
| THE "SIX DAYS BEFORE THE PASSOVER" (John XII, 1) | Tuesday (3) | 28 April | 11 ,, | Wednesday | 12 ,, | 25 ,, | 11 ,, | ,, 188 |
| | Wednesday (4) | 29 April | 12 ,, | Thursday | 13 ,, | 26 ,, | 12 ,, | ,, 189 |
| The Last Passover | Thursday (5) | 30 April | 13 ,, | Friday | 14 ,, | 27 ,, | 13 ,, | ,, 190 |
| The Lord Crucified | Friday (6) | 1 May | 14 ,, | SABBATH | 15 ,, | 28 ,, | 14 ,, | ,, 191 |
| | Saturday | 2 May | 15 ,, | NOT RECKONED | | 29 ,, | 15 ,, | ,, 192 |
| Midnight—Jesus rises | Sunday | 3 May | 16 ,, | NOT RECKONED | | 30 ,, | 16 ,, | ,, 193 |
| "First (day) of the sabbaths" | Monday | 4 May | 17 ,, | Sunday | 16 ,, | 1 VIIIth | 17 ,, | ,, 194 |
| | Tuesday | 5 May | 18 ,, | Monday | 17 ,, | 2 ,, | 18 ,, | ,, 195 |
| "AFTER EIGHT DAYS" (John XX, 26) | Wednesday | 6 May | 19 ,, | Tuesday | 18 ,, | 3 ,, | 19 ,, | ,, 196 |
| | Thursday | 7 May | 20 ,, | Wednesday | 19 ,, | 4 ,, | 20 ,, | ,, 197 |
| | Friday | 8 May | 21 ,, | Thursday | 20 ,, | 5 ,, | 21 ,, | ,, 198 |
| | Saturday | 9 May | 22 ,, | Friday | 21 ,, | 6 ,, | 22 ,, | ,, 199 |
| | Sunday | 10 May | 23 ,, | Saturday | 22 ,, | 7 ,, | 23 ,, | ,, 200 |
| | Monday | 11 May | 24 ,, | Sunday | 23 ,, | 8 ,, | 24 ,, | ,, 201 |
| The Lord appears, Thomas present | Tuesday | 12 May | 25 ,, | Monday | 24 ,, | 9 ,, | 25 ,, | ,, 202 |
| The Fishing Episode of John XXI | Monday | 18 May | 1 IInd | Sunday | 30 ,, | 15 ,, | VIIITH | ,, 208 |
| The Ascension | SABBATH | 13 June | 27 ,, | Friday | 26 IInd | 12 IXTH | 27 ,, | 33 yrs. 233d. |
| Jews' Pentecost | Sunday | 21 June | 6 IIIrd | Saturday | 5 IIIrd | 20 ,, | 6 IXTH | |
| Descent of the Holy Spirit | Monday | 22 June | 7 ,, | Sunday | 6 ,, | 21 ,, | 7 ,, | |

The dates in Solar Months enclosed in boxes are those either named or traceable in the Bible. Where dates in other Calendars are so enclosed it is to emphasize their Biblical significance in that series of years.

# CHAPTER FOURTEEN

## THE PATHWAY ON EARTH OF OUR LORD AND SAVIOUR JESUS CHRIST DRAWS TO ITS CLOSE

HE ARRIVES AT BETHANY IN THE EARLY EVENING OF SUNDAY, 26TH APRIL, WHICH WAS "SIX DAYS BEFORE THE PASSOVER" OF THE JEWS AT WHICH HE LAID DOWN HIS LIFE.

THE THREEFOLD SIGNIFICANCE ATTACHING TO THE DATE OF 26TH APRIL A.D. 33 SHEDS A NEW AND BRILLIANT LIGHT UPON MARY'S ACT IN ANOINTING OUR LORD DURING THE SUPPER AT BETHANY.

AN OUTLINE OF EVENTS IN THE FOUR UNRECKONED DAYS – 26TH TO 30TH APRIL – BETWEEN MARY'S ANOINTING OF OUR LORD AS THE ANTITYPICAL PASCHAL LAMB AND THE PASSOVER OF JEHOVAH WHICH HE AND HIS DISCIPLES KEPT ON THE NIGHT BEFORE HIS CRUCIFIXION.

OUR LORD'S TRIUMPHAL ENTRY INTO JERUSALEM ON MONDAY, 27TH APRIL (NISAN 10TH), A.D. 33.

Read John XII, Matthew XXI to XXVI, 19, Mark XI to XIV, 16, and Luke XIX, 28 to XXII, 13.

On 30th April A.D. 33 – the day before His death – the age of our Lord Jesus Christ was 32 Solar years and 183 days or 33 Bible years and 189 days.

### PART I

TO FOLLOW our Lord Jesus Christ, that is, to be able to trace His steps during the last few days of His pathway on earth, with the accuracy now made possible by a correct understanding of the Scriptures, is a high and holy privilege which may now be entered upon by all who love Him sufficiently to be willing to apply their minds and their hearts in seeking to possess for themselves the true facts which have lain concealed beneath the surface of the Divine Records for 1,800 years.

If ever there was a time when we should advisedly remove our shoes from off our feet, as did Moses and Joshua on certain occasions, it is when we are tracing out the holy footsteps of the Son of God as He drew near to the Supreme Climax of His life on the earth in order to accomplish the Redemption of the human race, as foretold in the Garden of Eden at the time when "by one man sin entered into the world, and death by sin" (Rom. V, 12). In this connection, we may say that we are about to set forth facts from Holy Scripture which reveal a direct chronological relationship between events at the Bethany Supper and events in the Garden of Eden, as narrated in the third chapter of Genesis.

Our Lord and His disciples left Jericho at the close of the Sabbath which He had spent in the house of Zacchaeus. They arrived at Bethany – a distance of about 18 miles – in time for the evening meal on Sunday 26th April. We are wholly indebted to the Apostle John for this information which is gleaned from his statement with which the 12th chapter opens:

> "Then Jesus six days before the passover came to Bethany, where Lazarus was which had been dead, whom He raised from the dead. There they made Him a supper."

This reference to the "six days before the passover" is of the utmost importance as without it we should have no knowledge of when the Lord reached Bethany or when Mary anointed Him. Matthew (XXVI) and Mark (XIV), for the most excellent reason, place the Bethany Supper just before the last Passover. Luke makes no mention of it.

All Bible statements on time are inclusive unless the wording or context indicates otherwise. Consequently, these "six days before the passover" include the Sunday on which our Lord arrived at Bethany, the other five days being Monday, Tuesday, Wednesday, Thursday and Friday. This Friday was "the day of the preparation" for the Jews' Passover and the one in which our Lord was crucified. That John is referring to the Jews' Passover and not that of Jehovah, which our Lord took with

His disciples on the previous evening – Thursday – is proved by His reference to it just previously in Chapter XI, 55.

The Bible, as we shall learn, had a very vital reason for making it absolutely clear to all that our blessed Lord, with His disciples, reached Bethany during the latter part of Sunday, 26th April, and that the Supper at which Mary anointed Him was on that day between the hours of 3 P.M. and 6 P.M. John, by his statement about the "six days", lifts this point out of the realm of dispute unless anyone is willing to deny that our Lord died on a Friday, to do which would be to deny one of the most patently clear and unqualified statements in the Bible (see Mark XV, 42 and John XIX, 31).

Before proceeding we will ask our readers to turn to the Chart of the Five Calendars and carefully note these "six days" (which are numbered in brackets after the Solar month date) starting with Sunday, 26th April, which it will be seen and noted was the 10th day of the 1st month – Nisan – in the Divine Calendar, and the 9th day of the 7th month – Tishri – in the Years as measured from our Lord's Birth. Both these dates add an immense significance to the act of Mary in anointing our Lord.

With His perfect knowledge of the Pattern of Time ordained for Him by His God and Father, our Lord directed His steps to Bethany so as to be available there *at that time and on that day* because it had a THREE-FOLD CHRONOLOGICAL significance of such importance that it must be marked by an act which would be remembered and told out "wheresoever this gospel shall be preached throughout the whole world".

"There they made Him a supper"
John XII, 2.

We shall not dwell at any length upon the details of the Supper "they" made for our Lord at Bethany. The Bible gives us three accounts which may be read and pondered over. Matthew and Mark inform us that the Supper took place "in the house of Simon the leper". This fact, coupled with John's statement that "they made Him a supper", as well as his references to the presence of Martha, Mary and Lazarus, imply that it was in the nature of a communal occasion arranged by several in Bethany and that Simon's house was chosen because of its suitability for the purpose. Leprosy being in the Bible a type of sin, it must have been a part of the Divine plan that the Lord's anointing for death at this momentous point of time should take place in the house of one who typifies a forgiven sinner. Doubtless the Lord had cleansed Simon who probably was the leper mentioned in the first three Gospels as having been cleansed. It has been suggested with some reason that Matthew and Mark omit reference to Martha, Mary and Lazarus because they were living at the time when their Gospels were written and because Lazarus had earned the hatred of the Jews as the result of his resurrection which became the cause of many believing on Jesus (John XII, 10 and 11).

John's account of the anointing of our Lord Jesus Christ is as follows (XII, 3):

> "Then took Mary a pound of ointment of spikenard, very costly, and anointed the feet of Jesus, and wiped His feet with her hair: and the house was filled with the odour of the ointment."

Matthew and Mark refer to the fact that Mary poured the ointment "on His head". This, with John's statement that she anointed "the feet of Jesus", allows us to know that Mary anointed both His head and His feet. This is confirmed by our Lord's own words, "she hath poured this ointment on My body" (Matthew XXVI, 12).

Very much has rightly been made of Mary's whole-hearted and self-sacrificing devotion to our Lord Jesus Christ as evidenced by the costliness of the spikenard she used with which to anoint Him. We do not, however, hear so much about her high spiritual intelligence which, in the light of the facts we are about to set forth, must have equalled her devotion. We do not know how often she sat, learner-wise, at Jesus' feet but it must have been a frequent experience as He so often visited Bethany and loved each member of Martha's household (John XI, 5). It is not easy to assess the extent of Mary's understanding of the importance of the occasion and of the date on which she expended her sacrificial offering, but certain facts are quite clear. Let us examine these.

MARY'S ACT OF ANOINTING OUR LORD TOOK PLACE IN THE DIVINE CALENDAR ON THE 10TH DAY OF THE 1ST MONTH – THE DAY WHEN THE PASCHAL LAMBS WERE SET APART FOR DEATH AT THE PASSOVER FOUR DAYS THEREAFTER, I.E., ON THE 14TH OF THE 1ST MONTH.

(See Exodus XII, 3 to 6, and Calendar Chart)

John the Baptist had borne powerful witness to the fact that our Lord Jesus Christ was "the Lamb of God, which taketh away the sin of the world", that is, the Antitypical Paschal Lamb (John I, 29). This Mary knew right well. She also knew that the Lord had repeatedly announced that He was on the way to Jerusalem to suffer and die (Mark X, 32 to 34).

Like the Twelve Apostles, Mary also knew that the Lord would take the Passover on the day before the Jews took their Passover (Matthew XXVI, 17, etc.). In the year A.D. 33 the Jews' Passover was on Friday, 1st May. Therefore, Jehovah's Passover would be on Thursday, 30th April, four days after the anointing. This was the date on which the Lord at the close of the day sat down with the Twelve and took what is known as the Last Supper.

As the Lord was now to fulfil a most vital aspect of His mission to earth by taking His place as the Antitypical Passover Lamb of God's providing, nothing in the universe was so important as that someone in Israel on the 10th day of the 1st month in the Divine Calendar should set Him apart as such for death on the 14th day thereof. Here was a Divine requirement and without a doubt the Spirit of God, taking advantage of her devotion, moved Mary of Bethany to fulfil it by being the one in Israel to set the Lord apart for death as "the Lamb of God" Who, four days hence, would offer Himself up to take away the sin of the world.

## A VITAL PRINCIPLE EXPLAINED

As our theme is one of infinite solemnity and of measureless importance to all those whose eternal hopes rest on the Death and Resurrection of our Lord Jesus Christ, it is greatly to be desired that all should comprehend the whole truth, as set forth in Holy Scripture, concerning these great Events.

We have just shown from the facts given in the Bible that Mary of Bethany by her act of anointing our Lord set Him apart as the Paschal Lamb of God on the 10th day of the 1st month – our 26th April. Exactly FOUR DAYS later, at the close of the 14th day of the 1st month – our 30th April – at about 6 P.M., when the Passover Lambs were slain, our Lord sat down with His twelve disciples to eat the Passover. If this type from Exodus XII had been *literally* fulfilled, our Lord would have had to die at the end of these Four Days instead of partaking of the Passover Supper with His disciples. It is absolutely essential to see that in principle, that is, "in a figure", He did so die, else how could He, in instituting the Memorial Supper, say to the disciples, "Take, eat; this is My body . . . this is My blood of the new testament (covenant), which is shed for many for the remission of sins" (Matt. XXVI, 26 to 28)? Our Lord's words implied that He had already been sacrificed as the Antitypical Passover Lamb. As this fact cannot be evaded, we must seek an explanation.

The death of our Lord Jesus Christ was prefigured in all the sacrificial Offerings of the Levitical economy, such as the Paschal Offering, the Burnt Offering, the Meal Offering, the Sin Offering and the Trespass Offering, etc., etc. It will be manifest to all that as our Lord could, in the physical sense, ONLY DIE ONCE, only one of these many prefigurements of His sacrificial death could have A LITERAL FULFILMENT. This, as we will presently explain, was as the Antitype of the SIN-OFFERING (Leviticus IV), for it was as such that our Lord actually died "without the camp" at 3 P.M. on Friday, 1st May, in A.D. 33.

What then of the other typical sacrificial Offerings? How were they fulfilled in the antitypical sense? Each of these, including the Paschal Offering which we are now considering, was fulfilled in a figurative sense by our Lord Jesus Christ offering Himself to God as such *at the time and in the manner* prescribed by the terms of the type, as given in Holy Scripture. The fact that physical death did not take place with our Lord except as the Antitype of the Sin-Offering does not detract one iota from the value in God's sight of those offerings of Himself which were figurative fulfilments of other types, all of which preceded, and were anticipative of, His actual death on Calvary's Tree.

**THE ANOINTING OF OUR LORD BY MARY OF BETHANY TOOK PLACE EXACTLY FOUR "DAYS" OF A THOUSAND YEARS EACH FROM THE FALL OF ADAM WHEN THE LORD GOD FIRST MADE PROMISE OF A REDEEMER IN THE GARDEN OF EDEN.**

(Genesis III, 15 and II Peter III, 8)

We have shown that Sunday, 26th April A.D. 33, when the Lord was anointed during the Bethany Supper, was the 10th day of the 1st month in the Divine Calendar and that in accordance with the type our Lord was then set apart for death as the Antitypical Paschal Lamb at the end of Four Days, that is, in the evening of the 14th of the 1st month, our 30th April. We have seen that figuratively He did die and that He addressed His disciples as One Who in reality had died. Little though we may be able to enter into it because of our ignorance of God's ways, we must at least remember that the Apostle Paul enunciated a Divine principle when he stated that God "calleth those things which be not as though they were" (Rom. IV, 17).

In the Summary of Facts (Paragraph 16) at the beginning of this Treatise, we give particulars of the 6,000 Years which form the Chronology of Redemption. This series of years, which runs right through the Bible and will terminate with the setting up of the Kingdom, began on the day after the Fall of Adam when God made promise of the coming of One Who would redeem our race. We have mentioned frequently that the 4 days in every Redemption Year during which the Passover lambs were in keeping, namely, the 10th to the 14th of the 1st month, are a type of the 4,000 years between the Fall of Adam and the death (i.e. "in a figure") of our Lord as the Antitypical Paschal Lamb.

*It is a solemn yet wondrous fact that in the Chronology of Redemption, 4,000 years had elapsed from the Fall of Adam to the day and the hour when the Supper at Bethany took place and when Mary anointed our Lord and set Him apart for death as the Antitypical Paschal Lamb four literal days thereafter.*

These 4,000 years in Redemption Chronology must end on the 10th day of the 1st month, as the following 4 days in all such years were unreckoned and formed no part of the year. In effect, this meant that the end of the 10th day when the lambs were set apart and the end of the 14th day when they were sacrificed were viewed as the same point of time. Hence it is true to say that the 4,000 Years of Redemption terminated both at the time of Mary's anointing and four days later at the hour of 6 P.M. when our Lord figuratively died as the Antitypical Paschal Lamb.

Now it is in order to demonstrate that time is not reckoned by God between Mary's anointing of our Lord and the last Passover Supper, at which "in a figure" He died, that Matthew (XXVI) and Mark (XIV) both record the anointing as if it took place immediately before the last Passover, when in fact, as John reveals, it took place a full four days previously.

In our former Treatise, *The World in Liquidation*, we show that the Bible reveals with undeniable clarity that in the Chronology of Redemption there were 2,000 years from Adam to the Birth of Abram and 2,000 years from Abram to 26th April A.D. 33 – making a total of 4,000 years. The latter 2,000 years was divided as follows. From Abram to the Exodus, 500 years – the Exodus to the Dedication of Solomon's Temple, 500 years – the Dedication to Nehemiah's return to rebuild Jerusalem, 500 years and from Nehemiah to 26th April A.D. 33, 500 years.

We have said enough to show that the Bethany Supper witnessed the termination of this immensely important predetermined era of 4,000 years between the Fall of Adam and the presentation of Himself for death by our Lord Jesus Christ as the Lamb of God Who, in deep humility, allows Himself to be set apart as such by Mary's anointing of His body on the 10th day of the 1st month, according to the type, and four days before His death. What a confirmation this fact receives in Mark's quotation of our Lord's reference to Mary's act, which is as follows: "She is come aforehand to anoint My body to the burying" (XIV, 8). This statement envisages a future purpose, namely, the Lord's death after the four days.

We can but call attention to the deep significance to be found in the fact that it was a woman who was chosen of God to set the Lord apart for death as our Redeemer at the end of these 4,000 years which began with the act of another woman – Eve – who "being deceived was in the transgression" which involved our whole race in ruin and made the coming of a Redeemer our one and only hope of salvation and restoration.

No wonder our Lord commanded that Mary's act should be recounted "wheresoever this gospel shall be preached in the whole world . . . for a memorial of her" (Matt. XXVI, 13).

## SUNDAY, 26TH APRIL A.D. 33, BETWEEN THE HOURS OF 3 P.M. AND 6 P.M., WAS ALSO THE OPENING OF THE DAY OF ATONEMENT IN THE CALENDAR BASED UPON OUR LORD'S PERSONAL CHRONOLOGY AS MEASURED FROM HIS BIRTH.

We must now briefly refer to this third chronological marking of the Bethany Supper and Mary's act of anointing our Lord. If reference is made to the Chart of the Five Calendars, it will be seen that 26th April was the 9th day of the 7th month in our Lord's years as measured from His birth.

In Leviticus XXIII, 26 to 32, we are informed that the Day of Atonement began at even on the 9th day of the 7th month and continued until even on the 10th day. "Even" in each Bible day began at 3 P.M. and lasted until 6 P.M. or sundown.

It is therefore clear that the three hours – 3 P.M. to 6 P.M. – during which the Bethany Supper took place was the opening of the Day of Atonement in the calendar of our Lord's years as measured from His birth. This being so, it becomes self-evident that our Lord must then have presented Himself before God as the Antitype of the Offerings of the Day of Atonement, as set forth in Leviticus XVI. In other words, we have here another solemn expression of the Lord dying "in a figure" both as the Sin Offering and the Burnt Offering of the Day of Atonement.

This fact sheds yet further light on the significance of Mary's act. It was not a question here of her anticipating our Lord's death four days hence, but of viewing Him as having already died as the Antitype of the sacrificial Offerings of the Day of Atonement. That this was so is made perfectly clear from the statements, recorded by both Matthew and John, uttered by our Lord Jesus Christ in defence of Mary's act when she is ignorantly accused of wanton waste by Judas and others. In the Matthew record our Lord says, "In that she hath poured this ointment on My body, she did it for My burial" (XXVI, 12). The Greek word translated "burial" signifies "embalming".

In John's record we find these words, "Let her alone: against (lit. unto) the day of My burying (lit. embalming) hath she kept this" (XII, 7 and cf. Septuagint Trans. of Genesis L, 2).

Both of these statements exclude the thought of anticipative action, such as is indicated by Mark in the use of the word "aforehand", and fix our attention on the fact that the Lord viewed Mary's act as the embalming of a dead body. That is, He viewed Himself as having died "in a figure" as the Antitype both of the Sin Offering and the Burnt Offering of the Day of Atonement. The importance of this aspect of Mary's act no one but the Lord Himself can estimate. If these Antitypes had not then been fulfilled, they would have had to remain unfulfilled for ever. But as it is, they were fulfilled in the figurative sense on the appointed Day of Atonement and as such they were accepted by God the Father Who had foreplanned this occasion in its every detail.

We have yet to set forth one further chronological marking of the day when Mary anointed our Lord Jesus Christ.

## 26TH APRIL A.D. 33, WAS 1,300 DAYS FROM 5TH OCTOBER A.D. 29, WHEN OUR LORD WAS BAPTIZED IN THE JORDAN BY JOHN THE BAPTIST.

By now all will have realized the tremendous importance of the apparently simple words with which John XII opens – "Then Jesus six days before the passover came to Bethany". We have already seen that the day referred to by John in this statement has both a spiritual and chronological significance almost unequalled in the whole Bible. There is yet a fourth marking which is of profound and solemn interest because it embraces the whole period of our Lord's public life from His Baptism.

In Chapter IV of this Treatise, when writing on the Saviour's baptism, we pointed out that it was separated by exactly 1,300 Days from His anointing by Mary of Bethany on 26th April A.D. 33. What is so wonderful to behold in this design is that both at the beginning and end of these 1,300 days was a Day of Atonement. Our Lord, as we have shown from the Scriptures, was baptized by John on Israel's Day of Atonement in A.D. 29 – our 5th October and their 10th of the 7th month. The anointing by Mary we have just revealed was also at the opening of the Day of Atonement in our Lord's personal years.

The number "13" is indelibly associated with Atonement because it stands out in the Bible as the symbol of sin and rebellion against God; that which, apart from ATONEMENT, must lead to the eternal banishment of the sinner from God. The number "13" marks Christ and His work, whenever He is seen as the sinner's Substitute, as accomplishing ATONEMENT FOR SIN.

We pointed out in Chapter IV that the numerical value of our Lord's Names in the Old Testament – Jehovah, Adonai, Ha-Elohim and Messiah – all have "13" as their main factor. What is more remarkable still is that the Name given to our Lord in His humiliation and which in mockery formed part of Pilate's superscription on the Cross – "JESUS OF NAZARETH" – has a numerical value of 2197 which is 13×13×13. By this design God intends to convey to man that our Lord, in order to redeem us, had to be "NUMBERED WITH THE TRANSGRESSORS". The application of the number "13" to the sinless Son of God is therefore the proof of His absolute identification with our fallen race. Only by being our Kinsman could He be our REDEEMER (Leviticus XXV, 48, 49, Galatians IV, 4, 5, and Hebrews II, 14).

But not only is "13" associated with man viewed as a rebel against God, it is also associated with Satan, both as the instigator of man's rebellion and as the expression of his own rebellion as described in Ezekiel XXVIII and Isaiah XIV. The Greek words translated "called the Devil, and Satan", in Revelation XII, 9, have a numerical value of 2197 which, like that of "Jesus of Nazareth", is composed of 13×13×13 (see *Spiritual Arithmetic* by R. T. Naish). The "serpent of brass" which Moses lifted up is a type of our Lord Jesus Christ as the One Whom God "made to be sin for us" in order that He might "through death . . . destroy . . . the devil" in whom sin originated (Ezekiel XXVIII, 15 and 16) and by whose lies Eve, "the mother of all living", was deceived and led into transgression (see Numbers XXI, 9, John III, 14 and Hebrews II, 14 and 15).

Without developing this extremely solemn theme any further, it will be appreciated from what we have stated that it was none other than God Himself Who designed that the whole pathway of our Lord in His public life from His baptism (which in one aspect was itself an act of identification with our sinful race) to His being set aside for death as the Antitype of the Paschal Offering, should cover a period of 1,300 days in order to express the fact that throughout this period He had taken the place of being our Kinsman, thus identifying Himself with all in us which finds its symbolism in the number "Thirteen".

We may mention before passing on that the whole 47 days (7+40) from our Lord's Baptism to His emergence from the Forty Days of Temptation are separated by exactly 1,300 days from the 47 days which began with the anointing by Mary of Bethany and ended with the Ascension into Heaven. Thus the 40 Days of Temptation were separated by exactly 1,300 days from the 40 Days of our Lord's Resurrection Ministry.

| | | | |
|---|---|---|---|
| *A.D.* 29 | | | *A.D.* 33 |
| Oct. 5th | | | 26th-27th April (evening) |
| 7 days | | | 7 days |
| 12th Oct. | 47 DAYS | 1,300 DAYS | 3rd-4th May (midnight) |
| 40 days | | | 40 days |
| 21st Nov. | | | 13th June (morning) |

It is when we behold a design such as these 1,300 days linking the beginning of our Lord's public life with the end that we realize the infallible accuracy with which it has pleased God to record in the Scriptures the Pattern of Time by which the pathway of our Lord Jesus Christ on the earth was regulated. Could anyone possibly doubt the accuracy of the dates we have given from the Scriptures? Let it be understood that if one date were in error the whole plan would be vitiated because it would disjoint every other date. All rests upon the one great fact that our blessed Lord and Master was born of the Virgin Mary into this world on Friday, 29th October 1 B.C., the starting date of the "thirty years" of Luke III, 23. May all Christendom take account of this fact, and cease any longer to honour a date (25th December) which has no connection whatsoever with our Lord Jesus Christ, but which has a very direct connection with heathenism.

# PART II

## FIVE DAYS BEFORE THE JEWS' PASSOVER OUR LORD MAKES A ROYAL ENTRY INTO JERUSALEM IN FULFILMENT OF THE PROPHECY OF ZECHARIAH IX, 9

"Behold, thy King cometh unto thee"

MONDAY – APRIL 27TH, A.D. 33 – ISRAEL'S 10TH OF THE 1ST MONTH

Read Matthew XXI, Mark XI, Luke XIX and John XII

WE ARE indebted exclusively to the Gospel by John for the knowledge that our Lord made His Royal Entry into Jerusalem "on the next day" to the Supper at Bethany (XII, 12) which took place on Sunday evening, 26th April. The common notion that the Triumphal Entry was on a Sunday – the anniversary of which is called "Palm Sunday" – is therefore without substance. John's statement that it was "on the next day" after that of the Bethany Supper, which was "six days before the passover", is final in its authority. Its date in solar terms was therefore Monday, 27th April.

In the Jews' calendar, the Triumphal Entry into Jerusalem was on the 10th of Nisan which, after the Babylonian Captivity, was the name of the first month of their Sacred year. It was notable as the day when the Passover lambs were set apart for death, and in the Apocalypse our Lord as reigning is referred to many times as THE LAMB. Furthermore, it had a marked place in Israel's history as that on which Joshua led this people and their armies up out of the Jordan when they entered the Promised Land (Joshua IV, 19) and as that on which Ezekiel received his wonderful vision of the Millennial Temple (Ezek. XL, 1). That our Lord chose this day upon which to make His Royal Entry into Jerusalem, in fulfilment of the Prophecy of Zechariah, adds immeasurably to its great historic importance.

We shall not dwell upon the details of this notable occasion when our Lord, as Israel's King and Messiah, officially presents Himself to His people. Each of the four Gospels contains a full account of it and, taken together, these form a comprehensive setting-forth of the whole wonderful incident.

Trees in the Bible are symbolic of the nations. Luke records that in giving His parable of the Fig Tree in the Olivet Discourse our Lord began, "Behold the fig-tree, and all the trees" (XXI, 29). The "fig tree" being symbolic of Israel, "all the trees" must be symbolic of the other nations and presumably those contiguous to Israel. The branches of "palm trees" (John XII, 13) and other trees which the people "strawed" in our Lord's path and over which He rode essentially typify the Gentile nations which will be forcibly subjected to His rule when He sets up His Kingdom (see Daniel II, 44, 45 and Rev. XIX, 15).

It will be noted that there is no mention in any of the Four Gospels of the setting apart of lambs for the Jews' Passover, even though it was the 10th day of their 1st month.

It is most important to realize that our Lord's act in sending His disciples to fetch the ass and the colt was in order that He might officially present Himself to the nation of Israel as their King, in exact accord with the terms of the prophecy of Zechariah IX, 9, which He thereby fulfilled to the letter. The rulers of the guilty nation were thus forced to make a final decision concerning the One Whose advent in Jerusalem, riding upon an ass in lowly meekness, exactly as foretold, they had just witnessed. Furthermore, the intense discomfort of the rulers in Jerusalem was added to by the fact that the people, knowing of the resurrection of Lazarus (John XII, 18), acclaimed our Lord with rejoicing and accorded to Him His full Messianic rights as they cried out, "Hosanna to the Son of David: Blessed is He that cometh in the Name of the Lord; Hosanna in the Highest" (Matt. XXI, 8, 9 and Psalm CXVIII, 26).

There is another very important aspect of our Lord's action in presenting Himself in Jerusalem as Israel's King and Messiah exactly four days before His death. We know from Acts IV, 25 and 26 that the Second Psalm had a positive fulfilment when the Lord was rejected at the time of His trial and condemnation. It is in the Second Psalm that God declares:

> "Yet have I set My King upon My holy hill of Zion" (verse 6).

This was fulfilled in a very real, though tentative, way when our Lord made His Royal Entry into Jerusalem on Monday, 27th April – the Jews' 10th of Nisan. Our Lord was the Son of

David and God's Anointed King, and *He was present in Jerusalem as such for four whole days*, and all His actions were in keeping with the status granted to Him of God, irrespective of the fact that this was denied to Him by those whose rightful King He was. His cleansing of the Temple, His symbolic rejection of Israel for the age in the cursing of the Fig Tree, His exposure of the Pharisees, Sadducees and Herodians who sought to entrap Him with questions, and His long pronouncement of woes on "scribes and Pharisees, hypocrites", were all in keeping with His position as God's anointed King on His "holy hill of Zion".

Exactly four days (from Monday morning to Friday morning) after our Lord entered into Jerusalem as King, He is to be seen being led out of Jerusalem to be crucified as a convicted felon in company with two notorious malefactors – the Jewish rulers having sealed their rejection of Him by coercing their Roman overlords into pronouncing Him guilty after they had proved Him to be innocent of all their charges.

This is not the occasion to give a detailed exposition of the Holy Scriptures which relate to events in the Four Days – 27th April to 1st May – during which our Lord was God's King in Zion, but we must emphasize that it was an absolutely unique period of time in the history of the world. Man may not have recognized as King the meek and lowly One Who rode into Jerusalem on an ass and remained in or about the Holy City for Four Days, but God so recognized Him; and had He been received as such by official Jewry He could and would have subjected the whole world to His sway there and then. Quite astonishing evidence has come to light about God's attitude to these Four Days, for when measuring certain chronological eras related to Gentile Governmental Supremacy of the earth (that which began after the fall of the Kingdom of Judah) we discovered that He excludes them from all such measurements. This fact affords perfect proof that during these Four Days when our Lord was King on "His holy hill of Zion", Gentile governmental domination of the earth was suspended by God. It could not be otherwise as He had disowned, in the person of Nebuchadnezzar, Gentile rule of the earth (see Daniel IV). In effect, this meant that while allowing it to run its course, He could have no association with it. Therefore, when our Lord was King in Jerusalem for Four Days, God recognized no other Governmental Supremacy on the earth than that of His King. This is one of many occasions on which God expresses Himself on a moral issue by means of the time factors of His Word. Neither is the fact to be forgotten that immediately these Four Days had elapsed, Gentile rule distinguished itself by the greatest perversion of Justice in its long and awful history. It condemned the Son of God to death knowing Him to be guiltless.

"Then came there a Voice from Heaven"
(John XII, 28)

This Jewish 10th of Nisan, our 27th April A.D. 33, was not alone marked by our Lord's Royal Entry into Jerusalem for, later in the day, and for the third time in our Lord's life, the Voice of God is heard speaking out of Heaven.

On learning that there are Greeks, that is, Gentiles, who have declared their desire to see Him (John XII, 20), our Lord discourses in most solemn terms concerning His approaching death. Rejected as Messiah by Israel, He must now become God's Salvation to the end of the earth (Isaiah XLIX, 5 and 6), but this was not possible except He took His place as the true corn of wheat and fell into the ground and died. For man in his fallen state and with a corrupt nature He could do nothing, as four thousand years of human history had proved. Man must be born of the Spirit and receive a new nature before he could be changed. That new nature our Lord could only impart by union with Himself after He had risen from the dead. All who then received Him would become partakers of the Divine nature and these would constitute the "much fruit" resulting from His death.

Had He refused to die, He would have returned to Heaven alone with Israel ungathered and the Gentiles without hope of salvation. But our Lord was here to glorify God and not to please Himself in the way common to man. Nevertheless, the burden upon Him was great and He declares, "Now is My soul troubled; and what shall I say? Father, save Me from this hour: but for this cause came I unto this hour" (XII, 27). The occasion becomes a sort of preliminary to the conflict in Gethsemane. Could He lose sight of His objective in coming into the world? Never. So He at once declares, "Father, glorify Thy Name". Had He ever failed to glorify His Father's Name? Never once in all the thirty-three years of His life on the earth. Who knew this as did His Father in Heaven? Therefore, at once God the Father responds to the deep desire of the Son and His Voice is heard out of Heaven to say, "I have both glorified it, and will glorify it again".

Our Lord immediately bears witness to the fact that God had made this open communication for the sake of those who heard it, and not for His own sake. Without a doubt, God was referring in the first place to the resurrection of Lazarus, whose sickness and death the Lord had said was "for the glory of God" (XI, 4); and in the second place to our Lord's own coming resurrection expressed by the words "will glorify it again". God's glory could alone be manifested by that which triumphed over death which, as the result of sin, came into the world through the first man, Adam, and marred that which had been created for His glory. In resurrection our Lord would become Head of the New Creation by which God's glory, in the ultimate, would be eternally maintained throughout the Universe (see I Corinth. XV, 20 to 28).

It is to be noted that on this occasion our Lord's words, "Now is the judgment of this world: now shall the prince of this world be cast out", are a direct reference to His death on the Cross when He was to be "lifted up from the earth" (XII, 31, 32). The time when He uttered these words was exactly four days before His death upon the Cross. In Israel's calendar these four days between the 10th day of the 1st month and the 14th when our Lord was crucified are unreckoned for reasons we have already fully explained. Our Lord appears, therefore, to have spoken as if no time existed between when they were uttered and His death four days later by which the world came under judgment and its prince – Satan – was cast out and his power for ever annulled (see Heb. II, 14).

This most notable day – our Monday, 27th April and Israel's 10th day of the 1st month – ended by our Lord and His disciples at "eventide" withdrawing to Bethany (Mark XI, 11). There was no royal palace in Jerusalem for the King of Israel to reside in, but at Bethany there were loyal and loving hearts which always welcomed Him into their humble dwellings.

# PART III

# FOUR DAYS BEFORE THE JEWS' PASSOVER OUR LORD JESUS CHRIST CLEANSES THE TEMPLE FOR THE SECOND TIME

## THE FIG TREE CURSED FOR THE AGE

TUESDAY, 28TH APRIL A.D. 33, ISRAEL'S 11TH OF NISAN

Read Matthew XXI, 12 to 19; Mark XI, 12 to 19 and Luke XIX, 45 to 48.

IT IS INDEED beautiful to behold the clear manner in which the Gospels account for each day to our Lord's death from the beginning of the "six days before the passover" of the Jews, named in John XII, 1.

In Mark XI, 12, we read, "And on the morrow, when they were come from Bethany. . . ." The "morrow" after the day of the Triumphal Entry was Tuesday, 28th April – the Jews' 11th of Nisan.

On the way back to Jerusalem the Lord, being hungry, seeks fruit from a fig tree. "When He came to it, He found nothing but leaves; for the time of figs was not yet." Our Lord addresses the fig tree with the words, "No man eat fruit of thee hereafter for ever". The words "for ever" should have been translated "to the age".

Our Lord's action, though symbolic, is of course an official act of judgment upon the Jewish nation typified by the fig tree. It was a most solemn occasion as it revealed that the Jewish people were to be under judgment during the coming age which is called "the times of the Gentiles", and that from God's point of view they would remain barren and without fruit, being cast out of their Promised Land and "led away captive into all nations" (Luke XXI, 24).

On entering Jerusalem and the Temple our Lord Jesus Christ for the second time asserts His Messianic authority by cleansing His Father's House – the Temple. We read, He "began to cast out them that sold and bought in the temple, and overthrew the tables of the money-changers, and the seats of them that sold doves". He then levels a fearful indictment against the Jewish rulers in which He declares, "Is it not written, My House shall be called of all nations the house of prayer? but ye have made it a den of thieves" (Mark XI, 17). Our Lord's words are more severe in their condemnation than those He used in performing the same solemn task when He first entered Jerusalem for the Passover of A.D. 30, as recorded in John II, almost exactly 3 years previously. On each occasion this cleansing of the Temple immediately followed an official presentation of Himself to the Jewish nation as their Messiah.

Having with righteous indignation performed His judicial act of exposing the failure of official Jewry to maintain the honour and sacredness of His Father's House, our Lord turns again to works of mercy and grace, for we are told by Matthew that "the blind and the lame came to Him in the temple; and He healed them" (XXI, 14). Furthermore, children, who doubtless the previous day had heard Israel's King acclaimed with Hosannas as He rode into Jerusalem, lifted up their voices in the Temple crying, "Hosanna to the Son of David". To the embittered "chief priests and scribes" who objected to His being so acclaimed our Lord quotes the Eighth Psalm, saying, "Have ye never read, Out of the mouth of babes and sucklings Thou hast perfected praise?"

"And when even was come, He went out of the city" (Mark XI, 19). So ended another of the days in which God's King was to be seen by all on His holy hill of Zion.

# PART IV

# THREE DAYS BEFORE THE JEWS' PASSOVER OUR LORD JESUS CHRIST IS AGAIN IN JERUSALEM

THIS IS HIS LAST DAY OF CONFLICT WITH OFFICIAL JEWRY. HE REPLIES TO THE QUESTIONS OF THE HERODIANS, SADDUCEES AND PHARISEES AND WITH PERFECT WISDOM SILENCES THEM. HE UTTERS MANY IMPORTANT PARABLES

THE PROPHETIC DISCOURSE ON OLIVET AFTER HIS FINAL DEPARTURE FROM THE TEMPLE

WEDNESDAY, 29TH APRIL, ISRAEL'S 12TH OF NISAN

Read Matthew XXI, 19 (last sentence) to XXV, 46; Mark XI, 20 to XIII, 37 and Luke XX to XXI, 36

THE DATE of Wednesday, 29th April A.D. 33, is one of immeasurable solemnity, as anyone will quickly gather who reads one or more of the accounts given in the Gospels of all that took place on it. Firstly, we must take note of the fact that it was THE LAST DAY on which our blessed Lord and Master ministered publicly to the Jewish nation and its rulers. With this in mind we shall the better understand the limitless importance of all He then said and did. There is no record in the Gospels of any public ministry on the next day which was Thursday and that of the Passover of Jehovah which our Lord took with His disciples and in the night of which He was apprehended by the Jewish Authorities under the direction of Judas, the apostle who betrayed Him.

Luke informs us that our Lord did His teaching in the Temple and that "all the people came early in the morning . . . for to hear Him" (XXI, 37 and 38).

Our Lord was in Jerusalem as God's King and the fearlessness and authority with which He acted won Him the attention of the multitude. At the same time it so exasperated the Jewish rulers to see Him boldly teaching that which openly exposed the wickedness and folly of their own position that they "sought to destroy Him, and could not find what they might do: for all the people were very attentive to hear Him" (Luke XIX, 47 and 48).

It is important to realize that our Lord's teaching on this particular day dealt with the past, the present and the future of the Jewish people and that all that He said will yet be pondered over by that section of the Jews that will be the first to acknowledge the sin of their forefathers and, repenting of the same, be baptized in His Name, Whom their nation rejected and slew, as Cain did his brother Abel. The Jews' rejection of their Messiah is the greatest tragedy in human history and the day we are now reviewing through the Gospels was the last on which He ministered to them; not, indeed, with words of entreaty or of grace, but in terms of the most fearful exposure intermingled with stern predictions of the judgments which were about to overtake them as a nation. In effect, the Jews' rejection of their Messiah was the proof of their having turned away from God (John VIII, 42 to 47) and it was this that our Lord brought home to them in all the teaching He gave on this last day of His public Ministry.

Early in the morning of this day our Lord and His disciples return to Jerusalem from the Mount of Olives. Mark names the occasion thus, "In the morning, as they passed by, they saw the fig tree dried up from the roots" (XI, 20 to 26). Peter calls our Lord's attention to the fact, whereupon He gives them some blessed instruction on the question of having faith in God's power to answer prayer, even to the removal of mountains. It is solemn to contemplate that this dried-up fig tree is a symbol of the Jewish nation throughout "the times of the Gentiles", that is, the present age. Let us not forget, however, that Israel's national resurgence has taken place before our eyes and that it was on this very day that our Lord, in referring to this event, as typified by a fig tree shooting forth leaves in spring, said, "When ye see these things come to pass, know ye that the kingdom of God is nigh at hand" (Luke XXI, 29 to 33).

"By what authority doest Thou these things?"

It was impossible for the Jewish rulers any longer to stand by while our Lord Jesus Christ continued on His way teaching and preaching in the Temple with such authority that the people knew He must be a Prophet (Matt. XXI, 46). They, therefore, determined officially and unitedly to challenge His right to do and to say the things He did. We will quote from Luke (XX, 1 and 2):

> "And it came to pass, that on one of those days, as He taught the people in the temple, and preached the gospel, the chief priests and the scribes came upon Him with the elders, and spake unto Him, saying, Tell us, by what authority doest Thou these things? or who is he that gave Thee this authority?"

The expression "came upon Him" needs to be noted as it is inserted to show that they had a hostile intent (cf. Acts IV, 1). Our Lord, therefore, found Himself suddenly confronted with an official deputation, composed of the highest authorities in Jewry, whose object was to use their own position of authority in order to undermine His influence by showing the people that they regarded Him as an impostor. It was a dangerous proceeding for these Jewish rulers to set themselves in array against the Son of God and pose as being in a position to judge Him when, in fact, He was about to become their judge.

With a stroke of consummate wisdom the blessed Son of God turns the tables on His enemies by challenging them to declare whether the ministry of John the Baptist was "from heaven, or of men". This placed them, as He well knew, in a great predicament as, whichever way they answered, it would react to their disfavour. On hearing their admission that they could not answer His question, our Lord replies, "Neither tell I you by what authority I do these things". In other words, our Lord denied their competency to challenge Him as to the source of His authority, since they on their part were unable to say from whence had come the authority of John the Baptist whom "all hold . . . as a prophet" (Matt. XXI, 26).

Our Lord then, according to Matthew (XXI, 28), utters the Parable of the Two Sons in order to expose the attitude of official Jewry to John the Baptist whose preaching was heeded by both publicans and harlots who, He said, would be found in the Kingdom of God before the self-righteous Pharisees who refused to repent and believe the Gospel the Baptist had proclaimed. Official Jewry made great profession of obeying God, yet refused John the Baptist; while those who made no such profession repented and believed John's preaching because they accepted that He was sent from God.

This was followed by the Parable of the Householder demanding fruit from the husbandmen to whom he had let out his vineyard. Matthew, Mark and Luke all give this extremely important parable in full. As Isaiah states, "The vineyard of the Lord of hosts is the house of Israel" (V, 7). This Parable is too clear to call for interpretation as it so obviously refers to Israel's treatment of God's various messengers and was prophetic of how Israel was about to act towards the One Who was the well-beloved Son of the Owner of the vineyard. As the Parable states, "they caught him, and cast him out of the vineyard, and slew him" (Matt. XXI, 39).

This parable was one of the most solemn for Israel ever uttered by our Lord Jesus Christ. Its imprecations are terrible to contemplate and these apply to Israel at the end of the age as well as at the beginning when they fell against Christ the Stone and were "broken". That Stone has now become the Head of the corner. Woe be to any on whom that Stone shall fall at the end of the age for "it will grind him to powder".

These two parables, spoken by our Lord on God's behalf, could not be misunderstood by the Pharisees who "perceived that He spake of them". Defeated by His challenge as to John the Baptist and exposed as to their attitude to our Lord Himself by these two parables, "they sought to lay hands on Him" but feared to do so because the multitude "took Him for a prophet" (Matt. XXI, 45 and 46).

In Matthew XXII the Parable of the Marriage of the King's Son follows the above two Parables. This again relates first to Israel's attitude towards God's gracious invitation, through John the Baptist and the Apostles in our Lord's lifetime, to have part in the Wedding of His Son, and, secondly, through His last messengers, namely, the Apostles who after Pentecost sought to bring Israel to repentance but whom the latter ill-treated "and slew". Then comes the prediction of the Fall of Jerusalem before the armies of the Roman Empire in A.D. 70. This is as follows: "when the king heard thereof, he was wroth: and he sent forth his armies, and destroyed those murderers, and burned up their city" (verse 7). The latter part of this Parable refers to the spread of the Gospel among the Gentiles after Jerusalem fell, so that they might have part in the Marriage of the King's Son in the place of Israel who had despised their day of opportunity.

The man who was found at the Wedding "not having a wedding garment" represents that large mass of nominal Christians in Christendom who make a profession of owning Christ but who in fact have never parted with the rags of their own self-righteousness and consequently have never, as Paul expresses it, "put on the new man, which after God is created in righteousness and true holiness" (Ephes. IV, 22 to 24). Our Lord discloses the fearful prospect awaiting all such because, in effect, they treat His death, by which alone sinners of the Gentiles can be clothed with a garment of righteousness acceptable to a thrice-holy God, as unnecessary.

## THREE EFFORTS TO TEMPT OUR LORD JESUS CHRIST AND SO "ENTANGLE HIM IN HIS TALK" (Matthew XXII, 15 to 46)

It is quite clear that the Jewish authorities were determined if possible to lure our Lord into saying something which would incriminate Him with both the Roman rulers and the Sanhedrin. The Pharisees persuade the Herodians to tempt our Lord into saying that the Jews should not pay tribute to Caesar, as this would provide them with evidence with which to accuse Him of being a potential leader of an insurrection against Rome.

Our Lord's reply, as the result of being shown Caesar's image and superscription on a coin in current use, has become almost a commonplace in defining the relationship of the claims of God to those of the State. The Jews, through their sins, had been made subject to Gentile overlords, and the time had not yet come for this to be changed. Therefore they must render to Caesar his due as having been permitted of God to hold suzerainty over them and their land. In accepting the Roman yoke they were bowing before a judgment sent from God and one which in no wise hindered them from rendering to Him that which was His due. It is recorded that "when they had heard these words, they marvelled, and left Him, and went their way" (Matt. XXII, 22).

"The same day came to Him the Sadducees, which say that there is no resurrection, and asked Him" a question by which they hoped to make the idea of resurrection look foolish (see Matthew XXII, Mark XII and Luke XX). They quote Moses as saying that "If a man die, having no children, his brother shall marry his wife, and raise up seed unto his brother". Having supposed a case in which seven brothers married the same woman in turn, they ask, "In the resurrection, whose wife shall she be?" Our Lord exposes their ignorance and says, "Ye do err, not knowing the Scriptures, nor the power of God. For in the resurrection they neither marry, nor are given in marriage, but are as the angels of God in heaven . . . God is not the God of the dead but of the living". Our Lord thus showed that these Sadducees who denied the resurrection and the life to come were in hopeless ignorance of what the Scriptures reveal concerning these realities. Years after their death, God had declared to Moses, "I am the God of Abraham, and the God of Isaac, and the God of Jacob", and this proved that these, like all the patriarchs, were living and would one day inherit the promises made to them.

"When the Pharisees had heard that He had put the Sadducees to silence, they were gathered together. Then one of them, which was a lawyer asked . . . tempting Him . . . Master, which is the great commandment in the law?" (Matthew XXII, 34 to 40). This question is dealt with more fully in Mark's Gospel, Chapter XII, 28 to 34. Without quoting the exact words, we know that our Lord declared that wholehearted love for God must come before all; but after this we must love our neighbour as ourselves. Then He said, "On these two commandments hang all the law and the prophets".

Our Lord takes occasion, when He finds the Pharisees "gathered together", to put a question to them as regards His own position as Messiah (Matt. XXII, 41). He asks, "What think ye of Christ? Whose son is He?" They reply, "The Son of David". He then quotes from Psalm CX and asks, "How then doth David in Spirit call Him Lord, saying, The Lord said unto my Lord, Sit Thou on My right hand, till I make Thine enemies Thy footstool? If David then call Him Lord, how is He his Son?"

In effect, our Lord is bringing out His own position as

Messiah as it is revealed in the 110th Psalm. The Messiah, David's Son and Lord, must ascend up on High if the Scripture is to be fulfilled in which Jehovah saith to Him, "Sit Thou on My right hand, till I make Thine enemies Thy footstool". His enemies were those who rejected Him and so delayed the coming of the Kingdom. In the interval He must ascend into Heaven for His session on the right hand of the Throne of God. David foresaw our Lord's rejection as Messiah but the Pharisees were unable to see that their own rejection of Him was leading to the fulfilment of David's prediction. Rejected by the Jews, He would ascend and await the moment when God was ready to make His enemies the footstool of His feet.

All had now had enough of seeking to entangle our Lord in His talk and Matthew tells us that "no man was able to answer Him a word", that is, in regard to our Lord's question concerning the Messiah being David's Son and Lord. Furthermore, we are told, "Neither durst any man from that day forth ask Him any more questions" (XXII, 46). Each of these questions had had a wicked purpose behind it which was ignominiously defeated by our Lord's perfect wisdom. In each case His answer led to the entire discomfiture of those asking the question.

The 23rd Chapter of Matthew speaks for itself and needs to be read by anyone who would know the thoughts of God in regard to the Religious World of our Lord's day. When One Who knows what is in man sets about exposing what He knows and sees of the conduct of those who hold a special place of responsibility towards God, such as the Jewish leaders held and in which they had so miserably failed, we may expect to hear words which shed the light of Heaven into depths of wickedness which exceeded anything previously recorded. It is not an exposure of the grosser forms of iniquity, but of that form which was the direct result of unfaithfulness to God and His Law in those who were appointed to be Teachers and exponents of the Law – those in fact who "sit in Moses' seat".

Our Lord's fearful indictment of the Scribes and Pharisees is uttered to His disciples and to the multitude, showing clearly that He differentiated between the responsible leaders of the Jewish nation and the people whom they professed to lead (Matt. XXIII, 1).

As regards the people in general, Matthew XXIII forms the end of our Lord's public Ministry on earth. It looks on to the time when those who had now rejected Him as their Messiah would reject, persecute and kill those whom, in mercy, He would send to them (verse 34) not with a view to national recovery, which must wait until the end of the age, but with a view to the salvation of any who could discern in the crucified and risen Jesus of Nazareth the Saviour of the World. It was, as we well know, under our Lord's specific instructions that the Gospel was first to be preached to the Jews (Acts XIII, 46 and 47).

This Chapter (XXIII) ends with a touching lament in which our Lord expresses His deep sorrow at not having been able to gather together His beloved nation "even as a hen gathereth her chickens under her wings". As the nation refused His entreaties He could do nothing more for it. He, therefore, utters His last words of warning to those among whom He had lived and laboured for 33 years and more. This He does in the Temple which He is about to leave for the last time. So long as He was present, the Temple was His Father's House; but directly He left it, it ceased to be so: and within two days the veil which shrouded the Holy Place would be "rent in twain from the top to the bottom" as a sign that all that the Temple stood for as the House of God had passed away before the incoming of a New Order founded upon His death and resurrection (Heb. X, 19 and 20). So our Lord declares to the Jews:

"Behold, *your house* is left unto you desolate."

He then gives them His final word and it could not be more solemn. He would leave them and not return until, with repentant hearts, they desired Him and could say, "Blessed is He that cometh in the name of the Lord". This looked on to the end of the age and His Return in Glory after the fires of the great tribulation had subsided. Then, according to Zechariah, they would look upon Him "whom they have pierced, and . . . mourn for Him, as one mourneth for his only son" (XII, 10). Afterwards He will do for Israel all that is promised, for then "Israel shall blossom and bud, and fill the face of the world with fruit" (Isaiah XXVII, 6).

## THE PROPHETIC DISCOURSE ON OLIVET
### Matthew XXIV and XXV, Mark XIII and Luke XXI

In point of time we have now reached about the close of Wednesday, 29th April – the last day of our Lord's Public Ministry to Israel. His last utterance looked on to the end of the age when "the times of the Gentiles" would have run their course and when He would be sought for by the nation that now so callously rejected Him. His discourse on Olivet was concerned with events which would lead up to His Return and the repentance of a Remnant in preparation for it.

In Matthew XXIV, 1, we read, "And Jesus went out, and departed from the temple". This was a symbolic act and really sealed the doom of the Temple, for He then declared concerning it, "There shall not be left here one stone upon another, that shall not be thrown down". As all know, this was quite miraculously fulfilled by soldiers of the Roman Empire at the time when Jerusalem was taken in A.D. 70. Our Lord's prediction on this subject was as positive as words could make it and it was fulfilled to the very letter 37 years later.

The Olivet Discourse forms one of the most important prophecies in the Bible. It was uttered in response to three leading questions put to Him by His disciples. We will quote from Matthew XXIV, but Mark XIII and Luke XXI are parallel passages:

> "And as He sat on the mount of Olives, the disciples came unto Him privately, saying, Tell us, when shall these things be? and what shall be the sign of Thy coming, and of the end of the world (lit. age)?"

The Greek words translated "the end of the world" should have been translated "the consummation of the age", as given in the Revised Version Margin.

The first of these questions clearly refers to our Lord's remark as to the destruction of the Temple and it is this aspect which Luke is caused to feature throughout his account of our Lord's utterance. Matthew and Mark both exclude the Fall of Jerusalem in A.D. 70 and are caused to frame their accounts with the focus on our Lord's return and the period called "the consummation of the age" in which it takes place.

In our former Treatise, *The World in Liquidation*, we show from the chronology of Holy Scripture that "the consummation of the age" positively began in the year 1933 when the predetermined 6,000 Julian Years from Adam terminated, and when on the same day the 2,000 Bible Years of the Christian Dispensation also finished. From 1933 to the start of the Thousand Years' Reign of Christ an unreckoned interval or chronological hiatus, four times spoken of by our Lord as "the consummation of the age", runs its course (see Matthew XIII, 39 and 40).

In a more literal sense, the Olivet Discourse as recorded by Matthew and Mark delineates the course of events, as affecting the world in general and Israel in particular, during the last seven years of the age. These terminate with our Lord's return in power and glory as described in Matthew XXIV, verses 27 to 30 and also in Revelation XIX, etc., etc.

This prophecy of our blessed Lord and Master, as we have seen, was uttered at the moment when He had finished with Israel as a nation for the age. The seven years covered by the ministries of John the Baptist and Himself (A.D. 26 to 33) had failed to bring in the Kingdom and our Lord knew that God for this reason intended to cancel the period chronologically, with the purpose of bringing it in again as a period of retributive judgment after the Christian Dispensation had ended with His Second Appearing, as described in I Thessalonians IV, 13 to 18.

The events in these seven years occupy the Book of Revelation from Chapter IV to XIX. The first half is a period of 1,260 days (see Rev. XI, 3 and XII, 6) and the second half is 42 months (see Rev. XI, 2 and XIII, 5).

Matthew XXIV, verses 4 to 8, refers to the first half of the coming seven years of judgment. This period our Lord ominously defines as "the beginning of sorrows". Verses 9 to 14 lead up to the end of the second half of these seven years and apply strictly to the Jewish people. In verses 15 to 31 the Spirit of God, according to a principle common throughout Scripture, caused Matthew to refer again to the second half of the seven years but with much more detail. This begins with the words, "When ye therefore shall see the abomination of desolation, spoken of by Daniel the prophet, stand in the holy place". This reference is to the setting up of an idol in the rebuilt Temple at Jerusalem at the opening of the 42 months of Antichrist (see Rev. XIII). In verse 21 our Lord defines these 42 months as the period of the "great tribulation" and adds concerning it, "such as was not since the beginning of the world to this time, no, nor ever shall be". These are words of limitless solemnity to all mankind and our Lord makes it clear that unless this judgment period was shortened "there should no flesh be saved".

In verses 29 and 30 we are informed that our Lord's Appearing "in the clouds of heaven with power and great glory" will take place "immediately after the tribulation of those days". As it is not likely that anyone on the earth who then possesses the Scriptures could possibly fail to know when the period of "the great tribulation" is running its course, it is manifest that all such will know when our Lord is to appear, save only that "that day and hour" is to be kept a strict secret. In the face of our Lord's clear teaching as to His Advent in power and glory it is utterly unreasonable to invest the occasion with uncertainty as to its time when He Himself declares that He will come "*immediately after the tribulation*" – a period of time which will have unmistakable markings. This Appearing, however, must not be confused with His Second Appearing, when He comes to assemble the Church which is His body, in the manner set forth by the Apostle Paul in the First Thessalonian Epistle (IV, 13 to 18) and also John XIV, 2 and 3 and Hebrews IX, 28. The time of this Second Appearing is much more deeply concealed and this with the object of keeping the Church on the alert lest it should lapse into saying, like the wicked servant, "My lord delayeth his coming" (Matt. XXIV, 48). In Matthew XXIV, 32 and 33, and Luke XXI, 29 to 31, our Lord gives the Parable of the Fig Tree which puts forth its leaves when "summer is nigh". This "fig tree" is a symbol of the people of Israel at the end of the age. When the spirit of nationalism burst forth in their midst, after the long winter of the Dispersion, then all were to *know* that "the Kingdom of God is nigh at hand". The Nationalist or Zionist Movement began in 1897 and led to the establishment of the State of Israel in 1948. The Kingdom of God must therefore verily be "at the doors".

### THE THREE PARABLES OF MATTHEW XXV.

The Parable of the Ten Virgins embraces the whole Christian Profession and the preparedness of individuals within it for the Lord's Second Appearing when He comes as the Bridegroom. At a time when Christians of every class are asleep to the fact of the Bridegroom's imminent approach, a shrill Cry will be sounded announcing the Event. This will awaken all from their dishonouring slumbers and everyone will be looking to the state of his or her lamp of profession. Those who have the "oil", which is a type of the Holy Spirit, will be ready for the Bridegroom and go in with Him to the Marriage. All the others the Bridegroom will disown. This parable deals with individual preparedness for our Lord's Second Advent.

In the Parable of the Talents, faithfulness in service to our absent Lord is in question. We are told "after a long time the lord of those servants cometh, and reckoneth with them". Our Lord has bestowed on one and another gifts – "His goods" – according to His sovereign choice. Faithfulness, inspired by devotion to the absent Lord, marks those who receive both the five talents and the two talents. They trade with these gifts and make a profit for Him, and each hears the blessed commendation, "Well done, thou good and faithful servant . . . enter thou into the joy of thy lord". The servant with one talent (one fears he represents a very large class of professing servants of Christ) knows no devotion to his lord but assails him as one desiring to get something to which he is not entitled. He takes his talent and hides it, thus refusing to trade with the gift in a way calculated to benefit the one who bestowed it. This man, who typifies those who profess to be servants of Christ but who in fact have no true knowledge of Him, comes under severe rebuke and then judgment for his unfaithfulness in refusing to render any service to his absent lord.

The third Parable of Matthew XXV is that of the Sheep and Goats. It is prophetic of the occasion when our Lord sets up His Throne on the earth, following His return in power and glory. This parable envisages the Great Assize of the Nations, for we read in verses 31 and 32:

> "Then shall He sit upon the throne of His glory: and before Him shall be gathered all nations: and He shall separate

them one from another, as a shepherd divideth his sheep from the goats."

The nations typified by the "sheep" qualify for a welcome into our Lord's Kingdom and to them He says, "Come, ye blessed of My Father, inherit the kingdom prepared for you from the foundation of the world" (verse 34). Contrariwise, to those nations typified by the goats our Lord says, "Depart from Me, ye cursed, into everlasting fire, prepared for the devil and his angels" (verse 41).

The supreme test in both cases is the treatment meted out by the respective nations towards those whom our Lord calls "My brethren".

While unable to attempt a dissertation on this most important prophecy, as this is not the occasion for such, we must at least draw attention to its essential objective which is to establish the conditions under which a nation may qualify for entry into the Kingdom of our Lord Jesus Christ.

After the Christian Dispensation has ended, by the Second Appearing of our Lord for His Church which will be translated from the earth, our Lord authorizes a Remnant of the Jews, which repents and owns Him as their Messiah, to go forth and preach what He terms "the gospel of the kingdom" to all the nations. Let the words of Matthew XXIV, 14 be carefully noted:

> "And this gospel of the kingdom shall be preached in all the world for a witness unto all nations; and then shall the end come."

The Gospel of the Kingdom, which was preached in the seven years, A.D. 26 to 33, first by John the Baptist, and then by our Lord and His disciples (Matthew IX, 35 and X, 7), is to be again preached by Jewish disciples "for a witness unto all nations". The question of the salvation of the individual does not come into it at all. The "My Brethren" of the Parable are these Jewish disciples who will go forth into all the earth proclaiming, amidst awful outpourings of judgment, the Coming of Christ as King. Many Scriptures reveal that these Jewish disciples will become the object of outrageous assaults by the openly anti-christian nations. Other nations (i.e. the "sheep") will receive these Jewish messengers and befriend them; and their actions in so doing will be accepted by our Lord as if done to Himself; for to them He says, "Inasmuch as ye have done it unto one of the least of these My brethren, ye have done it unto Me" (verse 40, cf. Acts IX, 4).

In Matthew XXIV, 9 to 14, our Lord casts a lurid light upon the treatment that will be accorded by some nations to His Jewish disciples in the latter half of the seven years of judgment. This will form the test by which our Lord decides which nations are to have part with Israel in the Kingdom, and which are to "go away into everlasting punishment".

We cannot further develop this vast and important theme but its relevance in the present hour will be obvious to many.

## "YE KNOW THAT AFTER TWO DAYS IS THE . . . PASSOVER, AND THE SON OF MAN IS BETRAYED TO BE CRUCIFIED"

(Matthew XXVI, 2, cf. Mark XIV, 1.)

It was at the close of Wednesday, 29th April – Israel's 12th of Nisan – that our Lord uttered these significant and solemn words to His disciples. We are told that He did so when He "had finished all these sayings", which is a reference to the great Prophetic Discourse He had just given "as He sat upon the mount of Olives" (Matt. XXIV, 3).

Not a word ever fell from our Master's lips but had a purposed significance, for with Him there was "a time to keep silence, and a time to speak" (Eccles. III, 7). We therefore conceive it to be a matter of vital importance to understand fully the significance of His announcement concerning the forthcoming Passover at which He would be "betrayed to be crucified". We may say at once that it has, as He intended, an important bearing upon the whole subject of Time in relation to His Death and Resurrection.

The supremely important question that has to be settled in reference to our Lord's statement is, To what Passover did He refer? We need hardly remind our readers that the Scriptures irrefutably establish that our Lord and His disciples took the Passover Supper on the Thursday evening *before* His death and that the Jews took their Passover Supper on the Friday evening *after* His death.

Our Lord's very words reveal that He was referring to the

Passover which He took with His disciples, because all such expressions of time in the Bible are strictly inclusive. The expression, "after two days" clearly infers the existence of a third day. Our Lord made this statement late on Wednesday which with Thursday makes the "two days". The Passover was eaten after 6 P.M. on Thursday. This, in Bible reckoning, was the opening of Friday which was the third day inclusively reckoned. Furthermore, as everyone who has read the Gospels knows, our Lord was betrayed by Judas directly after this Passover and crucified the next morning in exact fulfilment of His statement.

It must be noted that our Lord prefaced this statement to the disciples with the words, "Ye know". This He did in order to convey the fact that it was well known to them that He would take the Passover at the appointed time, according to the moon, namely, on the true 14th of the 1st month (Leviticus XXIII, 5) and not as the Jews who took their Passover one day later, that is, on the 14th of the 1st month according to their calendar which was based on months starting at the phasis or first appearance of the moon (see Par. XIII of the Summary of Facts).

It is helpful to note the way the Bible avoids all possible confusion about these two Passovers. Matthew, Mark and Luke refer exclusively to the Passover of Jehovah which our Lord took with His disciples, *and never mention the Jews' Passover by name;* while John always refers by name or implication to the Jews' Passover. As we have already pointed out, John in using the expression, "six days before the passover", refers to that of the Jews which he had just previously named (John XI, 55).

It could hardly surprise anyone to be told that God reckons Time in relation to the death and resurrection of His beloved Son *solely according to the Divine Calendar*. If it is reckoned or expressed in terms of Israel's Calendar, the days of the week and of the month do not accord with the requirements of the Levitical types. This will become very clear in due course. Indeed, failure to understand the difference between Israel's Calendar and the Divine Calendar renders it quite impossible to reconcile many Bible statements on the subject of our Lord's death and resurrection. It will be noted that in His statement to the disciples our Lord refers to the Passover of Jehovah which is according to the Divine Calendar and makes no reference to the Jews' Passover.

We must recall that our Lord's taking of the Passover one day before the Jews' Passover is the outstanding Biblical proof that the Divine Calendar prior to His death was one day ahead of the Calendar of Israel; and that our Lord had instructed His disciples in the matter is proved by His words, "Ye know that after two days is . . . the passover".

The expression, "after two days", spoken by our Lord, extends to Friday and completes the six days from the Bethany Supper when He was anointed by Mary. John refers to the Sunday which was "six days before the passover", and also to the Monday which he calls "the next day" (John XII, 1 and 12). Mark takes up the account and indicates Tuesday, the day after the Monday of the Triumphal Entry into Jerusalem, with the expression, "on the morrow", and he also indicates the Wednesday with the words, "and in the morning" (Mark XI, 12 and 20). Our Lord then carries the record forward to Friday by His statement, "after two days is . . . the passover". That Friday is the sixth day of John XII, 1. So the Bible with meticulous care marks out every one of these six days which lead up to the Friday on which Jesus was "betrayed" and "crucified".

The Bible Narrative has now been followed to the end of Wednesday, 29th April A.D. 33 – Israel's 12th of Nisan and the Divine 13th of Nisan. For our Lord Jesus Christ this Wednesday, as we have seen, was a day of ceaseless activities from beginning to end. It was the last day of His Public Ministry and one of the most solemn in all His history on the earth. It was followed, as we shall see, by a day spent in private with His disciples and in quiet anticipation of the last Passover Supper and of His approaching Betrayal, Arrest, Trial and Death.

## NOTE

## TIME IN RELATION TO OUR LORD'S DEATH AND RESURRECTION

At this point in our Narrative we commence to unveil from the Holy Scriptures the long-concealed Truth concerning Time in relation to the Death and Resurrection of our Lord Jesus

Christ – a subject upon which confusion has reigned throughout Christendom since the Apostles of our Lord departed. That this confusion has existed and does still exist, in spite of endless efforts to arrive at the Truth, is proof positive that the Scriptures of the New Testament have been so written as *to conceal from view* certain important facts, without the knowledge of which it is *absolutely* impossible to reconcile our Lord's own statements as to the length of His session in death with the statements in the Gospels as to the time of His resurrection.

We are told in Proverbs XXV, 2, that "It is the glory of God to conceal a thing", and as we unfold the true facts on this subject from the Scriptures it will be realized that in no other sphere has God so excelled in the art of concealment as in that which relates to His Son's Death and Resurrection. It appears that each Evangelist contributed an appointed quota of facts on this subject, under the specific direction of the Holy Spirit, without reference to the contributions of the other three – the Holy Spirit alone knowing the effect on human minds created by the composite Record, formed under His direction, which appears in the Four Gospels.

That Record has successfully safeguarded the Sacred Secrets of our Lord's Passion for eighteen hundred years. Neither could any human being pierce the veil of secrecy unless permitted to do so under the direct guidance of the Spirit of God and this because the hour had come in the Divine counsels for such an unveiling.

We will not add more, but ask readers to refer again to the Introduction to this Treatise as it contains remarks as to why it has now pleased God to grant light on the long concealed Time factors of our Lord's death and resurrection.

# PART V

## TWO DAYS BEFORE THE JEWS' PASSOVER THURSDAY 30TH APRIL

IN ISRAEL'S CALENDAR THIS WAS 13TH OF NISAN; BUT IN THE DIVINE CALENDAR IT WAS THE 14TH NISAN AND "THE PREPARATION" OF THE PASSOVER TAKEN BY JESUS WITH HIS DISCIPLES

---

THE TIDE OF FRENZIED MALICE ON THE PART OF THE JEWISH RULERS REACHES HIGH-WATER MARK WITH A CONSPIRACY TO KILL JESUS "IN THE ABSENCE OF THE MULTITUDE"

---

SATAN, DEFEATED BY OUR LORD IN THE TEMPTATION, REAPPEARS AS THE MASTER OF FALLEN MAN BY ENTERING JUDAS ISCARIOT – "ONE OF THE TWELVE" – WHO THEN SELLS HIS MASTER FOR THIRTY PIECES OF SILVER

---

THE NINETY HOURS OF OUR LORD'S PASSION OPEN AT 6 A.M. ON THIS THURSDAY, 30TH APRIL

---

Read Matthew XXVI, 1 to 19; Mark XIV, 1 to 16 and Luke XXII, 1 to 13

AS WE HAVE already intimated, the day of Thursday, 30th April, A.D. 33, was uneventful as far as our Lord's personal activities were concerned and the Gospels record no incident during it, save the sending of the two disciples who "made ready the passover" – an event to which we will refer later. The absence of any other recorded incident allows us to assume that our blessed Lord and Master remained quietly hidden from the public gaze with His disciples. Where He and they spent the night of Wednesday we are not told, but it would either have been at Bethany or in the Mount of Olives (Luke XXI, 37).

Leaving our Lord and His disciples for the moment, we must turn our attention to the activities of three associated parties on this ominous 13th of Nisan in Israel's Calendar. We allude to Satan, the Jewish rulers and Judas Iscariot. This Thursday was a day of dark conspiracy against the Son of God, as the language of Scripture makes most clear. Satan, our Lord's arch-enemy, stood at the back of the scenes with determination now to strike a death-blow at the One Who had so ignominiously defeated him in the Forty Days of Temptation three and a half years before, and Who ever since had been spoiling "his goods". Trading on the malicious envy (Matt. XXVII, 18) of the Jewish rulers and the covetous dishonesty of Judas Iscariot (John XII, 6) he, who "was a murderer from the beginning" (John VIII, 44), found in them ready tools to his hand through which to vent his hatred of the only One, born of woman, Who would yield no response to his will.

In Matthew XXVI, 3 to 5, we read:

> "Then assembled together the chief priests, and the scribes, and the elders of the people, unto the palace of the high priest, who was called Caiaphas. And consulted that they might take Jesus by subtilty, and kill Him. But they said, Not on the feast day, lest there be an uproar among the people."

Mark and Luke both make similar statements and, taken together, these form a threefold cord of witness to the absolute determination of the Jewish rulers to lay hold of our Lord by "subtilty" or "craft" and kill Him "in the absence of the multitude" (Luke XXII, 6). Nothing is more clear, therefore, than that a cunning plot was set on foot by the Jewish rulers to kill our Lord Jesus Christ in such a way as to keep "the people" in ignorance until their blood-thirsty object had been attained. It would appear it was for this reason that our Lord was arrested about midnight, and that before or soon after dawn He had been condemned. He was in fact crucified at "the third hour" (8 A.M.) before many of "the people" could have realized what their rulers were doing.

Those who serve Satan may be assured of his help in their dark enterprises, so it is not surprising that we read in Luke XXII, 3 to 6:

> "Then entered Satan into Judas surnamed Iscariot, being of the number of the twelve. And he went his way, and communed with the chief priests and captains, how he might betray Him unto them. *And they were glad*, and covenanted to give him money. And he promised, and sought opportunity to betray Him unto them *in the absence of the multitude*."

Nothing succeeds like success, and for the Jewish rulers to have succeeded in extracting a binding promise from one of our Lord's twelve apostles that for thirty pieces of silver he would "conveniently" deliver Jesus of Nazareth into their hands, appeared to be a master-stroke of good fortune – it never occurring to them in their frenzied zeal to destroy Jesus that illicit bargains struck with traitors sometimes react with evil effect upon those who make them. Nevertheless, the Jewish rulers got what appeared to them to be their money's worth at the time, but at what sort of a price thereafter? Let the history of the Jewish people in A.D. 70 and since be the answer to that question; even as it also forms the sequel to the oath taken by those who before Pilate declared concerning Jesus, "His blood be on us, and on our children" (Matt. XXVII, 25).

As for Judas himself, it is enough to say that our Lord in addressing His Father refers to him as "the son of perdition" – an appellation only elsewhere applied to "the man of sin" or Antichrist (John XVII, 12; II Thess. II, 3 and Rev. XVII, 8 and 11).

So we have seen the power of Satan in using fallen man as his tool to do despite to the unresisting and obedient Son of God; we have seen the frenzied malice of the Jewish rulers against our Lord, and their willingness to consort with a traitor indwelt by Satan in order to accomplish their project; and we have seen an apostle, chosen by our Lord to be one of the twelve, fulfilling the Psalm which speaks of him thus: "Yea, mine own familiar friend, in whom I trusted, which did eat of my bread, hath lifted up his heel against me" (XLI, 9).

How rightly does the Psalmist declare, "Surely the wrath of man shall praise Thee" (LXXVI, 10), for in spite of all Satan's efforts to use man in his projects against the Son of God and in spite of man's willingness to be Satan's tool in seeking to encompass the destruction of the One against Whom his malice knew no limit, this consortium of evil-doers can in the end only succeed in performing the predestined will of God – they can in fact only "do whatsoever Thy hand and Thy counsel determined before to be done", as it is expressed in Acts IV, 28. Jesus must be betrayed and die by the hand of man if, as "the Lamb of God", He is to take away "the sin of the world"; but God's foreplanning of this event and man's wilful and sinful part in its execution are in no way related to each other; so we hear our Lord say concerning Judas, "The Son of Man indeed goeth, as it is written of Him: but woe to that man by whom the Son of Man is betrayed! good were it for that man if he had never been born" (Mark XIV, 21).

The act of betrayal which led to our Lord's arrest by the Jewish rulers we are not now concerned with as it occurred the next day and will come before us in due course. We therefore leave those who were conspiring against our Lord, in order to consider what He and His disciples were doing on this day.

It will have been noted that both Matthew and Mark introduce the anointing of our Lord by Mary of Bethany just before their accounts of Judas' visit to the chief priests, and of the preparation of the Passover. It is most important, when God lays great emphasis on a matter, to pay proper attention to His reasons for doing so. As we have pointed out many times (see the Summary of Facts, Pars. 5, 6, 7 and 8), the Bible's Sacred Chronology totally ignores the four days between the 10th and the 14th of the 1st month during which the Passover lambs were awaiting death. It is in conformity with this principle that Matthew and Mark are caused to make it appear as if the anointing of our Lord by Mary of Bethany took place just before the Passover at which He was present with His disciples and at which He presented Himself for death as the Lamb of God – dying as such "in a figure".

It will be remembered that Mary set our Lord apart for death late in the afternoon of the previous Sunday and that in the afternoon of Thursday, the day we are considering, exactly Four Days had elapsed. The time had, therefore, come when our Lord must figuratively be sacrificed as God's Paschal Lamb. In the Divine Calendar the Sunday of the anointing was the 10th of Nisan, and the Thursday was the 14th of the same. May the Chart of the Five Calendars be frequently referred to so that the order of days and of dates may be kept well in mind as we proceed. Neither let it be forgotten that every Time feature associated with the death and resurrection of our Lord Jesus Christ was designed by God to effect a particular purpose. Therefore, no one could possibly possess aught but a limited understanding of these great Events apart from a true knowledge of Time in its many aspects as related thereto.

## "THE FIRST DAY OF THE FEAST OF UNLEAVENED BREAD" OPENS AT 3 P.M. ON THURSDAY, 30TH APRIL

## OUR LORD SENDS PETER AND JOHN TO PREPARE THE PASSOVER

## WHY HOLY SCRIPTURE MARKS THIS AS THE STARTING-POINT OF THE CHRISTIAN DISPENSATION

Read Matt. XXVI, 17 to 19; Mark XIV, 12 to 16 and Luke XXII, 7 to 13

It could escape the attention of no one who reads the above Scriptures that the Holy Spirit caused each Evangelist to draw emphatic attention to the start of the Feast of Unleavened Bread, "when the passover must be killed". (See Summary of Facts, Par. 9.) Furthermore, each of these chapters begins with a reference to the Passover or Feast of Unleavened Bread which was at hand. It always behoves searchers after the Truth in Holy Scripture to take full account of any matter which is obviously being emphasized. We, therefore, rightly ask why such immense emphasis is being laid upon the fact that the first day of Unleavened Bread, "when they killed the passover", had been reached. Let us at once say that the hour of 3 P.M. on Thursday, 30th April, which was the opening of the First day of Unleavened Bread, was a turning-point of the utmost importance in God's relations with the human race. Our blessed Lord and Master perfectly understood this and marked the occasion with a symbolic act in keeping with it. For particulars of this we will quote the Evangelist Luke as he gives the most detail (XXII, 7 and 8):

> "Then came the day of unleavened bread, when the passover must be killed. And He sent Peter and John, saying, Go and prepare us the passover, that we may eat."

In Exodus XII, 18, we are informed that the Seven Days' Feast of Unleavened Bread began at even (i.e. about 3 P.M.) on the 14th of the 1st month (then called "Abib") and continued until even on the 21st day. Each Evangelist shows that our Lord made no move in the matter of preparing for the Passover until the "first day of unleavened bread" was reached at 3 P.M. on this Thursday, 30th April, which was the 14th of the 1st month in the Divine Calendar. But directly that point of time was reached, both He and the disciples (see Matthew and Mark) were aware that the hour had come to act in the matter.

This waiting until about 3 P.M. was all the more remarkable because this Thursday, from 6 A.M. to 6 P.M., was "the preparation of the passover". This expression is used in John XIX, 14 of the Jews' Passover but it is equally applicable to the Passover of Jehovah which our Lord took with His disciples at 6 P.M. It is certain that the whole of the 14th day of the 1st month was given up to the preparation of the Passover as it was not eaten until sunset, which was at the opening of the 15th day. In Chapter Two of this Treatise we show the obvious relationship between the 12 hours of the Preparation day for the Passover and the first 12 years of our Lord's life which ended to the day and hour by His being present in the Temple for the Passover which on that occasion was according to the Calendar of the Years of the Messiah.

Why then did our Lord and His disciples wait until the hour had arrived at which the Seven Days' Feast of Unleavened Bread officially began? The answer to this question is solemnly important to every Gentile believer in Christ. It is this. The Seven Days' Feast of Unleavened Bread which opened at 3 P.M. on the 14th of the 1st month and in which, at 6 P.M., the Passover was killed, is the outstanding type in the Bible of the Christian Dispensation, which, as we have previously shown, is always marked by the number "seven".

(Leaven, which is always a type of evil in the Bible, had to be excluded from all association with an Israelite's house during the Seven Days of the Feast of Unleavened Bread. In the Christian Dispensation believers are to feed upon Christ, the Bread that came down from Heaven, and not to corrupt the pure Truth of His Word by adding the leaven of their own or others' thoughts.)

We have, however, the direct testimony of the Bible to the fact that the Seven Days' Feast of Unleavened Bread is a type of the Christian Dispensation. In I Corinthians V, 7 and 8, we read: "Purge out therefore the old leaven. . . . For even Christ our passover is sacrificed for us: Therefore *let us keep the feast,* not with old leaven . . . but with the unleavened bread of sincerity and truth".

What could be more clear and simple? Our Lord Jesus Christ was THE ANTITYPE of every Passover lamb offered in Israel since the Exodus. (An antitype is the person or the thing which a type or symbol represents.) In accordance with the Law He had been anointed and set apart for death four days before by Mary of Bethany as "the Lamb of God, which taketh away the sin of the world". The typical Passover was killed at about 6 P.M. on the first day of the typical Feast of Unleavened Bread. *Now the hour had arrived* when the Antitypical Passover Lamb – God's beloved Son – must be offered up, and when the Antitypical Seven Days of Unleavened Bread, that is, THE CHRISTIAN DISPENSATION, must commence to run its course.

The 40 years of Israel in the Wilderness between Egypt and Canaan are a type of the 2,000 Bible years (50×40) of the Christian Dispensation (see I Corinth. X, 1 to 11). These typical 40 years began with the typical Passover in Egypt on the first day of Unleavened Bread. Therefore, the Antitypical 2,000 Bible years of the Christian Dispensation had to begin with the offering up of the Antitypical Passover Lamb on the first day. It thus becomes manifest that the true significance of the slaying of the Passover lambs, and of the Seven Days of Unleavened Bread which followed, lies solely in what they represented as types, namely, Christ, the Lamb of God, dying as the sinner's Substitute, and this followed by a Dispensation of Grace to all mankind.

It is to be carefully noted that our Lord had never before instituted a Feast of any kind according to the Divine Calendar and that His doing so on this occasion was a proof that He was setting aside the Jewish order and was ushering in a new Dispensation. This would now open with the offering up of Himself as the Antitypical Passover Lamb – an act which signified the bringing to an end of this Feast in its typical aspect until the Kingdom is restored to Israel, when it will become a Feast of remembrance, not of deliverance from Egypt, but of the death of our Lord Jesus Christ as the true Paschal Lamb. In the meanwhile, this new Dispensation, which found its type in the Seven Days' Feast of Unleavened Bread, would run its course.

It is quite clear that when the Spirit of God caused the three Evangelists to name the Feast of Unleavened Bread, He had in mind the Antitypical Feast, namely, the Christian Dispensation, and not merely the typical seven days. The Apostle Paul in writing to the Corinthians refers to the Christian Dispensation when he says, as quoted above, "let us keep the feast . . . with the unleavened bread of sincerity and truth".

### "A LARGE UPPER ROOM FURNISHED: THERE MAKE READY"

All that we have sought to explain above is perfectly illustrated by the symbolic nature of our Lord's instructions about the Preparation of the Passover.

It is Luke who tells us that Peter and John were the two disciples sent by our Lord for the purpose. Never before, but always afterwards, do we find these two Apostles acting together; and no doubt it was our Lord Who knit them together to take the place of leadership in the Christian Body that was formed by the descent of the Holy Ghost at Pentecost. Indeed, they were together at the tomb on the Resurrection morning (John XX, 2). In Acts we see them frequently acting together and it was these two Apostles whom the Church at Jerusalem sent to aid Philip in dealing with the converts in Samaria (Acts VIII, 14). We mention these well-known facts to show that our Lord nominated Peter and John to prepare the Passover because they would in future be found acting together in all that had reference to the New Dispensation which officially came into being from the very hour in which He sent them to make this preparation.

On enquiring where they are to go in fulfilment of their mission, our Lord instructs them with these words:

> "Behold, when ye are entered into the city, there shall a man meet you, bearing a pitcher of water; follow him into the house where he entereth in. And ye shall say unto the goodman of the house, The Master saith unto thee, Where is the guestchamber, where I shall eat the passover with My disciples? And he shall shew you a large upper room furnished: there make ready. And they went, and found it as He had said unto them: and they made ready the passover" (Luke XXII, 10 to 13).

The symbolism of all this is beautiful to behold when it is

realized that at this very hour the Christian Dispensation was opening and that this event was a prelude to the coming into being of the Church which is the body of our Lord Jesus Christ. No wonder that it was Peter and John who were the first to enter that Upper Room which was to witness the birth of the Church on the Day of Pentecost, fifty-three days later.

The man bearing a pitcher of water whom Peter and John are to follow into the house can be a type of none other than our Lord Himself, Who "took upon Him the form of a servant". The "water", as ever, typifies the Holy Spirit Whom the Lord bestowed upon the Church which is typically represented by "the house" into which the man enters with the pitcher of water. The Church, as we know, and every individual member of it, is indwelt by the Spirit (I Cor. III, 16 and VI, 19).

This whole incident is glorious when its typology is taken into account, for not alone was the hour that Peter and John entered that house the actual beginning of the Christian Dispensation as the antitype of the Feast of Unleavened Bread, but the house itself with its Upper Room witnessed the Last Passover with the Institution of the Memorial Supper to take its place, the Appearing of the Risen Lord on the evening of His resurrection, and, finally, on the day of Pentecost the actual birth of the Church, by the descent of the Holy Ghost on the assembled company of 120 disciples.

We do not know who the "goodman of the house" was but manifestly he was one whom the Lord knew and trusted and of whose hospitality He was willing to accept. Without doubt, the owner of the house typifies God Himself, for the Church is spoken of as "an habitation of God through the Spirit" (Ephesians II, 22). Neither can we doubt that the way the matter was brought about implies secrecy, for this Upper Room later became a veritable trysting place for the disciples of Jesus in Jerusalem, and Judas, who might have made it known to the Jewish rulers, had already died by his own hand.

In this Chapter we only concern ourselves with the last 3 hours of Thursday – our 30th April and the 14th of Nisan in the Divine Calendar – namely, 3 to 6 P.M. when this First Day of

Unleavened Bread opened. The remaining 21 hours to 3 P.M. on Friday, 1st May, will occupy us in the next Chapter and, as all know, this was the period of our Lord's deepest sufferings and death.

At 6 P.M. on the Thursday, when our Lord sat down with His disciples to eat the Passover, the 15th of Nisan, the 1st month, opened and all that took place with Him on that day was in fulfilment of the Law's typical requirements, as set forth in Numbers XXVIII, 16 to 23. To understand this is to possess the key to all that occurred on the day of our Lord's death.

The essence of what we have been considering may be summed up thus. Between the hours of 3 and 6 P.M. on Thursday, 30th April, which was the 14th of Nisan in the Divine Calendar, our Lord Jesus Christ orders the Preparation of that Passover at which He is to be present as THE ANTITYPICAL PASSOVER LAMB – thus bringing to AN END all the typical Passover sacrifices which were but shadows of His own perfect Sacrifice which He was now about to offer to God "for the sin of the world". At the same time, also, the typical Feast of Unleavened Bread would come to an end because that of which it was a type, even the Christian Dispensation of Grace to all mankind, was about to open with a Passover Sacrifice which was not a shadow but an efficacious Offering which would enable myriads to declare with the Apostle Peter:

> "Ye were not redeemed with corruptible things . . . but with the precious blood of Christ, as of a lamb without blemish and without spot: Who verily was foreordained before the foundation of the world. . . . This is the word which by the gospel is preached unto you" (I Peter I, 18 to 25).

As this Thursday closes, the blessed Saviour of the World wends His way back into the Holy City with His disciples. They go direct to the house where Peter and John had prepared the Passover.

As our Lord enters the large Upper Room to take the Passover with His disciples the day of His death, which is Friday, 1st May, opens. It will close, as we know, to find His body "lifted up from the earth", hanging lifeless on a Tree betwixt two malefactors at "a place called Golgotha".

## THE NINETY HOURS OF OUR LORD'S PASSION WHICH OPEN AT 6 A.M. ON THURSDAY, 30TH APRIL – "THE DAY OF THE PREPARATION" FOR JEHOVAH'S PASSOVER

The Bible day opens at 6 A.M. and closes at 6 P.M. Our Lord established this fact when He said, "Are there not twelve hours in the day?" (John XI, 9).

"The day of the preparation" for the Passover of Jehovah, which our Lord took on the evening prior to His death, opened at 6 A.M. on Thursday, 30th April. This day in the Divine Calendar was the 14th of Nisan – the day at the close of which, according to the Law, the Passover must be killed (Exodus XII, 6).

In His death our Lord Jesus Christ suffered the full judgment of God due to us on account of OUR SINS. The actual period of this judgment commenced at 6 A.M. on the Day of the Preparation for the Passover. (He was the antitypical Passover Lamb of God and as such He had been set apart by Mary of Bethany four days previously.) After 12 hours, that is, at 6 P.M., He dies "in a figure" at the last Passover. At 3 P.M. on Friday, after another 21 hours – that is, after 33 hours in all – He dies actually on Calvary's Tree. He rises, as we are about to show from Holy Scripture, after 57 hours "in the heart of the earth". This makes the total number of hours 90 (33+57). Not until these 90 hours had passed upon Him were the full judgment claims of God on account of OUR SINS met.

The number "9" in the Bible signifies "judgment" and the number "10" – "ordinal perfection" or "completeness". We may rightly say, therefore, that in the sight of God the number "90" (9×10) signifies *judgment satisfied.* It is not surprising, therefore, that there are other examples in the Bible where God uses the number 90 to mark a period during which judgment is being satisfied. One of the most notable of these is the period of 2,520 years during which the Throne of Judah is cast down and the Gentiles rule the earth. In 2,520 years there are 90 "hours" of 28 years each. At the end of these 90 "hours" the Throne of Judah will again be set up, as the period of Judah's judgment will have been satisfied.

Let it, therefore, be remembered that the Bible reckons that the period of our Lord's Passion began at 6 A.M. on the Thursday, which was "the day of the preparation" for Jehovah's Passover, and continued for 3 days and 18 hours, or 90 hours in all, to His resurrection.

## A NOTE

### WHAT THE BIBLE REVEALS CONCERNING THE DATE OF OUR LORD'S DEATH

The day on which our Lord Jesus Christ was crucified must ever remain the most solemn and important in the whole history of the Universe. No Christian would wish to dispute this fact because all know that apart from our Lord's one perfect atoning Sacrifice for sin, accomplished on the Cross of Calvary, there would be no Redemption for sinners, and we should all still be under the guilt and power of sin like those who do not believe *with their hearts* on our Lord Jesus Christ (Romans X, 9 and 10).

It is, therefore, a matter of the first importance that all believers in Christ should know exactly what is revealed in the Bible concerning the date of Friday, 1st May A.D. 33, which was the day in our calendar when our Lord and Saviour Jesus Christ was crucified by the Roman Authorities at the instigation of the religious rulers of the Jews.

First, let us recall that on 1st January 45 B.C., Julius Caesar inaugurated a solar calendar only slightly different to our present Gregorian calendar, and that throughout our Lord's life the whole civilized earth was using this calendar in which the months, in length and in name, were identical with our own (see the Summary of Facts – Par. 20). To the Romans 1st May was "the Kalends" of May. The year date "A.D. 33" was, of course, unknown to the Romans who reckoned time by a series of years which started with the Foundation of Rome in the eighth century B.C. The excellent B.C. and A.D. system of reckoning years was originated by an abbot, Dionysius Exiguus, in the sixth century after Christ but it was not generally adopted until some time later.

The dates of our Lord's death and resurrection have an immense Biblical significance because in the Apostolic era the Church, as we will later show from the Bible, kept the Lord's

Supper, the Resurrection and Pentecost on the solar anniversaries of these events in A.D. 33.

As we have stated previously, the calendar which appears on the surface of Holy Scripture is that given by God to the nation of Israel – the Old Testament from Genesis XII being, in one aspect, a history of that people. For particulars of this calendar we need only refer readers to the early paragraphs of the Summary of Facts at the beginning of this Treatise.

It will be seen from the Chart of the Five Calendars in operation during our Lord's Life (which precedes this Chapter) that the date of Friday, 1st May A.D. 33, was the 14th of the 1st month – a Friday or sixth day in the Jews' Calendar, and the 15th of the 1st month – a Sabbath – in the Divine Calendar. We learn from John XIX, 14, that to the Jews that day "was the preparation of the passover". It opened at 6 A.M. and ended at 6 P.M. when the Passover was killed and eaten.

Mark's Gospel informs us that the day on which our Lord died (XV, 42),

> "was the preparation, that is, the day before the sabbath" (Greek: PROSABBATON).

Therefore, in two aspects this 1st May was to the Jews a "day of . . . preparation". That the day was a "Friday" in the Jews' Calendar is also proved by the above quotation from Mark.

Luke's Gospel also states that our Lord Jesus Christ died on a Friday, as may be learnt from the following quotation (XXIII, 54):

> "that day was the preparation, and the sabbath drew on".

John's Gospel bears a similar testimony which is as follows (XIX, 31):

> "The Jews therefore, because it was the preparation, that the bodies should not remain upon the cross on the sabbath day, (for that sabbath day was an high [lit. great] day,) besought Pilate that their legs might be broken, and that they might be taken away.

Matthew's Gospel likewise names the day of our Lord's death as "the day of the preparation" (XXVII, 62).

Nothing, therefore, is more clear in the whole Bible than that the Saviour of the World laid down His sinless life on the day before the Jewish Sabbath – the sixth day of the week which we call "Friday". Furthermore, as we have seen, the Bible states that that Friday was both "the day of the preparation" for the Jews' weekly Sabbath and the Jews' Passover.

It will be advisable to mention before passing on that there are some sincere scholars who, in their great zeal to solve the problem of time in relation to our Lord's death and resurrection, have supposed His death to have taken place on Wednesday or Thursday. They arrive at this unfortunate conclusion by assuming that the Sabbath mentioned by Mark, Luke and John was not the weekly Sabbath or Seventh day, but an extra Sabbath on account of its being the first day of the Feast of Unleavened Bread – the 15th of the 1st month. To do this is a grave transgression, because the Bible *with the utmost precision* refuses to call the first day of Unleavened Bread a Sabbath, but does call it "a holy convocation" and this, verily, in order to distinguish it from a Sabbath – a term only applied to the distinctively Jewish feasts (whether holy convocations or not) of the 7th month, namely, Trumpets, the Day of Atonement, and Ingathering. (Please confirm this by reference to Leviticus XXIII, and compare verses 6 to 8 with verses 24, 32 and 39.) On a "holy convocation" an Israelite could do "no servile work". On a "sabbath" (except that of the Feast of Trumpets) he could do "no work" at all. Furthermore, the Feasts of Unleavened Bread and Pentecost have found their antitypes in the Christian Church which takes no account whatsoever of the Sabbath or Seventh day.

The statement in John XIX, 31, "that sabbath day was an high day", simply directs attention to the fact that the Jewish weekly Sabbath in question was also "an holy convocation" because it was the first day of Unleavened Bread. This constituted it "an high day" and formed an additional reason to the Jews for removing our Lord's body and those of the forgiven and unforgiven malefactors from their respective crosses.

In accepting that our Lord Jesus Christ died on a Friday according to the calendars of Israel and of the Roman earth, the Churches of Christendom have, therefore, acted strictly in accordance with what *on the surface* the Gospels assert with such unmistakable clearness.

This, however, is only a part of the truth and by no means the most important part. In fact, the whole problem of time in relation to the death and resurrection of our Lord Jesus Christ becomes utterly insoluble if He is viewed as dying on a Friday. The reason for this will be seen with vivid clearness when we have set forth all that the Bible reveals *beneath the surface* concerning this deeply mysterious problem which for eighteen hundred years has baffled every effort to find a solution which did not, in some sort, do violence to the text of Holy Scripture.

We cannot develop this aspect further until we have reached the point in our narrative when it is necessary to reveal from the Bible the time at which our Lord Jesus Christ came forth in triumph from the grave. At the moment we are engaged in showing what the Bible reveals as to the date of His death and of the impossibility of correctly discerning this by means of Israel's Calendar *with which it has no direct connection whatsoever.* According to Israel's Calendar our Lord died at 3 P.M. on Friday, the 14th of Nisan – the day of preparation for the Passover – and, viewed in this light, His death would have no Biblical significance of any kind whatever, since there were no typical sacrifices offered on that day of which His death on account of sin could form an antitype.

This brings us back to what we affirmed at the end of Part IV in our last Chapter, namely, that it is impossible to suppose that God could measure time in relation to His well-beloved Son other than by means of the Divine Calendar which, let it be remembered, records TRUE TIME. As we stated in the Summary of Facts (please read Paragraphs 13 and 14), the Divine Calendar runs concurrently with the Calendar of Israel except that in it the days of the month and the days of the week were, until the Cross, ONE DAY AHEAD of those in Israel's Calendar. Consequently, our Lord and His disciples took the Passover the evening before His death because *it was the true 14th day of the 1st moon or month;* while the Jews took their Passover on the evening after His death because it was the 14th day of the 1st month in their Calendar. Likewise, as in Israel's Calendar the day of our Lord's death was a Friday, we know that in the Divine Calendar it must have been the Sabbath.

Let it therefore be clearly understood from this point that in reckoning time in relation to our Lord's death and resurrection the Bible views Him as dying on THE HOLY SABBATH. *This is the first great fact to be laid hold of by anyone who would understand what the Scriptures reveal on this subject.*

Before proceeding, it will be well to draw attention to the fact that, because of its immense importance, the Bible affords prima facie evidence that God reckons time in relation to the death and resurrection of Christ solely according to the Divine Calendar. In relation to the days of the month this is proved, as we have just shown, in that our Lord kept the last Passover with His disciples on the evening before the Jews kept their Passover. It must be obvious to all that our Lord kept this on the true 14th of the 1st month according to the Law. This affords undeniable evidence that the Divine Calendar was one day of the month ahead of the Calendar of Israel. In relation to the days of the week, as we are about to show, Matthew in his Gospel actually names the Sabbath as the day of our Lord's death; while Mark, Luke and John all name the day of His death as the day before the Sabbath – the day which we call Friday. Both, of course, are absolutely correct, but Matthew employs the Divine Calendar while the other three Evangelists employ that of Israel which is one day of the week behind the Divine Calendar.

## MATTHEW PRESENTS OUR LORD AS DYING ON THE SABBATH

The fact that our Lord Jesus Christ died on the SABBATH in Divine time is openly stated in Matthew's Gospel; but before this can be understood it is necessary to realize that the Holy Spirit designated that this Evangelist should exclusively employ the Divine Calendar in recording the time factors of our Lord's death and resurrection. On the other hand, Mark, Luke and John each employ Israel's Calendar in all their time references to our Lord's death though they are compelled to use the Divine Calendar when naming the time of the Resurrection.

To anyone who does not know of Matthew's use of the Divine Calendar many of his statements as to time must appear to be absolutely incomprehensible. For this reason critics of the Bible have not been slow to light on some of these and in their ignorance to speak of them in scathing terms. At the moment we only draw attention to part of the verse which shows that according to Matthew our Lord died on a Sabbath.

In Matthew XXVIII, 1, we read:

"In the end of the sabbath . . . came Mary Magdalene and the other Mary to see the sepulchre."

(We omit in this verse reference to "the first day of the week" because it has to do with the Resurrection and is inexplicable apart from the knowledge of certain other facts which we will disclose in due course.)

This statement by Matthew concerning the visit of the two Marys to the sepulchre "in the end of the sabbath" is in perfect accord with similar statements by Mark and Luke, both of whom make it plain that this took place at the end of the day of our Lord's death.

Mark in Chapter XV, 47, states:

"And Mary Magdalene and Mary the mother of Joses beheld where He was laid."

Luke in Chapter XXIII, 55, states:

"And the women also, which came with Him from Galilee, followed after, and beheld the sepulchre, and how His body was laid."

Matthew, Mark and Luke in these statements all draw attention to the fact that at the close of the day of our Lord's death and following His burial in the rock-hewn sepulchre, certain women, including "Mary Magdalene and the other Mary", approach the sepulchre in order to note (for the purpose of embalming) how and where the body of their crucified Lord was laid. Matthew, because he is caused to employ Divine time, states that this took place "in the end of the sabbath"; whereas Mark and Luke, who adopt Israel's Calendar, state that it occurred at the end of Friday which was the day of "the preparation" for the (Jews') Sabbath (Mark XV, 42 and Luke XXIII, 54). Both statements are absolutely true and both refer to the day of our Lord's death which to God was the holy Sabbath but which to the Jews was their sixth day, which we call Friday. It will appear perfectly manifest to all in due course that our Lord Jesus Christ had to die on a Sabbath in fulfilment of the Levitical type of "the sheaf of the firstfruits" which had to be presented before the Lord "on the morrow after the sabbath".

Before passing on we must call attention to the fact that the majority of students who realize that our Lord's death took place in the year A.D. 33 have given the date of Friday, 3rd April because they assume it was the 14th of Nisan in the Jews' Calendar.

In our former Treatise, *The World in Liquidation* (Paper IV – "A Summary of Time from Creation"), we set forth an exact reproduction of time in the Bible from Creation which is astronomically accurate to an hour. We show that the Bible reveals, in a manner which no one could possibly refute, that the date of the Exodus of Israel from Egypt was 12th May 1639 B.C. and that this day was the 15th of the 1st month (then called Abib) in Israel's Calendar and, therefore, the 1st day of the Feast of Unleavened Bread; and that it was also the 15th of the 7th month in the Years of the Messiah – facts which in themselves afford independent proof of the correctness of this date which otherwise could never have been marked with this dual significance (see reference to this in Chapter One, under the section headed "The Date of the Nativity in the Years of the Messiah").

This being so, it would be impossible for any first month of the Sabbatic series of years which was instituted at the Exodus to start before 29th March. The New Moon of the 1st month at the Exodus was on 28th April and any 12th month which ended before 29th March would be followed by an intercalary month of 30 days, in order that the start of the New Year might be delayed until the Spring season, which was the main objective of the new calendar which God gave to Moses before the Exodus (see Exodus XII, 1, 2). There can be no possible doubt that the 1st of Nisan, A.D. 33, in the Jews' Calendar was on 18th April and that the 14th of Nisan was on 1st May.

In an article on "Months" in *Smith's Dictionary of the Bible* the writer states, "At present Nisan answers to March, but in early times it coincided with April". This fact we have proved from the Bible.

This is the sum of what we have thus far set forth concerning the day of our Lord's death. This was called,

In the Roman Calendar: Calends of May (i.e., the 1st), A.D. 33,

In the Jews' Calendar: Sixth day (i.e., Friday) Nisan 14th, A.D. 33,

IN THE DIVINE CALENDAR: THE SABBATH, NISAN 15TH, A.D. 33.

## WHY THE DAY OF OUR LORD'S DEATH HAD TO BE THE 15TH OF NISAN, THE FIRST MONTH

Read Numbers XXVIII, 16 to 23

We have already pointed out that the 14th of Nisan – the 1st month – which was the date in Israel's Calendar when our Lord was put to death, had no significance because it contained no offerings of any kind which were typical of His Sacrifice on account of sin. Search as you will, you will be unable to locate in the whole Levitical economy a single sacrifice for sin or trespass appointed for the 14th day of the 1st month. This fact should at once satisfy every enquirer who does not yet appreciate why God refuses to reckon time in relation to the death of His Son according to the Calendar of Israel. It was because the 14th of Nisan had no appointed sacrifices except the Morning and Evening Burnt Offerings which typify Christ, as Man, rendering His whole duty to God and which, therefore, have no element in them related to sin, sins or trespass.

When, however, we consider the sacrificial elements of the next day, namely, the 15th of the 1st month and the 1st day of the Feast of Unleavened Bread, we find it to be a day saturated with sacrifices. It opened with the sacrifice of the Passover at 6 P.M. and on the following morning the Law commanded that there should be the presentation of special Burnt Offerings with their Meat Offerings, together with a Sin Offering. Each of these Offerings forms a separate and typical aspect of the One Sacrifice offered by our Lord Jesus Christ on the Cross of Calvary on the 15th day of the 1st month in the year A.D. 33.

In Numbers XXVIII, verse 16, we read:

> "And in the fourteenth day of the first month is the passover of the Lord."

In Exodus XII, 6, and in other Scriptures, we are told that the Passover was to be killed "in the evening". According to the Hebrew this should have been translated, "between the evenings" – an expression which refers to a point of time between the last 3 hours of the 14th day, namely, 3 to 6 P.M., and the first 3 hours of the 15th day of the 1st month, namely, 6 to 9 P.M. This in practice meant that the Passover was to be killed at or about 6 P.M. which was the opening of the 15th of Nisan or Abib, as this month was called before the Babylonian Captivity.

Then in Numbers XXVIII, 17, we read:

> "In the fifteenth day of this month is the feast: seven days shall unleavened bread be eaten."

In previous pages we have shown that the Seven Days of the Feast of Unleavened Bread form one of the most enlightening types of the Christian Dispensation in the whole Bible. No wonder the Apostle Paul declares to the Christians at Corinth, "Purge out therefore the old leaven, that ye may be a new lump, as ye are unleavened. For even Christ our passover is sacrificed for us: therefore let us keep the feast . . . with the unleavened bread of sincerity and truth" (I Cor. V, 6 to 8).

It matters not whether it is the Passover at 6 P.M. – the opening hour of the 15th of Nisan – or the Burnt Offerings with their Meat Offerings and the Sin Offering of the following morning, as commanded by the Lord to Moses and recorded by him in Numbers XXVIII, all are typical of the One Sacrifice offered by our Lord Jesus Christ on Calvary's Cross on God's Holy Sabbath, the 15th of Nisan – our 1st May – in A.D. 33, which was the First Day of the antitypical Feast of Unleavened Bread, namely, the Christian Dispensation or Day of Grace to all mankind.

No one, therefore, could get a glimmer of Biblical understanding of our Lord's Sacrifice on Calvary on 1st May A.D. 33, without the help of this passage in Numbers XXVIII in which the typical sacrifices of the 15th of the 1st month – the day in the Divine Calendar on which our Lord was crucified – are set forth. We need add nothing further as to the day and date of the death of our Lord and Saviour Jesus Christ. All will know as we proceed that in the sight of God, Who ordained every detail as to its time and place, the Saviour of men died on the 15th day of the 1st month or moon – a Sabbath – in the 34th year of His life – the year being in our reckoning, A.D. 33.

# CHAPTER FIFTEEN

## A BRIEF REVIEW OF EVENTS ON FRIDAY, 1ST MAY, A.D. 33, THE DAY OUR LORD JESUS CHRIST ACCOMPLISHED HIS EXODUS OUT OF THIS WORLD

### PART ONE

6 P.M. UNTIL MIDNIGHT
(THE BIBLE DAY OF FRIDAY BEGAN AT 6 P.M., THURSDAY)
THE DAY OPENS WITH OUR LORD JESUS CHRIST TAKING THE PASSOVER OF JEHOVAH WITH HIS TWELVE APOSTLES

---

JUDAS, AFTER BEING NAMED AS BETRAYER, LEAVES THE SUPPER TABLE

---

OUR LORD, HAVING DIED FIGURATIVELY AS THE ANTITYPICAL PASSOVER LAMB, INSTITUTES THE CHRISTIAN ORDINANCE OF "THE LORD'S SUPPER"

---

HIS LAST DISCOURSES TO THE APOSTLES

---

THE CONFLICT IN GETHSEMANE WHEN OUR LORD PROSTRATES HIMSELF IN SUPPLICATION TO GOD THE FATHER

---

THE BETRAYAL AND ARREST ABOUT MIDNIGHT

---

Matthew XXVI, 20 to 56; Mark XIV, 17 to 52; Luke XXII, 14 to 54, and John XIV to XVIII, 12

WE NOW enter the last day of our Lord's life on the earth and our object is to set forth a brief summary of the events which marked His last hours, with special reference to those features which relate to Time, most of which, because of their sacredness to God, lie hidden beneath the surface of the Four Gospel Accounts of His sufferings and death.

No one could embark on such a project without feelings of the deepest emotion unless, of course, such a one was an entire stranger to the infinite and eternal blessings which have flowed to mankind as the result of the Events which occupied that day and which culminated with our Lord's expiry at Calvary after He had cried triumphantly, "It is finished" – a statement which had reference to the completion of the work of man's Redemption which, sent by God the Father, He had come into the world to accomplish (see John IV, 34; XVII, 4; XIX, 30).

If, as is often the case, we are deeply moved on hearing an account of some form of extreme suffering which has overtaken a human being, known or unknown to us, what should our feelings be when we read in the Gospels of the unutterable sufferings and humiliation of the sinless Son of God Who had come down from Heaven with no other object than to redeem our fallen race by the giving up of His own life in the manner recorded historically in the Four Gospels? If we are not moved by these to the depths of our being, it can only be that we have become so hardened by sin as to make us insensible of the supreme purpose of it all, as expressed by the Prophet Isaiah in these words, "He was wounded for our transgressions, he was bruised for our iniquities . . . and with his stripes we are healed" (LIII, 5). To believe *with the heart* on our Lord Jesus Christ as the One Who suffered as our SUBSTITUTE the inexorable judgment of God due to us on account of our sins, is to have obtained the forgiveness of our sins and God's priceless gift of eternal life (Acts XIII, 38 and 39; Romans VI, 23).

As we proceed may we, with subdued hearts, ever keep in mind that the One Whose sufferings and death we are about to review from the Gospels was, though Man, and born so of the Virgin Mary, nevertheless God manifest in human form – "the Word . . . made flesh" dwelling among men (John I, 1 and 14).

In Bible terms 33 years and 190 days had elapsed since our Lord's birth in Bethlehem of Judaea. In our reckoning this was 32 years and 184 days which is one day over 32½ years. Again, in Bible terms our Lord began His public service for God on 26th November A.D. 29, at 30 years of age, so that only 3 years, 6 months and 13 days had passed from thence to the day of His death on 1st May A.D. 33. How brief, therefore, was His sojourn among men, for, as Isaiah foresaw, "He was cut off out of the land of the living" (LIII, 8). He did not live to see even a half of man's allotted span of "three-score years and ten".

### THE DAY OF OUR LORD'S DEATH OPENS WITH HIS TAKING THE PASSOVER WITH HIS TWELVE APOSTLES AT THE CLOSE OF THE TRUE 14TH DAY OF THE MOON, ACCORDING TO THE LAW

### THE TRANSCENDENT SIGNIFICANCE OF THE DATE OF THIS LAST PASSOVER

One has to be extremely careful in reading the Holy Scriptures not to miss the importance of an event because of the paucity of words employed in recording it. For instance, Matthew, Mark and Luke in the briefest possible terms record the fact that the Lord and the twelve Apostles kept the Passover on the evening before He was put to death. In Luke XXII, 13 and 14, we read, "and they made ready the passover. And when the hour was come, He sat down, and the twelve apostles with Him" (see also Matt. XXVI, 20 and Mark XIV, 17). The importance of this occasion – because of the place it holds in God's plan for the redemption of mankind – it is impossible to estimate. Never before had our Lord and Master been Host at one of the Levitical Feasts and, doubtless, He alone knew the true significance of the occasion. But He was not only the Host Who provided the Offering; He Himself was the Offering, seeing that He was present as "the Lamb of God, which taketh away the sin of the world" (John I, 29). He was in fact present as THE ANTITYPE of every Passover lamb that had ever been sacrificed in Israel since the Exodus in 1639 B.C. – 1,671 years previously. This Passover in A.D. 33 was not, therefore, another typical Passover which pointed on to the coming of the Messiah to accomplish the Redemption of our race, IT WAS THE ANTITYPICAL PASSOVER and THE MESSIAH was now present as God's Passover Lamb and would that very day be sacrificed for us "that He might redeem us from all iniquity" (Titus II, 14).

It is to John's Gospel in the main that we have to turn in order to obtain light upon the events which transpired in the upper room during the hours which were spent over the Supper table by our Lord and His Apostles. This is the more remarkable because John never names the Passover that the Lord took but refers to it merely as "Supper". The reasons for this are two. In the first place, John makes reference to "the Jews' passover", (XI, 55) and to name another would cause confusion. In this connection it is also to be carefully noted that for the same reason Matthew, Mark and Luke refer exclusively to the Passover which our Lord took with His Apostles and are silent as to the Jews' Passover.

The second reason for which John never names the Last Supper as the Passover is because his Gospel opens with our Lord figuratively dying and rising again as "the Lamb of God" (see John I, 29 and 36). This fact we have dealt with fully in Part III of Chapter Four of this Treatise. All will recall how that in the first chapter of his Gospel John presents Christ as already rejected by "His own". It would, therefore, be utterly inconsistent for John to present Christ again as the antitypical Passover Lamb of God. Because, at the beginning of his Gospel, our Lord is viewed as having died and risen again, John is able to present Him throughout as the One Who dispenses eternal life, which is a gift only made possible by His having been lifted up "as Moses lifted up the serpent in the wilderness" (John III, 14, 15).

Nevertheless, as we have said, it is to John we have to turn in order to glean light on what took place at the Last Passover Supper.

Matthew (XXVI, 21 to 25), Mark (XIV, 18 to 21) and Luke (XXII, 21 to 23) each make reference to the consternation of the Apostles when our Lord announced at the table that one of their number would betray Him; and they each record our Lord's "Woe unto that man". Luke refers to the strife which developed among the Apostles as to who "should be accounted the greatest" (XXII, 24 to 30).

John's account of the last Supper is found in Chapter XIII. It is most touching to note his reference to the Lord's love for His own and how He expressed that love when He knew "His hour was come that He should depart out of this world unto the Father" (verse 1).

It is unfortunate that the Authorized Version adopts the

expression in verse 2, "And supper being ended". The Revised Version corrects this to "during supper". Another translation is, "Supper having been served". From this we may infer that our blessed Lord's act of extreme humility in taking the place of a bond-slave and washing His disciples' feet was performed at the beginning of the Supper, and this, no doubt, as the prelude to this last act of fellowship with His Apostles. It was a touching scene and an expression of His great love for the band of men who had continued with Him in His temptations (Luke XXII, 28). But it was more than this (see verse 7) since it expressed His future love and care for His Church when, as our great High Priest in Heaven, He would keep His members cleansed from defilements contracted in the world that He was about to leave, by the application of the water of the Word of God in the power of the Spirit to our hearts and consciences (Ephes. V, 26). By this means He would maintain the members of His Church during His absence in fellowship with the Father and with Himself, the Son (I John I, 3 and 9). How solemn the warning of verse 8, "If I wash thee not, thou hast no part with Me".

It was following the episode of the feet-washing and after Jesus "was set down again" that "He was troubled in spirit, and testified, and said, Verily, verily, I say unto you, that one of you shall betray Me" (verses 12 and 21). It is at this point that the other three Gospels harmonize with John's account. The Apostles in their agitation press the Lord to name the betrayer, each of them saying, according to Mark, "Is it I?" John, "lying on Jesus' breast", at the behest of Peter, asks the Lord, "Who is it?" Then the Lord exposes the traitor openly by handing a sop to Judas Iscariot into whom "Satan entered" at once. "Then said Jesus unto him, That thou doest, do quickly", and Judas "went immediately out: and it was night" – darkness and evil deeds ever going together (John III, 19).

The words of our Lord Jesus Christ at the departure of Judas from the company denote that a supreme crisis in His Passion had thereby been reached. Aforetime it had been written, "He that eateth bread with me hath lifted up his heel against me" (Ps. XLI, 9). Therefore, until Satan openly showed himself as the master of fallen human nature by his conquest of Judas, one of the twelve, and until Judas – Satan's chosen vessel – had gone forth out of the midst to perform his fearful task, the predicted means by which our Lord was to be delivered up to be crucified were not in evidence. But directly Judas had gone out our Lord knew the hour had come in which, through His death upon the Cross, He would for ever annul Satan's power over man, obliterate sin from the universe, and destroy death which held the whole human race in bondage (II Tim. I, 10; Heb. II, 14, 15). For these reasons, and very many more, He declared when Judas departed, "Now is the Son of Man glorified, and God is glorified in Him". Now, by the work of Redemption the Son would glorify the Father here on earth before all men; and in due course would Himself be glorified by the Father when He returned to Heaven as Head of the New Creation. Yet how great the mystery that Satan, using fallen man in the person of Judas Iscariot as his tool, must be the one to set in motion those fearful circumstances which actually brought our Lord down into death at Calvary. Assuredly this was the fulfilling of the first prophecy of the Bible, which the Lord God addressed to Satan when He said, "Thou shalt bruise His heel". Little did Satan realize, however, that he was, through Judas, really encompassing his own final overthrow, for the same prophecy foretold that Christ – "the seed of the woman" – should "bruise" his head, and this we know was accomplished through His death upon the Cross (Genesis III, 15).

We must now briefly consider the last Passover in its historical setting.

## THE IMMENSE CHRONOLOGICAL SIGNIFICANCE OF THE PASSOVER WHICH OUR LORD JESUS CHRIST TOOK WITH HIS APOSTLES ON THURSDAY EVENING, 30TH APRIL A.D. 33

All should know that God's plan for man's redemption began in the Garden of Eden directly after Satan had seduced our first parents whom God had created exactly forty days previously. It was then that God gave promise of a Redeemer – One Who is spoken of as the Seed of the Woman – Who would in due season overthrow Satan and annul his power. Until the triumph of the Redeemer the race, now fallen, would remain subject to the power of Satan, except in the case of those few who would obey God according to the revelation He might make to their generation and who by faith would live in anticipation of the coming of the promised Redeemer.

We have many times in this Treatise been obliged to point out that when God first instructed Moses and Aaron in regard to the ordinance of the Passover, He specified in the clearest possible terms that the Passover lambs were to be gathered and set apart FOUR DAYS before they were to be sacrificed (Exodus XII, 3 to 6). On the 10th of the 1st month they were to be set apart and on the 14th day at even they were to be offered. To mark the immense importance in His sight of these FOUR DAYS between the 10th and the 14th of the 1st month, God ordained that they should never be reckoned in Sacred or Redemption Chronology. He ordained that the Sacred Year should begin on the 15th of the 1st month with the killing of the Passover lambs, and end with the 10th of the 1st month in the next year, so that under NO CIRCUMSTANCES should the 11th, 12th, 13th and 14th of the 1st month find any place in the Chronology of Redemption which was, therefore, composed of years of 350 days each – the civil lunar year being 354 days in length (see Paragraphs 5, 6, 7 and 8 in the Summary of Facts).

It will be remembered that in our previous chapter (XIV, Part I) we showed that Mary of Bethany anointed our Lord and set Him apart to be sacrificed, as the Antitypical Passover Lamb of God's providing, FOUR DAYS thereafter, namely, at the hour when our Lord sat down with His twelve Apostles to take the Passover which was the exact opening of the 15th day of the 1st month in the Divine Calendar. We pointed out that Mary's act was performed exactly FOUR THOUSAND YEARS FROM THE FALL in the Bible's Sacred or Redemption Chronology – a series of 6,000 Years which began after the Fall and will continue until the Kingdom of the Messiah, our Lord and Saviour Jesus Christ, is established over the earth (see Par. 16; Summary of Facts). Mary's anointing of Christ for death as the Lamb of God was at the close of 26th April, which was the true 10th of Nisan and, therefore, the day appointed for the setting apart of the Passover lambs (see Chart of the Five Calendars). As the following FOUR DAYS are unreckoned in Sacred Chronology, it is equally true to say that the 4,000 Years from the Fall were completed when our Lord and His twelve Apostles sat down to take the Passover as it is to say that they were completed at the time of Mary's act of devotion.

How wondrous and solemn, therefore, to realize that the One Who was both Host and Victim at the Last Passover had Himself been present at the Assize in the Garden of Eden after the Fall, and had there and then been set apart by the Lord God to die as our Redeemer at the end of FOUR "DAYS" OF A THOUSAND YEARS each. The Apostle Peter bears witness to this fact when he writes,"Ye know that ye were not redeemed with corruptible things . . . but with the precious blood of Christ, as of a lamb without blemish and without spot: Who verily was foreordained before the foundation of the world, but was manifest in these last times for you" (I Peter I, 18 to 20).

So when our Lord Jesus Christ entered the Upper Room in the early evening of Thursday, 30th April, which was the opening of the 15th of the 1st month in A.D. 33, in order to keep the Passover of Jehovah with His Apostles, He knew that the allotted span of 4,000 Redemption Years had passed and that He was there as the Lamb of God to take away the sin of the world; or, in other words, He was there to accomplish our redemption by the shedding of His own blood. Furthermore, He knew He had been anointed precisely 4 days previously at the Bethany Supper and had been thus set apart for death just as the typical lambs were on every 10th of Nisan. What a meaning these facts give to our Lord's message to the owner of the house, when He said, "My time is at hand; I will keep the passover at thy house with My disciples" (Matt. XXVI, 18).

These are the true facts about the hour at which our Lord entered the Upper Room to keep the Passover of Jehovah with His disciples. In the eye of God He was there to die on behalf of the whole human race, that is, to be sacrificed and to shed His blood for our redemption. Furthermore, in the sight of God "Who . . . calleth those things which be not as though they were", Jesus is viewed as having then died as the true Antitype of every previously-offered Paschal sacrifice. To the Lord Himself this was so also; consequently He was able to say at the institution of His Supper: "This is My body" and "This . . . My blood, which is shed for you" – words which prove that He viewed Himself as having died and as having shed His blood. We express such a matter by saying that He died "in a figure" –

an expression used in reference to Isaac's "death and resurrection" after he was offered up by Abraham (Heb. XI, 19). There is, however, in the Ordinance of the Passover, as recorded in Exodus XII, a feature which appears to be a link between that event and the following morning. In verse 10 we read, "and that which remaineth of it until the morning ye shall burn with fire". It would appear to be lawful, therefore, to view our Lord's crucifixion the next morning at "the third hour" (8 to 9 A.M.) as the burning of "that which remaineth of it until the morning". "Burning" in the Bible signifies judgment. If this is so, then we may view our Lord's crucifixion as making real His death "in a figure" the previous evening, when He offered Himself as "the Lamb of God, which taketh away the sin of the world". We must ever remember that it was as the true Passover Lamb of God that our Lord Jesus Christ effected our REDEMPTION; just as in a typical way the Passover lambs whose blood was sprinkled on the houses of the Israelites in Egypt effected their redemption and saved them from the sword of the Destroying Angel which slew all the first-born of the Egyptians (Exodus XII, 12, 13; XV, 13).

## THE RELATION BETWEEN THE FIRST PASSOVER IN EGYPT IN 1639 B.C. AND THE LAST PASSOVER TAKEN BY OUR LORD AND HIS DISCIPLES IN A.D. 33

It is a remarkable and an ominous fact that the Bible only records two Passovers as having been celebrated at the close of the true 14th day of the 1st moon or month, namely, that which preceded the Exodus of Israel from Egypt in the evening of Thursday, 11th May 1639 B.C., and that which preceded our blessed Lord's Exodus out of this world on the evening of Thursday, 30th April A.D. 33. In no other instance does the Bible record a Passover being kept by Israel other than at the close of the 14th day of the 1st month in Israel's Calendar, which was reckoned by months starting at the phasis or first appearance of the moon (see Par. 13; Summary of Facts).

In a real sense, therefore, the Passover kept in Egypt formed the true TYPE and that kept by our Lord with His Apostles its ANTITYPE. The former of these effected the Redemption of the people of Israel from Egyptian bondage (Exod. XV, 13) and the latter effected the Redemption of the whole human race from the bondage of sin and death, for Christ, we are told, "gave Himself a ransom for all" (I Tim. II, 6).

It is a matter of great chronological importance that the Passover in Egypt and that taken by our Lord with His Apostles were in Redemption Chronology to the day 1,500 years apart. These 1,500 years are composed of 1,470 years and 30 years of Jubile. Jacob lived 147 years; so his seed, the people of Israel, before being "cut off" had a national existence of ten times 147 years. In Secular Chronology the period between these two Passovers was 1,671 years, but Redemption Chronology omits the 131 years of chastisement in the days of the Judges and Samuel, and also the 70 years' Captivity in Babylon. (1,671 less 131+70=1,470 years.)

It is a fact of the utmost significance that, by design of God, the days of the week during which Israel's Exodus from Egypt was being effected after the taking of the Passover in the night of Thursday, 11th May 1639 B.C., were absolutely identical with those which witnessed our Lord's Exodus after the Last Passover taken on Thursday night, 30th April A.D. 33.

In this connection, let it be remembered that Luke in his account of the Transfiguration is caused by the Spirit of God to tell us that Moses and Elijah "spake of His decease which He should accomplish at Jerusalem". The Greek word translated "decease" is "EXODOS", from which we get our word "exodus" which could very profitably have been used by the translators, since it was adopted by Luke to bring out the relation between Israel's Exodus from Egypt and our Lord's Exodus from this world. The mystical relationship between Israel and Israel's Messiah, our Lord Jesus Christ, is again brought out by Matthew's use of the Hosea prophecy, "Out of Egypt have I called My Son" – words which apply in the first instance to Israel but which the Spirit applies to our Lord, when Joseph took Him and His Mother into Egypt (Hosea XI, 1 and Matt. II, 15).

In our former Treatise, *The World in Liquidation*, we trace in Paper IV the exact course of time in the Bible from the first day of Creation to 12th June 1933, when as we there irrefutably establish, the Six Thousand Years of Man terminated to an hour. We there show in the appropriate section that the Exodus Passover was kept in the night of the true 14th of the 1st month in the year 1639 B.C. The day was Thursday. Israel, we are informed in Exodus XIII and XIV, began the Exodus the next day – Friday – and after three days crossed the Red Sea during the night of Sunday. The three days were the 15th, 16th and 17th of the 1st month – our 12th, 13th and 14th May.

It is common knowledge that Israel's crossing of the Red Sea is a type of our Lord's triumphant resurrection. For Israel this meant deliverance from slavery and the seeing of all their enemies destroyed by the mighty power of God.

How filled with meaning is the fact that Israel's Messiah, our own blessed Lord and Saviour, made His own Exodus out of this world, like Israel, on Friday the 15th of the 1st month, and that (as we shall in due course prove) He rose in triumph over all His enemies after the same three days, at Midnight on Sunday. Chronologically, therefore, the Exodus of Israel from Egypt on Friday, Saturday and Sunday – the 15th, 16th and 17th of the 1st month in 1639 B.C. – constituted a divine prefigurement or type of the death and resurrection of Israel's Messiah, our Lord Jesus Christ, which took place on exactly the same days of the week and month in A.D. 33.

If our Lord had risen, as has been erroneously supposed for so long, early on Sunday morning, this precious similitude would not exist; but, as it is, Israel's crossing of the Red Sea in the night of the 17th-18th of the 1st month forms a perfect type, both spiritually and chronologically, of our Lord's triumphant resurrection at Midnight on the Sunday following His Exodus on the Friday.

### OUR LORD JESUS CHRIST INSTITUTES THE SUPPER WHICH FOR CHRISTIANS IS TO BE THE MEMORIAL OF HIS DEATH

---

### HE ANNOUNCES THE PUTTING AWAY OF THE PASSOVER "UNTIL THE KINGDOM OF GOD SHALL COME"

Matthew XXVI, 26 to 29; Mark XIV, 22 to 25;
Luke XXII, 15 to 20

The words employed by our Lord Jesus Christ in these passages must have made it intensely clear to His disciples that they were as Jews eating their last Passover until the coming of the Kingdom when, as Ezekiel reveals (XLV, 21), it will again be partaken of by the restored nation of Israel as a memorial of our Lord's death as the true Antitype of the Paschal lamb. In Luke XXII, 15, we read that our Lord said, "With desire I have desired to eat this passover with you before I suffer: for I say unto you, I will not any more eat thereof, until it be fulfilled in the kingdom of God". He used similar words as to the taking of "the fruit of the vine" which formed a feature of the Passover.

The Passover being the remembrance of an event in Israel's history could have no meaning in the Christian Dispensation which that very day was to begin its own history by the sacrifice of Christ – the shedding of Whose blood was not only for Israel but "for many for the remission of sins", that is, for the Gentiles as well. And if the Christian Dispensation was then beginning, the times of Israel, as God's elect nation, must in the meanwhile be going to lapse, like the Passover which our Lord had put away until the Kingdom.

But were the disciples of Jesus, whether Jews or Gentiles, to have no such ordinance as the Passover? Was the Church, which would form Christ's mystical Body, to have no memorial of the day when He, out of love, "gave Himself for it" (Ephes. V, 25)? Was not our Lord the Merchantman of Whom the parable speaks Who, having "found one pearl of great price, went and sold all that he had, and bought it"? And was there to be no memorial of the day when He paid that great price with blood most precious? (Matthew XIII, 46).

The reasonableness of these postulates our Lord Himself recognized as soon as He had abolished the Passover which had now found its true Antitype in Himself, the Lamb of God, Whose shed blood would from that day bring in a New Order affecting all mankind.

We are informed that in the course of the Passover meal, quite clearly after Judas had withdrawn into the night, the Saviour

> "took bread, and gave thanks, and brake it, and gave unto them, saying, This is My body which is given for you: this do in remembrance of Me.
>
> "Likewise also the cup after supper, saying, This cup is the new testament (i.e. covenant) in My blood, which is shed for you" (Luke XXII, 19 and 20).

Similar words to these are recorded in Matthew and Mark. John is silent as to the institution of the Memorial Supper because he is silent as to the Passover, the place of which it was to take during the interval of the Christian Dispensation.

If to the above quotation from Luke we add such further details as may be found in the Apostle Paul's reference to the subject in I Corinthians XI (that which he received directly from the Lord) we have all that the text of Holy Scripture has to say on the subject – one, by the way, that has been more contorted and more the cause of division in Christendom than all else in the Bible put together.

To a mind exclusively governed by the statements of Holy Scripture, and unembarrassed by adhesion to traditions of one kind or another, it must be as obvious as it was to the eleven Jewish Apostles that our blessed Lord instituted His Memorial Supper to take the place of the Passover – the latter being a memorial of an Event and the former the memorial of a Person – "This do in remembrance of Me". If our Lord substituted His Supper for the Passover, His disciples, failing His giving them any alternative directions, could never have entertained any thought other than that they were to keep it, like the Passover, *once a year* on the anniversary of the occasion when our Lord instituted it. This fact is borne out by the way our Lord reminds Paul of when this first occasion was, namely, on "the (same) night in which He was betrayed". With this we must take account of the significant fact that we can learn nothing from recorded Apostolic practice as the New Testament contains no account of any occasion when the Lord's Supper was partaken of except at its Institution by our Lord. In Acts XX, as we will prove later from Scripture, the Church at Troas, with the Apostle Paul and his company present, "came together to break bread" – "on the first (day) of the sabbaths" at midnight in celebration of the Lord's resurrection – a very different purpose to remembering Him in death, and one which manifestly shows that "the Lord's supper" and "the breaking of bread" are entirely different ordinances.

The Apostle Paul in I Corinthians XI, 26, clearly upholds the annual celebration of the Lord's Supper by stating that in keeping it thus, "ye do shew (lit. proclaim – as in R.V.) the Lord's death till He come". It is, indeed, unheard of to hold a memorial of an event other than at the return of the date when it took place. The daily papers bear solemn witness to this fact by their "In Memoriam" notices of loved ones killed in the two Great Wars which always appear on the anniversary of the day when they made the supreme sacrifice for their king and country. But anniversaries are also a divine institution and form a most vital element in the Levitical order of worship. The Feasts were all annual celebrations, as may be seen from Leviticus XXIII. From the very beginning the Church has celebrated the Resurrection of Christ and Pentecost as anniversaries. Why not the Lord's Death? It is manifest, therefore, that our Lord's intention was that, by His Church in each locality coming together to take His Memorial Supper on the Solar anniversary of the night of His betrayal, which was the opening of the day of His death, the people of the world might receive a forceful reminder that there was a never-to-be-forgotten day in its history when the Son of God hung 'twixt heaven and earth on a Tree outside the Holy City, "being made a curse for us" that He might redeem us "from the curse of the law" (Gal. III, 13).

Just as the Israelites fed at the Passover on the roast flesh of a slain lamb, because it was emblematic of those lambs whose sprinkled blood sheltered their forefathers in Egypt from death by the Destroying Angel who "passed over them", so in the Lord's Supper believers are invited to partake of the bread which is emblematic of the given body of Christ, their Passover Lamb, Whose blood, symbolized by the wine, had redeemed them, and for ever sheltered them from judgment on account of their sins.

Nothing is more clear from the words uttered by our Lord Jesus Christ in instituting His Memorial Supper than that this annual celebration of His death was to form a personal link of a most precious nature between His every disciple and Himself. He well knew that "the bread" and "the wine" which He had selected as emblems of His body given and His blood shed would constitute eloquent memorials of His intense sufferings and of His death upon the Tree, which was followed by the piercing of His side from whence His life-blood had then flowed in expiation of our sins. All sincere hearts would be bowed in worship and thanksgiving and feel the close union with the One, present by the Spirit, Whom they were remembering in His death. Furthermore, this union with our Lord Jesus Christ would have the effect of uniting each and all in bonds of holy fellowship and love with one another and with all the members of the Church which is His mystical body. It is to be noted that our Lord's words, as recorded in the Gospels and as given to the Apostle Paul for the Gentiles in I Corinthians XI, are in the nature of a command, more than a mere request. Neither was a man to absent himself because of a sense of wrong-doing, but to judge himself and then partake of the ordinance in the deep consciousness that the very memorials themselves bore testimony to his sins being forgiven and to his having a right to obey our Lord's command, "this do in remembrance of Me".

We must now turn again to events in the Upper Room, remembering that the Passover Supper was over and that our Lord had now instituted the first Christian ordinance – "the cup" being partaken of "after supper". We will briefly recall His last and most precious intercourse with His disciples while still in the Upper Room and also on the way to the Garden of Gethsemane. These sayings constitute, as it were, His last will and testament for His own in the world and they contain riches untold for all willing to conform to His conditions for partaking of them, the first of which is to be found in the saying, "If a man love Me, he will keep My words".

We must not forget that while our Lord Jesus Christ was holding this holy converse with the eleven disciples, Judas, who had left their midst, was consummating his plans to betray Him into the hands of His enemies. Mark tells us, Judas "sought how he might conveniently betray Him" (XIV, 11), and Luke, that he "sought opportunity to betray Him unto them *in the absence of the multitude*" (XXII, 6). The Jewish rulers, even before Judas became their tool, had "consulted that they might take Jesus by subtilty, and kill Him. But . . . not on the feast day, lest there be an uproar among the people" (Matt. XXVI, 4 and 5). So, as we shall learn, all was carried out under cover of darkness; and before "the people" had hardly begun to go about their labours on the Feast Day, that is, "the day of the preparation" for their Passover, our Lord Jesus Christ, in perfect submission to His Father's will, had bowed to the will of His enemies, and allowed them to take Him and to hold their mock assize, condemn and crucify Him, because He knew it was according to "the determinate counsel and foreknowledge of God" that it should be so (Acts II, 23).

## SOME BRIEF COMMENTS ON OUR LORD'S FAREWELL DISCOURSES TO THE ELEVEN APOSTLES

## HIS DEPARTURE TO HEAVEN IS TO BECOME THE OCCASION OF THE ADVENT OF THE HOLY SPIRIT

## PETER RECEIVES A SOLEMN WARNING OF SATAN'S EFFORT TO POSSESS HIM

Read Matthew XXVI, 30 to 35; Mark XIV, 26 to 31; Luke XXII, 28 to 38; and John XIV to XVII

From a comparison of John's account of Peter's declaration of willingness to follow Christ unto death with those given in the other three Gospels, it appears to be perfectly manifest that it preceded our Lord's discourse as given in John XIV (cf. XIII, 36 and 38). Matthew and Mark inform us that all the Apostles put their amen to Peter's affirmation of willingness to die for Christ. Mark records that after the Lord had warned him of Satan's purpose to possess him and of how he would deny him thrice, "before the cock crow twice", Peter "spake the more vehemently, If I should die with Thee, I will not deny Thee in any wise. Likewise also said they all" (XIV, 30, 31).

Against this profession of carnal confidence in the strength of their own affection for their Master we need only put Matthew's bald statement, "Then all the disciples forsook Him, and fled" (XXVI, 56), in order to learn why it was necessary for the Holy Spirit to come and indwell these and all other disciples, if they were going to be faithful witnesses for our Lord, Who was about to depart out of this world unto the Father. There can be no doubt that our Lord took the occasion of this well-intentioned but carnal profession of fidelity towards Himself on the part of Peter and his fellow disciples to unfold in His last hours with them teaching which was calculated to make them understand, either then or later, that no one in His absence could faithfully follow Him in this world, which was the domain of Satan, except by the possession of a power which entirely transcended all human power and which would lovingly link the disciples, not only with Himself, but with God the Father. So we hear our Lord say to them, "At that day ye shall know that I am in My Father, and ye in Me, and I in you" (XIV, 20).

If we may put this into plainer language, we should say that the whole purpose of our Lord's last discourses to His disciples was to remove all self-confidence and to reveal the utterly supernatural nature of that which would presently come to be called Christianity. Our Lord in these chapters of John's Gospel (XIV to XVII) discloses to the Apostles, and to "them also which shall believe on (Him) through their word", some of the deepest and most important of Divine principles. No longer would the Apostles feel that the Lord in departing from them was expecting great things *of them*; for, in fact, they heard Him say, "without Me ye can do nothing" (XV, 5). And how willing after their self-confidence had been broken to shivers by their unfaithfulness, were they to obey the risen Saviour's command, "Tarry ye in the city of Jerusalem, until ye be endued with power from on high" (Luke XXIV, 49).

We might well ask ourselves before proceeding, if there is any portion of Holy Scripture so badly and so sadly needed in the present day of decaying discipleship as these chapters in John's Gospel. Collective and sectarian forms of Christianity may flourish as a green bay tree in the sight of man, but the basis of everything which is of value in the sight of God must find its source in the faithful lives of individual men and women whose discipleship and personal obedience to our Lord Himself takes precedence over all human associations, howsoever orthodox or highly esteemed among men they may be.

At the end of John XIII we learn how the Lord impressed His disciples with the fact that He was going to leave them. It was this that made Peter say He would follow Christ even if it meant dying. Chapter XIV opens with words calculated to console the disciples in regard to our Lord's departure from them. He was going to His Father's House to prepare a place for His own. When ready He would "come again" and receive them unto Himself so that they might dwell with Him above. This is one of the grandest of His promises and the first in the New Testament to speak in plain terms of His coming for His own, that is, for His Church. Previous statements, except that of the Parable of the Ten Virgins, had made reference to His coming to judge and to reign which is a third coming (compare I Thess. IV, 16, 17 with Matthew XXIV, 27 to 37 and II Thess. I, 7 to 10). The way to Heaven was through Jesus Himself for He was "the way, the truth, and the life" and no one could ever come to the Father except by way of Jesus.

Then the Lord blessedly reveals through Philip's request (verse 8) that He and the Father are One; and to have seen Jesus was to have seen the Father. This Philip should have known after so long a time with Jesus. Did Philip not know that it was God Who spoke through Him and God Who did "the works" by Him, our Lord asks.

These "works" would not cease when the Lord left the earth to join the Father. Believers in Jesus would carry them on and even do "greater works" (verse 12) because "whatsoever" they asked in His Name would now be granted and thus they would be the means of glorifying the Father "in the Son" – no mean favour.

How could such a thing be? Our Lord says He would "pray the Father, and He shall give you another Comforter, that He may abide with you for ever" (verse 16). This could mean nothing less than an eternal union of the believer with the Spirit of Truth, Whom the disciples knew as present with them but would presently know as dwelling in them (verse 17).

The people of the world, who walk only by sight, cannot receive the Spirit, because they cannot see Him or even know of His existence. To the believer it is said, "after that ye believed, ye were sealed with that Holy Spirit of promise" (Ephes. I, 13).

"At that day" (in verse 20) looks on to the period after Pentecost when the Holy Ghost will have descended to take up His abode in the disciples of Christ who form His Church. Then, by the presence of the Spirit, we should know that Christ was in the Father, we in Christ and Christ in us. Here we touch a realm which is utterly beyond human conception – a revelation of the utmost blessedness and all made living and real to believers by the presence in them of the Holy Ghost.

In verses 21 to 25, our Lord sets forth the fact that the essence of all this holy relationship is based upon our obedience to His "commandments" or "words". Love for Him and obedience to things He has declared go hand in hand. To say we love Him and yet disobey what He says is a contradiction in terms. Furthermore, if there was a disposition to disobey Him, let all remember "that the word which ye hear is not Mine, but the Father's which sent me" (verse 24). In actuality, therefore, to disobey Him was also to disobey God Whom all profess to fear. Manifestation to the believer, either by the Father or the Son, is the precious reward of obedience to the words of Christ and impossible without it. Many now mourn the lack of manifestation by both the Father and the Son. This can only be the result of the almost universal habit of treating the words of Christ with indifference.

There was yet much more to be revealed after the Lord's pathway on earth had closed, so He again alludes to the coming of "the Comforter, which is the Holy Ghost" Who would "teach (them) all things, and bring all things to (their) remembrance", whatsoever He had said to them (verse 26). The Holy Ghost would be an infallible Teacher and He it was Who would interpret the Scriptures; and it was obedience to the Scriptures, not as interpreted by man who would make them conform to his own wishes, but as interpreted by the One Who is "the Spirit of Truth" – the One Who indited the whole body of Holy Scripture. If it were left to the believer to interpret the Word of God, then he would cloak his disobedience by a wishful interpretation. The true disciple is to know only one Teacher of the Holy Oracles of God and He is the Holy Ghost Who came down from Heaven for the purpose when our Lord Jesus Christ had been glorified (John VII, 39 and I John II, 27).

The statement in John XIV, 26, "He shall . . . bring all things to your remembrance, whatsoever I have said unto you", is of the utmost importance as it accounts for every recorded statement set forth in the Gospels of the words uttered by our blessed Lord. Take, for instance, these very chapters in John's Gospel – a Gospel said to have been written fifty or sixty years after our Lord ascended into Heaven – how could any human being recall in every detail words uttered so long before? What, indeed, are the Gospels but a living evidence of the truth of the Lord's promise that the Holy Ghost would restore to their minds ALL THINGS "whatsoever I have said unto you"? Neither has anyone who is indwelt by the Holy Spirit ever doubted for a second that words credited to our Lord in the Gospels were uttered by Him. There are those who do not believe His words and to these our Lord says, "He that . . . receiveth not My words, hath one that judgeth him: the word that I have spoken, the same shall judge him in the last day" (John XII, 48 to 50).

Finally, the departing Saviour bestows upon His faithful followers His peace – the peace which had kept Him, amidst the turmoil of earth, in unbroken communion with His Father during the thirty-three and a half years which composed His life among men. The world knew no such peace and could not bestow it. Therefore He again consoles them with the words, "Let not your heart be troubled, neither let it be afraid" (XIV, 27).

If they really loved their Master they would not indulge in self-pity because He was leaving them, but rather rejoice with Him in His portion in that He was going to the Father, "Who", He says, "is greater than I" (verse 28). What a lesson for them to learn! To put the interests of Christ before their own convenience.

Our Lord, knowing all things, then informs them (verse 30) of the approach of the Adversary – "the prince of this world" – whom He realized was summoning up all his strength for a final assault which, as we know, took place in the Garden of Gethsemane. The Lord had no sin in Him, so Satan could not deal with Him as with man for He had nothing in Him to which to appeal; but that did not mean there would be no conflict, since the mighty work of man's Salvation had yet to be accomplished if the world was to be freed from the tyranny of its usurper prince. One last opportunity presented itself to the Adversary, whose ready tools – Judas and the Jewish rulers – were now being supplied by Him with the energy and courage needed to make the final onslaught which he hoped would destroy the One Who had thus far proved Himself to be the "Stronger than he"; and Who had, since His triumph in the Forty Days' Temptation, been engaged in spoiling his (i.e. Satan's) goods and releasing his captives (Luke XI, 21 and 22).

With all this said, our Lord, in entire dependence on the Father, prepares to go forth, though well knowing what awaits Him. He says, "Arise, let us go hence", and with this the evening in the Upper Room is brought to a close; but not without a note of deep pathos, for Matthew tells us that after "they had sung an hymn, they went out into the mount of Olives" (XXVI, 30).

Virtually this brought to a close our Lord's earthly association with His chosen Apostles – the hour must have been about 9 to 10 P.M. and the second watch of the night.

### OUR LORD CONTINUES TO DISCOURSE TO HIS DISCIPLES ON THE WAY TO THE MOUNT OF OLIVES AND GETHSEMANE

Read John XV and XVI

It is impossible on this occasion to offer more than a few very brief comments on these chapters which have been the subject of so vast an amount of devotional literature.

Our blessed Lord presents Himself as "the true vine" because in many places in Scripture the vine is used as a symbol for Israel, and Israel had miserably failed as a vine to produce fruit for God in the earth. In Psalm LXXX we get a historical reference to Israel as a vine in these words, "Thou hast brought a vine out of Egypt". The same could be said of our Lord as "the true vine", for of Him Matthew quotes the words of Hosea XI, 1, "Out of Egypt have I called My Son". The above-quoted Psalm, with many such references from the Prophets, reveals that though Israel was a vine in God's sight, she bore no fruit in the earth (Isaiah V, 1 to 7; Jer. II, 21; Ezek. XV, 2 to 6, etc.). In a sense, our Lord as "the true vine" represents that Israel that will in a coming day, through union with Himself, be found fruitful. This is according to the prophecy, "Israel shall blossom and bud, and fill the face of the world with fruit" (Isaiah XXVII, 6).

As regards the immediate purpose of our Lord, the whole discourse is to put the Apostles who are "the branches" into a place of entire dependence upon Himself if they are to bear fruit which will glorify His Father. He says, "Herein is My Father glorified, that ye bear much fruit; so shall ye be My disciples" (verse 8). He had obeyed His Father while on earth and consequently had abode in His love – they must do the same in keeping the commandments He had given them if they would abide in His love (verse 10).

No longer would He regard them as "servants" but as "friends", and in proof of His friendship He had kept back nothing from them of all that He had received from His Father.

They must realize that they had not chosen Him but that He had acted sovereignly in choosing them to be His Apostles, and had ordained that they should go and bring forth fruit, and also that they should use His Name in making their requests to the Father Who would accordingly grant them.

Their position as His disciples would invoke the hatred of the world out of which He had chosen them to be His witnesses. As for "the world", it was now in the unenviable position of having rejected both the Father and the Son. Furthermore, by our Lord having openly spoken to the world of its sin, he had taken away any hope of its pretending to cover it up. Because He had told the truth He was hated by the world, and to hate Him was to hate the One Who sent Him. Then our Lord concludes, "If I had not done among them the works which none other man did, they had not had sin: BUT NOW they have both seen and hated both Me and My Father" – a fearful indictment (verses 18 to 24).

In Chapter XV, 26 and 27, the Saviour again reminds them of the coming of the Comforter "Whom (says He) I will send unto you from the Father, even the Spirit of Truth, which proceedeth from the Father". Then He brackets the testimony of the Spirit to Himself with the witness of the twelve Apostles who had been with Him "from the beginning". Consequently, after Pentecost we hear the Apostle Peter say, "we are His witnesses of these things; and so is also the Holy Ghost, Whom God hath given to them that obey Him" (Acts V, 32). Obviously, the testimony of the twelve Apostles who had been with the Lord in His earthly path transcended all other human testimony, so the Scripture declares, "their sound went into all the earth, and their words unto the ends of the world" (Romans X, 18).

Our Lord (in Chapter XVI, 1 to 4) warns the Apostles again of the sort of treatment they would get from the world and of how in their wilful ignorance some would actually think they were serving God by killing them. It was needful for Him to say these things now so that they would not be stumbled when they came to pass. While He was with them He could protect them, but now that He was going away they must boldly face the exacting terms of their Apostleship.

In verses 7 to 15, our Lord devotes further words of the greatest importance to the mission of the Holy Spirit in the earth. First, it was expedient for Him to depart as otherwise the Comforter could not come and perform that work which was to be the appointed outcome of His own work of Redemption. This statement of our Lord's gives immense importance to the Spirit's operations in this Dispensation.

The Spirit would convict mankind in a threefold way:

(I) of sin, in refusing to believe on our Lord as sent of God;

(II) of righteousness, because the Son of God, having been rejected by the world which would see Him no more, had in righteousness been received up into Heaven by the Father and had been accorded the place of highest honour at His right hand;

(III) of judgment, because the world, political and religious, had acted with Satan its Prince in killing the Son of God and had thereby become involved as an accomplice in the judgment which was to be Satan's portion as the instigator of this greatest of all crimes.

It is quite clear from our Lord's words that when the day of judgment comes the people of this Dispensation who are called to give an account will be speechless with guilt because their rejection of Christ will have taken place while the Holy Ghost is in the earth convicting all in this threefold manner.

Our Lord then again relates the ministrations of the Holy Spirit to the needs of the Apostles and those who would follow after them. There were "many things" He would like to have unfolded to them but as yet they were not spiritually equipped to receive them. When the Spirit came, and by virtue of His presence in them, they would be guided "into all truth" (verses 12 to 15). He would not speak out from Himself but He would speak that which was given Him to speak; just as the Lord when on the earth had only spoken words given to Him by His Father (XII, 49). The Spirit would also show them "things to come" and He would glorify Christ by taking "the things" of Christ and showing them to the Apostles and all believers.

Our Lord's final conversation with the eleven Apostles is to be found in verses 16 to 33 in Chapter XVI. The subject is again His departure from them. The "little while" is the period of His absence in Heaven with the Father. For all who would be faithful to Him while He was away from the earth it would be a time of lament and tribulation, while the world would forget its coming judgment and regard Christ's absence as an occasion for rejoicing. However, the tables would be turned for the time would come when, like a woman rejoicing at the delivery of a son, the purpose of the Dispensation would reach maturity and the body of Christ be completed, and thus "a Man" – the Christ – be born into the world. This clearly refers to Revelation XII, 5, where we read, "She brought forth a man child (=a son, a male), who was to rule all nations with a rod of iron: and her child was caught up unto God, and to His throne".

When this is about to take place our Lord will return, for He says, "I will see you again, and your heart shall rejoice, and your joy no man taketh from you" (verse 22).

After leading the Apostles into a full and clear understanding that, just as He had come forth from the Father, He was now going back again to the Father, and hearing from them that they understood, He warned them that they were about to be scattered and return to their own homes, leaving Him (as we say) to His fate. But though left by them (and this in spite of their profession of fidelity) He would not be left by His Father. Nevertheless, happen what might to them in the world, they were to "be of good cheer" because, said He, "I have overcome the world" – a note of ultimate triumph based upon His approaching death and resurrection which would "destroy" Satan's power as "prince of this world", over which our Lord will presently reign as King of kings and Lord of lords. But for the believer, Christ's triumph over the world may be a present possession, as the Apostle John declares when he writes, "this is the victory that overcometh the world, even our faith", that is, our faith that "Jesus is the Son of God" (I John V, 4 and 5).

Our Lord's prayer in John XVII is an intimate unveiling of the thoughts and desires of His heart, firstly, for His chosen vessels of testimony to the world, and then for us who, through "their word", have come to believe on Him. Death lay before our blessed Master Who had now "finished the work" He had been sent into the world to accomplish. His last act, that is, His death, would crown His life of suffering and obedience and glorify God above everything else. So He petitions His Father, saying, "Now, O Father, glorify Thou Me with Thine own self with the glory which I had with Thee before the world was" (verse 5). Having laid aside His Godhead glories in order to come into the world and become our Saviour, and having humbled Himself even to the death of the Cross, Our Lord, looking beyond death to His resurrection, petitions the return of His pre-Creation glories which He had enjoyed with the Father.

Our Lord Jesus Christ then pleads for "the men which Thou gavest Me out of the world" (verse 6). For the world He did not pray but only for His own, saying, "Holy Father, keep through Thine own name those whom Thou hast given Me, that they may be one, as we are" (verse 11). This request for this perfect unity of His own in the world is the first of five occasions in this one prayer (see verses 21, 22 and 23).

In verses 14 to 18 our Lord reveals that the antipathy of the world for His own is a living proof that "they are not of the world, even as (He says) I am not of the world". Sanctified by the truth, which is the Word of God, our Lord commissions His Apostles, even as He Himself had been commissioned by God Who sent Him.

Then our Lord prays for us, that is, all who have come to believe on Him through the spoken and written word of the Apostles. He prays chiefly for our UNITY because of its effect in convincing the world that He had been sent of God to save it. The prayer closes, "I have declared unto them Thy Name, and will declare it: that the love wherewith Thou hast loved Me may be in them, and I in them".

This is a portion rather for meditation than interpretation. There is nothing else like it in the whole Bible and the realization that it was uttered just before our Lord's apprehension by Judas and the officers sent to arrest Him reveals how utterly devoid of all self-concern He was. His thoughts are centred on the small band of men He is about to leave and these He commits to His Father's keeping while He bows His head in death.

## IN THE GARDEN OF GETHSEMANE

Matt. XXVI, 36 to 46; Mark XIV, 32 to 42;
Luke XXII, 40 to 46; John XVIII, 1

The narrative in John's Gospel – Chapter XVIII, 1 – continues thus:

> "When Jesus had spoken these words, He went forth with His disciples over the brook Cedron, where was a garden, into the which He entered, and His disciples."

As regards events in the Garden of Gethsemane John remains absolutely silent until the arrival of the betrayer and his band. Matthew and Mark give the fullest accounts of our Lord's immeasurable sufferings and conflict – Luke gives a less full but much more poignant account of the same. The reason John omits any account of our Lord's agony is because to do so would be utterly inconsistent with the aspect of His death which he is caused to present in his Gospel. After commenting on events at the time of the Crucifixion and Death of our Lord and Master, we shall write briefly on the reason for the immense difference between John's aspect of the same and that of Matthew, Mark and Luke. It will then be seen how out of keeping it would have been for John to have recorded events connected with our Lord's experience in Gethsemane.

As it has pleased Almighty God to lift the veil for people to know what our Lord Jesus Christ passed through in the Garden of Gethsemane, it is both the duty and solemn privilege of every believer in Christ to seek to understand a little of the cause of His tremendous perturbation, if we may use such a word to describe what He passed through in order to win eternal blessedness for us.

Before referring briefly to the circumstances of the occasion, we must recall the fact that we are told that after the Temptation, "the devil . . . departed from Him for a season" (Luke IV, 13). It is clear from this reference and our Lord's statement, "the prince of this world cometh, and hath nothing in Me" (John XIV, 30), that Satan returned at Gethsemane to make his final and most desolating assault upon Christ in order, if it were possible, to prevent Him from finishing the work of

Redemption He had come into the world to accomplish. It is, therefore, of the utmost importance to realize that in Gethsemane our Lord is to be seen enduring Satan's direst assault and coming out of it in triumph, but only through His perfect submission to His Father's Will, and after a conflict so terrible that "His sweat was as it were great drops of blood falling down to the ground" (Luke XXII, 44).

It is clear from the Gospels that after entering the Garden our Lord left the eight Apostles and advanced further with Peter, James and John whom He besought to tarry and watch, while He went "about a stone's cast" ahead to pray, because, said He, "My soul is exceeding sorrowful, even unto death". These words might have stirred the three Apostles into the realization that their Master was about to pass through a supreme test; and the more so, when they saw that He fell with His face toward the ground and was lying prostrate in an agony of prayer.

What a spectacle for human beings to behold! We may well enquire Who was the One Who had prostrated Himself in such a posture of fervent supplication? It was none other than "the Word . . . made flesh" – the Creator – the One by Whom all things were made, and without Whom "was not any thing made that was made" (John I, 1 to 3). To the three witnesses of His agony it was Jesus of Nazareth Whom they now knew was Israel's Messiah – the Christ of God – and Who but 33 days before they had seen transfigured so that when "He prayed, the fashion of His countenance was altered, and His raiment was white and glistering . . . and . . . they saw His glory" (Luke IX, 29 to 32). Then He had appeared in kingly majesty, but now they were beholding Him as a suppliant entreating His Father to deliver Him, *if such a thing were possible*, from taking that last but terrible step in His pathway, here on earth, of unfaltering obedience to His will. It was at the moment when the Saviour (Who Himself was sinless and need never experience death) was faced with SIN and DEATH as His portion that Satan the prince of this world, and the one who had the power of death, came upon Him with untold fury in an assault upon His spirit. In the Temptation our Lord had met Satan and thrice, by the skilful use of "the sword of the Spirit, which is the word of God", had triumphed over him. Satan's effort then was to persuade our Lord to use His power as the Son of God and not as dependent Son of Man – the place He had taken in infinite grace and humility at His incarnation.

Our Lord knew that Satan had perfected his plans to kill Him and without a doubt would do so. This fact Satan used with all its terror; neither could our Lord resist it for He knew He was purposed to die and had come to do so. Was Satan then to be a victor over Him? Could He *willingly* drink a cup which meant ignominy and defeat before the world He had come to save? Could He *willingly* be made sin and die forsaken of His God and Father? His own thrice-uttered prayer, "If it be possible, let this cup pass from Me", shows that He was not willing, except *on one condition.* (See also Mark XIV, 36.) Could He, as perfect Man, wish to meet death as the wages of sin – our sin? His whole Being revolted before such a prospect and the more so as Satan was present to overwhelm His spirit by pressing home the fact that he was the one who, with fallen man, would bring His death to pass. What a cup!

It was one thing to triumph over Satan, as in the Temptation, but quite another to submit to a death which Satan and his earthly accomplices both willed and would accomplish. It is this prospect that our Lord carries to His Father Whom this once He addresses with the personal pronoun, saying, "O My Father, if it be possible, let this cup pass from Me: nevertheless not as I will, but as Thou wilt" (Matt. XXVI, 39 and Mark XIV, 36).

Luke tells us that, as in the Temptation, "there appeared an angel unto Him from Heaven, strengthening Him" (XXII, 43). The vehemence of His supplication was evidently such that one of the angels, who was beholding the scene, had to come to strengthen Him lest death should overtake Him. Nevertheless, the victory was not yet secured and twice more He returns to plead for the removal of the cup. Luke tells us that "being in an agony He prayed more earnestly: and His sweat was as it were great drops of blood falling down to the ground" (XXII, 44).

Just as in the Temptation, Satan had three times tried to get our Lord to forsake the path of dependent Man and use His power as the Son of God, so now in Gethsemane our Lord had to meet three successive assaults by Satan before He gained the final triumph which enabled Him to rise up and meet the awful series of events which culminated in His expiry on Calvary's Tree – His soul being made "an offering for sin" and He being "numbered with the transgressors" (Isaiah LIII).

Our blessed Lord's triumph in Gethsemane lay in His submission to His Father's will by the acceptance of that bitter cup which made His holy soul recoil with terror at the prospect of having to drink it. That cup He would receive from one Hand only and that His Father's. Satan, Judas, and His enemies among Israel's rulers, might plot His death but He, now as always, could acknowledge no second causes. If God His Father handed to Him the cup which meant shame, dishonour and apparent defeat for Him and apparent triumph for His enemies, He would drink it, not because He wished it (how could He!) but because it was HIS FATHER'S WILL that He should do so. That was motive enough. This cup He would take from no other hand. Hence we hear Him say to Peter after His arrest, "The cup which My Father hath given Me, shall I not drink it" (John XVIII, 11). What a triumph!

We must face the fact that in Gethsemane our Lord Jesus Christ had to decide, as "the last Adam", whether He would undo the evil wrought by "the first man Adam" and thus accomplish the Redemption of the whole human race. In Gethsemane our Lord was brought face to face with the terrific cost of obedience, namely, that He should be made SIN for us and that He should then go down into the dark and terrible waters of death and thus atone for our sin. It is beside the mark to say, "Of course He would obey His Father; He always did". There is no "of course" about Gethsemane. Never before had our Lord been confronted with this supreme issue and Satan, who had the power of death, was there to enlarge upon its terrors and we doubt not intended, had it been possible, so to overwhelm our Lord that He would turn back and, instead of bowing before the will of His enemies because they were the allowed instruments to bring about His atoning death for sinners, claim deliverance from them, and so fail in the purpose for which He had come into the world (Psalm XXII, 5).

In all this we can see how our Lord, as the last Adam, in the Garden of Gethsemane, perfectly triumphed where the first Adam, in the Garden of Eden, miserably failed by yielding to Satan's temptation to disobey God. How true, therefore, the statement, "As by one man's disobedience (in Eden) many were made sinners, so by the obedience of One (in Gethsemane) shall many be made righteous" (Romans V, 19).

We, with our natures, are quite unable to enter in to what our Lord passed through in Gethsemane, or even to understand the issue with which He was faced; but those Christians who have themselves actually experienced conflict with the powers of darkness such as is named in Ephesians VI will be the best able to conceive some idea as to how these powers, under Satan their leader, sought to overwhelm our Saviour and Redeemer on this occasion. Not to understand Gethsemane is to be unable to appreciate the true nature of the Sacrifice of Calvary – in the former the victory was gained and in the latter it was displayed as in patient obedience our Lord drank to the dregs the cup His Father had put into His hand.

We have not thus far referred to the sad conduct of Peter, James and John, or of how the Lord in His deep conflict of soul would have valued their support and the knowledge that they were praying – at the least this would have given Him some consolation of heart. Did He not ask for this when He said to them, "Tarry ye here, and watch with Me"? When, however, after praying the first time He returned, it was to find all three asleep. In gentle rebuke to Peter, who had so recently boasted of his ability to follow Jesus to death, He says, "What, could ye not watch with Me one hour? Watch and pray, that ye enter not into temptation: the spirit indeed is willing, but the flesh is weak" (Matt. XXVI, 40 and 41). After His second season of conflict our Lord finds the disciples asleep again "for their eyes were heavy"; and yet again so after His third conflict; but then the victory had been gained, and if they wished to sleep they could do so now. But for our Lord and Master there would be no sleep, for, said He, "Behold, the hour is at hand, and the Son of Man is betrayed into the hands of sinners. Rise, let us be going: behold, he is at hand that doth betray Me" (Matt. XXVI, 45 and 46).

So in Gethsemane our Lord counted the cost of our Redemption. For Him this meant laying aside ALL RESISTANCE and allowing Himself to be "crucified through weakness" and to be brought "as a lamb to the slaughter" by His enemies and this to their supreme satisfaction. So He leaves the Garden holding the cup His Father had put into His hand, and this He carries with Him until He has emptied it and the last drop of blood has flowed out of His sacred veins, on behalf of those whose sins He had now expiated, for,

In weakness and defeat
He won the meed and crown,
Trod all our foes beneath His feet
By being trodden down.

As for Peter, James and John, the witnesses in part of His sufferings in Gethsemane, history records that they in turn each received a cup which meant for them a violent death on behalf of their now risen Master and Lord; but by then He had taken the sting out of death by Himself being made sin for us, for is it not written, "the sting of death is sin" (I Cor. XV, 56)? And who has not heard of the noble army of martyrs, each member of which received a like cup to that of Peter, James and John, before passing in triumph, dry-shod, through death to be "with Christ" by virtue of the fact that He himself by dying had dried up its swelling waters?

## THE BETRAYAL

OUR LORD JESUS CHRIST IS ARRESTED ABOUT MIDNIGHT BY A FORCE COMPOSED OF ROMAN SOLDIERS UNDER A CAPTAIN AND OFFICERS OF THE TEMPLE, GUIDED BY THE EX-APOSTLE, JUDAS

Read Matthew XXVI, 47 to 56; Mark XIV, 43 to 52; Luke XXII, 47 to 53; and John XVIII, 3 to 11

The humble and lowly Sufferer of Gethsemane had hardly taken the cup from His Father's Hand before it fell to His lot to have to take a draught from it; for the Scripture records that immediately after He had said to the disciples, "Rise, let us be going: behold, he is at hand that doth betray Me", Judas and "a great multitude with swords and staves, from the chief priests and elders of the people" arrived upon the scenes in order to lay hands upon Jesus and take Him as their prisoner.

The time would have been about Midnight for our Lord and

His disciples must have been at least an hour in the Garden, and the many events in the Upper Room and the Discourses on the way to the Garden would have covered the intervening hours from the time, about sunset, when they sat down to eat the Passover. As the Lord rose three days later at Midnight it is safe to assume that these three days form one of several such periods connected with His Passion.

It is important to take solemn account of the time and manner of our Lord's apprehension by the Jewish and Roman Authorities. First, let us recall that Matthew states that the Jewish rulers "consulted that they might take Jesus by subtilty, and kill Him" (XXVI, 4). Mark uses the expression "by craft" (XIV, 1). In keeping with this we are told by Mark that Judas, after he has struck his fearful bargain with the chief priests, "sought how he might conveniently betray Him", to which Luke adds, "in the absence of the multitude".

It is not, therefore, difficult to understand why our blessed Lord was apprehended in the dead of night. Because of the dark and fearful nature of their designs the Jewish rulers feared "an uproar among the people", and specially so as multitudes from all over Palestine had assembled in Jerusalem for the Jews' Passover (Matt. XXVI, 5; Mark XIV, 2). Among these multitudes there would have been many thousands who had either seen or experienced our Lord's miracles of healing or been blessed through His teaching.

It is, therefore, clear that the Jewish rulers, rather than delay the matter, determined to put up a case to the Roman Governor to have our Lord arrested under cover of darkness – no doubt representing Him to be a dangerous leader of revolt who purposed to carry out His designs during the Feast, which was a possibility the Romans carefully guarded against by the presence of additional soldiers in the fortress adjoining the Temple.

Needless to remark, these Jewish rulers were quite ignorant of the fact that they were but doing what was according to "the determinate counsel and foreknowledge of God" in thus taking Jesus into their custody. In the counsels of God our Lord had to die as the Sin Offering of the true 15th of the 1st month in the year A.D. 33, in order to make atonement for our sins. Therefore, God allowed the wickedness of man, directed and energized by

Satan, to perform in relation to the death of His Son only that which He had "determined before to be done" (Acts II, 23 and IV, 28).

John, in his account of our Lord's betrayal, tells us (XVIII, 2) that Judas "knew the place: for Jesus ofttimes resorted thither with His disciples". Doubtless, it was a sort of trysting place which served many purposes, one of which was for resting at night when, as so often, it was spent on the Mount of Olives. Judas, having ascertained that our Lord and His disciples had left the Holy City, knew well where he could find them and no doubt purposed to come upon them while in sleep.

It is difficult to believe, though it is a fact, that "the great multitude" which came under the guidance of Judas to arrest Jesus was mainly composed of soldiers. John says (XVIII, 3) that Judas "received a band of men and officers from the chief priests and Pharisees" and that these came "with lanterns and torches and weapons" – the latter being "the swords and staves" named by Matthew and Mark. This detachment of soldiers, which probably numbered 200 or a third of a cohort, was under a captain. (The presence of this important officer or Chiliarch indicated that the Romans, influenced by what they had heard from the Jewish rulers, attached great importance to the arrest of our Lord.) In addition, there were "captains of the Temple" and a body of elders who no doubt came as representing the Sanhedrin. It is clear, therefore, that the Jews must have impressed the Roman Governor with the desirability of at once seizing Jesus of Nazareth lest He turn the country into revolt! No doubt all this was a part of their Satanically-inspired subtlety to kill Jesus, as how otherwise could they have persuaded Pilate to put Him on trial so early in the morning?

Whilst this considerable force of soldiers and Temple guards was being assembled and led forth armed as if to encircle a band of dangerous robbers, our Lord was in Gethsemane passing through a fearful conflict with the unseen forces of darkness and giving Himself to "prayers and supplications with strong crying and tears unto Him that was able to save Him from death" (Hebrews V, 7). It was just when He had submitted Himself to obey His Father's will and to go unresistingly down into death at the hands of His enemies that Judas arrived with this "great multitude" to arrest Him.

It is beyond understanding how Satan could so capture the heart and will of Judas that he could add the direst insult to the untold injury of betraying Christ by approaching Him with a kiss – using it as a sign to the band of soldiers to mark out Him Whom they were to take and "hold . . . fast" (Matt. XXVI, 48). As a consequence Judas heard from our Lord the following words which stamp him with immortal shame, "Judas, betrayest thou the Son of Man with a kiss?" (Luke XXII, 48).

The most remarkable of all the facts recorded in the Four Gospels connected with our Lord's arrest is that which John brings out in presenting his aspect of the matter (see XVIII, 4 to 8). John, in keeping with his view of our Lord's death, does not see Jesus being forcibly taken, as that would not be consistent with what the Lord stated when He said of His life (as recorded by the Apostle), "No man taketh it from Me, but I lay it down of Myself" (X, 18). Consequently, John takes no account of Judas' kiss or of other details but refers at length to an incident not mentioned in the other Gospels.

It appears that when our blessed Lord saw this considerable body of soldiers, led by a Chiliarch, together with the Temple officials and religious leaders, advancing towards Him and His disciples, He went forth and, ignoring Judas, asked them, "Whom seek ye?" Not only did this action reveal that our Lord was fearless but by it He suddenly became the Dominant Figure in the whole scene. For a brief but precious moment the majestic Glory of His Person as the Son of God must have shone forth in such a way as to make all present feel their own utter moral inferiority. Having heard their reply, "Jesus of Nazareth", He "saith unto them, I AM (He). . . . As soon then as He had said unto them, I AM (He), they went backward, and fell to the ground" (verse 6). For the moment the transcendent superiority of His Divine Person had robbed them of all power to take our Lord, and if He had wished to escape out of their hands as He had done before (see John VIII, 59 and X, 39) because His hour had not yet come, He could then have done so with ease. But His hour had now come and the bitter cup He was to drink was already in His hand, as received from His Father.

Taking note of their discomfiture and inability to take any initiative against Him, our Lord again challenges them with the question, "Whom seek ye?" They again reply, "JESUS OF

NAZARETH". He then chides them by saying, "I have told you that I AM (He): if therefore ye seek ME, let these go their way" (verse 8).

Thus did our Lord give Himself up to His enemies because He had accepted the cup from His Father's Hand which involved His doing so as the first step in His Humiliation, Suffering and Death for sinners. And in thus giving Himself up He was able to secure the freedom of His disciples and so protect them from the wrath of His enemies. Furthermore, He must suffer alone as none could share His portion as the Good Shepherd that was about to give His life for the sheep.

It is John who tells us that after this incident Peter, who had gathered up courage by the manifestation of His Master's moral supremacy over His enemies, "having a sword drew it, and smote the high priest's servant, and cut off his right ear". In reply to this act of ill-placed zeal, our Lord Jesus Christ gently rebukes His impetuous Apostle by asking the solemn question, "The cup that My Father hath given Me, shall I not drink it?" In Luke XXII, 51, we learn that Jesus at once healed the ear of the High Priest's servant.

Luke records that after this Jesus addressed "the chief priests, and captains of the temple, and the elders, which were come to Him" as follows:

> "Be ye come out, as against a thief, with swords and staves? When I was daily with you in the temple, ye stretched forth no hands against Me: but this is your hour, and the power of darkness" (XXII, 52 and 53).

This was a fearful exposure of the cowardice of Israel's rulers who could only accomplish their nefarious plot against our Lord under cover of darkness for fear of "the people".

Having given Himself up to them it only remained for the assembled force to bind our Lord, so we read in John XVIII, 12:

> "Then the band and the captain and officers of the Jews took Jesus, and bound Him, and led Him away. . . ."

We may well add, "as a lamb to the slaughter", according to the Prophecy of Isaiah LIII, 7.

Matthew and Mark, who, according to their aspect of our Lord's death, view Him as taken by force, record the fact that when the soldiers bound our Lord "all the disciples forsook Him, and fled" (Matt. XXVI, 56; Mark XIV, 50). So it was that our Lord's warning prediction, uttered to the Apostles after leaving the Upper Room, was fulfilled when He said, "All ye shall be offended because of Me this night: for it is written, I will smite the Shepherd, and the sheep of the flock shall be scattered abroad. But after I am risen again, I will go before you into Galilee" (Matt. XXVI, 31, 32). As for the Lord, His own words concerning Himself, which He uttered to the twelve Apostles on the last journey to Jerusalem, had become true. These were:

> "Behold, we go up to Jerusalem; and the Son of Man shall be betrayed unto the chief priests and unto the scribes" (Matt. XX, 18).

Our blessed Lord and Master was now a Captive Prisoner in the hands of the Roman Empire of His own volition; and the rulers of the nation of Israel, to which He had come as Messiah, were about to be ranged against Him in open court – the accusers and traducers of their God.

So we bring Part I to a close with its brief commentary on the events in our Lord's path during the six hours from 6 P.M. to Midnight on Thursday, 30th April A.D. 33 – the period which forms the first 6 hours in the Bible day of Friday, 1st May, or in the Divine Calendar the Sabbath, Nisan 15th – the day of our Lord's arrest, trials and death.

N.B. The incident of the "certain young man" who followed our Lord and fled when the soldiers sought to lay hold of him, as exclusively recorded in Mark XIV, 51 and 52, is referred to later on because of its relation to events yet to be commented upon.

# PART II

## OUR LORD JESUS CHRIST IS PUT UPON TRIAL

HE IS FIRST ARRAIGNED BEFORE ANNAS WHO WAS CO-HIGH PRIEST WITH CAIAPHAS

HE IS THEN BROUGHT BEFORE CAIAPHAS AND THE JEWISH SANHEDRIN AND CONDEMNED TO BE WORTHY OF DEATH FOR ASSERTING THAT HE WAS THE SON OF GOD – ISRAEL'S MESSIAH

FINALLY, PILATE THE ROMAN GOVERNOR OF JUDAEA, AFTER PRONOUNCING OUR LORD TO BE GUILTLESS, YIELDS TO THE CLAMOUR OF THE JEWISH AUTHORITIES AND HANDS HIM OVER TO BE CRUCIFIED

PETER DENIES HIS MASTER THREE TIMES IN SPITE OF BEING WARNED

THURSDAY MIDNIGHT TO FRIDAY 8 A.M., 1ST MAY A.D. 33

Read Matthew XXVI, 57 to XXVII, 31; Mark XIV, 53 to XV, 20; Luke XXII, 54 to XXIII, 25 and John XVIII, 12 to XIX, 16

WE NOW seek to follow our Lord Jesus Christ from the moment of His arrest by a detachment of Roman soldiers in the Garden of Gethsemane to the hour when He was led forth to be crucified. In time only eight hours passed between these two stages in His Passion.

If we view the events which passed in these eight hours from a merely human standpoint, we shall be at a loss to find words with which to express our emotions at so dastardly a miscarriage of justice. In fact, it is an insult to the word "Justice" to associate it in any way with the so-called Trials at which our blessed Lord was forced to appear and hear Himself condemned. Apart from the hearing He received from Pilate, the Roman Governor, who admitted He was guiltless, our Lord's case was never examined or even presented. As everyone who has read the Gospels knows, the Jewish rulers had determined His death beforehand and these so-called Trials were merely part of a plan to dress up this determination with the barest semblance of conformity to the accepted processes of Law among civilized nations.

We may or should be filled with shame as we behold Jew and Gentile making common cause in order to destroy God's well-beloved Son, Who had come into "the world to save sinners" (I Tim. I, 15); but, on the other hand, we should be filled with wonder, praise and adoration as we behold His refusal to resist, while wicked men lay violent hands on Him because of His willingness to go down into death, so as to abolish it for all who believe on Him, and bring "life and immortality to light through the gospel" (II Tim. I, 10). Only as we behold our Lord's sufferings and death as the out-working of John III, 16, where we are told that "God so loved the world, that He gave His only begotten Son, that whosoever believeth in Him should not perish, but have everlasting life", can we understand why they were allowed. To the believer this is the all-sufficient answer and the only one which affords explanation for our Lord being allowed to be "betrayed into the hands of sinners" (Mark XIV, 41) in the manner we have just narrated from the Gospels.

It is to John's account of events after our Lord's apprehension that we must first turn if we would get the right sequence. In Chapter XVIII, verses 12 and 13, we read:

> "Then the band and the captain and officers of the Jews took Jesus, and bound Him, and led Him away to Annas first; for he was father-in-law to Caiaphas, which was the high priest that same year."

So our blessed Master returned to the Holy City a Prisoner bound (probably) with chains and under escort by a detachment of soldiers, as if He were an evil-doer of a dangerous order. The eleven Apostles had fled in order to avoid being made captives because associates of the One Who had been apprehended. Later, as "the great multitude" with its Victim bound made its way to the palace of the High Priest, "Peter followed afar off", and in due course reached the palace, as also did John, who refers to himself as "that other disciple" (XVIII, 16).

It is to be carefully noted that John informs us that our Lord was led to Annas "first". This he does with the object of correcting the impression left by Matthew, Mark and Luke in their accounts that He was taken direct to Caiaphas. John's account of events while before Annas is the only mention of this first ordeal through which the Saviour passed.

The Bible makes it perfectly clear that both Annas and Caiaphas were High Priests. In Luke III, 2 the expression occurs, "Annas and Caiaphas being the high priests"; and in Acts IV, 6, which is only a few weeks after the Crucifixion, we get the expression, "Annas the high priest, and Caiaphas, and John, and Alexander . . . were gathered together at Jerusalem".

We mention this because it has been held by some that the incident recorded in John XVIII, 19 to 23, took place in the presence of Caiaphas because the account starts with a reference to "the high priest". This reference is, of course, to Annas as the Bible would not record the visit to him if nothing had taken place during it.

Caiaphas was evidently the duly appointed *de facto* High Priest by the Roman Authorities that year. Annas was *de jure* High Priest and recognized as such by the Jews.

### OUR LORD IS BROUGHT BEFORE ANNAS THE HIGH PRIEST

Read John XVIII, 13 and 19 to 24

We have already noted that John is caused to inform us that our Lord's "first" examination was by Annas, who was one of the most powerful rulers in Jewry at that time. He proposes to question Jesus "of His disciples, and His doctrine". Our Lord in reply carefully avoids any reference to His disciples whom, no doubt, Annas wished to incriminate, but in answer to the second feature, namely, His Teaching, He says, "I spake openly to the world; I ever taught in the synagogue, and in the temple, whither the Jews always resort; and in secret have I said nothing. Why askest thou Me? Ask them which heard Me, what I have said unto them: behold, they know what I said".

The tone of our Lord's reply to Annas is very different from that which Matthew, Mark and Luke record of His replies to Caiaphas and the Jewish rulers assembled with him. John is caused to see our Lord laying down His life "of Himself" and not being driven to His death as a willing Victim by His enemies, as in the other Gospels. Consequently, only John records our Lord's reply to Annas which in effect is a rebuke ("Why askest thou Me?"). It is also an assertion that our Lord as Messiah had concealed nothing from His nation. Let Annas make enquiry from witnesses.

Annas apparently made no reply to our Lord's bold statement; but one of the officers of the Temple struck our Lord a cruel blow with his hand as he said, "Answerest Thou the high priest so?" This insulting blow was the first experience our Lord had had of what it meant for Him to be betrayed into the hands of sinners. But He was not silent under it and John records that He reasoned with the offender saying, "If I have spoken evil, bear witness of the evil: but if well, why smitest thou Me?" (XVIII, 23). All this is in perfect harmony with John's aspect of our Lord's sufferings and death, and entirely different from that of the other three Gospels in which we see the terms of Isaiah LIII fulfilled, one of which is, "He was oppressed, and He was afflicted, yet He opened not His mouth . . . as a sheep before her shearers is dumb, so He openeth not His mouth". As we have just seen, this was not so before Annas, as recorded by John, for our Lord is there seen acting in all the dignity of His Person and not as a submissive Victim of man's enmity towards Him. It appears likely that the Lord knew that Annas had no power to condemn Him on a capital charge such as lay with Caiaphas who was an appointee of Rome.

The sequel to our Lord's being brought before Annas was that the latter passed Him on for trial to Caiaphas. In John XVIII, 24, we read, "Now Annas had sent Him bound unto Caiaphas the high priest". This is a most unfortunate rendering of the Greek text which, according to Westcott (B.F.) and others, should be, "Annas, therefore, sent Him bound unto Caiaphas the high priest". The introduction of the word "had" to "sent" is responsible for creating the utterly false impression that the above incident took place with Caiaphas and not Annas.

As John, to be consistent with his aspect of our Lord's Passion, makes no reference to our Lord's trial before Caiaphas, we have to turn to the other three Gospels each of which omits the visit to Annas and presents the visit to Caiaphas as if it immediately followed the arrest in Gethsemane.

Before following our Lord Jesus Christ into the place where

Caiaphas the High Priest and the elders were assembled, we must delay to comment on the threefold denial of the Apostle Peter.

## THE FALL OF THE APOSTLE PETER

Read Matt. XXVI, 69 to 75; Mark XIV, 66 to 72; Luke XXII, 54 to 62, and John XVIII, 15 to 18 and 25 to 27

It is to be noted that God caused each of the Four Evangelists to record in detail the exact circumstances of Peter's denial of our Lord Jesus Christ. This is the more remarkable since the Lord had appointed Peter to the place of leadership and had given him authority to open the door into the Kingdom, first to his own nation and then, three years later (A.D. 36), to the Gentiles. This fact makes Peter's fall all the more serious since our Lord had said, "For unto whomsoever much is given, of him shall be much required" (Luke XII, 48).

Judas' betrayal of the Lord and Peter's denial of Him together form Satan's contribution towards the fulfilling of the first Bible prophecy, "Thou shalt bruise His heel" (Gen. III, 15). Both were chosen to be Apostles, yet in each case Satan was the source of energy that prompted the action and carried it through. In the case of Judas it succeeded because his heart was not right with the Lord and he was a thief; and in the case of Peter it succeeded because, though his heart was right with the Lord, his spring of confidence was in himself; and though walking with the Lord for three years he had never learnt the difference between the flesh and the spirit. Judas fell beyond recovery and his repentance was too late. Peter had the protection of the Saviour's prayers and his repentance was deep and real, as it needed to be; for his fall, in view of his position, was a terrible exhibition of what the human heart, though redeemed, is capable of. At the very time when his Master was being subjected to the most fearful indignities and cruelties, Peter was in the adjoining courtyard warming himself, and on occasions denying to those around him that he had any association with, or knowledge of, the One on trial for His life – the One Whom he had promised to follow even if it meant death.

It is not possible to conceive a more terrible collapse, but the whole episode is recorded in full four times in the Gospels as a warning, first of what man is by nature and then of Satan's immense power, even over a Christian, if the spring of confidence is in himself and not in God.

Whether or not Peter's threefold denial is symbolical of Israel's threefold denial of our Lord is a matter worthy of solemn consideration. The Jews first rejected John the Baptist's testimony to Jesus Christ. They then rejected the testimony of our Lord concerning Himself. Finally, they rejected the testimony of the Holy Ghost to our Lord through the twelve Apostles.

We shall not delay to compare the four accounts of Peter's denial but refer briefly to that of John's Gospel.

It is quite clear that Annas and Caiaphas both had their headquarters in a large building in which there was a court. This is called "the palace of the high priest", but the word signifies it was a courtyard. For this reason John's account of Peter's use of this court agrees with that of the other three Gospels which, however, associate it with Caiaphas. It was in fact a court common to both parts of the building.

It was while Peter was warming himself by the servants' fire that the damsel who kept the door from the courtyard into the council chamber where our Lord was on trial first accused him of being a disciple of Jesus – Peter replying to her "I am not" (XVIII, 17). He then continued to enjoy the warmth which he shared with the servants of the high priest until he was challenged again. This time more than one accused him and again "he denied it, and said, I am not" (XVIII, 25).

Finally, a kinsman of the man whose ear Peter cut off in the Garden said to him, "Did I not see thee in the garden with Him?" This Peter denied, making a third occasion (XVIII, 26 and 27).

Mark tells us that on this third occasion Peter "began to curse and to swear, saying, I know not this man of whom ye speak". It was then the cock crew a second time. Suddenly there shot into Peter's memory what the Lord had said, "Before the cock crow twice, thou shalt deny Me thrice" (XIV, 70 to 72). Luke tells us that following this third denial "the Lord turned, and looked upon Peter", who "went out, and wept bitterly" (XXII, 62).

That "look" which Peter received from his Master not only broke Peter's heart but sustained his courage in the succeeding three days. Our Lord's prayer for Peter and that "look" kept him from the despair which otherwise would have overwhelmed him as he realized to what depths of iniquity his self-confidence had carried him. When he had fully learnt this lesson he had the promise from the Lord that he should "strengthen" his brethren (Luke XXII, 32).

We must now leave Peter and learn from the three Gospels of Matthew, Mark and Luke what took place with our Lord and Master when He was brought before Caiaphas and the Jewish Council.

## OUR LORD JESUS CHRIST IS BROUGHT BEFORE CAIAPHAS THE HIGH PRIEST AND THE WHOLE COUNCIL OF THE JEWS

Read Matthew XXVI, 57 to 68; Mark XIV, 53 to 65; Luke XXII, 54, 63 to 71, and John XVIII, 24

The appearance of our Lord Jesus Christ before Caiaphas the High Priest, and the whole body of the Sanhedrists which formed the Council of Jewish rulers, was an event of the greatest possible significance because of its official nature. Never before had our Lord been confronted with official Jewry in Council and never before had official Jewry heard from His own lips a testimony to His Messiahship. The outcome of such a confrontation must obviously in the circumstances prove decisive; and as all the world knows it became the means, allowed so of God, by which our Lord went to His death on the Cross of Calvary a few hours later. Another direct, though delayed, outcome of Jewry's actions at that Council was her own excision by God, and her national dismemberment by the Romans who in A.D. 70 came and took away her "place and nation" (John XI, 48).

The Bible does not suggest that this Council of the Jews condemned our Lord to death, as they had not the power to do such a thing (John XVIII, 31). What they did do was to agree among themselves, under the leadership of the High Priest, to confirm their original intention to have Jesus put to death. As John reminds us (XVIII, 14), it was Caiaphas who, after our

Lord had raised Lazarus from the dead, declared that "it is expedient for us, that one man should die for the people, and that the whole nation perish not". This meant that as a matter of political expediency the judicial murder of Christ was justified; and so John tells us, "from that day forth they took counsel together for to put Him to death" (XI, 53). The High Priest may have been moved to speak prophetically of our Lord's atoning sacrifice, but the proposition itself was intended to justify the judicial act of killing Jesus.

When, therefore, our Lord Jesus Christ stood before Caiaphas and the Council of Jews, He knew they intended to kill Him and that He was not there to be tried judicially, but rather that they might trump up a charge of a nature calculated to be effective with the Roman Authorities in bringing about His death. They must already have branded our Lord to the Romans as a dangerous disturber of the peace or they would not have undertaken His arrest by sending a high officer (Gr. CHILIARCHOS) and a detachment of soldiers to effect it.

In reality, may we say in passing, it was not the Son of God Who on this occasion was on trial before the rulers of the Jewish nation, but the Jewish nation that was on trial before the God of Israel as to what it would do with His Son, Whom He had sent, last of all, to gather the fruits of His vineyard. The Jewish rulers chose the occasion of our Lord's appearing before them to say, as it were, among themselves, "This is the heir; come, let us kill Him, and let us seize on His inheritance" (Matthew XXI, 38). The history of the Jewish people from the siege of Jerusalem by the Romans in A.D. 70 to 1945, when the Hitler holocaust ended, was, in fact, the God of Israel's reply to the Jewish rulers for their part in the rejection and crucifixion of His Son. All in Christendom know this to be a fact, but as yet the Jewish nation cannot see its way to admit it. Later our Lord will present Himself to them again, for, said Zechariah on His behalf, "They shall look upon Me Whom they have pierced" (XII, 10). But this will not occur until after the period of their worst tribulation.

Luke informs us that it was when the first streaks of light appeared, or as we would say, at daybreak, that "the elders of the people and the chief priests and the scribes came together, and led Him (that is, Jesus) into their council" (XXII, 66).

Matthew adds the following facts which are almost identical with Mark's account:

"Now the chief priests, and elders, and all the council, sought false witness against Jesus, to put Him to death; but found none: yea, though many false witnesses came, yet found they none. At the last came two false witnesses, and said, This fellow said, I am able to destroy the temple of God, and to build it in three days" (XXVI, 59 to 61).

During the whole of this examination of false witnesses by the Council, our blessed Lord maintained a dignified and absolute silence. Was it not written of Him, "as a sheep before her shearers is dumb, so He openeth not His mouth" (Isai. LIII, 7)? Besides, our Lord knew that His enemies had not succeeded in extracting a coherent charge against Him out of all the tales they had heard from these perjured witnesses.

Not only did this fact irritate the Jewish rulers but our Lord's absolute refusal to become involved by advancing any kind of defence to the false charges against Him added fuel to their indignation. So much was this the case that "the high priest arose, and said unto Him, Answerest Thou nothing? What is it which these witness against Thee?"

In spite of this effort of the High Priest to force our Lord to open His mouth, the record continues, "But Jesus held His peace" (Matt. XXVI, 62 and 63).

Thus defeated before the whole Council, the High Priest, no doubt in a rage, resorted to a means by which according to the Levitical Law he could compel our Lord to reply or break the Law. In Leviticus V, 1 a witness is warned that if he hear "the voice of swearing" (literally, "adjuration") he must utter it or "bear his iniquity".

The High Priest, therefore, said to our Lord:

"I adjure Thee by the living God, that Thou tell us whether Thou be the Christ, the Son of God."

With calm dignity our Lord replied:

"Thou hast said: nevertheless I say unto you, Hereafter shall ye see the Son of Man sitting on the right hand of power, and coming in the clouds of heaven" (Matt. XXVI, 64).

Luke's account adds some details, one of which is that the Council asked our Lord the direct question, "Art Thou then the Son of God"? To this He replied, "Ye say that I am", which form of speech constituted a strong affirmation of the fact (XXII, 70).

Everyone in the Council now knew that Jesus of Nazareth had stated openly *under oath* that He was the Christ – the Son of God. Furthermore, by inference, He officially predicted that the next time they saw Him He would be coming in "the clouds of heaven" from the right hand of God, as their Judge.

The effect of our Lord's bold pronouncement was instantaneous. He had committed Himself and there could be no retraction, so the record continues:

> "Then the high priest rent his clothes, saying, He hath spoken blasphemy; what further need have we of witnesses? behold, now ye have heard His blasphemy. What think ye? They answered and said, He is guilty of death" (Matt. XXVI, 65 and 66).

The seared consciences of these Religious Leaders were thus set at rest and for their part they now felt fully justified according to the Law in causing Jesus of Nazareth to be put to death for, as they alleged, blasphemously claiming *under oath* to be the Son of God. This charge, however, would avail little with the Civil Power but for themselves it was sufficient. They were now at liberty to go to any lengths to destroy so impious a pretender.

The action of the High Priest in rending his clothes was most ominous and needs to be taken note of. It was an absolutely unlawful act for under no condition was the High Priest to rend his clothes. In Leviticus X, 6, Moses says to Aaron and his sons, "Uncover not your heads, neither rend your clothes; lest ye die, and lest wrath come upon all the people". In Leviticus XXI, 10, this solemn warning is repeated.

Caiaphas was standing in the presence of God's High Priest Who had been anointed at His Baptism and Who soon was to enter the Heavenly Sanctuary; and at Whose death on that very day the veil of the Temple would be rent in twain from the top to the bottom, in order to signify that the Aaronic priesthood and Levitical order had passed away and that now, under the New Covenant, sealed with the blood of Jesus, every believer – Jew and Gentile, male and female – could enter into the Holiest "to offer up spiritual sacrifices, acceptable to God by Jesus Christ" (Hebrews X, 19, 20 and I Peter II, 5). No longer then would a priestly caste exist in the sight of God, since the whole Church would form "a holy priesthood".

The act of Caiaphas in unlawfully rending his garments clearly indicates his *unfrocking* in the sight of God and the end of the priesthood of which he – Caiaphas – was the last High Priest. From that day and hour the only High Priesthood *known to God* has been that of our Lord Jesus Christ concerning Whom the 110th Psalm declares, "Thou art a priest for ever after the order of Melchizedek".

After hearing our Lord's declaration and coming to the united decision that He had committed an act by that declaration which made Him worthy of death, the High Priest and Council evidently retired from the scene for a while, as the next point of time named is "when the morning was come" – which means when the sun had risen, which would be about 5 A.M. at that time of year.

With the restraint necessitated by the presence of the Religious Authorities removed, those that held our Lord as their Prisoner immediately took upon themselves to express their contempt for Him by the most abominable acts of violence towards His Person. This was the reflex of the attitude adopted by the Council which held out that our Saviour was an impostor of the most blasphemous type.

Matthew, Mark and Luke adopt similar wording in their accounts of this solemn phase of our Lord's humiliation, all of which He now accepted with an obedient heart because He knew it formed a part of the bitter cup which His Father had put into His hand and which He had promised to drink to the dregs. In Luke's account we read:

> "And the men that held Jesus mocked Him, and smote Him. And when they had blindfolded Him, they struck Him on the face, and asked Him, saying, Prophesy, who is it that smote Thee? And many other things blasphemously spake they against Him." (XXII, 63 to 65).

It is made very clear in the Gospels that early in the morning (i.e. about 4 A.M.) there was another gathering of the whole Jewish Council to determine upon a plan "against Jesus to put Him to death" (Matt. XXVII, 1). We will quote Mark's reference:

> "And straightway in the morning the chief priests held a consultation with the elders and scribes and the whole council" (XV, 1).

There can be no doubt that the object of this further gathering was to elicit the support of nearly every responsible member of the Sanhedrin in making a plan to hand our Lord Jesus Christ over to the Roman Authorities who alone had the power to condemn and crucify a malefactor. So Mark's account continues:

"and bound Jesus, and carried Him away, and delivered Him to Pilate" (XV, 1).

John's account is as follows:

"Then led they Jesus from Caiaphas unto the hall of judgment: and it was early" (XVIII, 28).

In this manner were the words of Jesus fulfilled which He spake to His disciples on their last journey to Jerusalem, when He said, "The Son of Man shall be betrayed unto the chief priests and unto the scribes, and they shall condemn Him to death, and shall deliver Him to the Gentiles to mock, and to scourge, and to crucify Him" (Matt. XX, 18, 19, etc.).

Without a doubt the Jewish rulers, in taking the step of carrying our Lord to Pilate the Roman Governor, were confident of their power to force his hand and make him do their will. In all probability Pilate's own failings as a Governor left him open to charges being preferred against him by the Jews before the authorities at Rome.

Before following, as it were, our blessed Lord and Master into the presence of Pilate in the Hall of Judgment, we must comment briefly upon the Scriptures which inform us of Judas' end.

## THE SUICIDE OF JUDAS ISCARIOT

The name "Judas" is simply another form of the name "Judah". It was Judas who became Satan's tool to betray our Lord Jesus Christ into the hands of the Jews. The Jews are the people of Judah who, with the Tribe of Benjamin, were responsible for our Lord's crucifixion. The martyr Stephen accuses his own nation of being "the betrayers and murderers" of "the Just One" (Acts VII, 52). He thus links together Judas and Judah in the matter of our Lord's death.

All that we know about Judas' end is to be found in Matthew XXVII, 3 to 10 and Acts I, 16 to 19. When he saw what good value the Jewish rulers were getting for their thirty pieces of silver in that his former Master, Whom he had so successfully betrayed, was undoubtedly going to be put to death, he regretted his act, which is what the Greek word used here for "repented" implies. No doubt Judas was now fearful for the consequences of his sin, and perhaps hoped for some mitigation of the penalty if he renounced his gain. So he brought the thirty pieces of silver (which the chief priests refused to accept) and cast them down in the Temple and said to the chief priests and elders, "I have sinned in that I have betrayed the innocent blood". That was the last thing on earth that they wished to hear, so they replied, "What is that to us? See thou to that" (Matt. XXVII, 3 and 4).

If we combine the facts given by Matthew as to Judas' suicide with Peter's statement in Acts I, 18, we are able to know how fearful an end he came to. In his case, sin paid full wages almost at once. No sin named in the whole Bible equals in heinousness the sin of Judas because he was called to be an apostle of our Lord and Saviour, Who says of him, "He that eateth bread with Me hath lifted up his heel against Me" (John XIII, 18 and Ps. XLI, 9).

We are told that the Jewish rulers "took counsel" as to what to do with Judas' silver pieces, so they bought a field to bury strangers, that is, foreigners, in. This field became known as "the field of blood" and formed a monumental reminder of the day when the rulers of the Jews fulfilled the prophecy of Zechariah concerning their Messiah which says, "So they weighed for My price thirty pieces of silver" (XI, 12). Judas learnt too late that Satan is a cruel master to serve.

## OUR LORD JESUS CHRIST, FINALLY REJECTED BY HIS OWN NATION, IS BY IT DELIVERED BOUND TO THE GENTILES

---

### HE IS BROUGHT BEFORE PILATE, IMPERIAL ROME'S REPRESENTATIVE IN THE SUBJECT LAND OF JUDAH

Read Matt. XXVII, 1, 2 and 11 to 26; Mark XV, 1 to 16; Luke XXIII, 1 to 25, and John XVIII, 28 to XIX, 16

The Jewish rulers had now parted with Jesus, Whom they had handed over as a Prisoner to the Roman Governor for trial – an act which did but prove that they themselves, like their nation, were but vassals of Imperial Rome – the then proud Mistress of the civilized earth. This world-dominance of Rome was by right of charter granted by the Most High God to the Empires of the Image of Daniel II – of which she was the Fourth and last – after that, through sin, the Throne of Judah fell before the armies of Babylon under Nebuchadnezzar, the divinely-appointed Head of the Gentile Empires. (See Daniel II, 37 and 38.)

Before Pilate now stood the King of Israel – the rightful Claimant, as Son and Heir of David, to the Throne of Judah. Four days previously, in the early morning of Monday, 27th April, the Jews' 10th of Nisan, our Lord Jesus Christ had fulfilled literally the prophecy of Zechariah IX, 9, which runs thus:

> "Rejoice greatly, O daughter of Zion; shout, O daughter of Jerusalem: behold, thy King cometh unto thee: He is just, and having salvation; lowly, and riding upon an ass, and upon a colt the foal of an ass."

In a preliminary sense, also, the Second Psalm had been fulfilled, for God had set His King on His "holy hill of Zion".

This presentation by God to the Jewish nation of His Son as their King, in fulfilment of the above prophecies, was His final test of their relationship to Himself. Our Lord had said to the Pharisees, who objected to His self-evident popularity, "I tell you that, if these should hold their peace, the stones would immediately cry out" (Luke XIX, 40).

It was not, however, the rulers of the nation that had acclaimed Jesus of Nazareth when, as God's King, He rode in triumph into Jerusalem, but "the whole multitude of the disciples". The rulers had been sullen onlookers at this glorious spectacle (John XII, 19) since after the raising of Lazarus on the previous Monday (20th April) they had taken counsel to put Jesus to death (John XI, 53).

So God's final test of the Jewish nation did but prove abortive and this was fully manifested by the fact that it had handed our Lord over to the Gentiles to be put to death, saying, in terms of the Parable of the Pounds, "We will not have this man to reign over us" (Luke XIX, 14). The Jewish nation had therefore been tried and found grievously wanting, and its national excision was inevitable apart from an act of national repentance in keeping with the heinousness of their offence.

The solemn question now arose, What would be the response of the Gentile Empire, which by God's permission now ruled the earth, when His Son, the true King of Israel, appeared before its Representative in the land of Judah, charged with a series of palpably false accusations by His own nation? That question finds its full but fatal answer in the four Gospel accounts of our Lord's appearance before Pilate in the Hall of Judgment.

It is to John's Gospel we must first turn as he gives some facts not appearing in the other Gospels. In Chapter XVIII, verses 28 to 32, we get this exclusive account of the first phase of the trial of our Lord before Pilate:

> "Then led they Jesus from Caiaphas unto the hall of judgment: and it was early; and they themselves went not into the judgment hall, lest they should be defiled; but that they might eat the passover.
>
> "Pilate then went out unto them, and said, What accusation bring ye against this man?
>
> "They answered and said unto him, If He were not a malefactor, we would not have delivered Him up unto thee.
>
> "Then said Pilate unto them, Take ye Him, and judge Him according to your law. The Jews therefore said unto him, It is not lawful for us to put any man to death:
>
> "That the saying of Jesus might be fulfilled, which He spake, signifying what death He should die."

This concise record speaks for itself. The time was the early morning, about 5 A.M. Though engaged upon so solemn a task as laying a capital charge against a prisoner, these Jewish rulers were prevented by their religious punctiliousness from accompanying Him into the place where His examination before Pilate must be held.

Pilate had, therefore, to suffer the inconvenience of questioning our Lord and then going outside to His accusers. It was very evident that these Jewish rulers had to evade Pilate's direct question, "What accusation bring ye against this Man?" They could not, they said, judge Him as His as yet unstated offence demanded the death penalty by crucifixion which they, as a subject people, were not allowed to carry out. John here adds a reference to the fact that the Lord had declared that He would be crucified by the Gentiles (Matt. XX, 19).

After this, John tells us Pilate entered the Hall of Judgment again (XVIII, 33), but we have to turn to Luke to learn how the question of our Lord's Kingship arose. In Chapter XXIII, 2, we read:

> "And they began to accuse Him, saying, We found this fellow perverting the nation, and forbidding to give tribute to Caesar, saying that He himself is Christ a king."

Though it was a series of abominable lies, this statement constituted a most serious charge. It will be noted that it was so skilfully worded as to remove the whole case out of the realm of the Jewish religion into that of politics. In other words, our Lord Jesus Christ was presented to Pilate as a Conspirator against the Roman Empire and as One Who claimed kingly rights which He intended to enforce.

The effect of this statement on Pilate was immediate and, as all the Gospels state, he at once challenged our Lord on the subject of His kingship. It is John's account that gives the fullest details, most of which are exclusive to it and most important, so we will quote the same in full (Chapter XVIII, 33 to 38):

> "Then Pilate entered into the judgment hall again, and called Jesus, and said unto Him, Art Thou the King of the Jews?
>
> "Jesus answered him, Sayest thou this thing of thyself, or did others tell it thee of Me?
>
> "Pilate answered, Am I a Jew? Thine own nation and the chief priests have delivered Thee unto me: what hast Thou done?
>
> "Jesus answered, My kingdom is not of this world: if My kingdom were of this world, then would My servants fight that I should not be delivered to the Jews: but now is My kingdom not from hence.
>
> "Pilate therefore said unto Him, Art Thou a king then? Jesus answered, Thou sayest that I am a king. To this end was I born, and for this cause came I into the world, that I should bear witness unto the truth. Every one that is of the truth heareth My voice.
>
> "Pilate saith unto Him, What is truth?"

There is not a follower of our Lord Jesus Christ who is not

bowed with thanksgiving as he reads this bold testimony concerning Himself which our Lord rendered before Pilate. No wonder the Apostle Paul, some thirty years later, looks back to this occasion and reminds Timothy that "Christ Jesus . . . before Pontius Pilate witnessed a good confession" (I Tim. VI, 13).

The accusation implied a measure of jurisdiction over the Jews ("forbidding to give tribute to Caesar"), therefore Pilate framed his question upon the assumption that Jesus claimed to be the King of the Jews. Though our Lord was a Prisoner at the bar, His whole bearing and disdainful silence towards His accusers no doubt made Pilate realize that the One before him was no common malefactor. He must therefore elicit more information from Him. The nation and its rulers had handed Jesus over as a political miscreant, showing that they utterly disapproved of His alleged political intentions. Pilate, therefore, asks our Lord, "What hast Thou done?" That is, to have turned "Thine own nation and the chief priests" into such virulent opposers.

Our Lord's reply affords a perfect explanation. The Kingdom over which He ruled was not of this world, like other kingdoms. It had its source in Heaven; it was, in fact, the Kingdom of Heaven, where spiritual and moral values transcended all human values. Such a Kingdom the Jewish rulers did not want because they were morally unfitted to be its citizens and unwilling to admit the emptiness of their religious profession. They, therefore, rose up against Him and wished to cast Him out of His inheritance; for though His Kingdom was not *of this world*, this world was a part of His Kingdom and the nations were His inheritance (Ps. II, 8). If His Kingdom were "of this world", that is, based on the principle of force by which each worldly kingdom maintained its existence, then "His servants", loyal to a degree, would see to it that He was not made a prisoner of the Jews. The time had, however, not yet come for the manifestation of His Kingdom in power over this world. He must first defeat the moral and spiritual foes of mankind by Himself acting upon the principles which were to govern His Kingdom; and for Him that meant dying on behalf of men that in resurrection He could impart to all in His Kingdom His own heavenly life. All this was implied in the words He had spoken to a Jewish ruler when He said, "As Moses lifted up the serpent in the wilderness, even so must the Son of Man be lifted up: that whosoever believeth in him should not perish, but have eternal life" (John III, 14, 15).

As our Lord had spoken of "My Kingdom" and "My servants", Pilate says to Him, "Art Thou a King then?" or, rather, "a King Thou art, then".

In answering this our blessed Lord brings out some most vital facts. He refers to His pre-existence in the words, "for this cause came I into the world". He refers also to His Incarnation – "To this end was I born". The object of His birth was kingship and Micah had foretold that from Bethlehem "shall He come forth unto Me that is to be ruler in Israel" (V. 2). Furthermore, He was to "bear witness unto the truth". The whole system which governed men's thoughts was erroneous, whether about themselves or about God. Our Lord had declared, "Thy word is truth". He was the Incarnate Word and therefore the living manifestation of Truth. John had declared, "grace and truth came by Jesus Christ". There were those who were "of the truth" and, unlike His enemies, these heard His voice and were of a condition of heart to obey what they heard.

It will be obvious to all that our Lord Jesus Christ in addressing Pilate dealt with principles which are of universal importance and He did not hesitate to reveal that the supreme test to which all human beings would be subjected was their relationship to Himself.

This conversation between our Lord and Pilate ended with the latter's remark, "What is truth?"

The result thus far of our Lord's trial before Pilate is summed up in Pilate's own words, "I find in Him no fault at all" (XVIII, 38 and Luke XXIII, 4).

Pilate's attitude enraged the Jewish rulers who forthwith launched a series of random accusations against our Lord. Luke states, "And they were the more fierce, saying, He stirreth up the people, teaching throughout all Jewry, beginning from Galilee to this place" (XXIII, 5). Matthew and Mark both tell us that Pilate marvelled at the silence of our Lord and that he said to Him, "Hearest Thou not how many things they witness against Thee?" To this our Lord made no reply, "insomuch that the governor marvelled greatly" (Matt. XXVII, 12 to 14 and Mark XV, 3 to 5).

## OUR LORD JESUS CHRIST IS TAKEN BEFORE HEROD ANTIPAS

Read Luke XXIII, 6 to 12

The progress of our Lord's trial was beginning to prove a great embarrassment to Pilate, who was already satisfied that the Jews had made out no case for the death of their Victim Whom he had now examined at length and Whose answers made it perfectly clear that He was no political intriguer. Furthermore, the general bearing of our Lord and His refusal to reply to the obviously ill-founded and wicked accusations of His enemies made him reluctant to condemn Him on any score. Hearing that Jesus was from Galilee, Pilate, hoping to be relieved of giving a verdict, at once sent Him to Herod who ruled that province and under whose jurisdiction our Lord came. Luke alone records this incident.

Herod the Idumaean, the murderer of John the Baptist at the whim of an embittered woman, had often hoped to see our Lord perform some miracle, as he had heard so much about Him. To his many questions our Lord made not one reply and by His silence revealed His contempt for a ruler who had so transgressed against His herald – "a man sent from God". We are told "the chief priests and scribes stood and vehemently accused Him". Then Herod and his men of war, who were doubtless enraged by our Lord's silence, "mocked Him, and arrayed Him in a gorgeous robe, and sent Him again to Pilate" (XXIII, 11 and 12). But it is to be carefully noted that Herod refused to pass any form of sentence upon our Lord such as the Jews desired. Pilate later takes account of this fact in his effort to set our Lord free.

## OUR LORD JESUS CHRIST AGAIN BROUGHT BEFORE PILATE

### THE FINAL PHASE AND CONDEMNATION

### BARABBAS SET FREE

Read Matt. XXVII, 15 to 31; Mark XV, 6 to 20; Luke XXIII, 13 to 25, and John XVIII, 39 to XIX, 16

It is not easy to realize that the One Who was now being tried for His life held the future destiny of the whole human race in His hands. From Heaven the Father was watching the Son, now a meek Prisoner in the hands of the Gentiles. What wondrous sustainment of soul came to our Lord as He trod the path appointed for Him to the Cross, by virtue of doing His Father's will, and thereby rendering to Him that perfect obedience which no other one on the earth had ever rendered. Our Lord had once said to a lawyer, in reply to his enquiry as to the greatest commandment, "Thou shalt love the Lord thy God with all thy heart, and with all thy soul, and with all thy mind" (Matt. XXII, 37). Now our Lord was putting these three moral capacities in man into practice; and in spite of the utterly evil circumstances it gave Him ineffable joy to yield Himself up to the doing of His Father's will, knowing well that the work in hand was the Redemption of the world and the bringing of the human race back on to a footing whereby those who were enemies by nature could be reconciled to God and eternally blessed. It is said of Abraham and Isaac, when the latter was offered up, "they went both of them together" (Gen. XXII, 6 and 8). So now in all that follows, with its gruesome tale of man's wickedness and untold cruelty to our Lord and Saviour, may we realize that it was God the Father and God the Son moving along the appointed path together in unhindered communion, in order to accomplish our Redemption by the Son's limitless sacrifice of Himself.

It is to Luke's Gospel we must turn for information as to events directly after our Lord had been sent back by Herod to Pilate – the two potentates turning the occasion into a means of settling a feud of long standing (Luke XXIII, 12). The following verses give Luke's account of events at this point:

> "And Pilate, when he had called together the chief priests and the rulers and the people, said unto them, Ye have brought this Man unto me, as one that perverteth the people: and, behold, I, having examined Him before you, have found no fault in this Man touching those things whereof ye accuse Him: no, nor yet Herod: for I sent you to him; and, lo, nothing worthy of death is done unto Him.
>
> "I will therefore chastise Him, and release Him" (XXIII, 13 to 16).

This is an extremely important statement as it officially informed the Jewish rulers that their case had failed and that neither Herod the King nor Pilate the Governor had found our Lord at fault in the matter of the accusations they had brought against Him. Pilate, therefore, proposes to chastise our Lord, according to custom, and then to release Him. He had really no alternative. Furthermore, it was a custom at the Passover for the Governor to grant an amnesty to some notorious prisoner and to Pilate, knowing our Lord to be guiltless, this afforded an additional reason for pressing a claim for His discharge.

Matthew, Mark and John in their accounts make a great feature of Pilate's effort to use this customary release of a prisoner to set Jesus free. All the Gospels name Barabbas who was a notable prisoner who had made an insurrection and in the course of it had committed murder (Mark XV, 7).

In Matthew's account we get this statement:

> "Therefore when they were gathered together, Pilate said unto them, Whom will ye that I release unto you? Barabbas, or Jesus which is called Christ? For he knew that for envy they had delivered Him" (XXVII, 17 and 18).

From thenceforth, according to the four Accounts, Pilate was at pains to use his power to set Jesus free but, says Matthew, "the chief priests and elders persuaded the multitude that they should ask Barabbas, and destroy Jesus" (XXVII, 20).

It was at this critical juncture, as Matthew informs us, that Pilate had a message from his wife telling of a dream she had just had concerning Jesus. Her message was, "Have thou nothing to do with that just man: for I have suffered many things this day in a dream because of Him" (XXVII, 19). This message greatly added to Pilate's discomfiture because it perfectly confirmed his own view about Jesus that He was guiltless. But the chief priests and elders were inciting the mob, which had gathered outside the Hall of Judgment, to urge the release of Barabbas and to demand that Jesus be crucified.

A few weeks later the Apostle Peter, restored and filled with the Holy Ghost, charged Israel's rulers in these terms: "Ye delivered up, and denied Him (i.e., Christ) in the presence of Pilate, when he was determined to let Him go. But ye denied the Holy One and the Just, and desired a murderer to be granted unto you" (Acts III, 13 and 14).

It is only as we read the four Accounts given in the Gospels that it is possible fully to comprehend the fearful conflict that raged around the Person of our blessed Lord at this juncture. Pilate, not only knowing that Jesus was without guilt but also knowing that the Jews "had delivered Him for envy", sought by every means to persuade them to accept Jesus for the Passover release. We will continue the above quotation from Luke's account, but the parallel passages in Matthew XXVII, 20 to 24 and Mark XV, 11 to 14 should be read also. After Pilate's expressed intention of releasing our Lord when He had been chastised, Luke continues:

> "And they cried out all at once, saying, Away with this man, and release unto us Barabbas: (Who for a certain sedition made in the city, and for murder, was cast into prison). Pilate therefore, willing to release Jesus, spake again to them. But they cried, saying, Crucify Him, crucify Him.
>
> "And he said unto them the third time, Why, what evil hath He done? I have found no cause of death in Him: I will therefore chastise Him, and let Him go. And they were instant with loud voices, requiring that He might be crucified. And the voices of them and of the chief priests prevailed." (XXIII, 18 to 23).

Before this fearful clamour that Jesus should be crucified and the robber, Barabbas, released, Pilate's resolve began to give way. No voice was raised in favour of Jesus and the cry, "Not this Man, but Barabbas", filled the air. Pilate must make his own decision; and he evidently felt the weight of the occasion to be greater than his moral being could stand. The whole of influential Jewry was against him in his desire to do justice to an obvious Victim of Jewish religious pride and hatred. So Pilate weakens to the point of releasing Barabbas and seeks to release himself from the guilt of yielding to the pressure of the Jewish rulers by fastening the responsibility on them for what he well knew would be a judicial murder.

We will quote Matthew XXVII, 24 to 26:

> "When Pilate saw that he could prevail nothing, but that rather a tumult was made, he took water, and washed his hands before the multitude, saying, I am innocent of the blood of this just person: see ye to it.
>
> "Then answered all the people, and said, His blood be on us, and on our children. Then released he Barabbas unto them: and when he had scourged Jesus, he delivered Him to be crucified."

The "tumult" made by inciting the mob to demand that our Lord be crucified and Barabbas released was what caused the breakdown of Pilate's morale. It may have been vain for Pilate to wash his hands but the Jews perfectly understood the symbolism of this act by which he claimed to establish his own innocency in what was to become the greatest crime in human history. The Jews' response, "His blood be on us, and on our children", has proved to be the costliest statement that ever fell from human lips; and the history of the Jews ever since has been one of ceaseless blood-flowing and suffering – a historical fact which it is impossible to dissociate from the terrible events we are now tracing in the Scriptures.

After the release of Barabbas the scourging of our Lord Jesus Christ by the soldiers of Pilate, as the customary preliminary to crucifixion, took place. This scourging of our Lord, which was done in public after He had been stripped and tied to a stake, is so terrible to contemplate that one is bowed with shame to think that human beings could so act towards One Who had come down from Heaven and taken a body of flesh and blood in order that He might as Man – sinless Man – redeem us from all iniquity. How deep the mystery that man's sin must reach its greatest height in his hatred and violence toward the One Who was now about to put away sin by the sacrifice of Himself. How important, therefore, for all who own allegiance to Him to remember that our Lord's scourging was a part of His redemptive Sacrifice. Isaiah foresaw this and declared:

"But He was wounded for our transgressions,
He was bruised for our iniquities:
The chastisement of our peace was upon Him;
And with His stripes we are healed" (LIII, 5).

Though Pilate had released Barabbas and had now allowed Jesus to be cruelly scourged, he had not yet handed Him over to be crucified. It is from John's Gospel that we learn the precise details of what transpired after the scourging – though Matthew and Mark add certain details. It is quite clear that Pilate yet hoped to turn the Jewish rulers away from their determination to kill Jesus, and this fact the following passage from John's Gospel establishes:

"And the soldiers platted a crown of thorns, and put it on His head, and they put on Him a purple robe, and said, Hail, King of the Jews! and they smote Him with their hands. Pilate therefore went forth again, and saith unto them, Behold, I bring Him forth to you, that ye may know that I find no fault in Him. Then came Jesus forth, wearing the crown of thorns, and the purple robe. And Pilate saith unto them, Behold the man!

"When the chief priests therefore and officers saw Him, they cried out, saying, Crucify Him, crucify Him. Pilate saith unto them, Take ye Him, and crucify Him: for I find no fault in Him. The Jews answered him, We have a law, and by our law He ought to die, because He made Himself the Son of God" (XIX, 2 to 7).

The unresisting Son of God had now become an object for the sport and malice of the common soldiers who put on Him a purple robe (emblem of Gentile rulers) and a crown of thorns (emblem of the curse). They then carry their mockery further by placing a reed (emblem of weakness) in His hand and addressing Him, "Hail, King of the Jews!" When Pilate saw our Lord with His bruised and bleeding body, wearing the crown of thorns and affording so terrible a spectacle of suffering and humiliation, he evidently hoped it might satisfy the hate and blood-lust of the Jewish rulers and that he might set our Lord free.

It is to be noted that Pilate twice declares, "I find no fault in Him"; and on the first occasion gives that as the reason for bringing our Lord forth, with the words, "Behold the Man!" As, however, the Jews still demanded our Lord's crucifixion, Pilate tells them to go and do it and says a second time, "for I find no fault in Him".

What a fearful guilt all this places on the heads of the Jewish rulers. Our Lord's perfect Goodness and His devastating exposure from time to time of the Scribes, the Pharisees and the Sadducees for their abominable "hypocrisy" had engendered an undying hatred in their wicked hearts which could only be solaced by seeing Him put to death by crucifixion.

When Pilate heard that our Lord Jesus Christ lay claim to being the Son of God, "he was the more afraid". To a heathen Gentile who had closely observed our Lord's meek yet majestic bearing while under the stress of a Trial, it was not a matter for scorn that He made such a claim but one which could not be cast aside. Pilate, therefore, "went again into the judgment hall, and saith unto Jesus, Whence art Thou?" To this our Lord made no reply. Pilate is amazed at His silence and reminds Him that he has power either to crucify or release Him. Our Lord's reply to this once again reveals that He recognized no second causes. He, therefore, says to Pilate, "Thou couldst have no power at all against Me, except it were given thee from above: therefore he that delivered Me unto thee hath the greater sin" (XIX, 8 to 11).

On the strength of this statement of our Lord we are told "from thenceforth Pilate sought to release Him". The Jews, noting this firm attitude of Pilate, resort to a political subterfuge. They triumphantly declare:

> "If thou let this man go, thou art not Caesar's friend: whosoever maketh himself a king speaketh against Caesar" (XIX, 12).

[The time was now about 6 A.M. and the opening of "the day of the preparation" for the Jews' Passover – Friday, Nisan 14th in their Calendar, but the Sabbath, Nisan 15th in the Divine Calendar (XIX, 14)]

The record in John continues thus:

> "When Pilate therefore heard that saying, he brought Jesus forth, and sat down in the judgment seat in a place that is

called the Pavement, but in the Hebrew, Gabbatha . . . and he saith unto the Jews, Behold your king! But they cried out, Away with Him, away with Him, crucify Him. Pilate saith unto them, Shall I crucify your king? The chief priests answered, WE HAVE NO KING BUT CAESAR" (XIX, 13 to 15).

The perfidy of these last words is beyond conception when it is realized that the Jews were groaning under the yoke of Caesar and often made insurrections to free themselves and obtain their independence for which they longed.

The end of the trial of our Lord before Pilate had now come. The chief priests and rulers, aided by a multitude whom they incited to the point of a tumult, forced Pilate's hand and though we know well Pilate should have acted in the light of his own consciousness that our Lord was guiltless and the Victim of Jewish envy, he was not strong enough to risk his own position as a ruler by embittering the whole Jewish hierarchy and so endangering his own status with the Authorities at Rome. So Jesus had to be sacrificed on the altar of Pilate's personal well-being.

The record ends thus:

"Then delivered he Him therefore unto them to be crucified. And they took Jesus, and led Him away" (XIX, 16).

Mark's statement is as follows:

"And when they had mocked Him, they took off the purple from Him, and put His own clothes on Him, and led Him out to crucify Him" (XV, 20).

# PART III

## THE CRUCIFIXION, DEATH, AND BURIAL OF OUR LORD AND SAVIOUR, JESUS CHRIST

8 A.M. TO 6 P.M., FRIDAY, 1st MAY A.D. 33

OUR LORD, IN COMPANY WITH THE TWO MALEFACTORS, IS LED IN PROCESSION, UNDER ESCORT OF ROMAN SOLDIERS, OUTSIDE THE HOLY CITY TO A PLACE CALLED CALVARY WHERE "THEY CRUCIFIED HIM"

THE SON OF MAN WAS THUS "LIFTED UP FROM THE EARTH", EXACTLY AS HE HAD FORETOLD

PILATE'S DEEPLY SIGNIFICANT TRILINGUAL SUPERSCRIPTION OVER THE CROSS OF JESUS ANGERS THE JEWISH RULERS

TO ADD TO HIS HUMILIATION OUR LORD JESUS CHRIST IS REVILED, MOCKED AND TAUNTED BY HIS MURDERERS WHILE SILENTLY ENDURING THE AGONIES OF THE CRUCIFIXION

THE REPENTANT THIEF OWNS JESUS AS THE MESSIAH AND BECOMES THE FIRST FORGIVEN SINNER TO BE UNITED WITH HIM IN PARADISE

FOR THE THREE HOURS – NOON TO 3 P.M. – WHILE OUR SAVIOUR AND SUBSTITUTE IS SUFFERING THE JUST AND AWFUL JUDGMENT OF GOD FOR OUR SINS, THE SUN IS DARKENED IN THE HEAVENS

HIS WORK FOR GOD IN THE REDEMPTION OF THE WORLD BEING COMPLETED, OUR LORD DISMISSES HIS SPIRIT AND DIES

HIS SACRED BODY REMAINS FOR THREE HOURS (3 TO 6 P.M.) UPON THE TREE AFTER HIS EXPIRY. PIERCED AND BLEEDING, IT IS THEN REMOVED BY LOVING HANDS AND BURIED IN A NEW SEPULCHRE – THE PROCEEDINGS BEING CAREFULLY WATCHED BY "THE WOMEN ALSO, WHICH CAME WITH HIM FROM GALILEE"

"THOU WILT NOT . . . SUFFER THINE HOLY ONE
TO SEE CORRUPTION"
(PSALM XVI, 10)

# THE CRUCIFIXION OF OUR LORD JESUS CHRIST

"After that they . . . led Him away to crucify Him"
(Matthew XXVII, 31)

". . . And so it fell,
That Jew and Gentile making common cause
Against the Sinless One joined guilty hands,
Sealing the world's rejection of its God"

*Lyra Christi*

WE ARE now to comment upon the historic events narrated in the Holy Scriptures which came to pass in the TEN HOURS between 8 A.M. and 6 P.M. on FRIDAY, 1ST MAY A.D. 33 – the day of the CRUCIFIXION, DEATH AND BURIAL OF OUR LORD AND SAVIOUR, JESUS CHRIST.

Some will approach these events with a deep sense of personal concern because of the existence of a known (or, possibly, a desired) relationship with the One Who on that day allowed Himself to be put to death; but Who is now "ALIVE FOR EVERMORE". Others will approach them with a merely superficial concern like those who, having witnessed the Crucifixion, "smote their breasts, and returned", unaffected, to their own homes (Luke XXIII, 48). It is, however, self-evident that no one can, with impunity, adopt a neutral position in regard to the death of God's beloved Son – the One by Whom all things were created. We must be either FOR HIM and against His enemies OR AGAINST HIM and for His enemies. If we are FOR HIM, it will be because we believe with deep conviction that ON CALVARY'S TREE HE WAS FOR US, that we might receive from God, through His vicarious Sacrifice, the forgiveness of our sins and the gift of eternal life (Romans VI, 23).

* * *

## THE PROCESSION TO GOLGOTHA

The iniquity of the human race reached fullness and displayed the fact in unmistakable terms when, in unsanctified collaboration, "Herod, and Pontius Pilate, with the Gentiles, and the people of Israel, were gathered together" – "against the Lord and against His Christ", on the morning of Friday, 1st May A.D. 33, when Jesus of Nazareth, the Son of God, was led forth out of the Holy City to the place where criminals were publicly executed and which was termed in the Greek "Calvary" – and in the Hebrew – "Golgotha".

The sequel to the Incarnation of the Son of God was, according "to the determinate counsel and foreknowledge of God", His death on Calvary. Our Lord came into the world to die, and the manner of His death was foreknown to God and foretold in His Word in every detail. This fact, however, was unknown to (and therefore without influence upon) any of those who instigated His death or had part in its execution. Pilate acted according to the dictates of his own self-interest when "he delivered Jesus to their will", that is, to that of the Jewish rulers (Luke XXIII, 24, 25). It is, indeed, deeply mysterious to note the way in which man's act of supreme wickedness in killing God's beloved and only begotten Son became the means of fulfilling the Divine counsels of mercy to the world. By no other way could sin be atoned for than by the Sacrifice and blood-shedding of our Lord Jesus Christ on Calvary's Tree. Our Lord had been, at the beginning, acclaimed by John the Baptist as "the Lamb of God, which taketh away the sin of the world", and now THE DAY had arrived when the Lamb of God must be literally sacrificed. This could not be accomplished within the precincts of the Holy City as, in Leviticus IV, the type of the Sin Offering forbad it; so we read:

> "the bodies of those beasts, whose blood is brought into the sanctuary by the high priest for sin, are burned without the camp. Wherefore Jesus also, that He might sanctify the people with His own blood, suffered without the gate" (Hebrews XIII, 11, 12).

It was the counsels of God, therefore, and not the will of man merely that decreed that our Lord should shed His sacred blood outside Jerusalem at Golgotha, where the two malefactors were to be crucified.

We learn from Matthew and Mark that the soldiers of the Governor removed "the purple robe", with which they had mocked our Lord, and restored "His own raiment" to Him, before leading Him out to crucify Him.

It is painful in the extreme to contemplate our Lord's physical state when, with infinite humiliation, He joined the Procession with the two malefactors and the military escort, as it left the Governor's Palace to wend its way through the narrow and densely populated streets to the Gate of the City through which it must pass on its way to Golgotha.

Our Lord's body was a human body in every respect, otherwise the Scripture could not say of Him, "Wherefore in all things it behoved Him to be made like unto His brethren" (Heb. II, 17). However painful, it is not, therefore, difficult to form a correct judgment of His physical state after the inhuman brutalities, which He suffered at the hands of His captors, had taken their toll of His bodily strength. Added to the appalling sufferings consequent upon His being scourged by Pilate's soldiers – which included being stripped and tied to a post and lashed with a nail-laden scourge – our Saviour was subjected to smitings and buffetings which He received without a murmur because they formed a part of His one redemptive Sacrifice. (See Matt. XXVI, 67, 68; Luke XXII, 63, 64, and Matt. XXVII, 27 to 30.)

The prophet Isaiah appears to foresee, and express in words, our Lord's physical state before He was led out to be crucified. In the Authorized English Version, in Chapter LII, we read in verse 14, "His visage was so marred more than any man, and His form more than the sons of men". In the Margin of the Revised Version this is rendered, "His visage was so marred from that of man, and His form from that of the sons of men". This Scripture is given to convey the fact that the Saviour of the world before being crucified was so disfigured in face and form as to be almost unrecognizable as a man. Speaking through Isaiah, our Lord is heard to say, "I gave My back to the smiters, and My cheeks to them that plucked off the hair: I hid not My face from shame and spitting" (L, 6). There can be no doubt that this Scripture was fulfilled, like every other Scripture touching our Lord's sufferings and death; or else He could not have declared to His disciples, "All things that are written by the prophets concerning the Son of Man shall be accomplished" (Luke XVIII, 31).

## WHY OUR LORD HAD TO SUFFER SO BEFORE HIS CRUCIFIXION

May we not fail to remember in referring to our Lord's sufferings that they were *substitutional*, like His death. How else could Isaiah declare,

> "He was wounded for *our* transgressions,
> He was bruised for *our* iniquities:
> The chastisement of *our* peace was upon Him;
> And with His stripes *we* are healed" (LIII, 5)

This prediction affords the only explanation for our Lord's sufferings at the hands of men prior to His death upon the Cross when "His soul" was made "an offering for sin". The words used by the Prophet make it clear beyond dispute that these sufferings were vicarious and that they were borne by our Saviour, in infinite grace, as our Substitute. In other words, "our transgressions" and "our iniquities" were the direct cause of the "wounds" and the "bruises" and the "stripes" which He endured.

Why, it will be asked, was this necessary, seeing that the Saviour was that very day going to offer on the Tree an atoning Sacrifice for all our sins? Why should God require more than this? The answer is that the Law of God demanded that, before a man could present an offering to atone for an offence which caused INJURY to a fellow-being, he must first submit to the punishment which the Law enacted against his person or his possessions for such an offence. The justice of this is obvious otherwise the offender would go free and the injured person would go unavenged and the injury done him be unrequited.

The Saviour knew that He could not atone for the GUILT of our sins unless the demands of the Law for every act of violence or other injury inflicted by us upon our fellow-beings had been satisfied. The terms of God's Law in such matters were as just as they were inflexible. In Exodus XXI, verses 24 and 25, we read, "Eye for eye, tooth for tooth, hand for hand, foot for foot, burning for burning, wound for wound, stripe for stripe".

The above quotation from Isaiah LIII, 5, reveals how our blessed Saviour met the hopelessness of our position. From it we learn that before dying an atoning death upon the Cross *He assumed in His Person the massed sins committed by men against their fellows* (with special reference to acts of violence), none of which had ever been requited in accordance with God's holy and inexorable Law. Having thus taken upon Himself "our transgressions" and "our iniquities", He had to bear the full penalties which we had incurred for the same. Hence His "wounds", His "bruises", His "chastisement" and His "stripes" by which we are healed.

The Apostle Peter refers to this aspect of our Lord's Sacrifice when he says of Him, "Who His own self bare (Greek: carried up) our sins in His own body on the tree" (I Peter II, 24). This statement perfectly establishes that our Lord, having made "our transgressions" and "our iniquities" His own *by imputation*, and having suffered the punishment for the same in His own Person, carried them up with Him, that is, in His own body, on to the Tree, where He made atonement for them, as well as for our every sin, whether against God or man, by the shedding of His precious blood and the offering up of His life. Thus our Lord and Saviour, after He had perfectly met the claims of the Law against us for the unrequited injuries done to our fellow-men, atoned for the same on the Cross and so freed us from all guilt as before God.

In all this our blessed Lord was the Antitype of the Trespass Offering of Leviticus V and VI, in that He first made amends for our acts of trespass against our fellows before offering Himself on the Cross to atone for our guilt. All who value our Lord's Sacrifice will wish to enter more fully into this aspect of the same as revealed in the Holy Scriptures.

More we need not add as to our Lord's physical state as, worn out in body and disfigured in face and form, He takes His place in the Procession with the two malefactors (Luke XXIII, 32), He and they each being guarded by four soldiers. According to custom, the Procession would be led by the Centurion in charge and inscription boards announcing the offences for which each prisoner was to be executed would be carried before them. In the case of our Lord, Pilate could name *no offence* but evidently was caused to write what he did write and this no doubt was carried in the Procession, before being placed over the Cross on which Jesus was crucified.

The Procession leaves with our Lord carrying His own Cross, like the two malefactors, according to custom. We are not told the reason why the soldiers "compel" Simon the Cyrenian to bear Jesus' cross, but we dare not assume it was an act of sympathy on their part. Without a doubt our Lord Jesus had become physically incapable of carrying such a weight any longer. Simon was met "coming out of the country" and from this we can infer that the Saviour bore His cross until the Procession had passed through the Gate of the Holy City. Matthew (XXVII), Mark (XV) and Luke (XXIII) all refer to Simon's contribution in bearing the Cross of Jesus. John purposely omits the fact because it does not accord with his aspect of the Lord's death – a subject to which we will refer later.

1st May A.D. 33 was the Jews' Passover day and, though shops and bazaars would be closed, the city would be thronged with pilgrims from all over the Land.

It is worthy of note that our Lord's Crucifixion took place on the very day the Jewish rulers wished to avoid. They had said, "Not on the feast day, lest there be an uproar among the people" (Matt. XXVI, 5). The choice of the day, however, rested with God and not the Jewish rulers. No doubt, had the multitudes who had seen our Lord's miracles and heard His teaching realized in time what was happening there would have been an uproar, but His condemnation had been sealed and the plans for His crucifixion made before the public could have known anything about it.

As the Procession moved along it must have awakened untold interest, even if only of a morbid nature. Our Lord had long been, as we say, a public Figure. Luke alone records the following facts in relation to the journey to Calvary:

> "And there followed Him a great company of people, and of women, which also bewailed and lamented Him. But Jesus turning unto them said, Daughters of Jerusalem, weep not for Me, but weep for yourselves, and for your children. For, behold, the days are coming, in the which they shall say, Blessed are the barren, and the wombs that never bare, and the paps which never gave suck. Then shall they begin to say to the mountains, Fall on us; and to the hills, Cover us. For if they do these things in a green tree, what shall be done in the dry?" (XXIII, 27 to 31).

Jesus had already announced the destruction of Jerusalem and the Temple when speaking to His disciples, but on this occasion He gives warning in the light of what the Jewish rulers were that day doing in rejecting and crucifying their Messiah. The truth of His words is now known to the Jewish nation by what happened in A.D. 70, when Jerusalem and the Temple were laid in ruins after the most terrible siege in all human history.

It may rightly be inferred from a statement by the Evangelist Mark that our Lord had to be helped or actually carried the latter part of the journey to Golgotha. Mark states, "And they bring Him unto the place Golgotha" (XV, 22). The Greek word for "bring" used by Mark means "bear" or "carry" and it is so translated in Luke XXIII, 26, in reference to Simon being made to "bear" the Cross of Jesus. This fact sheds a yet more solemn light on the effect of our Lord's intense physical sufferings between His arrest and His Crucifixion. Oh that men might realize before it is too late that it was for them He allowed Himself to suffer such brutalities at the hands of wicked men. To Him all these sufferings were a part of the bitter cup which God the Father had placed in His hand in Gethsemane and which He, in obedience, had determined from that hour to drink to the dregs.

## A NECESSARY DIGRESSION
## WAS OUR LORD CRUCIFIED ON A CROSS OR A TREE?
## THE EVIDENCE OF HOLY SCRIPTURE

Before commenting further on the events recorded in the four Gospels which took place when our Lord Jesus Christ was being put to death with the two malefactors, we must digress briefly to show from the Holy Scriptures that *our Lord was not hung upon a cross*, that is, a wooden stake with a transverse cross-bar; but upon a single stake to which His hands and feet were nailed. The Romans called this single stake, which was often used for the crucifixion of the lowest criminals, "crux simplex".

The facts which we will now give in support of this most solemn statement will appeal only to those who make a sharp distinction between Truth and Tradition – Truth being what is written in the Holy Scriptures and Tradition being additions or, as in this case, contradictions, thereto. This is not a question where opinion has any place and certainly not prejudice, but where FACTS must rule with all who love our Lord Jesus Christ in sincerity.

In the current edition of the *Encyclopaedia Britannica* (printed in U.S.A.) which can be seen in any local Library, under the article – "The Cross and Crucifixion", these statements appear:

> "The Cross has been used both as a religious symbol and as an ornament from the dawn of man's civilization."

Under a sub-title, "Early Christian Crosses", this statement appears:

> "It was, however, not until the time of Constantine (A.D. 312) that the Cross was publicly used as the symbol of the Christian religion."

The cross in one form or another was evidently in constant use as a symbol of the religions of many of the nations of the earth, notably Egypt, Persia and India, before the Christian Era.

In the Greek language, from which the existing copies of the New Testament were translated, there is no word which represents our English word "cross", which is derived solely from the Latin word "crux". The Greek noun translated "cross" in the English Authorized Version is "STAUROS" which all lexicons, including Liddell and Scott, translate as, "upright pale, stake or pole". "The cross" is given as a later meaning and this evidently to conform with its use in the Holy Scriptures. In this connection we are advised that throughout the Greek classics the word "STAUROS" is exclusively used for a pole or stake, that is, a single piece of wood. (The verb "STAUROŌ", translated in the A. V. "crucify" means "to drive stakes".) There can be no doubt that the translation 28 times of "STAUROS" as "cross" was to make Scripture conform with the traditional view of our Lord's death, which came into public acceptance through the Emperor Constantine in the fourth century; and this as the direct result of the Emperor's very dubious account of an apparition which took the form of a cross in the sky and which he said was later confirmed to him in a dream. As Constantine was not then a true convert to Christianity, though favourably disposed towards it as a state religion, few would accept that he became the subject of a divine revelation. If this were the occasion, we could quote many authorities in the Churches of Christendom who deplore the devastating effect that Constantine's adoption of Christianity, as a state religion, had upon the true Christian Faith. At any rate, it cannot be denied that the Cross as a symbol of the Christian religion came into public use two or three hundred years after the Apostles had departed and that not a trace of it is to be found in the first century; and *this no doubt for the excellent reason that our Lord Jesus Christ was not crucified* but put to death by being nailed to a single stake, which the Romans termed "crux simplex". Few can doubt that the linking of our blessed Lord's death with a symbol (the cross) which had been for two or three thousand years used in reference to the false deities of heathendom was a master-stroke of the great Adversary who has succeeded in making it the highly respected symbol of official Christianity – it being displayed as such in and on religious buildings and on the devotees of several Christian communions.

So much for the negative aspect of this most solemn matter. For the positive aspect we must turn to the Holy Scriptures, which ordain that our Lord and Master had to be hung upon a tree in order to redeem us "from the curse of the law".

The Apostle Peter three times alludes to this fact and the Apostle Paul twice; and on each occasion they are referring to the actual mode of Christ's death. In Acts V, 30, Peter states, "the God of our fathers raised up Jesus, Whom ye slew and hanged on a tree". Again, in Acts X, 39, in addressing Gentiles, Peter refers to Jesus of Nazareth "Whom they slew and hanged on a tree". Then in I Peter II, 24, we read of our Lord "Who His own self bare (lit. carried up) our sins in His own body on the tree". In Acts II, 23, Peter states of our Lord, "Ye have taken, and by wicked hands have crucified and slain". The Greek word, "PROSPEGNUMI", here translated "crucified", means "to fix or fasten anything" and has no actual relation to crucifixion which is inferred by the translators in accord with tradition.

The Apostle Paul in Acts XIII, 29, says, "When they had fulfilled all that was written of Him, they took Him down from the tree, and laid Him in a sepulchre". Finally, in writing to the Galatians, Paul establishes the reason why the Saviour had to die on a tree. In Chapter III, verse 13, we read:

"Christ hath redeemed us from the curse of the law, being

made a curse for us: for it is written, Cursed is every one that hangeth on a tree."

A tree is not a cross which is an artificial structure composed of pieces of wood placed crosswise.

The Greek word used for "tree" in all these cases is "XULON" and it is to be found in the Septuagint Version of Deuteronomy XXI, 22, 23, which Paul quotes to the Galatians, and also in Joshua X in relation to the five kings which Joshua "hanged . . . on five trees".

Let the final witness be our Lord Himself. In His conversation with Nicodemus in John III, He says:

"And as Moses lifted up the serpent in the wilderness, even so must the Son of Man be lifted up: that whosoever believeth in Him should not perish, but have eternal life."

When we turn to Numbers XXI, we read, "And the Lord said unto Moses, Make thee a fiery serpent, and put it upon a pole (R. V. "standard"): and it shall come to pass, that every one that is bitten, when he looketh upon it, shall live" (verses 8, 9).

It is a fact to be solemnly noted that this serpent of brass set upon a pole became an idol to the people of Israel, for we read in II Kings XVIII, 4, that Hezekiah, King of Judah, "brake in pieces the brasen serpent that Moses had made: for unto those days the children of Israel did burn incense to it: and he called it Nehushtan".

Has not Christendom done likewise with the antitype? No sooner had the deception been foisted upon people that Christ had been put to death on a Cross ( † ) than it became, not merely an emblem, but a charm and an object for the abject veneration of people who adopted the Christian Faith as a formal religion. The Bible, which is God's own Word, is absolutely clear in its testimony to the fact that our Lord and Saviour was nailed by His hands and His feet to a single stake, which both Peter and Paul refer to as a tree. The cross is a pagan symbol, and to affirm that our Lord died on one is both contrary to the facts given in Holy Scripture and a concession to the great Adversary who introduced it as an idol, in order to lower Christianity to the level of pagan religions. Unfortunately, all translations of the New Testament are based upon Manuscripts nearly all of which are of a later date than the fourth century when the "cross" theory of the Saviour's death had begun to be generally accepted.

As throughout the Greek classics the word "STAUROS" signifies a "stake" or "pole", it is impossible to translate it "cross" which is a form of structure uniting two pieces of wood and an entirely different thing. To translate "XULON" as "tree" is not to depart from its original meaning of "wood". Both words apply to the stake to which our Lord was nailed when He was put to death.

The Bible, therefore, disallows the notion that our Lord Jesus Christ was put to death on a cross; and no doubt for this reason there exists a large body of true Christians in whom there has been wrought an innate antipathy to the exhibition of crosses as symbols of the Christian Faith. We will now again take up the Narrative.

## THE DEATH OF OUR LORD JESUS CHRIST

### THE SAVIOUR OF THE WORLD IS NAILED TO A TREE AND DIES AFTER SEVEN HOURS OF AGONY

### AS SON OF MAN OUR LORD IS "LIFTED UP FROM THE EARTH" IN ORDER TO ACCOMPLISH OUR REDEMPTION

John III, 14; VIII, 28; XII, 32

The arrival of the Procession at Golgotha, Mark tells us, was at "the third hour" which in Bible time was 8 to 9 A.M. (XV, 25). It was the opening of the last day of our Lord's life in a body of flesh and blood, for, as we explained in Chapter I, all His days began at 8 A.M. In Divine Time it was God's holy Sabbath and the 15th day of the 1st month which was the 1st day of Unleavened Bread. In Israel's Calendar it was Friday the 14th of the 1st month and the "day of the preparation", both for the Sabbath and the Passover which was to be celebrated at about 6 o'clock that evening. In the Gentile or Roman Calendar the day was the Calends of May (i.e. the 1st) and the year A.D. 33, in our terms.

Four thousand Sacred or Redemption Years had passed to the day from the scene in the Garden of Eden when, immediately after the Fall, the Lord God promised that the woman's "Seed", that is, Christ Jesus our Lord, would "bruise" the serpent's head, and when in fact the evil wrought by the serpent would be turned to man's highest blessing and God's eternal Glory. For this Friday, 1st May A.D. 33, was the Day of Man's Redemption and in it our Lord and Saviour, by the giving up of His own life and the shedding of His own precious blood as an offering for sin, "obtained eternal redemption for us", that is, for all who believe on Him (Heb. IX, 12).

However great the Saviour's bodily weakness may have been when the Procession arrived at the place of execution, that is, Calvary or Golgotha, He was in the enjoyment of perfect peace of mind and perfect communion with His Father in Heaven. The bitter cup received in Gethsemane from His Father (and from none other) was firmly grasped even though, as He well knew, He was about to drink its bitterest portion.

The Bible is silent as to any details relating to the fearful task of nailing the hands and feet of our blessed Lord to the stake upon which His sacred body was about to be suspended when ("as Moses lifted up the serpent in the wilderness") He, the Son of Man, was "lifted up" from the earth (John III, 14). The preparations obviously necessitated the infliction of appalling suffering upon the victims of this cruellest form of execution; but as the Bible is silent and spares those who would rightly be deeply harassed in their feelings by such details we, no doubt, will be well advised to avoid any imaginative comment.

There are, however, two preliminary events of historic importance recorded for us. The first of these is that, according to custom, when our Lord reached Golgotha He was offered "wine mingled with myrrh". This was to deaden the senses. Matthew and Mark both mention the incident. The former Evangelist records the fact that "when He had tasted thereof, He would not drink" (Matt. XXVII, 34 and Mark XV, 23). Our Lord well knew that if He was to suffer the judgment of God for our sins, He could not possibly take what was a soporific, as to do so would be to shun the suffering by making His faculties insensible to all He was called upon of God to pass through. Never, indeed, were our Lord's mental and spiritual faculties more alert than when He was experiencing, without a murmur, the unspeakable agonies of hanging nailed by hands and feet to a tree.

The other recorded event was His prayer to God on behalf of His murderers. Luke alone advises us of this (XXIII, 34). It appears that it was uttered as He was being nailed to the tree on which He was presently to die.

How strange His gracious words, "Father, forgive them; for they know not what they do", must have sounded to the rough soldiery engaged in putting to death One Who was as meek as He was sinless. Little did they realize that they were taking part in the world's most terrible crime. Without a doubt this prayer of our blessed Lord and Saviour was answered in that the Apostle Peter was commissioned to extend another offer of mercy to the Jewish rulers after the descent of the Holy Ghost.

### THE FOUR HOURS – 8 A.M. UNTIL NOON

Matthew, Mark and Luke all inform us that the stake or tree bearing our Lord and Saviour was placed in the earth between the two malefactors, "one on the right hand, and the other on the left" (Luke XXIII, 33). But John also says, "on either side one, and Jesus in the midst" (XIX, 18). What a solemn fulfilment this was of Isaiah's prophecy: "He was numbered with the transgressors" (LIII, 12) – a fact pointed out by Mark. No doubt the Roman records of that day included our Lord's Name – Jesus of Nazareth – with those of the two thieves put to death with Him. Every prediction of the prophets concerning the Saviour's death was fulfilled to the letter. To be our Kinsman-Redeemer, our Lord had to be wholly identified with our fallen race – so He was numbered with notorious sinners though He Himself was sinless.

According to custom the accusation against the offender was placed (presumably nailed) on the stake above him. All the Gospels refer to the "superscription" over our Lord and each gives a different version of its wording. There is nothing remarkable in this and obviously there is no contradiction but rather a confirmation of one another. Each account includes the words "THE KING OF THE JEWS" which shows that this was the feature that stood out most prominently. Mark and Luke limit themselves to this suggestive title; while Matthew adds the preface, "THIS IS JESUS", and John that of "JESUS OF NAZARETH" (Matt. XXVII, 37; Mark XV, 26; Luke XXIII, 38, and John XIX, 19).

It is John who informs us of the visit to Pilate of "the chief priests of the Jews" in order to persuade him to change the superscription and add, "He said, I am" to the "King of the Jews". Pilate, however, stood firm, saying, "What I have written I have written" – words which clearly imply that he had chosen this title with deliberation, partly no doubt because he had a measure of real belief that Jesus was a King on account of our Lord's own words, "To this end was I born"; and partly to anger the Jewish rulers who had forced his hand by compelling him to sentence to death One Whom he knew was not guilty.

Directly after our Lord had been "lifted up" on the tree or stake to which He had been nailed, the four soldiers, according to custom, laid claim to the garments which had covered His Sacred Body prior to His being stripped for execution. All the Evangelists refer to this event, but John gives the fullest account of the same. In Chapter XIX, 23, 24, we read, "Then the soldiers, when they had crucified Jesus, took His garments, and made four parts, to every soldier a part; and also His coat: now the coat was without seam, woven from the top throughout. They said therefore among themselves, 'Let us not rend it, but cast lots for it, whose it shall be:' that the scripture might be fulfilled, which saith, 'They parted My raiment among them, and for My vesture they did cast lots'. These things therefore the soldiers did". The Scripture referred to is in Psalm XXII, which so graphically and with such precision portrays our Lord's sufferings on the tree. That four Gentiles should have possessed themselves of our Lord's garments at the time of His death seems to pre-figure this Dispensation, when Gentiles the world over (the four points of the compass) have, by virtue of His death and resurrection, been clothed with that wondrous garment – "the righteousness of God which is by faith of Jesus Christ unto all and upon all them that believe" (Rom. III, 22).

## OUR LORD IS TAUNTED AND REVILED WHILE HANGING ON THE TREE

"Jesus . . . for the joy that was set before Him endured the cross (lit. stake), despising the shame" (Heb. XII, 2)

To contemplate the Son of God, by Whom all things were created, hanging on a stake to which He had been nailed and bound, and this between two common malefactors suffering a like execution, is a sight which ought to humble the proudest of human beings; for of Him it is written, "And being found in fashion as a man, He humbled Himself, and became obedient unto death, even the death of the cross (Gk. STAUROS) – (Phil. II, 8). To contemplate the impaled Christ of God, lifted up from the earth, is the only place to learn true humility. (Philippians II, 5 to 8.)

To add to His shame and, if possible, to humiliate Him even beyond that of dying a felon's death under the superscription, "This is Jesus the King of the Jews" (Matt. XXVII, 37), "the chief priests mocking Him, with the scribes and elders" further vented their spleen upon Him in these most shocking terms:

> "He saved others; Himself He cannot save. If He be the King of Israel, let Him now come down from the cross (Gk. stake), and we will believe Him. He trusted in God; let Him deliver Him now, if He will have Him: for He said, I am the Son of God" (Matt. XXVII, 41 to 43).

Not a word in this statement but savours of the hiss of the serpent; for who better than Satan, the master of these revilers, knew that the Holy Son of God was dying a felon's death in order to destroy the evil wrought in the Garden of Eden and so to save the human race from total destruction (see I John III, 8). Was Jesus not the King of Israel? Verily, He was. But it was not kingly power that could change the evil in human hearts, but self-sacrificing and immortal LOVE. There could be no remission of our sins without the shedding of His blood. Was not that the lesson of the Passover in Egypt? And did not the Law declare, "It is the blood that maketh an atonement for the soul" (Lev. XVII, 11)? But, blinded by their hate of Eternal Good, these Jewish rulers sense nothing of the fearful crime that is being enacted; nor do they realize they are involving their own people in judgments more terrible than any yet visited upon them or others.

But, for our blessed Saviour, the bitterest of all the evil things that were visited upon Him in His dying hours was that to all appearances God, in Whom He trusted with a perfect faith, disowned Him and refused to acknowledge or deliver Him. What better evidence could His enemies wish for in proof that His claim to be the Son of God was false and He an impostor?

Thus armed, they gloated over His extremity and thereby gave proof to the Universe that what Jesus had said of them was true, namely, "Ye are of your father the devil, and the lusts of your father ye will do. He was a murderer from the beginning" (John VIII, 44). It was these Jewish rulers who were the murderers of Jesus, as their own kinsman, the martyr Stephen, declared a few months later when he said, "of Whom ye have been now the betrayers and murderers" (Acts VII, 52; and see also I Thess. II, 14 to 16).

Added to the bitter taunts of the rulers were the ignorant gibes of those who said, "Thou that destroyest the temple, and buildest it in three days, save Thyself" – "If Thou be the Son of God, come down from the cross" (Gk. stake). Matthew (XXVII) and Mark (XV) both record this utterance. As we pointed out when writing of the Passover on 4th May A.D. 30, our Lord's statement as to the Temple was a positive prediction of His death at the hands of the Jews. This, which was given in answer to their request for a sign, was, "Destroy this temple, and in three days I will raise it up" – to which John adds, "But He spake of the temple of His body" (John II, 19 to 21).

The statement of His revilers was, therefore, a travesty of what our Lord had said and a perfect example of what malice can do in deliberately distorting facts. At that very moment the Jewish rulers, to whom our Lord had uttered His intimation, were actively putting it into effect. They were, in fact, then and there destroying "the temple" of which He spake. Little did they realize that "in three days" He would "raise it up". Actually, as we are about to show, our Lord rose from the dead on 4th May, exactly THREE YEARS to the day from His statement to the Jews on 4th May A.D. 30, when asked by them for a sign. Without doubt, our Lord's words embraced both these 3 years and the literal 3 days His spirit was absent from His body.

It is to be carefully noted that John in his Gospel makes no reference to the fearful mockery of our Lord when He was hanging on the Tree; nor does he direct attention in any way to the Lord's sufferings. This is due to the fact that this Evangelist presents an aspect of the Saviour's Sacrifice entirely different from that of the first three Gospels. This subject we shall refer to in Part IV of this Chapter.

## THE TWO MALEFACTORS

### THEIR RESPECTIVE ATTITUDES TO CHRIST ARE REPRESENTATIVE OF HUMANITY IN GENERAL

"Some believed . . . and some believed not" (Acts XXVIII, 24)

It is clear from Matthew and Mark that both the thieves, who were being executed with God's beloved Son, joined for a time in execrating our Lord in company with the heartless revilers who were watching the proceedings from around (Matt. XXVII and Mark XV). It is Luke alone who records the fact that a sudden and most exalted change of attitude came over one of them (XXIII, 39 to 43). This man's conversion was probably the most remarkable in the whole Bible; and it must have been the one and only relief that came to our Saviour in His hours of agony on the Tree.

On hearing his companion rail against Jesus and say, "If Thou be (the) Christ, save Thyself and us", the repentant thief rebuked him with the words, "Dost not thou fear God, seeing thou art in the same condemnation? And we indeed justly; for we receive the due reward of our deeds: but this Man hath done nothing amiss". In these words we can detect a most glorious work of God in this man's heart. To fear God, we are told in Proverbs (I), "is the beginning of knowledge" and in the Psalms (CXI), "the beginning of wisdom", and it would appear that this man had evidently at one stroke acquired both through the fear of God. These malefactors were Jews who had probably been brought up to know the Law and the Messianic hope. How remarkable that just as his nation was putting "the Hope of Israel" to death, the bright flame of that Hope should spring up in the heart of so deep-dyed a sinner and enable him to behold in his co-Sufferer the Messiah Himself.

We first get from this repentant thief his own confession of guilt and the acceptance of his punishment as lawful; after this comes his perfect testimony to the Saviour: "This Man hath done nothing amiss" – words which were akin to Pilate's, "I find in Him no fault at all".

It is to be remarked also that this man sought no relief in his present sufferings, like the other thief; nor indeed in the immediate future, for when he addresses the Saviour he only looks on to having part with Him in the Kingdom, whenever that might be. He says to Jesus, "Lord, remember me when Thou comest into Thy kingdom", words which prove that, unlike the Jewish rulers whose eyes were blinded by hypocrisy, his eyes had been opened wide, like his compatriot in the 9th Chapter of John, to the fact that Jesus, his co-Sufferer, was the Christ, Whose Kingdom would presently be set up over all the earth.

Our Lord's reply must have come to this forgiven sinner as an untold and unexpected refreshment of mind and soul. Jesus was then dying for this man's sins, not as Messiah but as Saviour and Redeemer – yea, for the sins of all the world was He then dying. His sins thus atoned for by the shedding of the blood of his sinless co-Sufferer, *this man in a few hours would enter upon eternal bliss*. So the Saviour is able to adjust His companion's viewpoint as to a future blessing in the Kingdom with the words of unspeakable grace affecting the immediate present, "Verily I say unto thee, To-day shalt thou be with Me in Paradise". And let us not forget that our Lord's one perfect Sacrifice removed this man's sins from him so completely that he entered Paradise as sinless as the One Who had that day made expiation for his sins by dying by his side on the Tree, accursed of God.

### OUR LORD JESUS CHRIST PLACES HIS MOTHER IN THE KEEPING OF JOHN, "THE DISCIPLE WHOM JESUS LOVED"

We have not as yet made reference to the considerable number of people known to our Lord who gathered around the scene of His execution.

Luke tells us that "All His acquaintance, and the women that followed Him from Galilee, stood afar off, beholding these things" (XXIII, 49).

Mark is more specific. He says, "There were also women looking on afar off: among whom was Mary Magdalene, and Mary the mother of James the less and of Joses, and Salome; (who also, when He was in Galilee, followed Him, and ministered unto Him;) and many other women which came up with Him unto Jerusalem" (XV, 40, 41).

Matthew speaks in a similar way in Chapter XXVII, 55, 56.

John alone records the fact that Mary, the beloved mother of our Lord, was among the many women who had been drawn to Golgotha when they heard early in the morning that Jesus had been condemned to death and was already being led forth to the place where public executions were held. When these women arrived is not said, but most would have done so to see the One they so loved and honoured as their Messiah already hanging nailed to the Tree. Their grief and bewilderment must have known no bounds, and the greatest distress must have marked every countenance. It would appear that, like the disciples, "they knew not the scripture, that He must rise again from the dead" (John XX, 9). This being so, death to them would be the end, save for a far-off resurrection of the just at the last day. A deep affection for our Lord marked these women, all of whom were His disciples and many of whom had ministered to Him of their substance. Prominent among these women were Mary Magdalene and Mary the mother of James and Joses and the mother of James and John, the sons of Zebedee. We hear nothing of the presence at Golgotha of Mary and Martha and Lazarus their brother whom the Lord had raised from the dead only twelve days before. Neither is there mention of any of the eleven disciples witnessing our Lord's death, save John, whose devotion to his Master forbad an absence, though it was evidently according to a Divine ordering that he should be present.

We read in John XIX, "Now there stood by the cross (stake) of Jesus His mother, and his mother's sister, Mary the wife of Cleophas, and Mary Magdalene". (At a later point these women moved "afar off", as stated by Matthew, Mark and Luke. That would have been during the Three Hours of darkness.) "When Jesus therefore saw His mother, and the disciple standing by, whom He loved, He saith unto His mother, Woman, behold thy son! Then saith He to the disciple, Behold thy mother"! Though the Eternal Son of God, our Lord was, in human terms, Mary's First-born Son, and as such He owned the human responsibility of making provision for His mother, who was doubtless then a widow. Our Lord had a perfect human love for His mother as He also had for John, His disciple. So He, as a last act of loving care for His mother, places her in John's guardianship. The Scripture continues, "and from that hour that disciple took her unto his own home" (verses 25 to 27). Whether John at once led Mary away from the scene of her beloved Son's exodus from this world we cannot tell, but it appears likely that she was thus spared this fearful ordeal. Calvary was the place where the words of Simeon to our Lord's mother were fulfilled when he said to her, "Yea, a sword shall pierce through thy own soul also" (Luke II, 35).

Four hours had now passed since the arrival at Golgotha and the hour had come when our Lord must pass under the rod of Divine wrath which was to be visited upon Him as He paid the full price for our redemption. For the next three hours the sun would hide its face and the earth be darkened while the sword of Divine judgment was unsheathed and buried itself in the sinless bosom of God's beloved Son.

These Four Hours terminated at Noon. During this period our Lord's great sufferings were essentially those which fell upon Him from man in his lowest estate as the accomplice of Satan, whose works our Lord had been manifested to destroy, and was in fact now in process of so doing through His death.

If we would enter in some small measure into what our Lord and Saviour passed through or, if we would gain some glimmer of His thoughts when suffering thus at the hands of those He came to save, we must turn to such Psalms as XXII and LXIX, which are so obviously expressive of His sufferings and death, when impaled upon the stake to which His sacred body had been nailed at the behest of the rulers of His own beloved nation – Israel.

The following lines, written by one now departed, may prove a help to those who would glean a more intimate knowledge of events in the hours before Noon. This writer views these as starting at the end of the ninth hour which is 9 A.M.

"... In His deep need
The Lord appeals to none. The grief, the pain
He bears alone. Among the gaping throng
Foregathered for His death there was not one
That pitied Him. He looked for comforters,
And found them not. They gave Him gall for meat,
And in His thirst they offered Him for drink
The thirst-provoking *homec* of the poor.
"I am poured out like water", thus He plained

Unto His full soul in the silences,
"And all My bones are out of joint. Like wax
"My heart melts in My bowels; and My strength
"Is dried up like a potsherd. I am faint
"By reason of My crying; and My tongue
"Cleaves to My jaws. My throat is dried: Mine eyes
"Fail with a long expectance still prolonged;
"And swelling floods of waters whelm My soul."

Noon was approaching. The fierce Syrian sun
For three full hours had poured his pitiless beams
Upon the Holy One. For three tense hours
The Prince of Life, Creator, Sovereign Lord,
Lifted twixt earth and heaven, had been the song
Of drunkards, scorn of perjured legalists,
Meek gazing-stock of lewd unfeeling men,
And butt of ribald soldiers; yet, sustained
As perfect Man by perfect trust in God
In fellowship unbroken, and consoled
By love – His love Whose bosom ever was
His dwelling-place – all yet was light within.
Three hours of shame; three hours of bitter pain;
By man inflicted, suffered patiently
Out of great love for man, and in the strength
Of the uplifting solace of a joy
Proceeding not from man but love's pure Source –
These passed, and at the sixth hour came a change.

(*Lyra Christi*—A. E. Knight)

THE SUN IS DARKENED IN THE HEAVENS "FROM THE SIXTH HOUR . . . UNTO THE NINTH HOUR"

NOON TO 3 P.M.

OUR LORD JESUS CHRIST NOW BECOMES THE ANTITYPE OF THE SIN OFFERING OF THE 15TH DAY OF THE 1ST MONTH
(Numbers XXVIII, 17 and 22)

IN THESE THREE HOURS OF DARKNESS OUR LORD, AS THE REDEEMER OF THE WORLD, SUFFERS THE WRATH OF GOD IN OUR STEAD, AND DIES FORSAKEN AFTER BEING "MADE . . . SIN" FOR US

"Now once in the end of the world (ages) hath He appeared to put away sin by the sacrifice of Himself"
(Hebrews IX, 26)

Read Numbers XXVIII, 17 to 25; Matt. XXVII, 45; Mark XV, 33, and Luke XXIII, 44, 45

We now reach the last Three Hours of our Lord's life on the earth. As far as the Gospels are concerned, we learn nothing of what transpired in them, save that a preternatural darkness enveloped the earth. We are, however, not left to our imagination because by making recourse to other Scriptures we are able to learn much as to what our Saviour passed through in them; though none but God Himself could ever measure the depth of the sufferings He endured ON OUR BEHALF during these last Three Hours of His earthly pathway.

It will be noted by all that it is the manifest intention of the three Gospels to make the period of darkness from Noon to 3 P.M. stand out by itself. This indicates that it was of a distinctly different order from the four hours to Noon when man, as the tool of Satan, was busy hurling his taunts and malicious insults at the impaled Son of God, as He hung nailed by hands and feet to the Tree on which He was about to be "made a curse for us" (Gal. III, 13).

It was when the hour of Noon was reached that our departing Saviour entered upon those particular sufferings the anticipation of which had caused Him such inexpressible agony in the

Garden of Gethsemane when, "with strong crying and tears", He made supplication to God for the removal of so bitter a cup – "if it be possible". When, after His third petition, He learnt that it was His Father's will that He should drink that cup, He, as ever, perfect in obedience, took it from His Father's hand and left the Garden a Captive in the hands of His enemies.

We have followed Him from the Garden to His trials before the Jewish Sanhedrin, Herod and Pilate. We have witnessed the unheard-of brutalities practised upon Him including a scourging so terrible that His face and form became distorted. We have seen His efforts to bear the Stake (crux simplex) on which He was to be impaled and break down under it, so that Simon the Cyrenian had to be compelled to carry it for Him; while He Himself had to be borne to the place of execution called Golgotha by the rough Roman soldiery. We have seen Him nailed and bound to the Tree after refusing a soporific to kill the pain caused thereby. Finally, we have watched Him hanging there beneath the truthful superscription – "Jesus of Nazareth the King of the Jews" – while His enemies taunt Him with invitations to give proof that He was the Son of God by coming down from the Tree. We have heard no word of retaliation escape from His lips, for "when He was reviled, (He) reviled not again" (I Peter II, 23).

As we have often remarked, our Lord's pathway on earth was according to a programme of Time, and in that programme these Three Hours from Noon to 3 P.M. held a place of unequalled importance and solemnity. To mark the occasion God darkened the sun and brought a pall of heavy darkness over the earth so that His enemies might be prevented from gloating over the sufferings of His beloved Son in His darkest hour.

In Divine Time the day on which our Lord died was the 15th of the 1st month – the first Day of Unleavened Bread. It was, as we have pointed out previously, the first day of the Christian Dispensation, of which era the Seven Days of Unleavened Bread form an outstanding type. The day had opened the evening before at 6 o'clock when our Lord and the twelve Apostles sat down to take the Passover Supper. (It must always be kept in mind that the Bible only measures the period of our Lord's death and resurrection according to Divine Time. This 15th of the 1st month was in Israel's Calendar the 14th of the same.)

We learn from Numbers XXVIII, verses 17 to 25, that on every 15th day of the 1st month the Law required the presentation of several burnt-offerings and ONE SIN-OFFERING to mark the occasion. All these sacrifices were typical of the Sacrifice offered by our Lord Jesus Christ on this 15th day of the 1st month in the year A.D. 33, and *were designed of God in anticipation of that event.* These many burnt-offerings and the one sin-offering represent two entirely different aspects of our Lord's death on the Tree. The burnt-offering aspect (see Leviticus I) is set forth by the Apostle John in his Gospel – a fact we explain in detail in a Note at the end of this Chapter.

The Sin-offering aspect (see Leviticus IV) is set forth by each of the other three Gospels, and it is this aspect which was fulfilled in the Three Hours of darkness. *Nothing is more clear or certain than that Matthew, Mark and Luke present our Lord's death as the Antitype of the Sin-offering of the 15th day of the 1st month, named in Numbers XXVIII, 17 and 22.* It hardly needs saying that to be the Antitype of this Sin-offering our Lord Jesus Christ had not only to bear our sins, but had to be, and was, "made . . . sin for us", that is *by imputation.* Our blessed Redeemer so completely identified Himself with our fallen race that He could present Himself to God *as one of us* (though He Himself was sinless) and be accepted *on our behalf.* In this way *He took our sin and died with it upon Himself,* thus paying the full penalty required by Divine justice in order to free us from all guilt. So we read in Hebrews IX, 26, "Now once in the end of the world (R. V., ages) hath He appeared to put away sin by the sacrifice of Himself" – a statement which reveals that our Lord came to put away sin, not by teaching us to observe His own sinless life, but by the deliberate sacrificing of that life in order to meet the claims of God's holy Law which demanded the death of all sinners, since "it is appointed unto men once to die, but after this the judgment" (Heb. IX, 27).

It is almost impossible for us to understand what our Lord's Sacrifice meant to Him. No one, however, who has considered the words of supplication He used in Gethsemane could have a doubt that there were elements in His Sacrifice which were so dreadful as to make His holy soul recoil with terror and cause Him to pray "more earnestly" for the removal of the cup from

Him. It is perhaps not difficult to detect the particular element which caused our Lord such great distress. To discern this we must contemplate the relationship that from the past ages of eternity had existed between God the Father and God the Son, and which had continued after His Incarnation throughout His earthly pathway until the actual start of these Three Hours of darkness. This relationship was one of ceaseless and unalloyed communion and of cloudless love – the Father finding ineffable joy in beholding His well-beloved Son on the earth, as He "went about doing good, and healing all that were oppressed of the devil" (Acts X, 38) – a statement to which the inspired writer, with deep meaning, adds "for God was with Him".

When the hour of Noon arrived a melancholy darkness exchanged places with the extreme brightness of noonday under the glaring Syrian sun. Now for the first time a dark and fearful cloud of horror and separation began to pass over the stainless soul of the One Who hung on Calvary's Tree. Now Redemption's price must be paid IN FULL – and the word of the Prophet Isaiah be fulfilled, "*Thou* shalt make His soul AN OFFERING FOR SIN" (LIII, 10); and, yet again, the word of the Psalmist, "*Thou* hast brought me into the dust of death" (XXII, 15).

As we have previously remarked, the Son of God knew no second causes (John XIX, 11). The chief priests, the Roman rulers and the howling mob that demanded His death might all contribute their quota, but for Him there was only One Who could have ordained His being nailed and bound to the Tree and that was His God and Father Who had sent Him into the world.

With darkness now covering the earth, Calvary became a scene from which all human elements were excluded. Like Abraham of old who went alone when he took Isaac his son to offer him up on Mount Moriah, it could now be said of God the Father and God the Son, "and they went both of them together" (Gen. XXII, 6, 8). The task in hand was the Redemption of the World by our Lord Jesus Christ and the overthrow of the great Adversary who had induced the first man, Adam, to disobey and thereby bring SIN and DEATH into the world. Now, "by the obedience of One (should) many be made righteous" (Romans V, 19). Well may we sing:

"O loving wisdom of our God!
When all was sin and shame,
A second Adam to the fight
And to the rescue came.

O wisest love! that flesh and blood,
Which did in Adam fail,
Should strive afresh against their foe,
Should strive and should prevail."

(J. H. Newman)

Our blessed Lord was the Second Man or Last Adam, and it was His perfect and unfaltering obedience that had now brought Him "as a lamb to the slaughter". Was He not "the Lamb of God, which taketh away the sin of the world" (John I, 29)? How else could sin be taken away, except by the giving of His life and the shedding of His precious blood? Did not God's inexorable Law declare, "the life of the flesh is in the blood: and I have given it to you upon the altar (type of Calvary) to make an atonement for your souls: for it is the blood that maketh an atonement for the soul" (Lev. XVII, 11)?

It was not, however, death and the shedding of His blood that had caused our Saviour to plead for the removal of the cup in Gethsemane, but the knowledge that in bearing our sins, and in being "made . . . sin" for us, He would not only forfeit the unclouded communion He had ever enjoyed with God the Father, *but would actually become a Subject of His wrath, which would be visited upon Him without limit as our Sin-Bearer*. That is, the wrath which would have been our portion would be gathered up and poured upon the head of Christ, exactly as if He had Himself committed all our sins. What this must have meant to One Who was as guiltless as He was sinless, who can tell?

At Calvary then our blessed Saviour and Redeemer exchanged places with us. Even thus was it with the Israelite who had sinned and desired atonement. He brought his unblemished sin-offering from the herd or flock. Before this animal was killed, he who presented it laid his hand upon its head to signify his identification with it. The sin of the offerer was thereby transferred to the offering which was killed in his place. This was God's law of Substitution and by means of it the sinning Israelite received atonement and forgiveness for his sin (Levit.

IV). Our Lord Jesus Christ in His death on Calvary became the Antitype of every sin-offering and this gave perfect validity to an atonement based upon the shedding of the blood of an animal which, apart from its typical significance, had no intrinsic merit (Heb. X, 4).

For our Lord Jesus Christ then the Three Hours of darkness which preceded His death was a period of unspeakable suffering at the hands of His God and Father Who visited upon Him the untold wrath due to us for our sins. No human mind can conceive the nature of the communications that passed between the Father and the Son when our every sin was being laid upon our Substitute. The Psalmist, however, is allowed to anticipate our Lord's very words at this time of His deepest woe:

> "Thou hast laid me in the lowest pit, in darkness, in the deeps. Thy wrath lieth hard upon me, and Thou hast afflicted me with all Thy waves. Selah . . . Thy fierce wrath goeth over me; Thy terrors have cut me off" (Psalm LXXXVIII, 6, 7 and 16).

### GOD ABANDONS HIS BELOVED SON, OUR LORD JESUS CHRIST

If a man would know what sin is in the sight of Almighty God, let him contemplate the Saviour of the World at the end of the Three Hours of darkness, abandoned by God, and His last bitter cry, "My God, My God, why hast Thou forsaken Me?" being uttered to a Heaven that had become brass to the One Who had once declared to His Father, "I know that Thou hearest Me always" (John XI, 42). *The wrath of God had now exhausted itself upon our Substitute, His own beloved Son,* Whom He gave out of love to the world, so that "whosoever believeth in Him should not perish, but have everlasting life" (John III, 16).

By identification with our fallen race, our Redeemer and Saviour had now, *by imputation,* been "made . . . sin" for us while hanging in the darkness upon Calvary's Tree. Now, *with our sin made His,* He is accursed *for us* as one who has broken God's Law; for only thus could He redeem us from the curse of the Law, which rests upon "every one that continueth not in all things which are written in the book of the law to do them" (Gal. III, 10 to 13).

It is, indeed, terrible to contemplate the end to which our Lord Jesus Christ came on account of our sins. He died with the full weight of them upon Him, forsaken of His God and Father, and made a curse for us, for "cursed is every one that hangeth on a tree". All this may be a deep, deep mystery to our shallow human hearts but one thing we know, namely, that when "He died, He died unto sin once" – our sin – and this He took with Him down into death and out of God's sight for evermore. Therefore may we ever remember that our Lord deliberately sacrificed His life to save us, and that in the fullest sense His death was vicarious, expiatory and redemptive. All who with their hearts believe on Him can now say in the words of the Apostle Paul to the Church at Colosse, "in Whom we have redemption through His blood, even the forgiveness of sins" (Col. I, 14).

## OUR LORD JESUS CHRIST DIES AFTER SEVEN HOURS UPON THE TREE

### THE HISTORIC FACTS AS RECORDED IN THE FOUR GOSPELS

As the death of the Son of God is the most important event in human history, the Bible records the facts related thereto with the utmost precision.

The Three Hours of darkness were just drawing to a close and the hour of 3 o'clock in the afternoon was at hand. Suddenly, the Holy Sufferer hanging on the Tree, between the forgiven and the unforgiven malefactors, uttered a loud cry. We will quote Matthew's Gospel, which is almost word for word the same as that of Mark:

> "And about the ninth hour Jesus cried with a loud voice, saying, Eli, Eli, lama sabachthani? that is to say, My God, My God, why hast Thou forsaken Me? Some of them that stood there, when they heard that, said, This man calleth for Elias.
>
> "And straightway one of them ran, and took a sponge, and filled it with vinegar, and put it on a reed, and gave Him to drink. The rest said, Let be, let us see whether Elias will come to save Him." (XXVII, 46 to 49; cf. Mark XV, 34 to 36).

From John's Gospel we learn that the giving of the vinegar to our Lord was in response to His last request, implied in the words, "I thirst". We will quote verses 28 and 29 of Chapter XIX:

> "After this, Jesus knowing that all things were now accomplished, that the Scripture might be fulfilled, saith, I thirst. Now there was set a vessel full of vinegar: and they filled a sponge with vinegar, and put it upon hyssop, and put it to His mouth."

The Scripture He referred to was Psalm LXIX, where in verse 21 we read, "And in my thirst they gave me vinegar to drink". With this fulfilled, our loving Saviour knew that not one prediction in the Old Testament concerning Himself remained to be accomplished. *His obedience was now complete.* There remained now but the act of expiry to accomplish His exodus from this world.

It is most blessed to note the manner in which the Spirit of God causes the four Gospel accounts to blend and amplify one another. Matthew, Mark and Luke each inform us that before His act of expiry our Lord "cried with a loud voice". This was the second time He had done so – the first being His cry, "My God, My God, why hast Thou forsaken Me?" It is, however, to John's Gospel we must turn if we would know for what reason the dying Saviour "cried with a loud voice" a second time. So we read:

> "When Jesus therefore had received the vinegar, He said, IT IS FINISHED" (XIX, 30).

The second loud cry was therefore an utterance of the utmost significance. These "loud" cries of the departing Saviour prove that, in spite of the intense bodily suffering of these Seven Hours on the Tree, He had retained to the bitter end an unclouded mental vigour, as well as the physical strength needed to make such cries.

Our Lord had come into the world to accomplish for God the work of Redemption and that we might be "reconciled to God by the death of His Son" (Rom. V, 10). His loud cry, "It is finished", was therefore the expression of a supreme triumph because His mighty task had been brought to an eternally successful completion. Every foe had been vanquished and now death itself would be wrested out of the hand of Satan and used to his destruction, just as David had seized the sword of Goliath and with it had slain him (see Heb. II, 14 and I Sam. XVII, 51).

## THE EXPIRY OF OUR LORD JESUS CHRIST

Matthew and Mark both inform us that after Jesus had cried with a loud voice, He "gave up the ghost". John states that after He had said, "It is finished", He "bowed His head, and gave up the ghost" (see Matt. XXVII, 50; Mark XV, 37, and John XIX, 30).

Luke, who had made no reference to our Lord's first loud cry or to the incident with the vinegar, alone informs us of the actual last words of our Lord on the Tree when He dismissed His spirit. We read in Chapter XXIII, verse 46:

> "And when Jesus had cried with a loud voice (i.e., "IT IS FINISHED"), He said, Father, into Thy hands I commend My spirit: and having said thus, He gave up the ghost."

The expression "gave up the ghost" here and in Mark means simply that He took His last breath. In Matthew and John it signifies that He dismissed His spirit.

How orderly and how perfect was our Lord's departure out of this world. His presence here undesired by man, He, Who was the Light of the World, departs out of it; for "this is the condemnation, that light is come into the world, and men love darkness rather than light, because their deeds were evil" (John III, 19). But if man had been allowed to extinguish that Light according to "the determinate counsel and foreknowledge of God", it was only that He Who was the Light might shine out in yet greater brilliance from another sphere – Heaven itself – upon this benighted world, until the day when He would return to it, not as a Lamb, but as "the Lion of the tribe of Juda" to reign over it in righteousness and bring peace to the warring nations, which should then learn war no more.

To the repentant thief the Saviour had said, "Verily I say unto thee, Today shalt thou be with Me in Paradise" and from this we know that the spirit of our Lord, when He vacated His body, went to that sphere of departed spirits called Paradise, which for "three days and three nights" was to be the scene of

His activities – for no one need imagine that in Paradise He would remain idle (I Peter III, 18 to 20).

As for the world He had left, there remained nought of Him save His untenanted body, which for a further three hours must remain hanging upon the Tree. How filled with significance are the words of the Law concerning one "put to death" by hanging "on a tree". In Deuteronomy XXI, 23, we read, "His body shall not remain all night upon the tree, but thou shalt in any wise bury him that day; (for he that is hanged is accursed of God;) that thy land be not defiled". So Jesus died accursed of God for us and in due course before the day closed His sacred body was buried, as the Law of God required.

## 3 P.M. TO 6 P.M.

### AFTER HIS EXPIRY, THE BODY OF THE SAVIOUR REMAINED HANGING FOR THREE HOURS ON THE TREE

### A RECORD OF EVENTS IN THESE THREE HOURS WHICH TERMINATED WITH HIS BURIAL IN A NEW ROCK-HEWN SEPULCHRE

Read Matt. XXVII, 51 to 61; Mark XV, 38 to 47; Luke XXIII, 45 to 56, and John XIX, 31 to 42

The Son of God had graced this earth with His presence for 33 Bible years, 190 days and 7 hours, or 32 Solar years, 184 days and 7 hours, before He departed out of it by way of a felon's Gibbet at 3 P.M. on Friday, 1st May A.D. 33. The world's last view of Jesus of Nazareth was to behold His bruised and bleeding Body hanging lifeless on a Stake between two thieves likewise suspended, but whose life was still in them. It is worth recalling that the world's next view of Jesus of Nazareth is to be as follows: "Behold, He cometh with clouds; and every eye shall see Him, and they also which pierced Him: and all kindreds of the earth shall wail because of Him" (Rev. I, 7). This is by the way.

It is very important to note how the Gospels fix the death of our Lord at 3 o'clock in the afternoon which was the hour of the Evening Sacrifice in the Temple. It was "AT THE NINTH HOUR" that our Lord gave the first loud cry according to Mark XV, 34, and 3 P.M. is the end of the ninth hour. It is Mark who informs us that our Lord was crucified at "the third hour". Inclusively this is a period of Seven Hours. It is also clear that from our Lord's first "loud cry" to His dismissal of His spirit was only a very brief season. It is at any rate most important to realize that the Bible fixes the hour of our Lord's death at 3 o'clock because it would otherwise be impossible to know exactly how long He was "in the heart of the earth". We shall see later that the Bible likewise perfectly establishes the time of His Resurrection. The reason for this is most solemn, namely, that our Lord's session in death was a typical period, the antitype of which is the time His mystical Body would remain in the sphere of death before the departed members are summoned from their graves at His Second Appearing (Heb. IX, 28 and I Thess. IV, 13 to 18).

## GOD'S FIRST ACTION FOLLOWING THE DEATH OF OUR LORD JESUS CHRIST

It is vividly clear both from the text of the Gospels of Matthew and Mark and because of its accord with the Divine counsels that, simultaneously with our Lord's exodus out of this world, that is, as His spirit left His body, God, as we would say, "went into action". Our Lord's death had instantly ushered in a vast and glorious change in God's relationship to the human race. Instead of dwelling in the utter darkness of "the most holy place" in the Temple, which could be visited only once in the year on the Day of Atonement by the High Priest (Heb. IX, 7), "the way into the Holiest" was now thrown wide open and every believer in Jesus could, by virtue of the forgiveness of his sins, now approach *without fear* into the very presence of our thrice Holy God. It was sin that drove man out of God's presence in the Garden of Eden; but now Jesus had shed His blood, and all who believe on Him could know that sin's terrible barrier had been removed by His death. So instantly and without a moment's delay, directly our Lord's death had taken place, God the Father gave command and (as recorded by Matthew and Mark),

> "The veil of the temple was rent in twain from the top to the bottom."

Who could measure the significance of God's act in thus sealing the death of His Son by tearing asunder the mighty Temple veil that barred man from any direct approach to his God? With the rent veil the whole Jewish system and priesthood came to an end in God's sight, "for the law made nothing perfect, but the bringing in of a better hope did; by the which we draw nigh unto God" (Heb. VII, 19). All this was due to the one great fact that Jesus Christ our Lord had in His death and the shedding of His most precious blood removed the sins (past, present and future) of every believer in Him from God's sight for ever. To all such the Apostle, in Hebrews, can say, "Having therefore, brethren, boldness to enter into the holiest by the blood of Jesus, by a new and living way, which He hath consecrated for us, through the veil, that is to say, His flesh; and having an high priest over the house of God; let us draw near . . ." et seq. (Heb. X, 19 to 22). And countless myriads since 1st May A.D. 33, have acted upon this word and are still doing so, God having made Himself directly available to every forgiven sinner – Jew or Gentile.

That the rending of the Temple veil was an act of God is made clear by the fact that the rending began at the top and ended at the bottom. To suggest that this was other than an act of God would be ludicrous – it was, in fact, God Himself addressing the whole earth in regard to what the death of His Son had accomplished, namely, the bringing in of a new order founded upon our Lord's mighty redemptive Sacrifice of Himself for sinners. So, it is written, "He taketh away the first, that He may establish the second" (Heb. X, 9).

## THE TESTIMONY OF THE ROMAN CENTURION

Matthew, Mark and Luke each record the testimony of the Roman centurion who was in charge at our Lord's execution. We will quote Luke's account first:

> "Now when the centurion saw what was done, he glorified God, saying, Certainly this was a righteous man" (XXIII, 47).

Matthew's account adds some details to this:

> "Now when the centurion, and they that were with him,

watching Jesus, saw the earthquake, and those things that were done, they feared greatly, saying, Truly this was the Son of God" (XXVII, 54).

From these accounts we learn much. This centurion was the first Gentile after His death to acknowledge our Lord as "the Son of God", that is, a Divine Person. From first to last he had witnessed our Lord's execution. He had heard every word that had fallen from the lips of Jesus as He hung upon the Tree. What he had heard and seen of the One, whose death by hanging on a Tree he had had to accomplish, convinced him that Jesus was a Divine Person – "a righteous Man". But when he "saw the earthquake" that accompanied the passing of the Lord's spirit from His body, he wanted no further evidence for he saw in it a preternatural confirmation that Jesus was not the impostor the Jews made out, but "a Son of God". The fact that Luke informs us that "he glorified God" is proof enough that he had there and then received a witness from the Spirit of God as to who Jesus really was. It was a glorious testimony this Gentile rendered and a first fulfilling of our Lord's word, "And I, if I be lifted up from the earth, will draw all men unto Me" (John XII, 32).

There was, therefore, a Jew (the repentant thief) and a Gentile brought to know Jesus during the hours of His agony on the Tree.

We shall later learn that there was a second earthquake which took place at the resurrection of our Lord.

## THE "STRANGE" WORDING OF MATTHEW XXVII, 51 TO 53

It is necessary at this juncture to refer briefly to the statement which accompanies Matthew's reference to the rending of the veil at our Lord's departure:

"And, behold, the veil of the temple was rent in twain from the top to the bottom; and the earth did quake, and the rocks rent; and the graves were opened; and many bodies of the saints which slept arose, and came out of the graves after His resurrection, and went into the holy city, and appeared unto many."

An advanced "modernist" prelate wrote in recent years that

if anyone believed this statement to be true history he could believe anything! It is of course true history, like all else in the Gospels, but it is an absolutely inexplicable statement until one knows why the Spirit of God caused Matthew to write it. Anyone can see at first sight that it is a mingling of the events at our Lord's death with those at or "after His resurrection". But with what object were they brought together in this fashion? We reply, with one of the utmost importance and without which no one could possibly know how to measure TIME in relation to the Lord's death and resurrection. It is indeed a key-statement, and taken with Matthew XXVIII, 1, *proves* two vital facts, which will in due course become vividly clear. The first of these is that the Spirit of God caused Matthew to adopt Divine Time in relation to our Lord's death and resurrection by naming the day of His death as "the sabbath" (XXVIII, 1); and the second is that God does not reckon time between our Lord's death and His resurrection for the same reason that we do not reckon time to one who has departed this life. In other words, these verses in Matthew XXVII and those of Matthew XXVIII, 1 and 2, *ignore time between our Lord's death and resurrection* by jumping from the one to the other just as if they had taken place in immediate succession.

We will add no more on this subject until later when we shall be obliged to consider these verses again because of their relation to the Resurrection of our Lord. Let it be realized that we are now unveiling Truth from the Scriptures which has been deliberately concealed by God therein since the departure of the Apostles, with the result that since those days no one has known how long the Saviour was "in the heart of the earth", or at what time He came forth in triumph from the grave.

## THE IMPALED BODY OF OUR LORD JESUS CHRIST IS PIERCED BY A ROMAN SOLDIER

(John XIX, 31 to 37)

The piercing of the Saviour's dead body is only recorded by the Apostle John who does so as an actual eye-witness. We will quote the whole passage before making any comments:

"The Jews therefore, because it was the Preparation, that

the bodies should not remain upon the cross (stake) on the sabbath day, (for that sabbath day was an high day,) besought Pilate that their legs might be broken, and that they might be taken away. Then came the soldiers, and brake the legs of the first, and of the other which was crucified with Him. But when they came to Jesus, and saw that He was dead already, they brake not His legs: but one of the soldiers with a spear pierced His side, and forthwith came there out blood and water.

"And he that saw it bare record, and his record is true: and he knoweth that he saith true, that ye might believe.

"For these things were done, that the scripture should be fulfilled, A bone of Him shall not be broken. And again another scripture saith, They shall look on Him Whom they pierced."

This passage speaks for itself and is informative to a degree. It confirms that our Lord Jesus Christ was slain on "the day of the Preparation" for the Jews' Sabbath, which on this occasion corresponded with "the holy convocation" of their first day of Unleavened Bread (Lev. XXIII, 7). It was this which made it "an high day". As we have already shown, the Law of God demanded that bodies hung on a tree should be removed before nightfall (Deut. XXI, 23). No doubt, the Jewish rulers were most anxious to see the Saviour's body taken down, in order to silence any possible clamour from those who honoured Him as a Prophet or more.

The heartless task of breaking the legs of the two malefactors (to the Romans, crurifragium) is duly performed as a means of inducing death. But God had no intention of such a thing happening to the body of His beloved Son Who had already died of His own volition. In Psalm XXXIV, verses 19 and 20, we read, "Many are the afflictions of the righteous . . . He keepeth all his bones: not one of them is broken". This is the Scripture which John, by the Spirit, affirms was fulfilled when the soldiers were prevented from treating the Son of God – "a righteous Man" as the Centurion declared – like the two malefactors. The reference, "a bone of Him shall not be broken", could not apply to Exodus XII, 46, where the breaking of a bone of the Paschal lambs is forbidden. Our Lord did not actually die as the Antitype of the Paschal lamb, but did so "in a figure" the previous night at the last Passover, which was at the close of the true 14th of the 1st month, according to the Law. Our Lord's actual death was on the true 15th of the 1st month and as such He was the Antitype of the Sin-Offering of that day. In another aspect – that presented by John – He died as the Antitype of all the Burnt-offerings of the 15th of the 1st month – a fact we hope to explain in due course.

The piercing of the Lord's body by one of the soldiers was an action as much controlled by God as was the diverting of the soldiers from breaking a bone in it. Both were matters named in Scripture which had to be fulfilled, as John declares.

In Zechariah XII, 10, we have a prophecy relating to the time when Israel will repent in great bitterness for their treatment of the Messiah. It is there recorded, "They shall look upon Me whom they have pierced, and they shall mourn for Him, as one mourneth for his only son". It is, therefore, quite clear why the soldier was allowed to take a spear and pierce the dead body of our Lord Who was Israel's Messiah. That the soldier's act caused a deep gaping wound may be inferred from the Lord's statement to Thomas, "thrust it (i.e., his hand) into My side" (John XX, 27).

It is by virtue of the death of our Lord Jesus Christ that we are cleansed from sin, so it is not surprising that the tokens of our cleansing had to flow out of a dead Saviour – the blood to cleanse us from *the stain* of sin, and the water (type of the Word of God) to cleanse us from *the defilement* of sin. Of "the blood" we read that it "cleanseth us from all sin"; and of "the water" we hear our Lord say, "If I wash thee not, thou hast no part with Me" (see I John I, 7; John XIII, 8, and cf. Ephes. V, 26). John alone makes mention of the piercing of the Saviour's side.

## THE BURIAL

### THE BODY OF OUR LORD IS REMOVED FROM THE TREE AND PLACED IN A NEW SEPULCHRE

Read Matt. XXVII, 57 to 60; Mark XV, 42 to 46; Luke XXIII, 50 to 53, and John XIX, 38 to 42

It is indeed most affecting to note how God Himself must have ordained every detail concerning the burial of His beloved

Son's body, for none but He could have reserved for the purpose two rich and influential disciples who until then had not chosen to declare themselves openly as the followers of Jesus of Nazareth. It was the fearfulness of the crime that the Jewish rulers had committed that compelled Joseph of Arimathaea and Nicodemus to come out into the open and act in such a way as to show to all that they had no part in it. Conscience would not allow inaction on such an occasion, as this might imply acquiescence; while affection for the departed Saviour demanded a positive form of practical expression. So it was that with loving hands the bruised and bleeding body of our Lord was taken down from the Tree and prepared for burial.

We will quote from John's Gospel so as to give one full account from Holy Scripture of the Saviour's burial:

> "And after this Joseph of Arimathaea, being a disciple of Jesus, but secretly for fear of the Jews, besought Pilate that he might take away the body of Jesus: and Pilate gave him leave. He came therefore, and took the body of Jesus.
>
> "And there came also Nicodemus, which at the first came to Jesus by night, and brought a mixture of myrrh and aloes, about an hundred pound weight. Then took they the body of Jesus, and wound it in linen clothes with the spices, as the manner of the Jews is to bury.
>
> "Now in the place where He was crucified there was a garden; and in the garden a new sepulchre, wherein was never man yet laid. There laid they Jesus therefore because of the Jews' preparation day; for the sepulchre was nigh at hand."

The burial of the Saviour was at the very close of the Friday, just about 6 o'clock. Luke states, "That day was the preparation, and the sabbath drew on" (XXIII, 54). The expression "drew on" signifies that the Sabbath was about to begin. Matthew and Mark speak of "even" having come. It must, therefore, have been in the early evening that Joseph "went in boldly unto Pilate, and craved the body of Jesus" (Mark XV, 43). Pilate, surprised that Jesus was already dead, and possibly suspicious that an effort was on foot to remove Him from the Tree while yet alive, takes cognizance of the matter with the centurion. After learning that the Lord was dead, Pilate gives Joseph – "an honourable counsellor, which also waited for the kingdom of God" – permission to take the body of Jesus and do with it what he will.

Nicodemus evidently meets Joseph at Calvary after the latter has obtained Pilate's permission. Together they remove the Lord's body from the Tree and enwrap it with the spices brought by Nicodemus "as the manner of the Jews is to bury". It was no accident that in that exact locality Joseph had prepared for himself a "new tomb, which he had hewn out in the rock" (Matt. XXVII, 60). Luke also informs us that in this tomb "never man before was laid".

Into this rock-hewn sepulchre these two faithful disciples of Jesus bear His sacred body. John's account closes the incident with these words, "There laid they Jesus therefore because of the Jews' preparation day; for the sepulchre was nigh at hand". We may infer from this that the placing of the Lord's body in this near-by sepulchre was not intended to be other than a temporary step on the part of Joseph, who would have no expectation of resurrection on "the third day".

Matthew informs us that Joseph "rolled a great stone to the door of the sepulchre".

It only remains to call attention to the words of the prophecy of Isaiah which were fulfilled in our Lord's burial. These are "He made His grave with the wicked, and with the rich in His death; because He had done no violence, neither was any deceit in His mouth" (LIII, 9). "The wicked" refers to the malefactors who would have been assigned to a special place apart in a Jewish cemetery. "The rich in His death" was wonderfully fulfilled by the action of Joseph who was "a rich man". No doubt, Nicodemus, who brought so expensive a weight of spices to embalm our Lord, was also a man of some wealth. How perfectly every Scripture concerning our Lord's death was fulfilled, the last of these being this one from Isaiah LIII.

So for the moment we leave the Sepulchre in which the tenantless body of the Saviour of the World is lying. How highly favoured were these two secret disciples in being allowed to be God's servants to render this last sacred service to His Son in His death.

## THE FAITHFUL WOMEN WHICH FOLLOWED JESUS FROM GALILEE

Because it is their due, the Gospels reveal how very important a part the women, who were our Lord's disciples, took in connection with His death and resurrection. Their deep devotion to the Saviour is made manifest and is a joy to behold, seeing that, apart from John, and Peter in his denials, the disciples are not heard of after "they all forsook Him, and fled". On every hand we meet this devotion of the women to our Lord and for this reason they are accorded a place of great importance in the Gospel narratives at the time of His death.

When our Lord addressed His Mother from the Tree, Mary Magdalene and Mary the wife of Cleophas were standing with her nearby. Afterward they moved away from the scene, no doubt overcome by its gruesome nature.

At the time of our Lord's expiry, Mary Magdalene and Mary the mother of James and Joses, and "many other women which came up with Him unto Jerusalem" (Mark XV, 40 to 42) are stated to be "beholding afar off" (see also Matthew XXVII, 55, 56).

Mary Magdalene and Mary the mother of James and Joses, also called "the other Mary", and other women evidently watched Joseph and Nicodemus as they carried the body of Jesus to the sepulchre. Luke states that they "followed after, and beheld the sepulchre, and how His body was laid" (see Mark XV, 47, and Luke XXIII, 55).

In Matthew XXVII, 61, we read, "And there was Mary Magdalene, and the other Mary, sitting over against the sepulchre".

In Matthew XXVIII, 1, we read, "In the end of the sabbath, as it began to dawn toward the first day of the week, came Mary Magdalene and the other Mary to see the sepulchre".

As we have already pointed out, the visit of Mary Magdalene and the other Mary to see (lit. to gaze upon) the sepulchre was at the close of the day of the Lord's death, which in Divine Time was "the sabbath". Mark refers to this in these terms, "Mary Magdalene and Mary the mother of Joses beheld where He was laid" (XV, 47). Matthew is caused to refer to the day of the Lord's resurrection *because in Divine Time the interval while our Lord was in death is not reckoned.* In other words (and may this fact be kept in mind), between verses 1 and 2 of Matthew XXVIII there exists the interval between the end of the day of the Lord's death and the moment of His resurrection at the opening of "the first day of the week" or, as it should be, according to the Greek, "the first (day) of the sabbaths".

### THE SEPULCHRE SEALED AND GUARDED
Matthew XXVII, 62 to 66

"Now the next day, that followed the day of the preparation, the chief priests and Pharisees came together unto Pilate, saying, Sir, we remember that that deceiver said, while He was yet alive, After three days I will rise again. Command therefore that the sepulchre be made sure until the third day, lest His disciples come by night, and steal Him away, and say unto the people, He is risen from the dead: so the last error shall be worse than the first.

"Pilate said unto them, Ye have a watch: go your way, make it as sure as ye can. So they went, and made the sepulchre sure, sealing the stone, and setting a watch."

These verses tell their own story and call for little comment. The Jewish rulers may have feared the possibility of the Lord rising again. Pilate's reply seems to carry a note of sarcasm: "Make it as sure as ye can". It is most important to note the way Matthew refuses to give a name to the day after our Lord's death but calls it, "the next day, that followed the day of the preparation". As he adopts only Divine Time, he could not call it "the sabbath", or even "the Jews' sabbath", because in Divine Time it did not exist, for reasons we have already given.

It is important also to notice that the Jews quote our Lord's statement in Mark VIII, 31, "and after three days rise again", and not the more common expression, "raised again the third day". So our Lord's sepulchre remained for three days guarded by soldiers. These, let it be said, might restrain anyone from entering the sepulchre but they were utterly powerless to hinder the One Whose body it held from rising again and coming forth from it.

# PART IV

## THE DEATH OF OUR LORD JESUS CHRIST AS IT IS PRESENTED BY THE APOSTLE JOHN IN HIS GOSPEL

### IN THIS ASPECT OUR LORD'S DEATH IS VIEWED EXCLUSIVELY AS THE ANTITYPE OF THE BURNT-OFFERING OF THE 15TH DAY OF THE FIRST MONTH

Read Numbers XXVIII, 17 to 21 and Leviticus I

WE HARDLY need repeat that in Divine Time the death of our Lord Jesus Christ took place on the 15th day of the first month in the year A.D. 33. In the Solar calendar this was 1st May and in Israel's calendar it was the 14th day of their first month (Nisan). As we have previously stated, the Bible only reckons our Lord's death in terms of the Divine calendar which up to then was always *one day ahead* of Israel's calendar. (See Summary of Facts, Pars 13 and 14.)

It will be seen from the above-named passage in Numbers XXVIII that the Law required that on the 15th day of the first month there should be no less than ten animals sacrificed as the Burnt-offering and "one goat for a sin offering to make an atonement for you". In all our previous comments on the Lord's sufferings and death our thoughts have been entirely centred on the aspect represented by this "one goat for a sin offering" on the 15th of the first month. With grateful, but solemnized, hearts we have beheld the Saviour of the World dying under the load of our sins as the Antitype of this "one goat for a sin offering" in order to accomplish the eternal redemption of our souls. Because this aspect meets man at the point of his direst need and opens for him the only way back into a direct relationship with his God, Matthew, Mark and Luke were each caused to adopt it. We therefore possess a three-fold testimony to our Lord's death as the Antitype of the Sin-offering of the 15th of the first month.

But whereas there was only one goat for a sin-offering to be sacrificed on that day, the Law called for the sacrifice of no less than a burnt-offering composed of "two young bullocks, and one ram, and seven lambs of the first year". This considerable burnt-sacrifice indicates that in GOD'S SIGHT the aspect of our Lord's death represented by them was of the first importance. In MAN'S SIGHT naturally enough the sin-offering aspect comes before any other; but not so with God Who found infinite satisfaction ("a sweet savour") in the Burnt-offering aspect of His beloved Son's sacrifice on Calvary.

Now it remained for the Apostle John alone to set forth the death of our Lord Jesus Christ as the Antitype of the Burnt-offering of the 15th day of the first month. Consequently, in John's Gospel we do not behold our blessed Lord being "brought as a lamb to the slaughter", which is the sin-offering aspect of His death; but rather as One passing along His way in all the majesty and dignity of His own Person as the Son of God, and as One Who possesses the right to offer up His own life voluntarily as a Sacrifice in the doing of His Father's will, and in no sense as One "crucified through weakness" (II Cor. XIII, 4). How manifestly clear this aspect becomes when we hear our Lord declare to those who intended, if possible, to stone Him to death (see John X, 17 and 18),

> "Therefore doth My Father love Me, because I lay down My life. . . . No man taketh it from Me, but I lay it down of Myself. I have power to lay it down, and I have power to take it again."

In these words of our Lord we have a perfect definition of His death as the Antitype of the Burnt-offering; for if we turn to Leviticus I, which defines the Burnt-offering, we read in verse 3, "he shall offer it of his own voluntary will".

Now the essential difference between the Burnt-offering and the Sin-offering lies in the fact that the former was *a purely voluntary act of worship* on the part of the offerer, and the latter a compulsory act of repentance for one who had sin to confess and wished to obtain God's forgiveness for the same (see Leviticus IV, 20, 26 and 31). These are obviously, therefore, two entirely different aspects of our Lord's one sacrifice on Calvary. But in each aspect He is to be seen as OUR REPRESENTATIVE. If our Lord is viewed as the Sin-offering, it is because He is suffering and dying IN OUR STEAD and ON OUR BEHALF; but if He is viewed as the Burnt-offering, it is because He is giving "Himself FOR US an offering and a sacrifice to God for a sweetsmelling savour", as the Apostle Paul expresses it (Ephes. V, 2). The word "FOR" in the Greek signifies here "on behalf of".

Our Lord in the voluntary sacrifice of Himself became the Antitype of, and gave validity to, every Burnt-offering in Old Testament times from Abel onwards. Until the Law was given on Sinai in 1639 B.C. the worship of God's people was solely by means of the Burnt-offering. We read in Genesis VIII, 20, that after the Flood, "Noah builded an altar unto the Lord; . . . and offered burnt-offerings on the altar. And the Lord smelled a sweet savour". We are told that Abraham, Isaac and Jacob did likewise. Then after the giving of the Law not only did the priests have to offer the continual Burnt-offering, morning and evening, every day throughout the year, but on every Sabbath, New Moon or Feast Day, additional Burnt-offerings were called for (see Numbers XXVIII and XXIX).

All these "burnt-offerings" were a sweet savour to God because they anticipated the coming into the world of His well-beloved Son, our Lord Jesus Christ, Whose death upon the Tree they foreshadowed; not, indeed, as paying the penalty for our sins but as voluntarily yielding up His life in whole-hearted devotion to God the Father, Whose glory in the earth He would come to uphold and in the doing of Whose will, even unto death, He would find His supreme delight.

We must briefly develop this aspect of our Lord's Sacrifice as it also constitutes the sole foundation of the Christian's worship of God if it is to be "in spirit and in truth" (John IV, 23, 24).

Man, as created by God and placed upon the earth for His glory and pleasure, was under two responsibilities. The first was to love, worship and serve his Creator, and the second was to love and serve his fellow-beings (our Lord positively avouched the Genesis record in Mark X, 6). The account of the Fall in Genesis III reveals that Satan got his way with our first parents by awakening in them *self-interest* which is the first cause of all human sin and misery. From that day to this every man born of woman into this world, *save our Lord Jesus Christ*, has been the slave of this dominating principle, which in effect means that man lives to and for himself, while robbing God and his neighbour of that which is due from him.

When the Law of God was promulgated on Sinai man became officially invested with the same two responsibilities.

This our Lord affirmed as, when asked to state which was the first commandment, He replied, "Thou shalt love the Lord thy God with all thy heart, and with all thy soul, and with all thy mind, and with all thy strength: this is the first commandment. And the second is like, namely this, Thou shalt love thy neighbour as thyself" (Mark XII, 28 to 34). There has only been ONE MAN in human history who perfectly loved and obeyed God and who perfectly loved and served His neighbour. As all know, this was THE MAN CHRIST JESUS, Who yielded up His sinless life on Calvary's Tree as a voluntary offering of Himself to God ON OUR BEHALF, and this as an expression of His supreme devotion to the doing of His will. The life of our Lord, from Bethlehem to His death on Calvary, was to God an odour of "a sweet-smelling savour"; and never more so than during the hours of immeasurable suffering, borne without a murmur, in which He hung twixt heaven and earth, the song of drunkards and the object of the reviling of His betrayers and murderers. No human intelligence, however enlightened, could possibly glean a fraction of the intense satisfaction brought to the heart of God as He beheld His beloved Son treading His way upon this earth, amidst the wreckage of four thousand years of human sin and failure, and in the end offering up His life as "a sacrifice for a sweetsmelling savour".

In the measure that we are able to enter in to the absolute perfection of the life, service and death of our Lord Jesus Christ as viewed by God shall we be able to comprehend the acceptability to Him of the typical offerings which the Old Testament saints presented when they came to worship. As typifying Christ each of these offerings had to be "without blemish" (Lev. I, 3 and IV, 3) and the offerer was accepted solely because of the acceptability of his offering as such.

The Burnt-offering then was a positive type of our Lord Jesus Christ rendering to God ON OUR BEHALF His whole duty AS MAN UNDER THE LAW and voluntarily laying down His sinless life out of devotion to God and in obedience to His will. Let it be carefully noted that our Lord's sacrifice in this aspect has no relation to our sins but is solely an expression of His own deep love to God the Father and of His delight to do His Father's will. No wonder, therefore, our Lord's sacrifice in this aspect was "a sweetsmelling savour" seeing that it was offered in a world peopled by those who were at enmity with God and who lived to glorify themselves or one another.

To be consistent with the presentation of our Lord's death as the Antitype of the Burnt-offerings of the 15th of the first month, the Apostle John had to omit many features which appear in the Gospels of his fellow-evangelists. It is in fact more by these omissions than by positive statements that we learn the Spirit's motive in John's account of our Lord's death. For instance, there is no mention whatever by John of our Lord's anticipations of His sufferings, such as we get in Matthew XX, 18, 19 (etc., etc.) where He says to the disciples, "Behold, we go up to Jerusalem; and the Son of Man shall be betrayed unto the chief priests and unto the scribes, and they shall condemn Him to death, and shall deliver Him to the Gentiles to mock, and to scourge, and to crucify Him". All such utterances of our Lord relate to His sufferings and death as the Antitype of the Sin-offering and the prominent feature in them is the enmity of men and the power allowed to them by God in accomplishing His Son's death. Who cannot see that this aspect is the absolute opposite of that expressed by the words, "I lay down My life. . . . No man taketh it from Me, but I lay it down of Myself" (John X, 17, 18).

The most notable omission in John's Gospel is his silence as to the Saviour's immeasurable agony in Gethsemane where He was compelled to face the cost He must pay in bearing our sins and in being "made sin" for us. Each other Gospel informs us of the Saviour's agonizing plea to His Father for the removal of the cup of bitterness which then faced Him; but of this John tells us nothing because as the Antitype of the Burnt-offering our Lord was wholly willing to die if it was His Father's will. He was not, however, wholly willing to be "made sin" for us. Neither was He wholly willing to die as a felon with all the shame attaching to such a death, though He would do so, and did do so, *rather than for once default in obedience to His Father's will.* But this aspect is the antithesis of His voluntarily offering Himself "through the eternal Spirit . . . without spot to God" (Heb. IX, 14).

Not only is John silent as to our Lord's pleas to the Father in the Garden of Gethsemane, but contrariwise he narrates an incident in it which presents Him as so completely overawing

His enemies that He has to urge them to take Him. We read in chapter XVIII, 4 to 8, "Jesus therefore, knowing all things that should come upon Him, went forth, and said unto them, Whom seek ye? They answered Him, Jesus of Nazareth. Jesus saith unto them, I AM (HE).... As soon then as He had said unto them, I AM (HE) they went backward, and fell to the ground. Then asked He them again, Whom seek ye? And they said, Jesus of Nazareth. Jesus answered, I have told you that I AM (HE): if therefore ye seek Me, let these go their way". This incident reveals our Lord acting as One determined to make a voluntary offering of Himself to God in the doing of His will. And in keeping with this on the same occasion He rebukes Peter's impulsive act in cutting off the ear of a servant of the High Priest with the words, "The cup which My Father hath given Me, shall I not drink it?"

Neither does John make any reference to the Three Hours of darkness. How could he do so and be consistent, seeing that it was then that our Lord had to bear the judgment of our sins at the hands of God? There could be no "sweetsmelling savour" when sin was being atoned for, even though our Lord as the Sin-Offering was "without blemish".

Very much more might be added to show that John's Gospel exclusively views our Lord's death as the Antitype of the Burnt-offerings of the 15th of the first month – the first day of Unleavened Bread and therefore of the Christian Dispensation. For instance, John makes no mention of Simon bearing the Stake upon which the Lord was to be nailed. He merely states, "He bearing His cross (lit. stake) went forth into a place . . . called in the Hebrew Golgotha". Here again John presents our Lord as One ordering His own way to the place of His Sacrifice and not as One being brought to Golgotha, as in Mark XV, 22.

Finally, the manner of the Saviour's departure as given by John reveals Him as One Who is acting according to the glory of His Person as the Son of God and Who has all the circumstances of it under His own control – a truly blessed picture! We read, "Jesus knowing that all things were now accomplished, that the Scripture might be fulfilled, saith, I thirst. . . . When Jesus therefore had received the vinegar, He said, IT IS FINISHED: and He bowed His head, and gave up the ghost"

(XIX, 28 to 30). The expression "gave up the ghost" in the Greek signifies "delivered up His spirit".

So every word and act in John's account of our Lord's departure is expressive of its voluntary nature. His death is viewed as the deliberate act of One sacrificing His life in obedience to God's will. John sees this Sacrifice to be the Antitype of the Burnt-offering and as such his narrative sets it forth. Having settled the question of His Mother's future, our Lord takes account of the fact that only one Scripture concerning Himself remained to be fulfilled. This done, He is able with a loud voice to proclaim that the purpose of His coming into the world was now complete. Therefore, as nothing remained for Him to do in the world that He had made and from which He was now departing unwanted, He, in perfect self-possession (as we would say) bows His head, which until then He evidently had held erect, and delivers up His spirit – THE SACRIFICE OF HIMSELF BEING NOW COMPLETE (John XIX, 28 to 30).

We are told that "no man knoweth who the Son is, but the Father" (Luke X, 22), and it is quite certain that "no man" in this life can estimate the infinite acceptability to God the Father of our Lord's voluntary sacrifice of Himself as the Antitype of the myriads of burnt-offerings which since the Creation had been offered, each one awaiting the seal of its validity as a typical offering by the Appearing and death of the Anti-type, "Who through the eternal Spirit offered Himself without spot to God" (Heb. IX, 14).

It should be noted that John alone records that "blood and water" flowed from the Saviour's side and this for the reason that in the type the priests were bidden to sprinkle the blood of the burnt-offering "round about upon the altar" (Levit. I, 5 and 11). Water also filled an important part in the sacrifice of the burnt-offering (see verse 9).

In the case of our Lord, Calvary was the Altar and it is of most solemn interest to note that we are informed that the Sin-offering must be killed at the same place as the Burnt-offering (Levit. VI, 25). For this reason our Lord's death as the Anti-type of both these offerings took place at Calvary for they really constituted but two aspects of His one Sacrifice of Himself FOR US.

It may rightly be asked, Was it necessary for our Lord Jesus

Christ to sacrifice His life in order to prove His devotion to God the Father? We reply that it was by no means necessary that He should do this for His own acceptance because He had no sin; but that it was absolutely necessary for Him to do it FOR OUR ACCEPTANCE, that is, for the members of His body, the Church. So we hear the Apostle Paul say to the Ephesian believers (V, 2):

> "Walk in love, as Christ also hath loved us, and hath given Himself FOR US an offering and a sacrifice to God for a sweet-smelling savour."

Our Lord's offering of Himself in sacrifice to God was therefore "FOR US", that is, "ON OUR BEHALF", and if our Lord had not perfectly fulfilled God's Law in every respect and been "obedient unto death, even the death of the cross" (Greek, stake), no believer in Christ could approach God in worship because, though he may be redeemed and enjoy the forgiveness of his sins, he still possesses a sinful nature which would make it impossible for God to accept his worship. This our blessed Lord perfectly understood when He identified Himself with our fallen race and it was for this reason that He offered Himself as a Sacrifice to God ON OUR BEHALF. He did this both FOR US and AS US; and as a direct and blessed consequence what He did is credited by God TO US who believe in Him, just as if we ourselves had offered perfect and acceptable sacrifices like that of our Lord. So we read in Hebrews XIII, 15, "By Him therefore let us offer the sacrifice of praise to God continually, that is, the fruit of our lips giving thanks to His Name".

This most blessed aspect of our Lord's Sacrifice as the Antitype of the Burnt-offering is made perfectly clear and plain by the Levitical type (see Leviticus I). The Israelite who desired to worship God, even though he belonged to a redeemed nation, had to make his approach with an unblemished burnt-offering from the herd or flock. Before his sacrifice was killed he laid his hand upon its head in order to identify himself with the perfection of his offering. The Law said, "It shall be accepted for him to make atonement for him" (verse 4). *This atonement was not for his sins but for his utter inability, as possessing a fallen nature, to approach his God.*

If then the Israelite was accepted of God by virtue of his

identification with an offering the merit of which solely lay in its being typical of our Lord's Sacrifice on Calvary, how much more shall we be accepted of God when we come as those on whose behalf that Sacrifice was directly offered (Ephes. V, 2). In other words, the Israelite presented to God the typical burnt-offering and was accepted of Him; while we, who are members of the Church which is Christ's body, present the Antitypical Burnt-Offering, namely, our Lord's voluntary offering of Himself to God on Calvary's Tree, and are accepted of Him.

This concludes these all too brief comments on John's presentation of our Lord's death as the Antitype of the Burnt-Offering of the 15th day of the first month in the Divine calendar.

NOTE. It may be thought that the above remarks on John's aspect of our Lord's death are rather more didactic than expository of the text. If this is to depart from the primary purpose of *The Restored Vision* we must plead as an excuse the desire to present to our fellow Christians an aspect of our Lord's sacrifice which is seldom entered into, and even if it is, is always made subsidiary to that aspect which relates solely to the question of our sins. As sinners we need to know Christ as our Sin-Offering, but as worshippers we need to know Him as our Burnt-Offering.

# CHAPTER SIXTEEN

## THE REVELATION OF HOLY SCRIPTURE CONCERNING "THE RESURRECTION OF JESUS CHRIST"

## THE MANIFESTATIONS OF THE RISEN LORD DURING FORTY DAYS

TIME

Midnight, Sunday, 3rd May to 8 A.M. Saturday, 13th June A.D. 33

Read Matthew XXVIII; Mark XVI, 1 to 8; Luke XXIV; John XX and XXI, and Acts I, 1 to 11

## PART I

## THE TIME OF OUR LORD'S RESURRECTION

THE DEEPLY CONCEALED SECRET RECOVERED FROM THE HOLY SCRIPTURES

"HE CHANGETH THE TIMES AND THE SEASONS" (DANIEL II)

THE MOON CEASES ITS NORMAL REVOLUTION FOR TWO WHOLE DAYS WHILE OUR LORD IS IN DEATH. THESE TWO DAYS NOT RECKONED IN DIVINE TIME

OUR LORD JESUS CHRIST RISES FROM AMONG THE DEAD AT EXACTLY MIDNIGHT ON SUNDAY, 3RD MAY, AFTER 57 HOURS OR "THREE DAYS AND THREE NIGHTS" IN DEATH

THE LITERAL ACCURACY OF EVERY STATEMENT MADE BY OUR LORD AS TO THE TIME OF HIS RESURRECTION

## ACTS XX REVEALS THAT THE CHURCH UNDER APOSTOLIC DIRECTION CELEBRATED THE RESURRECTION BY "BREAKING BREAD" AT MIDNIGHT ON THE SOLAR ANNIVERSARY OF THE SAME

---

## "THE FIRST DAY OF THE WEEK" NEVER ONCE MENTIONED IN THE NEW TESTAMENT. THE TRUE MEANING OF THE GREEK WORDS SO TRANSLATED IS "THE FIRST (DAY) OF THE SABBATHS"

WE WILL first allow our thoughts to revert for a moment to the scene on Calvary at the time of the expiry of our Lord Jesus Christ in order to recall that as He bowed His head in death His perfect trust in His God and Father never wavered, and that His last thoughts found expression in the following words of the 16th Psalm:

> "Therefore my heart is glad, and my glory rejoiceth: my flesh also shall rest in hope. For Thou wilt not leave my soul in hell (SHEOL); neither wilt Thou suffer Thine Holy One to see corruption" (verses 9 and 10).

Our Lord therefore died with perfect confidence that, having accomplished the work of Redemption for which He had come into the world, God the Father would not leave Him in the grave (SHEOL) or allow His now bloodless body to be defiled by corruption.

The Apostle Peter, seven and a half weeks later, when addressing the Jewish people on the Day of Pentecost, quotes much of this 16th Psalm in proof of the fact that David had prophesied our Lord's resurrection. He says, "He (David) seeing this before spake of the resurrection of Christ, that His soul was not left in hell (HADES), neither His flesh did see corruption. This Jesus hath God raised up, whereof we all are witnesses" (Acts II, 31, 32). This testimony of the Apostle Peter to the resurrection of "Jesus of Nazareth, a Man approved of God among you by miracles and wonders and signs, which God did by Him" was the means, as we well know, of leading no less than three thousand repentant men and women out of the Jewish fold by their being baptized "in the Name of Jesus Christ for the remission of sins" (Acts II). The Church of our Lord Jesus Christ, therefore, came into being as the result of the Apostolic testimony, in the power of the Holy Ghost, to the fact of our

Lord's resurrection, every detail of which was present to the minds of the Apostles since it was but nine days previously that they had beheld Him "carried up into Heaven" after "being seen of them forty days" (Acts I, 3).

It is, therefore, a self-evident fact that our fellow-Christians in the Apostolic Era were in possession of THE WHOLE TRUTH relating to our Lord's death and resurrection; that is, they knew the day, date and hour of His death, the exact length of His sojourn "in the heart of the earth", and the day, date and hour of His resurrection, as well as that of His presentation of Himself to God the Father as the Antitype of the "wave sheaf" on "the morrow after the sabbath" (Leviticus XXIII, 9 to 11). As one would expect, therefore, these facts, though deeply concealed, are to be found in the Four Gospels from which they have now, by God's infinite grace, been perfectly recovered. To say that they have been "recovered" is, of course, also to aver that they have at some time become lost to view. It may not be possible to say exactly when the times of our Lord's death and resurrection ceased to be known to His Church, but no evidence exists to indicate that anyone after the Apostles departed possessed this knowledge.

Before commenting on the events which followed the resurrection of our Lord and Master Jesus Christ, we will establish from the Holy Scriptures the exact hour it took place as with this knowledge we shall learn the precise length of time He was "in the heart of the earth". An event, however important, loses much of its historic value if unaccompanied by its true date. Neither must we forget that true Christianity is founded upon the historic facts to be found in the Gospels relating to the Person of our Lord and Saviour Jesus Christ. It should, therefore, be a cause for the deepest thanksgiving to God that it has pleased Him at this critical moment in human history to remove all uncertainty as to the dates of His beloved Son's death and resurrection by unveiling the Truth concerning them from His Word, in such a way as to remove the whole subject out of the sphere of human conjecture into that of perfectly-attested historic facts.

Without stopping to consider why it is so, we must advise the reader that it has become very evident that it was the intention of the Holy Spirit that the Four Evangelists should so present the facts touching the time of the Lord's resurrection as to make it impossible for anyone to discover the Truth by the process of natural reasoning. That this is so is made clear by the fact that until now no one since the days of the Apostles has been able to penetrate the veil of secrecy which enshrouds the subject or to harmonize all the many statements in the Four Gospels relating to it. It will be seen in due course that *the one factor* which harmonizes all the others is so deeply concealed in the Gospel narratives as to be beyond human reach. However, when the time had come in the Divine counsels for the Truth to be restored to the members of Christ's body on the earth, the Spirit of God by a most simple means wrought a disclosure of this deeply hidden factor, and at once the whole subject was illumined with the light of Heaven. That to which we refer is none other than *a change in time* wrought by God during the season that our Lord's sacred body lay untenanted in Joseph's rock-hewn sepulchre. The nature of this phenomenon we shall give in detail later.

## THE THREE PREDICTIONS OF OUR LORD JESUS CHRIST AS TO THE TIME OF HIS RESURRECTION

It is a most solemn fact that Religious Christendom, by accepting that the Saviour's resurrection took place early on the Sunday morning after His death at 3 P.M. on the Friday, makes each of the Three specific statements on the subject uttered by our Lord Himself appear grossly inaccurate. It is, therefore, a singular joy and a cause for much thanksgiving to be able to dispel the cloud of suspicion which has gathered around these Three statements by virtue of Christendom's willingness to accept and act upon a theory which does despite to each one of them. Every true Christian knows that our Lord could not err in any statement He made; but for eighteen centuries no one has been able to prove to the world from the Scriptures that each of His Three predictions was literally fulfilled. Rather have His statements been explained away than explained, and this often by those to whom the process must have caused much misgiving.

STATEMENT NO. I. Matthew XVI, 21, etc.

"From that time forth began Jesus to shew unto His disciples, how that He must go unto Jerusalem, and suffer many things of the elders and chief priests and scribes, and be killed, AND BE RAISED AGAIN THE THIRD DAY."

The expression "raised again the third day" appears no less than ten times, in one form or another, as follows: Matthew XVI, 21; XVII, 23; XX, 19; Mark IX, 31; X, 34; Luke IX, 22; XVIII, 33; XXIV, 7 and 46; I Corinth. XV, 4. This is by far the most frequent term used in reference to the time the Lord would be raised from the dead.

STATEMENT NO. II. Mark VIII, 31

"And He began to teach them, that the Son of Man must suffer many things, and be rejected of the elders, and of the chief priests, and scribes, and be killed, and AFTER THREE DAYS RISE AGAIN."

This statement "after three days" occurs only once in the Authorized Version but the Revised Version renders Mark IX, 31 and X, 34 as "after three days". It is also quoted in this form by the Jews to Pilate when they asked for a guard for the sepulchre. (See Matthew XXVII, 63 and also Luke XXIV, 21.)

STATEMENT NO. III. Matthew XII, 40

"For as Jonas was three days and three nights in the whale's belly; SO SHALL THE SON OF MAN BE THREE DAYS AND THREE NIGHTS IN THE HEART OF THE EARTH."

This statement is only recorded once in the Gospels.

This last Statement (No. III) is the most important of all because our Lord prefaced it with the words, "There shall no sign be given . . . but the sign of the prophet Jonas". If, therefore, our Lord was not *in the literal sense* "three days and three nights" in death, then His ONE SIGN to this "evil and adulterous generation" failed. To declare such a thing would be blasphemy. To evade the issue by accepting the notion that the expression used by our Lord was a Jewish idiom that need not be treated literally is a most dangerous slight upon Him which, if taken to its final analysis, would allow His critics all the leeway they wish when belittling His statements on other subjects. To be a true prediction, our Lord's session in death must have covered all or part of "three days" and all or part of "three nights"; and exactly the same terms would have applied to Jonah's session in "the whale's belly".

Obviously, our Lord intended these three statements covering THE TIME of His resurrection to be complementary one to the other. They are not purposeless and each one accomplishes a different object (Eccles. IV, 12). We will take them in turn.

"Raised again the third day" is an *exclusive* statement. From 3 P.M. on the Friday, when the Saviour died, to 3 P.M. Saturday is the *first* day. From 3 P.M. Saturday to 3 P.M. Sunday is the *second* day. From 3 P.M. Sunday to 3 P.M. Monday is the *third* day; and according to this statement our Lord could rise at any point of time between Sunday at 3 P.M. and Monday at 3 P.M. It will be noted that "the third day" excludes all of Sunday except the last 3 hours, namely, 3 to 6 P.M.

"And after three days rise again" is an *inclusive* statement. The *first* of these days, being inclusive, embraces all Friday – the day of our Lord's death. The *second* is all Saturday; and the *third* is all Sunday. Each of these days is composed of 24 hours, measured like all Bible days from 6 P.M. to 6 P.M. Therefore, "after three days" means any time after 6 P.M. Sunday when the fourth day began. *It will be noted that this statement excludes all Sunday as the day of the resurrection.*

"So shall the Son of Man be three days and three nights in the heart of the earth". This again is an *inclusive* statement. The *three* days are (I) 6 A.M. to 6 P.M. Friday; (II) 6 A.M. to 6 P.M. Saturday, and (III) 6 A.M. to 6 P.M. Sunday. The *three* nights are (I) 6 P.M. Friday to 6 A.M. Saturday; (II) 6 P.M. Saturday to 6 A.M. Sunday, and (III) 6 P.M. Sunday to 6 A.M. Monday. *This statement therefore positively restricts the time of the resurrection to the twelve hours of the third "night", namely,* 6 P.M. *Sunday to* 6 A.M. *Monday.*

As we are about to show from the Scriptures, our blessed Lord did rise in the middle of the third night. Therefore, His three predictions were all literally fulfilled because the resurrection took place on "the third day" – exclusively reckoned; "after three days" – inclusively reckoned; and in the third night of the "three days and three nights" – inclusively reckoned.

It is needless to make further comment as it must be perfectly obvious to all that these three statements of our Lord Jesus Christ above quoted finally dispose of the notion that He rose from the dead at any point of time on the Sunday which followed His death at 3 P.M. on the previous Friday, 1st May.

### "THE FIRST DAY OF THE WEEK" IS NEVER NAMED IN THE NEW TESTAMENT. A GRIEVOUS MIS-TRANSLATION

It will at once be asked, If our Lord's own statements completely rule out the Sunday following His death as the day of His resurrection, why does each of the Four Gospels state that He rose in the early morning of "the first (day) of the week"? The answer is that neither the Gospels nor any other part of Scripture makes any such statement, for if they did so it would contradict the One Who is the Incarnate Word, and that would mean that our blessed Lord and the Holy Spirit in the Evangelists were at variance on the matter, to say which would be to display culpable ignorance. No, it was the translators of the English Authorized and Revised Versions (etc., etc.), through their desire to conform with tradition, that stated that our Lord Jesus Christ rose on "the first day of the week"—and not the inspired Evangelists.

Knowing the great cost of their labour and acknowledging the general excellence of their work, it is painful to have to say that in this case the translators deliberately ignored accuracy and bowed to tradition when they translated, or rather interpreted, certain Greek words and gave "the first (day) of the week" as their meaning, in order to conform with the universally-held notion that our Lord rose early on a Sunday morning.

The expression "the first (day) of the week" occurs seven times as follows: Matthew XXVIII, 1; Mark XVI, 2; Luke XXIV,

1; John XX, 1 and 19. Each of these has reference to our Lord's resurrection. In Acts XX, 7 and I Corinthians XVI, 2, the same expression occurs in reference to the keeping of the solar anniversary of the Lord's resurrection.

The Greek words are the same in each of the above Scriptures. They are

"TĒ MIĀ TŌN SABBATŌN"

No serious person could possibly deny that these Greek words, which in each case refer to the day (or the anniversary) of our Lord's resurrection, can only be correctly translated as

"THE FIRST (DAY) OF THE SABBATHS"

(The word "day" is correctly interpolated as "MIĀ" ("first") is feminine and requires a feminine noun – "SABBATŌN" being neuter.)

To translate "SABBATŌN" as "week" is dishonest as it is a plural noun. If it had been translated "weeks", as in some versions, it would have been an erroneous translation, but a correct interpretation of the meaning (see Deuteronomy XVI, 9 and 10). Why, then, it will be asked, do the Four Gospels state that our Lord rose on "the first (day) of the sabbaths"? The answer to this, as most will know, is that the expression "sabbaths" refers to the seven sabbaths (or weeks) between the waving of "the sheaf of the firstfruits" (see Leviticus XXIII, 9 to 21) which is the pre-eminent type of our Lord in resurrection, and the waving of the two loaves of "the firstfruits" at Pentecost fifty days later. In other words, the Gospels state that our Lord rose on "the first day" of the seven weeks which elapsed between His resurrection and Pentecost. That day in our calendar was MONDAY, 4TH MAY A.D. 33.

When, in due course, we explain the change in time which God wrought when our Lord's untenanted body lay in the sepulchre, it will be seen that *this Monday became "the first day of the week" in Divine Time;* or in terms of the type in Leviticus XXIII, 11, "the morrow after the sabbath".

The sum of what we have thus far set forth is that our Lord's own plain statements as to the time of His resurrection absolutely exclude Sunday and fix that great Event as occurring after 6 P.M. Sunday and before 6 A.M. Monday. This Monday is named in each of the Four Gospels "the first (day) of the sabbaths", that is, the seven sabbaths or weeks between our Lord's resurrection and Pentecost in the year A.D. 33.

(NOTE. The reader will remember what we have previously stated, namely, that TIME in relation to our Lord's death and resurrection is only expressed in the Bible in terms of the Divine calendar. Israel's "first day of the sabbaths" was on the Sunday which was "the morrow after" their Sabbath – see Chart of the Five Calendars.)

We shall now proceed to show from the Scriptures that THE RESURRECTION OF OUR LORD JESUS CHRIST TOOK PLACE EXACTLY AT THE MIDNIGHT OF SUNDAY, MAY 3RD.

We have already shown how the Bible marks the hour of our Lord's death with the utmost precision. We shall now see that it marks the hour of His resurrection with equal precision. The Bible never indulges in vague or indefinite information, which in the sphere of chronology would be valueless. The time that our Lord, as Head of the Church, was in death was typical of the length of time that His mystical Body – the Church – will remain in the sphere of death before all its sleeping members are raised from the dead (see I Corinthians XV, 51 to 57).

As we have fully explained, each of the Four Evangelists asserts that the day of our Lord's resurrection was the first day of the seven sabbaths or weeks to Pentecost. In our calendar this was Monday – 4th May. In ordinary Bible terms this Monday would have begun at 6 P.M. on Sunday and ended at 6 P.M. on Monday. The Apostle John, however, is caused in this connection to reveal a most important fact, namely, that following our Lord's rejection and death and the rending of the Temple veil, God abandoned the ordinary Bible day as used by Israel from 6 P.M. to 6 P.M. and adopted the Gentile day which then, as now, is measured from Midnight to Midnight. No doubt, God did this because the Christian Dispensation, which opened on the day of our Lord's death ("the first day of unleavened bread"), was essentially to be a Gentile Era – it is in fact termed by our Lord in Luke XXI, 24, "the times of the Gentiles".

It is beautiful to see the simple way in which John is allowed to convey this important information. In Chapter XX, verse 1, we read according to the Greek:

"The first (day) of the sabbaths cometh Mary Magdalene

early, when it was yet dark, unto the sepulchre, and seeth the stone taken away from the sepulchre."

The Magdalene's visit here recorded must have taken place between 4 and 5 A.M. Thus far we only know that "the first (day) of the sabbaths" had opened some time previous to this. In the normal course we should rightly assume that this was at 6 P.M. the previous evening. To correct this impression and to reveal that God had abandoned the Jewish day and had taken up the Gentile day, John is caused in the same context to make a second reference to "the first (day) of the sabbaths".

In verse 19 of Chapter XX we read, according to the Greek:

"Then the same day at evening, being the first (day) of the sabbaths, when the doors were shut where the disciples were assembled for fear of the Jews, came Jesus and stood in the midst, and saith unto them, Peace be unto you."

Luke gives a more detailed account of this precious appearing of the Risen Saviour in the evening of "the first (day) of the sabbaths" – the day of our Lord's resurrection. He informs us that it was after the two disciples had returned from Emmaus which was "threescore furlongs", or about seven and a half miles, from Jerusalem. We are told in Chapter XXIV, 29, that these two disciples, when they constrained their unknown Guest to abide with them, said, "It is toward evening, and the day is far spent". This appearing of our Lord to the company in the Upper Room must therefore have been not earlier than 8 P.M., and probably much later, as the return from Emmaus to Jerusalem after sunset would have taken not less than three hours.

It will be noted that John is careful to inform us that this late appearing of our Lord was on "the same day" as His appearing to Mary Magdalene early in the morning and that it was "the first (day) of the sabbaths". These details are purposely given to make it evident that "the first (day) of the sabbaths" must now be regarded as beginning at Midnight, like all Gentile days. Consequently, it was current "when it was yet dark", that is, about 4 to 5 A.M., and still current about 8 to 10 o'clock that evening. (In the normal course a new Bible day would have opened at 6 P.M.) Incidentally, it is vital to remember that all "hours" quoted in John's Gospel relate to the Gentile day beginning at Midnight.

We need add no more as the fact must be patent to all that the day of our Lord's resurrection, that which is called "the first (day) of the sabbaths", began AT MIDNIGHT on Sunday, 3rd May, when Monday, 4th May opened, and ran its course of 24 hours to the next Midnight. In the early morning of this day the risen Saviour manifested Himself to Mary Magdalene and in the late evening of the "same day" He manifested Himself to the Ten disciples and "them that were with them" (Luke XXIV, 33).

At what exact point of time then did the Saviour actually part company with "the linen clothes" that had enwrapped His lifeless body, and "the napkin, that was about His head"? No human eye was allowed to behold that scene and no record exists as to it. But the hand of God was over it all for it was "according to the working of His mighty power" that Christ was "raised . . . from the dead". We are not, however, now considering the Event itself so much as THE TIME when it took place.

This the Scriptures reveal, like so much else, by means of a simple deduction to be drawn from the known facts. As Monday, 4th May A.D. 33 (the day which opened at Midnight on Sunday, 3rd May) was "the first (day) of the sabbaths" or weeks to Pentecost, it was utterly impossible for our Lord to remain even for one minute of it in death. These seven weeks or 49 days constituted the time of harvest which is the great symbol of resurrection. For there to be a harvest, grain has to "fall into the ground and die". On this very Monday, between 8 and 9 A.M., our Lord ascended to God the Father as a "sheaf of the firstfruits" of that great harvest of human souls which has yet to be gathered out of the earth as He was. The Apostle Paul, knowing this, declares "But now is Christ risen from the dead, and become the firstfruits of them that slept" (I Cor. XV, 20). Every minute of that Monday, from Midnight to Midnight, being the first day of the Harvest, when the firstfruits were presented to God, bespeaks resurrection – and it is a glorious fact that the moment it opened, yes, *exactly at Midnight*, the risen Christ came forth clothed with His body of glory, triumphant over death, and "loosed" from its pains, "*because it was not possible that He should be holden of it*" *for so much as one minute longer*.

This being so, we may be quite certain that the "great earthquake" named by Matthew (XXVIII, 2) and the descent of the Angel who "came and rolled back the stone from the door" both took place at Midnight as our Lord again entered His uncorrupted human body, now composed of "flesh and bones", and came forth "alive for evermore" (Rev. I, 18). Thus, as our Lord left His body, and as He returned to it, the earth was caused to quake in order to mark each of these momentous occasions.

Apart altogether from the deduction arrived at from the foregoing facts (the better these are understood, the more obvious will be the deduction), the Bible provides one independent and clear proof that our Lord's resurrection took place at Midnight. This it does by recording one occasion when a Church in the Apostolic Era met to celebrate our Lord's resurrection.

In Acts XX, 7, we read, according to the Greek:

> "And upon the first (day) of the sabbaths, when the disciples came together to break bread, Paul preached unto them . . . and continued his speech until midnight."

After Midnight and the raising of Eutychus, Paul broke the bread. Without going into the details, the fact stands out that the Church at Troas, with the Apostle Paul and his company present, met for the sole purpose of celebrating the Resurrection of the Lord on the solar anniversary of "the first (day) of the sabbaths" in A.D. 33, namely, the evening of 3rd May. From this incident we possess the incontestable evidence that it was the practice of the Churches in the Apostolic era to "break bread" at Midnight on each solar anniverary of "the first (day) of the sabbaths". For this purpose they met during the evening so that, when the hour of Midnight was reached and "the first (day) of the sabbaths" opened, they could with one heart and one voice lift up their praises to Him Who had raised up our Lord Jesus Christ from the dead and "set Him at His own right hand in the heavenly places" (Ephes. I, 20).

It must be remarked in passing that this incident at Troas constitutes Divine authority for the celebration by Christians of our Lord's resurrection and, seven weeks later, the day of Pentecost, which is named in verse 16, where we read that Paul "hasted, if it were possible for him, to be at Jerusalem the day of Pentecost" (see also I Cor. XVI, 2 and 8). The linking of this Pentecost with "the first (day) of the sabbaths" can leave no one in any doubt that the Church at Troas in this incident was celebrating our Lord's resurrection at Midnight with a "breaking of bread" or fellowship meal. The notion, therefore, that this was a Sunday or first day of a week and that the Church at Troas had met for "the Lord's Supper" or Holy Communion has not a single word to support it.

It is also to be carefully noted that this Midnight celebration of our Lord's resurrection and the opening of this "first (day) of the sabbaths" at Troas was no less than 19 days after the Jewish Passover and first day of Unleavened Bread (verse 6). This information is given to reveal that the time of this Christian ordinance has been fixed by God without any relation to the Jewish Passover which varied from year to year. It also reveals that the Church in the Apostolic era celebrated "the first (day) of the sabbaths" and Pentecost on solar anniversaries of these days in A.D. 33. This fixed these anniversaries to the same day of the month in every year, irrespective of the day of the week – not one of which is any different from any other as far as the Christian is concerned (see Galatians IV, 10 and Colossians II, 16).

(Naturally, as the State, since the days of Constantine, has set apart Sunday as a public holiday, Christians, freed from secular occupations, wish to use it to meet for the worship of God and to take part in various forms of Christian service. But the branding of "Sunday" as "the Lord's Day", because on it He is supposed to have risen from the dead, will cease with all those who desire to act in the light now afforded by the Holy Scriptures. The expression "the Lord's day" in Revelation I, 10, is simply an alternative form of "the day of the Lord" which is the Day of Judgment – the theme which occupies the Book from Chapter IV to XIX.)

The last occasion when "the first (day) of the sabbaths" is mentioned is in I Corinthians XVI, 2, where the Apostle Paul gives specific instructions to the Church at Corinth, as he had already given to "the churches of Galatia", that *in order to avoid collections* every Christian, on each anniversary of the Lord's resurrection, was to "lay by him in store, as God hath prospered him" a sum to be used solely for the Lord's work. Obviously, all the Churches knew when "the first (day) of the sabbaths" occurred, or the Apostle would not have given instructions to mark the anniversary of the Lord's resurrection by the setting apart of our substance for His service (cf. Deuteronomy XVI, 16, 17).

One further confirmation of the Lord's resurrection being at

Midnight is surely to be had in the action of Paul and Silas in the jail at Philippi. We read in Acts XVI, 25, "And at midnight Paul and Silas prayed, and sang praises unto God: and the prisoners heard them". No one could think that these two men of God would have needlessly disturbed their fellow-prisoners at Midnight if it had not been that they felt the irrepressible desire to celebrate the resurrection of our Lord, like the rest of the Churches were doing at that historic moment. We might add that it would have been equally unlikely that Paul would for any other reason have kept the hardworking believers at Troas up until Midnight to hear him discourse. Furthermore, at Philippi "there was a great earthquake, so that the foundations of the prison were shaken" (verse 26) and this surely provides confirmatory evidence, since the Lord's rising from the dead was also marked by such a sign.

There are several other "Midnights" in Holy Scripture which are directly or indirectly connected with the Midnight at which our Lord Jesus Christ turned His back upon death for Himself and His Church, but these the reader can seek out and interpret for himself. It is not surprising, in view of the fact that Holy Scripture reveals that the resurrection of our Lord Jesus Christ took place at Midnight and that Christians in the first century celebrated Easter by "breaking bread" together at that hour, to read in Ecclesiastical histories of sources other than the Bible which testify to the keeping of Easter by Midnight celebrations on the part of Christians in the early post-Apostolic centuries. To this very day the Greek Orthodox Church holds a Resurrection celebration at Midnight in the Athens Cathedral on Easter Eve which is attended by the leading people in the land. (The "church" which meets in the house of the writer has since 1939 returned to the Apostolic practice of "breaking bread" at the Midnight of 2nd May, which in our present calendar is the correct Anniversary of the Lord's resurrection in A.D. 33.)

## THE NINETY HOURS OF OUR LORD'S PASSION TERMINATED AT MIDNIGHT ON SUNDAY, 3RD MAY

In Chapter XIV, at the end of Part V, we wrote on the subject of the Ninety Hours of our Lord's Passion which began at

6 A.M. on Thursday, 30th April. This was the opening of "the day of the preparation" for the Passover of Jehovah which our Lord and His Apostles took twelve hours later at 6 P.M. We showed that there were 33 hours from this 6 A.M. Thursday to 3 P.M. Friday, when our Lord dismissed His spirit. These 33 hours were divided into 12 hours to the last Passover and 21 hours to His death – just as His 33 years were divided into 12 years to the Passover when He was twelve years of age and 21 years thereafter to His death – the last 7 years in one aspect being akin to the 7 hours He was hanging on Calvary's Tree. From our Lord's death at 3 P.M. on Friday to Midnight on Sunday when He arose is 57 hours – no more, no less. These 33 hours added to the 57 hours make a total of 90 hours, or 3 days and 18 hours. We refer readers back to Part V of Chapter XV for a fuller expression of this subject. It will, however, be seen that these 90 hours of our Lord's Passion terminated exactly at Midnight on Sunday. We shall later show that in the 9th hour (8 to 9 A.M.) after His resurrection our blessed Lord ascended to God the Father as the Antitype of "the sheaf of firstfruits". Thus, from 6 A.M. on Thursday to 9 A.M. on Monday there were 99 hours, and 99 is the numerical value of the word AMEN, translated "Verily", which our Lord used 99 times.

We must now proceed to show from the Holy Scriptures why in Divine Time God viewed Monday, 4th May A.D. 33, as "the morrow after the sabbath" or first day of a week in accordance with the type of our Lord's resurrection given in Leviticus XXIII, 11.

### GOD MARKS THE OCCASION OF THE DEATH OF HIS SON, OUR LORD JESUS CHRIST, BY SECRETLY CHANGING TIME

### HE CAUSES THE MOON TO CEASE IN ITS REVOLUTION AROUND THE EARTH FOR TWO WHOLE DAYS

### THE ASTRONOMICAL PROOF THAT THE MOON HAS LOST TWO DAYS SINCE THE INTRODUCTION OF THE JULIAN CALENDAR ON 1ST JANUARY 45 B.C.

It should not surprise anyone to learn that God the Father went to extraordinary lengths to mark the occasion of the death of His well-beloved Son, since it is the most important Event in the whole history of the Universe; for by means of it – and its sequel, the Resurrection – the whole Creation is soon going to be delivered from "the bondage of corruption" which now mars it, and be brought "into the glorious liberty of the children of God" (Romans VIII, 21). What will surprise all is that God could cause so mighty a "sign and wonder" as to suspend the Moon's revolution for two days without openly recording the fact in the Scriptures and without it becoming known and publicized by astronomers living at the time. In His acting thus we must take full account of the principle given in Proverbs XXV, 1 – "It is the glory of God to conceal a thing: but the honour of kings is to search out a matter". Assuredly, God has excelled in the way He has concealed this most remarkable of all lunar phenomena in the Scriptures. Needless to say, the Four Evangelists perfectly understood that God had wrought a change in Time, as otherwise the day of our Lord's resurrection and presentation to God the Father – Monday, 4th May – could not possibly conform with the requirements of the Levitical type of the "wave-sheaf" which had to be offered "on the morrow after the sabbath" – a day which must be both the first day of a week (our Sunday) and also "the first (day) of the sabbaths" or seven weeks to Pentecost (see Leviticus XXIII, 9 to 17).

In our previous section we had carried the subject of the time of our Lord's resurrection to the point that we saw from the Scriptures that it took place at the Midnight of Sunday, 3rd May, and that the day called in all the Gospels "the first (day) of the sabbaths" was Monday, 4th May – a day which, like all Gentile days, opened at Midnight and ran until the next Midnight.

*We now have to learn why this Monday was in Divine Time both "the morrow after the sabbath" and "the first (day) of the sabbaths" or seven weeks to Pentecost.* That it was so is proved by the fact that our risen Lord early in the morning sent Mary Magdalene with a message to His disciples, saying, "I ascend unto My Father, and your Father; unto My God, and your God" (John XX, 17). This ascent was as the Antitype of the Wave-Sheaf of Firstfruits, and as such our Lord could not present Himself on any other day without the type being broken as well as the Scripture of which it forms a part.

As it will be of interest to some to learn of the means by which light on this most vital subject was granted by God, we must ask forgiveness for the introduction of some features personal to those responsible for this Treatise.

In the Introduction we explained how in the year 1933 we engaged upon "a comprehensive research into the Holy Scriptures", in order to elucidate their Time mysteries.

By the latter part of the year 1935 we had succeeded for the first time in human history in reproducing from the Bible its astronomically perfect chronology, and with this an almost exact knowledge of time in our Lord's pathway. In due course we found ourselves confronted with the obviously unsolved problem of Time in relation to our Lord's death and resurrection – a state of things we felt to be most dishonouring and a weapon of great potency in the hands of the rationalist school which could glory over the Church's absolute ignorance, both of the date of the Saviour's death and of the length of time He was in the grave – not to mention the apparent irreconcilability of Scripture statements on the subject. We, therefore, felt the call to face this issue boldly and set about doing so, not by trying to find *a solution* so much as by patiently bringing together every relevant fact in Holy Scripture.

The result of this labour was, of course, the same as that experienced by all others who had made a genuine effort to reconcile the relevant Scriptures and obtain THE TRUTH as to the actual time of the Saviour's resurrection. We, therefore, had to admit that like everyone else we had reached *an absolute impasse* in our researches; for while Scripture unmistakably revealed that the day of our Lord's resurrection and presentation of Himself to God the Father as "the firstfruits" was the Monday after His death, the pre-eminent type fixed this event to "the morrow after the sabbath" – the day we call Sunday.

Conscious that it was our Lord's purpose that His Church on the earth should, before her departure at His Second Appearing, return to the Apostolic practice of keeping the appointed Ordinances related to His death and resurrection at their appointed times, and that for this it would be absolutely necessary for Him to restore to the Church from the Scriptures the deeply-concealed truth as to their true dates in the year A.D. 33, we gave ourselves to concerted and earnest supplication about the matter over many weeks.

In the early morning of 24th November 1935 (following a lengthy season of supplication of a most definite order the previous day in a lonely part of the mountains of Cumberland) one of our number was directed to the following words in Daniel II, 21 and 22: "He changeth the times and the seasons . . . He revealeth the deep and secret things: He knoweth what is in the darkness, and the light dwelleth with Him". These words appeared to be extremely applicable to the occasion and created the distinct impression that there might have been a change in time at our Lord's death by some manipulation of the great lights in the heavens, as in the days of Joshua and Hezekiah.

Later that day, while out walking in the early evening, an understanding was granted of the one incalculable factor in the problem of time as it is related to our Lord's death and resurrection.

The way in which this revelation came was simple in the extreme. It took the form of a brief dialogue with One Who drew near to the one walking. Said that One to him, "Do you count time to one who is dead?" The reply was, "No, Lord". Said He, "Neither do We". Nothing remained but to worship and give thanks to the One Who had drawn near, and Who "setteth an end to darkness . . . and the thing that is hid bringeth He forth to light" (Job XXVIII, 3 and 11). We well knew from that hour that *the unknown factor* in this great and solemn problem had been brought forth from its place of concealment in the Scriptures.

So it was by this simple means that God conveyed the knowledge that for the two unbroken days – our Saturday and Sunday – that our Lord was "in the heart of the earth" He refused to reckon time. Our Lord Jesus Christ was a Representative Man – "the last Adam" – and as such He represented ALL MEN in His death ("we thus judge, that if One died for all, then were all dead" – II Cor. V, 14). How could God go on reckoning time to such a One when He was no longer on the earth – the sphere of time? If we do not count time to a person after death, why should we expect God to do so?

It was not for several months after this that we obtained the proof that God had actually intervened to stay the Moon in its course around the Earth for these two days. We will, however, refer to that aspect a little later.

It will be remembered that we have often stated that the Bible only reckons our Lord's death and resurrection according to Divine Time and not according to Israel's calendar. In Divine Time our Lord Jesus Christ died on God's Sabbath (the Jews' Friday). The next two days of 24 hours each (the Jews' Sabbath and Sunday) are UNRECKONED because our Lord was absent from His body. Therefore, the following day (the Jews' Monday) was in literal fact, and according to true time, "the morrow after the sabbath" – the day on which the sheaf of firstfruits had to be waved according to the Law. So when our Lord presented Himself to God the Father, between 8 and 9 A.M. on the Monday morning as "the firstfruits of them that slept", He knew perfectly that in Divine Time – that is, Time as reckoned by God – the day was "the morrow after the sabbath" and also "the first day of the sabbaths" or seven weeks to Pentecost.

To simplify the matter we will tabulate the days of our Lord's Death and Resurrection, thus:

| IN DIVINE TIME | IN ISRAEL'S TIME |
|---|---|
| OUR LORD DIES ON GOD'S SABBATH | FRIDAY (6TH DAY) |
| (TIME UNRECKONED) | SATURDAY (SABBATH) |
| (TIME UNRECKONED) | SUNDAY (1ST DAY) |
| OUR LORD RISES "THE MORROW AFTER THE SABBATH" OR "THE FIRST (DAY) OF THE SABBATHS" | MONDAY (2ND DAY) |

As it is manifest in Matthew's Gospel that the whole of the interval between our Lord's death and resurrection is ignored in Divine Time, it may be asked why God only ceased reckoning time for Two Days when, as we have shown, our Lord was Two Days and Nine Hours in death. The answer is that Bible chronology never takes account of fractions of any unit of time. God was changing time and the day of 24 hours is the basic unit of the Bible calendar, as it is of our own and all calendars. Furthermore, it was the order of the days of the week that was being changed and this could not include an odd number of hours. These Two Days, when our Lord was absent from His body, are a positive type of the Two "Days" of a thousand years each, during which He, as Head, is absent from His Mystical Body – the Church. And not only is this so, but the statement in Hosea VI, 2, "after two days will He revive us", is a reference to the Jews in the same two thousand years during which they are dispersed over the earth. We have already given the exact measurement of these two thousand Bible years which ran from 12th October A.D. 33, to 12th June 1933, when the Christian Dispensation ended chronologically.

Apart from the Lunar phenomenon which God wrought when our Lord was in death and which we will now explain, we have nothing to add, as it will be plain to all that in our calendar the blessed Saviour of the World died on Friday, 1st May A.D. 33, and rose again at Midnight on Sunday, 3rd May; and that the Day of His Resurrection, when He appeared to Mary Magdalene and later (8 to 9 A.M.) ascended to present Himself to God the Father as "the firstfruits of them that slept", was Monday, 4th May. Finally, and most important of all, the Friday of our Lord's death was in Divine Time God's Sabbath and, therefore, the day of His resurrection was "the morrow after the sabbath" and also "the first (day) of the sabbaths", that is, of the seven sabbaths or weeks to Pentecost which in A.D. 33 was Monday, 22nd June, the 50th day from Monday, 4th May. These Mondays, and every Monday since, because of the change in the order of the days of the week wrought by God during our Lord's death, are in Divine Time "the first day of the week".

As we have seen, until the Lord's death the days of the week in Divine Time were ONE DAY AHEAD of Israel's time because of Joshua's long day (see Summary of Facts, Para. 14). Now, because the TWO DAYS of our Lord's death were not reckoned, the days of the week in Divine Time are ONE DAY BEHIND our days and those of the Jews. Some may think it remarkable that Christendom's Sunday, therefore, now corresponds to God's holy Sabbath; but for many reasons this has no significance for Christians who are to take no account of days of the week, and certainly not Sabbaths (Colossians II, 16).

# A MIGHTY ACT OF GOD

## THE MOON COMMANDED TO REMAIN FOR TWO WHOLE DAYS ENSHROUDED AND STATIONARY WHILE THE BODY OF CHRIST JESUS OUR LORD LIES UNTENANTED IN THE SEPULCHRE

## THE CHRONOLOGY OF THE BIBLE REVEALS THIS FACT AND ASTRONOMY AFFORDS CLEAR CORROBORATIVE EVIDENCE AS TO IT

"The sun shall be turned into darkness, and the moon into blood" (Peter on the day of Pentecost – Acts II)

The act of God in reference to the Moon during the death of our Lord ranks with His act in the days of Joshua when He caused the Sun and Moon to remain stationary for 24 hours while Israel completed its victory over the Southern half of Palestine (Joshua X). We are not concerned to know how the Creator made this great Light in the Heavens obey His will on the occasion of the death of His beloved Son, but to present the evidence of Holy Scripture and Astronomy in proof that He did so. We do not suppose that the combined erudition of all the astronomers in the world could elucidate the mystery of how such a thing could be done. Common sense, however, would rescue us from the dilemma of supposing that the Creator had set the heavenly Lights in motion without being able to control them and make them do His will.

As we stated earlier in this section, we had no knowledge of the fact that the Moon had been caused to cease for two days in its revolution around the Earth when it was first made known to us that God ceased reckoning time for the two days when our Lord was absent from His body. This fact came to light some months later in the following manner.

About the middle of the year 1936, after 3 years of patient research, we found ourselves in possession of an absolutely fault-less reproduction from the Bible of its astronomically perfect chronology of human history. This we had traced first in Bible years of 354 days and then coverted into days, solar years and lunations, or revolutions of the Moon. The absolute accuracy of this chronology was proved by the way it exactly agreed with the age of the Moon at the Flood, the Exodus, the Dedication of Solomon's Temple, the Last Passover, etc., etc., required by the terms of Holy Scripture. An error of one day would have made this impossible.

We found the first day of Genesis I to be 4th March 4075 B.C., and that the Moon was new at about 6 P.M., 3rd March, which was the starting-point of the first "evening and morning". We reached this date by measuring back from 1933 to A.D. 33; then from A.D. 33 to the Exodus in 1639 B.C. and from the Exodus to Adam in 4075 B.C., as Bible Chronology, by the nature of its composition, is divided into these three divisions.

We made the highly significant discovery that on 12th June in the year 1933 human history had run a course of 6,000 Julian years to the day and hour. This measurement, for reasons given in earlier pages, omitted the 7 years and 49 days which formed the period of the Ministries of John the Baptist and of our Lord up to His Ascension.

Between 4th March 4075 B.C., and 12th June 1933, there were 6,007 Julian years and 57 days. These contained 2,194,114 days. When converted into revolutions of the Moon at the universally accepted mean of 29 days, 12 hours, 44 minutes and 2.8 seconds, the result is 74,299 lunations, 21 days, 6 hours and 17 minutes.

This simply means that at the close of 12th June in 1933 the mean age of the Moon would be about 21 days and 6 hours. Not only is every one of these 2,194,114 days accounted for in the Bible, as we demonstrate in Paper IV of our former Treatise, *The World in Liquidation*, but the possibility of error is eliminated by the way the total has been built up, step by step, without a break of so much as a minute. In passing, we may mention that by virtue of the accuracy of the Bible's figures we learnt that our present Gregorian Calendar falls short by two days because Pope Gregory, when correcting the accumulated Julian error in 1582, should have omitted 12 days instead of 10 – a fact which is well known and has to be taken into account in all calculations since 1582.

Having learnt from the Bible that the age of the Moon at the close of 12th June 1933, should be about 21 days, we were considerably disturbed to find from the best Almanacs that it was only about 19 days. As our figures were accurate beyond any question, we consulted the leading authority in the country on

Calendar Astronomy to discover if it were in the realms of possibility for the Moon over 6,000 years to have retrogressed two days by some process of which we were ignorant. They assured us, after considering the matter, that this was impossible. We then realized that the discrepancy of two days in the age of the Moon and our figures from the Bible must mean that God had secretly stayed the Moon in its course while our Lord was in the grave. *All Bible Time being LUNAR, it was necessary for God to do this if, in fact, these two days were to have no place in Divine Time.* Apart from the Moon being thus actually stayed, the transaction would have been NOMINAL and not REAL, and that would not suit One Whose power is INFINITE. So we learnt that for the two days, 2nd and 3rd May A.D. 33, that our Lord was in death LUNAR TIME CEASED TO BE RECKONED BECAUSE THE MOON CEASED IN ITS REVOLUTION AROUND THE EARTH. With this adjustment the age of the Moon according to the Bible was, at the close of 12th June 1933, 19 days, like that given in all reputable Almanacs.

## THE ASTRONOMICAL PROOF THAT THE MOON HAS FALLEN BACK TWO DAYS SINCE 1ST JANUARY 45 B.C., WHEN JULIUS CAESAR INAUGURATED THE JULIAN CALENDAR

It stands to reason that if God caused the Moon to cease in its revolution for two days in May A.D. 33, corroborative evidence of the fact should be forthcoming from astronomical sources. That there is such is made plain by the following facts related to the institution of the Julian Calendar on 1st January 45 B.C.

Until the close of the year 46 B.C. (708 A.U.C.) the Roman Calendar was luni-solar, that is, the year was 355 days divided into 12 lunar months, each of which began with the phasis of the Moon. With this there was an intercalation of extra days as needed to keep the civil year in harmony with the solar year and seasons. The pontifices or priests watched for the phasis or first appearance of the Moon and then proclaimed the start of the month.

The system of intercalating extra days was so abused that by 46 B.C. the calendar had got into hopeless confusion. The famous Julius Caesar, as Pontifex Maximus in the year of his

3rd consulate, determined to abandon the luni-solar calendar and inaugurate a purely solar calendar of 365 days, with one extra day every 4th year.

Instead of starting this new order of years, as might be expected, at the winter solstice which occurred on 24th December in 46 B.C., he delayed doing so until 1st January because that was the day of the Moon's phasis when the first month of the New Year would normally have begun.

In confirmation of these facts which are well known, we will quote from *Smith's Dictionary of Greek and Roman Antiquities* (*Art. Calendarium*):

> "It was probably the original intention of Caesar to commence the year with the shortest day. The winter solstice at Rome, in the year 46 B.C., occurred on the 24th of December of the Julian Calendar. His motive for delaying the commencement for seven days longer, instead of taking the following day, was probably the desire to gratify the superstition of the Romans, by causing the first year of the reformed calendar to fall on the day of the new moon. Accordingly, it is found that the mean new moon occurred at Rome on the 1st of January 45 B.C., at 6h. 16m. P.M. In this way alone can be explained the phrase used by Macrobius: ANNUM CIVILEM CAESAR, HABITIS AD LUNAM DIMENSIONIBUS CONSTITUTUM, EDICTO PALAM PROPOSITO PUBLICAVIT. This edict is also mentioned by Plutarch."

It is clear from this quotation from Macrobius why Caesar ordained that the first solar year should start at the New Moon (AD LUNAM). Now it is perfectly obvious that this could not have been the astronomical New Moon (the time of which no one but a few astronomers would know) but at the phasis of the Moon, that is, the first appearance of the crescent in the sky, in the manner the Romans had for centuries been accustomed to at the start of their months. It will be noted, however, that the above article from *Smith's Dictionary* gives the time of the New Moon (meaning the time of the actual conjunction) as 6.16 P.M. on 1st January. This hour is confirmed very approximately by all astronomical tables. But if the Moon were only new in the evening of 1st January, its first appearance would not have been until the evening of 2nd January or later, in which case Caesar's desire to win the support of the populace, or at least to avoid their displeasure at the inauguration of the new Calendar, would have completely failed. Obviously, this was not the case.

What is the explanation? The writer of the article in *Smith's Dictionary*, like the authors of all astronomical tables, knew nothing about God's action in suspending the Moon's revolution for two days on 2nd and 3rd May A.D. 33, so consequently he gave the hour of the New Moon as the evening of 1st January 45 B.C. instead of the evening of 30th December 46 B.C.

(N.B. The effect of taking account of the Moon's ceasing its revolution for 2 days in May A.D. 33, is to make all New Moons previous thereto 2 days earlier than appear in Tables which take no account of this phenomenon.)

This being so, we are enabled to know that as the Moon was new in the evening of 30th December, the first appearance of the crescent would have been in the night of the 31st of December, or at the latest the evening of 1st January, exactly as Caesar intended.

No one could fail to realize that it is ludicrous to suggest that Caesar waited 8 days after the Solstice in order to start the new order of years at other than the Moon's phasis or first appearance. This, therefore, is proof that the astronomical New Moon of December 46 B.C. was in the evening of the 30th and as this is so we possess astronomical proof, which can be verified by a simple calculation, that at some point of time since then the Moon has fallen back two days. As there is no record of a Lunar phenomenon other than that to which we have directed attention, it is strictly according to reason to assert that it must have occurred, as the Scriptures clearly imply, when our Lord's body lay in the Sepulchre on Saturday, 2nd May, and Sunday, 3rd May A.D. 33.

We thus learn that God not only refused to reckon time during these two days, but that He rendered inoperative the great Time-Keeper in the Heavens so that time could not be registered by it – all Sacred Time being measured according to the Moon.

We have no doubt that yet more clear proof exists in the astronomical sphere as to this phenomenon on 2nd and 3rd May A.D. 33, and we trust that some who are learned in such matters will consider this worthy of their attention. In this connection we must mention that in his *Book of Almanacs* (published 1871) Augustus de Morgan who was Professor of Mathematics at London University, when indicating a system whereby it is possible to find out the age of the Moon on any day back to 2,000 B.C., twice states, without giving a reason, that the calculations will sometimes be found to be *two days* in error. It seems impossible to doubt that this unexplained error of two days is caused by the phenomenon of 2nd and 3rd May A.D. 33. It would appear that no calculation of Moons embracing these two days could fail to be in error if this phenomenon is not taken into account.

In calling attention to these astronomical aspects of God's action in staying the course of the Moon for two days we do not wish it to be thought that such a confirmation is necessary, even though it may be of great interest. The Bible by its perfect chronology proves that the Moon has lost these two days and the facts given in the Gospels, notably that of Matthew, make it perfectly clear that the Moon's course was stayed thus because God refused to reckon Time between our Lord's death and resurrection.

# PART II

## THE MANNER OF THE RESURRECTION OF OUR LORD JESUS CHRIST FROM AMONG THE DEAD

---

THE "TWO MEN . . . IN SHINING GARMENTS" WHO DESCEND FROM HEAVEN TO ATTEND UPON OUR LORD AND WITNESS HIS RESURRECTION ARE MOSES THE LAWGIVER AND ELIJAH THE PROPHET

---

WHO WERE "THE SAINTS" WHICH WERE RAISED "AFTER HIS RESURRECTION" AND "APPEARED UNTO MANY"?

---

THE EVIDENCE THAT MATTHEW EXCLUSIVELY FOLLOWS DIVINE TIME IN WRITING OF OUR LORD'S DEATH AND RESURRECTION

---

THE "YOUNG MAN" OF MARK XIV, 51 AND 52, WHO FLED NAKED

---

Read Matthew XXVII, 52, 53 to XXVIII; Mark XVI, 1 to 8; Luke XXIV, and John XX

HAVING written fully in Part One of this Chapter as to the time when our Lord Jesus Christ was raised from among the dead, namely, at the hour of Midnight of Sunday, 3rd May, after Two Days and Nine Hours "in the heart of the earth", we are in a position to proceed with some comments on the Event itself, and the happenings of the Forty Days which intervened between it and His Ascension into Heaven at the ninth hour on Saturday, 13th June A.D. 33.

The resurrection of our Lord from among the dead is surely to human beings the most glorious fact in the Universe. He, the Son of God, had become incarnate by the Holy Ghost in the womb of the Virgin Mary in order to rescue the human race from the power and penalty of sin – the penalty being death, and death being the end of human life with judgment as its sequel (Heb. IX, 27). So on Calvary's Tree the Human Life of our Lord, though in itself sinless and therefore immortal, came to an end as the inevitable result of His having, by imputation, been made sin for us – His death being God's judgment on account of our sins.

But, thank God, the matter did not end there for, as Peter declares on the Day of Pentecost:

> "This Jesus hath God raised up, whereof we all are witnesses."

If death is the end of human life, resurrection is the end of death, and when the risen Son of God came forth at Midnight clothed in His body of Glory, He had not only finished with death for Himself but had abolished it for all who believe on Him (see II Tim. I, 10). This fact forms the very essence of the glorious Gospel of Jesus Christ. So the Scripture declares:

> "But now is Christ risen from the dead, and become the firstfruits of them that slept. For since by man came death, by man came also the resurrection of the dead. For as in Adam all die, even so in Christ shall all be made alive."
> (I. Cor. XV, 20 to 22.)

When our Lord Jesus Christ left Paradise He again entered the body He had clothed Himself with in the womb of His Virgin Mother, and in which He had tabernacled on earth among men, because in the interval of Two Days and Nine Hours *it had seen no corruption;* though, as we very well know, it still retained, and will do so throughout all eternity, the marks of the nails in His sacred Hands and Feet and of the spear that pierced His Side. But though He came forth in the same body, now glorified, our Lord at His resurrection entered upon a transcendent new life – one which in no sense was a return to the life He had lived before His death on Calvary or to His pre-existent life before His Incarnation. As well as being the Son of God from all eternity, He was now the risen and glorified Son of Man and the Head of the New Creation – as the first man Adam had been of the Old Creation, which he brought down into ruin and death by his disobedience to his Creator. Now, as Head of the New Creation, our Lord could impart His own risen life to all in the thraldom of the Old Creation who would believe on Him; since by His death He had made expiation for their sins, borne their judgment and died in their stead. No wonder His first words to His assembled disciples were "Peace . . . unto you". And who can tell how many millions since His resurrection have entered into His peace – "peace with God" and "the peace of God" – by virtue of His triumph over sin, Satan and death? To His Name be eternal praise and glory.

## EVENTS AT THE MIDNIGHT OF THE RESURRECTION

The Evangelist Matthew is the only one to record the events which actually accompanied our Lord's resurrection at Midnight, so we will quote Chapter XXVIII, verses 2 to 4 in full:

> "And, behold, there was a great earthquake: for the (an) angel of the Lord descended from heaven, and came and rolled back the stone from the door, and sat upon it. His countenance was like lightning, and his raiment white as snow: and for fear of him the keepers did shake, and became as dead men."

It is most important to note that these three verses stand quite alone. The first verse of this chapter, as we have stated, refers to an event at the close of the day of our Lord's death. Unless it is realized that Matthew, because he adopts Divine Time, totally ignores the interval between our Lord's death and His resurrection at Midnight on the Sunday, when "the first (day) of the sabbaths" . . . "began to dawn", no one can possibly understand his meaning. Furthermore, the verses which follow this quotation refer to an event – the Angel's conversation with "the women" – which took place, as we will show later, about 8 A.M.

It is obvious that the "great earthquake" was sent to mark the actual occasion, we might safely say, the actual moment, that our blessed Lord re-entered His sacred body and emerged in it from "the linen clothes", so that they were left lying exactly as they were when they swathed His body – a feature of the utmost importance to which we shall refer again. The descent of "the (an) angel of the Lord" from Heaven, with its terrifying effect upon the morale of the soldier-guards must also have been AT MIDNIGHT as it is not conceivable that the stone which barred any entrance into the sepulchre could remain in its place for a minute after "the first (day) of the sabbaths" – the day of the Resurrection – had opened, because the lifeless body of Jesus was no longer there and *this fact must be in evidence* – a thing not possible so long as the stone remained in its place at the entrance of the sepulchre.

The act of "the Angel" in rolling back the "great stone" was in fact a pronouncement that the Saviour had risen and anyone who wished might find *the proof* of this by entering, as Peter and John did a little later. There is little need to comment upon the effect of the Angel's descent upon the guard who "became as dead men", save to remark how ludicrous and impotent human beings become in the presence of celestial beings. We noted that much the same happened to the soldiers who had come to arrest our Lord in the Garden of Gethsemane, just because they had caught a glimpse of His royal Majesty through the human veil which concealed it.

## A PARENTHESIS

### THE BRIBERY OF THE GUARD BY THE JEWISH RULERS

As we have made a reference to the soldiers who were sent to guard the sepulchre where our Lord's body lay, we may as well refer, before passing on, to the action of the chief priests when in the morning they heard from the soldiers of the preternatural happenings of the previous night. Matthew alone refers to this incident which must not be passed over as of little importance, as it really reveals how God allowed the Jewish rulers to be caught in their own trap. As we know, they went to Pilate and obtained a guard because they were afraid the disciples might get hold of our Lord's body and then proclaim that He had been raised from the dead. This they judged would recoil on their own heads so they took every precaution to prevent it. In Matthew XXVIII, 11 to 15, we get a full account of how the soldiers reported to the chief priests "all the things that were done". No doubt these Jewish rulers were deeply perturbed on hearing of the Angel's descent and action in rolling away the stone, not to mention the earthquake which accompanied it. They at once assemble the elders and take counsel. Rather than let it become known publicly that there had been a Divine interposition and that Jesus of Nazareth had been raised from the dead (the soldiers knew His body was gone from the unmoved grave clothes and bore witness to the fact) these Jewish rulers preferred to get out of their dilemma by themselves propagating the very story the guards had been installed to make impossible. So they bribe the soldiers with "large money" to say "His disciples came by night, and stole Him away while we slept" (verse 13, cf. XXVII, 64). This the soldiers did with the consequence that "this saying is commonly reported among the Jews until this day".

In actual fact God used these soldiers as His witnesses to the whole body of responsible Jewish rulers that the One Whose death they had occasioned had been raised from the dead; and that the event had been accompanied by a shaking of the earth and by the descent from Heaven of an angel, whose "countenance was like lightning, and his raiment white as snow", who had rolled away the stone and sat upon it. Thus the Jewish rulers were caught in their own trap in that they received from the soldiers evidence which could not be gainsaid that Jesus of Nazareth had been raised from the dead on "the third day" as He had said, and as they had said to Pilate. These facts greatly multiply the culpability of the Jewish rulers who, rather than repent of their sinful action in slaying their Messiah, resorted to the giving of heavy bribes to these soldiers to propagate lies which they hoped would keep the nation in ignorance of the fact that our Lord was risen.

## MOSES AND ELIJAH

## THE PRE-EMINENT REPRESENTATIVES OF THE LAW AND THE PROPHETS, HAVING RETURNED TO HEAVEN AFTER WITNESSING THE DEATH OF OUR LORD JESUS CHRIST, ARE AGAIN SENT BY GOD FROM HEAVEN TO BE WITNESSES OF HIS RESURRECTION AND TO ATTEND UPON HIM TO WHOM "ALL POWER . . . IN HEAVEN AND IN EARTH" HAD NOW BEEN GIVEN

---

### THE HEAVENLY VISITANTS NAMED IN THE GOSPELS AS PRESENT AT THE SEPULCHRE ARE IN EACH CASE MOSES AND/OR ELIJAH

---

Read Matthew XXVIII, 2 to 10; Mark XVI, 1 to 8; Luke XXIV, 1 to 12, and John XX, 11 and 12

It was the thought that God could not allow His well-beloved Son to rise from the dead, after Two Days and Nine Hours "in the heart of the earth", to find only ministering angels present to receive Him that caused us to turn again and consider every relevant Scripture, remembering, as we did so, how often very much of importance lies concealed beneath the surface for those who care, in dependence on the Holy Spirit, to search it out.

It had long been evident to us that the "two men . . . in shining garments" who addressed "the women" at the sepulchre, as recorded in Luke XXIV, 4 to 8, were the same "two men", even Moses and Elias, "who appeared in glory, and spake of His decease which He was about to accomplish at Jerusalem" when on the Mount of the Transfiguration (Luke IX, 30 to 32, R.V.). We felt equally sure that the "two men . . . in white apparel" who addressed the eleven disciples at the Ascension of our Lord into Heaven were also Moses and Elijah (Acts I, 10). Neither had we any doubt that this appearing of the Lawgiver of Sinai and the Prophet of Carmel at such a time was in relation to the testimony they are to render in a future day as predicted in Revelation XI, 3, where God speaks of them as "My two witnesses" who, "clothed in sackcloth", shall "prophesy a thousand two hundred and threescore days".

It was when we carefully considered the exact nature of the statements made by the celestial Visitants to "the women" at the Sepulchre that we detected that they were intended positively to convey the knowledge that the speakers had themselves been present and heard our Lord Jesus Christ say the things they quoted. This shed an entirely new light upon the whole subject and left no room for doubt that in each case the speakers were Moses and Elijah whom God had again sent down from Heaven that they might be WITNESSES OF OUR LORD'S RESURRECTION, even as three days before they had been WITNESSES OF HIS SUFFERINGS AND DEATH ON CALVARY'S TREE. Neither can there be any doubt that Moses and Elijah were sent by God in their official capacity to attend upon His risen Son, to Whom now "all power . . . in heaven and in earth" had been committed – the day of His humiliation being over and the day of His exaltation having arrived (Philipp. II, 6 to 11). So it was not ministering angels who had the honour of receiving our Lord and Saviour back from the grave, but the now glorified Representatives of the Law and the Prophets, concerning whom the Prophet Zechariah speaks thus: "These are the two anointed ones (Heb. 'sons of oil') that stand by the Lord of the whole earth" (IV, 14).

In our comments upon "The Transfiguration and its Prelude", in Chapter XI of this Treatise, we pointed out that it was the words uttered to "the women" at the Sepulchre by the "two men . . . in shining garments", as recorded by Luke, that first caused us to realize that the speakers must have been present on the occasion when our Lord, eight days before the Transfiguration and Forty Days before His death, first announced to His disciples that He would "be killed, and be raised again the third day" (Matt. XVI, 21 and Luke IX, 22). The words of the "two men" – "remember how He spake to you when He was yet in Galilee" – afford conclusive evidence that they and "the women" were present on that notable occasion which marked the opening of the last Forty Days before our Lord's death (Mark VIII, 32). With these facts before us, it was not difficult to understand that when, at the close of "these sayings", our Lord said, "But I tell you of a truth, there be some standing here, which shall not taste of death, till they see the kingdom of God", His eye was resting on the "two men" – Moses and Elijah – who that day had come down from Heaven, not to take part in, but to be witnesses of the solemn Events which would occupy the next Forty Days and notably so that of our Lord's death on the last of these.

(N.B. It should be explained that the whole truth concerning the appearing on earth of Moses and Elijah only came to light when writing our comments on the Resurrection. This made it necessary to re-write much of our comments in the Chapter on "The Transfiguration and its Prelude".)

It cannot be other than by design that whereas from Luke's quotation of what the "two men" told "the women" we learn that Moses and Elijah were present on earth on the first of the Forty Days leading up to our Lord's death, Matthew and Mark by their quotations reveal that they were present on the last of these Forty Days and must have witnessed all the Events that transpired in it.

In Mark XVI, verses 5 to 7, we learn that certain women who came to the Sepulchre "at the rising of the sun",

> "saw a young man sitting on the right side, clothed in a long white garment; and they were affrighted. And he saith unto them, Be not affrighted: Ye seek Jesus of Nazareth, which was crucified: He is risen; He is not here: behold the place where they laid Him. But go your way, tell His disciples and Peter that He goeth before you into Galilee: there shall ye see Him, *as He said unto you.*"

We learn from Mark XIV, 28 and Matthew XXVI, 32, that it was between leaving the Passover chamber and the arrival at Gethsemane in the evening before His death that our Lord said, "After I am risen (again), I will go before you into Galilee". This is the statement the "young man" quoted to "the women" and which he ended with the words, "*as He said unto you*". It is, therefore, manifest that the "young man" was present and heard what the Lord said to His disciples on the way to the Garden. "The women" were commissioned by the "young man" to bear the message to "His disciples and Peter", who would recall our Lord's words on that sad occasion.

In the Greek the word translated "young man" means a man in his prime. It is used by the Apostle John when he says, "I write unto you, young men" – a class of persons between "little children" and "fathers". It is obvious that "the women" in speaking of the occasion would refer to the celestial visitant who addressed them according to the impression left upon their own minds – to them he was "a young man . . . in a long white garment". We know of no means by which to discern whether the "young man", as "the women" spoke of him, was Moses or Elijah. It is probable that it is not ordained that they should be identified when one is acting apart from the other.

In Matthew XXVIII, verses 5 to 7, we have an account of what "the angel answered and said unto the women". It is an almost identical message with that of the "young man" in Mark XVI. In this case "the angel" uses the words "*as He said*" and "behold, He goeth before you into Galilee", thus showing that he, too, had been present on the way to Gethsemane and heard the Saviour say, "All ye shall be offended because of Me this night: for it is written, I will smite the shepherd, and the sheep of the flock shall be scattered abroad. But after I am risen again, I will go before you into Galilee" (Matt. XXVI, 31, 32). "The women" were commissioned to "go quickly" and bear this message to the disciples with its reminder of the very words our Lord uttered on the night of His betrayal.

The Greek word translated "angel" means in the first instance, "a messenger" and is so translated in the case of John the Baptist in Mark I, 2, – "Behold, I send My messenger before Thy face". When the messenger is of celestial origin the word is translated "angel". To "the women" of whom Matthew writes the celestial visitant was "an angel". Whether this "angel" was Moses or Elijah we know not, but we do know that like the "young man" he must also have been present on the way to Gethsemane and heard our Lord speak of going before into Galilee "after I am risen again".

To complete this picture we must briefly refer to John's statement that Mary Magdalene saw "two angels in white sitting, the one at the head, and the other at the feet, where the body of Jesus had lain. And they say unto her, Woman, why weepest thou?" (XX, 12 and 13). From this incident, which we have yet to comment upon, it would appear that as the risen Christ was engaged in solacing the grief of His faithful disciple, Moses and Elijah, here viewed by the Magdalene as "angels", kept in the background; and by sitting at the place, well known to her, where the Lord's body had lain, gave emphasis to the fact that He was risen – a matter she was about to receive perfect proof of direct from her Lord.

We have said sufficient to make it quite clear that the Holy Scriptures reveal that "the angel of the Lord" in Matthew, the "young man" in Mark, the "two men" in Luke and the "two angels" in John are terms adopted in order to veil for the time the actual identity of the heavenly visitants who were sent by God to receive our Lord and Saviour Jesus Christ when He came forth in His body of glory, after having "tasted death for every man". These, in fact, were none other than Moses, the servant of the Lord, and Elijah the Tishbite – the former, after being secretly buried by God, having been raised from the dead at an undisclosed time, but according to Jude (9) not without Satanic opposition; and the latter having been carried up "by a whirlwind into heaven".

So in the eight hours between His resurrection at Midnight and 8 A.M., when He presented Himself as the Antitype of "the sheaf of the firstfruits", that the Scripture might be fulfilled (Lev. XXIII, 10), the Risen Saviour of the World had as His attendants "the two anointed ones, that stand by the Lord of the whole earth", even Moses the Lawgiver and Elijah the Prophet (Zechariah IV, and Rev. XI, 3 to 12).

## SOME ADDITIONAL REMARKS ON THE FOREGOING SUBJECT

### MOSES AND ELIJAH WITNESS THE DEATH OF OUR LORD JESUS CHRIST ON CALVARY'S TREE

We have just shown that Moses and Elijah were present on the way to the Garden of Gethsemane when our Lord spoke of His going before into Galilee after He was risen. This was during the opening hours of Friday, 1st May, and our Lord was nailed to the Tree the next morning at "the third hour" which is 8 to 9 A.M. We know that on the Mount of the Transfiguration the subject about which Moses and Elijah talked was "His decease (lit. exodus) which He was about to accomplish at Jerusalem" (Luke IX, 31, R.V.). No doubt it was in order that they should be witnesses of our Lord's exodus from this world that Moses and Elijah had come down from Heaven, consequently that was the subject of their converse with Him on "the holy mount". Then again, they would be useless (in the terms of Revelation XI, 3) as witnesses to their own nation, upon which they are presently to fasten the guilt of killing their Messiah, unless they had witnessed the events with their own eyes, as required by the Law of Moses (Deut. XVII, 6 and XIX, 15).

It is, therefore, manifest that Moses and Elijah witnessed the whole tragedy of our Lord's death on Calvary. It is to be remarked that when the Saviour, in His dying moments, cried, "Eloi, Eloi, lama sabachthani", certain onlookers said, "Behold, He calleth Elias . . . Let alone; let us see whether Elias will come to take Him down" (Mark XV, 36). This is most striking because Elijah was present – a fact known to Satan who traded upon the ignorance of these onlookers in order to make it appear that our Lord, now *forsaken of God*, was seeking creature help in His extremity, when in fact He was quoting in Aramaic the first verse of Psalm XXII.

It will have been noted that in Matthew XXVIII, 2, we read, "For the (an) angel of the Lord descended from heaven, and came and rolled back the stone from the door, and sat upon it". This information enables us to know that after our Lord had expired on the Tree or Stake to which He had been nailed, Moses and Elijah must have returned to Heaven. As we have pointed out already, the interval between our Lord's death and resurrection, when the Moon was stayed in its course for Two Days, is a chronological type of this Dispensation when the Church which is His body is being called out and formed. Obviously, therefore, the Representatives of the Law and the Prophets returned to Heaven for this interval, but descended again to be present at our Lord's resurrection, at its close. This is in keeping with the fact that Moses and Elijah will descend from Heaven again at the end of this Dispensation to be God's witnesses in accordance with Revelation XI, 3. It appears that this descent will be with our Lord at His Second Advent.

## THE "YOUNG MAN" OF MARK XIV, 51 AND 52, WHO FLED – THE SAME AS THE "YOUNG MAN" OF MARK XVI, 5

When "they all forsook Him, and fled" at the time of our Lord's apprehension by the soldiers in Gethsemane, Mark, alone of the Evangelists, records that "there followed Him a certain young man, having a linen cloth cast about his naked body; and the young men (i.e., soldiers) laid hold on him: and he left the linen cloth, and fled from them naked".

The Bible is its own interpreter and it is not left to people to guess who this "young man" was, as every such speculation, whether it pointed to Mark himself or Lazarus or another, would leave one still in uncertainty because unconfirmed by Scripture itself. This apparently unimportant and unrelated incident has been a subject of much discussion among Bible students. To affirm that this "young man" was the same as the "young man . . . clothed in a long white garment" in Mark XVI, 5, who was either Moses or Elijah, may at first sound foolish; but sometimes truth is stranger than fiction and we need to be careful that our common-sense conclusions do not make void what the Word of God relates, however unlikely it may appear. We may well ask, Why is this incident recorded? It can be for no other reason than to raise the issue as to who this "young man" was who followed the Lord that night and suffered such a gross indignity to avoid arrest.

The first fact to bear in mind is what we have recorded above, namely, that the "young man" of Mark XVI, 5, was present and heard our Lord's words on the way to the Garden. It would be unreasonable to suppose that this "young man", who was either Moses or Elijah, did not remain near our Lord until the time of His arrest an hour or two later, since these "two men" had come to be witnesses of all that took place in the last Forty Days. Furthermore, "the angel" of Matthew XXVIII, as we have shown, was also present on the way to the Garden and he was either Moses or Elijah – so it is clear that both of these "two men" were following near our Lord at that time.

It appears that the counsels of God, for a very good reason, required that one of these "two men" should come into view for a brief moment. Their bodies being now of a heavenly character would require only to be clothed with a single garment. This "linen cloth" the soldiers laid hold of in seeking to arrest the occupant who fled and left it with them, since it was not the time for him to resist or openly disclose his identity.

If this course of conduct on the part of such as Moses or Elijah appears undignified, the fact must be faced that when they take up their position as God's "two witnesses" in a future day, and have finished their testimony, they will suffer the far greater indignity of being attacked and killed by "the beast that ascendeth out of the bottomless pit"; not to mention the fact that "their dead bodies shall lie in the street of the great city, which spiritually is called Sodom and Egypt, where also our (lit. their) Lord was crucified" (Rev. XI, 7 and 8). It is to be carefully noted, as it is of great significance, that the Greek reveals that "the linen cloth" (SINDON) covering the "young man" who fled was identical in type with that used by Joseph and Nicodemus to enwrap the Lord's body for burial (Mark XV, 46); while "the long white garment" (STOLE) which clothed the "young man" in the Sepulchre was identical in type with that named in Revelation as given to those who had passed through death into resurrection (VI, 11 and VII, 9, 13 and 14). This clearly implies, and is intended to do so, that Moses and Elijah came to be identified with our Lord in His death and resurrection. The marking may be faint but it is there and probably it is the purpose of this whole episode to bring out this fact.

This will become more obvious if attention is paid to another fact touching Moses and Elijah. It is clear from the relationship between Zechariah IV and Revelation XI, both of which speak of Moses and Elijah as "two olive trees" and "two candlesticks", that they have been appointed to "stand by the Lord of the whole earth" – "one upon the right side . . . and the other upon the left side" – to put the matter very briefly. Now we learn in the Gospels that James and John coveted these positions for themselves "in Thy glory". Our Lord, on hearing this request, challenged them thus, "Can ye drink of the cup that I drink of? and be baptized with the baptism that I am baptized with? And they said unto Him, We can", and, indeed, they were in due course, both being slain as martyrs. But the Lord did not stop there for He continued with these significant words, "But to sit on My right hand and on My left hand is not Mine to give; but it shall be given to them for whom it is prepared" (Mark X, 35 to 40, and Matt. XX, 20 to 28).

It is manifest that our Lord was referring to Moses and Elijah who in the Kingdom will be seated on either side of Him, as described in Zechariah IV; and no doubt that is the reason why they had to be present when our Lord was transfigured on "the holy mount" – an event which was an adumbration of the Kingdom. But before that high eminence is reached in the Kingdom both Moses and Elijah will have had to drink of the cup our Lord drank of and to be baptized with His death baptism, as described in Revelation XI, 7 to 12. They will, in fact, be slain in the place "where also their Lord was crucified"; and it is this positive identification with Him in death and resurrection that qualifies them to be on His right hand and on His left in the Kingdom, and to become the glorious channels through which the Holy Spirit (the golden oil) will render testimony in the Messianic Kingdom – they being pre-eminent as representatives of the Law and the Prophets, the two great sources of light to Israel.

If then we see a faint marking of that coming identification of Moses and Elijah with our Saviour and Redeemer in His death and resurrection implied by the clothing of the "young man" who fled and his change of clothing when "sitting on the right side" of the Sepulchre, we shall not be so readily disposed to return to speculating as to who the "young man" was who fled, but rather to admitting that "it is the glory of God to conceal a thing" (Prov. XXV, 2).

* * *

We must bring our comments on the appearing of Moses and Elijah in these two periods of Forty Days to a close. We have only dealt with the facts as they are revealed, or, as we might say, concealed in the Scriptures. The implications attaching to these appearances of God's faithful servants are immense and we have made no attempt to explore them. It might be asked why God has gone to such great lengths to conceal the presence of Moses and Elijah from view during these two periods of Forty Days. If it were not for the stated fact that they were with our Lord during His Transfiguration, the knowledge of their presence on earth would have been unattainable. As it is, this fact is the key which has unlocked the whole subject and brought all to light – as it was intended to do at the appointed time.

It is clear that there could be only One Person in view at such a time and that One the Holy Sufferer Who, after passing through death, became the mighty Victor over Satan, Sin and the Grave, even our Lord and Saviour Jesus Christ – the Son of God from all Eternity. It is, nevertheless, discernible from the facts given that Moses and Elijah filled a place behind the scenes of great importance to our Lord and Master, with Whom no doubt they maintained unbroken contact. On the Mount the disciples became incapacitated by sleep, so it must have been a cause of much consolation to our Lord that He could converse about His impending "exodus" with Moses and Elijah who perfectly entered into the immense solemnity of the issues involved.

It is noteworthy that the Old Testament ends with a reference to both Moses and Elijah in these terms:

> "Remember ye the law of Moses My servant, which I commanded unto him in Horeb for all Israel, with the statutes and judgments.
>
> "Behold, I will send you Elijah the prophet before the coming of the great and dreadful day of the Lord: and he shall turn the heart of the fathers to the children, and the heart of the children to their fathers, lest I come and smite the earth with a curse."

This prediction of Elijah's return is a reference to his association with Moses when they are to be God's "witnesses" in the land of Israel for 1,260 days, as stated in Revelation XI. "The great and dreadful day of the Lord" is the period of $3\frac{1}{2}$ years which immediately follow these 1,260 days.

It is also to be noted that both Moses and Elijah are closely related to Horeb – Moses for the giving of the Law and Elijah as the place where he received his last commission (I Kings XIX). Moses and Elijah were both empowered to anoint others and did so on many occasions. It is not surprising, therefore, that in Zechariah IV, 14, they are called "the two anointed ones" which in the Hebrew means "two sons of oil" – "oil" being a type of the Holy Spirit.

Finally, two notable periods of Forty Days are associated with Moses' past history and one such period with Elijah the Prophet (Deut. X, 10 and I Kings XIX, 8).

## THE EVIDENCE THAT MATTHEW EXCLUSIVELY FOLLOWS DIVINE TIME IN WRITING OF OUR LORD'S DEATH AND RESURRECTION

In Matthew XXVII we read:

51. "And, behold, the veil of the temple was rent in twain from the top to the bottom; and the earth did quake, and the rocks rent;

52. "And the graves were opened; and many bodies of the saints which slept arose,

53. "And came out of the graves after His resurrection, and went into the holy city, and appeared unto many."

In these verses, as we have previously remarked, we have a manifest instance of how the Spirit of God moved Matthew to record a series of events, some of which took place at the very time of the Saviour's death and others at the time of His resurrection, without giving any indication whatever of an interval between them lasting two days and nine or ten hours. The rending of the Veil, the quaking of the earth and rending of the rocks in verse 51 all took place at the very moment of the Lord's expiry. That this is so can be learnt from verse 54 which states, "Now when the centurion, and they that were with him, watching Jesus, saw the earthquake, and those things that were done, they feared greatly, saying, Truly this was the Son of God". Between verses 51 and 52 there is an interval of 57 hours, or 2 days and 9 hours. Matthew is forbidden to take any account of this interval because it was given to him to adopt Divine Time which ceased to be reckoned between the death and resurrection of our Lord. To emphasize this vital fact he writes of events at the death and at the resurrection as if they immediately followed one another.

It is precisely the same with verses 1 and 2 to 4 of Chapter XXVIII. The action of "Mary Magdalene and the other Mary" in coming "to see the sepulchre" took place at the close of the day of the Lord's death (about 6 P.M.) which in Divine Time was the Sabbath. Mark refers to this action in Chapter XV, 47, and Luke in Chapter XXIII, 55. But in verses 2 to 4 Matthew writes of the earthquake and the descent of the angel just as if they happened at the time of Mary's viewing of the sepulchre;

whereas they did not take place until Midnight, two days and about 6 hours later. Note how deliberately Matthew in verse 1 links "the end of the sabbath" (Israel's Friday) with the dawning of "the first (day) of the sabbaths" (Israel's Midnight on Sunday) when the earthquake, etc., took place.

Neither could "the women" of verse 5, who were addressed by the Angel, have been Mary Magdalene or the other Mary, as we will show a little later.

Another instance where Matthew reveals that he exclusively writes in terms of the Divine reckoning of time is in Chapter XXVII, verse 62. He is referring to the day which followed that of our Lord's death and in which the chief priests call upon Pilate for a guard to watch the sepulchre. In Divine Time that day did not exist, as Time had ceased to be reckoned when our Lord expired. *It therefore had no name*, so Matthew, in order to be coherent, calls it "the next day, that followed the day of the preparation". In actual fact, the day was the Jewish Sabbath, as all know, but Matthew refuses to adopt Israel's time, so to be consistent he calls it "the next day", etc.

It will be realized how important it is ever to keep in mind that our Lord's death and resurrection is only reckoned in the Bible by Divine Time and that Matthew is the only one of the Evangelists who was caused to adopt it. Thus in the Bible our Lord is viewed as dying on the Divine Sabbath at 3 P.M. and as rising at Midnight two days and nine hours later, at the opening of the Divine "first (day) of the sabbaths" – the intervening two days and nine hours being totally ignored. In Israel's Calendar and the Roman Calendar the day of our Lord's death was Friday and the hour of His resurrection Midnight the following Sunday. These facts can be perfectly understood by reference to the Chart of the Five Calendars placed at the end of Chapter XIII.

## WHO WERE "THE SAINTS" RAISED "AFTER HIS RESURRECTION"?

This is a most important enquiry. The subject is not mentioned elsewhere in the Bible. It is generally accepted, and quite rightly so, that if our blessed Lord in resurrection was the Antitype of "the sheaf of the firstfruits" in Leviticus XXIII, 9 to 13, it was needful that some should be raised from the dead with

Him, that is, at *about* the same time, as a "sheaf of the first-fruits" implies plurality.

It must be clearly understood that these "saints" were not raised at Midnight as our Lord was, otherwise the statement of the Apostle Paul that He was "the firstborn from the dead; that in all things He might have the pre-eminence" would not be true (Col. I, 18). The implication to be gathered from all the relevant facts in the Scriptures is that, whereas our Lord rose exactly at Midnight, these "saints" were raised exactly at the end of the first hour following Midnight, that is 1 A.M. on "the first (day) of the sabbaths". In other words, exactly one hour elapsed between His resurrection and theirs. Had it been in another unit of time our Lord and these saints could hardly have formed one sheaf of firstfruits. This may appear to be too fine a point but not so to those who have noted God's determined precision in matters of time throughout the Holy Scriptures. There is, however, another reason for there to be one hour between His and their resurrections.

These "saints" who were raised had in life formed a part of the faithful remnant of the Jews who acknowledged our Lord to be their Messiah. We think of the faithful ones at the time of His birth, such as Simeon and Anna, and "all them that looked for redemption in Jerusalem". We think of Elisabeth and Zacharias, the parents of John the Baptist, not to mention the Baptist himself who had been put to death. We think of Joseph, our Lord's legal father, who had evidently died before our Lord. And to these we may add not a few unnamed ones who believed on our Lord and had departed before His death.

Let it be realized that if these "believers" in Israel had lived on until after our Lord's death and resurrection they would, like the Apostles and the faithful among the Jews after Pentecost, have been brought into the Church, which is the body of Christ. In that case they would have waited in their graves and been among "the dead in Christ" who are to be raised at His Second Advent (see I Cor. XV, 51 to 53 and I Thess. IV, 13 to 17). But when they lived and died there was no Church of Jesus Christ, so they could not form a part of it. What then? Was their faith in Jesus as the Messiah to have no reward and must they be penalized, as it were, because they died before their fellow-members in the faithful remnant of Jews who lived on to

Pentecost and became a part of the Church? Not for a moment. Their faithfulness brought them a precious reward and it was these faithful ones, who died between our Lord's birth and His death, who were raised with Him, that is, at the end of the hour at the opening of which He Himself had been raised in a body of glory.

It is, therefore, clear that these "saints" who were raised about the same time as our Lord came in for a very favoured portion by becoming with Him a part of the "sheaf of the firstfruits" which meant for them being raised from their graves, clothed with their bodies of glory, at the opening of the Christian Dispensation, instead of at its close over nineteen centuries later.

It will, of course, be understood that the resurrection of these "saints", like that of any others, is the direct result of the Saviour's sacrificial death which had removed their sins from God's sight for ever.

The position of these raised "saints" was, therefore, entirely unique. We recommend those who desire to comprehend this matter more fully to study Leviticus XXIII, and take note of the following remarks related thereto.

We have seen that Christ risen and the saints raised after Him compose the Antitype of the "sheaf of the firstfruits" which had to be presented "on the morrow after the sabbath" – the day which is also "the first (day) of the sabbaths", that is, the seven Sabbaths or 49 days to the day of Pentecost. As all know, Christendom's Easter and Pentecost are derived from this type.

On the day of Pentecost, exactly seven weeks after the offering of "the sheaf of the firstfruits", the Israelite had to bring forth out of his dwelling "two wave loaves . . . baken with leaven" which were "the firstfruits unto the Lord" of the wheat harvest (verse 17 and Exodus XXXIV, 22). These "two loaves", which were offered on the day of Pentecost, form the official type of the Church, which is the body of Christ, which began its actual existence with the descent of the Holy Ghost on the day of Pentecost in A.D. 33. The "two wave loaves" represent the Jewish and Gentile members in regard to whom the Apostle Paul states in Ephesians II, "Christ Jesus . . . hath made both one . . . for through Him we both have access by one Spirit unto the Father" (verses 11 to 18).

The Jewish "wave loaf" is composed of every Jew that has become or will become a true believer in Christ between

Pentecost, A.D. 33, and the Second Appearing of our Lord. The Gentile "wave loaf" is composed of all true Gentile believers since Pentecost, A.D. 36, when the Holy Ghost first fell on the Gentiles, as recorded in Acts X and XI, and the Second Appearing of our Lord. At the Second Appearing of our Lord the whole body of Jewish and Gentile believers now departed will be raised from their graves and translated with all living believers to Heaven. When this takes place the whole type in Leviticus XXIII will have had its antitype. The Apostle Paul gives a perfect expression of this whole matter of the firstfruits in I Corinthians XV, 20 to 23. He says, "Now is Christ risen from the dead, and become the firstfruits of them that slept". This is a reference to our Lord and the saints raised with or just after Him who form the "sheaf of the firstfruits". Furthermore, they are "the first of the firstfruits" which, we are informed, have to be brought "unto the house of the Lord thy God" (Exodus XXXIV, 26). Later, the Apostle says "In Christ shall all be made alive. But every man in his own order: Christ the firstfruits; afterward they that are Christ's at His coming". The expression, "Christ the firstfruits", does not refer to our Lord Who is the Head, but to His body – the Church (see I Cor. XII, 12). The expression, "they that are Christ's at His coming", refers to the general resurrection (the main harvest as opposed to "the firstfruits") of the obedient in all ages at the Third Appearing of our Lord when He comes to reign.

So we have a complete picture of the three resurrections of believers in Christ since His birth. In our Lord's resurrection and those raised with Him we have "the first of the firstfruits". At our Lord's Second Appearing we have the Church – Jew and Gentile – called "Christ the firstfruits" raised from the dead. Finally, the main harvest, embracing the redeemed in all ages except our present one, defined as "they that are Christ's at His coming", that is, His coming to reign.

We trust this sets the resurrection of the faithful departed between our Lord's birth and death in the right perspective.

One point only remains for mention. On two occasions our Lord refers to this Dispensation as an "hour". In John IV, 23, we read that He said, "But the hour cometh, and now is, when the true worshippers shall worship the Father in spirit and in truth" (see also verse 21 and V, 25). Our Lord was not using a mere colloquialism when He three times referred to this Dispensation as an "hour". If the "saints" who were raised at the end of the hour, which began with the Midnight at which He was raised, are viewed, as they should be, as a type of the Church ("Christ the firstfruits") which is to be raised at the end of the age, then the hour between our Lord's resurrection and theirs is a type of this Dispensation, and accounts for our Lord's use of the term.

As forming a part with Christ of the "sheaf of the firstfruits" these saints would, of course, have ascended with Him at the ninth hour (8 to 9 A.M.) and been presented to God – a precious token of a great harvest yet to be gathered out of the earth as the result of our Lord's redemptive Sacrifice. It would seem probable that they remained with the risen Saviour during the Forty Days and that it was then that they "went into the holy city, and appeared unto many". If so, they would have ascended at the time our Lord did from Olivet. They would be the only group of human beings with glorified bodies in Heaven – a great and precious privilege.

# PART III

## THE DAY OF THE RESURRECTION OF OUR LORD JESUS CHRIST

---

### A RECORD OF EVENTS

---

### THE SCENE AT THE SEPULCHRE BETWEEN THE MIDNIGHT OF OUR LORD'S RESURRECTION AND THE HOUR OF 9–10 A.M.

---

### HIS ASCENSION TO PRESENT THE ANTITYPICAL "SHEAF OF THE FIRSTFRUITS" OF LEVITICUS XXIII, 9 TO 14

---

Read Matt. XXVIII, 1 to 10; Mark XVI, 1 to 8; Luke XXIV, 1 to 12; and John XX, 1 to 18

THE HOLY Scriptures, as we have shown, reveal that our blessed Redeemer and Lord rose from the dead exactly at the Midnight of Sunday, 3rd May A.D. 33, and that this was the opening moment of Monday, 4th May – the day called in the Gospels "the first (day) of the sabbaths", and not, as in our English Versions, "the first day of the week". As we have stated many times, this day, which was "Monday" in the Roman and Jewish Calendars, was "the morrow after the sabbath" or first day of the week in Divine Time – the day on which the "sheaf of the firstfruits" of the harvest had to be "waved before the Lord". It will be recalled that we pointed out that following the Jews' rejection of their Messiah, Whom they caused to be put to death, God commenced to use the Gentile day from Midnight to Midnight, because the Christian Dispensation was to be predominantly a Gentile era of blessing.

Our comments from henceforth will, therefore, be focused upon the events recorded in the Gospels that took place on this Monday, 4th May, which embraced the first 24 hours after our Lord rose from the dead and left the Sepulchre. In the eight hours between Midnight and 8 A.M. when He ascended to present the Antitypical "sheaf of the firstfruits" to God the Father, the Gospels record only one event concerning Him, namely, the meeting with Mary Magdalene, when He intervened to soothe her deep grief by revealing Himself to her, and this as a precious reward for her utter devotion to Himself.

It may, however, be assumed that as Moses and Elijah had come down from Heaven for the purpose of receiving Him back from the grave, holy converse, such as took place at His Transfiguration, was continued at His glorious resurrection; but, be that as it may, the prohibition which caused Him to forbid Mary Magdalene to touch Him, as did other women a little later, when they "held Him by the feet, and worshipped Him", operated to forbid Him from yet making any contact with mortals of the earth – the infinitely gracious exception with Mary affording but a proof of the rule. We shall return to this subject later, when commenting upon this incident.

It is not difficult to trace in the Four Gospels the exact order of events which took place in the early hours of this Monday morning with "the women", and with Peter and John, in their respective visits to the Sepulchre. We may be quite sure that as so much is written on the subject by the Four Evangelists, it is God's intention for His people to know exactly what took place and why it is recorded. To this end we have very carefully to compare Scripture with Scripture and, as we ourselves have found great help in having all the relevant passages from each Gospel before us in parallel columns, we will follow suit in these pages for the benefit of readers and in order to facilitate the exposition of the same. In doing this we shall take the liberty of omitting the utterly erroneous translation "the first day of the week" and in its place give the true rendering "the first (day) of the sabbaths".

## A HARMONY OF THE FOUR GOSPEL ACCOUNTS OF THE EARLY MORNING OF THE DAY OF OUR LORD'S RESURRECTION

| MATTHEW XXVII, 61 | MARK XV, 47 | LUKE XXIII, 55 | JOHN |
|---|---|---|---|
| And there was Mary Magdalene, and the other Mary, sitting over against the sepulchre. | And Mary Magdalene and Mary the mother of Joses beheld where He was laid. | And the women also, which came with Him from Galilee, followed after, and beheld the sepulchre, and how His body was laid. | |
| **MATTHEW XXVIII, 1 to 10** | **MARK XVI, 1 to 8** | **LUKE XXIV, 1 to 12** | **JOHN XX, 1 to 10** |
| (1) In the end of the sabbath, as it began to dawn toward the first (day) of the sabbaths, came Mary Magdalene and the other Mary to see the sepulchre. | (1) And when the sabbath was past, Mary Magdalene, and Mary the mother of James, and Salome, had bought sweet spices, that they might come and anoint Him. | (1) Now upon the first (day) of the sabbaths, very early in the morning, they came unto the sepulchre, bringing the spices which they had prepared, and certain others with them. | (1) The first (day) of the sabbaths cometh Mary Magdalene early, when it was yet dark, unto the sepulchre, and seeth the stone taken away from the sepulchre. |
| (2) And, behold, there was a great earthquake: for the angel of the Lord descended from heaven, and came and rolled back the stone from the door, and sat upon it. | (2) And very early in the morning the first (day) of the sabbaths, they came unto the sepulchre at the rising of the sun. | (2) And they found the stone rolled away from the sepulchre. | (2) Then she runneth, and cometh to Simon Peter, and to the other disciple, whom Jesus loved, and saith unto them, They have taken away the Lord out of the sepulchre, and we know not where they have laid Him. |

| | | | |
|---|---|---|---|
| (3) His countenance was like lightning, and his raiment white as snow: | (3) And they said among themselves, Who shall roll us away the stone from the door of the sepulchre? | (3) And they entered in, and found not the body of the Lord Jesus. | (3) Peter therefore went forth, and that other disciple, and came to the sepulchre. |
| (4) And for fear of him the keepers did shake, and became as dead men. | (4) And when they looked, they saw that the stone was rolled away: for it was very great. | (4) And it came to pass, as they were much perplexed thereabout, behold, two men stood by them in shining garments: | (4) So they ran both together: and the other disciple did outrun Peter, and came first to the sepulchre. |
| (5) And the angel answered and said unto the women, Fear not ye: for I know that ye seek Jesus, which was crucified. | (5) And entering into the sepulchre, they saw a young man sitting on the right side, clothed in a long white garment; and they were affrighted. | (5) And as they were afraid, and bowed down their faces to the earth, they said unto them, Why seek ye the living among the dead? | (5) And he stooping down, and looking in, saw the linen clothes lying; yet went he not in. |
| (6) He is not here: for He is risen, as He said. Come, see the place where the Lord lay. | (6) And he saith unto them, Be not affrighted: Ye seek Jesus of Nazareth, which was crucified: He is risen; He is not here: behold the place where they laid Him. | (6) He is not here, but is risen: remember how He spake unto you when He was yet in Galilee, | (6) Then cometh Simon Peter following him, and went into the sepulchre, and seeth the linen clothes lie, |
| (7) And go quickly, and tell His disciples that He is risen from the dead; and, behold, He goeth before you into Galilee; there shall ye see Him: lo, I have told you. | (7) But go your way, tell His disciples and Peter that He goeth before you into Galilee: there shall ye see Him, as He said unto you. | (7) Saying, The Son of man must be delivered into the hands of sinful men, and be crucified, and the third day rise again. | (7) And the napkin, that was about His head, not lying with the linen clothes, but wrapped together in a place by itself. |
| (8) And they departed quickly from the sepulchre with fear and great joy; and did run to bring His disciples word. | (8) And they went out quickly, and fled from the sepulchre; for they trembled and were amazed: neither said they anything to any man; for they were afraid. | (8) And they remembered His words. | (8) Then went in also that other disciple, which came first to the sepulchre, and he saw, and believed. |

(9) And as they went to tell His disciples, behold, Jesus met them, saying, All hail. And they came and held Him by the feet, and worshipped Him.

(10) Then said Jesus unto them, Be not afraid: go tell My brethren that they go into Galilee, and there shall they see Me.

(9) And returned from the sepulchre, and told all these things unto the eleven, and to all the rest.

(10) It was Mary Magdalene, and Joanna, and Mary the mother of James, and other women that were with them, which told these things unto the apostles.

(11) And their words seemed to them as idle tales, and they believed them not.

(12) Then arose Peter, and ran unto the sepulchre; and stooping down, he beheld the linen clothes laid by themselves, and departed, wondering in himself at that which was come to pass.

(9) For as yet they knew not the scripture, that He must rise again from the dead.

(10) Then the disciples went away again unto their own home.

Inexpressible sadness and gloom must have filled every heart among the disciples of Jesus from the moment that they saw His sacred and bruised body laid by loving hands in the rock-hewn sepulchre, after it had been "wound . . . in linen clothes with the spices, as the manner of the Jews is to bury" or entomb (John XIX, 40). This very action of Joseph and Nicodemus excluded the thought of resurrection except "at the last day"; as did also that of "the women" who had bought "spices and ointments" so "that they might come and anoint Him". Jesus was now to them the dead Messiah and with Him into death had gone every hope of Israel's redemption. One thing alone remained and that was the remembrance of Himself that lived in every heart; but their deep love for Him, certainly as far as "the women which came with Him from Galilee" were concerned, could only find expression in some tender ministration to His sacred body now lying lifeless in its silent grave. Perhaps with "the eleven" there was a nettled pride at the catastrophic collapse of all Kingdom hopes. Numbness and bewilderment and a sense of shocking unfaithfulness must have possessed all those who "forsook Him, and fled" when He was apprehended. The thought of the Saviour's resurrection, except in a far-off day, never seems to have had a place in the minds of any of our Lord's disciples – men or women. The bewildering circumstances probably upset any opportunity for quiet contemplation, otherwise the thoughts of "the eleven" would have turned to His oft-repeated declaration that after being killed He would rise again "the third day". Even the chief priests remembered hearing a report of what He had said about rising on the third day and had demanded a guard in consequence. Indeed, the absence of any thought of our Lord's resurrection as an immediate hope is proved by the fact that every action of the disciples was based upon the assumption that His death must be faced as a stern and awful reality. This being so, we can understand why they were so slow to give credence to the testimony of the Heavenly Visitants that Jesus was not in the sepulchre but was now risen (Luke XXIV, 11).

One quite obvious and very important query arises from the above Scriptures, namely, Why did Mary Magdalene and the other women come very early on this Monday morning to anoint the Saviour's body? They did not know that that Monday was viewed by God as "the first day of the sabbaths". Furthermore, they knew that the previous day – Sunday – was the Jews' "first (day) of the sabbaths". They knew nothing about the Moon ceasing in its normal revolution for two days or that the Saviour had died on the Sabbath in Divine reckoning. Why then did "the women" all come that Monday morning? Why did they not come on the Sunday morning? The expression, "they rested the sabbath day according to the commandment", has certainly induced the belief that they did come on Sunday morning, though there is nothing actually in the statement to warrant it. It is certain, however, that the Spirit of God Who caused Luke to write it, knew what its effect would be.

The answer is to be found in the reason which caused God to

appoint that our Lord should rise on "the third day" and be "in the heart of the earth" for "three days and three nights". Why did He not choose two days or four days? Because there was in Israel and the East generally an accepted and well-founded tradition that the final obsequies for a deceased person should not be performed until three days after death, because of the possibility that such a one might be only in a trance. There was also a Talmudic tradition that a person's spirit did not finally leave the body until the third day. Therefore, in electing that His beloved Son should rise "after three days" God took account of these traditions in order to remove any possibility of people saying that He had only been in a trance and that His alleged resurrection was a mere case of resuscitation. It will be appreciated by all that God had to exclude every possible avenue of attack on the actuality of our blessed Lord's death because of its mighty redemptive purpose and because otherwise the genuineness of His resurrection would be open to challenge.

This then is the answer to the question why "the women" came early on Monday morning with their "spices and ointments" to anoint our Lord's body. The third day after His burial began at 6 P.M. on Sunday and by coming "very early in the morning", even "when it was yet dark", on the Monday they would avoid publicity while accomplishing their sad but loving task. This Monday to them had no Biblical significance whatever and in coming then they were solely moved by the principle that the final act of embalming should not be performed until three days after death.

In this connection it is of deep and solemn interest to recall the words of our Lord when Mary of Bethany poured her precious ointment on His head at the supper table. He said to her critics, "she hath wrought a good work on Me . . . she is come aforehand to anoint My body to the burying" or embalming (Mark XIV, 6 to 8).

> "The women . . . beheld the sepulchre, and how His body was laid" (Luke XXIII, 55 and Mark XV, 47).

There are no redundant facts recorded in the Bible and in a matter such as we are now considering each one must be carefully noted if we wish to know *all* the Truth. The above-named

Scriptures and Matthew XXVIII, 1, reveal with what care Mary Magdalene and her fellow-companions from Galilee watched Joseph and Nicodemus as they placed the Sacred Body of the Saviour in the new rock-hewn sepulchre, just at the close of Friday at about 6 P.M. To Matthew, using Divine Time, that day was the Sabbath. The emphasis is on where and "how His body was laid". The importance of this we shall see as we proceed.

### MARY MAGDALENE ARRIVES AT THE SEPULCHRE "WHEN IT WAS YET DARK" (TIME ABOUT 5 A.M.). THE OTHER WOMEN, INCLUDING MARY THE MOTHER OF JAMES, SALOME AND JOANNA, ARRIVE "AT THE RISING OF THE SUN" (TIME ABOUT 5.30 A.M.)

It is self-evident from the various Scriptures given in the above Harmony that Mary Magdalene went on ahead of her companions, as John (XX, 1) states that she arrived at the Sepulchre "when it was yet dark"; whereas one group of her companions arrived, according to Mark, "at the rising of the sun" and another group, according to Luke, "very early in the morning". To avoid confusion, let it be noted that no actual mention of the time of the arrival of "the women" in Matthew XXVIII, 5, is given and that they are an entirely different company which, as we will show later, arrived about 8 – 9 A.M. We have, therefore, in the Gospels, four separate arrivals of women at the Sepulchre. Firstly, Mary Magdalene at about 5 A.M. (John XX); secondly, Mary the mother of James and Salome about 5.30 A.M. (Mark XVI); thirdly, an unnamed group of women, "which came with Him from Galilee", about 6 A.M. (Luke XXIV), and fourthly, the group of women referred to by Matthew.

Mary Magdalene on arrival at the Sepulchre "seeth the stone taken away". She at once realized that the Saviour's body was no longer in the Sepulchre. She had taken careful account of "how His body was laid" when it was brought into the Sepulchre, so she knew just where to look. She, however, noted nothing save that His body had gone, and this whether by friend or foe she knew not. What could she, a broken-hearted woman, do about it? Her mind travels at once to the two men who were closest to the Saviour – Peter and John – and her feet cannot carry her quickly enough as she runs to them to break the – to her – sad news, "They have taken away the Lord out of the sepulchre, and we know not where they have laid Him" (John XX, 2).

On hearing Mary's statement, with its implied earnest appeal for help, the two disciples are stirred to prompt action and both run to the Sepulchre in the manner described by John himself in Chapter XX, 3 to 5. Though in the meanwhile "Mary the mother of James and Salome" had arrived at the Sepulchre and had departed to bear their message to the other disciples, we will complete our comments on the visit of Peter and John first. We may mention in passing that Luke (XXIV, 12) only names Peter as running to the Sepulchre.

In John XX, 4 to 10, we have a first-hand account of exactly what transpired after Peter and John had arrived at the Sepulchre. The facts recorded in these verses are of the utmost importance because of their references to "the linen clothes" that had enwrapped the sacred body of the Saviour. The manner in which "the linen clothes" were left lying after He had emerged from them is of transcendent importance from two aspects.

John arrives first and sees "the linen clothes lying", but does not enter the Sepulchre. Peter then arrives and at once goes into the Sepulchre "and seeth the linen clothes lie, and the napkin, that was about His head, not lying with the linen clothes, but wrapped together in a place by itself". The record continues, "Then went in also that other disciple (i.e., John), which came first to the sepulchre, and *he saw, and believed*". What did he believe? It will be said, of course, he believed that Christ was risen. But we must note carefully, "he saw, and believed". What did he see that made him believe? He saw from the position in which "the linen clothes" were lying, laden as they were with "an hundred pound weight" of unguents, that the One raised had emerged from them without their having been disarranged an iota from their position when enwrapping His sacred body. In other words, John saw that our Lord's emergence from the heavily-laden grave-clothes was absolutely MIRACULOUS and in no sense a natural one. He saw that our Lord had not got up and removed them, or had them removed like Lazarus, but that He had disengaged Himself from them in such a way as to leave them lying undisturbed in precisely the same position as they were in when His body was enwrapped by them. By the use of exactly the same power our Lord, when risen, suddenly appeared to the eleven in a room with four walls and a shut door in the evening of the Resurrection day (Luke XXIV, 36). To suggest that One with such powers had to be "loosed" and "let go", like Lazarus had been, would be a slight upon His Deity.

Thus to John, and indeed to all the world, the position of "the linen clothes" was A CLEAR AND MANIFEST PROOF THAT JESUS HAD BEEN RAISED FROM THE DEAD. So John "saw, and believed"; and if Jesus had never again been seen on earth after He rose, the position of "the linen clothes" constituted for him an irrefragable proof that Christ had been miraculously "raised up from the dead by the glory of the Father" (Romans VI, 4).

John, inspired by the Holy Spirit, then makes this admission about Peter and himself, "for as yet they knew not the scripture, that He must rise again from the dead" (XX, 9). Had they known the Scriptures they would not have needed to "see" the evidence that Christ had been raised before believing. How applicable here are the Lord's words to Thomas, "Blessed are they that have not seen, and yet have believed" (XX, 29).

Peter and John then "went away again unto their own home". This statement was evidently caused to appear as a contrast to that which follows: "But Mary stood without at the sepulchre weeping". The disciples could await events in the comfort of their own home; but not so Mary whose heart was broken and who could find no comfort until she found the place to which her Lord's body had been removed, and then she would take it away. The deep, deep affection of these women who came with Him from Galilee stands out in bold relief against the desertion and cold unbelief of the disciples, none of whom apparently visited the Sepulchre except Peter and John, and this at the behest of the broken-hearted Mary who almost shamed them into action by her pronouncement that the Lord's body had been "taken away . . . out of the sepulchre". It is worthy of note that whereas the Heavenly Visitants – Moses and (or) Elijah – address three groups of women and later Mary Magdalene, they remain out of sight to the two disciples who could hardly have failed to recognize them, as they had done at the Transfiguration.

What a message John took back to our Lord's beloved Mother who, three days previously, had become a permanent and honoured guest in his house, by virtue of the simple words of command to him from the lips of the dying Saviour, "Behold thy mother". Not a word do we read about the reaction of Mary to the knowledge that her first-born Son had been raised from the dead, or that He ever again acknowledged the human link; but we may rest assured that more than any other she was filled with joy at hearing He was alive again. It is almost obvious that Mary was among "them that were with them" in "the upper room" when her risen Son appeared to "the eleven" on the evening of the resurrection (see Luke XXIV, 33).

## WHY "THE NAPKIN, THAT WAS ABOUT HIS HEAD" WAS "WRAPPED TOGETHER IN A PLACE BY ITSELF"
### John XX, 7

The relative positions of "the linen clothes" and "the napkin, that was about His head" are intended to convey a most precious and important fact to the people of God in this Dispensation or Church Age. We have learnt that the position of "the linen clothes" which were left lying just as they were when His body was enwrapped by them, affords a perfect proof that Jesus had been miraculously raised from the dead. That is one reason why our risen Lord did not disturb them or deal with them as He did with "the napkin, that was about His head". But there is another reason of even greater significance.

Our Lord's physical body with its sacred members forms a positive type of "the church, which is His (mystical) body". The Apostle Paul writes to the believers at Corinth thus – "Now ye are the body of Christ, and members in particular" (I Cor. XII, 12 and 27). Now if there is one certain fact about the members of Christ's mystical body, it is that they have not yet finished with death and the grave. To this very hour, and until our Lord's Second Appearing, every member of Christ's body who dies is buried in a grave as He was; and the bodies of myriads of such are now lying in the earth awaiting the moment when "the Lord Himself shall descend from heaven with a shout, with the voice of the archangel, and with the trump of God" for then, as the Scripture declares, "the dead in Christ shall rise first". Nothing, therefore, is more manifest than that Christ's mystical members have not finished with death as regards their bodies. For this reason our Lord left "the linen clothes" that had enwrapped His physical members lying as if they were still in use – it was a symbolical act with a most profound significance.

This becomes more apparent when we take account of the Lord's action in regard to "the napkin". John states what Peter had seen, namely, that "the napkin, that was about His head, (was) not lying with the linen clothes, but (was) wrapped together in a place by itself" (XX, 7). This act of the risen Saviour signified that He, as Head of the Body, the Church, had finished with death for ever and with all its trappings. When one has finished with a garment the natural thing is to wrap it up and put it away; and this is the exact meaning of our Lord's act in regard to "the napkin, that was about His head". Thus the whole scene in the Sepulchre after the Saviour had risen was as orderly as it was filled with significance for the Church and its every member.

Finally, the position of "the linen clothes", viewed as expressing symbolically the association of the members of Christ's mystical body – the Church – with death, carries with it the clear implication that the length of the session of the Head in death is a chronological type of the length of the session which His mystical members will remain in the sphere of death – a period corresponding to the length of the Christian Dispensation between our Lord's resurrection and the resurrection of the Church, which is His body, at His Second Appearing. Our Lord was in death for Two Days and Nine Hours but, as we have shown, He did not present Himself as "the firstfruits of them that slept" until the ninth hour (8 to 9 A.M.), so that between His death and His presentation the period was Two Days and Eighteen Hours. As we have shown in our former Treatise, *The World in Liquidation* (Paper V), the Two Days are a type of the 2,000 Bible Years from A.D. 33–36 to 1933–36. This type forms one of the many given in Holy Scripture to induce faithfulness in watching for Christ's return. It is not, however, a subject which can be presented in a few words and we only mention the matter because of its relation to "the linen clothes" which our Lord left lying as if to await the resurrection of His mystical body – the Church.

We must now take up the Narrative again and, having recorded Mary Magdalene's visit to the Sepulchre together with that of Peter and John, seek to trace in the Gospels the exact order of the visits of the three groups of women whose deep affection for our Lord impelled their steps thitherward so early on this "first (day) of the sabbaths".

## THE VISITS OF THE THREE GROUPS OF GALILEAN WOMEN TO THE SEPULCHRE BETWEEN SUNRISE AND 9 A.M. ON THE MORNING OF THE RESURRECTION

(I) Mark XVI, 1 to 8; (II) Luke XXIV, 1 to 9; (III) Matt. XXVIII, 1 to 10

It is not their faith but their devotion which marks these women disciples from Galilee as they concern themselves to do all that is humanly possible to express that devotion. If when alive it had been their exceeding privilege to minister of their substance to the Messiah, now that He was dead their only outlet was the Body in which He had tabernacled among them (Luke VIII, 3). To this they would minister by the purchase and application of costly unguents that they might embalm Him in a manner worthy of His position as their Messiah – His oft repeated promise that He would rise again "the third day" never having reached their understanding. So according to custom, when the third day from His death had arrived, these devoted women rise before daybreak to perform, as they think, their final act of devotion, and in small groups wend their way outside the city gates to the rock-hewn sepulchre in the garden near to Golgotha, where they had seen Him put to death on a Tree three days before.

It is not difficult to distinguish the three groups of women, as each group is addressed differently by the Heavenly Visitants who, as we now know, were Moses and Elijah. Furthermore, Mark refers to the first group to arrive, Luke to the second group and Matthew to the third.

## THE FIRST GROUP

We must first consider Mark XVI, 1 to 8. Mary Magdalene was evidently associated with Mary, the mother of James and Joses, and Salome in buying and preparing "sweet spices"; but as she had gone on ahead, evidently alone, and had returned after finding the Sepulchre empty to fetch Peter and John, Mary the mother of James and Salome must have arrived at the Sepulchre without her. This was "very early in the morning the first (day) of the sabbaths . . . at the rising of the sun", that is, about 5.30 A.M. Finding the stone which "was very great" already rolled away, they enter the Sepulchre. It was these two women who took fright when they saw "a young man sitting on the right side, clothed in a long white garment". This we know was either Moses or Elijah in heavenly garb. The "young man" addresses the women thus:

> "Be not affrighted: Ye seek Jesus of Nazareth, which was crucified: He is risen; He is not here: behold the place where they laid Him. But go your way, tell His disciples and Peter that He goeth before you into Galilee: there shall ye see Him, as He said unto you."

This was a truly glorious surprise and a commission of the highest possible order. First, the women are invited to "behold the place" where the body of Jesus had lain. This was that they might take account of the undisturbed position of the grave clothes and like John learn the truth they conveyed, namely, that Jesus had miraculously emerged from them and was now risen from the dead.

We have already shown that this "young man" had heard the Lord on the night of the betrayal say to His disciples that after rising He would go before them into Galilee. He, therefore, commissions the women to go and remind "His disciples and Peter" of what the Lord had said.

Mark records that the women "fled from the sepulchre; for they trembled and were amazed; neither said they any thing to any man; for they were afraid". No doubt they reported what they had seen and heard to the disciples but said nothing to anyone on the way. Mark's Gospel ends with this verse: for what reason we do not at present know.

(Whoever added the remaining verses of this chapter may

have recorded what he believed to be a true knowledge of events but *its accuracy is open to much question and it is certainly not inspired.* It appears to have been written after the notion prevailed that our Lord rose early on Sunday morning as verse 9 begins, "Now when (Jesus) was risen early the first (day) of the sabbath" (singular). In Mark XVI, 2, as in all other such quotations, the expression is "the first (day) of the sabbaths" (plural). The Bible reveals that our Lord rose at Midnight and not early in the morning. "The first day of the sabbath" is a meaningless statement, yet it is the only true translation of the received text of this addition to Mark's Gospel. Furthermore, in no other place in the New Testament is baptism made a condition for salvation as in verse 16.)

## THE SECOND GROUP

We will now consider Luke XXIV, 1 to 12. No names are attached to this company of women which is referred to in Chapter XXIII, 55, as "the women . . . which came with Him from Galilee". In XXIV, 1, we are told, "they came unto the sepulchre, bringing the spices which they had prepared, and certain (others) with them". This was "upon the first (day) of the sabbaths, very early in the morning". This must have been shortly after sunrise, between 5.30 and 6 A.M. Finding the stone rolled away "they entered in, and found not the body of the Lord Jesus". In their perplexity about this unexpected result to their efforts to embalm His body they find they are not alone in the sepulchre for "behold, two men stood by them in shining garments". They are filled with fear at the presence of these heavenly visitants and bow down before them with their faces to the earth. These "two men", as we have explained previously, were the same "two men", even Moses and Elijah, who had "appeared in glory" with our Lord on the Mountain during His Transfiguration and who were present at the opening of the last Forty Days and heard His pronouncement about His forthcoming death and that on "the third day" He would rise again (see Chapter XI). Of these facts the "two men" remind the women in the following terms (verses 5 to 8):

"Why seek ye the living among the dead? He is not here,

but is risen: remember how He spake unto you when He was yet in Galilee, saying, The Son of man must be delivered into the hands of sinful men, and be crucified, and the third day rise again.

"And they remembered His words."

(It was through understanding the real significance of these words of the "two men" to the women that we were led to see that they must have been Moses and Elijah.)

On hearing this statement which brought back to their minds what the Lord had said about His death and resurrection "when He was yet in Galilee", the women "returned from the sepulchre, and told all these things unto the eleven, and to all the rest".

The statement by Luke in verse 10 is of a general nature and does not specifically refer to "the women" in this second group. It mentions Mary Magdalene, Mary the mother of James (whom Matthew calls "the other Mary") and Joanna "the wife of Chusa, Herod's steward" (see Luke VIII, 3). Apparently the apostles and others to whom these women conveyed their news refused to believe what they heard and treated the subject "as idle tales". For the time their hearts appear to have been hardened by unbelief – an unbelief which only collapsed when the risen Lord appeared in Person and showed them His hands and His side.

Before commenting upon the third group of women who visited the Sepulchre, as recorded in Matthew XXVIII, we must make our comments upon the Appearing of the Risen Christ to Mary Magdalene which, for a very good reason, took place before He appeared to this third group of women as they left the Sepulchre about 9 to 10 A.M.

While the second group of women (those addressed by the "two men") were returning from the Sepulchre with their message, Peter and John arrived and made their investigation, as we have previously explained. This would have been between 6.30 and 7 A.M. Before they departed Mary Magdalene had returned to the Sepulchre without, so it appears, having met either of the other two groups of women from whom she might have learnt that the Lord was risen. Her meeting with our Lord must have taken place about 7 A.M.

## OUR LORD JESUS CHRIST AFTER HIS RESURRECTION APPEARS FIRST TO MARY MAGDALENE

Read John XX, 10 to 18

No woman has ever wept for a better reason than did Mary Magdalene as she stood "without, at the sepulchre weeping . . . where the body of Jesus had lain". Her tears, quite unrestrained, told out the deep devotion which lay in her heart for the One – Israel's Messiah – Who had set her free from a sevenfold possession by demons. It was, however, not alone what He had done for her but what He was in Himself that had won her heart and made her one of His most devoted disciples. She knew Him as the Shepherd of Israel and herself as one of His sheep for all eternity. His presence was Heaven itself to her emancipated being; but now He was gone and her heart was ravaged with inconsolable grief – a grief made more terrible by a certain lack of spiritual intelligence and a bewilderment caused by the suddenness of her bereavement of His presence.

One thought only possessed her, namely, What have they done with His body? Her love, so she thought, gave her some right to claim it as her own possession. Unmindful of all else, "as she wept, she stooped down and looked into the sepulchre". She knew exactly the position His body had occupied, for at the time of His burial she "beheld where He was laid". While in this posture she sees "two angels in white sitting, the one at the head, and the other at the feet, where the body of Jesus had lain". In answer to their gracious enquiry, "Woman, why weepest thou?" Mary, too prepossessed by her quest to be moved by their presence, replies with this vague imputation, "Because they (!) have taken away my Lord, and I know not where they have laid Him".

"Brought again from the dead, our Lord Jesus, that great Shepherd of the sheep", then drew near; and as He did so Mary intuitively "turned herself back, and saw Jesus standing, and knew not that it was Jesus" – her vision perhaps being blurred by her tears. The Saviour then uttered His first recorded words after rising from the dead. Not wishing at once to reveal Himself in order that His sorrowing disciple might unwittingly give expression to her devotion in His very presence, He, like the angels, enquires, "Woman, why weepest thou?" with the added personal touch, "Whom seekest thou?" The record then continues, "She, supposing Him to be the gardener, saith unto Him, Sir, if thou have borne Him hence, tell me where thou hast laid Him, and I will take Him away".

To this evidence of her deep devotion the risen Shepherd of Israel, Who "calleth His own sheep by name", responded by uttering the one word – "Mary". She, knowing full well Whose voice it was, instantly "turned herself" (no doubt as if now to face Him) and involuntarily exclaimed "RABBONI". What a fulfilling of the word, "I love them that love Me; and those that seek Me early shall find Me" (Prov. VIII, 17). And how true that "Weeping may endure for a night, but joy cometh in the morning" (Psalm XXX, 5). Mary's new-found joy must have far outweighed her deep sorrow when to her *first of all* the Lord revealed Himself after His resurrection. No one could receive a greater honour and no one was more worthy of it than Mary Magdalene or her name would not have found such prominence in the inspired Gospel records. Others might have knowledge or greater faith but none appear to have had such single-hearted devotion, yea, such selfless love for their Master Who both measured it and meted out the reward.

Our Lord's "Touch Me not" to the Magdalene may appear to be rather like an anti-climax to the scene we have just witnessed; but when understood it will be seen to add an infinitely precious touch to His act in thus solacing the deep grief of this devoted woman – one of many, judging from the number that visited the Sepulchre early on the morning of His Resurrection.

Many reasons have been advanced for the Lord's almost stern "Touch Me not" to Mary Magdalene, but the Scriptures only provide one reason and this is both simple and excludes all others.

We have stated many times that the Levitical "sheaf of the firstfruits" of the harvest in Israel constituted an official type of our Lord in resurrection. In I Corinthians XV, 20, we read, "But now is Christ risen from the dead, and become the firstfruits of them that slept". Now until this "sheaf of the firstfruits" had been waved "before the Lord" no one under any conditions whatsoever was permitted to partake of even one grain of the harvest. Hearken to God's ordinance on the subject in Leviticus XXIII, verse 14:

"And ye shall eat neither bread, nor parched corn, nor green ears, until the selfsame day that ye have brought an offering unto your God: it shall be a statute for ever throughout your generations in all your dwellings."

Such was the Law of God concerning the harvest and the offering of the typical "sheaf of the firstfruits". Obviously that Law operated in reference to Christ the Antitypical Sheaf – "the firstfruits of them that slept". Our Lord knew only too well that UNDER NO CONDITIONS WHATSOEVER could anyone in the universe partake of or worship Him – "the Firstborn from the dead" – until God the Father had had His portion. To effect this our Lord had to ascend to Heaven and present Himself to God as the Offering of the "firstfruits" of that vast harvest of human souls yet to be raised from the dead as the result of His own triumph over death. Until that had been accomplished "on the morrow after the sabbath", that is, between the hours of 8 and 9 A.M., on the morning of His resurrection, *no one under any conditions could touch Him or partake with Him of His glorious victory over death and the grave.*

It is when this is seen that our Lord's act towards Mary Magdalene is made to stand out as of wondrous grace. He, as it were, addressed her across this barrier in order that He might at once put an end to her sorrow; but more He could not do as nothing in the universe could induce Him to withhold from God His rightful portion which must be THE FIRST. After that was accomplished, all His own on earth might partake, and did do so; but not one "until the selfsame day" that He had ascended to present Himself as "the firstfruits of them that slept" unto God.

How easy of understanding then are His words to Mary, and yet how urgent the prohibition contained in the warning, "Touch Me not; for I am not yet ascended to My Father". The ascension to which He referred was the Antitype of the waving by the priest of "the sheaf of the firstfruits" before the Lord.

Could our Lord fail to keep the Law of His God in any detail? No, indeed. Therefore, under no conditions could Mary do what other women did an hour or two later when "they held

Him by the feet, and worshipped Him". And why not? Because in the meanwhile He had ascended to Heaven and there rendered to God His due portion, not merely because it was a fulfilling of the Law but because His heart was ever filled with perfect love toward His God and Father Whose glory in the earth He had come to restore.

Our Lord, unable therefore to do more than solace her grief at that time, sends Mary with one of the most meaningful messages in the whole Bible to His disciples. It is at once a perfect expression of the fruits of His own death and resurrection. Alone, as the true corn of wheat, He had fallen into the ground and died. His death was *for sin* and that He might remove the fearful barrier which kept man from His God. Now risen, all His own, and all who would yet own Him, may share the fruits of His triumph and know His Father and His God as their own – a deep but precious and eternal reality.

So the message Mary bears is "Go to My brethren, and say unto them, I ascend unto My Father and your Father; and to My God, and your God". How touching to note how our Lord can now refer to His disciples, with all their failure, as "My brethren". His own toil, suffering and death and the offering of Himself on our behalf to God has enabled Him to unite all who believe on Him into one Body, the Church – the members of which He now in infinite grace can own as "brethren".

We close our comments on this episode with the words of another concerning Mary Magdalene:

> "So, with the words still throbbing in her brain,
>   'Go, tell My brethren', Mary went her way,
> The gladdest of the glad that Easter morn
>   To find the Company and spread her joy."
>
> (*Lyra Christi*)

### THE THIRD GROUP

This group of women is referred to in Matthew XXVIII, 5 to 10. It is most important to understand that the women whom the angel addresses are not Mary Magdalene or the other Mary named in the first verse of this chapter, which refers to an event at the close of the day of our Lord's death, which Matthew, by using Divine time, calls the Sabbath. There is no indication in the Gospels as to who these women are who are referred to by Matthew. They were late-comers for on their way back from the Sepulchre "Jesus met them, saying, All hail! And they came and held Him by the feet, and worshipped Him" – *the very act He had forbidden Mary Magdalene to perform.* This proves that by this time our Lord had ascended and had performed His whole duty according to the Law, which meant that He was free to accept their worship. The hour when the "sheaf of the first-fruits" was waved before the Lord was 8 to 9 A.M. – the third hour in Jewish time and the ninth in Roman time (Acts II, 15 and X, 3 and 30). If these women of whom Matthew writes were met by the Lord between 9 and 10 A.M., they must have arrived at the Sepulchre between 8 and 9 A.M.

The angel, as the women thought him to be, addressed them in almost identical terms with those uttered by the "young man" in Mark XVI. Whether the angel was Moses or Elijah cannot be gleaned. We know it was one of them, as the speaker must have been present with the Lord and His disciples on the way to the Garden, seeing that he quotes what the Lord said at that time about going before into Galilee.

Perhaps, because the hour was already late, "the angel" commands them to "go quickly, and tell His disciples that He is risen from the dead; and, behold, He goeth before you into Galilee". The record continues, "And they departed quickly from the sepulchre with fear and great joy; and did run to bring His disciples word".

As they went the Lord met them, as we have just explained. This group of unnamed women had, therefore, the honour of being the first to worship the risen Son of God, Who confirms the angel's message with the words, "Go tell My brethren that they go into Galilee, and there shall they see Me".

The continual reference to Galilee is significant of the fact that our Lord after His resurrection had no intention of forming any links again with official Jewry. It was in Galilee among "the poor of the flock" that He had been received and thither would He go to renew His links with those who before His death had owned Him as their Messiah. He Himself had said "It cannot be that a prophet perish out of Jerusalem" (Luke XIII, 33).

Now the Holy City must be abandoned to its decreed judgment, "because", as He had said as He wept over it, "thou knewest not the time of thy visitation". On another occasion He said, "They shall fall by the edge of the sword, and shall be led away captive into all nations: and Jerusalem shall be trodden down of the Gentiles, until the times of the Gentiles be fulfilled" (Luke XXI, 24). Later we shall comment upon the post-resurrection Appearings of our Lord in Galilee whither He went after His second meeting with the eleven when Thomas was present.

This brings to a conclusion our comments on events between our Lord's Resurrection at the Midnight of Sunday/Monday, 3rd–4th May A.D. 33, and the hour of 9 to 10 A.M. when, having ascended to Heaven as "the Firstfruits of them that slept", He was greeted with worship by a company of "the women that followed Him from Galilee". Our next comments will cover events during the rest of the resurrection day which was "the first day of the sabbaths" and ended at Midnight after the Lord's first appearing to "the eleven . . . and them that were with them" (Luke XXIV, 33).

### THE THIRD APPEARING OF OUR LORD JESUS CHRIST ON THE DAY OF HIS RESURRECTION

---

### UNRECOGNIZED BY THEM, HE JOINS TWO DISCIPLES AS THEY JOURNEY FROM JERUSALEM TO EMMAUS – A DISTANCE OF SIXTY FURLONGS

---

### WHILE "AT MEAT" WITH THEM OUR LORD INSTITUTES "THE BREAKING OF BREAD" AS AN ORDINANCE FOR THE CHRISTIAN CHURCH. "HE WAS KNOWN OF THEM IN BREAKING OF BREAD"

---

### THESE TWO DISCIPLES ARE A TYPE OF THE CHURCH WHICH UNITES JEWS AND GENTILES IN ONE BODY

Read Luke XXIV, 13 to 35

The risen Saviour, having first revealed Himself to Mary Magdalene and in the second place to a group of women from

Galilee as they returned from visiting the empty Sepulchre, made a third Appearance by joining Himself to two disciples as they journeyed from Jerusalem to a village called Emmaus, which was threescore (60) furlongs distant. Apart from a reference in the unauthentic portion of Mark (XVI, 12), Luke alone records this event and this he does with much detail because of its importance, not merely in its historical setting but in its typical significance.

These two disciples, one of whom is named Cleopas, were not apostles but were ordinary folk attached to the company of the Apostles, like the faithful women "which were early at the sepulchre". They were serious men who were deeply moved by the manner of their Messiah's death and spoke together, as they walked, of their frustrated hopes. The record states, "And it came to pass, that, while they communed together and reasoned, Jesus Himself drew near, and went with them. But their eyes were holden that they should not know Him" (verses 15 and 16).

Sympathetically challenged by the unknown Stranger to give the reason for their sad demeanour, they express great astonishment that He should be ignorant of the "things" which were the cause of it. In replying to His question, "What things?" these two disciples answer, "Concerning Jesus of Nazareth, which was a Prophet mighty in deed and word before God and all the people". They then explain how He had been put to death through the action of "the chief priests and our rulers"; and following this they express what had been the hope of the faithful remnant which He had attached to Himself: "But we trusted that it had been He which should have redeemed Israel" (verses 19 to 21).

We learn from verses 22 to 24 that these two disciples had heard from "certain women" that the body of the Messiah was no longer in the Sepulchre and, furthermore, that they had seen a vision of angels there who declared the Messiah was alive. Verse 24 refers to the visit of Peter and John who confirm "the women's" story but "Him they saw not". It is quite clear that neither of these two disciples had made any contact with Mary Magdalene, or the other women who had seen our Lord. Perhaps, if they had received a direct testimony from those who had seen and spoken with the risen Christ, they would not have turned their backs on Jerusalem and gone to their home or homes at Emmaus, as Peter and John had done to theirs (John XX, 10).

Our Lord waited while His two disciples fully unburdened themselves before He exposed the fact that, had they known the Scriptures relating to the Messiah, they would have realized that all that had happened to Him was foretold therein. This our Lord sums up thus: "Ought not (the) Christ to have suffered these things, and to enter into His glory?" (verse 26). Then, in proof of this fact, "beginning at Moses and all the prophets, He expounded unto them in all the scriptures the things concerning Himself" (verse 27).

Nevertheless, the two disciples continued in ignorance of the identity of their Teacher, but more than ever their hearts were drawn to Him, and the contemplation of His parting from them made them urgent in their solicitations to Him to abide, for, said they, "it is toward evening, and the day is far spent". Yielding to their constraint, the risen Saviour enters their abode and accepts of their humble hospitality, sitting down to "meat with them". The unknown Stranger could not, however, long remain Guest because He was Lord of all and "the earth is the Lord's, and the fulness thereof", so assuming the place of Host, "He took bread, and blessed it, and brake, and gave to them" (verse 30). This act, so familiar to them, quickly revealed the identity of the Stranger, "and their eyes were opened, and they knew Him". Leaving the two disciples to finish their meal without Him, "He vanished out of their sight". Then "they said one to another, Did not our heart burn within us, while He talked with us by the way, and while He opened to us the scriptures?" (verse 32.)

No wonder, having themselves been for so long in the actual company of the risen Christ, they felt the strong desire to hasten back to Jerusalem to spread the good tidings and tell all the company "what things were done in the way, and how He was known of them in breaking of bread". But the company had already heard from the Apostle Peter of his meeting with our Lord and so, before they can rehearse the wonderful events of the afternoon they are told that "the Lord is risen indeed, and hath appeared to Simon" (verse 34).

But of all the Appearances of the risen Christ to His own, none were so highly favoured as these two disciples who enjoyed His company on the Emmaus road and who received from Him such personal and direct instruction from the Scriptures, not to mention His entering the home to accept of their hospitality.

Two features of this wondrous Appearing of the risen Saviour demand our most serious attention. The first is the significance of our Lord's act in "breaking bread"; and the second is the typical significance of the whole episode in relation to the end of the age.

### OUR LORD INSTITUTES "THE BREAKING OF BREAD" AS AN ORDINANCE OF THE CHRISTIAN CHURCH

We are told that "as He sat at meat with them, He took bread (i.e., the loaf), and blessed it, and brake, and gave to them" (verse 30). This action of the risen Christ was evidently one of the main objects of this whole episode. In commenting later on the typical significance of our Lord's meeting with these two disciples, we shall show that together they typify the Church of Christ – Jew and Gentile. This being so, we must realize that our Lord's act in breaking bread with them was an official one, by which we mean that He intended thereby to make "the breaking of bread" one of the ordinances of the Christian Church.

At the opening of the day of His death, when "in a figure" He had died as the true Paschal Lamb at the last Passover, He instituted as the Memorial of His death that which is called "the Lord's Supper" – with "the bread" as a symbol of His body given for us and with "the wine" as a symbol of His blood shed for the remission of our sins. This Memorial Supper was to take the place of the Passover which He set aside until the Kingdom, and which, as we have previously sought to show, was, like the Passover, to be a yearly celebration on the anniversary of "the same night in which He was betrayed" (I Cor. XI, 23). (See our previous remarks on the Lord's Supper in Chapter XV – Part I.)

Now on the day of His resurrection He institutes another ordinance which is wholly in keeping with the occasion, namely, "the breaking of bread". This, like the Memorial Supper, was to form part of a communal meal or fellowship gathering, Christ being in the midst, in fulfilment of His promise in Matthew XVIII, 20: "Where two or three are gathered together in My Name, there am I in the midst of them" – a promise never more literally fulfilled than at Emmaus when the Lord instituted this ordinance. The bread or loaf which the risen Saviour blessed and brake at Emmaus was not a type of His body given in sacrifice for us, as at the Lord's Supper, but a type of Himself now risen as the food and sustenance of His members – the antitype of "the bread of the firstfruits" or of "the old corn of the land", as partaken of by Israel after crossing the Jordan (II Kings IV, 42 and Joshua, V, 11). This "breaking of bread" at Emmaus expressed symbolically what our Lord had been doing on the journey thitherward with the two disciples, when "He expounded unto them in all the scriptures the things CONCERNING HIMSELF" (verse 27). This was food for their souls. Is there even a hint that wine formed a part of this first celebration of His resurrection? Not a syllable. To suggest that this "breaking of bread" with the risen Christ was the Lord's Supper, which is the memorial of His death, is a pathetic expression of how far people are prepared to go to make Holy Scripture appear to support the ill-founded tradition that the Lord's Supper and the Breaking of Bread are but one ordinance.

We say again that our blessed Lord, now risen, *officially instituted* the ordinance of "the breaking of bread" when He sat down to meat with these two disciples, who typify the Christian Church; and this at a place away from Jerusalem because the Church is not a Jewish body but a world-wide Organism mainly composed of Gentiles.

This is perfectly confirmed by the way this ordinance of "the breaking of bread" is put into practice at once by the Apostles. In Acts II, 42 to 47, which refers to the period immediately after Pentecost, we read: "They continued stedfastly in the apostles' doctrine and fellowship, and in *breaking of bread*, and in prayers . . . continuing daily with one accord in the temple and *breaking bread* from house to house (lit. at home), did eat their meat with gladness and singleness of heart, praising God, and having favour with all the people". This latter expression is no doubt inserted to show that the "breaking of bread" after Pentecost formed part of the communal meals which were held daily by the Church. No restriction of any kind existed as to how often believers might meet to break bread together. These occasions were termed "love-feasts" because they exhibited the love of those present for one another and for Christ.

In Acts XX, 7 to 12, we read how the Church at Troas with the Apostle Paul and his company present actually met on "the first (day) of the sabbaths" to *break bread* at Midnight in celebration of the Lord's resurrection at that hour and this on its solar anniversary in A.D. 59. Christians all over the world can testify that gatherings, where a meal is taken together with the object of fellowship and worship, have often proved the most fruitful and blessed form of service. May we, therefore, again learn the blessedness of keeping the ordinance of "the breaking of bread", as instituted by the risen Christ at Emmaus on the day of His resurrection.

## THE TYPICAL SIGNIFICANCE OF THE EMMAUS APPEARING OF THE RISEN CHRIST

We have already pointed out that the two disciples, only one of whom is named, form a type of the Church, which is the body of Christ. In exactly the same setting the two disciples of John, only one of whom is named, who followed Jesus and "abode with Him that day", are a type of the Church (John I, 35 to 39). As we pointed out in the appropriate section (Chapter IV, Part III), John's Gospel views our Lord as having died and risen before He goes forth in public ministry as the Dispenser of eternal life, and "that day" was, therefore, symbolically the day of His resurrection.

The fact of only one disciple being named in each of these instances is to emphasize the unity of the Church. In Ephesians II, 16, we read (of Jews and Gentiles), "that He might reconcile both unto God in *one body* by the cross". If two names had been given in either case the type would have been marred or remained unrecognized.

It must be remembered that the Church came into being as the result of our Lord's death and resurrection, and in the eye of God it is seen complete and perfect from the day and hour when He rose up out of death. This is the objective view to which living expression is given in a typical way by these two disciples being brought into association with our Lord on the day of His resurrection.

The key to the typology of the Emmaus incident is the distance from Jerusalem, namely, threescore or sixty furlongs. This is a chronological type of the Six Thousand Years from Adam to the Second Advent of Christ, when He comes as Bridegroom to take the Church, which is His Bride, to His Father's House, in which is the "place" He went away to prepare for her (John XIV, 1 to 3). In a chronological type there is always numerical affinity with the antitype. Thus, 60 may be a type of 600 or 6,000 – in this case the latter is the antitype.

As we have demonstrated in *The World in Liquidation*, the Bible divides human history into three periods of 2,000 Bible years, or 6,000 years in all. The first 2,000 elapsed between Adam and Abraham; the second 2,000 between Abraham and the death of Christ in A.D. 33; and the third 2,000 between A.D. 33 and 1933, when on 12 June in the latter year both the 6,000 years from Adam and the 2,000 years of the Christian Dispensation terminated to the day and hour. These most vital facts we have irrefutably established from the Holy Scriptures and set forth the proof thereof in full.

As our Lord did not come into the world until about the close of the second 2,000 years, we may assume that He joined the two disciples on the Emmaus Road after they had travelled about 40 furlongs – the last 20 furlongs being a type of the 2,000 years, A.D. 33 to 1933. The length of the Christian Dispensation is always given in the Bible as 2,000 Bible years.

It was while they covered these 20 furlongs that the Lord, "beginning at Moses and all the prophets . . . expounded unto them in all the scriptures the things concerning Himself;" and this is precisely what He, by the Holy Spirit, has been doing for the Church ever since Pentecost, A.D. 33.

In the chronological type Emmaus was reached, therefore, in 1933 when the extra-dispensational period, spoken of by our Lord as "the consummation of the age" or "time of harvest" began (Matthew XIII, 24 to 30 and 36 to 43). This consummating era of the Church's earthly history which has now lasted 23 years will terminate with our Lord's Appearing "a second time" (Heb. IX, 28). But before this the antitype of our Lord's unveiling of Himself to the two disciples "in the breaking of bread" must take place; and this clearly speaks of His revealing Himself in an exceptional way to the Church which is His body through the Scriptures – "the breaking of bread" at Emmaus thus having its true spiritual fulfilment.

It is to be noted that our Lord gave to the two disciples, not a general exposition of the Scriptures, but a selection of those particular parts which were directly "concerning Himself". What these disciples lacked was the understanding of the Scriptures which related to the Messiah's sufferings, rejection, death and resurrection as a prelude to His glory and manifestation in power. Coming at the end of the typical 60 furlongs, our Lord's action on this occasion is really prophetic of another such intervention at the close of the 6,000 years when also the Christian Dispensation would end. This would not be in relation to the interpretation of the Scriptures generally, for this would be quite unnecessary, but as to those parts, specially in the Gospels, which relate to Himself and His personal pathway here on earth, and which have remained concealed since the Apostles departed because of the apostasy which set in so soon thereafter.

It is at any rate a fact that in the year 1933, when the 6,000 years ended, our Lord commenced, under circumstances fully narrated in our former Treatise – *The World in Liquidation* – to give understanding of the Scriptures in the things which concern Himself to a few disciples (among whom were the authors of these pages) who for long had met as a "church in a house", believing it to be the only possible non-sectarian expression of the body of Christ (see Romans XVI, 5 and Philemon 2). This appeared to be an absolutely essential prerequisite, if our Lord was to grant new light upon the Scriptures in those parts which were "concerning Himself".

Leaving all other considerations aside, it is clear that if our Lord is to be known "in the breaking of bread" by the Church, as He was known to the two disciples at Emmaus, the Church will have to restore "the breaking of bread" to its rightful place as an ordinance instituted by the Lord on the day of His Resurrection and regularly practised by the Apostles and believers as such in the first century.

## THE RISEN SAVIOUR APPEARS TO SIMON PETER ALONE AND FORGIVES HIM FOR HIS THREEFOLD DENIAL OF HIS MASTER

When the two disciples returned from Emmaus, the first thing they heard on reaching the Company in the Upper Room was that "the Lord is risen indeed, and hath appeared to Simon" (Luke XXIV, 34). As these two disciples knew nothing of this Appearing, or indeed that the Risen One had appeared to either the Magdalene or "the women" as they returned from the Sepulchre, it must not be assumed that the Appearing to Peter was late in the day. There is no reason to doubt that our Lord's interview with Peter took place in the morning after He had met "the women" who worshipped Him and to whom He gave the message, "Go tell My brethren that they go into Galilee, and there shall they see Me" (Matt. XXVIII, 10).

The "young man" at the Sepulchre, of whom Mark writes (XVI, 5 to 7), tells "the women" to deliver his message to "His disciples and Peter"; and Peter must have received this message soon after he and John returned from the Sepulchre, having learnt of a certainty from the position of the "linen clothes" that the Saviour had been raised from the dead. It may be rightly inferred from the "young man's" message that Peter, after his fearful disowning of his Master with oaths and curses, had for the time forfeited, not only his leadership of the Apostles, but his actual discipleship (Matt. XXVI, 74). It could not be otherwise until the Lord forgave and restored him; and Peter must have known this. The "young man's" gracious message must, therefore, have quickened Peter's faith and given him the hope of being forgiven, even if not of being reinstated.

Our Lord would not have needlessly delayed making His Appearing to Peter, knowing what the state of his heart was. He had looked on Peter from the Judgment Hall and Peter had gone out to shed bitter tears when he realized that by his self-confidence he had made himself a victim of Satan's power and prowess.

It is clear that our Lord, with infinite grace, did not intend to meet Peter first in the company of others. He must meet him first alone. He Who had sustained the faith of His failing disciple by His prayers to the Father would now, in private loving converse, deal with the root-cause of Peter's downfall; and then restore him, and so heal the scars left in Peter's heart. Satan had done the sifting and the chaff in Peter's make-up had been exposed to all; but the wheat was there and the Saviour knew it; and He knew also that Satan had selected Peter as an object for his venom because He had appointed him to highest service. So in private our gracious risen Lord restored Peter to Himself, leaving for a later occasion his reinstatement in office before the company (see John XXI).

Paul, in I Corinthians XV, 5, places our Lord's Appearing to Cephas (i.e., Peter) as the first after His resurrection on "the third day", but this he does because he only names as witnesses of Christ's resurrection those calculated to impress doubters by virtue of their authoritative standing in the Church or, as in the case of the "five hundred brethren", the still existing collective testimony of a large proportion of those who had seen Him at one time. Nevertheless, Paul gives in the true order our Lord's Appearings to those he does mention, beginning with Peter and ending with himself on the Damascus road.

### OUR LORD JESUS CHRIST APPEARS ON THE EVENING OF HIS RESURRECTION TO THE COMPANY WHICH INCLUDED TEN APOSTLES

### HE GIVES AUTHORITATIVE EVIDENCE OF HIS RESURRECTION BY SHOWING TO ALL HIS HANDS AND HIS FEET

Read Luke XXIV, 36 to 48 and John XX, 19 to 23

Judging by the time it would have taken the two disciples to return to Jerusalem from Emmaus, some seven and a half miles, it must have been about 8 o'clock in the evening that our Lord appeared to the assembled company of His disciples in the Upper Room. It was as the two disciples were recounting to those present the events of the afternoon that "Jesus Himself stood in the midst of them, and saith unto them, Peace be unto you" (Luke XXIV, 36).

It was still "the first (day) of the sabbaths" because God had elected now to use the Gentile day which runs from Midnight to Midnight (John XX, 19). In our calendar it was Monday evening, 4th May A.D. 33, and in the Jews' calendar it was

Monday, Nisan 17th or, more accurately, Tuesday, Nisan 18th, as the new Jewish day had begun at 6 P.M.

It was this appearing of our blessed Lord in His body of glory in the midst of His own that finally dispelled the confusion and fears that beset them. John emphasizes the state all were in by saying that when Jesus appeared "the doors were shut where the disciples were assembled for fear of the Jews" (XX, 19). Until that moment the company had been like sheep without a shepherd, sheltering from a storm. But even when Jesus did appear and address them with the words, "Peace . . . unto you", we read that "they were affrighted, and supposed that they had seen a spirit" (Luke XXIV, 37). This shows that the testimonies of those who had both seen and spoken with the risen Saviour had had little effect upon the company in general which must have sadly discounted the reality of the things told them.

Perhaps the unexpected appearing of Jesus "in the midst" affected them, for He came through no door but unannounced was suddenly found standing among them. At Emmaus He had suddenly "vanished out of their sight" and now, with equal suddenness, "He stood in the midst".

Before proceeding, it may be of help to quote the words of another concerning our Lord's body after His resurrection:

> "The resurrection body of the Lord
> Was bound by no conditions save Himself.
> It was subservient to Him; and was used . . .
> As something in His power; an instrument
> Under His hands, that might be loosed at will
> From all restraints of matter; or, at will
> Conformed to them: a body knowable
> By human senses – hearing, vision, touch –
> Or hid from human ken, as He might choose,
> *And yet a real body.*"
>
> (*Lyra Christi* – A. E. Knight)

This Appearing of the risen Saviour to the Company soon developed into a most blessed reunion and with ineffable grace He quickly quieted all fears by using means to convince them that He was the same Jesus that they knew and loved though now, having passed through death and triumphed over it, He was clothed with a body of glory – a spiritual body – but, nevertheless a body formed, as before, of "flesh and bones". Let us hear His own gracious words as He stood in the midst:

"And He said unto them, Why are ye troubled? And why do thoughts arise in your hearts? Behold My hands and My feet, that it is I Myself: handle Me, and see; for a spirit hath not flesh and bones, as ye see Me have.

"And when He had thus spoken, He shewed them His hands and His feet." (Luke XXIV, 38 to 40)

Our Lord knew well that those present had no understanding of the resurrection of the body after death for He, after all, was the First One to be raised to die no more (Col. I, 18). He, therefore, sets their every fear at rest by giving them visible proof that the body He now dwelt in was the same body (though transfigured) as that which they had seen nailed by hands and feet to a Tree at the time of His expiry. To convince them of this He invites them not only to see the nail-prints in His hands and feet but actually to handle Him so that never again might they have a doubt that the One Who stood in their midst was the same Jesus of Nazareth as they had known from the beginning. And, as if to multiply proof by proof of this and to demonstrate His ability, though now glorified, to partake of food, He said unto them, "Have ye here any meat? And they gave Him a piece of a broiled fish, and of an honeycomb. And He took it, and did eat before them" (Luke XXIV, 41 to 43).

Now the hearts of all the company were at rest and filled with joyous wonder at having with them again the One Whom they so loved and had followed from Galilee. This accomplished, and the broken links of fellowship with His own perfectly repaired, our Lord proceeds to turn their thoughts to the Scriptures, just as a few hours before He had done with the two disciples on the Emmaus road. He was the Word Incarnate and, when with them, He had given them instruction in the Written Word concerning what would befall Him; but they had not understood because their minds were set on the Kingdom being restored to Israel at once. So again, with the Scriptures in hand, He leads their minds along the paths delineated therein concerning the events they had witnessed and concerning the future purposes of God in relation to them. He speaks thus:

"These are the words which I spake unto you, while I was

yet with you, that all things must be fulfilled, which were written in the law of Moses, and in the prophets, and in the psalms, concerning Me." (Luke XXIV, 44).

And, having opened "their understanding, that they might understand the Scriptures", He ends His dissertation by saying:

> "Thus it is written, and thus it behoved (the) Christ to suffer, and to rise from the dead the third day: and that repentance and remission of sins should be preached in His Name among all nations, beginning at Jerusalem."
>
> (Luke XXIV, 46, 47).

No doubt our Lord took His audience to Isaiah XLIX where His mission to Israel is viewed as having failed because of the nation's unbelief and unwillingness to accept a Messiah Who did not come with earthly pomp and glory; and where, as a result, He is presented as becoming "a light to the Gentiles", and God's "salvation unto the end of the earth" (verses 5 and 6).

By this means our Lord must have enlarged the scope of His Mission in the minds of this faithful remnant of the Jews so that they would see that by virtue of His atoning Sacrifice the Gospel could now be proclaimed "among all nations"; and the sphere to receive it first was to be Jerusalem, the very place where the Jews had caused Him to be put to death by the Gentiles, to whom they had been subject ever since they lost their Kingdom in 587 B.C. when Jerusalem fell to the armies of Nebuchadnezzar, King of Babylon.

It is not possible to say how many others were gathered with the ten Apostles in the Upper Room when the risen Saviour appeared. Luke refers to "them that were with them" (XXIV, 33). This would allow the thought that all "the women" which followed Him from Galilee were present and probably our Lord's mother and brethren, as in Acts I, 14, together with other disciples such as Cleopas and his associate from Emmaus.

We might say that the appearing of our Lord to this company of His Apostles and disciples was of an official nature in that He was at pains to render a final and conclusive testimony concerning His corporeal resurrection, so that future generations in His Church might possess evidence so irrefutable that it could only be gainsaid by wicked men whose object was to pervert the Gospel and destroy the precious hope of believers that they would in due season be raised, as our Lord was, with immortal bodies. In I Corinthians XV the Apostle Paul exposes the folly of those who say that our Lord Jesus Christ did not rise in a body by naming the Apostles and others who actually saw Him in His body after His resurrection. The Apostle Peter bears a like testimony in these words: "Him God raised up the third day, and shewed Him openly; not to all the people, but unto witnesses chosen before of God, even to us, who did eat and drink with Him after He rose from the dead" (Acts X, 40, 41).

## ADDED DETAILS FROM JOHN'S GOSPEL OF OUR LORD'S APPEARING IN THE EVENING OF THE DAY OF HIS RESURRECTION
(Chapter XX, verses 19 to 23)

The account of our Lord's Appearing on the evening of "the first (day) of the sabbaths", as given by the Apostle John contains facts omitted by Luke. In Luke we have what we might term the domestic scene, that is, our Lord being reunited with the Jewish remnant and giving at the same time positive evidence (to allay their doubts) that He had been raised from the dead in the same body, which did not see corruption while His spirit was absent from it, and which now had been transfigured into a body of glory. John confines himself to the bare fact of the Lord showing them "His hands and His side" and adds, "Then were the disciples glad, when they saw the Lord". Following this, our Lord again declares, "Peace (be) unto you" – a salutation which was full of the deepest meaning in that by his death and resurrection our Lord had overthrown, *for those who believe on Him*, every element in the Universe which could disturb their peace. Man was now reconciled to God and being justified by faith was at peace with God over the question of his sins, all enmity having been removed.

It is manifest that John views this assembly of our Lord's disciples gathered in the Upper Room (as no doubt they were) as the prototype or first expression of the Church, which is the body of Christ. It is, indeed, a glorious thought that on this very day that the Saviour rose triumphant over sin, death and the grave, He should gather around Himself a company of those Jewish disciples who presently would be merged into the mainly Gentile body of Christ but who, as so gathered together, formed in themselves a true Assembly in the New Testament sense (Matt. XVIII, 20). In another aspect this gathering of Jewish believers was the Church in embryo – an embryo that would be brought to the birth Fifty Days later, on the Day of Pentecost, by the descent of the Holy Spirit, Who would then take up His official residence in their Company, to which Three Thousand souls would be added on one day – their Company forming the nucleus of the Church, which is the body of Christ.

That this assembly of Apostles and believers was a prototype of those numerous assemblies which later would be found all over the earth, each of which would be an expression of the Church Universal, which is the body of Christ, is evidenced by our Lord's three acts on this occasion. We are told by John that He said, "As My Father hath sent Me, even so send I you" (XX, 21). This clearly was the granting of a Commission to His Church to continue and complete the Work He had been sent into the world to accomplish by His Father. What He had begun they must complete. Indeed, He had said at the Passover Supper, "He that believeth on Me, the works that I do shall he do also; and greater works than these shall he do; because I go unto My Father (XIV, 12).

This Commission could not be performed in the energy of the flesh or by the will of man. Before He Himself went forth to serve, the Baptist saw "the Spirit descending from heaven like a dove, and it abode upon Him" (John I, 32). So, following this Commission, "He breathed on them, and saith unto them, Receive ye (lit. take ye) the Holy Ghost". This act has been spoken of as a "pre-libation" of the Spirit and this it appears to be, for later, as Luke tells us, our Lord said, "And, behold, I send the promise of My Father upon you: but tarry ye in the city of Jerusalem, until ye be endued with power from on high" (XXIV, 49). The Son, now risen, could quicken whom He would, and that His disciples might enjoy the indwelling power of the Holy Ghost, while waiting the fifty days to Pentecost, our Lord imparted this Gift to them. Indeed, they could not form a prototype of the Church without being indwelt by the Spirit.

Immediately after bestowing this Gift upon them, our Lord added, "Whose soever sins ye remit, they are remitted unto them; and whose soever sins ye retain, they are retained" (John XX, 23). This was to endow the company with Authority, as set forth by our Lord in Matthew XVIII, 15 to 18. This passage signifies that the Church, when indwelt and empowered by the Holy Ghost and acting under Christ, its Head, has disciplinary powers over its members when they sin. An example of this is the Apostle Paul's urging of the Church at Corinth to deal with an incestuous member whose sin must not be remitted until repentance is in evidence (I Corinth. V). It is important to note how our Lord in resurrection confirms His previous instruction to the Church on this subject, as recorded in Matthew XVIII. The Church may, under certain conditions, absolve a sinning member, but it has no power to grant absolution to sinners – that belongs to God alone.

## PART IV

## "AFTER EIGHT DAYS" OUR LORD AGAIN APPEARS TO THE DISCIPLES

### THE APOSTLE THOMAS IS NOW PRESENT

THE PURPOSE OF THIS MEETING WAS TO MARK WITH A SIGN THE CHRONOLOGICAL END OF THE GREAT MESSIANIC TIME PROPHECY OF THE SEVENTY WEEKS OR 490 YEARS OF DANIEL IX, 24

"Thomas . . . reach hither thy hand, and thrust it into My side"
"They shall look upon Me Whom they have pierced."

Read John XX, 24 to 29 and Zechariah XII, 10 to 14

THE INCIDENT of our Lord's interview with the Apostle Thomas at His second Appearing to the disciples, after a lapse of EIGHT DAYS, is of the utmost significance both chronologically and prophetically, as Thomas is a type of Israel, when that nation repents of its unbelief and acknowledges our Lord Jesus Christ as the Messiah – the Sent One of God. It is clear that Thomas's absence on the resurrection evening when our Lord appeared, and his presence "after eight days" when He again appeared, was ordained of God Who used Thomas's unbelief in order to bring out a most important fact about the great

Messianic Time Prophecy of Daniel IX, 24 to 27, which, for the time, had an abortive ending through Israel's unbelief.

In John XX, verses 24 and 25, we read as follows:

> "But Thomas, one of the twelve, called Didymus, was not with them when Jesus came. The other disciples therefore said unto him, We have seen the Lord. But he said unto them, Except I shall see in His hands the print of the nails, and put my finger into the print of the nails, and thrust my hand into His side, I will not believe."

Thomas's unbelief about our Lord's resurrection appears to have been far more deep-seated than that of any other disciple, and his headstrong faithless vow that he would not believe our Lord was risen on the testimony of anyone, but that he must personally both see and feel the wounds in the Saviour's body before believing He was alive again, was a display of sheer human wilfulness.

As we have many times stated, the day of our Lord's resurrection, that is, "the first (day) of the sabbaths", was in Roman time, Monday, 4th May A.D. 33, and in Jewish time, Monday, Nisan 17th. The first Appearing of our Lord to the Company (when Thomas was absent) was in the evening of that day between 8 P.M. and Midnight – Nisan 18th having begun at 6 P.M.

We read in John XX, 26:

> "And after eight days again His disciples were within, and Thomas with them: then came Jesus, the doors being shut, and stood in the midst, and said, 'Peace be unto you'."

This wording is clearly intended to convey the simple fact that "after eight days" the events of the resurrection evening were repeated by the Appearing of the Lord with the same salutation of "Peace", but with the one difference that this time Thomas was present.

It is quite obvious, therefore, that if we wish to ascertain the date of our Lord's meeting with the disciples and Thomas we must measure forward eight days from His first meeting with the disciples in the evening of the day of His resurrection. This was Monday evening, 4th May, and in Bible time (from 6 P.M.) the 18th of the 1st month (Nisan). "After eight days" must, therefore, have been Tuesday evening, 12th May and in Bible time (from 6 P.M.) the 26th of the 1st month.

As we have previously shown, the Lord rose, according to His own statement, "after three days" (Mark VIII, 31). This inclusive reckoning embraced all Friday, Saturday and Sunday to 6 P.M. Therefore "after three days" means the 4th day, which opened at 6 P.M. on Sunday. The resurrection was therefore, in this reckoning, six hours into the 4th day, as it took place at Midnight. On the same principle "after eight days" is an inclusive reckoning which begins at 6 P.M. on Monday, 4th May, and ends at 6 P.M. on Tuesday, 12th May, which is 8 complete Bible days. The meeting with Thomas was, therefore, in the evening "after" 6 P.M. on Tuesday, 12th May, when the 8 days ended and the 9th day began. In Bible terms this was from the opening of the 18th of the 1st month to the opening of the 26th of the same.

We are about to show that this meeting of our Lord with His disciples and Thomas took place in the evening of the 26th of the 1st month for a reason of the utmost importance. But before doing so may we say that people generally allege that our Lord, having risen early on a Sunday, met His disciples and Thomas the following Sunday in order to mark that day with a special seal of Divine authority. This is a most grievous error as, to start with, the Bible makes it manifest that our Lord did not rise on a Sunday at all; but even if He had done so, "after eight days" could not be other than the next Monday week as "*after* eight days" cannot be made to mean *on* the eighth day which is after seven days. Furthermore, the manifest teaching of the Apostles is that Christianity involves no keeping of "days" as all the Sacred Anniversaries, such as the Memorial Supper, the Resurrection and Pentecost, are based on the true solar year and these, because of its incommensurability, must occur on a different day of the week each succeeding year (see Gal. IV, 9, 10 and Col. II, 16).

We cannot do better than quote John XX, verses 27 to 29, as they give all that may be known of our Lord's interview with Thomas. The record runs thus:

> "Then saith He to Thomas, Reach hither thy finger, and behold My hands; and reach hither thy hand, and thrust it into My side: and be not faithless, but believing.
>
> "And Thomas answered and said unto Him, My Lord and My God.

"Jesus saith unto him, Thomas, because thou hast seen Me, thou hast believed: blessed are they that have not seen, and yet have believed."

Our Saviour, knowing all things, took Thomas at his word by inviting him to fulfil the conditions he had himself laid down before he would "believe". It was a humbling moment for Thomas when the Saviour said to him "be not faithless, but believing". His words, "blessed are they that have not seen, and yet have believed", may have a meaning for those in this Dispensation who believe in Christ while He is absent in Heaven, but primarily they refer to a remnant of the Jews who repent and believe on Christ before the nation as a whole does so when He comes to reign. Thomas, who typifies the nation in its obstinate unbelief, becomes at once a spontaneous worshipper with the ejaculation, "My Lord and my God".

It is to be noted that directly after this incident John continues thus, "And many other signs truly did Jesus in the presence of His disciples" (verse 30). This statement carries with it the obvious implication that the incident with Thomas was intended as a "sign". So we must briefly consider the event of which it was a "sign".

### THE SEVENTY WEEKS OR 490 YEARS, THE GREAT MESSIANIC TIME PROPHECY OF DANIEL IX, 24 TO 27, TERMINATES TO THE HOUR ON THE 26TH DAY OF THE 1ST MONTH (NISAN) IN A.D. 33, WHEN "AFTER EIGHT DAYS" OUR LORD APPEARED TO THE DISCIPLES AND REVEALED HIMSELF TO THOMAS

Read Daniel – Chapter IX, 24 to 27

It should be obvious to all that if Holy Scripture so carefully dates our Lord's second Appearing to His disciples, when Thomas was present, it must have been with the object of directing attention to the relationship between the event and the time of its occurrence.

The prophecy of the Seventy Weeks or Four Hundred and Ninety Years of Daniel IX, to which we have had to direct attention so often, must be regarded as the foundation stone of all Bible prophecy. It was given to Daniel, in response to his urgent prayers and fasting and relates in a preliminary sense to a literal seventy weeks or 490 days from the day of his prayer to the keeping of the Day of Atonement in 536 B.C. by a remnant of Daniel's people – the Jews – who had returned to the Holy City from Babylon, where for 70 years they had been in captivity. The occasion is described in Ezra III.

The wording of the prophecy was, however, such as to give it a far more extensive meaning than could relate to a mere 490 days. Mention in it was made of the coming of the Messiah after "seven weeks, and threescore and two weeks" from "the going forth of the commandment to restore and to build Jerusalem" – a reference to the return of Nehemiah under the command of Artaxerxes in 458 B.C. It at once becomes apparent that in its enlarged interpretation these literal weeks of seven days are typical of years and that from Nehemiah's return to Jerusalem "unto the Messiah" would be 483 years ($7 \times 7 = 49$ plus $7 \times 62 = 434$, or 483 in all).

Reference should be made to Part III of Chapter I of this Treatise where it will be seen that these 483 years ended in A.D. 26 with the proclamation of the Kingdom by John the Baptist; and that the subsequent "week" or seven years from A.D. 26 to 33 must have brought the antitypical Seventy Weeks or 490 years to a conclusion.

It is unnecessary to give an exposition of this prophecy on this occasion but it is well known by all who have studied its terms in verse 24 that at the end of these 490 years the Kingdom of the Messiah would come into being and "everlasting righteousness" be established in the earth. At some unnamed point of time in the last seven years the Messiah would be "cut off" and for the time the whole purport of the prophecy would fail. History has shown that since the Messiah was put to death the whole Christian Dispensation, now 1,923 years, has intervened and the prophecy has remained in abeyance. In verse 27 there is mention of another "week" or seven years. Why is this? There is no mention of 497 years but only of 490 years.

In our former Treatise *The World in Liquidation* we show in Paper IV (pages 302 to 305) that the Bible reveals the actual day that this prophecy of the 490 years began, that is, the actual date when Artaxerxes, King of Persia, gave Nehemiah a commandment to "restore and to build Jerusalem" (Nehemiah II).

We dare not delay to give the simple evidence but must confine ourselves to the assertion that it was at the opening of the 26th day of the 1st month in the year 458 B.C. – a date which corresponded with our 26th April. *It was also the first day of the 1st month of the Messianic year 3,733.* In regard to the accuracy of this date no one need have a single doubt and our authority for saying this is THE BIBLE. In actual fact the date of our Lord's action "after eight days", with its symbolical marking of the end of the Seventy Weeks or 490 years, is itself a proof of the accuracy of the starting date.

We have just shown that our Lord's interview with Thomas was in the opening hours of the 26th day of the 1st month (Nisan) in A.D. 33. Between the 26th of the 1st month in 458 B.C. and the 26th of the 1st month in A.D. 33 is exactly 490 YEARS. *Therefore our Lord must have deliberately determined that His interview with Thomas should take place at the exact point when the great Messianic Time Prophecy of the Seventy Weeks or 490 years terminated chronologically.* Why did He do this? The answer is, In order to show how the prophecy of the Seventy Weeks would end in a far-off day by the repentance and restoration of the nation of Israel of which Thomas, in his stiff-necked unbelief and subsequent confession of faith, is a perfect type. But, it will be said, the Seventy Weeks or 490 years ended with Thomas's restoration and forgiveness. Truly enough; but the Messianic Kingdom and "everlasting righteousness" were not established; therefore the prophecy must have failed. Yes, through the action of the Jewish rulers it did then fail of accomplishment, but God had foreseen that this might be, and had made His plans accordingly. The last "week" or seven years from A.D. 26 to 33, which is left blank in the prophecy and which witnessed the rejected testimonies of John the Baptist and of our Lord Jesus Christ, would be CANCELLED and the prophecy be held in abeyance while the Christian Dispensation ran its course, after which the cancelled "week" or seven years, A.D. 26 to 33, would again run its course. Consequently it is these seven years which form the period of the Book of the Revelation and which are divided into 1,260 days and 42 months in Chapter XI. Instead of years of undiluted grace, as in A.D. 26 to 33, these re-lived seven years would witness retributive judgments on all Jewish and Gentile rejectors of our

Lord Jesus Christ. At the end of them, however, Israel's promised restoration and forgiveness would take place and of this Thomas's unbelief and restoration was a symbol. The wonderful restoration of Joseph's brethren to himself, the account of which occupies the last twelve chapters of the Book of Genesis, is also a type in graphic detail of Israel's return to their Messiah.

In Zechariah XII, 10, we read, "And they shall look upon Me Whom they have pierced, and they shall mourn for Him, as one mourneth for his only son, and shall be in bitterness for Him".

The solar date of 12th May, on which our Lord's symbolical action in regard to Thomas took place, is of great interest since it was the anniversary of Israel's Exodus from Egypt in 1639 B.C. and also of the Fall of Jericho in 1599 B.C. at the end of 40 Solar years – the latter fact being of great significance since the seven days' siege of Jericho forms a brilliant type of the last "week" or seven years of the Seventy Weeks when it is re-lived. Rahab and her household typify the Gentiles which are to be brought into the Messianic Kingdom with Israel. (See Matt. XXV, 34 and Rev. VII, 9.)

With this we must conclude our comments on our Lord's second Appearing to the disciples after His resurrection when Thomas was present with them. All will appreciate the exceptional importance of the occasion and of how our Lord reserved it for a date which marked the chronological end of a prophecy which, apart from the Jews' unbelief, must have witnessed the inauguration of His Kingdom – an event which then had to be relegated to a far-off day until which the Jews would "be led away captive into all nations: and Jerusalem . . . be trodden down of the Gentiles, until the times of the Gentiles be fulfilled" (Luke XXI, 24).

# PART V

## OUR LORD JESUS CHRIST NEXT APPEARS TO SEVEN DISCIPLES IN GALILEE BY THE SEA OF TIBERIAS

THIS WAS ON THE MORNING OF MONDAY, 18TH MAY A.D. 33, 14 DAYS AFTER HIS RESURRECTION

---

HE PERFORMS THE EIGHTH SIGN-MIRACLE OF JOHN'S GOSPEL

---

THE SYMBOLICAL DRAUGHT OF 153 GREAT FISHES

---

A POST-RESURRECTION SIGN WHICH EMBRACES THE WHOLE CHRISTIAN DISPENSATION FROM PETER'S ENTRY INTO THE HOUSE OF CORNELIUS IN ACTS X TO OUR LORD'S RETURN

---

THE RISEN SAVIOUR PUBLICLY RESTORES PETER TO LEADERSHIP OF THE APOSTLES

---

A NOTE ON THE IMPORTANCE OF THE DATE OF 18TH MAY A.D. 33

---

OTHER APPEARINGS OF THE RISEN CHRIST IN GALILEE

Read John XXI, 1 to 14 and 15 to 25; Acts X and XI

In verse 14 of John XXI we read, "This is now the third time that Jesus shewed Himself to His disciples, after that He was risen from the dead". The first time was in the Upper Room on the evening of His resurrection (Monday, 4th May); the second time was in the same place "after eight days" when Thomas was present (Tuesday, 12th May). It is this "third" Appearing to the disciples by the Sea of Tiberias or Galilee which we are now to consider in some detail, because of its great dispensational significance.

It is quite clear that the disciples were guided to delay their return to Galilee until after Thomas had been restored to faith. This was in the evening of Tuesday, 12th May. No doubt on this occasion the Lord intimated to the disciples that He would now fulfil the promise, "I will go before you into Galilee". We must also remember that He had bestowed the Holy Ghost upon His disciples at His first meeting with them and that the presence in them of the Comforter would ensure their being Divinely guided, as they manifestly were, in the interval before Pentecost.

It is quite clear from certain facts, which we will give in a Note at the end of our comments on John XXI, that the fishing episode took place during the night of Sunday, 17th–18th May. This was the sixth day after the meeting with Thomas. The journey from Jerusalem to Capernaum would not have taken more than four days for men in their prime who had every reason to reach without delay the locality where their risen Lord had engaged to meet them. (Capernaum was about 85 miles from Jerusalem. Eleven hours travelling per day, at an average of 2 miles per hour, would complete the distance in 4 days.)

The fact that this was "the third time" our Lord met with His disciples places the occasion before His Appearing to the "five hundred brethren", which preceded the meeting with James and "all the apostles" to which Paul refers in I Corinthians XV, 6 and 7. It was indeed to be expected that our Lord would meet with His disciples as soon as they had reached Galilee, and that this would be on a date in keeping with the purpose of such a meeting.

It is well known that John only records eight of all the miracles performed by our Lord Jesus Christ and that the miraculous draught of fishes in John XXI is the eighth of these. Each of these miracles was a sign (Greek: SĒMEION), as may be inferred from the Revised Version translation of John II, 11, which reads, "This beginning of His signs did Jesus in Cana of Galilee, and manifested His glory". The perfection of Divine order is seen in the fact that the one sign our Lord performed after His resurrection was the EIGHTH, and "eight" is the number always associated in the Bible with resurrection. The Scriptures, indeed, contain the record of eight resurrections only, the last of these being that of Eutychus in Acts XX.

It is also generally known that the first sign in John's Gospel – the Wedding at Cana in Chapter II – and the eighth sign – the Fishing expedition of Peter and six companions in Chapter XXI – are complementary one to the other as each embraces the whole Christian Dispensation and each takes note of events at the beginning and the ending of the same. Furthermore,

"Nathaniel of Cana in Galilee", who was present at the Cana Wedding, was also with Peter in the fishing episode and is never elsewhere referred to by name after his call by our Lord in John I.

It is impossible to exaggerate the importance to all Christians of understanding the symbolical significance of every detail in this eighth Sign of John's Gospel. It is a demonstration of the mighty wisdom of God in using natural circumstances to illustrate or prefigure future events – in this case those which were going to mark the beginning and the ending of the Christian Dispensation.

The first fact to be noted is that Peter was accompanied by six other disciples. We read in verse 2, "There were together Simon Peter, and Thomas called Didymus, and Nathaniel of Cana in Galilee, and the sons of Zebedee, and two other of His disciples". We shall learn, as we proceed, that this number of disciples forms a key-factor in the interpretation of this Sign.

As the result of the night's effort these seven disciples did not haul on board a single fish, for as John, who was present, states, "And that night they caught nothing" (verse 3).

It is quite erroneous to suggest that Peter and his fellow-disciples were acting in self-will or attempting to return to their old trade because they engaged in this fishing effort. Far better is it to assume that they were guided by the indwelling Spirit of God in initiating circumstances which were to develop into this pre-ordained Eighth Sign. It is not improbable that the disciples were in need after the secession of Judas with the bag, and that the Spirit of God used this fact to induce Peter to propose a night's fishing which, if blessed of God, might replenish their empty purses. Our Lord did not ask them if they had caught fish, but if they had anything to eat.

We will quote the Scripture record for the sequel to this night of abortive fishing:

> "But when the morning was now come, Jesus stood on the shore: but the disciples knew not that it was Jesus. Then Jesus saith unto them, Children, have ye any meat? They answered Him, No.
>
> "And He said unto them, Cast the net on the right side of the ship, and ye shall find. They cast therefore, and now they were not able to draw it for the multitude of fishes" (verses 4, 5 and 6).

Like the two disciples on the Emmaus road, these seven "knew not that it was Jesus" Who told them to "cast the net on the right side of the ship". But when John – "that disciple whom Jesus loved" – saw the effect of obeying the Stranger's instructions in the form of a net full of so many fishes that they could not draw it up into the boat, he realized intuitively Who the Stranger was and said to Peter, "It is the Lord".

The record continues, "Now when Simon Peter heard that it was the Lord, he girt his fisher's coat unto him (for he was naked), and did cast himself into the sea". A natural but, in this case, a quite wrong assumption is that Peter did this in order to reach the Lord before the others. Peter was moved to do this for two very good reasons which we shall name in due course, but in passing we must remark that Peter, who had not yet been publicly restored after his fall – a fall which followed his boast of having an affection for our Lord superior to that of all others – would have been most unlikely to take a course which would have appeared to be a display of greater affection than that possessed by his fellow-disciples whom he left to bring the net to the shore.

Peter's act in putting on his "fisher's coat" is again symbolic and the fact that he was not wearing it indicates that he had given up fishing. Had not the Lord said at his call, "Follow Me, and I will make you fishers of men" (Matt. IV, 19)? Therefore, directly Peter knew it was the Lord, his conscience smote him and he at once donned the garment of his Divine calling. The fact that Peter was not wearing his "fisher's coat" and that during the night they "caught nothing" cannot be disconnected, as we shall see when we interpret the symbolism of the whole episode.

As every detail in the following verses has a symbolical significance we are obliged to quote them in full:

> "And the other disciples came in a little ship; (for they were not far from land, but as it were two hundred cubits,) dragging the net with fishes. As soon then as they were come to land, they saw a fire of coals there, and fish laid thereon, and bread. Jesus saith unto them, Bring of the fish which ye have now caught. Simon Peter went up, and drew the net to land full of great fishes, an hundred and fifty and three: and for all there were so many, yet was not the net broken" (verses 8 to 11).

The larger fishing vessel could not be brought to the land, so the six disciples transfer to a small boat, which would probably have been attached to the larger ship. The mention of the "two hundred cubits" is most significant and implies that that was the distance from the shore where the whole episode took place including Peter's casting himself into the sea. It is to be noted that it is our Lord Who instructs them to draw the net to land, even as it was He Who had given the word, "Cast the net on the right side of the ship, and ye shall find". It was Peter's right to do this and to count the haul of 153 fishes – a number, as we shall see later, of the utmost significance.

We must now turn to consider what this episode prefigures, as all will realize that the many details given need to be seen in their symbolical significance to be really appreciated.

## THE INTERPRETATION OF THE FISHING EPISODE

We have said that this is the Eighth Sign of John's Gospel. Of what is it a sign or a symbol, or what does it prefigure? In a nutshell, it forms a Divine prefigurement of the Christian Church, the mystical body of Christ, from Pentecost, A.D. 33, to our Lord's return with the Apostle Peter at the end of the age, after the last member has been "caught" in the Gospel net and the Church has been brought to fullness – a fact expressed symbolically by the number of fishes in the net, namely, 153.

This episode focuses our attention upon certain events at the beginning of the Church's history, and then jumps over the Christian era and does the same in regard to events at the end – a phase we are now in and one, therefore, which makes our subject literally one of present concern.

That part of the episode which leads up to Peter and his companions obeying our Lord's instruction, "Cast the net on the right side of the ship", covers the opening phase of the Church's history, namely, the period of exactly three years between the descent of the Holy Ghost upon the Jewish believers at Pentecost in A.D. 33, and His descent upon the Gentiles in the house of Cornelius at Pentecost in A.D. 36. There are three positive types of this interval of 3 years in the Bible of which the most simple is the three days of Israel's journey from the Red

Sea to Marah, where Moses casts a "tree" into the bitter waters – an obvious and precious type of Peter first preaching the Gospel of Christ to the Gentiles in the house of Cornelius at Pentecost in A.D. 36, as fully recorded in Acts X and XI. When it is remembered that "water" in the Bible is often used as a type of the Gentiles, we are not surprised to read that the Israelites "went three days in the wilderness, and found no water" (Exodus XV, 22 to 25). This statement expresses typically exactly what happened between Pentecost, A.D. 33, and Pentecost, A.D. 36, in that the Jewish Apostles or their adherents never made any effort to reach the Gentiles with the Gospel and consequently not one Gentile was converted in this interval. This state of things was in the eyes of the Lord a most serious offence and one which called loudly for His intervention. In the Upper Room on the evening of His resurrection He had told the assembled company that, as the result of His sufferings, death and resurrection, "repentance and remission of sins should be preached in His name among *all nations*, beginning at Jerusalem", and, said He, "Ye are witnesses of these things" (Luke XXIV, 46 to 48). Our Lord, following His rejection by the Jews, had become "a light to the Gentiles" and God's "salvation unto the end of the earth" (Isai. XLIX, 6). How solemn, therefore, that our Lord's Apostles should so utterly fail to carry out their Commission – a major responsibility falling upon Peter as the one who held the key of the door by which alone the Gentiles could enter the Kingdom of God.

This condition of things is manifested typically by the statement in the fishing episode, "And that night they caught nothing" – "that night" referring to the three years, A.D. 33 to 36. Now the prophet Jonah is a clear and positive type of this remnant of Jewish believers which included the Apostles, in that they, as he, refused to go to the Gentiles when commanded to do so by our Lord. The name "Jonah" means a "dove" and the dove is a type of the Holy Spirit. This Jewish remnant had already received the Holy Ghost Who was now waiting to descend upon the Gentiles, but could not do so until Peter used the "keys" of the Kingdom to preach to them the glorious tidings of eternal salvation and the remission of sins for all who believe on our Lord and Saviour Jesus Christ.

Like Jonah with those in the ship, this remnant of Jewish

disciples brought a storm of trouble down upon their own heads by delaying to obey our Lord's command to carry the Gospel to the Gentiles. It was the cause of a great storm of persecution arising against all converted Jews. In Acts VIII, I, we read, "And at that time there was a great persecution against the church which was at Jerusalem; and they were all scattered abroad throughout the regions of Judaea and Samaria, except the apostles". Then in Acts XI, 19, we read, "Now they which were scattered abroad . . . travelled as far as Phenice, and Cyprus, and Antioch, *preaching the word to none but unto the Jews only*".

These words contain a damning indictment of the Jewish believers who, led by the Apostles, allowed their Jewish prejudice to rule out for the time the clear command and deep desire of the risen Saviour to see Gentiles brought into His Kingdom.

As we show in detail in our former Treatise, the Christian Dispensation, or "the times of the Gentiles", began chronologically on 12th October A.D. 33, which was the end of the year of clemency to the Jewish nation named in Luke XIII, 8. Our Lord waited until four days before Pentecost in A.D. 36 before adopting extraordinary means to compel Peter to do his duty and carry the Gospel to the Gentiles. It has pleased God to give us a most comprehensive account of our Lord's actions in this matter and this occupies some 48 verses in Acts X and 18 verses in Acts XI which should be read with care.

In essence, Acts X, with its long account of how our Lord appeared first to Cornelius, the Roman Centurion, and then to Peter with a vision which contained this rebuke, "What God hath cleansed (i.e., the Gentiles), that call not thou common", we have the antitypical fulfilling of the word uttered by the risen Christ from the lake shore, "Cast the net on the right side of the ship, and ye shall find". In other words, this was our Lord telling Peter and the Jewish remnant in typical language to go to the Gentiles. In the Messianic Psalm (XLV) the Church, which is mainly a Gentile body is typified by the Queen of whom it is said, "Upon Thy right hand did stand the queen in gold of Ophir" (verse 9).

How amazing that Peter, who held the leadership of the Apostles, should have been found by our Lord at Joppa, the very place to which Jonah went to take ship that he might flee "from the presence of the Lord" (Jonah I, 3). Who cannot see the relationship of Jonah to this Jewish remnant led by Peter in their refusal to go to the Gentiles? The book of Jonah and John XXI, 1 to 14, are both typical of Acts X which, as we have shown, is an account of how our Lord induced Peter to do his duty, compelling him to go to the house of Cornelius, the Roman Centurion, and proclaim the Gospel so that upon believing Gentiles the Holy Ghost might descend, as He already had upon the Jewish disciples; and that thus the Church, which is His body, might be formed and Jew and Gentile be "reconciled . . . unto God in one body by the cross", and that "both (might) have access by one Spirit unto the Father" (Ephes. II, 11 to 18).

We said above that the number of Peter's companions on this fishing expedition formed a key-factor in its interpretation. In Acts XI, 12, Peter, in the course of his detailed account which he had to give to the Church at Jerusalem in explanation, when they "contended with him, saying, Thou wentest in to men uncircumcised, and didst eat with them", says, "The Spirit bade me go with them, nothing doubting. Moreover these six brethren accompanied me, and we entered into the man's (i.e., Cornelius') house". So in the typical fishing episode Peter took as his companions six fellow-disciples, and in the antitypical fulfilment he did precisely the same – a fact which blessedly seals the relationship between John XXI and Acts X.

How beautifully the thought of Peter and his six companions casting the net into the sea and gathering into it a haul of great fishes accords with the words of James, at the first great Church Conference, when he says, "Simeon (i.e., Peter) hath declared how God at the first did visit the Gentiles, *to take out of them a people for His Name*" (Acts XV, 14). The sea in the Bible is usually a symbol of the Gentile nations, that is, of all peoples other than the elect nation of Israel (Numbers XXIII, 9). The true Church of our Lord Jesus Christ is composed of people who have been "called out" from the "sea" of the nations to follow Christ, and the Greek word translated "Church" (EKKLESIA) means "that which is called out", and nothing else.

It is most important to notice that as soon as Peter had opened the door of the Kingdom for the Gentiles to enter, all the persecution of Jewish believers ceased for the time. In Acts IX, 31, which refers to a period which was after Paul's first visit to Jerusalem and his return to Tarsus in the year A.D. 37, we read, "Then had the churches rest throughout all Judaea and Galilee and Samaria, and were edified; and walking in the fear of the Lord, and in the comfort of the Holy Ghost, were multiplied". This was after Peter had figuratively "cast himself into the sea". This perfectly accords with Jonah's experience, for we read in Chapter I, 15, "So they took up Jonah, and cast him forth into the sea: and the sea ceased from her raging".

Another key-factor in the interpretation of John XXI is the "two hundred cubits" which was the distance from the shore where the haul of 153 fishes was made (verse 8). These 200 cubits typically accomplish a double purpose. In the first place, they typify the 2,000 years of the Christian Dispensation which throughout the Bible is designated as being of that duration. The "two thousand cubits" of Joshua III, 4, the "two days" in Samaria of John IV, the "two days" of Hosea VI, 2, and the "two pence" of Luke X, 35, are each types of the 2,000 Bible years of the Christian Dispensation which began on 12 October A.D. 33, with the martyrdom of Stephen and the cutting down of the useless "fig tree", typically the Jewish nation, referred to in Luke XIII, 6 to 9. We shall refer to the ending of these 2,000 Bible years when we give the second typical meaning of the 200 cubits. The dragging of the net by the six disciples over the two hundred cubits is a simple type of how the Gospel has been preached to the Gentiles down through the 2,000 Bible years of the Christian Dispensation, ever since Peter and his six companions first carried it to Cornelius and his household, and when first the Holy Ghost fell upon the Gentiles in A.D. 36 as He had fallen upon the Jewish disciples in A.D. 33. Obviously, Peter could not have remained in the little ship while it traversed the 200 cubits to the shore, as he was not going to remain on earth during the Dispensation. The six disciples who brought the net to the shore form a type of all the faithful down through the Christian era who have had part in dragging the Gospel net through the sea of the nations.

We must now answer the question, Why did Peter cast himself into the sea? To do this we must realize that Peter filled two roles when he went into the house of the Gentile Cornelius, which was the antitype of the fishing episode. In the first place, he represented the whole body of Jewish believers and was their leader; in the second place, he was appointed by our Lord to hold and use "the keys of the kingdom of heaven" which gave him the headship of the Apostolic administration. In a real sense it was Peter's net that was cast into the sea of the nations in the house of Cornelius and this gave him a right to be present when finally that net was drawn to the shore with the instruction of our Lord, "Bring of the fish which ye have now caught".

Peter, in the first instance, was caused to cast himself into the sea in order to express typically *the merging of the Jewish remnant of believers with the Gentile body*. Until Pentecost, A.D. 36, this Jewish remnant composed the Church; but once the Holy Ghost had fallen upon the Gentiles it became merged with the predominantly Gentile body of Christ. Jonah, cast into the sea, is simply another type of this Spirit-indwelt remnant of the Jews being merged with the Gentiles, and the "three days and three nights" of his session in the fish's belly is not only typical of our Lord's session in death but of the whole course of the Christian Dispensation – a subject which lies beyond the confines of our present deliberations. Nevertheless, it will be well to remember that our Lord said, "There shall no sign be given (to this evil and adulterous generation) . . . but the sign of the prophet Jonas" (Matt. XII, 39).

The second reason for which Peter cast himself into the sea was not only that the type forbad his being in the little ship for the typical 200 cubits, but that it required him to be present with our Lord when the little ship reached the shore and the net full of great fishes had to be drawn in. It was to Peter that our Lord had given the keys of the Kingdom and as it was he who first cast the net of the Gospel into the sea of the nations it must be he who draws up the net at the last. So when our Lord says, "Bring of the fish which ye have now caught", it was Peter who "went up, and drew the net to land full of great fishes"; even as presently, when our Lord returns, He will bring Peter with Him, so that he may receive the haul of Gentile believers composing the Church which have been gathered out of the nations ever since he first cast in the net in the house of the Gentile Cornelius at Pentecost, A.D. 36.

## THE SIGNIFICANCE OF THE NUMBER 153

There is a glorious significance attaching to the number 153. It represents typically the number of the elect who form the Church, which is the body and bride of Christ, when brought to fullness; or, as the Apostle Paul expresses it, when "the fulness of the Gentiles be come in" (Romans XI, 25). It should be a matter of solemn interest to all Christians that God should concern Himself to insert in the account of this typical fishing expedition a number with a mystical significance such as 153. It is common knowledge that if we set out in a perpendicular column all the numbers from 1 to 17, the total will add up to 153. This fact indicates how every believer in Christ, however insignificant, throughout succeeding generations forms a part of the total number which when reached brings in "the fulness of the Gentiles".

The number 153 is composed of 7 plus 10, multiplied by 9. The number "seven" in the Bible denotes what is spiritually perfect. The number "ten" denotes what is numerically perfect. So, "seven" and "ten" together express in this case a body of people whom God views as being spiritually and numerically perfect. The number "nine" in the Bible signifies finality, being the last of the digits. The word "AMEN" has a numerical value in the Greek of 99, and our Lord is said to have used it (i.e., "verily") 99 times. So in reality when God sees the Church at the time of our Lord's return, it will be stamped with the number 153 which signifies that as a body she has reached FINALITY, being SPIRITUALLY PERFECT and NUMERICALLY COMPLETE. The fact that the net did not break shows that every member of Christ's body, the Church, will be found in his or her place when our Lord appears to raise "the dead" and to translate those "which are alive and remain" to meet Him in the air (I Thess. IV, 13 to 18).

It is also a wonderful fact that the numerical value of the Greek word both for "fishes" (ICHTHUES) and "the net" (TO DIKTUON) in John XXI is 1224 which is exactly 8 times 153. As "8" is the number of resurrection, its combination with "153" indicates that when complete the Church will have a glorious resurrection. There are many other words or phrases in the Bible relating to believers which have the number 153 as a factor in their numerical value, but we have said enough to show why it pleased God to bring it into this portion of His Word.

### "AS IT WERE TWO HUNDRED CUBITS"
### (John XXI, 8)

We stated previously that the "two hundred cubits" of John XXI had a two-fold signification. We have already shown that they typify the 2,000 years of the Christian Dispensation – there being numerical affinity between two hundred and two thousand. We are now going to see that they also typify the last 200 days leading up to the termination of these 2,000 years.

As we explained previously, we are now in the very end phase of the typical fishing episode of John XXI; and we have solemn reason to believe that our Lord is about to return with the Apostle Peter to receive the completed Church, as typified by the 153 fishes in the net which Peter drew to shore and counted in the presence of the risen Saviour.

The 2,000 Bible years of the Christian Dispensation or "times of the Gentiles" officially began on 12th October A.D. 33. Without going into details we may say that these 2,000 Bible years are just 120 days less than 1,900 Solar years and that they came to an end on 12th June in the year 1933. As we have perfectly proved from the Scriptures (the facts are given in our former Treatise, *The World in Liquidation*) the 6,000 Years of man's sin and failure also ended by design of God on the same day of 12th June 1933. As God refuses to reckon time between the end of the 6,000 years and the beginning of the seventh thousand years, which is the Millennial Reign of Christ, the world must then have entered a chronological hiatus, or extra-dispensational period, on 12th June 1933. This period was named by our Lord, "the consummation of the age" (Matt. XIII, 39 and 40, R.V. Margin).

The fact that has to be borne in mind is that the Two Thousand Years of the Christian Dispensation began on 12th October, A.D. 33, and terminated chronologically on 12th June 1933. This is an irrefutable mathematical fact for which the Bible supplies the evidence. *That for 23 or 24 years since there has been a chronological hiatus which constitutes an extra-dispensational era does not affect the position.* The Two Thousand Years of the Christian Dispensation, as typified by the 200 cubits of John XXI, have officially ended.

In the Second Paper of *The World in Liquidation* we give an account of a Meeting we held in London on 25th November 1932, in which we announced that in 200 days, that is, on 12th June 1933, the nations of Christendom would be "cut off" and the Christian Dispensation be brought to an end. We cannot here go into details but this we must say, that no one could have been more clearly guided than we were in making this pronouncement to our fellow-Christians. Two features linked our action with John XXI. The first was that six male disciples of our Lord were responsible for calling the Meeting; and the second that exactly 153 persons attended it – a feature over which we had no control.

To our astonishment when 12th June 1933, the last of the 200 days, arrived, God had assembled the Governments of every nation under Heaven to London for the greatest World Conclave ever held in human history. Features connected with this world gathering made it perfectly clear that the nations of Christendom had been brought together by God in order that sentence of excision might be pronounced, as forewarned by the Apostle Paul when he wrote in the Roman Epistle as follows:

"I speak to you Gentiles, inasmuch as I am the apostle of the Gentiles . . . Be not highminded, but fear: . . . Behold therefore the goodness and severity of God: on them which fell (i.e., the Jews) severity; but toward thee, goodness, if thou continue in His goodness: *otherwise thou also shalt be cut off* "(Romans XI, 13 to 25). Neither could anything be more manifest than that God required us to give warning to Christendom of its forthcoming excision 200 days prior thereto.

We cannot add more on this occasion but from what we have said it should be clear that the 200 cubits of John XXI typified also the last 200 days of the 2,000 years of the Christian Dispensation which terminated chronologically with the excision of Christendom on 12th June 1933. (Full details of this whole matter may be found in Paper Two of *The World in Liquidation.*)

## THE SEVEN DISCIPLES HAVE BREAKFAST WITH THEIR RISEN LORD AND MASTER ON THE LAKE SHORE

It is not easy to define the typical significance of the wondrous provision made by our Lord for the comfort of His seven disciples. Certainly it was a practical expression of His love and miraculous power but this one, like all His actions, was clothed with a deeper meaning than appeared on the surface.

The record states, "Jesus saith unto them, Come and break your fast" (verse 12, R.V.). This we do know, that our Lord Jesus Christ stated on one occasion, when challenged because His disciples did not fast, "As long as they have the bridegroom with them, they cannot fast. But the days will come, when the bridegroom shall be taken away from them, and then shall they fast" (Mark II, 19 and 20). This would indicate that the occasion is typical of the time when our Lord, as the Bridegroom, has come back again to fetch His bride. How perfect, therefore, that He should at once invite these seven disciples, who so clearly typify or represent the whole Church, to come and "break their fast".

No doubt when our Lord returns to fetch His bride He will give to His Church "meat in due season" in preparation for her departure to meet Him "in the air"; and it may be this which is concealed in the words of Peter, in his First Epistle, "Hope to the end for the grace that is to be brought unto you at the revelation (i.e., unveiling) of Jesus Christ" (I, 13).

Whether in some mystical sense this breakfast on the lake shore with the risen Christ covers the years of this extra-dispensational era since 1933, it is not possible to say with certainty. In due course all will be made clear.

## OUR LORD PUBLICLY RESTORES PETER'S LEADERSHIP OF THE APOSTLES

"So when they had broken their fast" (verse 15, R.V.)

On the night of the Saviour's betrayal Peter had said, "Though all men shall be offended because of Thee, yet will I never be offended" (Matt. XXVI, 33). It was this boast of a superior affection that was Peter's undoing. When, therefore, the time had come for the risen Saviour to restore Peter to his leadership ("for the gifts and calling of God are without repentance"), He sternly reminds him of his former boast with the words, "Simon, son of Jonas, (dearly) lovest thou Me *more than these?*" It is well known that Peter, in his reply to our Lord's three questions, falls back on a Greek word which means "fond of", because, knowing now his own weakness, he dare not affirm that he deeply loved His Master.

A threefold denial demanded a threefold confirmation of affection to which our Lord responded with a threefold restoration of authority – "Feed My lambs", and twice, "Feed My sheep". This was all carried out in the presence of the six other disciples, in order that the fact might be conveyed to all that Peter had been freely forgiven and officially restored to his leadership and the possession of "the keys of the kingdom of heaven".

Following this the Saviour makes a most solemn intimation to Peter about his martyrdom. Peter had said, "Lord, I am ready to go with Thee, both into prison, and to death" (Luke XXII, 33). In effect, our Lord takes Peter at his word in "signifying by what death he should glorify God". Said the Saviour, "When thou shalt be old, thou shalt stretch forth thy hands", that is, in a vain appeal for help that is not forthcoming, "and another shall gird thee, and carry thee whither thou wouldest not" (verse 18). (Peter, according to several writers, was put to death on a stake outside Rome about A.D. 65.)

Peter, having been now restored publicly, feels free to ask our Lord about John's future – "What shall this man do?" In effect our Lord tells Peter that this is not his concern – "If I will that he tarry till I come, what is that to thee? Follow thou Me". We know from John himself that this statement led to the general belief that John would not die and, as so often, the intention of our Lord's words was completely lost. Why did our Lord make this statement about John? For the simple reason that He wished to convey the intimation that John's ministry – unlike Peter's and Paul's – would reach right up to the time when He would come again. The proof of this is to be found throughout John's Gospel in the eight signs, all of which either embrace the whole Christian Dispensation or else events at the end of it, like the raising of Lazarus, which typifies that which took place in 1948 when, exactly 4 "days" of a thousand years each from God's covenant with Abram and his seed, the State of Israel came into being. John's ministry, like Daniel's, was both prophetic and contained many time measurements indicative of the end of the age and the return of our Lord. In Daniel I, 21, we read, "And Daniel continued even unto the first year of King Cyrus" – a statement which is intended to convey the fact that Daniel's prophecies reach right down the ages to the return of Christ – the antitypical "Cyrus" of Isaiah XLV. That this statement does not directly refer to Cyrus, King of Persia, is proved by the statement in Daniel X, 1, that Daniel's last vision was given in that Cyrus' "third year".

At any rate nothing is more clear, as we have sought to show, than that Peter's fishing expedition, as recorded in John XXI, embraces the whole Christian Dispensation from Pentecost, A.D. 33, to the return of our Lord Jesus Christ from Heaven when, with Peter, He will be present here on earth to receive His Church, then spiritually perfect through the infinite merits of His own Sacrifice, and numerically complete through the faithful and mighty activities of the Holy Ghost Who gathered her out from the sea of the nations.

## A NOTE ON THE SIGNIFICANCE OF THE DATE OF MONDAY, 18TH MAY A.D. 33, WHEN THE EVENTS RECORDED IN JOHN XXI TOOK PLACE

"There is . . . a time to every purpose under the heaven" (Eccles. III, 1)

The date of Monday, 18th May, stands out vividly as that upon which our Lord Jesus Christ performed His only post-resurrection Miracle – the Eighth Sign of John's Gospel.

If reference is made to the Chart of the Five Calendars, it will be seen that Monday, 4th May – the day of our Lord's resurrection – was the *1st day of the 8th month* in the Years of the Messiah. If the solar month dates are followed down to Monday, 18th May, when the Fishing episode of John XXI took place, it will be seen that in the calendar based upon the Years of our Lord's Life from His Nativity, the date was again the *1st day of the 8th month* – our Lord's age, from 29th October, 1 B.C., being 33 Bible years and 208 days which is 7 months and 1 day. We need hardly remark on the significance of an event connected with the risen Saviour taking place on the first day of an 8th month, as the number "8" is indelibly associated with Him and is also the number in the Bible which denotes "resurrection".

The most remarkable feature is that 18th May A.D. 33, is the 1,671st anniversary of Israel's arrival at Marah on 18th May 1639 B.C. It was at Marah that Moses cast a tree into the bitter waters, an event which, as mentioned above, was a positive type of Peter's taking the Gospel to the Gentiles in the house of Cornelius – of which the casting of the net into the sea, as recorded in John XXI, is also a type. We thus see that, by design of God, both these types of the events recorded in Acts X were wrought on the same month date of 18th May in the solar or Gentile calendar. But that is not the only similitude because in each case these types were preceded by an event which took place on 12th May, the interval of six days being occupied with a journey – in the case of the Exodus, that from Rameses to Marah and in that of the seven disciples from Jerusalem to the Lake of Tiberias.

Another remarkable feature about 18th May A.D. 33, is that it is exactly 1,260 days from 5th December A.D. 29, when our Lord Jesus Christ turned the water into wine at the Cana Wedding. Thus there were exactly 1,260 days between the "beginning of His signs" in John II and the last of these, the eighth, in John XXI. Periods of 1,260 days appear frequently in the Scriptures and we could name several between events in the seven years, A.D. 26 to 33, but will confine ourselves to the mention of the one between the start of the Ministry of John the Baptist on 25th April A.D. 26, and 5th October A.D. 29, when our Lord was baptized of John in Jordan. In Revelation XI and XII there are two references to 1,260 day periods of time, the former being the length of the testimony of Moses and Elijah as God's Two Witnesses.

Every date in the pathway on earth of our Lord Jesus Christ was designed by God the Father with a purpose known to Him, and it is the privilege of His people to search these dates out and learn what their purpose is. We need to be careful that in our ignorance we do not lightly esteem that which God in His infinite wisdom and forethought has designed for the glory of His Son, our Lord Jesus Christ. The Bible contains a faultless chronology of human history and this we have been allowed to reproduce and set forth in our former Treatise. An instance of its accuracy may be seen in the date of Israel's arrival at Marah, and more especially in that of the Exodus of Israel from Egypt six days prior thereto on Friday, 12th May 1639 B.C. Possessing this knowledge, we were able to make the fact known that the new State of Israel rose in 1948 on the 3,586th anniversary of Israel's crossing of the Red Sea on the night of 14th to 15th May. On both occasions Egypt came in pursuit and was ignominiously overthrown.

## THE APPEARINGS OF THE RISEN CHRIST IN GALILEE

## HIS MEETING WITH "THE ELEVEN" IN A MOUNTAIN WHICH HE "HAD APPOINTED"

## THE COMMISSION TO TEACH ALL NATIONS RELATES TO THE MILLENNIAL KINGDOM

## WHY MATTHEW MAKES NO MENTION OF OUR LORD'S ASCENSION

No one can fail to be struck by the way our Lord Jesus Christ on the evening before His death informed His disciples that after He was risen He would go before them into Galilee (Matt. XXVI, 32). As we have already noted, "the angel" in Matthew and the "young man" in Mark each send messages through "the women" to remind the disciples of this which our Lord had said to them (Matt. XXVIII and Mark XVI). This can only mean that our Lord in resurrection purposed to renew His links with the many in Galilee who had received Him and believed the Gospel of the Kingdom which He had preached to them. Traditional Judaism had now done its worst and the Jews nationally would not see Him again until, as He told them, "ye shall say, Blessed is He that cometh in the name of the Lord" (Matt. XXIII, 39). This would not apply in Galilee where "the poor of the flock" had received Him as Messiah, that is, as Emmanuel (Zech. XI, 11). Here, Paul tells us, "He was seen of above five hundred brethren at once" (I Cor. XV, 6). All this was a yet further fulfilment of Isaiah's prophecy touching "Galilee of the nations" when he declared, "The people that walked in darkness have seen a great light . . . upon them hath the light shined" (IX, 1 and 2).

After our Lord's second meeting with the disciples in Jerusalem when Thomas was present, He must have gone before them into Galilee, as He had said. The disciples, as we show in our comments on John XXI, arrived at Lake Tiberias on 17th May. No doubt "the women that followed Him from Galilee" had already returned thither, having heard with such emphasis what the Lord had planned to do.

It appears from I Corinthians XV, 7, that after the meeting with over five hundred brethren, "He was seen of James" – "the Lord's brother" as Paul writes of him. There is something most pleasing about this statement because until after His death and resurrection John tells us "neither did His brethren believe in Him" (VII, 5). No doubt James on this occasion became a worshipper and entered into the fact that Jesus was not born in the way he and his brothers and sisters had been, but was "God . . . manifest in the flesh" and conceived by His Mother in her virginal state by the power of God. In Acts I we learn that "Mary the mother of Jesus, and . . . His brethren" were present in "the upper room" with the disciples awaiting "the promise of the Father", that is, the descent of the Holy Ghost at Pentecost. In Acts XV we read of James as the presiding Elder at the first great Church conference, and Paul links him with Peter and John as "pillars" of the Church (Gal. II, 9).

Paul also tells us that after the meeting with James our Lord was seen "of all the apostles" (I Cor. XV, 7). It is this meeting to which Matthew refers thus, "Then the eleven disciples went away into Galilee, into a mountain where Jesus had appointed them" (XXVIII, 16).

It was in Galilee that our Lord commissioned the Twelve Apostles in the terms set forth in Matthew X. Now He re-commissions them (or, rather their successors in a far-off day) with entirely different terms, as follows:

"And Jesus came and spake unto them, saying, All power

is given unto Me in heaven and in earth. Go ye therefore, and teach all nations, baptizing them in the name of the Father, and of the Son, and of the Holy Ghost: teaching them to observe all things whatsoever I have commanded you: and, lo, I am with you alway, even unto the end of the world (lit. age)."

The expression "teach all nations" means "disciple all nations" and is a different word from that used in the expression "teaching them to observe all things", etc. Our Lord makes no suggestion about preaching the Gospel so as to convert "nations", but of going to "teach" *already converted nations* "all things whatsoever I have commanded you". No Gospel statement has been more misconstrued than this. We must, therefore, be allowed to explain its meaning.

As all know, Matthew's Gospel is for the Jewish people – the one which presents Jesus as Messiah, the Son of David. As such it covers every phase of the Messiah's relationship with Israel, from John the Baptist's proclamation of the Kingdom to the Kingdom's establishment at "the end of the age" after our Lord's return to reign.

In Matthew X, verses 1 to 15, the immediate purpose of sending out the Twelve Apostles is covered and they are to go exclusively to "the lost sheep of the house of Israel". From verse 16 our Lord's words go beyond the mission of the Twelve. Thus in verse 23 He jumps right over the Christian Dispensation to the end of the last seven years of the age and declares "Ye shall not have gone over the cities of Israel, till the Son of Man be come". To understand this we have to turn to Matthew XXIV or Mark XIII where our Lord refers to these last seven years of the Apocalyptic era – the seven years which immediately precede His return as the Son of Man to take over the Government of the earth. During these seven years – exactly as during the seven years A.D. 26 to 33, when first John the Baptist and then our Lord and His Apostles were testifying – that which our Lord terms "this gospel of the kingdom" is to be "preached in all the world for a witness unto all nations". It is the Jewish disciples of our Lord, referred to in Revelation VII, 1 to 8, and converted after the Church, which is the body of Christ, has left the earth, who, like their forbears, will preach "the gospel of the kingdom" in all the world.

When our blessed Lord returns to reign He at once gathers "all nations" before "the throne of His glory" as described in Matthew XXV, 31 to 46. The "sheep" nations are those who believe the Gospel of the Kingdom and befriend the despised and persecuted Jewish disciples of Jesus – to do which is to accept the coming King. The "goat" nations are those which refuse these Jewish messengers and their message – to do which is to refuse the coming King.

In Revelation XXI, 23 and 24, we read of "the nations of them which are saved" and of "the kings of the earth" which have their part in the Kingdom, and these are the same as "the sheep" nations of Matthew XXV.

This brief and very condensed survey of the history of our Lord's dealings with Israel through the various phases of testimony by His disciples has been necessary in order to explain the actual purpose of His commission above quoted in Matthew XXVIII. The Bible is never to be added to, and when the time of the Kingdom comes there will appear Jewish disciples who through understanding the purpose of this commission will go forth to the converted and blessed nations of the earth and precisely instruct them, *not in the Law of Moses*, but as the risen Saviour said,

> "teaching them to observe all things whatsoever I have commanded you".

This statement, while it is very comprehensive, must in the first instance refer to our Lord's wondrous Kingdom discourse on Olivet which Matthew, alone of the Evangelists, records in full, the subject embracing three long chapters (V, VI and VII).. How certainly this shows that Matthew ever has the King Messiah and the Kingdom in view.

The peoples of all these saved nations will then be baptized, not in the Name of Jesus Christ as practised by the Apostles in this Dispensation (see Acts II, 38 and X, 48 R.V.), but "in the name of the Father, and of the Son, and of the Holy Ghost" which is exclusively the Kingdom formula for baptism – a Christian now being baptized into Jesus Christ, that is, "into His death" (Romans VI, 3).

So in Matthew we find no account of our Lord's Appearings to the disciples which had any typical or embryonic relationship to the Church, as Matthew totally ignores the interval of the

Christian Dispensation and is concerned solely with the Israel aspect of the Messianic testimony. Not only is Matthew silent as to the Ascension of our Lord into Heaven, but he ends his Gospel with the words of our Lord, "And, lo, I am with you alway, even unto the consummation of the age" (R.V. Margin).

# CHAPTER SEVENTEEN

## THE ASCENSION OF OUR LORD JESUS CHRIST INTO HEAVEN ON THE SABBATH, 13TH JUNE, A.D. 33

THE PATHWAY IN TIME OF JESUS OF NAZARETH, THE ETERNAL SON OF GOD, CLOSES WITH HIS RETURN TO HEAVEN FROM MOUNT OLIVET AFTER 33 BIBLE YEARS AND 233 DAYS IN THE WORLD

THE FORTY DAYS' RESURRECTION MINISTRY OF OUR LORD JESUS CHRIST HAVING BEGUN ON MONDAY, 4TH MAY, TERMINATES ON SATURDAY, 13TH JUNE A.D. 33, WITH HIS ASCENSION INTO HEAVEN

DISALLOWED OF MEN, AND REJECTED FROM THE EARTH HE HAD CREATED, OUR LORD, AS SON OF MAN, IS EXALTED TO GOD'S RIGHT HAND; THE HIGHEST PLACE IN THE UNIVERSE – "A PRIEST FOR EVER AFTER THE ORDER OF MELCHIZEDEK"

(Ps. CX, 4)

OUR LORD ASCENDS WHILE IN THE ACT OF BLESSING HIS ELEVEN APOSTLES

MOSES AND ELIJAH, THE "TWO MEN . . . IN WHITE APPAREL", ARE AGAIN PRESENT TO WITNESS OUR LORD'S ASCENSION. THEY ASSURE THE APOSTLES THAT HE WILL RETURN "IN LIKE MANNER" TO THAT OF HIS DEPARTURE JUST EFFECTED

Read Luke XXIV, 49 to 53; Acts I, 1 to 12, and Psalm CX, 1

OUR LORD Jesus Christ, in every sense of the word, belonged to Heaven. By His Incarnation He came from Heaven *into* this world to accomplish God's will in the Redemption of the human race. Before expiring on Calvary's Tree He had cried with a loud voice, "It is finished", in order to denote that the purpose of His coming into the world had been accomplished. Before His death He had made it clear to His disciples that He was going to leave the world. On the last evening He had said to them, "I came forth from the Father, and am come into the world: again, I leave the world, and go to the Father" (John XVI, 28).

Our Lord's Ascension into Heaven was a great historic Event affecting the whole Universe and its implications are so vast as to be beyond the limits of human expression. The Apostle Peter writes of it thus, "Jesus Christ: Who is gone into heaven, and is on the right hand of God; angels and authorities and powers being made subject unto Him" (I Peter III, 22).

Our Lord left Heaven as the Son of God and as such came into the world; but when He returned to Heaven at His Ascension He was not only the Son of God but also the Son of Man, as He said to Nicodemus, "No man hath ascended up to heaven, but He that came down from heaven, even the Son of Man which is in heaven" – a statement made in anticipation of His Ascension but which, being in the present tense, also expressed the fact that John's Gospel was a foreshadowing of this Dispensation when the Son of Man is in Heaven (John III, 13).

It is a truth worthy of all acceptation that He Who was a Babe in the manger at Bethlehem, even Jesus of Nazareth, the firstborn Son of the Virgin Mary, after His Ascension into Heaven was exalted to the right hand of God, from whence He is now administering the Universe on God's behalf, pending His return to reign over the earth as KING OF KINGS, AND LORD OF LORDS (Psalm CX, 1; Matthew XXVIII, 18, and Rev. XIX, 16).

The Fishing episode of John XXI having taken place on Monday, 18th May, twenty-six days would elapse before the Ascension of our Lord on Saturday, 13th June, which was Forty Days from Monday, 4th May, when He rose from the dead. The Bible does not supply us with any specific information concerning events in these 26 days except that they were spent in Galilee and included a meeting with "above five hundred brethren at once" and after that with James, our Lord's brother (I Cor. XV, 6 and 7). In Matthew XXVIII, 16, we learn that the disciples assembled themselves in "a mountain (in Galilee) where Jesus had appointed them". There can be no doubt that our Lord's meetings with the disciples were frequent for it was then that He spoke with them "of the things pertaining to the kingdom of God" (Acts I, 3).

It is manifest that the counsels of God decreed that our Lord Jesus Christ should render a Testimony after His resurrection lasting Forty Days in order to provide the human race with irresistible proof that He had been raised from the dead as He had said. The Bible records eight instances when forty days were adopted as a period of testing, testimony or probation. The number "forty" so used implies adequacy.

We are exclusively indebted to the Evangelist Luke for our knowledge that the Lord's resurrection testimony lasted for forty days. This is to be found in Luke's second treatise, called "The Acts of the Apostles", or, more correctly, "The Acts of the Ascended Christ through the Apostles". In Chapter I, verses 1 to 3, we read:

> "The former treatise have I made, O Theophilus, of all that Jesus began both to do and teach, until the day in which He was taken up, after that He through the Holy Ghost had given commandments unto the apostles whom He had chosen: to whom also He shewed Himself alive after His passion by many infallible proofs, being seen of them forty days, and speaking of the things pertaining to the kingdom of God."

It is beautiful to note how Luke here links his Gospel with the Acts – the former embracing the whole of our Lord's life up to the very day of His Ascension. In the above quotation, with which the Acts opens, it will be noted that the Apostles were the chosen witnesses of the Saviour's resurrection and to them "He shewed Himself alive after His passion by many infallible proofs, being seen of them forty days". Our Lord never once showed Himself after His resurrection to the world but only to His disciples. Peter, when he first addressed the Gentiles in the house of the Roman centurion Cornelius, affirmed this fact in these words:

> "Him God raised up the third day, and shewed Him openly; not to all the people, but unto witnesses chosen before of God, even to us, who did eat and drink with Him after He rose from the dead" (Acts X, 40 and 41).

In electing Matthias to fill the apostolate of the fallen Apostle Judas, Peter declares that the one so chosen "must . . . be ordained to be a witness with us of His resurrection" (Acts I, 22).

At Antioch the Apostle Paul, when referring to our Lord's resurrection, states, "He was seen many days of them which came up with Him from Galilee to Jerusalem, who are His witnesses unto the people" (Acts XIII, 30 and 31).

The testimony of the Twelve Apostles to the fact that Jesus of Nazareth was raised from the dead and that He was seen by them over a period of Forty Days, and that they did both eat and drink with Him after His resurrection, places the whole human race under responsibility to God "because", as Paul affirmed on Mars' Hill, "He hath appointed a day, in the which He will judge the world in righteousness by that Man Whom He hath ordained; whereof He hath given assurance unto all men, IN THAT HE HATH RAISED HIM FROM THE DEAD" (Acts XVII, 31).

We must now comment briefly on the facts given in Holy Scripture relating to the Ascension of our Lord Jesus Christ into Heaven.

## THE ASCENSION

We may well give thanks for the simple and direct statements of Holy Scripture concerning the act of our Lord's Ascension. These contain no human embellishments, being limited to statements of unadorned fact.

In Luke XXIV, verses 50 and 51, we read:

> "He led them out as far as to Bethany, and He lifted up His hands, and blessed them. And it came to pass, while He blessed them, He was parted from them, and carried up into heaven."

In Acts I, 9, we read,

> "And when He had spoken these things, while they beheld, He was taken up; and a cloud received Him out of their sight."

It was thus that the Forty Days of sweet and holy communion between the risen Christ and the faithful band of eleven men, who had followed Him for three and a half years, ended. Whether they knew the purpose of His leading them out along the familiar road that led to Bethany and the Mount of Olives we do not know; but His precise instructions to them to wait in

Jerusalem for "the promise of the Father", that is, the descent of the Holy Ghost, would have been warning enough that He was about to fulfil His many intimations concerning His departure from them.

It was as God's High Priest that the departing Saviour "lifted up His hands, and blessed" His eleven Apostles to whom He declared, "Ye shall be witnesses unto Me both in Jerusalem, and in all Judaea, and in Samaria, and unto the uttermost part of the earth" (Acts I, 8).

The manner of our Lord's ascent into Heaven could not be other than it was. Whether we read that He was "carried up into Heaven" or "taken up", we know that the power to ascend was in Himself and that He was not the subject of some extraneous force like that implied in the words "caught up" (lit. snatched away) which are used in reference to the translation to Heaven of the members of the body of Christ in I Thessalonians IV, 17, and Revelation XII, 5.

## MOSES AND ELIJAH ARE WITNESSES OF OUR LORD'S ASCENSION

Once again "two men", who are Moses and Elijah, are found to be present as our Lord Jesus Christ ascends up into Heaven. Having witnessed the Transfiguration, Death and Resurrection of our blessed Lord, it was to be expected that they would tarry by Him during the Forty Days to His Ascension. If presently they are to be God's Two Witnesses in Jerusalem either to convict or convert their own nation, they must be able to bear a first-hand testimony concerning all that overtook the Messiah as the result of His being rejected by them and delivered to the Gentiles to be put to death.

We read in Acts I, verses 10 and 11:

> "And while they looked stedfastly toward heaven as He went up, behold, two men stood by them in white apparel; which also said, Ye men of Galilee, why stand ye gazing up into heaven? this same Jesus, which is taken up from you into heaven, shall so come in like manner as ye have seen Him go into heaven."

These "two men" in celestial garments are the same as the "two men" named by Luke on the Mount of Transfiguration

(IX, 30 and 32) and at the Sepulchre on the morning of the Resurrection (XXIV, 4). It is important to note that in each of these instances we find it stated that the "two men . . . stood" – an expression which is intended to assist us in identifying them as the same persons on each occasion.

We have already written at considerable length on the reason for these appearings of Moses and Elijah during the two periods of Forty Days – the one preceding the death of our Lord and the other following His resurrection – so we will refer readers back to what we have previously written on the subject.

## MOSES AND ELIJAH PREDICT OUR LORD'S SECOND ADVENT (Acts I, 10 and 11)

The statement, "this same Jesus, which is taken up from you into heaven, shall so come in like manner as ye have seen Him go into heaven", is one of the most positive predictions of our Lord's Second Advent to be found in the New Testament. The expression, "in like manner", limits the prediction to the Second Advent when our Lord Jesus Christ comes in person to raise His sleeping members from their graves, and to transmute His living members "which are alive and remain", before summoning His whole Church to meet Him in the air, as precisely described by the Apostle Paul in I Thessalonians IV, 13 to 18 and I Corinthians XV, 51 to 57.

The statement, "in like manner", could not possibly refer to our Lord's return in power and glory to reign over the earth *which is His Third Advent.* That "coming", we are told in II Thessalonians I, 8, is "in flaming fire taking vengeance on them that know not God, and that obey not the gospel of our Lord Jesus Christ". In Revelation I, 7, our Lord's Third Coming is described thus, "Behold, He cometh with clouds; and every eye shall see Him, and they also which pierced Him: and all kindreds of the earth shall wail because of Him" (see also Revelation XIX, 11 to 21).

As the Lord Jesus Christ departed to Heaven so will He return. We are told in I Thessalonians IV that "the Lord Himself shall descend from heaven" – words which perfectly comport with "This same Jesus . . . shall so come in like manner as ye have seen Him go into heaven". In Hebrews IX, 26 to 28, we read, "But now once in the end of the world (lit. ages) hath He appeared to put away sin by the sacrifice of Himself . . . and unto them that look for Him shall He appear THE SECOND TIME without sin unto salvation". It is, therefore, this SECOND APPEARING to which Moses and Elijah referred when they addressed the Apostles as our Lord ascended.

## THE DAY AND DATE OF THE ASCENSION PROVE THAT OUR LORD JESUS CHRIST ROSE FROM THE DEAD ON A MONDAY

### THE FORTY DAYS END AT 8–9 A.M. ON THE SABBATH – 13TH JUNE, A.D. 33

We have no means of knowing from Scripture at what time the disciples left Galilee to return to Jerusalem, but it may be assumed it was only just prior to the Ascension. We are informed in Acts I, 12, that the eleven Apostles "returned . . . unto Jerusalem from the mount called Olivet, which is from Jerusalem A SABBATH DAY'S JOURNEY". The mention of "a sabbath day's journey" in this context has been a source of great perplexity to commentators, for the simple reason that one and all have been in bondage to the universally held tradition that our Lord rose from the dead early on a Sunday morning. If this were true then, as a mathematical fact, the Ascension must have taken place on a Friday which is five weeks and five days (i.e., 40 days) from the alleged Sunday of the Resurrection. Why then this mention of a Sabbath day's journey? Furthermore, this is the only place in the New Testament where this expression occurs.

As we have abundantly proved from the Holy Scriptures, our Lord and Saviour Jesus Christ rose from the dead at the Midnight of Sunday, 3rd May; and Monday, 4th May, was "the morrow after the sabbath", when "the wave sheaf" had to be presented before the Lord and when our Lord, as the Antitype of the same, ascended to God the Father as "the firstfruits of them that slept". This being so, the Forty Days of our Lord's Resurrection Ministry began at 8 to 9 A.M. on Monday, 4th May, and ended at 8 to 9 A.M. on Saturday,

13th June, when "He was taken up; and a cloud received Him out of their (the apostles') sight".

Not only need we seek no further for a reason why the Spirit of God caused Luke to introduce this reference to the "sabbath day's journey", but, knowing that it was inserted for no other reason than to make plain that the day of the Ascension was a Sabbath, *we possess a positive mathematical proof by this reference that our Lord rose on a Monday.*

It is worthy of mention that Chrysostom, who was Patriarch of Constantinople (A.D. 398) and a great writer on the Holy Scriptures, made no attempt to escape the obvious conclusion from Luke's mention of "a sabbath day's journey" that the Ascension was on a Sabbath day. His actual statement is "DOKEI MOI EN SABBATŌ GEGONENAI TAUTA" – "It seems to me that these things happened on the Sabbath" (Bishop C. Wordsworth's Commentary – Acts I, 12).

To those who have laboured to lift this precious subject off the ever-shifting sands of human conjecture on to the rock-foundation of Holy Scripture this mention of "a sabbath day's journey" in Acts I constituted a divine endorsement of the fact that they are "rightly dividing the word of truth" in establishing that the resurrection of Jesus Christ from the dead took place on a Monday – a Monday which was, nevertheless, in Divine Time, "the morrow after the sabbath" and, therefore, the first day of a week.

## THE 1,300 DAYS BETWEEN THE FORTY DAYS OF OUR LORD'S TEMPTATION AND THE FORTY DAYS OF HIS RESURRECTION MINISTRY

In Chapter XIV of this Treatise we demonstrated the chronological fact that the 7 days and 40 days of the Temptation which began with the Saviour's Baptism in Jordan on 5th October A.D. 29, were separated by exactly 1,300 days from the 7 days and the 40 days of His Resurrection Ministry which followed His Anointing by Mary of Bethany on 26th April A.D. 33. Thus Saturday, 13th June A.D. 33, when our Lord ascended into Heaven in triumph, was exactly 1,300 days from Monday, 21st November A.D. 29, when He emerged from the 40 days of the Temptation by dispelling Satan with the words, "Get thee hence, Satan: for it is written, Thou shalt worship the Lord thy God, and Him only shalt thou serve" (Matt. IV, 10).

We shall not comment further on this subject, but ask the reader to refresh his memory by turning back to Chapter XIV where it is dealt with in detail. The mention of these facts will, however, once again serve as a reminder of the existence in our Lord's life of a programme of Time designed by God the Father in which He walked while here on earth in humble obedience, from His Nativity at Bethlehem to His Ascension into Heaven from Bethany and the Mount of Olives, when He was, in terms of our years, but thirty-two years and two hundred and twenty-seven days of age.

## THE SPIRITUAL ASPECT OF THE ASCENSION OF OUR LORD JESUS CHRIST BRIEFLY CONSIDERED

> "We have . . . an High Priest, Who is set on the right hand of the throne of the Majesty in the heavens . . . now to appear in the presence of God for us" (Hebrews VIII, 1 and IX, 24).

When our blessed Lord and Master again entered Heaven at His Ascension He was greeted by God the Father with the opening words of the 110th Psalm: "Sit Thou at My right hand, until I make thine enemies Thy footstool". Exalted thus to the highest place in the Universe, the lowly One, Whose pathway in Time we have been tracing, began His session in Heaven as our Great High Priest on 13th June A.D. 33, for which Office He had been anointed with the Holy Ghost immediately after He had been baptized of John in the river Jordan on 5th October A.D. 29 – 1,300 and 47 days previously.

It must have occurred to some to ask why our Lord Jesus Christ did not remain on the earth to build His Church instead of leaving His Apostles to do it. The answer to that question is to be found in His own words, when He said,

> "Nevertheless I tell you the truth; It is expedient for you that I go away: for if I go not away, the Comforter will not come unto you; but if I depart, I will send Him unto you" (John XVI, 7).

These words make it perfectly clear that our Lord's Ascension into Heaven was in order that the Holy Ghost might descend from Heaven and take up His abode on the earth in the bodies of all true believers in Himself (see I Cor. VI, 19). It was not, however, our Lord's Ascension that made the descent of the Holy Ghost possible but His glorification at God's right hand. This fact is stated as a parenthesis in John VII, 39, thus, "for the Holy Ghost was not yet (given); because that Jesus was not yet glorified". Peter confirms this on the day of Pentecost thus: "Therefore being by the right hand of God exalted, and having received of the Father the promise of the Holy Ghost, He hath shed forth this, which ye now see and hear" (Acts II, 33).

When here on earth the Lord Jesus was *with* His disciples but not *in* them. After He had ascended and had again been glorified with the glory He had "before the world was", He bestowed the Holy Spirit upon all believers and in this manner fulfilled His promise, "I will not leave you comfortless (orphans): I will come to you . . . at that day ye shall know that I am in My Father, and ye in Me, and I in you" (John XIV, 16 to 20).

It is thus perfectly clear that as long as our Lord was on the earth He could not receive His disciples into union with Himself. This could only be accomplished by the Holy Spirit's indwelling of them as the result of our Lord's glorification at God's right hand. Ever since the first day of Pentecost the Holy Ghost has been revealing the Ascended Christ as dwelling *in* all true believers. The Apostle Paul refers to this indwelling of Christ as "the mystery which hath been hid from ages and from generations, but now is made manifest to His saints . . . which is Christ in you, the hope of glory" (Colossians I, 26 and 27).

Rejected from the earth, our Lord Jesus Christ has been accorded by God the place of supreme power in the Universe. This is defined by the Apostle Paul in the Ephesian Epistle as follows:

> "God . . . raised Him from the dead, and set Him at His own right hand in the heavenly places, far above all principality, and power, and might, and dominion . . . and hath put all things under His feet, and gave Him to be head over all things to the Church, which is His body, the fulness of Him that filleth all in all" (Ephesians I, 20 to 23).

With the account of the Ascension of our Lord and Master, Jesus Christ, into Heaven on Saturday, 13th June A.D. 33, the immediate purpose of *The Restored Vision* is completed, because His "Pathway in Time" was thereby brought to an end. What follows in the few remaining pages may be correctly entitled, "The Pathway in Time of the Mystical Body of Christ, the Church". This will furnish the reader with an exact knowledge of Time in relation to the Church from Pentecost, A.D. 33, to the present time.

OUR LORD JESUS CHRIST, HAVING BEEN BORN OF THE VIRGIN MARY INTO THE WORLD ON FRIDAY, 29TH OCTOBER, 1 B.C., WAS 33 BIBLE YEARS AND 233 DAYS, OR 32 SOLAR YEARS AND 227 DAYS, OF AGE, WHEN HE DEPARTED OUT OF IT TO "GO TO THE FATHER"

ON SATURDAY, 13TH JUNE A.D. 33

# CHAPTER EIGHTEEN

## THE PATHWAY IN TIME OF THE MYSTICAL BODY OF CHRIST—THE CHURCH

"This is a great mystery . . . Christ and the church"
(Ephesians V, 30, 32)

THE SIGNIFICANCE OF THE TEN DAYS BETWEEN THE ASCENSION OF OUR LORD AND THE DESCENT OF THE HOLY GHOST AT PENTECOST, A.D. 33

THE FINAL YEAR OF CLEMENCY TO THE JEWS, NAMED IN LUKE XIII, 8, ENDS ON 11TH OCTOBER A.D. 33, WITH THE MARTYRDOM OF STEPHEN

THE DESCENT OF THE HOLY GHOST UPON THE GENTILES IN THE HOUSE OF CORNELIUS ON THE DAY OF PENTECOST IN A.D. 36, AS DESCRIBED IN ACTS X AND XI

THE DISPENSATION OF GRACE OR "TIMES OF THE GENTILES" BEGINS ON 12TH OCTOBER A.D. 33 AND RUNS ITS COURSE OF TWO THOUSAND YEARS TO 12TH JUNE 1933 WHEN THE GENTILES ARE "CUT OFF", AS FOREWARNED BY THE APOSTLE PAUL IN ROMANS XI, 22

MANKIND – JEW AND GENTILE – NOW PASSING THROUGH "THE CONSUMMATION OF THE AGE" PENDING THE SECOND ADVENT OF OUR LORD JESUS CHRIST

With the Ascension of our Lord Jesus Christ into Heaven a new phase opened in the history of the human race – a phase which will continue until the day and hour when He again comes out of Heaven in fulfilment of the prediction uttered by

Moses and Elias to the disciples, as they watched their Master ascend up in the clouds, "This same Jesus, which is taken up from you into heaven, shall so come in like manner as ye have seen Him go into heaven."

This phase of human history, between our Lord's Ascension and His Second Appearing, is called "the dispensation of the grace of God" (Ephesians III, 2) during which, under our Lord's specific instructions,

> "repentance and remission of sins should be preached in His Name among all nations, beginning at Jerusalem." (Luke XXIV, 46, 47).

This plainly means that having been rejected by His own nation – Israel – the Kingdom of God would not now be set up in visible form and power; but in its place another purpose predicted by the Prophet Isaiah would be accomplished. This is defined in the following words which are addressed to our Lord after His mission to Israel had failed through its unbelief:

> "I will also give Thee for a light to the Gentiles, that Thou mayest be My salvation unto the end of the earth" (Chap. XLIX, 6).

This did not mean that the Gentile world was to be converted from heathenism to Christianity; but rather that the peoples of "all nations" were to hear of the sufferings, death and resurrection of our Lord Jesus Christ and be given an opportunity to repent and receive the remission of their sins by believing on His Name.

That this did not imply world conversion is proved by the statement of the Apostle James at the first great Church Council at Jerusalem in A.D. 51, when he said, "Simeon (i.e. Simon Peter) hath declared how God at the first did visit the Gentiles, *to take out of them a people for His Name*" (Acts XV, 14).

We shall learn presently that all, whether Jews or Gentiles, who in their hearts believe on our Lord and Saviour Jesus Christ, and who as a result have received the remission of their sins, become members of the Church which is His mystical Body, and this by virtue of the action of the Holy Ghost Who indwells every such one (I Cor. XII, 3) – the word "Church" (EKKLESIA) in the Greek simply signifying a company of "those called out".

May the fact then be clearly understood that the Bible marks off the period of time between our Lord's Ascension and His Second Appearing as that during which a vast assemblage of "saved" men, women and children is being called together by the Holy Spirit into ONE BODY – the Church of our Lord Jesus Christ of which He is THE HEAD (Ephesians I, 22, 23). This Body came into being on the day of His Resurrection, and embraced all then living who believed on Him Whom God had raised from the dead. The Dispensation, however, did not officially begin, indeed, could not, until the descent of the Holy Ghost on the day of Pentecost, which was the tenth day after our Lord's Ascension.

The Eleven Apostles of our Lord Jesus Christ must have returned from the scene of His Ascension from Olivet with His last command occupying their hearts and minds. This was "that they should not depart from Jerusalem, but wait for the promise of the Father", for, said He, "Ye shall be baptized with the Holy Ghost not many days hence" (Acts I, 4, 5). Consequently, they "returned to Jerusalem with great joy" and remained there for nine days until the day of Pentecost.

We shall presently direct attention to an aspect of these 9 or 10 days which is of phenomenal importance and absorbing interest because of its relationship to future events, *now impending*, connected with the return of "this same Jesus" at His Second Appearing.

It is most instructive to read in Acts I, 14, that during these nine days of waiting for the descent of the Holy Ghost the eleven Apostles "continued with one accord in prayer and supplication, with the women, and Mary the mother of Jesus, and with His brethren".

No doubt our Lord's absence was keenly felt by all. He had from the beginning shepherded His little flock and led them out of the Jewish fold. We are told by the Apostle John that on the night of the resurrection, when the Risen One appeared, "the doors were shut where the disciples were assembled for fear of the Jews" (XX, 19). The possibility that the Jewish rulers would follow up their successful removal of the One they hated by an assault upon His followers must have been ever present to all hearts; and this sense of dependence expressed itself by continual prayer and supplication. No doubt this "upper room" proved to be a divinely-provided haven where all the disciples of Jesus could meet in safety. Their number, we are told, was "about an hundred and twenty".

It is most touching to know that the Lord's Mother was to be found in the midst, and that His brethren after the flesh now realized Who their Mother's Firstborn Son really was, and wished to be associated with the faithful disciples who had believed on Him from the beginning.

The account of the election of a twelfth apostle given in Acts I is complete in itself and calls for no comment. The suggestion that the Eleven might have waited for the Apostle Paul to fill the vacant apostolate is beside the mark for, as we have previously stated, the candidate must "have companied" with the other eleven "all the time that the Lord Jesus went in and out among (them), beginning from the baptism of John, unto that same day that He (Jesus) was taken up". Paul could not qualify under such terms as he was not converted until after the martyrdom of Stephen. Matthias is duly elected and is "numbered with the eleven apostles" – our Lord having ordained that their number should be twelve. Peter, knowing this, delayed not to act in the light of the Psalms which refer to Judas' fall (LXIX, 25 and CIX, 8).

## THE DAY OF PENTECOST

### MONDAY, 22ND JUNE A.D. 33

### THE HOLY GHOST DESCENDS UPON THE JEWISH DISCIPLES OF OUR LORD JESUS CHRIST AT JERUSALEM

"The same day there were added unto them about three thousand souls"

Read Acts II, 1 to 47 and Leviticus XXIII, 9 to 22

The Day of our Lord's resurrection was Monday, 4th May A.D. 33. All four Gospels affirm that this was "the first (day) of the Sabbaths", that is, the seven Sabbaths or weeks to Pentecost, which was the 50th day, or "morrow after the seventh sabbath". The Greek word for "fiftieth" is "PENTEKOSTĒ". The Day of Pentecost was, therefore, Monday 22nd June, being the 50th day from Monday, 4th May.

It will be remembered that the Bible only records our Lord's death and resurrection in terms of the Divine Calendar which, up to His death, was *one day ahead* of Israel's Calendar, but which after His death, because the Moon ceased its normal revolution for Two Days, was *one day behind* Israel's Calendar. If reference is made to the Chart of the Five Calendars, between Chapters XIII and XIV, it will be seen that the "Descent of the Holy Spirit" took place on 22nd June in the Solar Calendar and that this was Monday, the 7th of the 3rd month in the Jews' Calendar, and Sunday, the 6th of the 3rd month in the Divine Calendar.

One of the most beautiful types of the Holy Spirit in the Old Testament is to be seen in Eliezer of Damascus, the servant of Abraham, whom he sent into Mesopotamia to fetch a bride for his son Isaac, as recorded in Genesis XXIV. The primary objective that God had in sending the Holy Spirit down from Heaven was that He might, through the preaching of the Gospel, gather out, first from Israel and then from the Gentiles, that vast assemblage which would form the Church of our Lord Jesus Christ which, in one most important aspect, is viewed as His Bride. In other words, what Eve was to "the first man Adam" the Church is to be to "the last Adam", that is, our Lord Jesus Christ. (See Ephesians V, 25 to 33, etc., etc.) So we may view the descent of the Holy Ghost on the day of Pentecost as the true birthday of the Church which, in the ultimate, is to be the Bride and Eternal Helpmeet of Christ, Who "loved the Church, and gave Himself for it" at Calvary.

We do not purpose to comment on the details given in Acts II of events on the day of Pentecost. A multitude of tomes has been published on the subject. It will suffice to say that in his first and second sermons, as recorded in Acts II and III, the Apostle Peter, in the energy and power of the newly-descended Holy Spirit, drove home to the Jews from all over the world gathered at Jerusalem that "Jesus of Nazareth, a Man approved of God", Who had been "taken, and by wicked hands . . . crucified and slain", had been raised up by God from death, "because it was not possible that He should be holden of it". In each case Peter called for the repentance of the Jewish nation for what its rulers had done in rejecting and crucifying their Messiah, God's beloved Son. In the first instance, three thousand Jews are baptized "in the name of Jesus Christ for the remission of sins" and receive the Holy Ghost, and in the second instance "the number of the men was about five thousand".

It will be remembered that our Lord gave to Peter "the keys of the Kingdom of Heaven", as recorded in Matthew XVI, 19. On the day of Pentecost in A.D. 33 Peter used the "key" which opened the door for repentant Jews to enter the Kingdom, and 3,000 did so. That door still remains open to all repentant Jews.

As the Bible views the descent of the Holy Ghost on the Jews at Jerusalem in A.D. 33 and His descent upon the Gentiles at Caesarea in A.D. 36 AS ONE DESCENT, we will at once refer to the latter event as recorded in much detail in Acts X and XI.

## THE DAY OF PENTECOST
### FRIDAY, 22ND JUNE A.D. 36

THE HOLY GHOST DESCENDS UPON THE GENTILES ASSEMBLED IN THE HOUSE OF THE ROMAN CENTURION, CORNELIUS, AT CAESAREA

"While Peter yet spake these words, the Holy Ghost fell on all them which heard the word"

There are three manifestly clear types in the Bible which reveal that THREE YEARS intervened between the descent of the Holy Ghost on the Jews at Jerusalem and His descent upon the Gentiles at Caesarea, which was the Roman capital in Palestine. We cannot now give an exposition of these types which are as follows:

(I) The *three years* between the death of Sarah and the marriage of Isaac to Rebekah (Genesis XVII, 17; XXIII, 1; XXV, 20),

(II) The *three days* of Israel's journey from the Red Sea to Marah, where Moses cast a tree into the bitter waters which "were made sweet" (Exodus XV, 22 to 25),

(III) The healing of the waters of Jericho by Elisha with a new cruse and salt, *three days* after Elijah's ascension (II Kings II, 16 to 22).

(The Bible frequently employs days to typify years, as in II and III.)

That the descent of the Holy Ghost upon the Gentiles likewise took place on the day of Pentecost is obvious from the type of Leviticus XXIII, as also is the fact that the descent on the Jews and on the Gentiles is one descent, and not two – otherwise that on the Gentiles cannot be viewed as on the 50th day from our Lord's resurrection, in which case it would be invalid. For this reason TIME IS NOT RECKONED in relation to this type between Pentecost, A.D. 33, and Pentecost, A.D. 36.

It is painfully clear from many Scriptures that the Jewish Apostles and believers in general ignored our Lord's command to proclaim the Gospel to "all nations". In Acts XI, 19, we are informed that those who were scattered abroad in the persecution following Stephen's martyrdom "travelled as far as Phenice, and Cyprus, and Antioch, *preaching the word to none but unto the Jews only*".

Not only is this state of things revealed typically in the refusal of the prophet Jonah to go to the Gentiles, but Peter, whom our Lord addresses in John XXI as "son of Jonas", is actually found at Joppa where Jonah took ship to flee from the Lord rather than obey His command to go to Nineveh. And so it is at Joppa that our Lord visited a firm rebuke upon Peter in the vision He gave him, as recorded so fully in Acts X which should be read with care. Following the vision of the sheet let down from Heaven and the rebuke contained in the words, "What God hath cleansed, that call not thou common", Peter is sought by messengers from Cornelius the Roman Centurion. The Spirit commands Peter to go with these messengers "doubting nothing".

We referred to this episode in writing on John XXI in which the fishing incident in all its details is a foreshadowing of Peter's going to the Gentiles as recorded in Acts X.

As Peter was preaching to these Gentiles and declaring "that through His (Jesus') Name whosoever believeth in Him shall receive remission of sins", the Holy Ghost "fell on all them which heard the word". No wonder we read next, "And they of the circumcision (i.e. Jews) which believed were astonished . . . because that on the Gentiles also was poured out the gift of the Holy Ghost".

It was thus that Peter for a second time used "the keys of the Kingdom of Heaven" and this in order to throw open wide the door of mercy to the Gentiles.

Let the fact be noted that baptism preceded the incoming of the Holy Ghost upon the Jews and that with the Gentiles it came afterwards.

Let it also be noted that prior to the descent of the Holy Ghost upon the Gentiles Peter raised Dorcas to life. Clearly Dorcas' death and resurrection were typical of our Lord's and probably occurred on the anniversaries of the same – a fact which reveals that the gracious gift of the Holy Ghost was a direct outcome of our Lord's one perfect Sacrifice and Oblation offered for our sins on Calvary's Tree.

## WHY OUR LORD ASCENDED AFTER FORTY DAYS

---

## THE TEN DAYS TO PENTECOST YET TO BE LIVED BY CHRIST AND HIS CHURCH AT THE SECOND ADVENT IN FULFILMENT OF THE LEVITICAL TYPE

---

Read Leviticus XXIII, 9 to 22

The subject we are about to consider is of the utmost importance to all believers in our Lord Jesus Christ because it relates to events at His now impending Second Appearing.

All the great Christian Communities celebrate the Fifty Days between Easter and Pentecost because this number of days elapsed between our Lord's resurrection and the day of Pentecost in A.D. 33, when the Holy Ghost came down to form the Church, which is the mystical Body of Christ. If reference is made to Leviticus XXIII, 16, it will be seen that these fifty days are specifically named as the period between the offering of "a sheaf of the firstfruits . . . on the morrow after the sabbath" (verses 10 and 11) and the offering of the "two wave loaves" on "the morrow after the seventh sabbath".

In writing on the day of the Lord's resurrection we showed that in the fulfilment of the type of "the sheaf of the firstfruits" this took place "on the morrow after the sabbath". For this reason our Lord is referred to as "the firstfruits of them that slept" in I Corinthians XV, 20. It is equally well known that the "two wave loaves", which have to be offered on the fiftieth day after the offering of "the sheaf of the firstfruits", form a simple and beautiful type of the Church – Jew and Gentile – which is Christ's mystical Body. It will be noted that both offerings are "firstfruits". The reason for this is that Christ's resurrection and that of the Church at His Second Advent are "the firstfruits" or token of that great harvest of human souls which presently are to be raised from the dead.

It will be obvious to all that this Levitical type positively requires, if taken literally, that the completed Church, which is the antitype of the "two wave loaves", should be offered on the 50th day or "morrow after the seventh sabbath"; just as Christ, Who is the Anti-type of "the sheaf of the firstfruits", was offered to God on the first of these fifty days, that which is called in all the Gospels "the first (day) of the sabbaths", that is, the seven Sabbaths to Pentecost.

It will be equally clear to all that on the day of Pentecost in A.D. 33, which was the 50th day after Christ's resurrection, there were no "two wave loaves" to offer to God, as the Church, which they typify, on that day only began to be formed by the descent of the Holy Ghost. Did the type, therefore, fail? If so, the Scripture is broken. This, however, cannot be so as our Lord said, "The Scripture cannot be broken" (John X, 35). What then?

When forty of these fifty days between our Lord's resurrection and Pentecost had passed He left the earth and ascended up to Heaven. His doing so was a vital part of a perfect plan – *the effect of His Ascension being to suspend the course of the fifty days when ten had yet to run.*

Apart from this suspension of the typical fifty days, our Lord, as the risen Head of the Church, would have had to remain on earth with His believing members until the day of Pentecost, when He would have presented them as an offering to God at their translation to Heaven. What then would have happened to the world-wide commission to preach repentance and remission of sins to all nations? The answer is obvious. It would never have been accomplished.

To meet this situation God devised the plan that our Lord should ascend to Heaven after forty days. During His session at God's right hand and until the day of His return, the course of the typical fifty days would be suspended. In other words, between the actual day and hour of our Lord's Ascension and the actual day and hour of His Second Advent *there would be a vast chronological hiatus or suspension of the type.*

The type requires, and Divine order demands, that our Lord's Second Advent shall occur on the solar anniversary of His Ascension in order that the interval of His absence should be an exact number of solar years, without any fractions thereof – the solar year being incommensurable.

In effect, this means that our Lord's Second Appearing will take place on the same day in the solar year as His Ascension; and that when He returns it will be to find the Church, which is His body, complete – "the fulness of the Gentiles" having been reached.

From the moment of our Lord's return to the earth He, together with His completed Church, will pass through the nine days required to reach the fiftieth day or day of Pentecost. That day of Pentecost will, in Divine reckoning (which totally ignores the hiatus) be THE FIFTIETH DAY FROM THE RESURRECTION OF OUR LORD JESUS CHRIST, and in it the Church, which is the antitype of the "two wave loaves", will ascend to Heaven with Christ to be presented to God as "the firstfruits" – Christ the Head and Christ the Body forming "THE CHRIST" – an immortal and incorruptible and eternal company of redeemed men, women and children, gathered out of the nations and Israel to dwell in Heaven for evermore.

The Holy Scriptures supply all the details needed to see how this wondrous plan will be effected.

In the first place it is important to note the way Moses and Elijah link our Lord's return with His Ascension when they address the disciples. It is not only to be in "like manner", but on the anniversary of the Ascension.

When we turn to the Bible's most detailed account of our Lord's Second Advent in I Thessalonians IV, 13 to 18, we find it perfectly comports with what we have set forth above. In verses 16 and 17 we read:

> "The Lord Himself shall descend from heaven with a shout, with the voice of the archangel, and with the trump of God: and the dead in Christ shall rise first: then (Greek: 'afterward') we which are alive and remain shall be caught up together with them in the clouds, to meet the Lord in the air."
>
> (See also I Corinthians XV, 51 to 53.)

How perfect a plan! As our Lord descends the departed members of His Church are raised in bodies of glory from their graves. At once by this act the exact conditions of the forty days after our Lord's resurrection again obtain.

In those days there were with Christ some who had been raised from the dead after His resurrection and on the earth a large number of disciples still in their mortal bodies. When our Lord descends and "the dead in Christ" rise it will be so again and will continue so for nine days until the day of Pentecost. Then, that is, after nine days, all the members of Christ's Body, the Church, who are alive on the earth, will be "changed, in a moment, in the twinkling of an eye" and be "caught up together with" the raised members to meet our Lord "in the air".

It is important to see that during the whole fifty days Christ and the Church are together and, being "firstfruits" of the Harvest, death has no place in their midst – Christ and His members having passed through death physically into resurrection life – the exception being those who "are alive and remain" unto His coming, who without dying will be miraculously changed into immortality when summoned "at the last trump" – "to meet the Lord in the air" (see also Philippians III, 20, 21).

We may have very inadequately expounded this most important subject, but we trust we have said enough to enable all who wish to follow it through in greater detail. One thing is quite certain and that is that our Lord Jesus Christ will return to the earth at His Second Advent and remain with His Church for nine days before summoning her to meet Him in the air. This fact gives a true meaning to those many Scriptures which speak of His Appearing, such as, "Unto them that look for Him shall He appear the second time without sin unto salvation"; and "Hope to the end for the grace that is to be brought unto you at the revelation (lit. unveiling) of Jesus Christ"; and "Abide in Him; that, when He shall appear, we may have confidence, and not be ashamed before Him at His coming" (Heb. IX, 28; I Peter I, 13; I John II, 28, etc., etc.).

It has been the habit of some sections of the Christian Community to affirm that our Lord's Second Coming and the Translation of the Church to Heaven are to be secretly accomplished "at any moment". Nothing could be further from the facts given in the Holy Scriptures. The whole world is to know when our Lord descends "a second time", and that He is present on the earth. The Greek word for "coming" is PAROUSIA which means "presence" in contradistinction to "absence" (see Phil. II, 12). Neither will our Lord come "at any moment" but on the solar anniversary of His Ascension, which in our present calendar is 12th June and nine days before Pentecost, which is 21st June.

The great distinguishing mark of the nine days in A.D. 33 between the Ascension and Pentecost was the absence of a Divine Person on the earth. This is the only occasion when it will have been so between our Lord's First and Second Advents. In Revelation VII, 2, it would appear there is a reference to our Lord (viewed as an "Angel") in the act of escorting the Holy Spirit ("the Seal of the living God") back to Heaven at His Second Advent – The Spirit's work of forming the Church being then complete.

Finally, let the simple but vital fact be kept in mind that the type of the Fifty Days, given in Leviticus XXIII, embraces the whole history of the Church, which is the Body of Christ, from His presentation to God as "the firstfruits" on the morning of His resurrection to the presentation of the completed Church, the antitype of the "two wave loaves", on that day of Pentecost which will occur nine days after our Lord's Second Advent.

## THE MARTYRDOM OF STEPHEN ON SUNDAY, 11TH OCTOBER, A.D. 33

---

## THE JEWISH NATION "CUT DOWN" FOR THE AGE

---

## "THE TIMES OF THE GENTILES" BEGIN THEIR COURSE OF TWO THOUSAND BIBLE YEARS ON 12TH OCTOBER A.D. 33, AND TERMINATE ON 12TH JUNE 1933

Read Luke XIII, 6 to 9; Acts VI and VII, and Luke XXI, 24

The date of Sunday, 11th October A.D. 33 has, according to the Holy Scriptures, a fearful pre-eminence in the history of the Jewish nation. It was the last day of the final year of clemency granted by our Lord to His beloved nation and it became the occasion for it to seal its rejection of Himself, in spite of the pleadings of the Holy Ghost through the Apostles, by stoning to death Stephen, one of the seven deacons and "a man full of faith and of the Holy Ghost".

We must turn again to the Parable of the Barren Fig Tree in Luke XIII, 6 to 9. We have shown in previous pages that the "three years" of our Lord's seeking fruit from Israel ran from 26th November A.D. 29, when He attained thirty Bible years of age, to 23rd October A.D. 32, when He uttered this parable. The Dresser of the Vineyard asks for one further opportunity in these terms: "Lord, let it alone this year also, till I shall dig about it, and dung it: And if it bear fruit, well: and if not, then after that Thou shalt cut it down". In effect, this plea of the Dresser refers to the efforts of the Holy Ghost through the Apostles after Pentecost to persuade the Jewish rulers and the nation to repent of their sinful act in rejecting their Messiah. Peter's charge was in these terms: "Ye denied the Holy One and the Just, and desired a murderer to be granted unto you: and killed the Prince of life, Whom God hath raised from the dead . . . repent ye therefore" (Acts III, 14 to 20).

We know that instead of repenting the Jewish rulers persecuted the Apostles and sought to stop them preaching the Gospel to their own nation.

This state of things continued from Pentecost, on 22nd June to 11th October – the last day of the Jews' sixth month – a period of 111 days.

Stephen's address given in Acts VII was God's last message to the Jewish nation. In effect, their response is given in the Parable of the Pounds, in these terms: "But his citizens hated him, and sent a message after him, saying, We will not have this man to reign over us" (Luke XIX, 14). It was given to Stephen to take this message with him when he went to be with Christ, after they had cruelly stoned him to death. Like his Master, Stephen in his death "cried with a loud voice", and again like his Master he pleads for his persecutors, saying, "Lord, lay not this sin to their charge".

It is a remarkable fact that Sunday, 11th October A.D. 33 was the 14th day of the 1st month in the Messianic Calendar and, therefore, the day of the Passover. No doubt God allowed that this last day of the year of clemency to the Jews should be marked by the slaying of the first martyr of the Christian

Church on the same Feast day as that of our Lord's death, namely, the Passover.

There can be no question that the Jews' act in stoning Stephen sealed their own doom for the age and that there and then judgment was executed as forewarned in the Parable of the Fig Tree – "If it bear fruit, well: and if not, then after that THOU SHALT CUT IT DOWN".

It is also a fact of terrible significance that this 11th October, which was the last day of the Jews' 6th month, was also *the last day* of the 490 years which began on the "first day of the seventh month" in 458 B.C., just after Nehemiah's return to rebuild Jerusalem, when the Seventy Weeks or 490 years of Daniel IX, 24 began (see Nehemiah II and VIII).

### "THE TIMES OF THE GENTILES" BEGAN ON MONDAY, 12TH OCTOBER A.D. 33

Israel having now been finally rejected *for the age*, God entered into covenant relations with the Gentile nations that compose Christendom. In Romans XI Paul, the Apostle to the Gentiles, discourses in much detail about the Jews' rejection and the consequent bringing of the Gentiles into covenant relations with God. This needs to be carefully read by anyone wishing to know the position of the Jews and Gentiles in this Dispensation.

The expression "times (or, seasons) of the Gentiles" was used by our Lord in reference to the downtreading of Jerusalem by Gentiles from A.D. 70, when the Romans laid it low, until His purposes for the Gentiles had been fulfilled at the end of the age. A like expression is used by Paul in Romans XI where we are told that Israel's blindness will continue "until the fulness of the Gentiles be come in".

When our Lord uttered this statement, "the times of the Gentiles" had not begun; but He knew they would do so as soon as the Jews had sealed their rejection of Himself by refusing to repent under the preaching of His Apostles.

"The times of the Gentiles" cover a period of Two Thousand Bible Years and they constitute the third such period in Sacred History. The Bible reveals that from Adam to Abram's birth there were 2,000 Bible years and that from Abram's birth to the death of Christ in A.D. 33 there were 2,000 Bible years. This latter period might well be named "the times of the nation of Israel". From 12th October A.D. 33 – the day following the Jews' rejection as a nation – "the times of the Gentiles" began their appointed course of 2,000 Bible years and ran without a break to 12th June 1933. In our former Treatise, *The World in Liquidation*, we narrate in detail how we were caused forty days before this 12th June, that is, on 2nd May 1933, to announce at a large Public Meeting and in the Press that Christendom would be "cut off" in 40 days, "as forewarned by the Apostle Paul", because it had not continued "in the goodness of God" but wholly apostatised from Him. (See Romans XI, 22.) To effect His intention now to "cut off" the Gentiles, God caused the governments of every nation under heaven to assemble in London for the greatest World Conference ever held. This took place on 12th June 1933, exactly forty days after our warning.

We learnt in the course of our researches after giving this warning to Christendom that on 12th June 1933 the great span of man's 6,000 years from Adam, which is typified by the six days of the Creation, terminated to the day and hour. This we may affirm is an absolutely irrefutable fact which can be verified from the Holy Scriptures with the data given in our former Treatise.

It then became evident that, with the completion of the 2,000 years of "the times of the Gentiles", or Christian Dispensation, and the 6,000 years of man's sinful failure from Adam, the World then entered a period of time called by our Lord on several occasions "the consummation of the age" – a translation given in the Revised Version Margin in the place of the incorrect "end of the world" (see Matthew XIII, 39, 40, 49 and XXIV, 3). This era, so named by our Lord, lies between the end of the 6,000 Years of Man on 12th June 1933 and the beginning of the Seventh Thousand Years or Millennial Reign of Christ, when His Kingdom is set up following His Third Advent, as described in Revelation XIX, etc., etc.

May it be recalled that we have many times stated that the seven years, A.D. 26 to 33, were cancelled chronologically by God because of the rejection by the Jewish nation of both our Lord and His herald, John the Baptist. The seven years of the Apocalypse, referred to as "1,260 days" and "42 months" in Chapter XI, take the place of these seven cancelled years,

A.D. 26 to 33. This whole subject we have dealt with in our former Treatise and only mention it now that all who have read our present Treatise may realize the immeasurable solemnity of the present hour.

## SOME CONCLUDING FACTS

We have reason to believe that the Conversion of the Apostle Paul took place in A.D. 34, on the anniversary of our Lord's birth which was 29th October. We cannot on this occasion take the time to give our reasons for this conclusion, but will say that the evidence in favour of this date is to us conclusive.

The only date in the Acts of the Apostles given on the surface is that of Paul's visit to Troas recorded in Chapter XX. From the number of days between the end of the days of Unleavened Bread and the start of "the first (day) of the sabbaths", on the Anniversary of our Lord's resurrection – which the Church at Troas had met to celebrate at Midnight – it is easy to calculate that the year was A.D. 59. This fact enables us to know that Paul came to Ephesus, as recorded in Acts XIX, in A.D. 56 – three years previously. In His Seven Addresses to the Churches of Asia our Lord begins with that to Ephesus and it is not surprising, therefore, that in the events recorded in Acts XIX we have a set of circumstances which correspond to the beginning of the Dispensation in A.D. 33 – the twelve men who had only "John's baptism" being in the exact position of the Twelve Apostles. Acts XIX is like a new beginning of the Dispensation because it was not until the Apostle Paul went to Ephesus that the grand truth of the Church, as the mystical body of Christ, was made known.

As Paul's visit to Troas was in A.D. 59, then his imprisonment at Caesarea began after Pentecost in that year and continued for two years to the late summer of A.D. 61. He must have arrived in Rome after the shipwreck in the spring of A.D. 62, and remained for two years until the spring of A.D. 64, when no doubt he was released and this just before the great fire of Rome in July that year which Nero credited to the Christians. That Paul, after extensive travels, was again made a prisoner is quite clear and that he died a martyr's death in A.D. 66 or possibly 67 is certain – his desire, expressed to the Philippians of "being made conformable unto His (i.e. Christ's) death" being granted to him, as it was to Peter, as our Lord had predicted.

## CONCLUSION

WE HAVE now completed our commission which was to trace "The Pathway in Time of Jesus of Nazareth, the Eternal Son of God" as it is set forth in the Holy Scriptures, from whence it has now been perfectly recovered, never again to be lost to view as during the past 1,800 years.

Howsoever faulty the form of expression may appear, we are fully assured that the more critically the dating of events we give in our Lord's life is examined, the more certain it will become that they are those to be found in the Holy Scriptures – not, indeed, lying on the surface thereof, but beneath it and now brought to light according to the good pleasure of "God our Saviour; Who will have all men to be saved, and to come unto the knowledge of the truth" concerning His well-beloved Son, our Lord Jesus Christ.

Assuredly this knowledge of Time in the Saviour's pathway on earth constituted the essential element in "the faith which was once (for all) delivered unto the saints" by the Apostles of our Lord under the guidance of the Holy Spirit. May all, therefore, who love our Lord Jesus Christ in sincerity receive it again as such and amend their practice of Christianity accordingly; as anything less would constitute an act of gross disrespect to our Lord and be calculated to defeat the very purpose for which it has pleased Almighty God to restore to His children knowledge which was the cherished possession of our fellow-Christians in Apostolic times.

It is our hope and prayer that some who were strangers to the Voice of the Good Shepherd when they began to read these pages can now confidently adopt the clear testimony of the Samaritans in John IV, concerning our Lord Jesus Christ; and say:

> "*Now we believe*, not because of Thy saying: for we have heard Him ourselves, and *know* that this is indeed . . . THE SAVIOUR OF THE WORLD."

# APPENDIX A

# THE CHRONOLOGY OF THE WORLD AND THE CHRONOLOGY OF REDEMPTION

THIS CHART FORMS A PART OF "THE SUMMARY OF TIME" WHICH IS PAPER FOUR OF "THE WORLD IN LIQUIDATION"

| SECULAR CHRONOLOGY | | | | EVENTS OR EPOCHS | | REDEMPTION CHRONOLOGY | | | | | |
|---|---|---|---|---|---|---|---|---|---|---|---|
| | | SOLAR YEARS B.C. | YEARS OF SCRIPTURE | | | TIME UNRECKONED | YEARS OF REDEMPTION | YEARS OF JUBILE | | | |
| | | 4075 | | THE CREATION (March 4th-9th) | | | | | | | |
| | | | | FALL OF ADAM AND EVE (April 19th) | | 47d. | | | | | |
| | | 4028 | 48 | BIRTH OF ABEL AT 1ST JUBILE | | | 48 | | | 1960 YEARS & 40 JUBILE YEARS | |
| | | 3996 | 82 | DEATH OF ABEL (33½ years old) | | YEARS | 82 | | | | |
| | | 3949 | 130 | BIRTH OF SETH (after 48½ years) | | 48 | 82 | | | | |
| | | 2470 | 1656 | THE FLOOD | Gen. VII. | 147d. | 1608 | | | | |
| THE | | 2129 | 2008 | THE BIRTH OF ABRAM | Gen. XI | | 1960 | 40th | | | |
| | 430 YEARS of Exod. XII | 2056 | 2083 | ABRAM ENTERS CANAAN | Gen. XII. | | 2035 | | | | |
| | | 2047 | 2093 | ABRAM MARRIES HAGAR | ,, XVI. | | 2045 | | 490 YEARS | | |
| SIX | | 2032 | 2108 | BIRTH OF ISAAC-2109TH YEAR | ,, XXI. | YEARS 15 | 2045 | | | | |
| | | 1639 | 2513 | THE EXODUS OF ISRAEL | Ex. XII. | 4d. | 2450 | 50th | | | THE |
| THOUSAND | | 1599 | 2553 | ISRAEL ENTERS CANAAN | Jos. VI. | | 2490 | | | | |
| | | 1592 | 2560 | DIVISION OF THE LAND | ,, XIV. | YEARS | 2497 | | | | |
| | 450 YEARS of Acts XIII. 20 | 1564 | 2588 | 1st Servitude ends | Jud. III. | 8 | 2517 | | | | |
| (SECULAR) | | 1506 | 2646 | 2nd ,, ,, | ,, III. | 18 | 2557 | 480 YEARS of I Kgs. VI. 1. | | | |
| | | 1406 | 2746 | 3rd ,, ,, | ,, IV. | 20 | 2637 | | | | |
| | | 1359 | 2793 | 4th ,, ,, | ,, VI. | 7 | 2677 | | | | |
| YEARS | | 1253 | 2899 | 5th ,, ,, | ,, X. | 18 | 2765 | | 490 YEARS | | SIX |
| | | 1182 | 2970 | 6th ,, ,, | ,, XIII. | 40 | 2796 | | | | |
| | | 1142 | 3010 | TIME OF SAMUEL BEGINS | ISam. VII. | | | | | | |
| OF | | 1122 | 3030 | 7th Servitude ends | ,, VII. | 20 | 2836 | | | | |
| | | 1112 | 3040 | SAUL'S REIGN BEGINS | ,, VII. | | 2846 | | | | |

HISTORY FROM THE CREATION OF ADAM TO JUNE 12TH A.D.1933

IV. — OR 2520 YEARS — THE "SEVEN TIMES"

| B.C./A.D. | A.M. | Event | | Sacred | | | |
|---|---|---|---|---|---|---|---|
| 720 | 3432 | CAPTIVITY OF ISRAEL IIKgs. XVIII | | 3238 | | JUBILE YEARS | |
| 606 | 3546 | JUDAH'S CAPTIVITY-70 Years Jer. XXV. | | 3352 | 490 YEARS | | |
| 588 | 3564 | JERUSALEM BESIEGED Ezek. XXIV. | | | | | |
| 536 | 3616 | CYRUS' RESTORATION DECREE Ezra I. | 70 | 3352 | | | (SACRED) |
| 458 | 3694 | NEHEMIAH REBUILDS JERUSALEM | | 3430 | 70th | | |
| 409 | 3743 | JERUSALEM RESTORED (after 49 years—see Dan.IX.25) | | 3479 | 483 YEARS | | |
| B.C. 1 | 4152 | BIRTH OF JESUS CHRIST——Friday, October 29th Luke II. | | 3888th | | | |
| A.D. 26 | 4177 | TESTIMONY OF JOHN THE BAPTIST | | 3913 | | | YEARS |
| 26 | 4177 | THE 3½ YEARS MINISTRY OF JOHN ENDS WITH BAPTISM OF JESUS | | | THE CANCELLED 7 YEARS | | |
| 29 | 4180 | THE 3½ YEARS MINISTRY OF JESUS CHRIST OPENS—Nov. 26th | 7 YEARS | | | | |
| 33 | 4184 | CRUCIFIXION OF CHRIST—May 1st | | (3920) | (80th Jubile not reckoned) | | |
| | | THE RESURRECTION—May 4th | | | | | |
| | | THE ASCENSION—June 13th | 49d. | | | | OF |
| 33 | 4184 | PENTECOST IN JERUSALEM—June 22nd | | 3913 | | | |
| | | "THE TIMES OF THE GENTILES" BEGIN—Oct. 12th | 121d. | | A.D.33 Oct. 12th | | |
| 36 | 4187 | PENTECOST IN CAESAREA Acts X. | | 3916 | | | |
| 70 | 4222 | DESTRUCTION OF JERUSALEM | | 3951 | 2000 BIBLE YEARS | 1960 YEARS & 40 JUBILE YEARS | |
| 1917 | 6128 | BALFOUR DECLARATION—JEWISH RESTORATION DECREED | | 5857 | | | REDEMPTION |
| 1923 | 6134 | PALESTINE MANDATE CONFIRMED | | 5863 | | | |
| 1933 | 6144 | JUNE 12TH—6000 YEARS END | | 5873 | | | |
| | | THE CONSUMMATION OF THE AGE An unreckoned interval precedes the opening of the Millennial Kingdom of our Lord Jesus Christ | | | | | |
| | | THE APOCALYPTIC ERA OF 7 YEARS OF JUDGMENT REPLACES THE CANCELLED 7 YEARS, A.D.26 TO 33, AND COMPLETES REDEMPTION CHRONOLOGY AND THE "SEVEN TIMES". | | 5873 – 5880 | 120th | 7 YEARS | |

THIS CHART IS AN ABRIDGMENT OF A LARGER CHART (42 × 24 INCHES) BY THE SAME AUTHORS, ENTITLED "THE CHRONOLOGY OF THE WORLD".

## APPENDIX B

# THE TESTIMONY OF ANCIENT HISTORY TO THE YEAR 1 B.C. BEING THAT IN WHICH OUR LORD JESUS CHRIST WAS BORN

A LETTER FROM HUGH J. SCHONFIELD, D.S.LITT. THE JEWISH SCHOLAR AND AUTHOR OF "THE AUTHENTIC NEW TESTAMENT", ETC., ETC., CONCERNING "THE RESTORED VISION"

BEING desirous of obtaining independent testimony from an authoritative Jewish source as to the accuracy of our interpretation of Biblical Times, and knowing Dr. Hugh Schonfield's perfect acquaintance with the text of the New Testament, as the result of making an excellent translation of it from the Greek, we submitted the typed manuscript of *The Restored Vision* to him for his opinion. This he gives in brief in the following letter.

Highgate,
London, N.6
25th December 1956

Dear Mr. Ware,

I have carefully examined the data given in your book *The Restored Vision*, and note with satisfaction that you have been at pains to represent correctly the method of time-reckoning in use among the Jews in Bible Times.

As you know, I am a historian, and am therefore bound to relate where relevant the Biblical statements to the secular data available. I am not able consequently to confirm the date of 29th October 1 B.C. which you give for the Nativity. I agree that the birth of Jesus was probably about the time of the Feast of Tabernacles.

It does, however, appear from the date of the Nativity which you give that you have succeeded in reproducing from the Gospels a chronological pattern which will be both interesting and instructive to those who accept the Bible as the only criterion.

Yours faithfully,

(*Signed*) HUGH J. SCHONFIELD, *D.S. Litt.*

Dr. Schonfield warned us that while he would read *The Restored Vision* with great care and an open mind, he would have to remain absolutely true to his convictions as a historian in giving his opinions. We were not aware of the fact when we approached him that he was already committed by notes, etc., in his *Authentic New Testament*, to a system of dating Gospel events in accordance with the findings of modern Biblical scholarship, which in general acts upon the principle that historical data in the Bible can only be accepted as accurate if it can be confirmed from secular sources where available.

We make bold to say that it would be impossible for anyone who accepts the Bible *as the only criterion* to deny, in the light of the facts we have given from the Bible, that our Lord Jesus Christ was born on Friday, 29th October 1 B.C., which was the 1st day of the Feast of Tabernacles in the Bible's Sacred or Redemption Year 3888 from the Fall of Adam, and the 1st day of the Feast of Unleavened Bread in the Messianic Year 4205 from Adam. If this were not the actual date of our Lord's birth, that is, if another date could be advanced for any reason, then every feature in the wonderful Time Pattern of His life which we have set forth would be marred. Nevertheless we fear that, as in the case of Dr. Schonfield, no person or group of persons, who demand that this date, to be accepted, must first be shown to be in agreement with the findings of modern historical scholarship, will be likely to allow its authenticity because, by their adhesion to unreliable sources extraneous to the Scriptures, all such have formed the settled conviction that the birth of Christ took place three, four, five or even seven years before the start of the Christian Era as established in the sixth century by the well-instructed Dionysius Exiguus as 1st January A.D. 1.

The Gospels name certain historical events, such as the

taxing or enrolment decreed by Augustus Caesar, (which sent Mary and Joseph to Bethlehem), the rulership of Syria by Cyrenius (Luke II – 1 and 2) and the death of Herod the Great (Matthew II – 19), which it connects with our Lord's birth. These were not recorded for chronological purposes. The mention of the taxing and when it took place is simply given to establish Mary and Joseph's connection with the Davidic dynasty; and the death of Herod to afford the reason for bringing our Lord back from Egypt in fulfilment of the prophecy "Out of Egypt have I called My Son". To suggest that secular history must settle the dates of these events before we can learn the date of the Nativity is a gross afront to the Holy Scriptures and their Author. In actual fact the Bible itself gives the dates of each of them with absolute accuracy as we have shown; while secular history has never yet been able to speak with unanimity on any one of them, as any modern encyclopaedia which deals faithfully with the subject makes plain (e.g., *Encyclopaedia Biblica.* Cheyne & Black. Art: Chronology).

Some will understand us when we say that it is not surprising that secular history has never been able to establish the date of Christ's birth from these three named events, because it was in the Divine counsels that this date should remain concealed until the present critical hour in human history.

It is, indeed, also true to say that no date for the birth of Christ could be universally accepted unless proof for it could be produced from the Scriptures themselves. This is what we have done and no one who accepts the Bible *as the only criterion* can deny it.

## SOME TESTIMONIES FROM ANCIENT HISTORY WHICH CONFIRM THE YEAR 1 B.C. AS THAT OF OUR LORD'S BIRTH

It stands to reason as the Bible reveals our Lord was born on 29th October 1 B.C. that some among the earliest writers in the Christian Church would make some mention of the fact. No doubt it was from such documents that the worthy Dionysius Exiguus arrived at the conclusion that our Lord was born in the year that is now known as 1 B.C.

## TERTULLIAN (A.D. 160 TO 220)

Tertullian is called the father of Latin theology. He was a learned man and a prolific writer. We do not, however, have to concern ourselves with anything he wrote except that which relates to the year of Christ's birth. We will quote from *The Chain of Ages* by Rev. W. B. Galloway (pages 523-4,) who gives the Latin quotations in full and their source.

He says "Tertullian, who flourished in the second century and in the beginning of the third, places the Nativity of Christ in the fifteenth year before the death of Augustus, that is 1 B.C., and in the thirtieth year before the close of the fifteenth year of Tiberius Caesar, that is also 1 B.C."

It is common knowledge that Augustus Caesar died in August A.D. 14 and, as Galloway says, the 15th year previous must have been 1 B.C. Again, the 15th year of the reign of Tiberius Caesar, measured from the death of Augustus, was from August A.D. 28 to August A.D. 29, so that the thirtieth year prior thereto must have been 1 B.C. These measurements are expressed in the form common at the time with the Romans.

## EUSEBIUS

### *Bishop of Caesarea about A.D. 325*

Eusebius is said to be the father of Church History and spiritual adviser to Constantine. His *Ecclesiastical History* is said to have "a very high value as a careful collection of facts". In this work in Book I, Chapter IX we read:

> "The same author [i.e., Josephus], in the eighteenth book of his Antiquities, says, 'that about the twelfth year of the reign of Tiberius, Pontius Pilate was appointed over Judea, and remained there upon the whole ten years.' "

Eusebius, therefore, accepts that Pilate was appointed in A.D. 26 which is the 12th year of Tiberius, reckoned from his accession in August A.D. 14 when Augustus died.

In Book I, Chapter X, we read:

> "It was about the fifteenth year of the reign of Tiberius, according to the Evangelist, in the fourth year that Pilate was procurator of Judea . . . when our Lord and Saviour

Jesus Christ was in His thirtieth year, that He came to the baptism of John, and then made the beginning of promulgating His Gospel."

This latter measurement is the same as that given above in the quotation by Tertullian. The 15th year of Tiberius when, as Eusebius says, our Lord was in His thirtieth year was between August A.D. 28 and August A.D. 29. He must, therefore, have been born in 1 B.C. In actual fact as we have shown in this treatise our Lord reached 30 Bible years of age on 26th November A.D. 29.

We will again quote W. B. Galloway's *The Chain of Ages* to show that Eusebius declares that our Lord died in A.D. 33. (Chapter XIII, Section I):

> "But Eusebius in the Greek of his *Chronica* assigns it [i.e., the death of Christ] to the nineteenth year of Tiberius . . . ."

*The Chronicon Paschale* also gives expressly the nineteenth year of the reign of Tiberius as the year of our Lord's crucifixion.

The 19th year of the reign of Tiberius was August A.D. 32 to August A.D. 33. The Bible reveals that our Lord died on Friday 1st May A.D. 33 when He was 32 solar years and 184 days or 33 Bible years and 190 days.

Concerning the date of Herod's death, Galloway writes this: (page 585, *The Chain of Ages*):

> "I am at a loss to know what ancient authority can be produced in support of the assumption that Herod died four years before the recognized Christian Era. Eusebius places his death in the second or third year of the 195th Olympiad, A.D. 2 or 3."

As we have shown in Chapter I Herod could not have died until the Spring of A.D. 3 as the Wise Men from the East only visited Nazareth at the Feast of Tabernacles in the autumn of A.D. 2 and Herod then slew all male children under two years.

The Roman-Jewish historian, Josephus, gives thirty-seven years for the reign of Herod as measured, not from his titular designation by the Senate in 40 B.C., but from his actual investiture by Antony after the capture of Jerusalem from Antigonus, which was more than three years later. The date of the investiture must have been delayed until 35 B.C. or Herod's 37 years would not have ended in A.D. 3 as the Bible clearly concludes. The reason for this delay would be related to the position of Herod's enemy Antigonus, who was not put to death for about three years after his defeat by Herod and the capture of Jerusalem (see Josephus, *Wars of the Jews*, Book I).

It is a remarkable fact that the Rev. W. B. Galloway in his comprehensive treatise *The Chain of Ages* solely by means of ancient history and a painstaking weighing up of all the facts connected with the dates of our Lord's birth and death given therein, arrives at exactly the same results as we have, except for one month – our information having been obtained solely from the Holy Scriptures.

Galloway's conclusion is that our Lord was born on 29th September 1 B.C. whereas the Bible reveals that it was on 29th October 1 B.C. – just one month later. He concluded also that our Lord died on Friday 3rd April A.D. 33 whereas the Bible reveals that He died on Friday 1st May A.D. 33.

This difference of one month is entirely due to the fact that Galloway failed to realize that the Bible's first month in Bible Times came later than that in current use among the Jews.

So we may conclude by saying that Ancient History, *properly understood and interpreted*, is found to be in absolute agreement with the Holy Scriptures as to the dates of the birth and death of our Lord and Saviour Jesus Christ. Why should modern historical and Biblical scholarship be in disagreement?

# INDEX

Entries under the following headings are chronological rather than alphabetical.

**Burial of Jesus**
**Crucifixion**
**Crucifixion 8am to Noon**
**Crucifixion Noon to 3pm**
**Death of Jesus**
**Gethsemane**
**Last Supper**
**Ministry and Itinary of Jesus**
**Nativity**
**Passion Week**
**Resurrection of Jesus**
**Resurrection Day**
**Resurrection Appearances**
**Trial of Jesus**

Brackets ( ) indicate that there is not a direct reference to the subject in the text.

**R**